SSH, the Secure Shell

The Definitive Guide

SSH, the Secure Shell

The Definitive Guide

Daniel J. Barrett and Richard E. Silverman

O'REILLY®

Beijing · Cambridge · Farnham · Köln · Paris · Sebastopol · Taipei · Tokyo

SSH, the Secure Shell: The Definitive Guide
by Daniel J. Barrett and Richard E. Silverman

Printed in the United States of America.

Published by O'Reilly & Associates, Inc., 101 Morris Street, Sebastopol, CA 95472.

Editor: Mike Loukides

Production Editor: Mary Anne Weeks Mayo

Cover Designer: Ellie Volckhausen

Printing History:

February 2001: First Edition.

ISBN: 0-596-00011-1 [8/01]

[M]

Table of Contents

Preface

Privacy is a basic human right, but on today's computer networks, privacy isn't guaranteed. Much of the data that travels on the Internet or local networks is transmitted as plain text, and may be captured and viewed by anybody with a little technical know-how. The email you send, the files you transmit between computers, even the passwords you type may be readable by others. Imagine the damage that can be done if an untrusted third party—a competitor, the CIA, your in-laws— intercepted your most sensitive communications in transit.

Network security is big business as companies scramble to protect their information assets behind firewalls, establish virtual private networks (VPNs), and encrypt files and transmissions. But hidden away from all the bustle, there is a small, unassuming, yet robust solution many big companies have missed. It's reliable, reasonably easy to use, cheap, and available for most of today's operating systems.

It's SSH, the Secure Shell.

Protect Your Network with SSH

SSH is a low-cost, software-based solution for keeping prying eyes away from the data on a network. It doesn't solve every privacy and security problem, but it eliminates several of them effectively. Its major features are:

- A secure, client/server protocol for encrypting and transmitting data over a network
- Authentication (recognition) of users by password, host, or public key, plus optional integration with other popular authentication systems, including Kerberos, SecurID, PGP, TIS Gauntlet, and PAM

- The ability to add security to insecure network applications such as Telnet, FTP, and many other TCP/IP-based programs and protocols
- Almost complete transparency to the end user
- Implementations for most operating systems

Intended Audience

We've written this book for system administrators and technically minded users. Some chapters are suitable for a wide audience, while others are thoroughly technical and intended for computer and networking professionals.

End-User Audience

Do you have two or more computer accounts on different machines? SSH lets you connect one to another with a high degree of security. You can copy files between accounts, remotely log into one account from the other, or execute remote commands, all with the confidence that nobody can intercept your username, password, or data in transit.

Do you connect from a personal computer to an Internet service provider (ISP)? In particular, do you connect to a Unix shell account at your ISP? If so, SSH can make this connection significantly more secure. An increasing number of ISPs are running SSH servers for their users. In case your ISP doesn't, we'll show you how to run a server yourself.

Do you develop software? Are you creating distributed applications that must communicate over a network securely? Then don't reinvent the wheel: use SSH to encrypt the connections. It's a solid technology that may reduce your development time.

Even if you have only a single computer account, as long as it's connected to a network, SSH can still be useful. For example, if you've ever wanted to let other people use your account, such as family members or employees, but didn't want to give them unlimited use, SSH can provide a carefully controlled, limited access channel into your account.

Prerequisites

We assume you are familiar with computers and networking as found in any modern business office or home system with an Internet connection. Ideally, you are familiar with the Telnet and FTP applications. If you are a Unix user, you should be familiar with the programs *rsh*, *rlogin*, and *rcp*, and with the basics of writing shell scripts.

System-Administrator Audience

If you're a Unix system administrator, you probably know that the Berkeley r-commands (*rsh, rcp, rlogin, rexec,* etc.) are inherently insecure. SSH provides secure, drop-in replacements, eliminates *.rhosts* and *hosts.equiv* files, and can authenticate users by cryptographic key. SSH also can increase the security of other TCP/IP-based applications on your system by transparently "tunneling" them through SSH encrypted connections. You will love SSH.

Prerequisites

In addition to the end-user prerequisites in the previous section, you should be familiar with Unix accounts and groups, networking concepts such as TCP/IP and packets, and basic encryption techniques.

Reading This Book

This book is roughly divided into three parts. The first three chapters are a general introduction to SSH, first at a high level for all readers (Chapters 1 and 2), and then in detail for technical readers (Chapter 3).

The next nine chapters cover SSH for Unix. The first two (Chapters 4 and 5) cover SSH installation and serverwide configuration for system administrators. The next four (Chapters 6–9) cover advanced topics for end users, including key management, client configuration, per-account server configuration, and forwarding. We complete the Unix sequence with our recommended setup (Chapter 10), some detailed case studies (Chapter 11), and troubleshooting tips (Chapter 12).

The remaining chapters cover SSH products for Windows and the Macintosh, plus brief overviews of implementations for other platforms (Chapter 13).

Each section in the book is numbered, and we provide cross-references throughout the text. If further details are found in Section 7.1.3.2, we use the notation [7.1.3.2] to indicate it.

Our Approach

This book is organized by concept rather than syntax. We begin with an overview and progressively lead you deeper into the functionality of SSH. So we might introduce a topic in Chapter 1, show its basic use in Chapter 2, and reveal advanced uses in Chapter 7. If you would prefer the whole story at once, Appendix B presents all commands and their options in one location.

We focus strongly on three levels of server configuration, which we call compile-time, serverwide, and per-account configuration. Compile-time configuration

(Chapter 4) means selecting appropriate options when you build the SSH clients and servers. serverwide configuration (Chapter 5) applies when the SSH server is run and is generally done by system administrators, while per-account configuration (Chapter 8) can be done any time by end users. It's vitally important for system administrators to understand the relationships and differences among these three levels. Otherwise, SSH may seem like a morass of random behaviors.

Although the bulk of material focuses on Unix implementations of SSH, you don't have to be a Unix user to understand it. Fans of Windows and Macintosh may stick to the later chapters devoted to their platforms, but a lot of the meaty details are in the Unix chapters so we recommend reading them, at least for reference.

Which Chapters Are for You?

We propose several "tracks" for readers with different interests and skills:

System administrators
: Chapters 3–5 and 10 are the most important for understanding SSH and how to build and configure servers. However, as the administrator of a security product, you should read the whole book.

Unix users (not system administrators)
: Chapters 1–2 provide an overview, and Chapters 6–9 discuss SSH clients in depth.

Windows end users
: Read Chapters 1, 2, and 13–16, for starters, and then others as your interests guide you.

Macintosh end users
: Read Chapters 1, 2, 13, 16, and 17, for starters, and then others as your interests guide you.

Users of other computer platforms
: Read Chapters 1, 2, and 13, for starters, and then others as your interests guide you.

Even if you are experienced with SSH, you will likely find value in Chapters 3–12. We cover significant details the Unix manpages leave unclear or unmentioned, including major concepts, compile-time flags, server configuration, and forwarding.

Supported Platforms

This book covers Unix, Windows, and Macintosh implementations of SSH. Products are also available for the Amiga, BeOs, Java, OS/2, Palm Pilot, VMS, and Windows CE, and although we don't cover them, their principles are the same.

This book is current for the following Unix SSH versions"

SSH1	1.2.30
F-Secure SSH1	1.3.7
OpenSSH	2.2.0
SSH Secure Shell (a.k.a. SSH2)	2.3.0
F-Secure SSH2	2.0.13

The F-Secure products for Unix differ little from SSH1 and SSH2, so we won't discuss them separately except for unique features. See Appendix B for a summary of the differences.

Version information for non-Unix products is found in their respective chapters.

Disclaimers

We identify some program features as "undocumented." This means the feature isn't mentioned in the official documentation but works in the current release and/or is clear from the program source code. Undocumented features may not be officially supported by the software authors and can disappear in later releases.

Conventions Used in This Book

This book uses the following typographic conventions:

`Constant width`
: For configuration files, things that can be found in configuration files (such as keywords and configuration file options), source code, and interactive terminal sessions.

`Constant width italic`
: For replaceable parameters on command lines or within configuration files.

Italic
: For filenames, URLs, hostnames, command names, command-line options, and new terms whre they are defined.

A_K
: In figures, the object labeled A has been secured using a cryptographic key labled K. "Secured" means encrypted, signed, or some more complex relationship, depending on the context. If A is secured using multiple keys (say K and L), they will be listed in the subscript, separated by commas: $A_{K, L}$

The owl icon designates a note, which is an important aside to the nearby text.

The turkey icon designates a warning relating to the nearby text.

Comments and Questions

The information in this book has been tested and verified, but you may find that features have changed (or even find mistakes!). You can send any errors you find, as well as suggestions for future editions, to:

O'Reilly & Associates, Inc.
101 Morris Street
Sebastopol, CA 95472
(800) 998-9938 (in the United States or Canada)
(707) 829-0515 (international/local)
(707) 829-0104 (fax)

There is a web page for this book, which lists errata, examples, or any additional information. You can access this page at:

http://www.oreilly.com/catalog/sshtdg/

To comment or ask technical questions about this book, send email to:

bookquestions@oreilly.com

For more information about books, conferences, software, Resource Centers, and the O'Reilly Network, see the O'Reilly web site at:

http://www.oreilly.com/

Acknowledgments

First and foremost, we'd like to thank O'Reilly & Associates for the opportunity to write this book, especially our editor, Mike Loukides, who let us stretch the schedule to cover advanced topics in depth. We thank Frank Willison for believing in our idea, Christien Shangraw for administrative excellence and for heroically performing the first typesetting pass, Mike Sierra for tools and advice, and Rob Romano for turning our hasty sketches into polished illustrations.

We thank our excellent technical review team for their thorough reading and insightful comments: Anne Carasik, Markus Friedl, Joseph Galbraith, Sergey Okhapkin, Jari Ollikka, Niels Provos, Theo de Raadt, Jim Sheafer, Drew Simonis, Mike Smith, and Dug Song.

Big thanks to the vendors and developers of SSH products who provided us with free copies and answered our questions: Tatu Ylönen, Anne Carasik, and Arlinda Sipilä (SSH Communication Security, Ltd.); Sami Sumkin, Heikki Nousiainen, Petri Nyman, Hannu Eloranta, and Alexander Sayer (F-Secure Corporation); Dan Rask (Van Dyke Technologies, Inc.); Gordon Chaffee (Windows SSH port); Ian Goldberg (Top Gun SSH); Douglas Mak (FiSSH); Jonas Walldén (NiftyTelnet SSH); and Stephen Pendleton (sshCE). SSH Communication Security also gave us permission to include the *sshregex* manpage (Appendix A) and the *sshdebug.h* error codes (Table 5-6).

We thank Rob Figenbaum, James Mathiesen, and J.D. Paul for tips and inspirations incorporated into the text; and Chuck Bogorad, Ben Gould, David Primmer, and Brandon Zehm for their web pages about SSH on NT. Richard Silverman would like to thank his co-workers at *the company formerly known as*, especially Michelle Madelien, for being very flexible and accommodating with his erratic hours and behavior while working on this tome. He would also like to thank Deborah Kaplan for her judicious and inspired application of the LART. Lastly, we thank the many contributors to *comp.security.ssh* on Usenet, for asking good questions that improved the book, especially Chapter 12.

1
Introduction to SSH

In this chapter:
- *What Is SSH?*
- *What SSH Is Not*
- *The SSH Protocol*
- *Overview of SSH Features*
- *History of SSH*
- *Related Technologies*
- *Summary*

Many people today have multiple computer accounts. If you're a reasonably savvy user, you might have a personal account with an Internet service provider (ISP), a work account on your employer's local network, and one or more PCs at home. You might also have permission to use other accounts owned by family members or friends.

If you have multiple accounts, it's natural to want to make connections between them. For instance, you might want to copy files between computers over a network, log into one account remotely from another, or transmit commands to a remote computer for execution. Various programs exist for these purposes, such as *ftp* and *rcp* for file transfers, *telnet* and *rlogin* for remote logins, and *rsh* for remote execution of commands.

Unfortunately, many of these network-related programs have a fundamental problem: they lack security. If you transmit a sensitive file via the Internet, an intruder can potentially intercept and read the data. Even worse, if you log onto another computer remotely using a program such as *telnet*, your username and password can be intercepted as they travel over the network. Yikes!

How can these serious problems be prevented? You can use an *encryption program* to scramble your data into a secret code nobody else can read. You can install a *firewall*, a device that shields portions of a computer network from intruders. Or you can use a wide range of other solutions, alone or combined, with varying complexity and cost.

1.1. What Is SSH?

SSH, the Secure Shell, is a popular, powerful, software-based approach to network security.* Whenever data is sent by a computer to the network, SSH automatically encrypts it. When the data reaches its intended recipient, SSH automatically decrypts (unscrambles) it. The result is *transparent* encryption: users can work normally, unaware that their communications are safely encrypted on the network. In addition, SSH uses modern, secure encryption algorithms and is effective enough to be found within mission-critical applications at major corporations.

SSH has a client/server architecture, as shown in Figure 1-1. An SSH *server* program, typically installed and run by a system administrator, accepts or rejects incoming connections to its host computer. Users then run SSH *client* programs, typically on other computers, to make requests of the SSH server, such as "Please log me in," "Please send me a file," or "Please execute this command." All communications between clients and servers are securely encrypted and protected from modification.

Our description is simplified but should give you a general idea of what SSH does. We'll go into depth later. For now, just remember that SSH clients communicate with SSH servers over encrypted network connections.

An SSH-based product might include clients, servers, or both. Unix products generally contain both clients and servers; those on other platforms are usually just clients, though Windows-based servers are beginning to appear.

If you're a Unix user, think of SSH as a secure form of the Unix r-commands: *rsh* (remote shell), *rlogin* (remote login), and *rcp* (remote copy). In fact, the original SSH for Unix includes the similarly named commands *ssh*, *scp*, and *slogin* as secure, drop-in replacements for the r-commands. Yes, you can finally get rid of those insecure *.rhosts* and *hosts.equiv* files! (Though SSH can work with them as well, if you like.) If you're still using the r-commands, switch to SSH immediately: the learning curve is small, and security is far better.

1.2. What SSH Is Not

Although SSH stands for Secure Shell, it is not a true shell in the sense of the Unix Bourne shell and C shell. It is not a command interpreter, nor does it provide wildcard expansion, command history, and so forth. Rather, SSH creates a chan-

* "SSH" is pronounced by spelling it aloud: S-S-H. You might find the name "Secure Shell" a little puzzling, because it is not, in fact, a shell at all. The name was coined from the existing *rsh* utility, a ubiquitous Unix program that also provides remote logins but is very insecure.

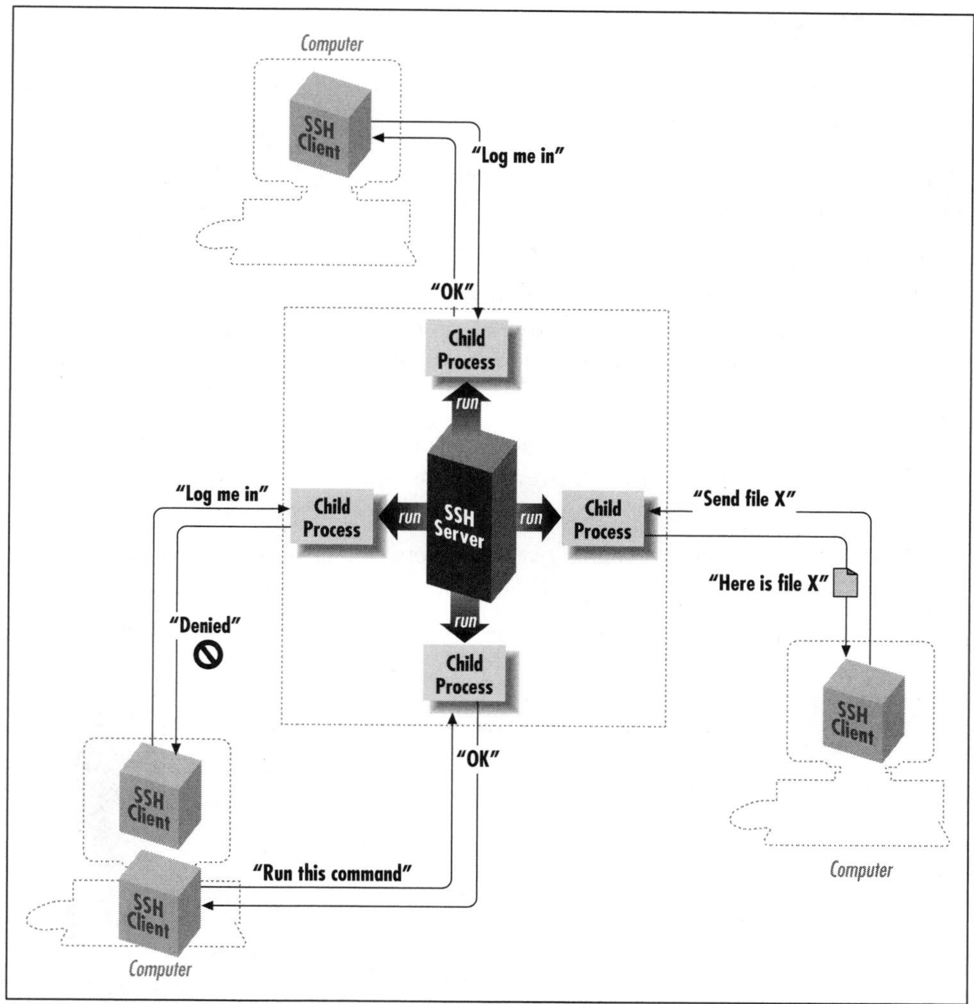

Figure 1-1. SSH architecture

nel for running a shell on a remote computer, in the manner of the Unix *rsh* command, but with end-to-end encryption between the local and remote computer.

SSH is also not a complete security solution—but then, nothing is. It won't protect computers from active break-in attempts or denial-of-service attacks, and it won't eliminate other hazards such as viruses, Trojan horses, and coffee spills. It does, however, provide robust and user-friendly encryption and authentication.

1.3. The SSH Protocol

SSH is a *protocol,* not a product. It is a specification of how to conduct secure communication over a network.*

The SSH protocol covers authentication, encryption, and the integrity of data transmitted over a network, as shown in Figure 1-2. Let's define these terms:

Authentication
: Reliably determines someone's identity. If you try to log into an account on a remote computer, SSH asks for digital proof of your identity. If you pass the test, you may log in; otherwise SSH rejects the connection.

Encryption
: Scrambles data so it is unintelligible except to the intended recipients. This protects your data as it passes over the network.

Integrity
: Guarantees the data traveling over the network arrives unaltered. If a third party captures and modifies your data in transit, SSH detects this fact.

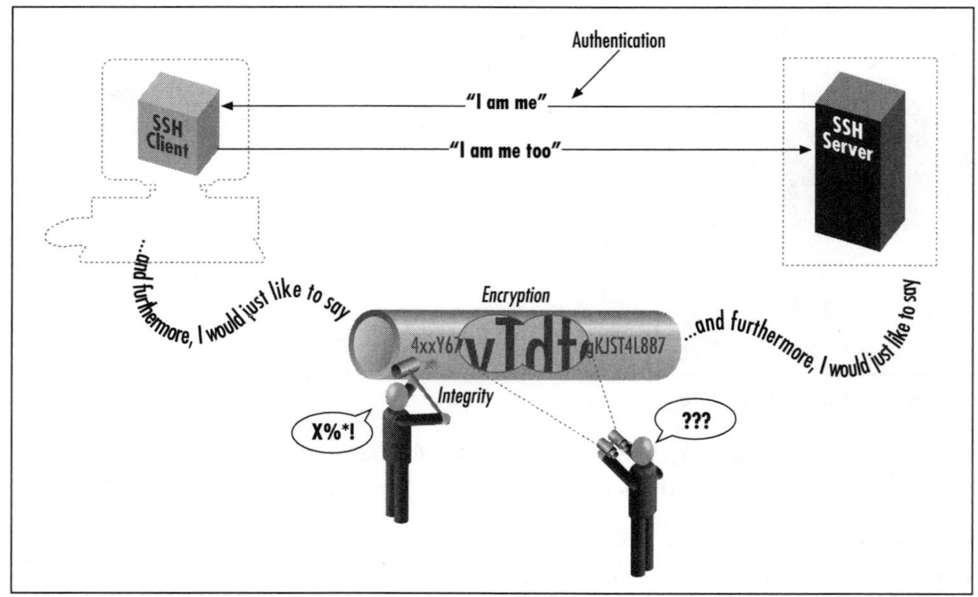

Figure 1-2. Authentication, encryption, and integrity

* Although we say "the SSH protocol," there are actually two incompatible versions of the protocols in common use: SSH-1 (a.k.a SSH-1.5) and SSH-2. We will distinguish these protocols later.

In short, SSH makes network connections between computers, with strong guarantees that the parties on both ends of the connection are genuine. It also ensures that any data passing over these connections arrives unmodified and unread by eavesdroppers.

1.3.1. Protocols, Products, Clients, and Confusion

SSH-based products—i.e., products that implement the SSH protocol—exist for many flavors of Unix, Windows, Macintosh, and other operating systems. Both freely distributable and commercial products are available. [13.3]

The first SSH product, created by Tatu Ylönen for Unix, was simply called "SSH." This causes confusion because SSH is also the name of the protocol. Some people call Ylönen's software "Unix SSH," but other Unix-based implementations are now available so the name is unsatisfactory. In this book, we use more precise terminology to refer to protocols, products, and programs, summarized in the sidebar "Terminology: SSH Protocols and Products." In short:

- Protocols are denoted with dashes: SSH-1, SSH-2.
- Products are denoted in uppercase, without dashes: SSH1, SSH2.
- Client programs are in lowercase: *ssh*, *ssh1*, *ssh2*, etc.

1.4. Overview of SSH Features

So, what can SSH do? Let's run through some examples that demonstrate the major features of SSH, such as secure remote logins, secure file copying, and secure invocation of remote commands. We use SSH1 in the examples, but all are possible with OpenSSH, SSH2, and F-Secure SSH.

1.4.1. Secure Remote Logins

Suppose you have accounts on several computers on the Internet. Typically, you connect from a home PC to your ISP, and then use a *telnet* program to log into your accounts on other computers. Unfortunately, *telnet* transmits your username and password in plaintext over the Internet, where a malicious third party can intercept them.* Additionally, your entire *telnet* session is readable by a network snooper.

---

* This is true of standard Telnet, but some implementations add security features.

Terminology: SSH Protocols and Products

SSH
: A generic term referring to SSH protocols or software products.

SSH-1
: The SSH protocol, Version 1. This protocol went through several revisions, of which 1.3 and 1.5 are the best known, and we will write *SSH-1.3* and *SSH-1.5* should the distinction be necessary.

SSH-2
: The SSH protocol, Version 2, as defined by several draft standards documents of the IETF SECSH working group. [3.5.1]

SSH1
: Tatu Ylönen's software implementing the SSH-1 protocol; the original SSH. Now distributed and maintained (minimally) by SSH Communications Security, Inc.

SSH2
: The "SSH Secure Shell" product from SSH Communications Security, Inc. (*http://www.ssh.com*). This is a commercial SSH-2 protocol implementation, though it is licensed free of charge in some circumstances.

ssh (all lowercase letters)
: A client program included in SSH1, SSH2, OpenSSH, F-Secure SSH, and other products, for running secure terminal sessions and remote commands. In SSH1 and SSH2, it is also named *ssh1* or *ssh2*, respectively.

OpenSSH
: The product OpenSSH from the OpenBSD project (see *http://www.openssh.com/*), which implements both the SSH-1 and SSH-2 protocols.

OpenSSH/1
: OpenSSH, referring specifically to its behavior when using the SSH-1 protocol.

OpenSSH/2
: OpenSSH, referring specifically to its behavior when using the SSH-2 protocol.

SSH completely avoids these problems. Rather than running the insecure *telnet* program, you run the SSH client program *ssh*. To log into an account with the username smith on the remote computer *host.example.com*, use this command:

```
$ ssh -l smith host.example.com
```

Terminology: Networking

Local computer (local host, local machine)
: A computer on which you are logged in and, typically, running an SSH client.

Remote computer (remote host, remote machine)
: A second computer you contact from your local computer. Typically, the remote computer is running an SSH server and is contacted via an SSH client. As a degenerate case, the local and remote computers can be the same machine.

Local user
: A user logged into a local computer.

Remote user
: A user logged into a remote computer.

Server
: An SSH server program.

Server machine
: A computer running an SSH server program. We will sometimes simply write "server" for the server machine when the context makes clear (or irrelevant) the distinction between the running SSH server program and its host machine.

Client
: An SSH client program.

Client machine
: A computer running an SSH client. As with the server terminology, we will simply write "client" when the context makes the meaning clear.

~ or $HOME
: A user's home directory on a Unix machine, particularly when used in a file path such as *~/filename*. Most shells recognize ~ as a user's home directory, with the notable exception of Bourne shell. $HOME is recognized by all shells.

The client authenticates you to the remote computer's SSH server using an encrypted connection, meaning that your username and password are encrypted before they leave the local machine. The SSH server then logs you in, and your entire login session is encrypted as it travels between client and server. Because the encryption is transparent, you won't notice any differences between *telnet* and the *telnet*-like SSH client.

1.4.2. Secure File Transfer

Suppose you have accounts on two Internet computers, *me@firstaccount.com* and *metoo@secondaccount.com*, and you want to transfer a file from the first to the second account. The file contains trade secrets about your business, however, that must be kept from prying eyes. A traditional file-transfer program, such as *ftp*, *rcp*, or even email, doesn't provide a secure solution. A third party can intercept and read the packets as they travel over the network. To get around this problem, you can encrypt the file on *firstaccount.com* with a program such as Pretty Good Privacy (PGP), transfer it via traditional means, and decrypt the file on *secondaccount.com*, but such a process is tedious and nontransparent to the user.

Using SSH, the file can be transferred securely between machines with a single secure copy command. If the file were named *myfile*, the command executed on *firstaccount.com* might be:

```
$ scp myfile metoo@secondaccount.com:
```

When transmitted by *scp*, the file is automatically encrypted as it leaves *firstaccount.com* and decrypted as it arrives on *secondaccount.com*.

1.4.3. Secure Remote Command Execution

Suppose you are a system administrator who needs to run the same command on many computers. You'd like to view the active processes for each user on four different computers—*grape*, *lemon*, *kiwi*, and *melon*—on a local area network using the Unix command */usr/ucb/w*. Traditionally, one could use *rsh*, assuming that the *rsh* daemon, *rshd*, is configured properly on the remote computers:

```
#!/bin/sh                                     This is a shell script.
for machine in grape lemon kiwi melon         On each of these four machines in turn...
do
  rsh $machine /usr/ucb/w                     invoke the "/usr/ucb/w" program, which
done                                          prints a list of all running processes.
```

Although this method works, it's insecure. The results of */usr/ucb/w* are transmitted as plaintext across the network; if you consider this information sensitive, the risk might be unacceptable. Worse, the *rsh* authentication mechanism is extremely insecure and easily subverted. Using the *ssh* command instead, you have:

```
#!/bin/sh
for machine in grape lemon kiwi melon
do
  ssh $machine /usr/ucb/w                     Note "ssh" instead of "rsh"
done
```

The syntax is nearly identical, and the visible output is identical, but under the hood, the command and its results are encrypted as they travel across the network, and strong authentication techniques may be used when connecting to the remote machines.

1.4.4. Keys and Agents

Suppose you have accounts on many computers on a network. For security reasons, you prefer different passwords on all accounts; but remembering so many passwords is difficult. It's also a security problem in itself. The more often you type a password, the more likely you'll mistakenly type it in the wrong place. (Have you ever accidently typed your password instead of your username, visible to the world? Ouch! And on many systems, such mistakes are recorded in a system log file, revealing your password in plaintext.) Wouldn't it be great to identify yourself only once and get secure access to all the accounts without continually typing passwords?

SSH has various authentication mechanisms, and the most secure is based on *keys* rather than passwords. Keys are discussed in great detail in Chapter 6, but for now we define a key as a small blob of bits that uniquely identifies an SSH user. For security, a key is kept encrypted; it may be used only after entering a secret *passphrase* to decrypt it.

Using keys, together with a program called an *authentication agent*, SSH can authenticate you to all your computer accounts securely without requiring you to memorize many passwords or enter them repeatedly. It works like this:

1. In advance (and only once), place special files called *public key files* into your remote computer accounts. These enable your SSH clients (*ssh*, *scp*) to access your remote accounts.
2. On your local machine, invoke the *ssh-agent* program, which runs in the background.
3. Choose the key (or keys) you will need during your login session.
4. Load the keys into the agent with the *ssh-add* program. This requires knowledge of each key's secret passphrase.

At this point, you have an *ssh-agent* program running on your local machine, holding your secret keys in memory. You're now done. You have password-less access to all your remote accounts that contain your public key files. Say goodbye to the tedium of retyping passwords! The setup lasts until you log out from the local machine or terminate *ssh-agent*.

1.4.5. Access Control

Suppose you want to permit another person to use your computer account, but only for certain purposes. For example, while you're out of town you'd like your secretary to read your email but not to do anything else in your account. With SSH, you can give your secretary access to your account without revealing or changing your password, and with only the ability to run the email program. No system-administrator privileges are required to set up this restricted access. (This topic is the focus of Chapter 8.)

1.4.6. Port Forwarding

SSH can increase the security of other TCP/IP-based applications such as *telnet*, *ftp*, and the X Window System. A technique called *port forwarding* or *tunneling* reroutes a TCP/IP connection to pass through an SSH connection, transparently encrypting it end-to-end. Port forwarding can also pass such applications through network firewalls that otherwise prevent their use.

Suppose you are logged into a machine away from work and want to access the internal news server at your office, *news.yoyodyne.com*. The Yoyodyne network is connected to the Internet, but a network firewall blocks incoming connections to most ports, particularly port 119, the news port. The firewall does allow incoming SSH connections, however, since the SSH protocol is secure enough that even Yoyodyne's rabidly paranoid system administrators trust it. SSH can establish a secure tunnel on an arbitrary local TCP port—say, port 3002—to the news port on the remote host. The command might look a bit cryptic at this early stage, but here it is:

```
$ ssh -L 3002:localhost:119 news.yoyodyne.com
```

This says "*ssh*, please establish a secure connection from TCP port 3002 on my local machine to TCP port 119, the news port, on *news.yoyodyne.com*." So, in order to read news securely, configure your news-reading program to connect to port 3002 on your local machine. The secure tunnel created by *ssh* automatically communicates with the news server on *news.yoyodyne.com*, and the news traffic passing through the tunnel is protected by encryption. [9.1]

1.5. History of SSH

SSH1 and the SSH-1 protocol were developed in 1995 by Tatu Ylönen, a researcher at the Helsinki University of Technology in Finland. After his university network was the victim of a password-sniffing attack earlier that year, Ylönen whipped up SSH1 for himself. When beta versions started gaining attention, however, he realized that his security product could be put to wider use.

In July 1995, SSH1 was released to the public as free software with source code, permitting people to copy and use the program without cost. By the end of the year, an estimated 20,000 users in 50 countries had adopted SSH1, and Ylönen was fending off 150 email messages per day requesting support. In response, Ylönen founded SSH Communications Security, Ltd., (SCS, *http://www.ssh.com/*) in December of 1995 to maintain, commercialize, and continue development of SSH. Today he is chairman and chief technology officer of the company.

Also in 1995, Ylönen documented the SSH-1 protocol as an Internet Engineering Task Force (IETF) Internet Draft, which essentially described the operation of the SSH1 software after the fact. It was a somewhat ad hoc protocol with a number of problems and limitations discovered as the software grew in popularity. These problems couldn't be fixed without losing backward compatibility, so in 1996, SCS introduced a new, major version of the protocol, SSH 2.0 or SSH-2, that incorporates new algorithms and is incompatible with SSH-1. In response, the IETF formed a working group called SECSH (Secure Shell) to standardize the protocol and guide its development in the public interest. The SECSH working group submitted the first Internet Draft for the SSH-2.0 protocol in February 1997.

In 1998, SCS released the software product "SSH Secure Shell" (SSH2), based on the superior SSH-2 protocol. However, SSH2 didn't replace SSH1 in the field, for two reasons. First, SSH2 was missing a number of useful, practical features and configuration options of SSH1. Second, SSH2 had a more restrictive license. The original SSH1 had been freely available from Ylönen and the Helsinki University of Technology. Newer versions of SSH1 from SCS were still freely available for most uses, even in commercial settings, as long as the software was not directly sold for profit or offered as a service to customers. SSH2, on the other hand, was a commercial product, allowing gratis use only for qualifying educational and non-profit entities. As a result, when SSH2 first appeared, most existing SSH1 users saw few advantages to SSH2 and continued to use SSH1. As of this writing, three years after the introduction of the SSH-2 protocol, SSH-1 is still the most widely deployed version on the Internet, even though SSH-2 is a better and more secure protocol.

This situation promises to change, however, as a result of two developments: a loosening of the SSH2 license and the appearance of free SSH-2 implementations. As this book went to press in late 2000, SCS broadened the SSH2 license to permit free use by individual contractors working for qualifying noncommercial entities. It also extends free use to the Linux, NetBSD, FreeBSD, and OpenBSD operating systems, in any context at all including a commercial one. At the same time, OpenSSH (*http://www.openssh.com/*) is gaining prominence as an SSH implementation, developed under the auspices of the OpenBSD project (*http://www.openbsd.org/*) and freely available under the OpenBSD license. Based on the last free release of the original SSH, 1.2.12, OpenSSH has developed rapidly.

Though many people have contributed to it, OpenSSH is largely the work of software developer Markus Friedl. It supports both SSH-1 and SSH-2 in a single set of programs, whereas SSH1 and SSH2 have separate executables, and the SSH-1 compatibility features in SSH2 require both products to be installed. While OpenSSH was developed under OpenBSD, it has been ported successfully to Linux, Solaris, AIX, and other operating systems, in tight synchronization with the main releases. Although OpenSSH is relatively new and missing some features present in SSH1 and SSH2, it is developing rapidly and promises to be a major SSH flavor in the near future.

At press time, development of SSH1 has ceased except for important bug fixes, while development of SSH2 and OpenSSH remains active. Other SSH implementations abound, notably the commercial versions of SSH1 and SSH2 maintained and sold by F-Secure Corporation, and numerous ports and original products for the PC, Macintosh, Palm Pilot, and other operating systems. [13.3] It is estimated there are over two million SSH users worldwide, including hundreds of thousands of registered users of SCS products.

Sometimes we use the term "SSH1/SSH2 and their derivatives." This refers to SCS's SSH1 and SSH2, F-Secure SSH Server (Versions 1 and 2), OpenSSH, and any other ports of the SSH1 or SSH2 code base for Unix or other operating systems. The term doesn't encompass other SSH products (SecureCRT, NiftyTelnet SSH, F-Secure's Windows and Macintosh clients, etc.).

1.6. Related Technologies

SSH is popular and convenient, but we certainly don't claim it is the ultimate security solution for all networks. Authentication, encryption, and network security originated long before SSH and have been incorporated into many other systems. Let's survey a few representative systems.

1.6.1. rsh Suite (R-Commands)

The Unix programs *rsh*, *rlogin*, and *rcp*—collectively known as the *r-commands*—are the direct ancestors of the SSH1 clients *ssh*, *slogin*, and *scp*. The user interfaces and visible functionality are nearly identical to their SSH1 counterparts, except that SSH1 clients are secure. The r-commands, in contrast, don't encrypt their connections and have a weak, easily subverted authentication model.

An r-command server relies on two mechanisms for security: a network naming service and the notion of "privileged" TCP ports. Upon receiving a connection from a client, the server obtains the network address of the originating host and translates it into a hostname. This hostname must be present in a configuration file on the server, typically */etc/hosts.equiv*, for the server to permit access. The server also checks that the source TCP port number is in the range 1–1023, since these port numbers can be used only by the Unix superuser (or root uid). If the connection passes both checks, the server believes it is talking to a trusted program on a trusted host and logs in the client as whatever user it requests!

These two security checks are easily subverted. The translation of a network address to a hostname is done by a naming service such as Sun's Network Information Service (NIS) or the Internet Domain Name System (DNS). Most implementations and/or deployments of NIS and DNS services have security holes, presenting opportunities to trick the server into trusting a host it shouldn't. Then, a remote user can log into someone else's account on the server simply by having the same username.

Likewise, blind trust in privileged TCP ports represents a serious security risk. A cracker who gains root privilege on a trusted machine can simply run a tailored version of the *rsh* client and log in as any user on the server host. Overall, reliance on these port numbers is no longer trustworthy in a world of desktop computers whose users have administrative access as a matter of course, or whose operating systems don't support multiple users or privileges (such as Windows 9x and the Macintosh).

If user databases on trusted hosts were always synchronized with the server, installation of privileged programs (setuid root) strictly monitored, root privileges guaranteed to be held by trusted people, and the physical network protected, the r-commands would be reasonably secure. These assumptions made sense in the early days of networking, when hosts were few, expensive, and overseen by a small and trusted group of administrators, but they have far outlived their usefulness.

Given SSH's superior security features and that *ssh* is backward-compatible with *rsh* (and *scp* with *rcp*), we see no compelling reason to run the r-commands any more. Install SSH and be happy.

1.6.2. Pretty Good Privacy (PGP)

PGP is a popular encryption program available for many computing platforms, created by Phil Zimmerman. It can authenticate users and encrypt data files and email messages.

SSH incorporates some of the same encryption algorithms as PGP, but applied in a different way. PGP is file-based, typically encrypting one file or email message at a time on a single computer. SSH, in contrast, encrypts an ongoing session between networked computers. The difference between PGP and SSH is like that between a batch job and an interactive process.

PGP and SSH are related in another way as well: SSH2 can optionally use PGP keys for authentication. [5.5.1.6]

More PGP information is available at *http://www.pgpi.com/*.

1.6.3. Kerberos

Kerberos is a secure authentication system for environments where networks may be monitored, and computers aren't under central control. It was developed as part of Project Athena, a wide-ranging research and development effort at the Massachusetts Institute of Technology (MIT). Kerberos authenticates users by way of *tickets,* small sequences of bytes with limited lifetimes, while user passwords remain secure on a central machine.

Kerberos and SSH solve similar problems but are quite different in scope. SSH is lightweight and easily deployed, designed to work on existing systems with minimal changes. To enable secure access from one machine to another, simply install an SSH client on the first and a server on the second, and start the server. Kerberos, in contrast, requires significant infrastructure to be established before use, such as administrative user accounts, a heavily secured central host, and software for network-wide clock synchronization. In return for this added complexity, Kerberos ensures that users' passwords travel on the network as little as possible and are stored only on the central host. SSH sends passwords across the network (over encrypted connections, of course) on each login and stores keys on each host from which SSH is used. Kerberos also serves other purposes beyond the scope of SSH, including a centralized user account database, access control lists, and a hierarchical model of trust.

Another difference between SSH and Kerberos is the approach to securing client applications. SSH can be easily integrated with programs that use *rsh* in the background, such as Pine, the popular mail reader. [11.3] Configure it to use *ssh* instead of *rsh*, and the program's remote connections are transparently secure. For programs that open direct network connections, SSH's port-forwarding feature provides another convenient form of integration. Kerberos, on the other hand, contains a set of programming libraries for adding authentication and encryption to other applications. Developers can integrate applications with Kerberos by modifying their source code to make calls to the Kerberos libraries.* The MIT Kerberos distribution comes with a set of common services that have been "kerberized," including secure versions of *telnet*, *ftp*, and *rsh*.

If the features of Kerberos and SSH both sound good, you're in luck: they've been integrated. [11.4] More information on Kerberos can be found at:

> *http://web.mit.edu/kerberos/www/*
> *http://nii.isi.edu/info/kerberos/*

1.6.4. IPSEC

Internet Protocol Security (IPSEC) is an evolving Internet standard for network security. Developed by an IETF working group, IPSEC comprises authentication and encryption implemented at the IP level. This is a lower level of the network stack than SSH addresses. It is entirely transparent to end users, who don't need to use a particular program such as SSH to gain security; rather, their existing insecure network traffic is protected automatically by the underlying system. IPSEC can securely connect a single machine to a remote network through an intervening untrusted network (such as the Internet), or it can connect entire networks (this is the idea of the "Virtual Private Network," or VPN).

SSH is often quicker and easier to deploy as a solution than IPSEC, since SSH is a simple application program, whereas IPSEC requires additions to the host operating systems on both sides if they don't already come with it, and possibly to network equipment such as routers, depending on the scenario. SSH also provides user authentication, whereas IPSEC deals only with individual hosts. On the other hand, IPSEC is more basic protection and can do things SSH can't. For instance, in Chapter 11, we discuss in detail the difficulties of trying to protect the FTP protocol using SSH. If you need to secure an existing insecure protocol such as FTP, which isn't amenable to treatment with SSH, IPSEC is a way to do it.

IPSEC can provide authentication alone, through a means called the Authentication Header (AH), or both authentication and encryption, using a protocol called Encapsulated Security Payload (ESP). Detailed information on IPSEC can be found at:

> *http://www.ietf.org/ids.by.wg/ipsec.html*

---

* SSH2 has moved toward this model as well, organized as a set of libraries implementing the SSH2 protocol and accessed via an API.

1.6.5. Secure Remote Password (SRP)

The Secure Remote Password (SRP) protocol, created at Stanford University, is a security protocol very different in scope from SSH. It is specifically an authentication protocol, whereas SSH comprises authentication, encryption, integrity, session management, etc., as an integrated whole. SRP isn't a complete security solution in itself, but rather a technology that can be a part of a security system.

The design goal of SRP is to improve on the security properties of password-style authentication, while retaining its considerable practical advantages. Using SSH public-key authentication is difficult if you're traveling, especially if you're not carrying your own computer, but instead are using other people's machines. You have to carry your private key with you on a diskette and hope that you can get the key into whatever machine you need to use. Oops, you've been given an X terminal. Oh well.

Carrying your encrypted private key with you is also a weakness, because if someone steals it, they can subject it to a dictionary attack in which they try to find your passphrase and recover the key. Then you're back to the age-old problem with passwords: to be useful they must be short and memorable, whereas to be secure, they must be long and random.

SRP provides strong two-party mutual authentication, with the client needing only to remember a short password which need not be so strongly random. With traditional password schemes, the server maintains a sensitive database that must be protected, such as the passwords themselves, or hashed versions of them (as in the Unix */etc/passwd* and */etc/shadow* files). That data must be kept secret, since disclosure allows an attacker to impersonate users or discover their passwords through a dictionary attack. The design of SRP avoids such a database and allows passwords to be less random (and therefore more memorable and useful), since it prevents dictionary attacks. The server still has sensitive data that should be protected, but the consequences of its disclosure are less severe.

SRP is also intentionally designed to avoid using encryption algorithms in its operation. Thus it avoids running afoul of cryptographic export laws, which prohibits certain encryption technologies from being shared with foreign countries.

SRP is an interesting technology we hope gains wider acceptance; it is an excellent candidate for an additional authentication method in SSH. The current SRP implementation includes secure clients and servers for the Telnet and FTP protocols for Unix and Windows. More SRP information can be found at:

> *http://srp.stanford.edu/*

1.6.6. Secure Socket Layer (SSL) Protocol

The Secure Socket Layer (SSL) protocol is an authentication and encryption technique providing security services to TCP clients by way of a Berkeley sockets-style API. It was initially developed by Netscape Communications Corporation to secure the HTTP protocol between web clients and servers, and that is still its primary use, though nothing about it is specific to HTTP. It is on the IETF standards track as RFC-2246, under the name "TLS" for Transport Layer Security.

An SSL participant proves its identity by a *digital certificate*, a set of cryptographic data. A certificate indicates that a trusted third party has verified the binding between an identity and a given cryptographic key. Web browsers automatically check the certificate provided by a web server when they connect by SSL, ensuring that the server is the one the user intended to contact. Thereafter, transmissions between the browser and the web server are encrypted.

SSL is used most often for web applications, but it can also "tunnel" other protocols. It is secure only if a "trusted third party" exists. Organizations known as *certificate authorities* (CAs) serve this function. If a company wants a certificate from the CA, the company must prove its identity to the CA through other means, such as legal documents. Once the proof is sufficient, the CA issues the certificate.

For more information, visit the OpenSSL project at:

> *http://www.openssl.org/*

1.6.7. SSL-Enhanced Telnet and FTP

Numerous TCP-based communication programs have been enhanced with SSL, including *telnet* (e.g., SSLtelnet, SRA telnet, SSLTel, STel) and *ftp* (SSLftp), providing some of the functionality of SSH. Though useful, these tools are fairly single-purpose and typically are patched or hacked versions of programs not originally written for secure communication. The major SSH implementations, on the other hand, are more like integrated toolsets with diverse uses, written from the ground up for security.

1.6.8. stunnel

stunnel is an SSL tool created by Micha Trojnara of Poland. It adds SSL protection to existing TCP-based services in a Unix environment, such as POP or IMAP servers, without requiring changes to the server source code. It can be invoked from *inetd* as a wrapper for any number of service daemons or run standalone, accepting network connections itself for a particular service. *stunnel* performs authentication and authorization of incoming connections via SSL; if the connection is allowed, it runs the server and implements an SSL-protected session between the client and server programs.

This is especially useful because certain popular applications have the option of running some client/server protocols over SSL. For instance, both Netscape Communicator and Microsoft Internet Explorer allow you to connect POP, IMAP, and SMTP servers using SSL. For more *stunnel* information, see:

http://mike.daewoo.com.pl/computer/stunnel/

1.6.9. Firewalls

A *firewall* is a hardware device or software program that prevents certain data from entering or exiting a network. For example, a firewall placed between a web site and the Internet might permit only HTTP and HTTPS traffic to reach the site. As another example, a firewall can reject all TCP/IP packets unless they originate from a designated set of network addresses.

Firewalls aren't a replacement for SSH or other authentication and encryption approaches, but they do address similar problems. The techniques may be used together.

1.7. Summary

SSH is a powerful, convenient approach to protecting communications on a computer network. Through secure authentication and encryption technologies, SSH supports secure remote logins, secure remote command execution, secure file transfers, access control, TCP/IP port forwarding, and other important features.

In this chapter:

- *A Running Example*
- *Remote Terminal Sessions with ssh*
- *Adding Complexity to the Example*
- *Authentication by Cryptographic Key*
- *The SSH Agent*
- *Connecting Without a Password or Passphrase*
- *Miscellaneous Clients*
- *Summary*

2

Basic Client Use

SSH is a simple idea, but it has many complex parts. This chapter is designed to get you started with SSH quickly. We cover the basics of SSH's most immediately useful features:

- Logging into a remote computer over a secure connection
- Transferring files between computers over a secure connection

We also introduce authentication with cryptographic keys, a more secure alternative to ordinary passwords. Advanced uses of client programs, such as multiple keys, client configuration files, and TCP port forwarding, will be covered in later chapters.

We use SSH1 and SSH2 (and occasionally OpenSSH) for all examples. If the syntax differs among the products, we'll discuss each of them.

2.1. A Running Example

Suppose you're out of town on a business trip and want to read your email, which sits on a Unix machine belonging to your ISP, *shell.isp.com*. A friend at a nearby university agrees to let you log into her Unix account on the machine *local.university.edu*, and then remotely log into yours. For the remote login you could use the *telnet* or *rlogin* programs, but as we've seen, this connection between the machines is insecure. (No doubt some subversive college student would grab your password and turn your account into a renegade web server for pirated software and Ani DiFranco MP3s.) Fortunately, both your friend's Unix machine and your ISP's have an SSH product installed.

In the example running through the chapter, we represent the shell prompt of the local machine, *local.university.edu*, as a dollar sign ($) and the prompt on *shell.isp.com* as `shell.isp.com>`.

2.2. Remote Terminal Sessions with ssh

Suppose your remote username on *shell.isp.com* is "pat". To connect to your remote account from your friend's account on *local.university.edu*, you type:

```
$ ssh -l pat shell.isp.com
pat's password: ******
Last login: Mon May 24 19:32:51 1999 from quondam.nefertiti.org
You have new mail.
shell.isp.com>
```

This leads to the situation shown in Figure 2-1. The *ssh* command runs a client that contacts the SSH server on *shell.isp.com* over the Internet, asking to be logged into the remote account with username pat.* You can also provide *user@host* syntax instead of the *–l* option to accomplish the same thing:

```
$ ssh pat@shell.isp.com
```

Figure 2-1. Our example scenario

On first contact, SSH establishes a secure channel between the client and the server so all transmissions between them are encrypted. The client then prompts for your password, which it supplies to the server over the secure channel. The server authenticates you by checking that the password is correct and permits the login. All subsequent client/server exchanges are protected by that secure channel, including the contents of the email you proceed to read using a mail program on *shell.isp.com.*

It's important to remember that the secure channel exists only between the SSH client and server machines. After logging into *shell.isp.com* via *ssh*, if you then *telnet* or *ftp* to a third machine, *insecure.isp.com*, the connection between

* If the local and remote usernames are identical, you can omit the *–l* option (*–l pat*) and just type `ssh shell.isp.com`.

shell.isp.com and *insecure.isp.com* is not secure. However, you can run another *ssh* client from *shell.isp.com* to *insecure.isp.com*, creating another secure channel, which keeps the chain of connections secure.

We've covered only the simplest use of *ssh*. Chapter 7 goes into far greater depth about its many features and options.

2.2.1. File Transfer with scp

Continuing the story, suppose that while reading your email, you encounter a message with an attached file you'd like to print. In order to send the file to a local printer at the university, you must first transfer the file to *local.university.edu*. Once again, you reject as insecure the traditional file-transfer programs, such as *ftp* and *rcp*. Instead, you use another SSH client program, *scp*, to copy the file across the network via a secure channel.

First, you write the attachment to a file in your home directory on *shell.isp.com* using your mail client, naming the file *print-me*. When you've finished reading your other email messages, log out of *shell.isp.com*, ending the SSH session and returning to the shell prompt on *local.university.edu*. You're now ready to copy the file securely.

The *scp* program has syntax much like the traditional Unix *cp* program and nearly identical to the insecure *rcp* program. It is roughly:

```
scp name-of-source name-of-destination
```

In this example, *scp* copies the file *print-me* on *shell.isp.com* over the network to a local file in your friend's account on *local.university.edu*, also called *print-me*:

```
$ scp pat@shell.isp.com:print-me print-me
```

The file is transferred over an SSH-secured connection. The source and destination files may be specified not only by filename, but also by username ("pat" in our example) and hostname (*shell.isp.com*), indicating the location of the file on the network. Depending on your needs, various parts of the source or destination name can be omitted, and defaults values used. For example, omitting the username and the "at" sign (pat@) makes *scp* assume that the remote username is the same as the local one.

Like *ssh*, *scp* prompts for your remote password and passes it to the SSH server for verification. If successful, *scp* logs into the pat account on *shell.isp.com*, copies your remote file *print-me* to the local file *print-me*, and logs out of *shell.isp.com*. The local file *print-me* may now be sent to a printer.

The destination filename need not be the same as the remote one. For example, if you're feeling French, you could call the local file *imprime-moi*:

```
$ scp pat@shell.isp.com:print-me imprime-moi
```

The full syntax of *scp* can represent local and remote files in powerful ways, and the program also has numerous command-line options. [7.5]

2.3. Adding Complexity to the Example

The preceding example session provided a quick introduction to the most often-used client programs—*ssh* and *scp*—in a format to follow while sitting at your computer. Now that you have the basics, let's continue the example but include situations and complications glossed over the first time. These include the "known hosts" security feature and the SSH escape character.

If you're following at the computer as you read, your SSH clients might behave unexpectedly or differently from ours. As you will see throughout the book, SSH implementations are highly customizable, by both yourself and the system administrator, on either side of the secure connection. Although this chapter describes common behaviors of SSH programs based on their installation defaults, your system might be set up differently.

If commands don't work as you expect, try adding the *–v* ("verbose") command-line option, for example:

```
$ ssh -v shell.isp.com
```

This causes the client to print lots of information about its progress, often revealing the source of the discrepancy.

2.3.1. Known Hosts

The first time an SSH client encounters a new remote machine, it does some extra work and prints a message like the following:

```
$ ssh -l pat shell.isp.com
Host key not found from the list of known hosts.
Are you sure you want to continue connecting (yes/no)?
```

Assuming you respond **yes** (the most common response), the client continues:

```
Host 'shell.isp.com' added to the list of known hosts.
```

This message appears only the first time you contact a particular remote host. The message is a security feature related to SSH's concept of *known hosts.*

Suppose an adversary wants to obtain your password. He knows you are using SSH, and so he can't monitor your connection by eavesdropping on the network.

Instead, he subverts the naming service used by your local host so that the name of your intended remote host, *shell.isp.com*, translates falsely to the IP address of a computer run by him! He then installs an altered SSH server on the phony remote host and waits. When you log in via your trusty SSH client, the altered SSH server records your password for the adversary's later use (or misuse, more likely). The bogus server can then disconnect with a preplanned error message such as "System down for maintenance—please try again after 4:00 p.m." Even worse, it can fool you completely by using your password to log into the real *shell.isp.com* and transparently pass information back and forth between you and the server, monitoring your entire session. This hostile strategy is called a man-in-the-middle attack. [3.10.4] Unless you think to check the originating IP address of your session on the server, you might never notice the deception.

The SSH *known-host mechanism* prevents such attacks. When an SSH client and server make a connection, each of them proves its identity to the other. Yes, not only does the server authenticate the client, as we saw earlier when the server checked pat's password, but the client also authenticates the server by public-key cryptography. [3.4.1] In short, each SSH server has a secret, unique ID, called a *host key*, to identify itself to clients. The first time you connect to a remote host, a public counterpart of the host key gets copied and stored in your local account (assuming you responded "yes" to the client's prompt about host keys, earlier). Each time you reconnect to that remote host, the SSH client checks the remote host's identity using this public key.

Of course, it's better to have recorded the server's public host key before connecting to it the first time, since otherwise you are technically open to a man-in-the-middle attack that first time. Administrators can maintain system-wide known-hosts lists for given sets of hosts, but this doesn't do much good for connecting to random new hosts around the world. Until a reliable, widely deployed method of retrieving such keys securely exists (such as secure DNS, or X.509-based public-key infrastructure), this record-on-first-use mechanism is an acceptable compromise.

If authentication of the server fails, various things may happen depending on the reason for failure and the SSH configuration. Typically a warning appears on the screen, ranging from a repeat of the known-hosts message:

```
Host key not found from the list of known hosts.
Are you sure you want to continue connecting (yes/no)?
```

to more dire words:

```
@@@@@@@@@@@@@@@@@@@@@@@@@@@@@@@@@@@@@@@@@@@@@@@@@@@@@@@
@    WARNING: HOST IDENTIFICATION HAS CHANGED!       @
@@@@@@@@@@@@@@@@@@@@@@@@@@@@@@@@@@@@@@@@@@@@@@@@@@@@@@@
IT IS POSSIBLE THAT SOMEONE IS DOING SOMETHING NASTY!
Someone could be eavesdropping on you right now (man-in-the-middle attack)!
It is also possible that the host key has just been changed.
```

```
Please contact your system administrator.
Add correct host key in <path>/known_hosts to get rid of this message.
Agent forwarding is disabled to avoid attacks by corrupted servers.
X11 forwarding is disabled to avoid attacks by corrupted servers.
Are you sure you want to continue connecting (yes/no)
```

If you answer `yes`, *ssh* allows the connection, but disables various features as a security precaution and doesn't update your personal known-hosts database with the new key; you must do that yourself to make this message go away.

As the text of the message says, if you see this warning, you aren't necessarily being hacked: for example, the remote host may have legitimately changed its host key for some reason. In some cases, even after reading this book, you won't know the cause of these messages. Contact your system administrator if you need assistance, rather than take a chance and possibly compromise your password. We'll cover these issues further when we discuss personal known hosts databases and how to alter the behavior of SSH clients with respect to host keys. [7.4.3]

2.3.2. The Escape Character

Let us return to the *shell.isp.com* example, just after you'd discovered the attachment in your remote email message and saved it to the remote file *print-me*. In our original example, you then logged out of *shell.isp.com* and ran *scp* to transfer the file. But what if you don't want to log out? If you're using a workstation running a window system, you can open a new window and run *scp*. But if you're using a lowly text terminal, or you're not familiar with the window system running on your friend's computer, there is an alternative. You can temporarily interrupt the SSH connection, transfer the file (and run any other local commands you desire), and then resume the connection.

ssh supports an *escape character*, a designated character that gets the attention of the SSH client. Normally, *ssh* sends every character you type to the server, but the escape character is caught by the client, alerting it that special commands may follow. By default, the escape character is the tilde (~), but you can change it. To reduce the chances of sending the escape character unintentionally, that character must be the first character on the command line, i.e., following a newline (`Control-J`) or return (`Control-M`) character. If not, the client treats it literally, not as an escape character.

After the escape character gets the client's attention, the next character entered determines the effect of the escape. For example, the escape character followed by a `Control-Z` suspends *ssh* like any other shell job, returning control to the local shell. Such a pair of characters is called an *escape sequence*. Table 2-1 summarizes the supported escape sequences. It's followed by a list that describes each sequence's meaning.

Table 2-1. ssh Escape Sequences

Sequence	Example with <ESC> = ~	Meaning
`<ESC> ^Z`	`~ ^Z`	Suspend the connection (`^Z` means `Control-Z`)
`<ESC> .`	`~ .`	Terminate the connection
`<ESC> #`	`~ #`	List all forwarded connections[a]
`<ESC> &`	`~ &`	Send *ssh* into the background (when waiting for connections to terminate)[a]
<ESC> r	~ r	Request rekeying immediately (SSH2 only)
<ESC><ESC>	~ ~	Send the escape character (by typing it twice)
`<ESC> ?`	`~ ?`	Print a help message
`<ESC> -`	`~ -`	Disable the escape character (SSH2 only)
`<ESC> V`	`~ V`	Print version information (SSH2 only)
`<ESC> s`	`~ s`	Print statistics about this session (SSH2 only)

[a] For SSH2, this option is documented but not implemented as of Version 2.3.0.

- "Suspend the connection" puts *ssh* into the background, suspended, returning control of the terminal to the local shell. To return to *ssh*, use the appropriate job control command of your shell, typically *fg*. While suspended, *ssh* doesn't run, and if left suspended long enough, the connection may terminate since the client isn't responding to the server. Also, any forwarded connections are similarly blocked while *ssh* is suspended. [9.2.9]
- "Terminate the connection" ends the SSH session immediately. This is most useful if you have lost control of the session: for instance, if a shell command on the remote host has hung and become unkillable. Any X or TCP port forwardings are terminated immediately as well. [9.2.9]
- "List all forwarded connections" prints a list of each X forwarding or TCP port forwarding connection currently established. This lists only active instances of forwarding; if forwarding services are available but not currently in use, nothing is listed here.
- "Send ssh into the background," like the "suspend connection" command, reconnects your terminal to the shell that started *ssh*, but it doesn't suspend the *ssh* process. Instead, *ssh* continues to run. This isn't ordinarily useful, since the backgrounded *ssh* process immediately encounters an error.* This escape sequence becomes useful if your *ssh* session has active, forwarded connections when you log out. Normally in this situation, the client prints a message:

* The error occurs as *ssh* attempts to read input from the now disconnected pseudo-terminal.

```
Waiting for forwarded connections to terminate...
The following connections are open:
X11 connection from shell.isp.com port 1996
```

as it waits for the forwarded connections to close before it exits. While the client is in this state, this escape sequence returns you to the local shell prompt.

- "Request rekeying immediately" causes the SSH2 client and server to generate and use some new internal keys for encryption and integrity.
- "Send the escape character" tells the client to send a real tilde (or whatever the escape character is) to the SSH server as plaintext, not to interpret it as an escape. "Disable the escape character" prevents further escape sequences from having any effect. The rest of the escape sequences are self-explanatory.

To change the *ssh* escape character, use the *–e* command-line option. For example, type the following to make the percent sign (%) the escape character when connecting to *shell.isp.com* as user pat:

```
$ ssh -e "%" -l pat shell.isp.com
```

2.4. Authentication by Cryptographic Key

In our running example, the user pat is authenticated by the SSH server via login password. Passwords, however, have serious drawbacks:

- In order for a password to be secure, it should be long and random, but such passwords are hard to memorize.
- A password sent across the network, even protected by an SSH secure channel, can be captured when it arrives on the remote host if that host has been compromised.
- Most operating systems support only a single password per account. For shared accounts (e.g., a superuser account), this presents difficulties:
  - Password changes are inconvenient because the new password must be communicated to all people with access to the account.
  - Tracking usage of the account becomes difficult because the operating system doesn't distinguish between the different users of the account.

To address these problems, SSH supports *public-key authentication*: instead of relying on the password scheme of the host operating system, SSH may use cryptographic *keys*. [3.2.2] Keys are more secure than passwords in general and address all the weaknesses mentioned earlier.

2.4.1. A Brief Introduction to Keys

A key is a digital identity. It's a unique string of binary data that means, "This is me, honestly, I swear." And with a little cryptographic magic, your SSH client can prove to a server that its key is genuine, and you are really you.

An SSH identity uses a pair of keys, one private and one public. The *private key* is a closely guarded secret only you have. Your SSH clients use it to prove your identity to servers. The *public key* is, like the name says, public. You place it freely into your accounts on SSH server machines. During authentication, the SSH client and server have a little conversation about your private and public key. If they match (according to a cryptographic test), your identity is proven, and authentication succeeds.

The following sequence demonstrates the conversation between client and server. [3.4.1] (It occurs behind the scenes, so you don't need to memorize it or anything; we just thought you might be interested.)

1. Your client says, "Hey server, I'd like to connect by SSH to an account on your system, specifically, the account owned by user smith."
2. The server says, "Well, maybe. First, I challenge you to prove your identity!" And the server sends some data, known as a *challenge,* to the client.
3. Your client says, "I accept your challenge. Here is proof of my identity. I made it myself by mathematically using your challenge and my private key." This response to the server is called an *authenticator*.
4. The server says, "Thanks for the authenticator. I will now examine the smith account to see if you may enter." Specifically, the server checks smith's public keys to see if the authenticator "matches" any of them. (The "match" is another cryptographic operation.) If so, the server says, "OK, come on in!" Otherwise, the authentication fails.

Before you can use public-key authentication, some setup is required:

1. You need a private key and a public key, known collectively as a *key pair.* You also need a secret passphrase to protect your private key. [2.4.2]
2. You need to install your public key on an SSH server machine. [2.4.3]

2.4.2. Generating Key Pairs with ssh-keygen

To use cryptographic authentication, you must first generate a key pair for yourself, consisting of a private key (your digital identity that sits on the client machine) and a public key (that sits on the server machine). To do this, use the *ssh-keygen* program. Its behavior differs for SSH1, SSH2, and OpenSSH. On an SSH1 system, the program is called *ssh-keygen* or *ssh-keygen1*. When you invoke it, *ssh-keygen* creates an RSA key pair and asks you for a secret passphrase to protect the private key.*

```
$ ssh-keygen1
Initializing random number generator...
Generating p:  .................................++ (distance 1368)
Generating q:  ....++ (distance 58)
Computing the keys...
Testing the keys...
Key generation complete.
Enter file in which to save the key (/home/pat/.ssh/identity):
Enter passphrase: **************
Enter the same passphrase again: **************
Your identification has been saved in identity.
Your public key is:
1024 35 11272721957877936880509167858732970485872567486703821636830\
1950099934876023218886571857276011133767701853088352661186539160906\
9214986989240214507621864063548908730298546478215446737245984456708\
9631066077107611074114663544313782992987840457273825436579285836220\
249339573064845129660159434497929045742180923 6729 path@shell.isp.com
Your public key has been saved in identity.pub.
```

On SSH2 systems, the command is either *ssh-keygen* or *ssh-keygen2*, and its behavior is a bit different and produces either a DSA key (the default) or an RSA key:

```
$ ssh-keygen2
Generating 1024-bit dsa key pair
   1 ..oOo.oOo.oO
   2 o.oOo.oOo.oO
   3 o.oOo.oOo.oO
   4 o.oOo.oOo.oO
Key generated.
1024-bit dsa, created by pat@shell.isp.com Mon Mar 20 13:01:15 2000
Passphrase : **************
Again      : **************
Private key saved to /home/pat/.ssh2/id_dsa_1024_a
Public key saved to /home/pat/.ssh2/id_dsa_1024_a.pub
```

The OpenSSH version of *ssh-keygen* also can produce either RSA or DSA keys, defaulting to RSA. Its operation is similar to that of *ssh-keygen1*.

Normally, *ssh-keygen* performs all necessary mathematics to generate a key, but on some operating systems you might be asked to assist it. Key generation requires some random numbers, and if your operating system doesn't supply a random-number generator, you may be asked to type some random text. *ssh-keygen* uses the timings of your keystrokes to initialize its internal random-number generator. On a 300-MHz Pentium system running Linux, generating a 1024-bit RSA key takes about three seconds; if your hardware is slower than this or heavily loaded,

* RSA is an encryption algorithm for SSH keys, among other things. [3.9.1] DSA is another, as you'll see later.

generation may take significantly longer, up to a minute or more. It can also take longer if the process runs out of random bits, and *ssh-keygen* has to wait to collect more.

ssh-keygen then creates your local SSH directory (*~/.ssh* for SSH1 and OpenSSH or *~/.ssh2* for SSH2) if it doesn't already exist, and stores the private and public components of the generated key in two files there. By default, their names are *identity* and *identity.pub* (SSH1, OpenSSH) or *id_dsa_1024_a* and *id_dsa_1024_a.pub* (SSH2). SSH clients consider these to be your default identity for authentication purposes.

Never reveal your private key and passphrase to anyone else. They are just as sensitive as your login password. Anyone possessing them can log in as you!

When created, the identity file is readable only by your account, and its contents are further protected by encrypting them with the passphrase you supplied during generation. We say "passphrase" instead of "password" both to differentiate it from a login password, and to stress that spaces and punctuation are allowed and encouraged. We recommend a passphrase at least 10–15 characters long and not a grammatical sentence.

ssh-keygen has numerous options for managing keys: changing the passphrase, choosing a different name for the key file, and so forth. [6.2]

2.4.3. Installing a Public Key on an SSH Server Machine

When passwords are used for authentication, the host operating system maintains the association between the username and the password. For cryptographic keys, you must set up a similar association manually. After creating the key pair on the local host, you must install your public key in your account on the remote host. A remote account may have many public keys installed for accessing it in various ways.

Returning to our running example, you must install a public key into the "pat" account on *shell.isp.com*. This is done by editing a file in the SSH configuration directory: *~/.ssh/authorized_keys* for SSH1 and OpenSSH* or *~/.ssh2/authorization* for SSH2.

* OpenSSH uses *authorized_keys2* for SSH-2 connections. For simplicity, we'll discuss OpenSSH later. [8.2.3]

For SSH1 or OpenSSH, create or edit the file *~/.ssh/authorized_keys* and append your public key, i.e., the contents of the *identity.pub* file you generated on the local machine. A typical *authorized_keys* file contains a list of public key data, one key per line. The example contains only two public keys, each on its own line of the file, but they are too long to fit on this page. The line breaks inside the long numbers are printing artifact; if they were actually in the file, it would be incorrectly formatted and wouldn't work:

```
1024 35 8697511247987525784866526224505474204292260357215616159982327587956883143
362147028876494426516682677550219425827002174890309672203219700937187777979705864
107549106608811204142046600066790196940691100768682518506600601481676686828742807
11088849408310989234142475694298520575977312478025518391 my personal key
1024 37 1140868200916227508775331982659387253607752793422843620910258618820621996
941824516069319525136671585267698112659690736259150374130846896838697083490981532
877352706061107257845462743793679411866715467672826112629198483320167783914580965
674001731023872042965273839192998250061795483568436433123392629 my work key
```

These are RSA public keys: the first number in each entry is the number of bits in the key, while the second and third are RSA-specific parameters called the *public exponent* and *modulus*. After these comes an arbitrary amount of text treated as a comment. [8.2.1]

For SSH2, you need to edit two files, one on the client machine and one on the server machine. On the client machine, create or edit the file *~/.ssh2/identification* and insert a line to identify your private key file:

```
IdKey id_dsa_1024_a
```

On the server machine, create or edit the file *~/.ssh2/authorization*, which contains information about public keys, one per line. But unlike SSH1's *authorized_keys* file, which contains copies of the public keys, the *authorization* file lists only the filename of the key:

```
Key id_dsa_1024_a.pub
```

Finally, copy *id_dsa_1024_a.pub* from your local machine to the remote SSH2 server machine, placing it in *~/.ssh2*.

Regardless of which SSH implementation you use, make sure your remote SSH directory and associated files are writable only by your account:*

```
# SSH1, OpenSSH
$ chmod 755 ~/.ssh
$ chmod 644 ~/.ssh/authorized_keys

# OpenSSH only
$ chmod 644 ~/.ssh/authorized_keys2
```

* We make files world-readable and directories world-searchable, to avoid NFS problems. [10.7.2]

```
# SSH2 only
$ chmod 755 ~/.ssh2
$ chmod 644 ~/.ssh2/id_dsa_1024_a.pub
$ chmod 644 ~/.ssh2/authorization
```

The SSH server is picky about file and directory permissions and may refuse authentication if the remote account's SSH configuration files have insecure permissions. [5.4.2.1]

You are now ready to use your new key to access the "pat" account:

```
# SSH1, SSH2, OpenSSH; output shown is for SSH1
$ ssh -l pat shell.isp.com
Enter passphrase for RSA key 'Your Name <you@local.org>': ************
Last login: Mon May 24 19:44:21 1999 from quincunx.nefertiti.org
You have new mail.
shell.isp.com>
```

If all goes well, you are logged into the remote account. Figure 2-2 shows the entire process.

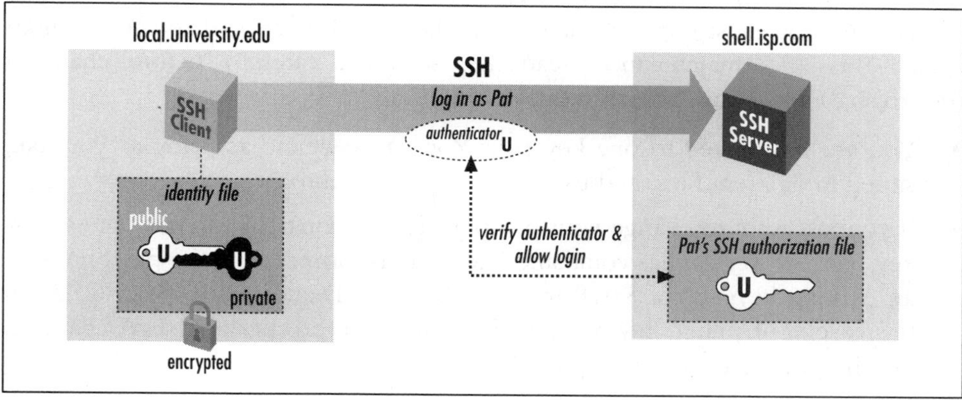

Figure 2-2. Public-key authentication

Note the similarity to the earlier example with password authentication. [2.2] On the surface, the only difference is that you provide the passphrase to your private key, instead of providing your login password. Underneath, however, something quite different is happening. In password authentication, the password is transmitted to the remote host. With cryptographic authentication, the passphrase serves only to decrypt the private key to create an authenticator. [2.4.1]

Public-key authentication is more secure than password authentication because:

- It requires two secret components—the identity file on disk, and the passphrase in your head—so both must be captured in order for an adversary to access your account. Password authentication requires only one component, the password, which might be easier to steal.

- Neither the passphrase nor the key is sent to the remote host, just the authenticator discussed earlier. Therefore, no secret information is transmitted off the client machine.
- Machine-generated cryptographic keys are infeasible to guess. Human-generated passwords are routinely cracked by a password-guessing technique called a *dictionary attack*. A dictionary attack may be mounted on the passphrase as well, but this requires stealing the private key file first.

A host's security can be greatly increased by disabling password authentication altogether and permitting only SSH connections by key.

2.4.4. If You Change Your Key

Suppose you have generated a key pair, *identity* and *identity.pub*, and copied *identity.pub* to a bunch of SSH server machines. All is well. Then one day, you decide to change your identity, so you run *ssh-keygen* a second time, overwriting *identity* and *identity.pub*. Guess what? Your previous public key file is now invalid, and you must copy the new public key to all those SSH server machines again. This is a maintenance headache, so think carefully before changing (destroying!) a key pair. Some caveats:

- You are not limited to one key pair. You can generate as many as you like, stored in different files, and use them for diverse purposes. [6.4]
- If you just want to change your passphrase, you don't have to generate a new key pair. *ssh-keygen* has command-line options for replacing the passphrase of an existing key: *–p* for SSH1 and OpenSSH [6.2.1] and *–e* for SSH2 [6.2.2]. In this case your public key remains valid since the private key hasn't changed, just the passphrase for decrypting it.

2.5. The SSH Agent

Each time you run *ssh* or *scp* with public-key authentication, you have to retype your passphrase. The first few times you might not mind, but eventually this retyping gets annoying. Wouldn't it be nicer to identify yourself just once and have *ssh* and *scp* remember your identity until further notice (for example, until you log out), not prompting for your passphrase? In fact, this is just what an *SSH agent* does for you.

An agent is a program that keeps private keys in memory and provides authentication services to SSH clients. If you preload an agent with private keys at the beginning of a login session, your SSH clients won't prompt for passphrases. Instead, they communicate with the agent as needed. The effects of the agent last until you terminate the agent, usually just before logging out. The agent program for SSH1, SSH2, and OpenSSH is called *ssh-agent*.

Generally, you run a single *ssh-agent* in your local login session, before running any SSH clients. You can run the agent by hand, but people usually edit their login files (for example, *~/.login* or *~/.xsession*) to run the agent automatically. SSH clients communicate with the agent via the process environment,* so all clients (and all other processes) within your login session have access to the agent. To try the agent, type:

```
$ ssh-agent $SHELL
```

where SHELL is the environment variable containing the name of your login shell. Alternatively, you could supply the name of any other shell, such as *sh*, *bash*, *csh*, *tcsh*, or *ksh*. The agent runs and then invokes the given shell as a child process. The visual effect is simply that another shell prompt appears, but this shell has access to the agent.

Once the agent is running, it's time to load private keys into it using the *ssh-add* program. By default, *ssh-add* loads the key from your default identity file:

```
$ ssh-add
Need passphrase for /u/you/.ssh/identity ('Your Name <you@local.org>').
Enter passphrase: ************
Identity added: /u/you/.ssh/identity ('Your Name <you@local.org>').
```

Now *ssh* and *scp* can connect to remote hosts without prompting for your passphrase. Figure 2-3 shows the process.

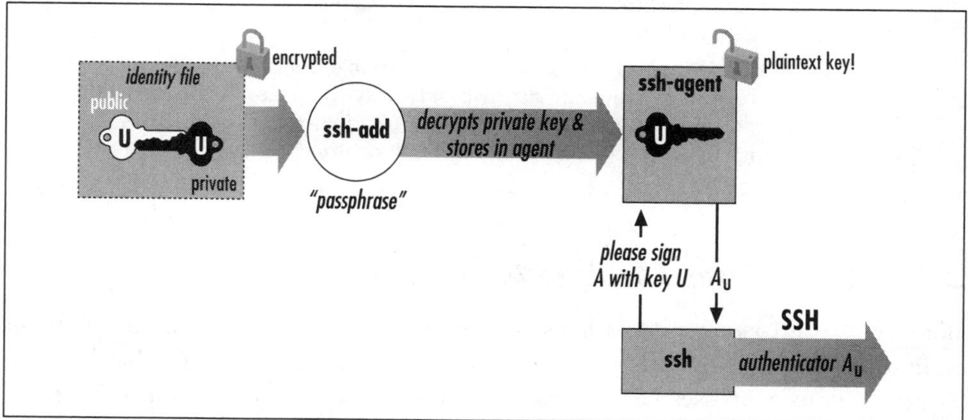

Figure 2-3. How the SSH agent works

* In Unix, they talk to the agent over a named pipe whose filename is stored in an environment variable. [6.3.2]

ssh-add reads the passphrase from your terminal by default or optionally from standard input noninteractively. Otherwise, if you are running the X Window System with the DISPLAY environment variable set, and standard input isn't a terminal, *ssh-add* reads your passphrase using a graphical X program, *ssh-askpass*. This behavior is useful when calling *ssh-add* from X session setup scripts.*

ssh-add has further capabilities, particularly in SSH2, and can operate with multiple identity files. [6.3.3] For now, here are a few useful commands. To load a key other than your default identity into the agent, provide the filename as an argument to *ssh-add*:

```
$ ssh-add my-other-key-file
```

You can also list the keys the agent currently holds:

```
$ ssh-add -l
```

delete a key from the agent:

```
$ ssh-add -d name-of-key-file
```

or delete all keys from the agent:

```
$ ssh-add -D
```

When running an SSH agent, don't leave your terminal unattended while logged in. While your private keys are loaded in an agent, anyone may use your terminal to connect to any remote accounts accessible via those keys, without needing your passphrase! Even worse, a sophisticated intruder can extract your keys from the running agent and steal them.

If you use an agent, make sure to lock your terminal if you leave it while logged in. You can also use `ssh-add -D` to clear your loaded keys and reload them when you return. In addition, *ssh-agent2* has a "locking" feature that can protect it from unauthorized users. [6.3.3]

2.5.1. Other Uses For Agents

Because *ssh* and *rsh* command lines have such similar syntax, you naturally might want to replace *rsh* with *ssh*. Suppose you have an automation script that uses *rsh* to run remote processes. If you use *ssh* instead, your script prompts for passphrases, which is inconvenient for automation. If the script runs *ssh* many times, retyping that passphrase repeatedly is both annoying and error-prone. If you run an agent, however, the script can run without a single passphrase prompt. [11.1]

* To force *ssh-add* to use X to read the passphrase, type `ssh-add < /dev/null` at a command line.

2.5.2. A More Complex Passphrase Problem

In our running example, we copied a file from the remote to the local host:

```
$ scp pat@shell.isp.com:print-me imprime-moi
```

In fact, *scp* can copy a file from remote host *shell.isp.com* directly to a third host running SSH on which you have an account named, say, "psmith":

```
$ scp pat@shell.isp.com:print-me psmith@other.host.net:imprime-moi
```

Rather than copying the file first to the local host and then back out again to the final destination, this command has *shell.isp.com* send it directly to *other.host.net*. However, if you try this, you will run into the following problem:

```
$ scp pat@shell.isp.com:print-me psmith@other.host.net:imprime-moi
Enter passphrase for RSA key 'Your Name <you@local.org>': ************
You have no controlling tty and no DISPLAY.  Cannot read passphrase.
lost connection
```

What happened? When you run *scp* on your local machine, it contacts *shell.isp.com* and internally invokes a second *scp* command to do the copy. Unfortunately, the second *scp* command also needs the passphrase for your private key. Since there is no terminal session to prompt for the passphrase, the second *scp* fails, causing the original *scp* to fail. The SSH agent solves this problem: the second *scp* command simply queries your local SSH agent, so no passphrase prompting is needed.

The SSH agent also solves another more subtle problem in this example. Without the agent, the second *scp* (on *shell.isp.com*) needs access to your private key file, but the file is on your local machine. So you have to copy your private key file to *shell.isp.com*. This isn't ideal; what if *shell.isp.com* isn't a secure machine? Also, the solution doesn't scale: if you have a dozen different accounts, it is a maintenance headache to keep your private key file on all of them. Fortunately, the SSH agent comes to the rescue once again. The remote *scp* process simply contacts your local SSH agent, authenticates, and the secure copy proceeds successfully, through a process called agent forwarding.

2.5.3. Agent Forwarding

In the preceding example, the remote instance of *scp* has no direct access to your private key, since the agent is running on the local host, not the remote. SSH provides *agent forwarding* [6.3.5] to address this problem.

When agent forwarding is turned on,* the remote SSH server masquerades as a second *ssh-agent* as shown in Figure 2-4. It takes authentication requests from

* It is on by default in SSH1 and SSH2, but off in OpenSSH.

your SSH client processes there, passes them back over the SSH connection to the local agent for handling, and relays the results back to the remote clients. In short, remote clients transparently get access to the local *ssh-agent.* Since any programs executed via *ssh* on the remote side are children of the server, they all have access to the local agent just as if they were running on the local host.

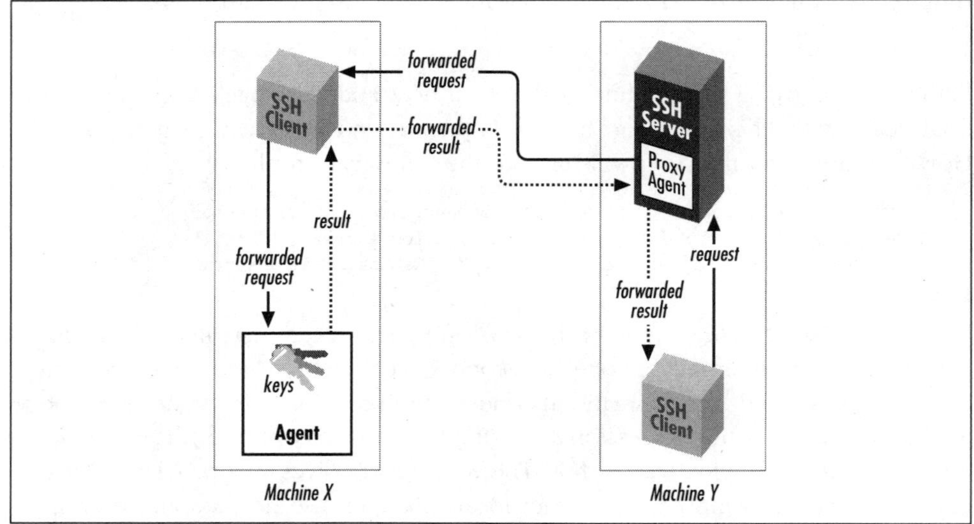

Figure 2-4. How agent forwarding works

In our double-remote *scp* example, here is what happens when agent forwarding comes into play (see Figure 2-5):

1. You run the command on your local machine:

```
$ scp pat@shell.isp.com:print-me psmith@other.host.net:imprime-moi
```

2. This *scp* process contacts your local agent and authenticates you to *shell.isp.com.*

3. A second *scp* command is automatically launched on *shell.isp.com* to carry out the copy to *other.host.net.*

4. Since agent forwarding is turned on, the SSH server on *shell.isp.com* poses as an agent.

5. The second *scp* process tries to authenticate you to *other.host.net* by contacting the "agent" that is really the SSH server on *shell.isp.com.*

6. Behind the scenes, the SSH server on *shell.isp.com* communicates with your local agent, which constructs an authenticator proving your identity and passes it back to the server.

7. The server verifies your identity to the second *scp* process, and authentication succeeds on *other.host.net*.
8. The file copying occurs.

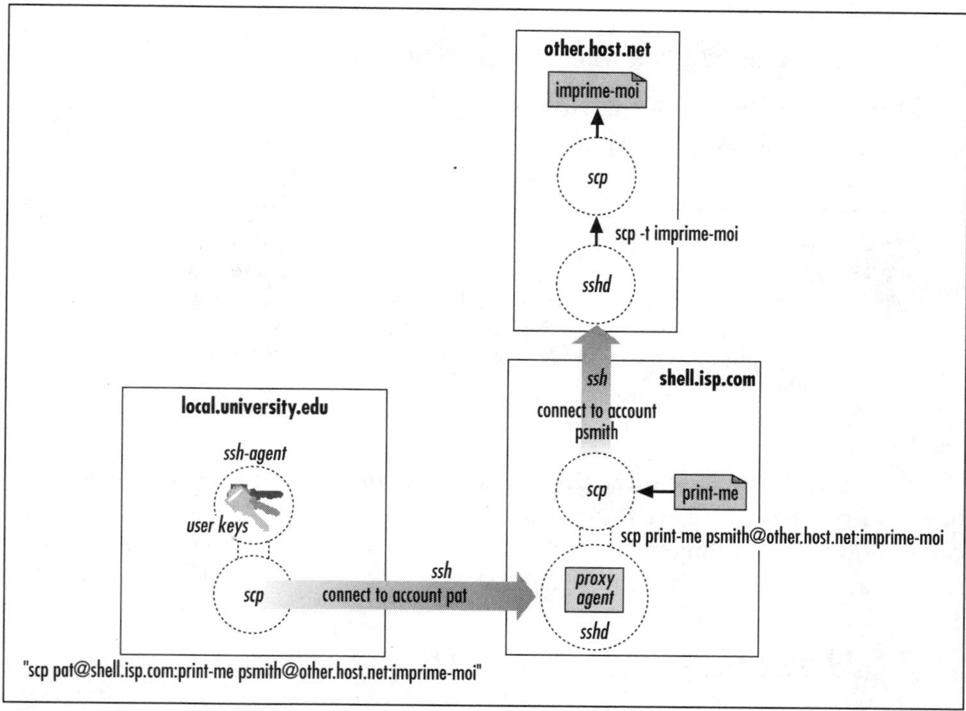

Figure 2-5. Third-party scp with agent forwarding

Agent forwarding works over multiple connections in a series, allowing you to *ssh* from one machine to another, and then to another, with the agent connection following along the whole way. These machines may be progressively less secure, but since agent forwarding doesn't send your private key to the remote host but rather relays authentication requests back to the first host for processing, your key stays safe.

2.6. Connecting Without a Password or Passphrase

One of the most frequently asked questions about SSH is: "How can I connect to a remote machine without having to type a password or passphrase?" As you've seen, an SSH agent can make this possible, but there are other methods as well, each with different tradeoffs. Here we list the available methods with pointers to the sections discussing each one.

To use SSH clients for *interactive sessions* without a password or passphrase, you have several options:

- Public-key authentication with an agent [2.5] [6.3]
- Trusted-host authentication [3.4.2.3]
- Kerberos authentication [11.4]

Another way to achieve password-less logins is to use an unencrypted private key with no passphrase. Although this technique can be appropriate for automation purposes, never do this for interactive use. Instead, use the SSH agent, which provides the same benefits with much greater security. Don't use unencrypted keys for interactive SSH!

On the other hand, noninteractive, unattended programs such as *cron* jobs or batch scripts may also benefit from not having a password or passphrase. In this case, the different techniques raise some complex issues, and we will discuss their relative merits and security issues later. [11.1]

2.7. Miscellaneous Clients

Several other clients are included in addition to *ssh* and *scp*:

- *sftp*, an *ftp*-like client for SSH2
- *slogin*, a link to *ssh*, analogous to the *rlogin* program
- Hostname links to *ssh*

2.7.1. sftp

The *scp* command is convenient and useful, but many users are already familiar with FTP (File Transfer Protocol), a more widely used technique for transferring files on the Internet.* *sftp* is a separate file-transfer tool layered on top of SSH. It was developed by SSH Communications Security and was originally available only in SSH2, but other implementations have since appeared (e.g., client support in SecureFX, and both a client and server in OpenSSH). The OpenSSH *sftp* can run

* Due to the nature of the FTP protocol, FTP clients are difficult to secure using TCP port forwarding, unlike most other TCP-based clients. [11.2]

over either SSH-1 or SSH-2, whereas the SSH2 version runs over SSH-2 only due to implementation details.

sftp is advantageous for several reasons:

- It is secure, using an SSH-protected channel for data transfer.
- Multiple commands for file copying and manipulation can be invoked within a single *sftp* session, whereas *scp* opens a new session each time it is invoked.
- It can be scripted using the familiar *ftp* command language.
- In other software applications that run an FTP client in the background, you can try substituting *sftp*, thus securing the file transfers of that application.

You may need an agent when trying this or similar FTP replacements, since programs that use FTP might not recognize the prompt *sftp* issues for your passphrase, or they might expect you to have suppressed FTP's password prompt (using a *.netrc* file, for example).

Anyone familiar with FTP will feel right at home with *sftp*, but *sftp* has some additional features of note:

- Command-line editing using GNU Emacs-like keystrokes (`Control-B` for backward character, `Control-E` for end of line, and so forth)
- Regular-expression matching for filenames, as documented in the *sshregex* manpage supplied with SSH2 and found in Appendix A
- Several command-line options:

  –b filename
  : Read commands from the given file instead of the terminal

  –S path
  : Locate the *ssh2* program using the given path

  –h Print a help message and exit

  –V Print the program version number and exit

  –D module=level
  : Print debugging output [5.8.2.2]

Also, *sftp* doesn't have the separate ASCII and binary transfer modes of standard FTP, only binary. All files are transferred literally. Therefore, if you copy ASCII text files between Windows and Unix with *sftp*, end-of-line characters aren't translated properly. Normally, FTP's ASCII mode translates between Windows' "carriage return plus newline" and Unix's newline, for example.

2.7.2. slogin

slogin is an alternative name for *ssh*, just as *rlogin* is a synonym for *rsh*. On Unix systems, *slogin* is simply a symbolic link to *ssh*. Note that the *slogin* link is found in SSH1 and OpenSSH but not SSH2. We recommend using just *ssh* for consistency: it's found in all these implementations and is shorter to type.

2.7.3. Hostname Links

ssh for SSH1 and OpenSSH also mimics *rlogin* in another respect: support for hostname links. If you make a link to the *ssh* executable, and the link name isn't in the set of standard names *ssh* recognizes,* *ssh* has special behavior. It treats the link name as a hostname and attempts to connect to that remote host. For example, if you create a link called *terpsichore.muses.org* and then run it:

```
$ ln -s /usr/local/bin/ssh terpsichore.muses.org
$ terpsichore.muses.org
Welcome to Terpsichore!  Last login January 21st, 201 B.C.
terpsichore>
```

It's equivalent to running:

```
$ ssh terpsichore.muses.org
Welcome to Terpsichore!  Last login January 21st, 201 B.C.
terpsichore>
```

You can create a collection of these links for all commonly used remote hosts. Note that support for hostname links has been removed in SSH2. (We have never found them to be very useful, ourselves, but the capability does exist in SSH1 and OpenSSH.)

2.8. Summary

From the user's point of view, SSH consists of several client programs and some configuration files. The most commonly used clients are *ssh* for remote login and *scp* for file transfer. Authentication to the remote host can be accomplished using existing login passwords or with public-key cryptographic techniques. Passwords are more immediately and easily used, but public-key authentication is more flexible and secure. The *ssh-keygen*, *ssh-agent*, and *ssh-add* programs generate and manage SSH keys.

* These are *rsh, ssh, rlogin, slogin, ssh1, slogin1, ssh.old, slogin.old, ssh1.old, slogin1.old,* and *remsh*.

3

Inside SSH

SSH secures your data while it passes over a network, but how exactly does it *work*? In this chapter, we move firmly onto technical ground and explain the inner workings of SSH. Let's roll up our sleeves and dive into the bits and bytes.

This chapter is written for system administrators, network administrators, and security professionals. Our goal is to teach you enough about SSH to make an intelligent, technically sound decision about using it. We cover the SSH-1 and SSH-2 protocols separately since they have important differences.

Of course, the ultimate references on SSH are the protocol standards and the source code of an implementation. We don't completely analyze the protocols or recapitulate every step taken by the software. Rather, we summarize them to provide a solid, technical overview of their operation. If you need more specifics, you should refer to the standards documents. The SSH Version 2 protocol is in draft status on the IETF standards track; it is available at:

http://www.ipsec.com/tech/archive/secsh.html
http://www.ietf.org/

The older protocol implemented in SSH1 and OpenSSH/1 is Version 1.5 and is documented in a file named *RFC* included in the SSH1 source package.

3.1. Overview of Features

The major features and guarantees of the SSH protocol are:

- *Privacy* of your data, via strong encryption
- *Integrity* of communications, guaranteeing they haven't been altered
- *Authentication,* i.e., proof of identity of senders and receivers
- *Authorization,* i.e., access control to accounts
- *Forwarding* or *tunneling* to encrypt other TCP/IP-based sessions

3.1.1. Privacy (Encryption)

Privacy means protecting data from disclosure. Typical computer networks don't guarantee privacy; anyone with access to the network hardware, or to hosts connected to the network may be able to read (or *sniff*) all data passing over the network. Although modern switched networks have reduced this problem in local area networks, it is still a serious issue; passwords are regularly stolen by such sniffing attacks.

SSH provides privacy by encrypting data that passes over the network. This end-to-end encryption is based on random keys that are securely negotiated for that session and then destroyed when the session is over. SSH supports a variety of encryption algorithms for session data, including such standard ciphers as ARCFOUR, Blowfish, DES, IDEA, and triple-DES (3DES).

3.1.2. Integrity

Integrity means assuring that data transmitted from one end of a network connection arrives unaltered on the other side. The underlying transport of SSH, TCP/IP, does have integrity checking to detect alteration due to network problems (electrical noise, lost packets due to excessive traffic, etc.). Nevertheless, these methods are ineffective against deliberate tampering and can be fooled by a clever attacker. Even though SSH encrypts the data stream so an attacker can't easily change selected parts to achieve a specific result, TCP/IP's integrity checking alone can't prevent, say, an attacker's deliberate injection of garbage into your session.

A more complex example is a *replay attack.* Imagine that Attila the Attacker is monitoring your SSH session and also simultaneously watching over your shoulder (either physically, or by monitoring your keystrokes at your terminal). In the course of your work, Attila sees you type the command `rm -rf *` within a small directory. He can't read the encrypted SSH session data, of course, but he could correlate a burst of activity on that connection with your typing the command and capture the packets containing the encrypted version of your command. Later, when you're working in your home directory, Attila inserts the captured bits into your SSH session, and your terminal mysteriously erases all your files!

Attila's replay attack succeeds because the packets he inserted are valid; he could not have produced them himself (due to the encryption), but he can copy and replay them later. TCP/IP's integrity check is performed only on a per-packet basis, so it can't detect Attila's attack. Clearly, the integrity check must apply to the data stream as a whole, ensuring that the bits arrive as they were sent: in order and with no duplication.

The SSH-2 protocol uses cryptographic integrity checking, which verifies both that transmitted data hasn't been altered and that it truly comes from the other end of the connection. SSH-2 uses keyed hash algorithms based on MD5 and SHA-1 for this purpose: well known and widely trusted algorithms. SSH-1, on the other hand, uses a comparatively weak method: a 32-bit cyclic redundancy check (CRC-32) on the unencrypted data in each packet. [3.9.3]

3.1.3. Authentication

Authentication means verifying someone's identity. Suppose I claim to be Richard Silverman, and you want to authenticate that claim. If not much is at stake, you might just take my word for it. If you're a little concerned, you might ask for my driver's license or other photo ID. If you're a bank officer deciding whether to open a safe-deposit box for me, you might also require that I possess a physical key, and so on. It all depends on how sure you want to be. The arsenal of high-tech authentication techniques is growing constantly and includes DNA-testing microchips, retina and hand scanners, and voice-print analyzers.

Every SSH connection involves two authentications: the client verifies the identity of the SSH server (*server authentication*), and the server verifies the identity of the user requesting access (*user authentication*). Server authentication ensures that the SSH server is genuine, not an impostor, guarding against an attacker's redirecting your network connection to a different machine. Server authentication also protects against man-in-the-middle attacks, wherein the attacker sits invisibly between you and the server, pretending to be the client on one side and the server on the other, fooling both sides and reading all your traffic in the process!

There is difference of opinion as to the granularity of server authentication: should it be distinguish between different server hosts, or between individual instances of the SSH server? That is, must all SSH servers running on a particular host have the same host key, or might they have different ones? The term "host key," of course, reflects a bias towards the first interpretation, which SSH1 and OpenSSH follow: their known-hosts lists can only associate a single key with any particular hostname. SSH2, on the other hand, uses the second approach: "host keys" are actually associated with individual listening sockets, allowing multiple keys per host. This may reflect a pragmatic need rather than a considered change in principle. When SSH2 first appeared, it supported only DSA host keys, whereas SSH-1 supports only RSA keys. It was therefore impossible, as a matter of implementation, for a single host to run both SSH-1 and SSH2 servers and have them share a host key.

User authentication is traditionally done with passwords, which unfortunately are a weak authentication scheme. To prove your identity you have to reveal the password, exposing it to possible theft. Additionally, in order to remember a password, people are likely to keep it short and meaningful, which makes the password easier for third parties to guess. For longer passwords, some people choose words or sentences in their native languages, and these passwords are likely to be crackable. From the standpoint of information theory, grammatical sentences contain little real information (technically known as *entropy*): generally less than two bits per character in English text, far less than the 8–16 bits per character found in computer encodings.

SSH supports authentication by password, encrypting the password as it travels over the network. This is a vast improvement over other common remote-access protocols (Telnet, FTP) which generally send your password in the clear (i.e., unencrypted) over the network, where anyone with sufficient network access can steal it! Nevertheless, it's still only simple password authentication, so SSH provides other stronger and more manageable mechanisms: per-user public-key signatures, and an improved *rlogin*-style authentication, with host identity verified by public key. In addition, various SSH implementations support some other systems, including Kerberos, RSA Security's SecurID tokens, S/Key one-time passwords, and the Pluggable Authentication Modules (PAM) system. An SSH client and server negotiate to determine which authentication mechanism to use, based on their configurations. SSH2 can even require multiple forms of authentication.

3.1.4. Authorization

Authorization means deciding what someone may or may not do. It occurs after authentication, since you can't grant someone privileges until you know who she is. SSH servers have various ways of restricting clients' actions. Access to interactive login sessions, TCP port and X window forwarding, key agent forwarding, etc., can all be controlled, though not all these features are available in all SSH implementations, and they aren't always as general or flexible as you might want. Authorization may be controlled at a serverwide level (e.g., the */etc/sshd_config* file for SSH1), or per account, depending on the authentication method used (e.g., each user's files *~/.ssh/authorized_keys*, *~/.ssh2/authorization*, *~/.shosts*, *~/.k5login*, etc.).

3.1.5. Forwarding (Tunneling)

Forwarding or tunneling means encapsulating another TCP-based service, such as Telnet or IMAP, within an SSH session. This brings the security benefits of SSH (privacy, integrity, authentication, authorization) to other TCP-based services. For example, an ordinary Telnet connection transmits your username, password, and the rest of your login session in the clear. By forwarding *telnet* through SSH, all of this data is automatically encrypted and integrity-checked, and you may authenticate using SSH credentials.

SSH supports three types of forwarding. General TCP port forwarding operates as described earlier for any TCP-based service. [9.2] X forwarding comprises additional features for securing the X protocol (i.e., X windows). [9.3] The third type, agent forwarding, permits SSH clients to access SSH public keys on remote machines. [6.3.5]

3.2. A Cryptography Primer

We've covered the basic properties of SSH. Now we focus on cryptography, introducing important terms and ideas regarding the technology in general. There are many good references on cryptographic theory and practice, and we make no attempt here to be comprehensive. (For more detailed information, check out Bruce Schneier's excellent book, *Applied Cryptography*, published by John Wiley & Sons.) We introduce encryption and decryption, plaintext and ciphertext, keys, secret-key and public-key cryptography, and hash functions, both in general and as they apply to SSH.

Encryption is the process of scrambling data so that it can't be read by unauthorized parties. An *encryption algorithm* (or *cipher*) is a particular method of performing the scrambling; examples of currently popular encryption algorithms are RSA, RC4, DSA, and IDEA. The original, readable data is called the *plaintext*, or data in the clear, while the encrypted version is called the corresponding ciphertext. To convert plaintext to ciphertext, you apply an encryption algorithm parameterized by a key, a string that is typically known only to you. An encryption algorithm is considered secure if it is infeasible for anyone to read (or *decrypt*) the encrypted data without the key. An attempt to decrypt data without its key is called *cryptanalysis*.

3.2.1. How Secure Is Secure?

It's important to understand the word "infeasible" in the previous paragraph. Today's most popular and secure ciphers are vulnerable to *brute-force* attacks: if you try every possible key, you will eventually succeed in decryption. However, when the number of possible keys is large, a brute-force search requires a great deal of time and computing power. Based on the state of the art in computer hardware and algorithms, it is possible to pick sufficiently large key sizes so as to render brute-force key search infeasible for your adversary. What counts as infeasible, though, varies depending on how valuable the data is, how long it must stay secure, and how motivated and well-funded your adversary is. Keeping something secret from your rival startup for a few days is one thing; keeping it secret from a major world government for 10 years is quite another.

Of course, for all this to make sense, you must be convinced that brute force is the only way to attack your cipher. Encryption algorithms have structure and are susceptible to mathematical analysis. Over the years, many ciphers previously thought secure have fallen to advances in cryptanalysis. It isn't currently possible to *prove* a practical cipher secure. Rather, a cipher acquires respectability through intensive study by mathematicians and cryptographers. If a new cipher exhibits good design principles, and well-known researchers study it for some time and fail to find a practical, faster method of breaking it than brute force, then people will consider it secure.*

3.2.2. Public- and Secret-Key Cryptography

Encryption algorithms as described so far are called *symmetric* or *secret-key* ciphers; the same key is used for encrypting and decrypting. Examples are Blowfish, DES, IDEA, and RC4. Such a cipher immediately introduces the key-distribution problem: how do you get the key to your intended recipient? If you can meet in person every once and a while and exchange a list of keys, all well and good, but for dynamic communication over computer networks, this doesn't work.

Public-key, or *asymmetric,* cryptography replaces the single key with a pair of related keys: public and private. They are related in a mathematically clever way:

* In his pioneering works on information theory and encryption, the mathematician Claude Shannon defined a model for cipher security and showed there is a cipher that is perfectly secure under that model: the so-called *one-time pad*. It is perfectly secure: the encrypted data gives an attacker no information whatsoever about the possible plaintexts. The ciphertext literally can decrypt to any plaintext at all with equal likelihood. The problem with the one-time pad is that it cumbersome and fragile. It requires that keys be as large as the messages they protect, be generated perfectly randomly, and never be reused. If any of these requirements are violated, the one-time pad becomes extremely insecure. The ciphers in common use today aren't perfectly secure in Shannon's sense, but for the best of them, brute-force attacks are infeasible.

data encrypted with the public key may be decrypted with its private counterpart, and it is infeasible to derive the private key from the public one. You keep your private key, well... private, and give the public key to anyone who wants it, without worrying about disclosure. Ideally, you publish it in a directory next to your name, like a telephone book. When someone wants to send you a secret message, they encrypt it with your public key. Other people may have your public key, but that won't allow them to decrypt the message; only you can do that with the corresponding private key. Public-key cryptography goes a long way towards solving the key-distribution problem.*

Public-key methods are also the basis for *digital signatures:* extra information attached to a digital document to provide evidence that a particular person has seen and agreed to it, much as a pen-and-ink signature does with a paper document. Any asymmetric cipher (RSA, ElGamal, Elliptic Curve, etc.) may be used for digital signatures, though the reverse isn't true. For instance, the DSA algorithm, which is used by the SSH-2 protocol for its keys, is a signature-only public-key scheme and can't be used for encryption.†

Secret- and public-key encryption algorithms differ in another way: performance. All common public-key algorithms are enormously slower than secret-key ciphers—by orders of magnitude. It is simply infeasible to encrypt large quantities of data using a public-key cipher. For this reason, modern data encryption uses both methods together. Suppose you want to send some data securely to your friend Bob Bitflipper. Here's what a modern encryption program does:

1. Generate a random key, called the *bulk key,* for a fast, secret-key algorithm such as 3DES (a.k.a the *bulk cipher*).
2. Encrypt the plaintext with the bulk key.
3. Secure the bulk key by encrypting it with Bob Bitflipper's public key, so only Bob can decrypt it. Since secret keys are small (a few hundred bits long at most), the speed of the public-key algorithm isn't an issue.

To reverse the operation, Bob's decryption program first decrypts the bulk key, and then uses it to decrypt the ciphertext. This method yields the advantages of both kinds of encryption technology, and in fact, SSH uses this technique. User data crossing an SSH connection is encrypted using a fast secret-key cipher, the key for which is shared between the client and server using public-key methods.

* There is still the issue of reliably determining whose public key is whose; but that gets into public-key infrastructure, or PKI systems, and is a broader topic.

† That's the idea, anyway, although it has been pointed out that it's easy to use a general DSA implementation for both RSA and ElGamal encryption. That was not the intent, however.

3.2.3. Hash Functions

In cryptography (and elsewhere in computing and network technology), it is often useful to know if some collection of data has changed. Of course, one can just send along (or keep around) the original data for comparison, but that can be prohibitively expensive both in time and storage. The common tool addressing this need is called a *hash function*. Hash functions are used by SSH-1 for integrity checking (and have various other uses in cryptography we won't discuss here).

A hash function is simply a mapping from a larger set of data values to a smaller set. For instance, a hash function *H* might take an input bit string of any length up to 50,000 bits, and uniformly produce a 128-bit output. The idea is that when sending a message *m* to Alice, I also send along the hash value *H(m)*. Alice computes *H(m)* independently and compares it to the *H(m)* value I sent; if they differ, she concludes that the message was modified in transit.

This simple technique can't be completely effective. Since the range of the hash function is strictly smaller than its domain, many different messages have the same hash value. To be useful, *H* must have the property that the kinds of alterations expected to happen to the messages in transit, must be overwhelmingly likely to cause a change in the message hash. Put another way: given a message *m* and a typical changed message *m'*, it must be extremely unlikely that $H(m) = H(m')$.

Thus a hash function must be tailored to its intended use. One common use is in networking: datagrams transmitted over a network frequently include a message hash that detects transmission errors due to hardware failure or software bugs. Another use is in cryptography, to implement digital signatures. Signing a large amount of data is prohibitively expensive, since it involves slow public-key operations as well as shipping along a complete encrypted copy of the data. What is actually done is to first hash the document, producing a small hash value, and then sign that, sending the signed hash along instead. A verifier independently computes the hash, then decrypts the signature using the appropriate public key, and compares them. If they are the same, he concludes (with high probability) that the signature is valid, and that the data hasn't changed since the private key holder signed it.

These two uses, however, have different requirements, and a hash function suitable for detecting transmission errors due to line noise might be ineffective at detecting deliberate alterations introduced by a human attacker! A cryptographic hash function must make it computationally infeasible to find two different messages having the same hash or to find a message having a particular fixed hash. Such a function is said to be *collision-resistant* (or *collision-proof*, though that's a bit misleading), and *pre-image-resistant*. The Cyclic Redundancy Check hash commonly used to detect accidental data changes (e.g., in Ethernet frame transmissions) is an example of a non-collision-resistant hash. It is easy to find CRC-32 hash collisions, and the SSH-1 insertion attack is based on this fact. [3.10.5] Examples of cryptographically strong hash functions are MD5 and SHA-1.

3.3. The Architecture of an SSH System

SSH has about a dozen distinct, interacting components that produce the features we've covered. [3.1] Figure 3-1 illustrates the major components and their relationships to one another.

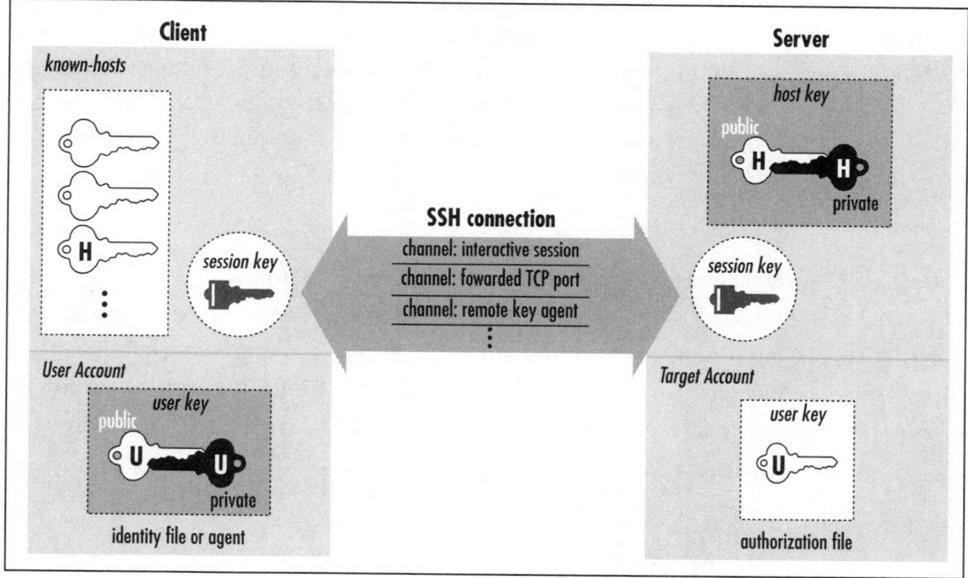

Figure 3-1. SSH architecture

By "component" we don't necessarily mean "program:" SSH also has keys, sessions, and other fun things. In this section we provide a brief overview of all the components, so you can begin to get the big picture of SSH:

Server
: A program that allows incoming SSH connections to a machine, handling authentication, authorization, and so forth. In most Unix SSH implementations, the server is *sshd*.

Client
: A program that connects to SSH servers and makes requests, such as "log me in" or "copy this file." In SSH1, SSH2, and OpenSSH, the major clients are *ssh* and *scp*.

Session

An ongoing connection between a client and a server. It begins after the client successfully authenticates to a server and ends when the connection terminates. Sessions may be interactive or batch.

Key

A relatively small amount of data, generally from tens to one or two thousand bits, used as a parameter to cryptographic algorithms such as encryption or message authentication. The use of the key binds the algorithm operation in some way to the key holder: in encryption, it ensures that only someone else holding that key (or a related one) can decrypt the message; in authentication, it allows you to later verify that the key holder actually signed the message. There are two kinds of keys: symmetric or secret-key, and asymmetric or public-key. [3.2.2] An asymmetric key has two parts: the public and private components. SSH deals with four types of keys, as summarized in Table 3-1 and described following the table.

Table 3-1. Keys, Keys, Keys

Name	Lifetime	Created by	Type	Purpose
User key	Persistent	User	Public	Identify a user to the server
Session key	One session	Client (and server)	Secret	Protect communications
Host key	Persistent	Administrator	Public	Identify a server/machine
Server key	One hour	Server	Public	Encrypt the session key (SSH1 only)

User key

A persistent, asymmetric key used by clients as proof of a user's identity. (A single user may have many keys/identities.)

Host key

A persistent, asymmetric key used by a server as proof of its identity, as well as by a client when proving its host's identity as part of trusted-host authentication. [3.4.2.3] If a machine runs a single SSH server, the host key also uniquely identifies the machine. (If a machine is running multiple SSH servers, each may have a different host key, or they may share.) Often confused with the server key.

Server key

A temporary, asymmetric key used in the SSH-1 protocol. It is regenerated by the server at regular intervals (by default every hour) and protects the session key (defined shortly). Often confused with the host key. This key is never explicitly stored on disk, and its private component is never transmitted over the connection in any form; it provides "perfect forward secrecy" for SSH-1 sessions. [3.4.1]

Session key

A randomly generated, symmetric key for encrypting the communication between an SSH client and server. It is shared by the two parties in a secure manner during the SSH connection setup, so that an eavesdropper can't discover it. Both sides then have the session key, which they use to encrypt their communications. When the SSH session ends, the key is destroyed.

SSH-1 uses a single session key, but SSH-2 has several: each direction (server to client, and client to server) has keys for encryption and others for integrity checking. In our discussions we treat all SSH-2's session keys as a unit and speak of "the session key" for convenience. If the context requires it, we specify which individual key we mean.

Key generator

A program that creates persistent keys (user keys and host keys) for SSH. SSH1, SSH2, and OpenSSH have the program *ssh-keygen.*

Known hosts database

A collection of host keys. Clients and servers refer to this database to authenticate one another.

Agent

A program that caches user keys in memory, so users needn't keep retyping their passphrases. The agent responds to requests for key-related operations, such as signing an authenticator, but it doesn't disclose the keys themselves. It is a convenience feature. SSH1, SSH2, and OpenSSH have the agent *ssh-agent,* and the program *ssh-add* loads and unloads the key cache.

Signer

A program that signs hostbased authentication packets. We explain this in our discussion of trusted-host authentication. [3.4.2.3]

Random seed

A pool of random data used by SSH components to initialize software pseudo-random number generators.

Configuration file

A collection of settings to tailor the behavior of an SSH client or server.

Not all these components are required in an implementation of SSH. Certainly servers, clients, and keys are mandatory, but many implementations don't have an agent, and some even don't include a key generator.

3.4. Inside SSH-1

Now that we've seen the major features and components of SSH, let's delve into the details of the SSH-1 protocol. SSH-2 is covered separately. [3.5] The architecture of SSH-1 is summarized in Figure 3-2. We will cover:

- How the secure session is established
- Authentication by password, public key, or trusted host
- Integrity checking
- Data compression

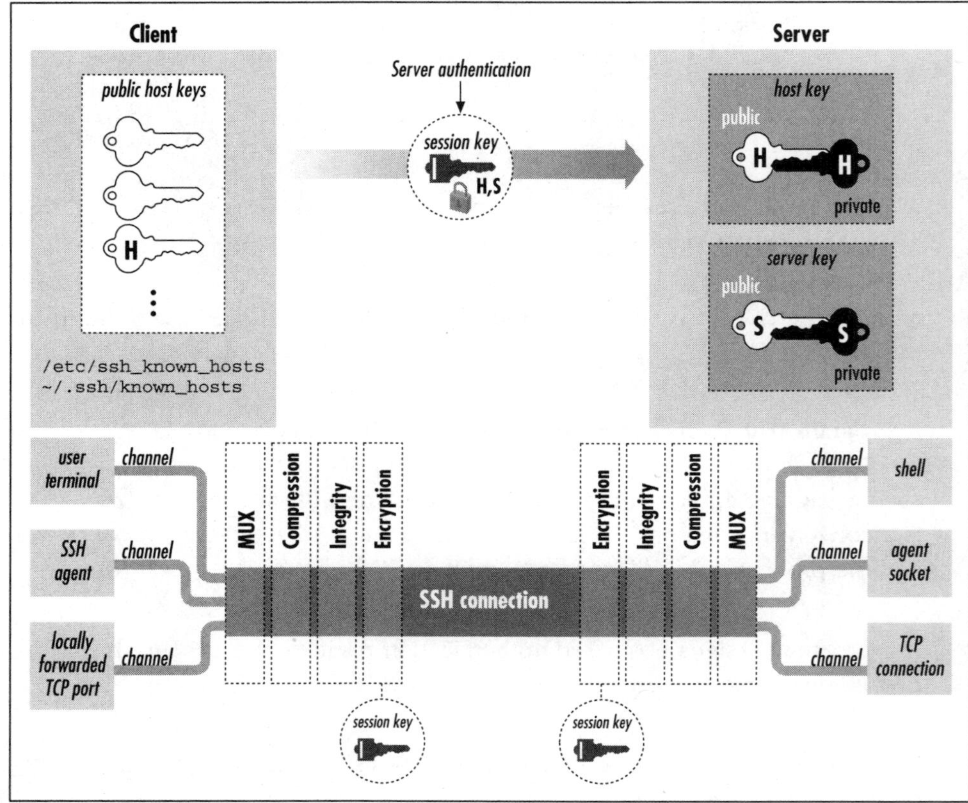

Figure 3-2. SSH-1 architecture

3.4.1. Establishing the Secure Connection

Before meaningful interaction can take place, the SSH client and server must establish a secure connection. This lets them share keys, passwords, and ultimately, whatever data they transmit to each other.

We will now explain how the SSH-1 protocol guarantees security of a network connection. Through a multistep process, starting from scratch, the SSH-1 client and server agree on an encryption algorithm and generate and share a secret session key, establishing a secure connection:

1. The client contacts the server.
2. The client and server disclose the SSH protocol versions they support.
3. The client and server switch to a packet-based protocol.
4. The server identifies itself to the client and provides session parameters.
5. The client sends the server a secret (session) key.
6. Both sides turn on encryption and complete server authentication.
7. The secure connection is established.

Now the client and server can communicate by encrypted messages. Let's examine each step in detail; the complete process is summarized in Figure 3-3.

1. *The client contacts the server.*

   This is done without fanfare, simply by sending a connection request to the server's TCP port, which is port 22 by convention.

2. *The client and server disclose the SSH protocol versions they support.*

   These protocols are represented as ASCII strings, such as "SSH-1.5-1.2.27", which means SSH protocol Version 1.5 as implemented by SSH1 Version 1.2.27. You can see this string by connecting to an SSH server port with a Telnet client:

   ```
   $ telnet server 22
   Trying 192.168.10.1
   Connected to server (192.168.10.1).
   Escape character is '^]'.
   SSH-1.5-1.2.27
   ```

   The implementation version (1.2.27) is just a comment and is optional in the string. But, some implementations examine the comment to recognize particular software versions and work around known bugs or incompatibilities.*

   If the client and server decide their versions are compatible, the connection process continues; otherwise either party may decide to terminate the connection. For instance, if an SSH-1-only client encounters an SSH-2-only server, the client disconnects and prints an error message. Other actions are

* Some system administrators remove the comment, preferring not to announce their software package and version to the world, which provides clues to an attacker.

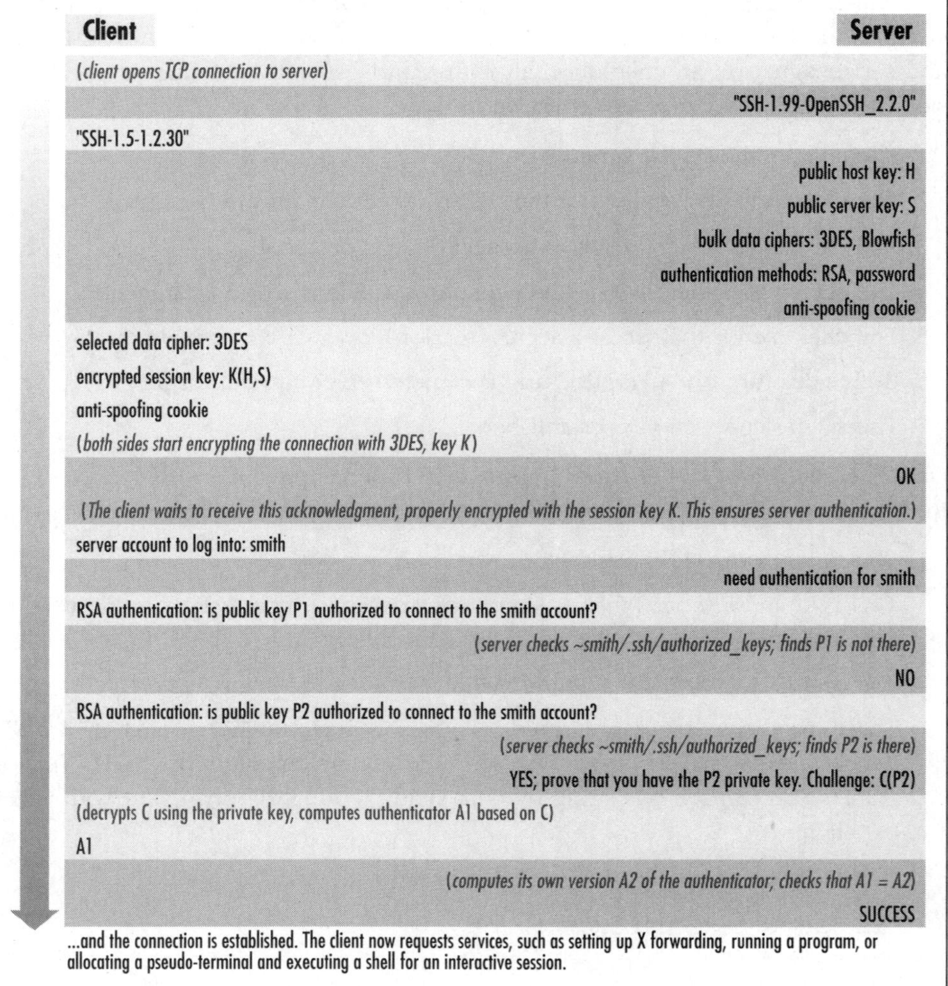

Figure 3-3. SSH-1 protocol exchange

possible: for example, the SSH-2-only server can invoke an SSH-1 server to handle the connection.

3. *The client and server switch to a packet-based protocol.*

   Once the protocol version exchange is complete, both sides switch to a packet-based protocol over the underlying TCP connection. Each packet consists of a 32-bit length field, 1–8 bytes of random padding to foil known-plaintext attacks, a one-byte packet type code, the packet payload data, and a four-byte integrity check field.

UNIVERSITY

BOOK STORE-DOWNTOWN

RETAIN THIS RECEIPT

2001-2002

6 702 81386 528331 Sale

6317906 RED HAT LINUX SURVIVA	39.99	
503 91 SSH THE SECURE SHELL	39.95	
Subtotal	79.94	
Total Tax	7.03	
Total	86.97	*
Bankcard Online	86.9[illegible]	

Account: 5471XXXXXXXX2492

Expiration Date:# 0403

Authorization: 006558

Referance: 38713007

Control#: 6..702.81386.47581

13:02 03/06/02

THANK YOU FOR SHOPPING AT

UNIVERSITY BOOK STORE!

4. *The server identifies itself to the client and provides session parameters.*

   The server sends the following information to the client (all still unencrypted):

   — Its host key, used to prove the server host identity later.

   — Its server key, which helps establish the secure connection.

   — A sequence of eight random bytes, called *check bytes*. The client must include these check bytes in its next response, or the server rejects the response. This measure protects against some IP spoofing attacks.

   — Lists of encryption, compression, and authentication methods that the server supports.

   At this point, both sides also compute a common 128-bit *session identifier*, which is used in some subsequent protocol operations to uniquely identify this SSH session. This is an MD5 hash of the host key, server key, and check bytes taken together.

   When the client receives the host key, it asks the question: "Have I spoken with this server before, and if so, what was its host key then?" To answer this question, the client consults its known hosts database. If the newly arrived host key matches a previous one in the database, all is well. However, there are two other possibilities: the server might not appear in the known hosts database, or it might be present but with a different host key. In each of these cases, the client elects to trust the newly arrived key or to reject it. [7.4.3.1] Human guidance may be needed: for example, the client's user can be prompted to accept or reject the key.

   If the client rejects the host key, the connection ends. Let's assume the host key is acceptable and continue.

5. *The client sends the server a secret (session) key.*

   Now the client randomly generates a new key for a bulk cipher [3.2.2] that both client and server support; this is called the session key. Its purpose is to encrypt and decrypt messages sent between the client and the server. All that's needed is to give this session key to the server, and both sides can turn on encryption and begin communicating securely.

   Of course, the client can't simply send the session key to the server. Encryption isn't operating yet, and if a third party intercepts this key, it can decrypt the client's and server's messages. Goodbye security! So the client must send the session key securely. This is done by encrypting it twice: once with the server's public host key and once with the server key. This step ensures that only the server can read it. After the session key is double-encrypted, the client sends it to the server, along with the check bytes and a choice of algorithms (picked from the server's list of supported algorithms sent in Step 4).

6. *Both sides turn on encryption and complete server authentication.*

   After sending the session key, both sides begin encrypting the session data with the key and the selected bulk cipher. Before sending anything further, though, the client waits for a confirmation message from the server, which (like all subsequent data) must be encrypted with the session key. This final step provides the server authentication: only the intended server can have decrypted the session key, since it was encrypted with the host key verified earlier against the known hosts list.

   Without the session key, an impostor server can't decrypt the subsequent protocol traffic or produce valid traffic in return, and the client will notice and terminate the connection.

   Note that server authentication is implicit; there's no explicit exchange to verify the server host key. Therefore it's important for the client to wait for a valid server response using the new session key before sending anything further, in order to verify the server's identity before proceeding. The SSH-1 protocol isn't specific about this point, but SSH-2 requires it when server authentication is implicit in the session key exchange.

   Encrypting the session key a second time with the server key provides a property called *perfect forward secrecy*. This means there are no persistent keys lying around whose disclosure can jeopardize the secrecy of past or future SSH sessions. If the server host key alone is used to protect the session key, then disclosure of the host private key compromises future communications and allows decryption of old, recorded sessions. Using the server key in tandem for this purpose removes this weakness, as it is temporary, never explicitly stored on disk, and replaced periodically (by default, once an hour). Having stolen the server private key, an interloper must still perform an active man-in-the-middle or server spoofing attack to compromise a session.

7. *The secure connection is established.*

   Since both the client and server now know the session key, and nobody else does, they can send each other encrypted messages (using the bulk cipher they agreed on) only they can decrypt. Also, the client has completed server authentication. We're ready to begin client authentication.

3.4.2. Client Authentication

Once the secure connection is established, the client attempts to authenticate itself to the server. The client may try any authentication methods at its disposal until one succeeds, or all have failed. For example, the six authentication methods defined by the SSH-1.5 protocol, in the order attempted by the SSH1 implementation, are:

1. Kerberos*
2. Rhosts
3. RhostsRSA
4. Public-key
5. TIS*
6. Password (flavors: host login password, Kerberos, SecurID, S/Key, etc.)

F-Secure SSH Client for Windows (see Chapter 16) tries these in order:

1. Public-key
2. Password

Knowing the order for your client is a good idea. It helps to diagnose problems when authentication fails or acts unexpectedly.

3.4.2.1. Password authentication

During password authentication, the user supplies a password to the SSH client, which the client transmits securely to the server over the encrypted connection. The server then checks that the given password is acceptable for the target account, and allows the connection if so. In the simplest case, the SSH server checks this through the native password-authentication mechanism of the host operating system.

Password authentication is quite convenient because it requires no additional setup for the user. You don't need to generate a key, create a *~/.ssh* directory on the server machine, or edit any configuration files. This is particularly convenient for first-time SSH users and for users who travel a lot and don't carry their private keys. You might not want to use your private keys on other machines, or there may be no way to get them onto the machine in question. If you frequently travel, you should consider setting up SSH to use one-time passwords if your implementation supports them, improving the security of the password scheme. [3.4.2.5]

On the other hand, password authentication is inconvenient because you have to type a password every time you connect. Also, password authentication is less secure than public-key because the sensitive password is transmitted off the client host. It is protected from snooping while on the network but is vulnerable to capture once it arrives at the server if that machine has been compromised. This is in contrast with public-key authentication, as even a compromised server can't learn

* This method isn't available by default; it must be requested at compile time.

your private key through the protocol. Therefore, before choosing password authentication, you should weigh the trustworthiness of the client and the server, as you will be revealing to them the key to your electronic kingdom.

Password authentication is simple in concept, but different Unix variants store and verify passwords in different ways, leading to some complexities. OpenSSH uses PAM for password authentication by default, which must be carefully configured. [4.3] Most Unix systems encrypt passwords with DES (via the `crypt()` library routine), but recently some systems have started using the MD5 hash algorithm, leading to configuration issues. [4.3] The behavior of password authentication also changes if Kerberos [5.5.1.7] or SecurID support [5.5.1.9] is enabled in the SSH server.

3.4.2.2. Public-key authentication

Public-key authentication uses public-key cryptography to verify the client's identity. To access an account on an SSH server machine, the client proves that it possesses a secret: specifically, the private counterpart of an authorized public key. A key is "authorized" if its public component is contained in the account's authorization file (e.g., *~/.ssh/authorized_keys*). The sequence of actions is:

1. The client sends the server a request for public-key authentication with a particular key. The request contains the key's modulus as an identifier.*

   The key is implicitly RSA; the SSH-1 protocol specifies the RSA algorithm particularly and exclusively for public-key operations.
2. The server reads the target account's authorization file, and looks for an entry with the matching key. If there is no matching entry, this authentication request fails.
3. If there is a matching entry, the server retrieves the key and notes any restrictions on its use. The server can then reject the request immediately on the basis of a restriction, for example, if the key shouldn't be used from the client host. Otherwise, the process continues.
4. The server generates a random 256-bit string as a challenge, encrypts it with the client's public key, and sends this to the client.
5. The client receives the challenge and decrypts it with the corresponding private key. It then combines the challenge with the session identifier, hashes the result with MD5, and returns the hash value to the server as its response to the challenge. The session identifier is mixed in to bind the authenticator to the current session, protecting against replay attacks taking advantage of weak or compromised random-number generation in creating the challenge.

* An RSA key consists of two parts: the *exponent* and the *modulus*. The modulus is the long number in the public key (*.pub*) file.

The hashing operation is there to prevent misuse of the client's private key via the protocol, including a chosen-plaintext attack.* If the client simply returns the decrypted challenge instead, a corrupt server can present any data encrypted with the client's public key, and the unsuspecting client dutifully decrypts and returns it. It might be the data-encryption key for an enciphered email message the attacker intercepted. Also, remember that with RSA, "decrypting" some data with the private key is actually the same operation as "signing" it. So the server can supply chosen, *unencrypted* data to the client as a "challenge," to be signed with the client's private key—perhaps a document saying, "OWAH TAGU SIAM" or something even more nefarious.

6. The server computes the same MD5 hash of the challenge and session ID; if the client's reply matches, the authentication succeeds.

The public-key method is the most secure authentication option available in SSH, generally speaking. First of all, the client needs two secrets to authenticate: the private key, and the passphrase to decrypt it. Stealing either one alone doesn't compromise the target account (assuming a strong passphrase). The private key is infeasible to guess and never leaves the client host, making it more difficult to steal than a password. A strong passphrase is difficult to guess by brute force, and if necessary, you can change your passphrase without changing the associated key. Also, public-key authentication doesn't trust any information supplied by the client host; proof of possession of the private key is the sole criterion. This is in contrast to RhostsRSA authentication, in which the server delegates partial responsibility for the authentication process to the client host: having verified the client host's identity and privilege of the client running on it, it trusts the client software not to lie about the user's identity. [3.4.2.3] If someone can impersonate a client host, he can impersonate any user on that host without actually having to steal anything from the user. This can't happen with public-key authentication.†

Public-key authentication is also the most flexible method in SSH for its additional control over authorization. You may tag each public key with restrictions to be applied after authentication succeeds: which client hosts may connect, what commands may be run, and so on. [8.2] This isn't an intrinsic advantage of the public-

* In a *chosen-plaintext* attack, the cryptanalyst is allowed to examine plaintext/ciphertext pairs of her choosing, encrypted with the key she's trying to break. The RSA algorithm is particularly vulnerable to chosen-plaintext attacks, so it's important for a protocol using RSA to avoid them.

† Don't confuse *impersonating* the client host with *compromising* it, however. If you actually break into the client host and compromise its security, all bets are off; you can then steal the keys, passwords, etc., of any users on that host. SSH doesn't protect against host compromise.

key method, of course, but rather an implementation detail of SSH, albeit an important one.*

On the down side, public-key authentication is more cumbersome than the other methods. It requires users to generate and maintain their keys and authorization files, with all the attendant possibilities for error: syntax errors in *authorized_keys* entries, incorrect permissions on SSH directories or files, lost private key files requiring new keys and updates to all target accounts, etc. SSH doesn't provide any management infrastructure for distributing and maintaining keys on a large scale. You can combine SSH with the Kerberos authentication system, which does provide such management, to obtain the advantages of both. [11.4]

One technical limitation regarding public-key authentication arises in connection with the RSAref encryption library. [3.9.1.1] RSAref supports key lengths only up to 1024 bits, whereas the SSH internal RSA software supports longer keys. If you try to use a longer key with SSH/RSAref, you get an error. This can happen with either user or host keys, perhaps preexisting ones if you've recently switched to RSAref, or keys transferred from systems running the non-RSAref version of SSH. In all these cases, you have to replace the keys with shorter ones.

3.4.2.3. Trusted-host authentication (Rhosts and RhostsRSA)

Password and public-key authentication require the client to prove its identity by knowledge of a secret: a password or a private key particular to the target account on the server. In particular, the client's location—the computer on which it is running—isn't relevant to authentication.

Trusted-host authentication is different.† Rather than making you prove your identity to every host that you visit, trusted-host authentication establishes trust relationships between machines. If you are logged in as user andrew on machine A, and you connect by SSH to account bob on machine B using trusted-host authentication, the SSH server on machine B doesn't check your identity directly. Instead, it checks the identity of host A, making sure that A is a trusted host. It further checks that the connection is coming from a trusted program on A, one installed by the system administrator that won't lie about andrew's identity. If the

* We wish this were done differently. Rather than entangling the authentication and authorization functions in this way, SSH should be able to apply any restriction to any connection, regardless of the authentication method. However, no implementation of SSH, to our knowledge, keeps authentication and authorization truly orthogonal.

† The term "trusted-host" is our own; it refers to the Rhosts, SSH-1 RhostsRSA, and SSH-2 hostbased authentication methods as a related group.

connection passes these two tests, the server takes A's word you have been authenticated as andrew and proceeds to make an authorization check that andrew@A is allowed to access the account bob@B.

Let's follow this authentication process step by step:

1. The SSH client requests a connection from the SSH server.
2. The SSH server uses its local naming service to look up a hostname for the source address of the client network connection.
3. The SSH server consults authorization rules in several local files, indicating whether particular hosts are trusted or not. If the server finds a match for the hostname, authentication continues; otherwise it fails.
4. The server verifies that the remote program is a trusted one by following the old Unix convention of *privileged ports*. Unix-based TCP and UDP stacks reserve the ports numbered 1 through 1023 as privileged, allowing only processes running as root to listen on them or use them on the local side of a connection. The server simply checks that the source port of the connection is in the privileged range. Assuming the client host is secure, only its superuser can arrange for a program to originate such a connection, so the server believes it is talking to a trusted program.
5. If all goes well, authentication succeeds.

This process has been practiced for years by the Berkeley r-commands: *rsh*, *rlogin*, *rcp*, *rexec*, etc. Unfortunately, it is a notoriously weak authentication method within modern networks. IP addresses can be spoofed, naming services can be subverted, and privileged ports aren't so privileged in a world of desktop PCs whose end users commonly have superuser (administrator) privileges. Indeed, some desktop operating systems lack the concept of a user (such as MacOS), while others don't implement the privileged-port convention (Windows), so any user may access any free port.

Nevertheless, trusted-host authentication has advantages. For one, it is simple: you don't have to type passwords or passphrases, or generate, distribute, and maintain keys. It also provides ease of automation. Unattended processes such as *cron* jobs may have difficulty using SSH if they need a key, passphrase, or password coded into a script, placed in a protected file, or stored in memory. This isn't only a potential security risk but also a maintenance nightmare. If the authenticator ever changes, you must hunt down and change these hard coded copies, a situation just begging for things to break mysteriously later on. Trusted-host authentication gets around this problem neatly.

Since trusted-host authentication is a useful idea, SSH1 supports it in two ways. *Rhosts authentication* simply behaves as described in Steps 1–5, just like the Berkeley r-commands. This method is disabled by default, since it is quite insecure, though it's still an improvement over *rsh* since it provides server host authentication, encryption, and integrity. More importantly, though, SSH1 provides a more secure version of the trusted-host method, called *RhostsRSA authentication,* which improves Steps 2 and 4 using the client's host key.

Step 2 is improved by a stronger check on the identity of the client host. Instead of relying on the source IP address and a naming service such as DNS, SSH uses public-key cryptography. Recall that each host on which SSH is installed has an asymmetric "host key" identifying it. The host key authenticates the server to the client while establishing the secure connection. In RhostsRSA authentication, the client's host key authenticates the client host to the server. The client host provides its name and public key, and then must prove it holds the corresponding private key via a challenge-response exchange. The server maintains a list of known hosts and their public keys to determine the client's status as a known, trusted host.

Step 4, checking that the server is talking to a trusted program, is improved again through use of the client's host key. The private key is kept protected so only a program with special privileges (e.g., setuid root) can read it. Therefore, if the client can access its local host key at all—which it must do to complete authentication in Step 2—the client must have those special privileges. Therefore the client was installed by the administrator of the trusted host and can be trusted. SSH1 retains the privileged-port check, which can't be turned off.* SSH2 does away with this check entirely since it doesn't add anything.

Trusted-host access files. Two pairs of files on the SSH server machine provide access control for trusted-host authentication, in both its weak and strong forms:

- */etc/hosts.equiv* and *~/.rhosts*
- */etc/shosts.equiv* and *~/.shosts*

The files in */etc* have machine-global scope, while those in the target account's home directory are specific to that account. The *hosts.equiv* and *shosts.equiv* files have the same syntax, as do the *.rhosts* and *.shosts* files, and by default they are all checked.

If any of the four access files allows access for a particular connection, it's allowed, even if another of the files forbids it.

* SSH1 has a `UsePrivilegedPort` configuration keyword, but it tells the client not to use a privileged port in its source socket, which renders the session unusable for rhosts or RhostsRSA authentication. The purpose of this feature is to get around firewalls that might block connections coming from privileged ports and requires that some other authentication method be used.

The */etc/hosts.equiv* and *~/.rhosts* files originated with the insecure r-commands. For backward compatibility, SSH can also use these files for making its trusted-host authentication decisions. If using both the r-commands and SSH, however, you might not want the two systems to have the same configuration. Also, because of their poor security, it's common to disable the r-commands, by turning off the servers in your *inetd.conf* files and/or removing the software. In that case, you may not want to have any traditional control files lying around, as a defensive measure in case an attacker managed to get one of these services turned on again.

To separate itself from the r-commands, SSH reads two additional files, */etc/shosts.equiv* and *~/.shosts*, which have the same syntax and meaning as */etc/hosts.equiv* and *~/.rhosts*, but are specific to SSH. If you use only the SSH-specific files, you can have SSH trusted-host authentication without leaving any files the r-commands would look at.*

All four files have the same syntax, and SSH interprets them very similarly—but not identically—to the way the r-commands do. Read the following sections carefully to make sure you understand this behavior.

Control file details. Here is the common format of all four trusted-host control files. Each entry is a single line, containing either one or two tokens separated by tabs and/or spaces. Comments begin with #, continue to the end of the line, and may be placed anywhere; empty and comment-only lines are allowed.

```
# example control file entry
[+-][@]hostspec  [+-][@]userspec  # comment
```

The two tokens indicate host(s) and user(s), respectively; the *userspec* may be omitted. If the at-sign (@) is present, then the token is interpreted as a netgroup (see the sidebar "Netgroups"), looked up using the `innetgr()` library call, and the resulting list of user or hostnames is substituted. Otherwise, the token is interpreted as a single host or username. Hostnames must be canonical as reported by `gethostbyaddr()` on the server host; other names won't work.

If either or both tokens are preceded by a minus sign (–), the whole entry is considered negated. It doesn't matter which token has the minus sign; the effect is the same. Let's see some examples before explaining the full rules.

The following *hostspec* allows anyone from *fred.flintstone.gov* to log in if the remote and local usernames are the same:

```
# /etc/shosts.equiv
fred.flintstone.gov
```

* Unfortunately, you can't configure the server to look at one set but not the other. If it looks at *~/.shosts*, then it also considers *~/.rhosts*, and both global files are always considered.

Netgroups

A netgroup defines a list of (*host, user, domain*) triples. Netgroups are used to define lists of users, machines, or accounts, usually for access-control purposes; for instance, one can usually use a netgroup to specify what hosts are allowed to mount an NFS filesystem (e.g., in the Solaris *share* command or BSD *exportfs*).

Different flavors of Unix vary in how they implement netgroups, though you must always be the system administrator to define a netgroup. Possible sources for netgroup definitions include:

- A plain file, e.g., */etc/netgroup*
- A database file in various formats, e.g., */etc/netgroup.db*
- An information service, such as Sun's YP/NIS

On many modern Unix flavors, the source of netgroup information is configurable with the Network Service Switch facility; see the file */etc/nsswitch.conf*. Be aware that in some versions of SunOS and Solaris, netgroups may be defined only in NIS; it doesn't complain if you specify "files" as the source in *nsswitch.conf*, but it doesn't work either. Recent Linux systems support */etc/netgroup*, though C libraries before *glibc* 2.1 support netgroups only over NIS.

Some typical netgroup definitions might look like this:

```
# defines a group consisting of two hosts: hostnames "print1" and
# "print2", in the (probably NIS) domains one.foo.org and two.foo.com.
print-servers         (print1,,one.foo.com) (print2,,two.foo.com)
# a list of three login servers
login-servers         (login1,,foo.com) (login2,,foo.com) (login1,,foo.com)
# Use two existing netgroups to define a list of all hosts, throwing in
# another.foo.com as well.
all-hosts             print-servers login-servers (another,,foo.com)
# A list of users for some access-control purpose.  Mary is allowed from
# anywhere in the foo.com domain, but Peter only from one host.  Alice
# is allowed from anywhere at all.
allowed-users         (,mary,foo.com) (login1,peter,foo.com) (,alice,)
```

When deciding membership in a netgroup, the thing being matched is always construed as an appropriate triple. A triple (x, y, z) matches a netgroup N if there exists a triple (a, b, c) in N which matches (x, y, z). In turn, you define that these two triples match if and only if the following conditions are met:

—Continued—

> $x = a$ or x is null or a is null
>
> and:
>
> $y = b$ or y is null or b is null
>
> and:
>
> $z = c$ or z is null or c is null
>
> This means that a null field in a triple acts as a wildcard. By "null," we mean missing; that is, in the triple (, *user, domain*), the host part is null. This isn't the same as the empty string: ("", *user, domain*) . In this triple, the host part isn't null. It is the empty string, and the triple can match only another whose host part is also the empty string.
>
> When SSH matches a username *U* against a netgroup, it matches the triple (, *U*,); similarly, when matching a hostname *H*, it matches (*H*, ,) . You might expect it to use (, *U, D*) and (*H*, , *D*) where *D* is the host's domain, but it doesn't.

The following *hostspecs* allow anyone from any host in the netgroup "trusted-hosts" to log in, if the remote and local usernames are the same, but not from *evil.empire.org*, even if it is in the trusted-hosts netgroup.

```
# /etc/shosts.equiv
-evil.empire.org
@trusted-hosts
```

This next entry (*hostspec* and *userspec*) allows *mark@way.too.trusted* to log into any local account! Even if a user has *-way.too.trusted mark* in *~/.shosts*, it won't prevent access since the global file is consulted first. You probably never want to do this.

```
# /etc/shosts.equiv
way.too.trusted mark
```

On the other hand, the following entries allow anyone from *sister.host.org* to connect under the same account name, except mark, who can't access any local account. Remember, however, that a target account can override this restriction by placing `sister.host.org mark` in *~/.shosts*. Note also, as shown earlier, that the negated line must come first; in the other order, it's ineffective.

```
# /etc/shosts.equiv
sister.host.org -mark
sister.host.org
```

This next *hostspec* allows user wilma on *fred.flintstone.gov* to log into the local wilma account:

```
# ~wilma/.shosts
fred.flintstone.gov
```

This entry allows user fred on *fred.flintstone.gov* to log into the local wilma account, but no one else—not even *wilma@fred.flintstone.gov*:

```
# ~wilma/.shosts
fred.flintstone.gov fred
```

These entries allow both fred and wilma on *fred.flintstone.gov* to log into the local wilma account:

```
# ~wilma/.shosts
fred.flintstone.gov fred
fred.flintstone.gov
```

Now that we've covered some examples, let's discuss the precise rules. Suppose the client username is C, and the target account of the SSH command is T. Then:

1. A *hostspec* entry with no *userspec* permits access from all *hostspec* hosts when T = C.
2. In a per-account file (*~/.rhosts* or *~/.shosts*), a *hostspec userspec* entry permits access to the containing account from *hostspec* hosts when C is any one of the *userspec* usernames.
3. In a global file (*/etc/hosts.equiv* or */etc/shosts.equiv*), a *hostspec userspec* entry permits access to any local target account from any *hostspec* host, when C is any one of the *userspec* usernames.
4. For negated entries, replace "permits" with "denies" in the preceding rules.

Note Rule #3 carefully. You never, ever want to open your machine to such a security hole. The only reasonable use for such a rule is if it is negated, thus disallowing access to any local account for a particular remote account. We present some examples shortly.

The files are checked in the following order (a missing file is simply skipped, with no effect on the authorization decision):

1. */etc/hosts.equiv*
2. */etc/shosts.equiv*
3. *~/.shosts*
4. *~/.rhosts*

SSH makes a special exception when the target user is root: it doesn't check the global files. Access to the root account can be granted only via the root account's */.rhosts* and */.shosts* files. If you block the use of those files with the `IgnoreRootRhosts` server directive, this effectively prevents access to the root account via trusted-host authentication.

When checking these files, there are two rules to keep in mind. The first rule is: the first accepting line wins. That is, if you have two netgroups:

```
set     (one,,) (two,,) (three,,)
subset  (one,,) (two,,)
```

the following */etc/shosts.equiv* file permits access only from host three:

```
-@subset
@set
```

But this next one allows access from all three:

```
@set
-@subset
```

The second line has no effect, because all its hosts have already been accepted by a previous line.

The second rule is: if any file accepts the connection, it's allowed. That is, if */etc/shosts.equiv* forbids a connection but the target user's *~/.shosts* file accepts it, then it is accepted. Therefore the sysadmin can't rely on the global file to block connections. Similarly, if your per-account file forbids a connection, it can be overridden by a global file that accepts it. Keep these facts carefully in mind when using trusted-host authentication.*

Netgroups as wildcards. You may have noticed the rule syntax has no wildcards; this omission is deliberate. The r-commands recognize bare + and – characters as positive and negative wildcards, respectively, and a number of attacks are based on surreptitiously adding a "+" to someone's *.rhosts* file, immediately allowing anyone to *rlogin* as that user. So SSH deliberately ignores these wildcards. You'll see messages to that effect in the server's debugging output if it encounters such a wildcard:

```
Remote: Ignoring wild host/user names in /etc/shosts.equiv
```

However, there's still a way to get the effect of a wildcard: using the wildcards available in netgroups. An empty netgroup:

```
empty  # nothing here
```

matches nothing at all. However, this netgroup:

```
wild  (,,)
```

* By setting the server's `IgnoreRhosts` keyword to `yes`, you can cause the server to ignore the per-account files completely and consult the global files exclusively instead. [5.5.1.3]

matches everything. In fact, a netgroup containing (,,) anywhere matches everything, regardless of what else is in the netgroup. So this entry:

```
# ~/.shosts
@wild
```

allows access from any host at all,* as long as the remote and local usernames match. This one:

```
# ~/.shosts
way.too.trusted @wild
```

allows any user on *way.too.trusted* to log into this account, while this entry:

```
# ~/.shosts
@wild @wild
```

allows any user access from anywhere.

Given this wildcard behavior, it's important to pay careful attention to netgroup definitions. It's easier to create a wildcard netgroup than you might think. Including the null triple (,,) is the obvious approach. However, remember that the order of elements in a netgroup triple is (*host,user,domain*). Suppose you define a group "oops" like this:

```
oops        (fred,,) (wilma,,) (barney,,)
```

You intend for this to be a group of usernames, but you've placed the usernames in the host slots, and the username fields are left null. If you use this group as the userspec of a rule, it will act as a wildcard. Thus this entry:

```
# ~/.shosts
home.flintstones.gov @oops
```

allows anyone on *home.flintstones.gov,* not just your three friends, to log into your account. Beware!

Summary. Trusted-host authentication is convenient for users and administrators, because it can set up automatic authentication between hosts based on username correspondence and inter-host trust relationships. This removes the burden of typing passwords or dealing with key management. However, it is heavily dependent on the correct administration and security of the hosts involved; compromising one trusted host can give an attacker automatic access to all accounts on other hosts. Also, the rules for the access control files are complicated, fragile, and easy to get wrong in ways that compromise security. In an environment more concerned with eavesdropping and disclosure than active attacks, it may be

* If strong trusted-host authentication is in use, this means any host verified by public key against the server's known hosts database.

acceptable to deploy RhostsRSA (SSH-2 "hostbased") authentication for general user authentication. In a more security-conscious scenario, however, it is probably inappropriate, though it may be acceptable for limited use in special-purpose accounts, such as for unattended batch jobs. [11.1.3]

We don't recommend the use of weak ("Rhosts") trusted-host authentication at all in SSH1 and OpenSSH/1. It is totally insecure.

3.4.2.4. Kerberos authentication

SSH1 and OpenSSH provide support for Kerberos-based authentication; SSH2 doesn't yet.* [11.4] Table 3-2 summarizes the support features in these products.

Table 3-2. Kerberos Authentication Support in SSH

Product	Kerberos Version	Tickets	Password Authentication	AFS	Forwarding
SSH1	5	Yes	Yes	No	Yes
OpenSSH	4	Yes	Yes	Yes	Only with AFS

The following list explains the columns:

Tickets
: Performs standard Kerberos authentication. The client obtains a ticket for the "host" (v5) or "rcmd" (v4) service on the server and sends that to the SSH server as proof of identity; the server validates it in the standard fashion. Both SSH1 and OpenSSH do Kerberos mutual authentication. This isn't strictly necessary given that SSH has already authenticated the server as part of connection setup, but the extra check can't hurt.

Password Authentication
: Option to perform server-side password authentication using Kerberos. Instead of checking the password using the operating system's account database, the SSH server instead attempts to obtain Kerberos initial credentials for the target user (a "ticket-granting-ticket" or TGT). If this succeeds, the user is authenticated. Also, the server stores the TGT for the session so that the user has access to it, thus removing the need for an explicit *kinit*.

AFS
: The Andrew File System (*http://www.faqs.org/faqs/afs-faq/*), or AFS, uses Kerberos-4 in a specialized way for its authentication. OpenSSH has extra support for obtaining and forwarding AFS credentials. This can be critical in environments using AFS for file sharing. Before it performs authentication, *sshd*

* At press time, experimental Kerberos support is being integrated into SSH2 2.3.0.

must read the target account's home directory, for instance to check *~/.shosts,* or *~/.ssh/authorized_keys.* If the home directory is shared via AFS, then depending on AFS permissions *sshd* might not be able to read it unless it has valid AFS credentials for the owning user. The OpenSSH AFS code provides this, forwarding the source user's Kerberos-4 TGT and AFS ticket to the remote host for use by *sshd.*

Forwarding

Kerberos credentials are normally usable only on the machine to which they are issued. The Kerberos-5 protocol allows a user to forward credentials from one machine to another on which he has been authenticated, avoiding the need for repeated *kinit* invocations. SSH1 supports this with the `KerberosTgtPassing` option. Kerberos-4 doesn't do ticket forwarding, so OpenSSH doesn't provide this feature—unless it is using AFS, whose modified Kerberos-4 implementation provides a form of ticket forwarding.

OpenSSH provides Kerberos support only when using the SSH-1 protocol.

3.4.2.5. One-time passwords

Password authentication is convenient because it can be used easily from anywhere. If you travel a lot and use other people's computers, passwords might be your best bet for SSH authentication. However, it's precisely in that situation that you're most concerned about someone stealing your password—by monitoring keyboard activity on a hacked computer or by old-fashioned shoulder-surfing. One-time password, or OTP systems, preserve the convenience of password access while mitigating the risk: each login requires a different, unpredictable password. Here are the properties of some OTP systems:

- With the free S/Key software OTP system, you carry a printed list of passwords or calculate the next one needed using a piece of software on your laptop or PDA.
- With the SecurID system from RSA Security, Inc., you carry a small hardware token (credit-card or key-fob size) with an LCD screen, which displays a passcode that changes frequently and is synchronized with the SecurID server, which verifies the passcode.
- The OTP system from Trusted Information Systems, Inc. (TIS) is a variant called *challenge-response*: the server displays a challenge, which you type into

your software or hardware token. The token supplies the corresponding response, which you supply to be authenticated.

SSH1 supports SecurID as a variant behavior of password authentication, and TIS as a separate method with the `TISAuthentication` configuration keyword (as noted earlier, this is actually a separate authentication type in the SSH-1 protocol). OpenSSH doesn't support TIS but instead reuses the TIS message types in the SSH-1 protocol to implement S/Key. This works because both TIS and S/Key fit the model of a challenge/response exchange.

Using these systems involves obtaining the requisite libraries and header files, compiling SSH with the appropriate *configure* switches, enabling the right SSH authentication method, and setting up the system according to its instructions. If you are using SecurID or TIS, the requisite libraries and header files should have come with the software or be available from the vendor. S/Key is widely available on the Net, though it has diverged into many versions, and we don't know a canonical site for it. One popular implementation is found in the *logdaemon* package by Wietse Venema; see *http://www.porcupine.org/wietse/*. The details of these external packages are mostly outside the scope of SSH proper, so we won't delve into them.

3.4.3. Integrity Checking

The SSH-1 protocol uses a weak integrity check: a 32-bit cyclic redundancy check or CRC-32. This sort of check is sufficient for detecting accidental changes to data, but isn't effective against deliberate corruption. In fact, the "insertion attack" of Futoransky and Kargieman specifically targets this weakness in SSH-1. [3.10.5] The use of the CRC-32 integrity check is a serious inherent weakness in SSH-1 that helped prompt the evolution of SSH-2, which uses cryptographically strong integrity checking invulnerable to this attack.

3.4.4. Compression

The SSH-1 protocol supports compression of session data using the "deflate" algorithm of the GNU *gzip* utility (*ftp://ftp.gnu.org/pub/gnu/gzip/*). Packet data bytes in each direction are compressed separately, each as a single large stream without regard to packet boundaries.

While not typically needed on LAN or fast WAN links, compression can improve speed noticeably over slower links, such as an analog modem line. It is especially beneficial for file transfers, X forwarding, and running curses-style programs in a terminal session, such as text editors. Also, since compression is done before encryption, using compression can reduce delays due to encryption. This may be especially effective with 3DES, which is quite slow.

3.5. Inside SSH-2

In this section, we discuss the design and internals of SSH-2, focusing particularly on its differences and improvements as compared to SSH-1. We won't repeat the information common to the two protocols. We also compare the products SSH1 and SSH2, their software implementation differences, and their protocol support. Figure 3-4 summarizes the architecture of SSH-2.

The most important distinction between SSH1 and SSH2 is that they support different, incompatible versions of the SSH protocol: SSH-1.5 and SSH-2.0. [1.5] These products also have important implementation differences, some due to the differing protocols, but many are simply omissions due to SSH2's being a complete rewrite.

3.5.1. Protocol Differences (SSH-1 Versus SSH-2)

SSH-1 is monolithic, encompassing multiple functions in a single protocol. SSH-2, on the other hand, has been separated into modules and consists of three protocols working together:

- SSH Transport Layer Protocol (SSH-TRANS)
- SSH Authentication Protocol (SSH-AUTH)
- SSH Connection Protocol (SSH-CONN)

Each of these protocols has been specified separately, and a fourth document, SSH Protocol Architecture (SSH-ARCH), describes the overall architecture of the SSH-2 protocol as realized in these three separate specifications.

Figure 3-5 outlines the division of labor between these modules and how they relate to each other, application programs, and the network. SSH-TRANS is the fundamental building block, providing the initial connection, packet protocol, server authentication, and basic encryption and integrity services. After establishing an SSH-TRANS connection, an application has a single, secure, full-duplex byte stream to an authenticated peer.

Next, the client can use SSH-AUTH over the SSH-TRANS connection to authenticate itself to the server. SSH-AUTH defines three authentication methods: publickey, hostbased, and password. Publickey is similar to the SSH-1 "RSA" method, but it is more general and can accommodate any public-key signature algorithm. The standard requires only one algorithm, DSA, since RSA until recently was encumbered by patent restrictions.* Hostbased is similar to the SSH-1 RhostsRSA method, providing trusted-host authentication using cryptographic assurance of the

* RSA entered the public domain in September 2000, after many years as a patented algorithm.

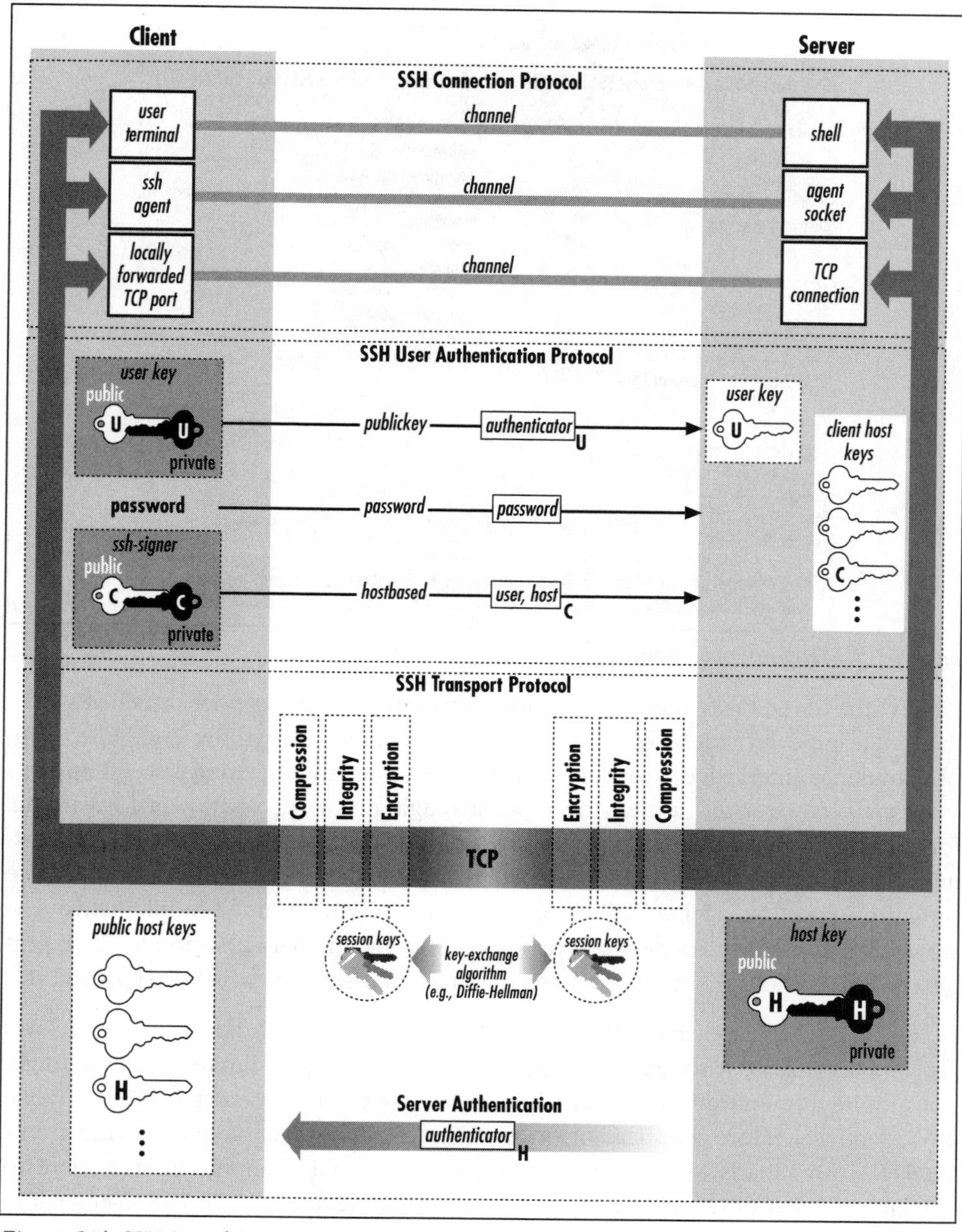

Figure 3-4. SSH-2 architecture

client host's identity. The password method is equivalent to SSH-1's password authentication; it also provides for changing a user's password, though we haven't seen any implementations of this feature. The weak, insecure Rhosts authentication of SSH-1 is absent.

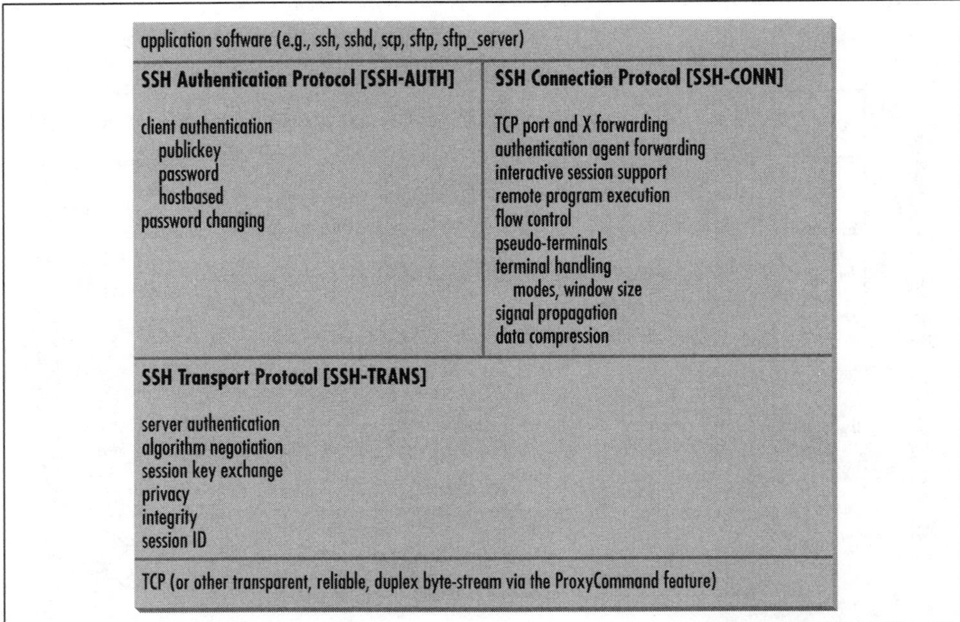

Figure 3-5. SSH-2 protocol family

Finally, the SSH-CONN protocol provides a variety of richer services to clients over the single pipe provided by SSH-TRANS. This includes everything needed to support multiple interactive and noninteractive sessions: multiplexing several streams (or *channels*) over the underlying pipe; managing X, port, and agent forwarding; forwarding application signals across the connection (such as SIGWINCH, indicating terminal window resizing); terminal handling; data compression; and remote program execution. Unlike SSH-1, SSH-CONN can handle multiple interactive sessions over the same connection, or none. This means SSH-2 supports X or port forwarding without the need for a separate terminal session, which SSH-1 can't do.

Note that SSH-CONN isn't layered on SSH-AUTH; they are both at the same level above SSH-TRANS. A specialized SSH server for a particular, limited purpose might not require authentication. Perhaps it just prints out "Nice to meet you!" to anyone who connects. More practically, an anonymous *sftp* server might provide freely available downloads to all comers. Such a server could simply allow a client to engage in SSH-CONN immediately after establishing an SSH-TRANS connection, whereas a general login server would always require successful authentication via SSH-AUTH first.

We now survey the major differences between SSH-1 and SSH-2. These include:

- Expanded algorithm negotiation between client and server
- Multiple methods for key-exchange

- Certificates for public keys
- More flexibility with authentication, including partial authentication
- Stronger integrity checking through cryptography
- Periodic replacement of the session key ("rekeying")

3.5.1.1. Algorithm choice and negotiation

A nice feature of SSH-1 is *algorithm negotiation,* in which a client selects a bulk encryption cipher from among those supported by the server. Other algorithms within SSH-1, however, are hardcoded and inflexible. SSH-2 improves upon this by making other algorithms negotiable between client and server: host key, message authentication, hash function, session key exchange, and data compression. SSH-2 requires support of one method per category to ensure interoperability and defines several other recommended and optional methods. [3.9]

Another improvement of SSH-2 is an extensible namespace for algorithms. SSH-1 identifies the negotiable bulk ciphers by a numerical code, with no values set aside for local additions. In contrast, SSH-2 algorithms (as well as protocols, services, and key/certificate formats) are named by strings, and local definitions are explicitly supported. From SSH-ARCH:

> Names that do not contain an at-sign (@) are reserved to be assigned by IANA (Internet Assigned Numbers Authority). Examples include 3des-cbc, sha-1, hmac-sha1, and zlib. Additional names of this format may be registered with IANA [and] MUST NOT be used without first registering with IANA. Registered names MUST NOT contain an at-sign (@) or a comma (,). Anyone can define additional algorithms by using names in the format name@domainname, e.g., ourcipher-cbc@ssh.fi. The format of the part preceding the at sign is not specified; it *must* consist of US-ASCII characters except at-sign and comma. The part following the at-sign *must* be a valid fully qualified internet domain name [RFC-1034] controlled by the person or organization defining the name. Each domain decides how it manages its local namespace.

This format allows new, nonstandard algorithms to be added for internal use without affecting interoperability with other SSH-2 implementations, even those with other local additions. OpenSSH makes use of this ability, defining an integrity-checking algorithm called `hmac-ripemd160@openssh.com`.

3.5.1.2. Session key exchange and the server key

Recall that the *session key* is the shared symmetric key for the bulk data cipher—the one used directly to encrypt user data passing over the SSH connection. [3.3] In SSH-1, this key is generated by the client and passed securely to the server by double-encrypting it with the server key and server's host key. The server key's purpose is to provide perfect forward secrecy. [3.4.1]

In keeping with its design, SSH-2 introduces a more general mechanism to accommodate multiple key-exchange methods, from which one is negotiated for use. The chosen method produces a shared secret that isn't used directly as the session key, but rather is input to a further process that produces the session key. The extra processing ensures that neither side can fully determine the session key (regardless of the exchange method used) and provides protection against replay attacks. [3.1.2] The key-exchange phase of the SSH-2 protocol is also responsible for server authentication, as in SSH-1.

SSH-2 currently defines only one key-exchange method, `diffie-hellman-group1-sha1`, and all implementations must support it. As the name implies, it is the Diffie-Hellman key-agreement algorithm with a fixed group,* together with the SHA-1 hash function. The Diffie-Hellman algorithm provides forward secrecy by itself, so no server key is needed. Also, independent of the processing just described, the Diffie-Hellman algorithm alone ensures that neither side can dictate the shared secret.

`diffie-hellman-group1-sha1` already provides forward secrecy, so SSH-2 implementations using it don't need a server key. Since other key-exchange methods may be defined for SSH-2, someone could conceivably implement the SSH-1 key-exchange algorithm, requiring a server key or similar method to provide perfect forward secrecy. But such a method hasn't been defined, so server keys are found only in SSH1 and OpenSSH/1. Therefore, an SSH-2-only server is more amenable to control by *inetd*, since it avoids the overhead of generating a server key on startup. [5.4.3.2] Examples are SSH2, or OpenSSH with SSH-1 support turned off.

3.5.1.3. Key/identity binding

In any public-key system, a crucial problem is verifying the owner of a key. Suppose you want to share encrypted messages with your friend Alice, but an intruder, Mallory, tricks you into accepting one of *his* public keys as Alice's. Now any messages you encrypt (supposedly) to Alice are readable by Mallory. Of course, you and Alice will quickly discover the problem when she finds that she can't decrypt your messages, but by then the damage is done.

The key-ownership problem is addressed using a technique called *public-key certificates*. A certificate is a data structure attesting that a *trusted third party* vouches for the key's owner. More precisely, the certificate attests to the binding between a public key and a particular identity (a personal or company name, email address, URL, etc.), or an ability (the right to access a database, modify a file, log into an account, etc.). The attestation is represented by a digital signature

* A *group* is a mathematical abstraction relevant to the Diffie-Hellman procedure; see references on group theory, number theory, or abstract algebra if you're curious.

from the third party. So in our example, you and Alice could arrange for a trusted third party, Pete, to sign your respective public keys, and you would therefore not believe Mallory's bogus, unsigned key.

This is all well and good, but who vouches for the voucher? How do you know the signer of Alice's key is really Pete? This problem continues recursively, as you need the signer's public key, and a certificate for that, and so on. These chains of certificates can be arranged in a hierarchy rooted at well-known Certificate Authorities, or they may be arranged in a decentralized network, the so-called "web of trust" used by PGP. Such arrangements, or trust models, are the basis for a public-key infrastructure (PKI).

In SSH, the key-ownership problem shows up in the bindings between hostnames and host keys. In all current SSH implementations, this is done using simple databases of hostnames, addresses, and keys which must be maintained and distributed by the user or system administrator. This isn't a scalable system. SSH-2 permits certificates to be included with public keys, opening the door for PKI techniques. The current SSH-2 specification defines formats for X.509, SPKI, and OpenPGP certificates, although no current SSH implementation supports their use.

Certificates, in theory, can also apply to user authentication. For instance, a certificate can bind a username to a public key, and SSH servers can accept valid certificates as authorization for the private key holder to access an account. This system provides the benefits of hostbased authentication without the fragile dependence on peer host security. If PKIs become more common, perhaps such features will appear.

3.5.1.4. Authentication

In order to authenticate, an SSH-1 client tries a sequence of authentication methods chosen from the set allowed by the server—public-key, password, trusted host, etc.—until one succeeds or all fail. This method is an all-or-nothing proposition; there's no way for a server to require multiple forms of authentication, since as soon as one method succeeds, the authentication phase ends.

The SSH-2 protocol is more flexible: the server informs the client which authentication methods are usable at any point in the exchange, as opposed to just once at the beginning of the connection, as in SSH-1. Thus, an SSH-2 server can, for example, decide to disallow public-key authentication after two unsuccessful attempts but still continue allowing the password method only. One use of this feature is interesting to note. SSH-2 clients usually first make an authentication request using a special method, "none." It always fails and returns the real authentication methods permitted by the server. If you see puzzling references in the SSH logs indicating that the method "none" has "failed," now you know what's going on (and it's normal).

An SSH-2 server also may indicate partial success: that a particular method succeeded, but further authentication is necessary. The server therefore can require the client to pass multiple authentication tests for login, say, both password and hostbased. The SSH2 server configuration keyword `RequiredAuthentications` controls this feature, which OpenSSH/2 currently lacks. [5.5.1]

3.5.1.5. Integrity checking

Improving on SSH-1's weak CRC-32 integrity check, SSH-2 uses cryptographically strong Message Authentication Code (MAC) algorithms to provide integrity and data origin assurance. The MAC methods and keys for each direction (separate from the session encryption keys) are determined during the key-exchange phase of the protocol. SSH-2 defines several MAC algorithms, and requires support for `hmac-sha1`, a 160-bit hash using the standard keyed HMAC construction with SHA-1. (See RFC-2104, "HMAC: Keyed-Hashing for Message Authentication.")

3.5.1.6. Hostbased authentication

An SSH server needs some sort of client host identifier to perform hostbased authentication. Specifically, it needs this for two operations:

- Looking up the client host key
- Matching the client host while performing authorization via the hostbased control files (*shosts.equiv*, etc.)

Call these operations the *HAUTH* process. Now, there is an important difference between trusted-host authentication in protocols 1 and 2: in SSH-2, the authentication request contains the client hostname, whereas in SSH-1 it doesn't. This means that SSH-1 is constrained to use the client IP address, or a name derived from the address via the naming service, as the identifier. Since the SSH-1 server's idea of the client host identity is tied to the client's network address, RhostsRSA authentication can't work completely (or sometimes at all) in the following common scenarios:

- Mobile client with a changing IP address (e.g., a laptop being carried around and connected to different networks)
- Client behind a network-visible proxy, such as SOCKS
- Client with multiple network addresses ("multihomed"), unless the corresponding DNS entries are arranged in a particular way

The SSH-2 protocol, on the other hand, doesn't impose this restriction: the hostbased authentication process is in principle independent of the client's network address. An SSH-2 server has two candidates at hand for the client identifier: the name in the authentication request, N_{auth} and the name looked up via the client's network address, N_{net}. It can simply ignore N_{net} altogether, using N_{auth} for *HAUTH* instead. Of course, the known-hosts list and hostbased authorization files must be maintained using that namespace. Indeed, N_{auth} can be chosen from any space of identifiers, not necessarily tied or related to the network naming service at all. For clarity's sake, it should probably continue to be the client's canonical hostname.

As currently implemented, SSH2 doesn't do this. *sshd2* behaves just as *sshd1* does, using N_{net} for *HAUTH* and uses N_{auth} only as a sanity check. If $N_{net} \neq N_{auth}$, *sshd2* fails the authentication. This is really backwards and causes hostbased authentication to be much less useful than it could be, since it continues to not work in the scenarios noted earlier. The authors have suggested to SCS to instead use N_{auth} for *HAUTH* and implement the $N_{net} = N_{auth}$ check as a per-host option. It makes sense as an extra bit of security, in cases where it's known that the client host address should never change. This is analogous to public-key authentication, which is independent of the client host address, but which admits additional restrictions based on the source address when appropriate (via the `"hosts="` *authorized_keys* option).

3.5.1.7. Session rekeying

The more data that's encrypted with a particular key and available for analysis, the better an attacker's chances of breaking the encryption. It is therefore wise to periodically change keys if large amounts of data are being encrypted. This isn't much of an issue with asymmetric keys, since they are typically used only to encrypt small amounts of data, producing digital signatures over hash values or encrypting symmetric keys. A key for the bulk data cipher of an SSH connection, however, might encrypt hundreds of megabytes of data, if it's being used to transfer large files or perform protected backups, for example. The SSH-2 protocol provides a way for either side of an SSH connection to initiate a re-keying of the session. This causes the client and server to negotiate new session keys and take them into use. SSH-1 doesn't provide a way to change the bulk cipher key for a session.

3.5.1.8. SSH-1/SSH-2: summary

Table 3-3 summarizes the important differences between Versions 1.5 and 2.0 of the SSH protocol.

Table 3-3. SSH-1 and SSH-2 Differences

SSH-2	SSH-1
Separate transport, authentication, and connection protocols.	One monolithic protocol.
Strong cryptographic integrity check.	Weak CRC-32 integrity check.

Table 3-3. SSH-1 and SSH-2 Differences (continued)

SSH-2	SSH-1
Supports password changing.	N/A
Any number of session channels per connection (including none).	Exactly one session channel per connection (requires issuing a remote command even when you don't want one).
Full negotiation of modular cryptographic and compression algorithms, including bulk encryption, MAC, and public-key.	Negotiates only the bulk cipher; all others are fixed.
Encryption, MAC, and compression are negotiated separately for each direction, with independent keys.	The same algorithms and keys are used in both directions (although RC4 uses separate keys, since the algorithm's design demands that keys not be reused).
Extensible algorithm/protocol naming scheme allows local extensions while preserving interoperability.	Fixed encoding precludes interoperable additions.
User authentication methods: • public-key (DSA, RSA, OpenPGP) • hostbased • password • (Rhosts dropped due to insecurity)	Supports a wider variety: • public-key (RSA only) • RhostsRSA • password • Rhosts (*rsh*-style) • TIS • Kerberos
Use of Diffie-Hellman key agreement removes the need for a server key.	Server key used for forward secrecy on the session key.
Supports public-key certificates.	N/A
User authentication exchange is more flexible and allows requiring multiple forms of authentication for access.	Allows exactly one form of authentication per session.
Hostbased authentication is in principle independent of client network address, and so can work with proxying, mobile clients, etc. (but see [3.5.1.6]).	RhostsRSA authentication is effectively tied to the client host address, limiting its usefulness.
Periodic replacement of session keys.	N/A

3.5.2. Implementation Differences

There are many differences among the current crop of SSH-1 and SSH-2 implementations. Some are direct results of the different protocols, such as the ability to require multiple forms of authentication or support of the DSA public-key algorithm. Others are feature differences that aren't dictated by the protocols, but are simply inclusions or omissions by the software authors. Here we discuss some nonprotocol-related design and feature differences among OpenSSH, SSH1, and SSH2:

- Host keys
- No fallback to *rsh*
- Setuid client
- SSH-1 backward compatibility

3.5.2.1. Host keys

SSH host keys are long-term asymmetric keys that distinguish and identify hosts running SSH, or instances of the SSH server, depending on the SSH implementation. This happens in two places in the SSH protocol:

1. Server authentication verifying the server host's identity to connecting clients. This process occurs for every SSH connection.*
2. Authentication of a client host to the server; used only during RhostsRSA or hostbased user authentication.

Unfortunately, the term "host key" is confusing. It implies that only one such key may belong to a given host. This is true for client authentication but not for server authentication, because multiple SSH servers may run on a single machine, each with a different identifying key.† This so-called "host key" actually identifies a running instance of the SSH server program, not a machine.

SSH1 maintains a single database serving both server authentication and client authentication. It is the union of the system *known_hosts* file (*/etc/ssh_known_hosts*), together with the user's *~/.ssh/known_hosts* file on either the source machine (for server authentication) or the target machine (for client authentication). The database maps a hostname or address to a set of keys acceptable for authenticating a host with that name or address. One name may be associated with multiple keys (more on this shortly).

SSH2, on the other hand, maintains two separate maps for these purposes:

- The *hostkeys* map for server host authentication
- The *knownhosts* map for client host authentication

Hooray, more confusing terminology. Here, the term "known hosts" is reused with slightly different formatting (knownhosts versus known_hosts) for an overlapping but not identical purpose.

---

* In SSH-1, the host key also encrypts the session key for transmission to the server. However, this use is actually for server authentication, rather than for data protection per se; the server later proves its identity by showing that it correctly decrypted the session key. Protection of the session key is obtained by encrypting it a second time with the ephemeral server key.

† Or sharing the same key, if you wish, assuming the servers are compatible with one another.

While SSH1 keeps host keys in a file with multiple entries, SSH2 stores them in a filesystem directory, one key per file, indexed by filename. For instance, a *knownhosts* directory looks like:

```
$ ls -l /etc/ssh2/knownhosts/
total 2
-r--r--r--    1 root     root         697 Jun  5 22:22 wynken.sleepy.net.ssh-dss.pub
-r--r--r--    1 root     root         697 Jul 21  1999 blynken.sleepy.net.ssh-dss.pub
```

Note that the filename is of the form *<hostname>.<key type>.pub.*

The other map, *hostkeys,* is keyed not just on name/address, but also on the server's TCP listening port; that is to say, it is keyed on TCP sockets. This allows for multiple keys per host in a more specific manner than before. Here, the filenames are of the form *key_<port number>_<hostname>.pub.* The following example shows the public keys for one SSH server running on *wynken,* port 22, and two running on *blynken,* ports 22 and 220. Furthermore, we've created a symbolic link to make "nod" another name for the server at *wynken*:22. End users may add to these maps by placing keys (either manually or automatically by client) into the directories *~/.ssh2/knownhosts* and *~/.ssh2/hostkeys.*

```
$ ls -l /etc/ssh2/hostkeys/
total 5
-rw-r--r--    1 root     root     757 May 31 14:52 key_22_blynken.sleepy.net.pub
-rw-r--r--    1 root     root     743 May 31 14:52 key_22_wynken.sleepy.net.pub
-rw-r--r--    1 root     root     755 May 31 14:52 key_220_wynken.sleepy.net.pub
lrwxrwxrwx    1 root     root      28 May 31 14:57 key_22_nod.pub ->
                                                    key_22_wynken.sleepy.net.pub
```

Even though it allows for multiple keys per host, SSH2 is missing one useful feature of SSH1: multiple keys *per name.* This sounds like the same thing, but there's a subtle difference: names can refer to more than one host. A common example is a set of load-sharing login servers hidden behind a single hostname. A university might have a set of three machines intended for general login access, each with its own name and address:

login1.foo.edu → 10.0.0.1
login2.foo.edu → 10.0.0.2
login3.foo.edu → 10.0.0.3

In addition, there is a single generic name that carries all three addresses:

login.foo.edu → {10.0.0.1, 10.0.0.2, 10.0.0.3}

The university computing center tells people to connect only to *login.foo.edu,* and the university's naming service hands out the three addresses in round-robin order (e.g., using round-robin DNS) to share the load among the three machines. SSH has problems with this setup by default. Each time you connect to *login.foo.edu,* you have a 2/3 chance of reaching a different machine than you reached last time, with a different host key. SSH repeatedly complains that the host key of *login.foo.com* has changed and issues a warning about a possible attack against your client. This soon gets annoying. With SSH1, you can edit the *known_hosts* file to associate the generic name with each of the individual host keys, changing this:

```
login1.foo.edu 1024 35 1519086808544755383...
login2.foo.edu 1024 35 1508058310547044394...
login3.foo.edu 1024 35 1087309429906462914...
```

to this:

```
login1.foo.edu,login.foo.edu 1024 35 1519086808544755383...
login2.foo.edu,login.foo.edu 1024 35 1508058310547044394...
login3.foo.edu,login.foo.edu 1024 35 1087309429906462914...
```

With SSH2, however, there's no general way to do this; since the database is indexed by entries in a directory, with one key per file, it can't have more than one key per name.

It might seem that you're losing some security by doing this, but we don't think so. All that's really happening is the recognition that a particular name may refer to different hosts at different times, and thus you tell SSH to trust a connection to that name if it's authenticated by any of a given set of keys. Most of the time, that set happens to have size 1, and you're telling SSH, "When I connect to this name, I want to make sure I'm connecting to this particular host." With multiple keys per name, you can also say, "When I connect to this name, I want to make sure that I get one of the following set of hosts." That's a perfectly valid and useful thing to do.

Another way to solve this problem is for the system administrators of *login.foo.com* to install the same host key on all three machines. But this defeats the ability for SSH to distinguish between these hosts, even if you want it to. We prefer the former approach.

3.5.2.2. No fallback to rsh

Not only does SSH1 support *rsh*-style authentication, but also *ssh* can invoke *rsh* automatically if a remote host has no SSH server running. Along with Rhosts authentication support, this feature is deliberately absent from SSH2, due to the poor security of *rsh*. [7.4.5.8]

3.5.2.3. Setuid client

The SSH1 client needs to be installed as setuid root in order to use RhostsRSA authentication. There are two reasons for this: host key access and privileged source ports. The privileged port requirement from the client is a holdover from *rsh*-style authentication that adds no security to RhostsRSA, and that requirement has been dropped from SSH2 hostbased authentication. [3.4.2.3]

The remaining reason for a setuid client is access to the private host key file. The host key is stored unencrypted, so SSH can access it without a human to type a passphrase. Therefore the file containing the private host key must be protected from general read access. The SSH server usually runs as root for other reasons, and so can read any file. The client, though, is run by ordinary users, yet must have access to the private host key to engage in trusted-host authentication. The file is usually installed as readable only by the root user, and so the client needs to be setuid root.

Now, on general security grounds, one tries to avoid installing setuid programs if at all possible—most especially those that setuid to root. Any such program must be carefully written to prevent abuse. Preferably, a setuid program should be small and simple with little user interaction. The big, complicated SSH client, which talks constantly with users as well as other machines, is definitely not a safe candidate.

SSH2 sidesteps this problem by introducing the *ssh-signer2* program. *ssh-signer2* factors into a separate program that portion of the client that requires access to the private host key. It speaks the SSH packet protocol on its standard input and output and takes as input a hostbased authentication request to be signed. It carefully checks the request for validity; most particularly, it checks that the username in the request is that of the user running *ssh-signer2*, and that the hostname is the canonical name of the current host. If the request is valid, *ssh-signer2* signs the request with the host key and returns it.

Since *ssh-signer2* is a relatively small and simple, it is easier to be confident that it is securely written and safe to make setuid. In turn, the SSH client itself is no longer setuid; when it needs to sign a hostbased authentication request, it runs *ssh-signer2* as a subprocess to get the signature.

Although the SSH2 installation process makes the private host key readable only by root, and *ssh-signer2* setuid root, there is no real need to use the root account for this purpose, and indeed every reason not to. It suffices to create a new, unprivileged user for this specific purpose, say, "ssh." It should be a locked account with no password and no way to log into it, and the account information should be stored in local files (e.g., */etc/passwd*, */etc/group*) rather than NIS. You should then make the host key file readable only by this account and make *ssh-signer2* setuid and owned by it. For example:

```
# chown ssh /etc/ssh_host_key
# chmod 400 /etc/ssh_host_key
# chown ssh /usr/local/bin/ssh-signer2
# chmod 04711 /usr/local/bin/ssh-signer2
```

This has the same effect as the default installation and is even less risky since it doesn't involve a setuid root program.

You can do the same thing with *ssh1*, but it renders trusted-host authentication unusable, since the server demands a privileged source port for the RhostsRSA mechanism.

3.5.2.4. SSH-1 backward compatibility

SSH2 can provide backward compatibility for the SSH-1 protocol if the entire SSH1 package is also installed on the same machine. The SSH2 client and server simply run their SSH1 counterparts when they connect to a partner running the older protocol. This is rather cumbersome. It's also wasteful and slow, since each new *sshd1* needs to generate its own server key, which otherwise the single master server only regenerates once an hour. This wastes entropy, sometimes a precious commodity, and can cause noticeable delays in the startup of SSH-1 connections to an SSH2 server. Further, it is an administrative headache and a security problem, since one must maintain two separate SSH server configurations and try to make sure all desired restrictions are adequately covered in both.

Beginning with Version 2.1.0, OpenSSH supports both SSH-1 and SSH-2 in a single set of programs, though the support isn't yet as complete as that found in SSH2. (For example, hostbased authentication is missing; this doesn't affect compliance with SSH-2, though, since that support is optional.) This technique avoids the problems inherent in the SSH2 mechanism. The SSH-1 protocol is still considered the primary option; if you're contacting a server that supports both protocols, the OpenSSH client uses SSH-1. You can force it to use SSH-2 with the *–2* switch, or the "protocol 2" configuration statement.

3.6. As-User Access (userfile)

The SSH server usually runs as root (as does the client, in some circumstances). At various points, SSH needs to access files belonging to the source or target accounts. The root account privilege overrides most access controls, but not all. For instance, the root account on an NFS client doesn't necessarily have any special access to files on a remote filesystem. Another example is POSIX access control lists (ACLs); only the file owner can change a file ACL, and root doesn't override this restriction.

In Unix, there is a way for a process to take on the identity of a different user than its current user ID: the setuid system call. Root can use this facility to "become" any user. However, this call is irreversible for the duration of the process; a program can't regain its previous privileges, making setuid unsuitable for SSH. Some

Unix implementations have a reversible form, seteuid (set effective user ID), but it isn't universally available and isn't part of POSIX.*

To aid in portability, SSH1 and SSH2 use the reliably available setuid system call. The first time they need to access a file as a regular user, they start a subprocess. The subprocess calls setuid to change (irrevocably) to the desired uid, but the main SSH program continues running as root. Then, whenever SSH needs file access as that user, the main program sends a message to the subprocess, asking it to perform the needed operation and return the results. Internally, this facility is called the *userfile* module.

Keep this behavior in mind when debugging an SSH process with SunOS *trace*, Solaris *truss*, Linux *strace*, or another process tracer. By default, these programs trace only the topmost process, so always remember to trace subprocesses as well. (See the tracer's manpage for the appropriate option, though it is usually *–f*.) If you forget to do this, and the problem is with file access, you might not see it, since the userfile subprocess performs the file-access system calls (`open`, `read`, `write`, `stat`, etc.).

3.7. Randomness

Cryptographic algorithms and protocols require a good source of random bits, or entropy. Randomness is used in various ways:

- To generate data-encryption keys
- As plaintext padding and initialization vectors in encryption algorithms, to help foil cryptanalysis
- For check bytes or *cookies* in protocol exchanges, as a measure against packet spoofing attacks

Randomness is harder to achieve than you might think; in fact, even defining randomness is difficult (or picking the right definition for a given situation). For example, "random" numbers that are perfectly good for statistical modeling might be terrible for cryptography. Each of these applications requires certain properties of its random input, such as an even distribution. Cryptography, in particular, demands *unpredictability* so an attacker reading our data can't guess our keys.

True randomness—in the sense of complete unpredictability—can't be produced by a computer program. Any sequence of bits produced as the output of a program eventually repeats itself. For true randomness, you have to turn to physical processes, such as fluid turbulence or the quantum dice of radioactive decay. Even

* Actually, POSIX does have the same feature under a different name, but it isn't always present, either.

there, you must take great care that measurement artifacts don't introduce unwanted structure.

There are algorithms, however, that produce long sequences of practically unpredictable output, with good statistical randomness properties. These are good enough for many cryptographic applications, and such algorithms are called pseudo-random number generators, or PRNGs. A PRNG requires a small random input, called the *seed*, so it doesn't always produce the same output. From the seed, the PRNG produces a much larger string of acceptably random output; essentially, it is a randomness "stretcher." So a program using a PRNG still needs to find some good random bits, just fewer of them, but they had better be quite unpredictable.

Since various programs require random bits, some operating systems have built-in facilities for providing them. Some Unix variants (including Linux and OpenBSD) have a device driver, accessed through */dev/random* and */dev/urandom*, that provides random bits when opened and read as a file. These bits are derived by all sorts of methods, some quite clever. Correctly filtered timing measurements of disk accesses, for example, can represent the fluctuations due to air turbulence around the drive heads. Another technique is to look at the least significant bits of noise coming from an unused microphone port. And of course, they can track fluctuating events such as network packet arrival times, keyboard events, interrupts, etc.

SSH implementations make use of randomness, but the process is largely invisible to the end user. Here's what happens under the hood. SSH1 and SSH2, for example, use a kernel-based randomness source if it is available, along with their own sampling of (one hopes) fluctuating system parameters, gleaned by running such programs such as *ps* or *netstat*. It uses these sources to seed its PRNG, as well as to "stir in" more randomness every once in a while. Since it can be expensive to gather randomness, SSH stores its pool of random bits in a file between invocations of the program, as shown in the following table:

	SSH1	SSH2
Server	*/etc/ssh_random_seed*	*/etc/ssh2/random_seed*
Client	*~/.ssh/random_seed*	*~/.ssh2/random_seed*

These files should be kept protected, since they contain sensitive information that can weaken SSH's security if disclosed to an attacker, although SSH takes steps to reduce that possibility. The seed information is always mixed with some new entropy before being used, and only half the pool is ever saved to disk, to reduce its predictive value if stolen.

In SSH1 and SSH2, all this happens automatically and invisibly. When compiling OpenSSH on platform without */dev/random*, you have a choice. If you have installed an add-on randomness source, such as the OpenSSH-recommended "Entropy Gathering Daemon" (EGD, *http://www.lothar.com/tech/crypto/*), you can tell OpenSSH to use it with the switch **`--with-egd-pool`**. If you don't specify a pool, OpenSSH uses an internal entropy-gathering mechanism. You can tailor which programs are run to gather entropy and "how random" they're considered to be, by editing the file */etc/ssh_prng_cmds*. Also, note that OpenSSH random seed is kept in the *~/.ssh/prng_seed file*, even the daemon's, which is just the root user's seed file.

3.8. SSH and File Transfers (scp and sftp)

The first thing to understand about SSH and file transfers, is that SSH doesn't do file transfers.

Ahem.

Now that we have your attention, what can we possibly mean by that? After all, there are entire sections of this book dedicated to explaining how to use *scp1*, *scp2*, and *sftp* for file transfers. What we mean is that there is nothing in the SSH protocol about transferring files: an SSH speaker can't ask its partner to send or receive a file through the protocol. And the programs we just mentioned don't actually implement the SSH protocol themselves nor incorporate any security features at all. Instead, they actually run the SSH client in a subprocess, in order to connect to the remote host and run the other half of the file-transfer process there. There is nothing very SSH-specific about these programs; they use SSH in much the same way as do other applications we cover, such as CVS and Pine.

The only reason it was necessary to come up with *scp1* in the first place was that there was no widely used, general-purpose file-transfer protocol available that operated over the single, full-duplex byte stream connection provided by the SSH remote program execution. If existing FTP implementations could easily be made to operate over SSH, there would be no need for *ssh*, but as we'll see, FTP is entirely unsuited to this. [11.2] So Tatu Ylönen wrote *scp1* and made it part of SSH1. The protocol it uses (let's call it "SCP1") remained entirely undocumented, even when Ylönen wrote the first RFC documenting the SSH-1 protocol.

Later, when SSH Communications Security was writing SSH2, they wanted to continue to include a file-transfer tool. They stayed with the model of layering it on top of SSH proper, but decided to entirely reimplement it. Thus, they replaced the "scp1 protocol" with the "SFTP protocol," as it is commonly known. The SFTP protocol is again simply a way to do bidirectional file transfers over a single, reliable, full-duplex byte stream connection. It happens to be based on the same packet protocol used as the substrate for the SSH Connection Protocol, presumably as a matter of convenience. The implementers already had a tool available for sending record-oriented messages over a byte pipe, so they reused it. SFTP remains an undocumented, proprietary protocol at press time, though there is work beginning in the IETF SECSH working group to document and standardize it.

The name SFTP is really unfortunate, because it confuses people on a number of levels. Most take it to stand for "Secure FTP." First, just as with *scp1*, as a protocol it isn't secure at all; the implementation derives its security by speaking the protocol over an SSH connection. And second, it has nothing whatsoever to do with the FTP protocol. It is a common mistake to think you can somehow use SFTP to talk securely to an FTP server—a reasonable enough supposition, given the name.

Another confusing aspect of file transfer in SSH2, is the relationship among the two programs *scp2* and *sftp*, and the SFTP protocol. In SSH1, there is a single file-transfer protocol, SCP1, and a single program embodying it: *scp1*. In SSH2, there is also a single, new file-transfer protocol: SFTP. But there are three separate programs implementing it and two different clients. The server side is the program *sftp-server*. The two clients are *scp2* and *sftp*. *scp2* and *sftp* are simply two different front-ends for the same process: each runs the SSH2 client in a subprocess to start and speak to *sftp-server* on the remote host. They merely provide different user interfaces: *scp2* is more like the traditional *rcp*, and *sftp* is deliberately similar to an FTP client.

None of this confusing terminology is made any easier by the fact that both SSH1 and SSH2 when installed make symbolic links allowing you to use the plain names "scp," "ssh," etc., instead of "scp1" or "ssh2." When we speak of the two SSH-related file-transfer protocols, we call them the SCP1 and SFTP protocols. SCP1 is sometimes also just called the "scp" protocol, which is technically ambiguous but usually understood. We suppose you could refer to SFTP as the "scp2 protocol," but we've never heard it and don't recommend it if you want to keep your sanity.*

3.8.1. scp1 Details

When you run *scp1* to copy a file from client to server, it invokes *ssh1* like this:

```
ssh -x -a -o "FallBackToRsh no" -o "ClearAllForwardings yes" server-host scp ...
```

This runs another copy of *scp* on the remote host. That copy is invoked with the undocumented switches *-t* and *-f* (for "to" and "from"), putting it into SCP1 server mode. This next table shows some examples; Figure 3-6 shows the details.

This client scp command:	Runs this remote command:
`scp foo server:bar`	`scp -t bar`
`scp server:bar foo`	`scp -f bar`
`scp *.txt server:dir`	`scp -d -t dir`

* Especially since *scp2* may run *scp1* for SSH-1 compatibility! Oy gevalt!

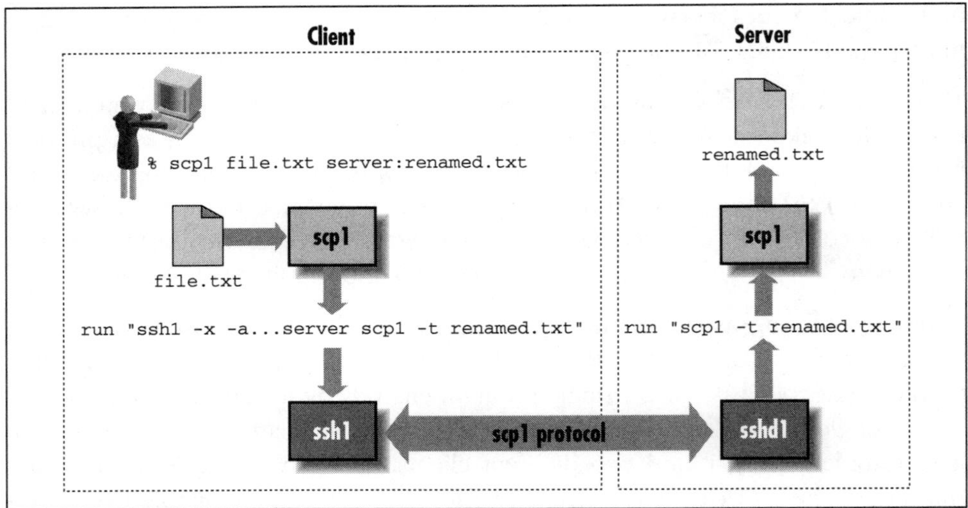

Figure 3-6. scp1 operation

If you run *scp1* to copy a file between two remote hosts, it simply executes another *scp1* client on the source host to copy the file to the target. For example, this command:

```
scp1 source:music.au target:playme
```

runs this in the background:

```
ssh1 -x -a ... as above ... source scp1 music.au target:playme
```

3.8.2. scp2/sftp Details

When you run *scp2* or *sftp*, they run *ssh2* behind the scenes, using this command:

```
ssh2 -x -a -o passwordprompt "%U@%H\'s password:"
           -o "nodelay yes"
           -o "authenticationnotify yes"
           server host
           -s sftp
```

Unlike *scp1*, here the command doesn't vary depending on the direction or type of file transfer; all the necessary information is carried inside the SFTP protocol.

Note that they don't start *sftp-server* with a remote command, but rather with the SSH2 "subsystem" mechanism via the *–s sftp* option. [5.7] This means that the SSH2 server must be configured to handle this subsystem, with a line like this in */etc/ssh2/sshd2_config*:

```
subsystem-sftp                  /usr/local/sbin/sftp-server
```

Assuming the *ssh2* command succeeds, *sftp* and *sftp-server* start speaking the SFTP protocol over the SSH session, and the user can send and retrieve files. Figure 3-7 shows the details.

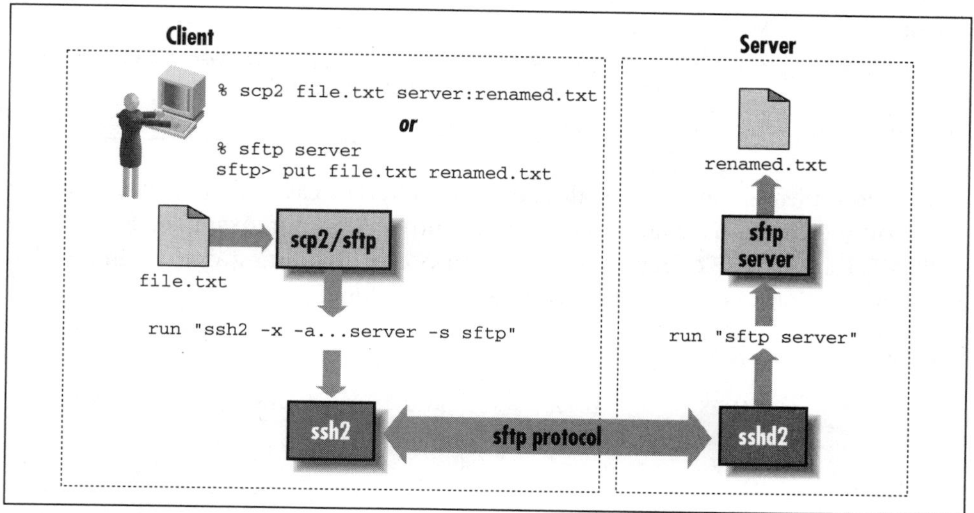

Figure 3-7. scp2/sftp operation

Our testing shows roughly a factor-of-four reduction in throughput from *scp1* to *scp2*. We observe that the SFTP mechanism uses the SSH packet protocol twice, one encapsulated inside the other: the SFTP protocol itself uses the packet protocol as its basis, and that runs on top of an SSH session. While this is certainly inefficient, it seems unlikely to be the reason for such a dramatic reduction in performance; perhaps there are simply implementation problems that can be fixed, such as bad interactions between buffering in different layers of the protocol code. We have not dug into the code ourselves to find a reason for the slowdown.

3.9. Algorithms Used by SSH

Tables 3-4 through 3-6 summarize the available ciphers in the SSH protocols and their implementations. Required algorithms are in bold;, recommended ones are italic; the others are optional. Parentheses indicate an algorithm not defined in the protocol, but provided in some implementation. The meanings of the entries are:

x The implementation supports the algorithm and is included in the default build.

o The implementation supports the algorithm, but it isn't included in the default build (it must be specifically enabled when compiling).

– The implementation doesn't support the algorithm.

Table 3-4. Algorithms in the SSH Protocols

	SSH-1.5	SSH-2.0
Public-key	RSA	**DSA**, **DH**
Hash	**MD5**, **CRC-32**	**SHA-1**, MD5
Symmetric	**3DES**, *IDEA*, *ARCFOUR*, DES	**3DES**, *Blowfish*, *Twofish*, CAST-128, IDEA, ARCFOUR
Compression	zlib	zlib

Note that Table 3-4 simply lists algorithms in different categories used in the two protocol specifications, without regard to purpose. So for example, SSH-1 uses both MD5 and CRC-32, but for different purposes; this listing doesn't imply that SSH-1 has option to employ MD5 for integrity checking.

Table 3-5. SSH-1 Ciphers

	3DES	IDEA	RC4	DES	(Blowfish)
SSH1	x	x	o	o	x
OpenSSH	x	–	–	–	x

Table 3-6. SSH-2 Ciphers

	3DES	Blowfish	Twofish	CAST-128	IDEA	RC4
SSH2	x	x	x	–	–	x
F-Secure SSH2	x	x	x	x	–	x
OpenSSH	x	x	–	x	–	x

Why are some algorithms unsupported by different programs? DES is often omitted from SSH-1 software as insufficiently secure. RC4 is omitted because of problems in the way it is used in the SSH-1 protocol, permitting vulnerabilities to active network-level attacks; this problem has been fixed in SSH-2. IDEA is omitted from OpenSSH and the noncommercial SSH1 and SSH2 because it is patented and requires royalties for commercial use. Twofish isn't in OpenSSH because it isn't yet part of the OpenSSL toolkit, which OpenSSH uses. CAST-128 is free, so we don't know why it is missing from the noncommercial SSH2.

The free version of SSH2 supports only the required DSA for public keys, while the commercial F-Secure SSH2 Server adds partial support for RSA keys for user authentication. [6.2.2]. The F-Secure server starts if its host key is RSA and reports that it successfully read the key. However, it still advertises its host key type as DSA in its key-exchange messages and then supplies the RSA key anyway, causing clients to fail when they try to read the supplied key. Of course, this problem masks the question of whether the client can handle an RSA host key even if it were properly identified. OpenSSH/2 doesn't contain RSA support at all, but now that the RSA patent has expired, the ssh-rsa key type will be added to the SSH-2 protocol, and support should follow shortly.

We now summarize each of the algorithms we have mentioned. Don't treat these summaries as complete analyses, however. You can't necessarily extrapolate from characteristics of individual algorithms (positive or negative) to whole systems without considering the other parts. Security is complicated that way.

3.9.1. Public-Key Algorithms

3.9.1.1. Rivest-Shamir-Adleman (RSA)

The Rivest-Shamir-Adleman public-key algorithm (RSA) is the most widely used asymmetric cipher. It derives its security from the difficulty of factoring large integers that are the product of two large primes of roughly equal size. Factoring is widely believed to be intractable (i.e., infeasible, admitting no efficient, polynomial-time solution), although this isn't proven. RSA can be used for both encryption and signatures.

Until September 2000, RSA was claimed to be patented in the United States by Public Key Partners, Inc., a company in which RSA Security, Inc. is a partner. (The algorithm is now in the public domain.) While the patent was in force, PKP claimed that it controlled the use of the RSA algorithm in the USA, and that the use of unauthorized implementations was illegal. Until the mid-1990s, RSA Security provided a freely available reference implementation, RSAref, with a license allowing educational and broad commercial use (as long as the software itself was not sold for profit). They no longer support or distribute this toolkit, though it is commonly available. Since RSA is now in the public domain, there's no longer any reason to use RSAref. It is no longer supported, some versions contain security flaws, and there are better implementations out there; we discourage its use.

The SSH-1 protocol specifies use of RSA explicitly. SSH-2 can use multiple public-key algorithms, but it defines only DSA. [3.9.1.2] The SECSH working group plans to add the RSA algorithm to SSH-2 now that the patent has expired. In the meantime, only the F-Secure SSH2 Server implements RSA keys in SSH2, using the global key-format identifier "ssh-rsa". This isn't yet part of the draft standard: to be technically correct it should use a localized name, e.g., *ssh-rsa@datafellows.com.* [3.5.1.1] However, this is unlikely to cause a real problem. The feature is useful for authentication to an SSH2 server with an existing SSH1 key, so you don't need to generate a new (DSA) key.

3.9.1.2. Digital Signature Algorithm (DSA)

The Digital Signature Algorithm (DSA) was developed by the U.S. National Security Agency (NSA), and promulgated by the U.S. National Institute of Standards and

Technology (NIST) as part of the Digital Signature Standard (DSS). The DSS was issued as a Federal Information Processing Standard, FIPS-186, in May 1994. It is a public-key algorithm, based on the Schnorr and ElGamal methods, and relies on the difficulty of computing discrete logarithms in a finite field. It is designed as a signature-only scheme that can't be used for encryption, although a fully general implementation may easily perform both RSA and ElGamal encryption.

DSA has also been surrounded by a swirl of controversy since its inception. The NIST first claimed that it had designed DSA, then eventually revealed that the NSA had done so. Many question the motives and ethics of the NSA, with ample historical reason to do so.* Researcher Gus Simmons discovered a subliminal channel in DSA that allows an implementor to leak information—for instance, secret key bits—with every signature.† Since the algorithm was to be made available as a closed hardware implementation in smart cards as part of the government's Capstone program, many people considered this property highly suspicious. Finally, NIST intended DSA to be available royalty-free to all users. To that end it was patented by David Kravitz (patent #5,231,668), then an employee of the NSA, who assigned the patent to the U.S. government. There have been claims, however, that DSA infringes existing cryptographic patents, including the Schnorr patent. To our knowledge, this issue has yet to be settled in court.

The SSH-2 protocol uses DSA as its required (and currently, only defined) public-key algorithm for host identification.

3.9.1.3. Diffie-Hellman key agreement

The Diffie-Hellman key agreement algorithm was the original public-key system, invented by Whitfield Diffie, Martin Hellman, and Ralph Merkle in 1976. It was patented by them in 1977 (issued in 1980, patent #4,200,770); that patent has now expired, and the algorithm is in the public domain. Like DSA, it is based on the discrete logarithm problem, and it allows two parties to derive a shared secret key securely over an open channel. That is, the parties engage in an exchange of messages, at the end of which they share a secret key. It isn't feasible for an eavesdropper to determine the shared secret merely from observing the exchanged messages.

* See James Bamford's book, *The Puzzle Palace* (Penguin), for an investigative history of the NSA.

† G. J. Simmons, "The Subliminal Channels in the U.S. Digital Signature Algorithm (DSA)." *Proceedings of the Third Symposium on: State and Progress of Research in Cryptography*, Rome: Fondazione Ugo Bordoni, 1993, pp. 35-54.

SSH-2 uses the Diffie-Hellman algorithm as its required (and currently, its only defined) key-exchange method.

3.9.2. Secret-Key Algorithms

3.9.2.1. International Data Encryption Algorithm (IDEA)

The International Data Encryption Algorithm (IDEA) was designed in 1990 by Xuejia Lai and James Massey,* and went through several revisions, improvements, and renamings before reaching its current form. Although relatively new, it is considered secure; the well-known cryptographer Bruce Schneier in 1996 pronounced it "the best and most secure block algorithm available to the public at this time."

IDEA is patented in Europe and the United States by the Swiss company Ascom-Tech AG.† The name "IDEA" is a trademark of Ascom-Tech. The attitude of Ascom-Tech towards this patent and the use of IDEA in the United States has changed over time, especially with regard to its inclusion in PGP. It is free for noncommercial use. Government or commercial use may require a royalty, where "commercial use" includes use of the algorithm internal to a commercial organization, not just directly selling an implementation or offering its use for profit. Here are two sites for more information:

http://www.ascom.ch/infosec/idea.html
http://www.it-sec.com/idea.html

3.9.2.2. Data Encryption Standard (DES)

The Data Encryption Standard (DES) is the aging workhorse of symmetric encryption algorithms. Designed by researchers at IBM in the early 1970s under the name Lucifer, the U.S. government adopted DES as a standard on November 23, 1976 (FIPS-46). It was patented by IBM, but IBM granted free worldwide rights to its use. It has been used extensively in the public and private sectors ever since. DES has stood up well to cryptanalysis over the years and is becoming viewed as outdated only because its 56-bit key size is too small relative to modern computing power. A number of well-publicized designs for special-purpose "DES-cracking" machines have been put forward, and their putative prices are falling more and more into the realm of plausibility for governments and large companies. It seems sure that at least the NSA has such devices. Because of these weaknesses, NIST is

* X. Lai and J. Massey, "A Proposal for a New Block Encryption Standard," *Advances in Cryptology—EUROCRYPT '92 Proceedings*, Springer-Verlag, 1992, pp 389-404.

† U.S. patent #5,214,703, 25 May 1993; international patent PCT/CH91/00117, 28 November 1991; European patent EP 0 482 154 B1.

currently in the process of selecting a successor to DES, called the Advanced Encryption Standard (AES).

3.9.2.3. Triple-DES

Triple-DES, or 3DES, is a variant of DES intended to increase its security by increasing the key length. It has been proven that the DES function doesn't form a group over its keys,* which means that encrypting multiple times with independent keys can increase security. 3DES encrypts the plaintext with three iterations of the DES algorithm, using three separate keys. The effective key length of 3DES is 112 bits, a vast improvement over the 56-bit key of plain DES.

3.9.2.4. ARCFOUR (RC4)

Ron Rivest designed the RC4 cipher in 1987 for RSA Data Security, Inc. (RSADSI); the name is variously claimed to stand for "Rivest Cipher" or "Ron's Code." It was an unpatented trade secret of RSADSI, used in quite a number of commercial products by RSADSI licensees. In 1994, though, source code claiming to implement RC4 appeared anonymously on the Internet. Experimentation quickly confirmed that the posted code was indeed compatible with RC4, and the cat was out of the bag. Since it had never been patented, RC4 effectively entered the public domain. This doesn't mean that RSADSI won't sue someone who tries to use it in a commercial product, so it is less expensive to settle and license than to fight. We aren't aware of any test cases of this issue. Since the name "RC4" is trademarked by RSADSI, the name "ARCFOUR" has been coined to refer to the publicly revealed version of the algorithm.

ARCFOUR is very fast but less studied than many other algorithms. It uses a variable-sized key; SSH-1 employs independent 128-bits keys for each direction of the SSH session. The use of independent keys for each direction is an exception in SSH-1, and crucial: ARCFOUR is essentially a pad using the output of a pseudorandom number generator. As such, it is important never to reuse a key because to do so makes cryptanalysis trivially easy. If this caveat is observed, ARCFOUR is considered secure by many, despite the dearth of public cryptanalytic results.

3.9.2.5. Blowfish

Blowfish was designed by Bruce Schneier in 1993, as a step toward replacing the aging DES. It is much faster than DES and IDEA, though not as fast as ARCFOUR, and is unpatented and free for all uses. It is intended specifically for implementation on large, modern, general-purpose microprocessors and for situations with

* K. W. Campbell and M. J. Wiener, "DES Is Not a Group," *Advances in Cryptology—CRYPTO '92 Proceedings*, Springer-Verlag, pp. 512-520.

relatively few key changes. It isn't particularly suited to low-end environments such as smart cards. It employs a variable-sized key of 32 to 448 bits; SSH-2 uses 128-bit keys. Blowfish has received a fair amount of cryptanalytic scrutiny and has proved impervious to attack so far. Information is available from Counterpane, Schneier's security consulting company, at:

http://www.counterpane.com/blowfish.html

3.9.2.6. Twofish

Twofish is another design by Bruce Schneier, together with J. Kelsey, D. Whiting, D. Wagner, C. Hall, and N. Ferguson. It was submitted in 1998 to the NIST as a candidate for the Advanced Encryption Standard, to replace DES as the U.S. government's symmetric data encryption standard. Two years later, it is one of the five finalists in the AES selection process, out of 15 initial submissions. Like Blowfish, it is unpatented and free for all uses, and Counterpane has provided uncopyrighted reference implementations, also freely usable.

Twofish admits keys of lengths 128, 192, or 256 bits; SSH-2 specifies 256-bit keys. Twofish is designed to be more flexible than Blowfish, allowing good implementation in a larger variety of computing environments (e.g., slower processors, small memory, in-hardware). It is very fast, its design is conservative, and it is likely to be quite strong. You can read more about Twofish at:

http://www.counterpane.com/twofish.html

You can read more about the NIST AES program at:

http://www.nist.gov/aes/

3.9.2.7. CAST

CAST was designed in the early 1990s by Carlisle Adams and Stafford Tavares. Tavares is on the faculty of Queen's University at Kingston in Canada, while Adams is an employee of Entrust Technologies of Texas. CAST is patented, and the rights are held by Entrust, which has made two versions of the algorithm available on a worldwide royalty-free basis for all uses. These versions are CAST-128 and CAST-256, described in RFC-2144 and RFC-2612, respectively. SSH-2 uses CAST-128, which is named for its 128-bit key length.

3.9.2.8. Speed comparisons

We ran some simple experiments to rank the bulk ciphers in order of speed. Since there is no single SSH package that contains all of the ciphers, we present two experiments to cover them all. Tables 3-7 and 3-8 show the time required to transfer a 5-MB file from a 300-MHz Linux box to a 100-MHz Sparc-20 over an otherwise unloaded 10-base-T Ethernet.

Table 3-7. Transferring with scp2 (F-Secure SSH2 2.0.13)

Cipher	Transfer Time (seconds)	Throughput (KB/second)
RC4	22.5	227.4
Blowfish	24.5	208.6
CAST-128	26.4	193.9
Twofish	28.2	181.3
3DES	51.8	98.8

Table 3-8. Same Test with scp1 (SSH-1.2.27)

Cipher	Transfer Time (seconds)	Throughput (KB/second)
RC4	5	1024.0
Blowfish	6	853.3
CAST-128	7	731.4
Twofish	14	365.7
3DES	15	341.3

This is necessarily a gross comparison, and we provide it only as a rough guideline. Remember that these numbers reflect the performance of particular implementations, not the algorithms themselves, tested in a single configuration. Your mileage may vary. Objects in mirror are closer than they appear.

Note that *scp1* is roughly four times faster than *scp2*. This is due to a major implementation difference: *scp1* uses the *scp1 –t* server, whereas *scp2* uses the SFTP subsystem. [7.5.9] Nonetheless, the relative cipher speed comparisons do agree where they overlap.

We must emphasize that we included RC4 in the SSH1 test only for completeness; due to security vulnerabilities, RC4 shouldn't ordinarily be used with the SSH-1 protocol.

3.9.3. Hash Functions

3.9.3.1. CRC-32

The 32-bit Cyclic Redundancy Check (CRC-32), defined in ISO 3309,* is a noncryptographic hash function for detecting accidental changes to data. The SSH-1 proto-

* International Organization for Standardization, *ISO Information Processing Systems—Data Communication High-Level Data Link Control Procedure—Frame Structure*, IS 3309, October 1984, 3rd Edition.

col uses CRC-32 (with the polynomial 0xEDB88320) for integrity checking, and this weakness admits the "insertion attack" discussed later. [3.10.5] The SSH-2 protocol employs cryptographically strong hash functions for integrity checking, obviating this attack.

3.9.3.2. MD5

MD5 ("Message Digest algorithm number 5") is a cryptographically strong, 128-bit hash algorithm designed by Ron Rivest in 1991, one of a series he designed for RSADSI (MD2 through MD5). MD5 is unpatented, placed in the public domain by RSADSI, and documented in RFC-1321. It has been a standard hash algorithm for several years, used in many cryptographic products and standards. A successful collision attack against the MD5 compression function by den Boer and Bosselaers in 1993 caused some concern, and though the attack hasn't resulted in any practical weaknesses, there is an expectation that it will, and people are beginning to avoid MD5 in favor of newer algorithms. RSADSI themselves recommend moving away from MD5 in favor of SHA-1 or RIPEMD-160 for future applications demanding collision-resistance.*

3.9.3.3. SHA-1

SHA-1 (Secure Hash Algorithm) was designed by the NSA and NIST for use with the U.S. government Digital Signature Standard. Like MD5, it was designed as an improvement on MD4, but takes a different approach. It produces 160-bit hashes. There are no known attacks against SHA-1, and, if secure, it is stronger than MD5 simply for its longer hash value. It is starting to replace MD5 in some applications; for example, SSH-2 uses SHA-1 as its required MAC hash function, as opposed to MD5 in SSH-1.

3.9.3.4. RIPEMD-160

Yet another 160-bit MD4 variant, RIPEMD-160, was developed by Hans Dobbertin, Antoon Bosselaers, and Bart Preneel as part of the European Community RIPE project. RIPE stands for RACE Integrity Primitives Evaluation;† RACE, in turn, was the program for Research and Development in Advanced Communications Technologies in Europe, an EC-sponsored program which ran from June 1987 to December 1995 (*http://www.race.analysys.co.uk/race/*). RIPE was part of the RACE effort, devoted to studying and developing data integrity techniques. Hence, RIPEMD-160 should be read as "the RIPE Message Digest (160 bits)." In particular, it

* RSA Laboratories Bulletin #4, 12 November 1996, *ftp://ftp.rsasecurity.com/pub/pdfs/bulletn4.pdf*.

† Not to be confused with another "RIPE," Réseaux IP Européens ("European IP Networks"), a technical and coordinating association of entities operating wide area IP networks in Europe and elsewhere (*http://www.ripe.net*).

has nothing to do with RIPEM, an old Privacy-Enhanced Mail (PEM) implementation by Mark Riordan (*http://ripem.msu.edu/*).

RIPEMD-160 isn't defined in the SSH protocol, but it is used for an implementation-specific MAC algorithm in OpenSSH, under the name `hmac-ripemd160@openssh.com`. RIPEMD-160 is unpatented and free for all uses. You can read more about it at:

> *http://www.esat.kuleuven.ac.be/~bosselae/ripemd160.html*

3.9.4. Compression Algorithms: zlib

zlib is currently the only compression algorithm defined for SSH. In the SSH protocol documents, the term "zlib" refers to the "deflate" lossless compression algorithm as first implemented in the popular *gzip* compression utility, and later documented in RFC-1951. It is available as a software library called ZLIB at:

> *http://www.info-zip.org/pub/infozip/zlib/*

3.10. Threats SSH Can Counter

Like any security tool, SSH has particular threats against which it is effective and others that it doesn't address. We'll discuss the former first.

3.10.1. Eavesdropping

An eavesdropper is a network snooper who reads network traffic without affecting it in any way. SSH's encryption prevents eavesdropping. The contents of an SSH session, even if intercepted, can't be decrypted by a snooper.

3.10.2. Name Service and IP Spoofing

If an attacker subverts your naming service (DNS, NIS, etc.), network-related programs may be coerced to connect to the wrong machine. Similarly, an attacker can impersonate a host by stealing use of its IP address(es). In either case, you're in trouble: your client program can connect to a false server that steals your password when you supply it. SSH guards against this attack by cryptographically verifying the server host identity. When setting up a session, the SSH client validates the server's host key against a local list associating server names and addresses with their keys. If the supplied host key doesn't match the one on the list, SSH complains. This feature may be disabled in less security-conscious settings if the warning messages get annoying. [7.4.3.1]

The SSH-2 protocol allows for including PKI certificates along with keys. In the future, we hope that implementation of this feature in SSH products along with more common deployment of PKI will ease the burden of key management and reduce the need for this particular security trade-off.

3.10.3. Connection Hijacking

An "active attacker"—one who not only can listen to network traffic but also can inject his own—can hijack a TCP connection, literally stealing it away from one of its legitimate endpoints. This is obviously disastrous: no matter how good your authentication method is, the attacker can simply wait until you've logged in, then steal your connection and insert his own nefarious commands into your session. SSH can't prevent hijacking, since this is a weakness in TCP, which operates below SSH. However, SSH renders it ineffective (except as a denial-of-service attack). SSH's integrity checking detects if a session is modified in transit, and shuts the connection down immediately without using any of the corrupted data.

3.10.4. Man-in-the-Middle Attacks

A *man-in-the-middle attack* is a particularly subtle type of active attack and is illustrated in Figure 3-8. An adversary sits between you and your real peer (i.e., between the SSH client and server), intercepting all traffic and altering or deleting messages at will. Imagine that you try to connect to an SSH server, but Malicious Mary intercepts your connection. She behaves just like an SSH server, though, so you don't notice, and she ends up sharing a session key with you. Simultaneously, she also initiates her own connection to your intended server, obtaining a separate session key with the server. She can log in as you because you used password authentication and thus conveniently handed her your password. You and the server both think you have a connection to each other, when in fact you both have connections to Mary instead. Then she just sits in the middle, passing data back and forth between you and the server (decrypting on one side with one key and re-encrypting with the other for retransmission). Of course, she can read everything that goes by and undetectably modify it if she chooses.

SSH counters this attack in two ways. The first is server host authentication. Unless Mary has broken into the server host, she is unable to effect her impersonation, because she doesn't have the server's private host key. Note that for this protection to work, it is crucial that the client actually check the server-supplied public host key against its known hosts list; otherwise, there is no guarantee that the server is genuine. If you connect for the first time to a new server and let *ssh* accept the host key, you are actually open to a man-in-the-middle attack. However, assuming you aren't spoofed that one time, future connections to this server are safe as long as the server host key isn't stolen.

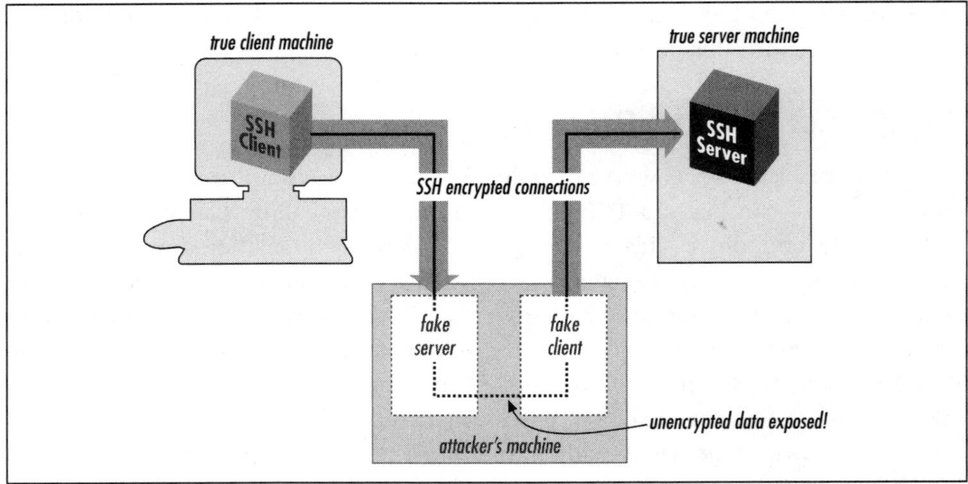

Figure 3-8. Man-in-the-middle attack

The second protection SSH affords is to limit the authentication methods vulnerable to this attack. The password method is vulnerable, but public-key and host-based/RhostsRSA are immune. Mary can't discover the session key simply by observing the key exchange; she must perform an active attack in which she carries out separate exchanges with each side, obtaining separate keys of her own with the client and server. In both SSH-1 and SSH-2,* the key exchange is so designed that if she does this, the session identifiers for each side will be diferent. When a client provides a digital signature for either public-key or trusted-host authentication, it includes the session identifier in the data signed. Thus, Mary can't just pass on the client-supplied authenticator to the server, nor does she have any way of coercing the client into signing the other session ID.

If you don't verify the server name/key correspondence, Mary can still perform the man-in-the-middle attack, even though she can't log in as you on the server side. Perhaps she can log into her own account or another she has cracked. With some cleverness, she might still deceive you long enough to do damage.

3.10.5. The Insertion Attack

Recall that SSH-1 uses a weak integrity mechanism. This weakness was exploited in a successful attack discovered by Ariel Futoransky and Emiliano Kargieman in June 1998; see *http://www.core-sdi.com/advisories/ssh-advisory.htm* for the gory

* At least, with the `diffie-hellman-group1-sha1` key exchange. We assume that if more exchange methods are added later, they will also have this property.

details. This "insertion" (or "compensation") attack allows an adversary who can perform an active network attack to insert arbitrary data into the plaintext data stream bound for either the client or server. That is, it allows insertion of encrypted data into the connection that then successfully decrypts to the attacker's desired plaintext and is delivered by SSH. The server direction is the most serious problem, since this lets the attacker insert arbitrary commands into a user's terminal session. Although not an especially easy attack to mount, this is a serious vulnerability. The attack results from composition properties of CRC-32 together with certain bulk ciphers in certain modes. The attack can be avoided altogether by using the 3DES cipher, which is immune.

SSH1 1.2.25, F-Secure SSH1 1.3.5, and later versions, as well as all versions of OpenSSH, include the *crc32 compensation attack detector*, designed to detect and prevent this attack. The detector renders the attack harder to mount, but doesn't prevent it entirely. SSH-2 uses cryptographically strong integrity checks to avoid such problems.

3.11. Threats SSH Doesn't Prevent

SSH isn't a total security solution. We'll now present some examples of attacks that SSH wasn't designed to prevent.

3.11.1. Password Cracking

SSH dramatically improves password security by encrypting your password as it passes over the network. Nevertheless, a password is still a weak form of authentication, and you must take care with it. You must choose a good password, memorable to you but not obvious to anyone else, and not easily guessable. You must also avoid having your password stolen, since possession alone is sufficient to grant access to your account. So watch out: the guy at the next terminal might be surreptitiously "shoulder-surfing" (watching as you type). That computer kiosk you're about to use may have been tricked up to log all keystrokes to Cracker Central Command. And the nice-sounding fellow who calls from Corporate IT and asks for your password to "fix your account" might not be who he claims.

Consider public-key authentication instead, since it is *two-factor*: a stolen passphrase is useless without the private key file, so an attacker needs to steal both. Of course, the SSH client on the computer you're borrowing can be rigged to squirrel away your key after you blithely supply your passphrase to decrypt it. If you're that worried, you shouldn't use strange computers. In the future, one hopes, cryptographic smartcards and readers will be ubiquitous and supported by SSH, so that you can carry your keys conveniently and use them in other computers without fear of disclosure.

If you must use password authentication because of its convenience, consider using a one-time password scheme such as S/Key to reduce risk. [3.4.2.5]

3.11.2. IP and TCP Attacks

SSH operates on top of TCP, so it is vulnerable to some attacks against weaknesses in TCP and IP. The privacy, integrity, and authentication guarantees of SSH limit this vulnerability to denial-of-service attacks.

TCP/IP is resistant to network problems such as congestion and link failure. If the enemy blows up a router, IP can route around it. It wasn't designed to resist an adversary injecting bogus packets into the network, however. The origin of TCP or IP control messages isn't authenticated. As a result, TCP/IP has a number of inherent exploitable weaknesses, such as:

SYN flood
: SYN stands for "synchronize," and is a TCP packet attribute. In this case, it refers to the initial packet sent to start the setup of a TCP connection. This packet often causes the receiver to expend resources preparing for the coming connection. If an attacker sends large numbers of these packets, the receiving TCP stack may run out of space and be unable to accept legitimate connections.

TCP RST, bogus ICMP
: Another TCP packet type is RST, for "reset." Either side of a TCP connection can send an RST packet at any time, which causes immediate teardown of the connection. RST packets may be injected easily into a network, immediately disconnecting any target TCP connection.

: Similarly, there is ICMP, the Internet Control Message Protocol. ICMP allows IP hosts and routers to communicate information about network conditions and host reachability. But again, there is no authentication, so that injecting bogus ICMP packets can have drastic effects. For instance, there are ICMP messages that say a particular host or TCP port is unreachable; forging such packets can cause connections to be torn down. There are also ICMP messages that communicate routing information (redirects and router discovery); forging such messages can cause sensitive data to be routed through unintended and possibly compromised systems.

TCP desynchronization and hijacking
: By clever manipulation of the TCP protocol, an attacker can desynchronize two sides of a TCP connection with respect to data byte sequence numbers. In this state, it is possible to inject packets that are accepted as a legitimate part of the connection, allowing the attacker to insert arbitrary information into the TCP data stream.

SSH provides no protection against attacks that break or prevent setup of TCP connections. On the other hand, SSH's encryption and host authentication are effective against attacks that involve inappropriate routing that would otherwise permit reading of sensitive traffic or redirect a connection to a compromised server. Likewise, attacks that hijack or alter TCP data will fail, because SSH detects them, but they also break the SSH connection, because SSH responds to such problems by termination.

Because these threats focus on problems with TCP/IP, they can be effectively countered only by lower, network-level techniques, such as hardware link encryption or IPSEC. [1.6.4] IPSEC is the IP Security protocol that is part of the next-generation IP protocol, IPv6, and available as an add-on to the current IP standard, IPv4. It provides encryption, integrity, and data origin-authentication services at the IP packet level.

3.11.3. Traffic Analysis

Even if an attacker can't read your network traffic, he can glean a great deal of useful information by simply watching it—noting the amount of data, the source and destination addresses, and timing. A sudden increase in traffic with another company might tip him off that an impending business deal is in the works. Traffic patterns can also indicate backup schedules or times of day most vulnerable to denial-of-service attacks. Prolonged silence on an SSH connection from a sysadmin's desktop might indicate that she's stepped out, and that now is a good time to break in, electronically or physically.

SSH doesn't address traffic-analysis attacks. SSH connections are easily identifiable as they generally go to a well-known port, and the SSH protocol makes no attempt to obfuscate traffic analysis. An SSH implementation could conceivably send random, no-op traffic over a connection when it's otherwise idle, to frustrate activity correlation, but we know of no SSH package with this feature.

3.11.4. Covert Channels

A *covert channel* is a means of signaling information in an unanticipated and unnoticed fashion. Suppose that one day, Sysadmin Sally decides her users are having too much fun, and she turns off email and instant messaging so they can't chat. To get around this, you and your friend agree to put messages to each other into world-readable files in your home directories, which you'll check every once a while for new messages. This unanticipated communication mechanism is a covert channel.

Covert channels are hard to eliminate. If Sysadmin Sally discovers your file-based technique, she can make all home directories unreadable and unsearchable by anyone but their owners, and prevent the owners from changing this restriction. While she's at it, she can also make sure you can't create files anywhere else, like */tmp*. (Most of your programs don't work now, but that doesn't matter to Sally.) Even so, you and your friend can still list each other's home directory nodes themselves, which reveals the directory modification date and number of files, so you devise a secret code based on these visible parameters and communicate by modifying them. This is a more complex covert channel, and you can imagine even more outlandish ones in the face of further restrictions from Sally.

SSH doesn't attempt to eliminate covert channels. Their analysis and control are generally part of highly secure computer systems, such as those designed to handle information safely at various security classification levels within the same system. Incidentally, the SSH data stream itself can be used perfectly well as a covert channel: the encrypted contents of your SSH session might be a recipe for chocolate chip cookies, while a secret message about an impending corporate merger is represented in Morse code using even/odd packet lengths for dashes and dots.

3.11.5. Carelessness

Mit der Dummheit kämpfen Götter selbst vergebens.
(Against stupidity, even the Gods struggle in vain.)
—Friedrich von Schiller

Security tools don't secure anything; they only help people to do so. It's almost a cliché, but so important that it bears any amount of repeating. The best cryptography or most secure protocols in the world won't help if users pick bad passwords, or write their passphrases on Post-it notes stuck to the undersides of their keyboards. They also won't help sysadmins who neglect other aspects of host security, allowing host-key theft or wiretapping of terminal sessions.

As Bruce Schneier is fond of saying, "Security is a process, not a product." SSH is a good tool, but it must be part of an overall and ongoing process of security awareness. Other aspects of host integrity must still be attended to; security advisories for relevant software and operating systems monitored, appropriate patches or workarounds applied promptly, and people educated and kept aware of their security responsibilities. Don't just install SSH and think that you're now secure; you're not.

3.12. Summary

The SSH protocol uses openly published, strong cryptographic tools to provide network connections with privacy, integrity, and mutual authentication. The SSH-1 protocol (a.k.a SSH-1.5) is wildly popular, despite being somewhat ad hoc: essentially a documentation of SSH1's program behavior. It has a number of shortcomings and flaws, of which the weak integrity check and resulting Futoransky/Kargieman insertion attack is perhaps the most egregious example. The current protocol version, SSH-2, is more practically flexible and fixes the known earlier problems but has unfortunately seen limited deployment due to licensing restrictions and the continued availability of the free SSH1 software for many commercial purposes.

SSH counters many network-related security threats, but not all. In particular, it is vulnerable to denial-of-service attacks based on weaknesses in TCP/IP, its underlying transport. It also doesn't address some methods of attack that may be of concern depending on the environment, such as traffic analysis and covert channels.

4

Installation and Compile-Time Configuration

In this chapter:
- *SSH1 and SSH2*
- *F-Secure SSH Server*
- *OpenSSH*
- *Software Inventory*
- *Replacing R-Commands with SSH*
- *Summary*

Now that you know what SSH is and how it works, where do you get it and how do you install it? This chapter surveys several popular and robust Unix implementations of SSH and explains how to obtain, compile, and install them:

SSH1 and SSH Secure Shell (SSH2)
: Products from SSH Communications Security, Ltd., that implement the SSH-1 and SSH-2 protocols, respectively.

F-Secure SSH Server
: F-Secure Corporation's versions of SSH1 and SSH2.

OpenSSH
: A free offshoot of SSH1 with independently implemented support for the SSH-2 protocol; part of OpenBSD.

Non-Unix implementations of SSH are covered in Chapters 13–17.

4.1. SSH1 and SSH2

SSH1 and SSH2 (a.k.a SSH Secure Shell) were written for Unix and have been ported to several other operating systems. Both products are distributed as source code that must be compiled before use, although precompiled executables for various platforms are also available.

SSH1 and SSH2 may be distributed without cost for noncommercial use. If you plan to use either for commercial purposes, then according to the license, you must purchase the software. Commercial versions are sold by SSH Communication

Security, Ltd., and F-Secure Corporation, and we'll be discussing these later. The precise terms for copying and using each version are spelled out in a file called *COPYING* (for SSH1) or *LICENSING* (for SSH2). Be sure to read and understand the terms before using the software. Also, because these products involve cryptography, your local laws may dictate whether you may use or distribute the software.

4.1.1. Features

SSH1 and SSH2 define the de facto standard for SSH features and have tremendous flexibility and power. Both products include:

- Client programs for remote logins, remote command execution, and secure file copying across a network, all with many runtime options
- A highly configurable SSH server
- Command-line interfaces for all programs, facilitating scripting with standard Unix tools (shells, Perl, etc.)
- Numerous, selectable encryption algorithms and authentication mechanisms
- An SSH agent, which caches keys for ease of use
- Support for SOCKS proxies
- Support for TCP port forwarding and X11 forwarding
- History and logging features to aid in debugging

4.1.2. Obtaining the Distribution

SSH1 and SSH2 are available by anonymous FTP from *ftp.ssh.com* in the directory */pub/ssh*, or equivalently from the URL:

ftp://ftp.ssh.com/pub/ssh/

You may reach this repository from the web site of SSH Communications Security:

http://www.ssh.com/

4.1.2.1. Extracting the files

Distributions are packaged in gzipped tar format. To extract the files, apply *gunzip* followed by *tar*. For example, to extract SSH1 Version 1.2.27 from the gzipped *tar* file *ssh-1.2.27.tar.gz*, type:

```
$ gunzip ssh-1.2.27.tar.gz
$ tar xvf ssh-1.2.27.tar
```

Alternatively, use a single command with a pipe:

```
$ gunzip < ssh-1.2.27.tar.gz | tar xvf -
```

Or, if you have GNU Tar (called *gtar* or *tar* on some systems), simply type:

```
$ gtar xzvf ssh-1.2.27.tar.gz
```

The result is a new subdirectory containing all files in the distribution.

4.1.2.2. Verifying with PGP

Along with each SSH1 and SSH2 distribution is a PGP signature file for Pretty Good Privacy that guarantees the distribution is genuine and has not been modified. [1.6.2] The file *ssh-1.2.27.tar.gz*, for example, is accompanied by *ssh-1.2.27.tar.gz.sig* containing the PGP signature. To verify the file is genuine, you need PGP installed. Then:

1. If you have not done so previously, obtain the PGP public keys for the distributions. Separate keys are used for verifying SSH1 and SSH2:

   ftp://ftp.ssh.com/pub/ssh/SSH1-DISTRIBUTION-KEY-RSA.asc
   ftp://ftp.ssh.com/pub/ssh/SSH2-DISTRIBUTION-KEY-RSA.asc
   ftp://ftp.ssh.com/pub/ssh/SSH2-DISTRIBUTION-KEY-DSA.asc

   Add them to your PGP key ring by saving each one to a temporary file and typing:

   ```
   $ pgp -ka temporary_file_name
   ```

2. Download both the distribution file (e.g., *ssh-1.2.27.tar.gz*) and the signature file (e.g., *ssh-1.2.27.tar.gz.sig*).
3. Verify the signature with the command:

   ```
   $ pgp ssh-1.2.27.tar.gz
   ```

   If no warning messages are produced, the distribution file is genuine.

Always check the PGP signatures. Otherwise, you can be fooled by a hacked version of SSH1 created by an untrusted third party. If you blindly install it without checking the PGP signature, you can compromise your system security.

4.1.3. Building and Installing SSH1

Generally, SSH1 is compiled and installed by the following steps. You should read any *README*, *INSTALL*, etc., documents in the distribution to see if there are any particular known problems or extras steps for installation in your environment.

1. Run the supplied *configure* script. [4.1.5] To accept all defaults, change the directory to the root of the SSH1 distribution and type:

   ```
   $ ./configure
   ```

2. Compile everything:

   ```
   $ make
   ```

3. Install everything. You need root privileges if you plan to install files in system directories:

   ```
   $ su root
   Password: ********
   # make install
   ```

   The following files are installed:

   — The server program, *sshd1*, and a link to it called *sshd*

   — The clients *ssh1* and *scp1*, and respective links called *ssh* and *scp*

   — The symbolic link *slogin1*, pointing to *ssh1*, and likewise a link called *slogin* pointing to *slogin1*

   — Support programs *ssh-add1*, *ssh-agent1*, *ssh-askpass1*, *ssh-keygen1*, and links to them called *ssh-add*, *ssh-agent*, *ssh-askpass*, and *ssh-keygen*, respectively

   — The support program *make-ssh-known-hosts*

   — A newly generated host key pair, created by *ssh-keygen* and placed by default into */etc/ssh_host_key* (private key) and */etc/ssh_host_key.pub* (public key)

   — The server configuration file, */etc/sshd_config* by default [5.3.1]

   — The client configuration file, */etc/ssh_config* by default [7.1.3]

   — Manpages for the various programs

4. Create the known hosts file. [4.1.6]

4.1.4. Building and Installing SSH2

SSH2 is compiled and installed much like SSH1, using the *configure* script and a pair of *make* commands:

1. Perform compile-time configuration as with SSH1. [4.1.5] To accept all defaults, simply change directory to the root of the SSH2 distribution and type:

   ```
   $ ./configure
   ```

2. Compile everything:

   ```
   $ make
   ```

3. Install everything, remembering to become root if you are installing files in system directories:

   ```
   $ su root
   Password: ********
   # make install
   ```

The following files are installed:

— The server programs *sshd2*, and a link to it called *sshd*

— The secure FTP server program *sftp-server*

— The clients *ssh2*, *scp2*, and *sftp2*, and links to them called *ssh*, *scp*, and *sftp*, respectively

— Support programs *ssh-add2*, *ssh-agent2*, *ssh-askpass2*, *ssh-keygen2*, *ssh-probe2*, and *ssh-signer2*, and links to them called *ssh-add*, *ssh-agent*, *ssh-askpass*, *ssh-keygen*, *ssh-probe*, and *ssh-signer*, respectively

— Additional support programs *ssh-dummy-shell* and *ssh-pubkeymgr*

— A newly generated host key pair, created by *ssh-keygen2* and placed by default into */etc/ssh2/hostkey* (private key) and */etc/ssh2/hostkey.pub* (public key)

— The server configuration file, */etc/ssh2/sshd2_config* by default [5.3.1]

— The client configuration file, */etc/ssh2/ssh2_config* by default [7.1.3]

— Manpages for the various programs

4.1.4.1. SSH1 and SSH2 on the same machine

Notice that SSH1 and SSH2, when installed, create some files with the same names, such as the link *sshd*. What happens if you install both SSH1 and SSH2 on the same machine? Happily, everything works out, even if you install them into the same *bin* and *etc* directories, provided you install the most recent versions. Each of their Makefiles is constructed to check for the existence of the other version and respond appropriately.

Specifically, both SSH1 and SSH2 create symbolic links called *sshd*, *ssh*, *scp*, *ssh-add*, *ssh-agent*, *ssh-askpass*, and *ssh-keygen*. If you install SSH1 and then SSH2, the SSH2 Makefile renames these files by appending the suffix *.old* and then creates new symbolic links pointing to its own SSH2 programs. For instance, *ssh* originally points to *ssh1*; after installing SSH2, *ssh* points to *ssh2*, and *ssh.old* points to *ssh1*. This is appropriate since SSH2 is considered a later version than SSH1.

On the other hand, if you install SSH2 and then SSH1, the SSH1 Makefile leaves SSH2's links untouched. As a result, *ssh* remains pointing to *ssh2*, and no link points to *ssh1*. This is consistent with the practice of installing SSH1 to allow SSH2 to provide fallback SSH1 support.

4.1.5. Compile-Time Configuration

Building SSH1 and SSH2 seems pretty simple, eh? Just type *configure* and a few *make* commands, and you're done. Well, not so fast. When building and installing a new security product, you shouldn't blindly accept its defaults. These SSH products have dozens of options that may be set at compile-time, and you should carefully consider each one. We call this process *compile-time configuration.*

Compile-time configuration is performed by running a script, called *configure*, just before compiling the distribution.* Roughly speaking, *configure* accomplishes two tasks:

- It examines the local computer, setting various computer-specific and operating system-specific options. For example, *configure* notices which header files and libraries are available and whether your C compiler is ANSI or not.
- It includes or excludes certain features found in the SSH source code. For example, *configure* can keep or remove support for Kerberos authentication.

We'll discuss only the second task, since it's SSH-specific, and cover only the configuration options that are directly related to SSH or security. For example, we won't cover flags that related to the compiler (e.g., whether warnings should be printed or suppressed) or operating system (e.g., whether particular Unix library functions should be used). To see the full set of *configure* flags, type:

```
$ configure --help
```

and also read the files *README* and *INSTALL* in the root of the distribution.

Incidentally, the behavior of SSH1 and SSH2 may be controlled at three levels. The first is compile-time configuration as discussed in this chapter. In addition, *server-wide configuration* (Chapter 5) controls global settings for a running SSH server, and *per-account configuration* (Chapter 8) controls settings for each user account accepting SSH connections. Figure 4-1 illustrates where compile-time configuration fits into the whole spectrum. We'll remind you of this picture each time we introduce a new type of configuration.

4.1.5.1. Configuration standards

The *configure* script accepts command-line flags, each beginning with a double dash (--), to control its actions. Flags are of two types:

With/without flags
: Include a package during compilation. These flags begin with `--with` or `--without`. For example, support for the X Window System may be included using the flag `--with-x` or omitted using `--without-x`.

* The *configure* script is generated by a Free Software Foundation package called *autoconf*. You don't need to know this to compile SSH1 or SSH2, but if you're interested in learning more about *autoconf*, visit the GNU web site at *http://www.gnu.org/*.

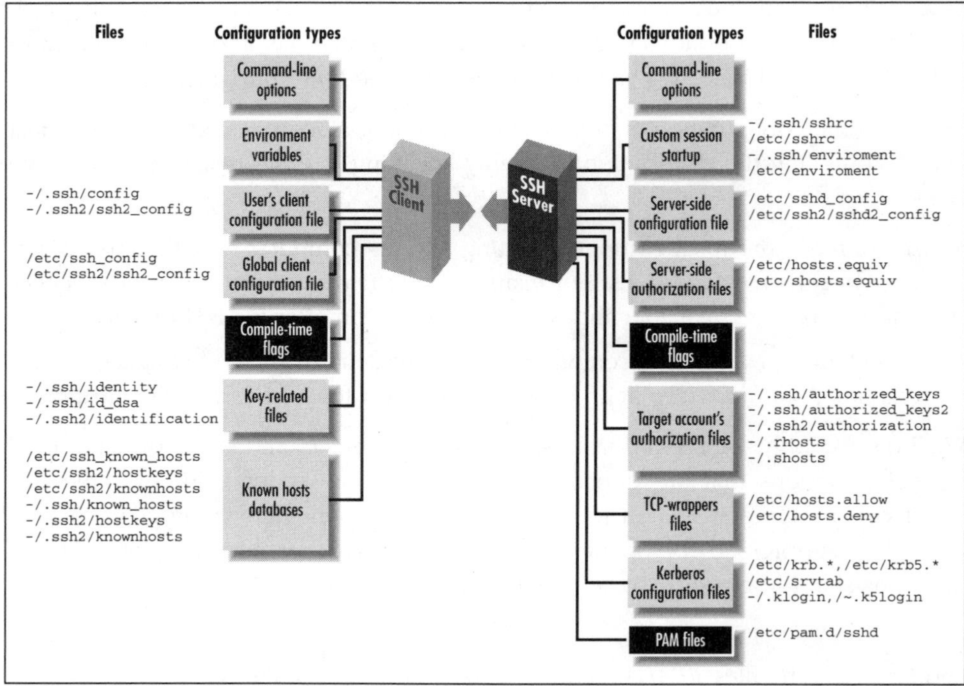

Figure 4-1. SSH compile-time configuration (highlighted parts)

Enable/disable flags

Set the default behavior of SSH1. These flags begin with `--enable` or `--disable`. For example, the X forwarding feature in SSH2 is enabled by the flag `--enable-X11-forwarding` or disabled with `--disable-X11-forwarding`. Some of these defaults may be overridden later by serverwide or per-account configuration.

Flags beginning with `--with` or `--enable` may optionally be followed by an equals sign and a string value, such as:

```
--with-etcdir=/usr/local/etc
--enable-X11-forwarding=no
```

Various string values are used, but the most common are `yes` and `no`. For a given package *P*, the flags `--with-`*P* and `--with-`*P*`=yes` are equivalent. The following tables illustrate the relationships:

If you write:	It's equivalent to:
`--with-P=yes`	`--with-P`
`--with-P=no`	`--without-P`

This next table shows the relationships for a given feature *F*:

If you write:	It's equivalent to:
`--enable-F=yes`	`--enable-F`
`--enable-F=no`	`--disable-F`

In the sections that follow, we show many examples of *configure* with different command-line flags. Most examples demonstrate only one flag at a time, so we use ellipses like this:

```
$ configure ... --enable-fancy-feature ...
```

to indicate other flags might be present on the command line. The proper way to run *configure* is just once, before compilation, with all desired flags on the same command line.

Be careful when choosing *configure* flags, or you might waste a lot of time. The *configure* script is not very smart, performing little or no sanity checking on its input. If you provide an invalid flag, *configure* can naively run for several minutes, handling a hundred other configuration options, before finally reaching the bad flag and dying. Now you have to run the script all over again.

Also, don't depend on flags' default values since they might differ among SSH implementations. For maximum security and control, specify all flags explicitly when running *configure*.

4.1.5.2. Installation, files, and directories

Let's begin our discussion of *configure*'s SSH-related flags. First, we discuss file-related flags for choosing installation directories, turning setuid bits on and off, and permitting files and directories to be group writable.

The SSH executables are installed in a directory of your choosing—*/usr/local* by default—within a subdirectory called *bin*. This is specified with the *configure* flag **`--prefix`**. For example, to place the bin directory in */usr/local/ssh* and install the executables in */usr/local/ssh/bin*:

```
# SSH1, SSH2, OpenSSH
$ configure ... --prefix=/usr/local/ssh ...
```

Some SSH-related system files are installed in the directory */etc*. This default location can be overridden with the *configure* flag **`--with-etcdir`**, supplying an alternative directory name (for OpenSSH, this is **`--sysconfdir`**):

```
# SSH1, SSH2
$ configure ... --with-etcdir=/usr/local/etc ...
```

The flag `--with-etcdir` is unique among flags because there is no corresponding `--without-etcdir` flag. SSH1 and SSH2 must have installation directories or their Makefiles will refuse to compile the software.

Next, certain executables are installed as setuid root by default: *ssh1* (for SSH1) and *ssh-signer2* (for SSH2). *ssh1* needs to be setuid root for trusted-host authentication (i.e., host-based authentication of various kinds), for the following reasons:

- To access the local host key, which is readable only by root
- To allocate a privileged port, which only root can do

In SSH2, privileged ports are no longer used, and the first function has migrated into a separate program, *ssh-signer2*, which signs authentication packets for trusted-host authentication. If you don't make this program setuid root, hostbased authentication will fail. [3.5.2.3]

SSH1's *ssh* client has its setuid root permissions controlled with the *configure* flags `--enable-suid-ssh` and `--disable-suid-ssh`:

```
# SSH1 only
$ configure ... --disable-suid-ssh ...
```

Similarly, the setuid bit of *ssh-signer2* for SSH2 is controlled by `--enable-suid-ssh-signer` and `--disable-suid-ssh-signer`; for example:

```
# SSH2 only
$ configure ... --disable-suid-ssh-signer ...
```

Finally, the SSH server requires certain permissions on files and directories in user accounts, such as the *.rhosts* file and the *authorized_keys* file.* In particular, group write and world write permissions are forbidden. Group write permission may be useful for shared accounts (so members of a group can conveniently modify the account's SSH files). This restriction may be relaxed using the `--enable-group-writeability` *configure* flag:†

```
# SSH1, SSH2
$ configure ... --enable-group-writeability ...
```

Now the server permits SSH connections to accounts with group-writable SSH files.

4.1.5.3. TCP/IP support

Most TCP/IP features of SSH1 and SSH2 are controlled by serverwide configuration [5.4.3], but a few are available through compile-time configuration. These

* Only if `StrictModes` is turned on in the server. [5.4.2.1]

† Yes, "writeability" is correct, even though it's a misspelling.

include the TCP NODELAY feature, TCP-wrappers, the SO_LINGER socket option, and a limit on the maximum number of connections.

If you plan to operate SSH over a wide-area network as opposed to a speedy Ethernet connection, you might consider disabling TCP/IP's NODELAY feature, a.k.a the Nagle Algorithm, for SSH connections. The Nagle Algorithm reduces the number of TCP segments sent with very small amounts of data, such as the small byte sequences of a terminal session. You may disable it at compile time with the `--disable-tcp-nodelay` flag:

```
# SSH1, SSH2
$ configure ... --disable-tcp-nodelay ...
```

Alternatively, you may enable or disable it during serverwide configuration using the `NoDelay` configuration keyword. [5.4.3.8]

TCP-wrappers is a security feature for applying access control to incoming TCP connections based on their source address. [9.4] For example, TCP-wrappers can verify the identity of a connecting host by performing DNS lookups, or it can reject connections from given addresses, address ranges, or DNS domains. Although SSH already includes some of this kind of control with features such as `AllowHosts`, `DenyHosts`, etc., TCP-wrappers is more complete. It allows some controls not currently implemented in any SSH version, such as restricting the source of forwarded X connections.

SSH1 and SSH2 both include support for TCP-wrappers if the flag `--with-libwrap` is given at compile time, providing the path to the wrapper library, *libwrap.a*:

```
# SSH1, SSH2
$ configure ... --with-libwrap=/usr/local/lib ...
```

If your Unix installation doesn't include the TCP-wrappers library, you can retrieve and compile it yourself from:

ftp://ftp.porcupine.org/pub/security/index.html

For more information on TCP-wrappers, read the manpages for *tcpd* and *hosts_access*.

A rather low-level option for SSH1 concerns the SO_LINGER socket flag, which may be turned on or off at compile time. Suppose SSH1 is communicating via an open socket, but the socket gets closed while data is still queued. What happens to the data? The setting of the SO_LINGER flag determines what should be done. With the flag enabled, the socket close "lingers" (delayed) until the data is delivered or until a specified timeout occurs. Monkeying with this flag requires a detailed knowledge of TCP/IP and socket behavior, so if you know what you're doing, use the `--enable-so-linger` flag:

```
# SSH1 only
$ configure ... --enable-so-linger ...
```

Finally, you may instruct *sshd2* to limit the maximum number of simultaneous connections it supports. By default it accepts an unlimited number of connections, but if you want to conserve resources on the server machine, you may set a limit. The appropriate flag is `--with-ssh-connection-limit` with a nonnegative integer argument; for example:

```
# SSH2 only
$ configure ... --with-ssh-connection-limit=50 ...
```

You may override this value at runtime with the serverwide configuration keyword `MaxConnections`. [5.4.3.6]

4.1.5.4. X window support

If you plan to use SSH to communicate between hosts running the X Window System, make sure to include support for X at compile time. (By default, it is included.) Conversely, if you never have anything to do with X, you can leave out the support and save some disk space. Use the flag `--with-x` or `--without-x` as desired:

```
# SSH1, SSH2
$ configure ... --without-x ...
```

Few people have a strong need to eliminate X support, but *configure* has a few other, more useful, X-related flags. Specifically, you may enable or disable support for X forwarding, which allows X applications opened on the SSH server machine to appear on the SSH client machine's display. [9.3]

For SSH1, X forwarding support is separately controllable for SSH clients and servers:

```
# SSH1 only
$ configure ... --disable-server-x11-forwarding ...
$ configure ... --disable-client-x11-forwarding ...
```

For SSH2, X forwarding support is controlled as a whole by the compile-time flag `--enable-X11-forwarding` (or `--disable-X11-forwarding`):

```
# SSH2 only
$ configure ... --disable-x11-forwarding ...
```

Remember, these enable/disable flags set only SSH's default behavior. X forwarding may be further enabled or disabled through serverwide configuration using the `X11Forwarding` (SSH1, OpenSSH) or `ForwardX11` (SSH2) configuration keywords. [9.3.3]

4.1.5.5. TCP port forwarding

Port forwarding enables SSH to encrypt the data passing through any TCP/IP-based program. [9.2] This feature can be disabled at compile time if desired. X window forwarding isn't affected by these general port-forwarding flags.

In SSH1, port forwarding can be disabled for the server, the clients, or both. To disable port forwarding on the SSH1 server, use the *configure* flag `--disable-server-port-forwarding`. Likewise, to prevent SSH1 clients from using port forwarding, use the *configure* flag `--disable-client-port-forwardings`. By default, port forwarding is enabled at compile time.

In SSH2, support for port forwarding isn't controlled separately for the clients and server. The *configure* flags `--enable-tcp-port-forwarding` and `--disable-tcp-port-forwarding`, respectively, enable or disable the feature.

4.1.5.6. Encryption and ciphers

SSH1 may be compiled with or without support for particular encryption algorithms, such as IDEA, Blowfish, DES, and ARCFOUR. (In SSH2, this support is controlled with the `Ciphers` keyword during serverwide configuration. [5.4.5]) Flags to include this support are:

`--with-idea`
: Include the IDEA algorithm

`--with-blowfish`
: Include the Blowfish algorithm

`--with-des`
: Include the DES algorithm

`--with-arcfour`
: Include the ARCFOUR algorithm

`--with-none`
: Permit unencrypted transmissions

To exclude support, use the `--without` form of the flag:

```
# SSH1 only
$ configure ... --without-blowfish ...
```

We recommend using `--without-none` to forbid unencrypted transmissions. Otherwise, an intruder who breaks into your server machine can turn off SSH encryption for clients by adding a simple line to a configuration file ("Ciphers None"). You may also incur other security risks. [5.4.5] If you need unencrypted transmissions for testing, build a second SSH1 server using `--with-none` and make it executable only by the system administrator. Also, be aware that with the SSH-1 protocol, turning off encryption doesn't just eliminate data privacy; it also renders the server authentication and data integrity features ineffective.

Some implementations of SSH include the RSA encryption algorithm for public-key authentication. [3.9.1.1] At press time, the algorithm is absent from some implementations because RSA was protected by patent until September 2000; it is now in the public domain. While the patent was in force, the company made available a "reference implementation" of RSA, called RSAREF, that was freely used for educational and noncommercial purposes and didn't run afoul of the patent. We suspect that RSAREF will fall into disuse now that other more popular RSA implementations are available to all. Furthermore, we discourage its use because it contains security flaws and is no longer supported. However, you may still instruct SSH1 to use RSAREF instead of its own implementation of RSA via the *configure* flag `--with-rsaref`:

```
# SSH1 only
$ configure ... --with-rsaref
```

Then, unpack the RSAREF package into a directory named *rsaref2* at the top of the SSH1 distribution. RSA encryption is used by default or if you specify the *configure* flag `--without-rsaref`. (There is no `--with-rsa` flag.) For more information about RSAREF, visit *http://www.rsa.com/*.

4.1.5.7. Authentication

SSH1 and SSH2 may be compiled with support for several optional authentication techniques. For SSH1, the techniques in question are Kerberos, SecurID, and the Gauntlet firewall toolkit from Trusted Information Systems (TIS). SSH2 can support authentication using OpenPGP keys.* There is also experimental code for Kerberos-5 authentication in SSH 2.3.0, although it is not yet supported, and the relevant definitions haven't yet been added to the SSH-2 draft standard.

* SecurID and Gauntlet-related flags are accepted by the SSH2 *configure* script, but at press time the source code contains no support for these techniques.

Kerberos [11.4] is an authentication mechanism that passes around *tickets*, small sequences of bytes with limited lifetimes, in place of user passwords. The configuration flags `--with-kerberos5` and `--without-kerberos5` control whether Kerberos support is included or excluded during the build.* The `--with-kerberos5` flag is optionally followed by a string value indicating the directory containing Kerberos files:

```
# SSH1 only
$ configure ... --with-kerberos5=/usr/kerberos ...
```

If the directory name is omitted from `--with-kerberos5`, the default location is */usr/local*. Additionally, the Kerberos feature of forwarding ticket-granting tickets is enabled by default by the flag `--enable-kerberos-tgt-passing`:

```
# SSH1 only
$ configure ... --enable-kerberos-tgt-passing ...
```

SecurID is an authentication mechanism in which users carry electronic cards, approximately the size of a credit card, that display randomly changing integers. During authentication, the user is prompted to type whatever number appears on the card at the time, in addition to a username and password.

To compile SSH1 with SecurID support, use the flag `--with-securid`, providing the path to the directory containing SecurID's header files and libraries:

```
# SSH1 only
$ configure ... --with-securid=/usr/ace ...
```

Gauntlet is a firewall toolkit containing an authentication server program, *authserv*. If you are running Gauntlet and want SSH1 to communicate with its authentication server, use the `--with-tis` flag, providing the path to your local Gauntlet directory:

```
# SSH1, SSH2
$ configure ... --with-tis=/usr/local/gauntlet ...
```

Pretty Good Privacy, or PGP, is a popular encryption and authentication program available for many computing platforms. [1.6.2] SSH2 optionally authenticates users based on their PGP keys, so long as those keys comply with the OpenPGP standard (RFC-2440, "OpenPGP Message Format"; some PGP versions, especially older ones, may not be OpenPGP-compliant). To include this support, compile using the flag `--with-pgp`:

```
# SSH2 only
$ configure ... --with-pgp ...
```

* Don't compile Kerberos support in SSH1 Version 1.2.27 or earlier because there is a serious security bug. [11.4.4.5] Use 1.2.28 or later. OpenSSH doesn't have this bug.

4.1.5.8. SOCKS proxy support

SOCKS is a network protocol for proxies. A *proxy* is a software component that masquerades as another component to hide or protect it. For example, suppose a company permits its employees to surf the Web but doesn't want the hostnames of its internal machines to be exposed outside the company. A proxy server can be inserted between the internal network and the Internet, so that all web requests appear to be coming from the proxy. In addition, a proxy can prevent unwanted transmissions from entering the internal network, acting as a firewall.

SSH1 and SSH2 both have SOCKS support, meaning that they can create connections passing through a SOCKS proxy server. With SSH1, this support is optionally enabled at compile time and can handle either Versions 4 or 5 of the SOCKS protocol. The SSH2 support is SOCKS4-only but is built in and always available (no external library or special compilation option needed).

SSH1 relies on an external SOCKS library for its SOCKS support, so you must install such a library before compiling SSH1 with SOCKS. We did our testing with the *socks5* package available from the NEC Networking Systems Laboratory (*http://www.socks.nec.com/*).*

There are three SSH1 SOCKS *configure* options:

`--with-socks4`
: Use SOCKS4

`--with-socks5`
: Use SOCKS5

`--with-socks`
: Use either SOCKS5 or SOCKS4, preferring SOCKS5 if both are available

The SSH2 SOCKS feature is controlled by the **`SocksServer`** client configuration option. [7.4.6] In addition to the usual methods of setting this in a configuration file or on the command line with *–o*, you can also set it using the SSH_SOCKS_SERVER environment variable.

`SocksServer` has an empty default value, causing SSH2 to assume there's no SOCKS server. The configuration flag:

```
--with-socks-server=string
```

gives nonempty default value to this parameter, allowing you to install an SSH2 that assumes the presence of a SOCKS server. Note that this isn't the same as using

* The NEC *socks5* reference implementation is licensed free of charge for "for noncommercial purposes only, such as academic, research and internal business use." The full text of the license is available on their web site.

the **SocksServer** directive in the global client configuration file, because the configuration parameter always overrides the value of the environment variable. If you use the compilation option, users can specify an alternate SOCKS server with SSH_SOCKS_SERVER; if you use the global file, they can't (although they can still override using their own **SocksServer** directive).

See [7.4.6] for a detailed discussion of how SSH SOCKS support works and *http://www.socks.nec.com/* for more information on SOCKS.

4.1.5.9. User logins and shells

Several aspects of logins and shells may be controlled during compile-time configuration. You may use a custom login program instead of */bin/login* and set the user's search path to something other than the system default.

When a user logs into a remote machine via *ssh* or *slogin*, the remote SSH server executes a process to accomplish the login. By default, the SSH1 server runs a login shell. Alternatively, the server can run a dedicated login program, either */bin/login* (by default) or another of your choosing, such as the Kerberos login program or a modified version of */bin/login* with additional features.

The choice of an alternative login program is made at compile time, using the *configure* flag **--with-login**, and providing the path to the program:

```
# SSH1 only
$ configure ... --with-login=/usr/local/bin/my-login ...
```

Your alternative login program must support the same command-line flags as */bin/login*, including *–h* (specify the hostname), *–p* (pass environment variables to the login shell), and *–f* (force login without checking the password). This is because *sshd1* spawns the login program using the command line:

```
name_of_login_program -h hostname -p -f --username
```

If you specify **--with-login**, and you wish to use the alternative login program, you must also turn on the **UseLogin** keyword during serverwide configuration: [5.5.3]

```
# Keyword in SSH1 server-wide configuration file
UseLogin yes
```

Login programs do useful things like set the default search path for users. If *sshd1* doesn't invoke a login program (i.e., it was compiled using **--without-login**), you can tell it to set the default search path for SSH-invoked sessions. This is done with the configuration flag **--with-path**:

```
# SSH1 only
$ configure ... --with-path="/usr/bin:/usr/local/bin:/usr/mine/bin" ...
```

If you don't specify **--with-path**, and your Unix environment doesn't provide a default path, the *sshd1* default is:

```
PATH="/bin:/usr/bin:/usr/ucb:/usr/bin/X11:/usr/local/bin"
```

4.1.5.10. Forbidding logins

The file */etc/nologin* has special meaning to many versions of Unix. If the file exists, all logins are disabled. *sshd* respects this file. However, you may instruct *sshd1* to bypass the */etc/nologin* file to permit designated users to log in. This is done by creating a second file, such as */etc/nologin.allow*, to contain exceptions: names of users who may log in even if */etc/nologin* exists. For example, placing system administrators' names in */etc/nologin.allow* might be a wise idea, to prevent them from being denied access to the machine. You must then enable the feature using the *configure* flag **--with-nologin-allow**, supplying the path to the file of exceptions:

```
# SSH1 only
$ configure ... --with-nologin-allow=/etc/nologin.allow ...
```

4.1.5.11. scp behavior

The secure copy client optionally prints statistics about its progress. During a file copy across the network, *scp* can display the percentage of the file transferred so far. The SSH1 distribution has several *configure* flags relating to these statistics. One pair of flags controls whether the statistics code is compiled into *scp*, and others control *scp*'s default behavior for displaying (or not displaying) statistics.

The flags **--with-scp-stats** and **--without-scp-stats** control whether the statistics code is included in *scp* at all. By default, the code is included. To prevent its inclusion:

```
# SSH1 only
$ configure ... --without-scp-stats ...
```

If the statistics code is included, further *configure* flags control *scp*'s default behavior for statistics display. The flags **--enable-scp-stats** and **--disable-scp-stats** set the default for single file transfers. If neither flag is used, statistics are enabled. To disable:

```
# SSH1 only
$ configure ... --disable-scp-stats ...
```

Likewise, the flags **--enable-all-scp-stats** and **--disable-all-scp-stats** set the default for multiple file transfers. Again, if neither flag is used, statistics are enabled. To disable:

```
# SSH1 only
$ configure ... --disable-all-scp-stats ...
```

Regardless of the configuration for single and multiple file transfers, statistics may be turned on or off using *scp*'s command-line options (*–Q* and *–a*) and user environment variables (SSH_SCP_STATS, SSH_NO_SCP_STATS, SSH_ALL_SCP_STATS, and SSH_NO_ALL_SCP_STATS). [7.5.7] Of course, the statistics code must be present (`--with-scp-stats`) for this runtime configuration to work.

4.1.5.12. R-commands (rsh) compatibility

In SSH1 and OpenSSH, if *ssh* can't achieve a secure connection to a remote host, then optionally an insecure connection is established using the r-commands (*rsh, rcp, rlogin*). This feature is helpful for backward compatibility but might be undesirable in a secure setting. SSH2 specifically doesn't include this insecure feature.

The SSH1 *configure* flags `--with-rsh` and `--without-rsh` determine whether *ssh* may establish connections by *rsh*. To permit use of *rsh*, provide a path to its executable:

```
# SSH1, OpenSSH
$ configure ... --with-rsh=/usr/ucb/rsh ...
```

If you include *rsh* support, individual users can selectively control it for clients launched in their accounts with the keywords `FallBackToRsh` and `UseRsh`. [7.4.5.8] Or, to prevent *ssh* from using *rsh* entirely, compile with:

```
# SSH1, OpenSSH
$ configure ... --without-rsh ...
```

4.1.5.13. SSH-1/SSH-2 agent compatibility

Agents [2.5] that use the protocols SSH-1 and SSH-2 are normally not compatible. That is, each can't store keys or forward connections from the other version. [6.3.2.4] However, the SSH2 agent has an optional feature to serve SSH-1 protocol applications if three criteria are met:

- Your SSH2 implementation must include RSA support, since SSH1 uses RSA to encrypt keys. At press time, the F-Secure SSH2 Server includes RSA support, but SSH2 doesn't.
- The SSH2 *configure* script must be run with the flag `--with-ssh-agent1-compat`:

```
# SSH2 only
$ configure ... --with-ssh-agent1-compat ...
```

- The SSH2 agent, *ssh-agent2*, must be run with the command line flag *–1* (that's a one, not a lowercase L):

```
# SSH2 only
$ ssh-agent2 -1
```

4.1.5.14. Debug output

SSH servers produce detailed debugging output on demand. [5.8] At compile time, you may enable different levels of debugging and optionally include support for the Electric Fence memory allocation debugger.

If desired, the SSH2 server may be compiled with or without two levels of debugging output. Without the debugging code, the programs may experience a slight increase in performance, but with it, the programs are easier to maintain. We recommend including at least some debugging code, because you never know when you'll need to diagnose a problem.

"Light" and "heavy" debugging are two levels of debugging that may be specified in the source code. Light debugging output is controlled by the *configure* flags `--enable-debug` and `--disable-debug` (the default). Heavy debugging output is controlled by the *configure* flags `--enable-debug-heavy` and `--disable-debug-heavy` (the default). For example:

```
# SSH2 only
$ configure ... --enable-debug --disable-debug-heavy ...
```

The two debug levels aren't mutually exclusive: you may select light, heavy, both, or neither. We recommend turning on heavy debugging; otherwise the messages contain too little information to be useful.

Finally, SSH2 memory allocations may be tracked by Electric Fence, a freely distributable memory allocation debugger created by Bruce Perens of Pixar. You must have Electric Fence installed on the server machine in order for this to work. The *configure* flags `--enable-efence` and `--disable-efence` (the default) control whether Electric Fence is used:

```
# SSH2 only
$ configure ... --enable-efence ...
```

This flag causes SSH2's programs to be linked with the Electric Fence library, *libefence.a*, which provides instrumented versions of `malloc()`, `free()`, and other memory-related functions. Electric Fence is available from:

http://sources.isc.org/devel/memleak/

4.1.6. Creating the Serverwide Known-Hosts File

After configuring and installing SSH1 on a host, it's time to create a machinewide known hosts file. [2.3.1] Normally */etc/ssh_known_hosts*, this file contains the public host keys of all hosts in the local domain or remote hosts that people in this domain connect to frequently via SSH1. For example, the known hosts file on *myhost.example.com* likely contains the host keys of all machines in the *example.com* domain and perhaps others.

You can get by without populating this file, if the SSH client is configured to add new host keys to users' personal *known_hosts* files. [7.4.3.1] However, it's better to fill the central file with as many common hosts as possible, for these reasons:

- It makes users' lives easier, avoiding the various prompts for adding keys.
- It's more secure. When you accept a key for a new SSH server, you are open to man-in-the-middle attacks. [3.10.4] If the remote host key is known in advance, and an intruder tries to masquerade as a remote host, the SSH client will detect the fake host key.

The known-hosts file is required for trusted-host authentication. [3.4.2.3] Only users connecting from hosts whose keys appear in the file may be authenticated by this method.

You can collect all the host keys by hand while or after you install SSH on your hosts. But if you have a large number of hosts, SSH1 comes with a utility to help with task: *make-ssh-known-hosts*. This Perl script queries the Domain Name Service (DNS) to find all hostnames in the local domain, and connects to them using SSH to obtain their host keys. The keys are then written to standard output as a list ready for inclusion in the known-hosts file.

In its simplest form, the program is invoked with one argument, the name of the local domain:

```
# SSH1 only
$ make-ssh-known-hosts example.com > /etc/ssh_known_hosts
```

make-ssh-known-hosts has quite a few command-line flags for tailoring its behavior. [4.1.6.1] In addition, you may limit which machines are queried by providing Perl-style regular expressions as arguments following the domain name. For example, to print the host keys of all hosts in *example.com* whose names begin with `z`:

```
$ make-ssh-known-hosts example.com '^z'
```

A second regular expression argument performs the opposite task: it excludes the keys of hosts that match the regular expression. You can extend the previous example to exclude hosts ending in `x`:

```
$ make-ssh-known-hosts example.com '^z' 'x$'
```

Just for fun, here's a command that produces no host keys at all:

```
$ make-ssh-known-hosts example.com mymachine mymachine
```

because it includes and excludes the same string.

4.1.6.1. make-ssh-known-hosts command-line flags

Each flag may appear in two forms, both of which we present in the discussion that follows:

- A full word preceded by a double-dash, such as `--passwordtimeout`
- An abbreviated form with a single dash, such as `-pa`

The following flags are related to program locations:

`--nslookup (-n)` *`path`*
: Inform the script of the full path to *nslookup*, a program to make DNS queries. The default is to locate *nslookup* in the shell's current search path.

`--ssh (-ss)` *`path`*
: Inform the script of the full path to the SSH client. You may also provide command-line options to *ssh* here. The default is to locate *ssh* in the shell's current search path.

These flags are related to timeouts:

`--passwordtimeout (-pa)` *`timeout`*
: How long to wait for the user to type a password, in seconds. The default is not to prompt for passwords. A value of `0` means prompt for a password with timeouts disabled.

`--pingtimeout (-pi)` *`timeout`*
: How long to wait for a ping response from a host's SSH port, in seconds. The default is 3 seconds.

`--timeout (-ti)` *`timeout`*
: How long to wait for an SSH command to complete, in seconds. The default is 60 seconds.

Here are flags related to domain information:

`--initialdns (-i)` *`nameserver`*
: Initial nameserver to query; otherwise, uses the resolver list. The first query is for the zone SOA record of the domain argument to *make-ssh-known-hosts*. It then does a zone transfer from the master nameserver listed in the SOA record.

`--server (-se)` *`nameserver`*
: If this is given, skip the SOA record lookup and immediately do the zone transfer from this nameserver.

`--subdomains (-su)` *`domain1,domain2,...`*
: Normally, *make-ssh-known-hosts* includes aliases for each host using all domain-name abbreviations starting from the leftmost label and moving to the

right, except for the second-to-last one. So for example, host *foo.bar.baz.geewhiz.edu* gets these names:

foo
foo.bar
foo.bar.baz
foo.bar.baz.geewhiz.edu

This option allows you to pick a subset of these subdomains to be included, instead of all of them.

`--domainnamesplit (-do)`
Create aliases for each host key in the output by splitting the domain name into prefixes. For example, domain name *a.b.c* is split into the prefixes *a*, *a.b*, and *a.b.c*, and each prefix is appended to each hostname to create an alias.

`--norecursive (-nor)`
Obtain keys only for the domain listed and not (recursively) its subdomains. The default is to examine subdomains.

These are flags related to output and debugging:

`--debug (-de)` *`level`*
Specify a nonnegative integer debugging level. The higher the level, the more debugging output is produced. The default is 5. At press time, the highest level used within *make-ssh-known-hosts* is 80.

`--silent (-si)`
Don't ring the terminal bell. The default is to make noise.

`--keyscan (-k)`
Print results in an alternative format used by *ssh-keyscan*, a program for gathering SSH public keys. *ssh-keyscan* is a separate piece of software, not part of SSH1. [13.4]

Finally, this flag is related to failure recovery:

`--notrustdaemon (-notr)`
make-ssh-known-hosts invokes *ssh host cat /etc/ssh_host_key.pub* to obtain a host's public key. If that command fails for some reason (e.g., the key file is elsewhere), SSH may still have gotten the key via the SSH protocol and stored it in the user's *~/.ssh/known_hosts* file. Normally, *make-ssh-known-hosts* uses that key; with `--notrustdaemon`, the key is included but commented out.

4.2. F-Secure SSH Server

F-Secure Corporation, formerly DataFellows, Ltd., a Finnish software company, produces commercial implementations of SSH derived from those of SSH

Communications Security. F-Secure's server product line, F-Secure SSH Server, runs on Unix, and SSH-1 and SSH-2 servers are available as separate products. They are repackagings of SSH1 and SSH2 with commercial licenses and a few added features:

- A manual covering F-Secure SSH products for all platforms (Unix, Windows, Macintosh)
- Additional encryption algorithms in the SSH-2 product, such as RSA and IDEA. (see the F-Secure manual for the current list)
- An additional SSH client, *edd* (Encryption Data Dump), a Unix filter that applies SSH encryption or decryption to standard input, writing the results to standard output
- A few additional options in SSH1 (see Appendix B)

4.2.1. Obtaining and Installing

F-Secure SSH Server is available from *http://www.f-secure.com/*. In addition to their commercial SSH products, which may be purchased and downloaded from the web site, free "evaluation versions" are available.

Except for the few additional features listed in the previous section, installation, configuration, and operation of F-Secure Unix SSH is almost identical to that of the SCS versions. SSH2 has moved ahead with new features not present in its F-Secure counterpart, however, so check the F-Secure documentation to see if particular features are available.

4.3. OpenSSH

OpenSSH is a free implementation of SSH-1 and SSH-2, obtained from the OpenSSH web site:

http://www.openssh.com/

Since it is developed by the OpenBSD Project, the main version of OpenSSH is specifically for the OpenBSD Unix operating system, and is in fact included in the base OpenBSD installation. As a separate but related effort, another team maintains a "portable" version that compiles on a variety of Unix flavors and tracks the main development effort. The supported platforms include Linux, Solaris AIX, IRIX, HP/UX, FreeBSD, and NetBSD (OpenSSH is included in FreeBSD as well). The portable version carries a "p" suffix. For example, 2.1.1p4 is the fourth release of the portable version of OpenSSH 2.1.1.

4.3.1. Prerequisites

OpenSSH depends on two other software packages: OpenSSL and zlib. OpenSSL is a cryptographic library available at *http://www.openssl.com/*; all the cryptography used in OpenSSH is pulled from OpenSSL. zlib is a library of data-compression routines, available at *http://www.info-zip.org/pub/infozip/zlib/*. Before compiling OpenSSH, you must obtain and install these packages.

4.3.2. Building

Building OpenSSH is similar to building SSH1 and SSH2, with the same *configure; make; make install* sequence. In some versions of OpenSSH prior to 2.2.0, though, *make install* didn't generate and install the host keys automatically. If your host keys are missing, you can install them with *make host-key*.

4.3.3. PAM

By default, OpenSSH uses PAM for password authentication. PAM, the Pluggable Authentication Modules system, is a generic framework for authentication, authorization, and accounting (AAA). The idea is that programs call PAM to perform AAA functions, leaving the sysadmin free to configure individual programs to use various kinds of authentication, via dynamically loaded libraries. Visit *http://www.kernel.org/pub/linux/libs/pam/* for more information on PAM.

Generally, if a program uses PAM, some host configuration is necessary to describe how PAM should behave for that program. The PAM configuration files are usually in the directory */etc/pam.d*.

On many operating systems that use PAM, including RedHat Linux, OpenSSH builds with PAM support by default (you can turn this off using `configure --without-pam`). However, you must then configure PAM on the host to know about *sshd*, or password authentication will not work. By default, PAM normally denies authentication for programs not specifically configured to use it.

PAM configuration for SSH is usually just a matter of copying the appropriate *sshd.pam* file from the distribution's *contrib* directory into place as */etc/pam.d/sshd*. Sample files are included for various flavors of Unix.

Note that you don't need to restart *sshd* when you change the PAM configuration; the configuration files are checked on every use of PAM.

4.3.4. Randomness

The main OpenSSH code base relies on the host operating system to provide a source of entropy, or randomness, via a device driver accessed through */dev/urandom*. This is because the OpenBSD operating system has this device. If you build OpenSSH on a platform lacking such a device, such as Solaris, it needs an alternative source of randomness. There are two choices:

- Use the built-in, "internal entropy-gathering" system
- Install the "Entropy Gathering Daemon" (EGD) package *(http://www.lothar.com/tech/crypto/)*

OpenSSH defaults to the first choice, the internal system, unless you configure it with EGD. The internal system uses a configurable set of commands that monitor changing aspects of the system operation, mixing their output together. You can control which commands are used and how, with the file */etc/ssh_prng_cmds*.

4.3.5. Compilation Flags

As with the other SSH implementations, OpenSSH has a number of compilation flags, many the same, some different. Here are the most important ones to know:

`--without-pam` *Disable PAM support*

Omit PAM support from OpenSSH. This flag isn't normally necessary, since the *configure* process detects whether the host has PAM, and if so, you probably want to use it.

`--with-md5-passwords` *Enable use of MD5 passwords*

`--without-shadow` *Disable shadow password support*

These options control OpenSSH's treatment of the Unix account database (passwd map). They are relevant only if OpenSSH isn't using PAM, since otherwise PAM deals with reading the account information, not the OpenSSH code proper.

Enable `--with-md5-passwords` if your system uses MD5 instead of the traditional *crypt* function to hash passwords, and you are not using PAM.

"Shadow passwords" refers to the practice of keeping the hashed password in a restricted file */etc/shadow* (*/etc/passwd* must be world-readable). Use `--without-shadow` to suppress reading of the */etc/shadow* file, should it be necessary.

`--with-ssl-dir=PATH` *Set path to OpenSSL installation*

If OpenSSL isn't installed in the usual place, */usr/local/ssl*, use this flag to indicate its location.

`--with-xauth=`*`PATH`* *Set path to xauth program*

In OpenSSH, the default location of the *xauth* program is a compile-time parameter.

`--with-random=`*`FILE`* *Read randomness from given file*

Specify the character device file providing a source of random bits, normally */dev/urandom.*

`--with-egd-pool=`*`FILE`* *Read randomness from EGD pool FILE (default none)*

If you install EGD as described earlier, use this flag to have OpenSSH use EGD as its randomness source.

`--with-kerberos4=`*`PATH`* *Enable Kerberos-4 support*

`--with-afs=`*`PATH`* *Enable AFS support*

These flags apply to Kerberos-4 and AFS. [3.4.2.4] Note that there's no Kerberos-5 support in OpenSSH.

`--with-skey` *Enable S/Key support*

Enable support for the S/Key one-time password system for password authentication. [3.4.2.5]

`--with-tcp-wrappers` *Enable TCP-wrappers support*

Equivalent to the SSH1 *configure* flag **`--with-libwrap`**. [4.1.5.3]

`--with-ipaddr-display` *Use IP address instead of hostname in $DISPLAY*

In X forwarding, use DISPLAY values of the form 192.168.10.1:10.0 instead of hostname:10.0. This flag works around certain buggy X libraries that do weird things with the hostname version, using some sort of IPC mechanism for talking to the X server rather than TCP.

`--with-default-path=`*`PATH`* *Default server PATH*

The default path OpenSSH uses when attempting to run a subprogram.

`--with-ipv4-default` *Use IPv4 unless "-6" is given*

`--with-4in6` *Check for and convert IPv4 in IPv6 mapped addresses*

OpenSSH supports IPv6, the next-generation TCP/IP protocol suite that is still in the development and very early deployment stages in the Internet (the current version of IP is IPv4). The default configuration of OpenSSH attempts to use IPv6 where possible, and sometimes this results in problems. If you encounter errors mentioning "af=10" or "address family 10," that's IPv6, and you should try the *–4* runtime option, or compiling **`--with-ipv4-default`**.

`--with-pid-dir=PATH` *Specify location of ssh.pid file*

Location of the OpenSSH pid file, where it stores the pid of the currently running daemon. The default is */var/run/sshd.pid.*

4.4. Software Inventory

Table 4-1 provides a reference to the many files and programs installed with SSH.

Table 4-1. Software Inventory

Component	SSH1	OpenSSH	SSH2
Server config	*/etc/sshd_config*	*/etc/sshd_config*	*/etc/ssh2/sshd2_config*
Global client config	*/etc/ssh_config*	*/etc/ssh_config*	*/etc/ssh2/ssh2_config*
Host private key	*/etc/ssh_host_key*	*/etc/ssh_host_dsa_key*	*/etc/ssh2/hostkey*
Host public key	*/etc/ssh_host_key.pub*	*/etc/ssh_host_dsa_key.pub*	*/etc/ssh2/hostkey.pub*
Client host keys	*/etc/ssh_known_hosts* *~/.ssh/ssh_known_hosts*	*/etc/ssh_known_hosts* *~/.ssh/ssh_known_hosts* *~/.ssh/ssh_known_hosts2*	*/etc/ssh2/hostkeys* *~/.ssh2/hostkeys/**
Remote host keys	*~/.ssh/ssh_known_hosts*	*~/.ssh/ssh_known_hosts* *~/.ssh/ssh_known_hosts2*	*~/.ssh2/knownhosts/**
libwrap control files	*/etc/hosts.allow* */etc/hosts.deny*	*/etc/hosts.allow* */etc/hosts.deny*	*/etc/hosts.allow* */etc/hosts.deny*
Authorization for login via public key	*~/.ssh/authorized_keys*	*~/.ssh/authorized_keys* *~/.ssh/authorized_keys2*	*~/.ssh2/authorization*
Authorization for login via trusted-host	*/etc/hosts.equiv* */etc/shosts.equiv* *~/.shosts* *~/.rhosts*	*/etc/hosts.equiv* */etc/shosts.equiv* *~/.shosts* *~/.rhosts*	*/etc/hosts.equiv* */etc/shosts.equiv* *~/.shosts* *~/.rhosts*
Default keypair for public-key authentication	*~/.ssh/identity{.pub}*	*SSH-1/RSA: ~/.ssh/identity{.pub}* *SSH-2/DSA: ~/.ssh/id_dsa{.pub}*[a]	*(No default)*
Random seed	*~/.ssh/random_seed* */etc/ssh_random_seed*	*~/.ssh/prng_seed*[b]	*~/.ssh2/random_seed* */etc/ssh2/random_seed*
Commands for generating randomness	–	*/etc/ssh_prng_cmds*	–
Kerberos	*/etc/krb5.conf* *~/.k5login*	*/etc/krb.conf* *~/.klogin*	–

Table 4-1. Software Inventory (continued)

Component	SSH1	OpenSSH	SSH2
Terminal client	*ssh1* *slogin link to ssh1*	*ssh* *slogin link to ssh*	*ssh2*
Secure file copy client	*scp1*	*scp*	*scp2*
Signer program	–	–	*ssh-signer2*
sftp2/*scp2* server	–	–	*sftp-server2*
Authentication agent	*ssh-agent1*	*ssh-agent*	*ssh-agent2*
Key generator	*ssh-keygen1*	*ssh-keygen*	*ssh-keygen2*
Key add/remove	*ssh-add1*	*ssh-add*	*ssh-add2*
Find SSH servers	–	–	*ssh-probe2*
Get passphrase via terminal or X	*ssh-askpass1*	–	*ssh-askpass2*
Server program	*sshd1*	*sshd*	*sshd2*

[a] This can't be changed using *–i* as it can with OpenSSH/1; use *–o Identity2=key_file* instead.

[b] Present only if using OpenSSH's internal entropy-gathering mechanism (i.e., no */dev/random* or equivalent on system). SSH1 and SSH2 use seed files even when */dev/random* exists.

4.5. Replacing R-Commands with SSH

SSH and the r-commands (*rsh*, *rcp*, *rlogin*) can coexist peacefully on the same machine. Since the r-commands are insecure, however, some system administrators prefer to replace them by their SSH counterparts (*ssh*, *scp*, *slogin*). This replacement has two parts:

- Installing SSH and removing *rsh*, *rcp*, and *rlogin*; requires some user retraining
- Modifying other programs or scripts that invoke the r-commands

The r-commands are so similar to their analogous SSH commands, you might be tempted to rename the SSH commands as the r-commands (e.g., rename *ssh* as *rsh*, etc.). After all, common commands like these are practically identical in syntax:

```
$ rsh -l jones remote.example.com
$ ssh -l jones remote.example.com

$ rcp myfile remote.example.com:
$ scp myfile remote.example.com:
```

Why not just rename? Well, the two sets of programs are incompatible in some ways. For example, not all versions of *ssh* support the "hostname link" feature of *rsh* [2.7.3], and some old versions of *rcp* use a different syntax for specifying remote filenames.

In the following sections, we discuss some common Unix programs that invoke the r-commands and how to adapt them to use SSH instead.

4.5.1. The /usr/hosts Directory

The program *rsh* has an interesting feature called *hostname links*. [2.7.3] If you rename the executable from "rsh" to something else, the program treats its new name as a hostname and connects to it by default. For example, if you rename *rsh* as "petunia," on invocation it executes *rsh petunia*. The renaming may be done literally or by creating a hard link or symbolic link to *rsh*:

```
$ ls -l petunia
lrwxrwxrwx  1 root       12 Jan 31  1996 petunia -> /usr/ucb/rsh
$ petunia
Welcome to petunia!
Last login was Wed Oct 6 21:38:14 from rhododendron
You have mail.
```

Some Unix machines have a directory, commonly */usr/hosts*, that contains symbolic links to *rsh* representing various hosts on the local network (or beyond):

```
$ ls -l /usr/hosts
lrwxrwxrwx  1 root       12 Jan 31  1996 lily -> /usr/ucb/rsh
lrwxrwxrwx  1 root       12 Jan 31  1996 petunia -> /usr/ucb/rsh
lrwxrwxrwx  1 root       12 Jan 31  1996 rhododendron -> /usr/ucb/rsh
...
```

If you eliminate */usr/ucb/rsh* from such a machine, obviously these links become orphaned. Delete them and replace them with links to *ssh*, perhaps with a shell script like this:

```
#!/bin/sh
SSH=/usr/local/bin/ssh
cd /usr/hosts
for file in *
do
  rm -f $file
  ln -s $SSH $file
  echo "Linked $file to $SSH"
done
```

4.5.2. Concurrent Version System (CVS)

CVS is a *version-control system*. It maintains a history of changes to sets of files, and helps coordinate the work of multiple people on the same files. It can use *rsh* to connect to repositories on remote hosts. For example, when you check in a new version of a file:

```
$ cvs commit myfile
```

if the repository is located on a remote machine, CVS may invoke *rsh* to access the remote repository. For a more secure solution, CVS can run *ssh* instead of *rsh*. Of course, the remote machine must be running an SSH server, and if you use public-key authentication, your remote account must contain your key in the appropriate place.*

To make CVS use *ssh*, simply set the environment variable CVS_RSH to contain the path to your *ssh* client:

```
# Bourne shell family
# Put in ~/.profile to make permanent.
CVS_RSH=/usr/local/bin/ssh
export CVS_RSH

# C shell family
# Put in ~/.login to make permanent.
setenv CVS_RSH /usr/local/bin/ssh
```

This approach has one problem: each time you check in a file, the logger's name is the remote account owner, which might not be your own. The problem is solved by manually setting the remote LOGNAME variable using the "environment=" option in your remote *authorized_keys* file. [8.2.6.1]

4.5.3. GNU Emacs

The Emacs variable `remote-shell-program` contains the path to any desired program for invoking a remote shell. Simply redefine it to be the full path to your *ssh* executable. Also, the *rlogin* package, *rlogin.el*, defines a variable `rlogin-program` you can redefine to use *slogin*.

4.5.4. Pine

The Pine mail reader uses *rsh* to invoke mail-server software on remote machines. For example, it might invoke the IMAP daemon, *imapd*, on a remote mail server. Another program may be substituted for *rsh* by changing the value of a Pine configuration variable, `rsh-path`. This variable holds the name of the program for opening remote shell connections, normally */usr/ucb/rsh*. A new value may be assigned in an individual user's Pine configuration file, *~/.pinerc*, or in the system-wide Pine configuration file, typically */usr/local/lib/pine.conf*. For example:

```
# Set in a Pine configuration file
rsh-path=/usr/local/bin/ssh
```

A second variable, `rsh-command`, constructs the actual command string to be executed for the remote mail server. The value is a pattern in the style of the C

* CVS also has a remote-access method involving its own server, called *pserver*. This mechanism can be secured using SSH port forwarding instead; see Chapter 9.

function `printf()`. Most likely, you won't need to change the value because both *rsh* and *ssh* fit the default pattern, which is:

```
"%s %s -l %s exec /etc/r%sd"
```

The first three "%s" pattern substitutions refer to the `rsh-path` value, the remote hostname, and the remote username. (The fourth forms the remote mail daemon name, which doesn't concern us.) So by default, if your username is *alice* and the remote mail server is *mail.example.com*, `rsh-command` evaluates to:

```
/usr/ucb/rsh mail.example.com -l alice ...
```

By changing the `rsh-path`, it becomes instead:

```
/usr/local/bin/ssh mail.example.com -l alice ...
```

As we said, you probably don't need to do anything with `rsh-command`, but just in case, we've included it for reference. We present a detailed case study of integrating Pine and SSH1 later. [11.3]

4.5.5. rsync, rdist

rsync and *rdist* are software tools for synchronizing sets of files between different directories on the same machine or on two different hosts. Both can call *rsh* to connect to a remote host, and both can easily use SSH instead: simply set the RSYNC_RSH for *rsync* and use the *–P* option with *rdist*. *rsync* with SSH is a particularly simple and effective method to securely maintain remote mirrors of whole directory trees.

4.6. Summary

SSH1, SSH2, F-Secure SSH Server, and OpenSSH may all be tailored in various ways by compile-time configuration with the *configure* script. We've covered the SSH-specific flags, but remember that other operating system-specific flags may also apply to your installation, so be sure to read the installation notes supplied with the software.

Once installed, SSH software may replace the insecure r-commands on your Unix system, not only when run directly, but also within other programs that invoke *rsh*, such as Emacs and Pine.

In this chapter:

5
Serverwide Configuration

After installing an SSH server (*sshd*), it's time to make informed decisions about your server's operation. Which authentication techniques should be permitted? How many bits should the server key contain? Should idle connections be dropped after a time limit or left connected indefinitely? These and other questions must be considered carefully. *sshd* has reasonable defaults, but don't accept them blindly. Your server should conform to a carefully planned security policy. Fortunately, *sshd* is highly configurable so you can make it do all kinds of interesting tricks.

sshd may be configured at three levels, and this chapter covers the second one: *serverwide configuration*, in which a system administrator controls the global runtime behavior of the server. This includes a large, rich set of features, such as TCP/IP settings, encryption, authentication, access control, and error logging. Some features are controlled by modifying a serverwide configuration file, and others by command-line options passed to the server at invocation.

The other two levels of configuration are compile-time configuration (Chapter 4), in which the server is compiled with or without certain functionality; and per-account configuration (Chapter 8), in which the server's behavior is modified by end users for their accounts only. We'll discuss the distinction between the three levels in more detail later in this chapter.

This chapter covers only the servers from SSH1/SSH2 and their derivatives OpenSSH and F-Secure SSH Server. Our reference implementations, however, are SSH1 and SSH2 for Unix. We've tried to indicate which features are found or not found in the various flavors of *sshd*, but these will certainly change as new versions appear, so read each product's documentation for the latest information.

5.1. The Name of the Server

The SSH server is named *sshd1* for SSH1, *sshd2* for SSH2, and *sshd* for OpenSSH. However, you may also be able to invoke *sshd1* or *sshd2* as *sshd*, because their Makefiles create a symbolic link called *sshd*. [4.1.3] [4.1.4] The link points to *sshd2* if it's installed, otherwise *sshd1* (the SSH1 Makefile doesn't supersede links installed by SSH2).

Some features in this chapter apply to *sshd1* only, *sshd2* only, OpenSSH's *sshd* only, or various combinations. We indicate this in the following ways:

- If a command-line option applies to only one package, e.g., SSH1, we present the example using *sshd1* and a comment. For instance, in SSH1 the *–d* option (debug mode) may appear alone:

  ```
  # SSH1 only
  $ sshd1 -d
  ```

- If a command-line option applies only to SSH2, we use *sshd2*. Its *–d* option requires an argument:

  ```
  # SSH2 only
  $ sshd2 -d 2
  ```

- We similarly identify OpenSSH-specific and F-Secure-specific features with comments:

  ```
  # OpenSSH only
  # F-Secure SSH only
  ```

- If a command-line option works for several packages, we refer to the server as *sshd*. For example, the *–b* option (set the number of bits in the server key) is the same for SSH1 and OpenSSH, so you write:

  ```
  # SSH1, OpenSSH
  $ sshd -b 1024
  ```

- Likewise, when we discuss configuration keywords, some apply to SSH1, SSH2, OpenSSH, or various combinations. We precede examples with a comment for clarity. For example, the `MaxConnections` keyword, which limits the number of available TCP/IP connections, is supported only by SSH2, so an example looks like:

```
# SSH2 only
MaxConnections 32
```

5.2. Running the Server

Ordinarily, an SSH server is invoked when the host computer is booted, and it is left running as a daemon. This works fine for most purposes. Alternatively, you can invoke the server manually. This is advantageous when you're debugging a server, experimenting with server options, or running a server as a nonsuperuser. Manual invocation requires a bit more work and forethought but might be the only alternative for some situations.

Most commonly, a computer has just one SSH server running on it. It handles multiple connections by spawning child processes, one per connection.* You can run multiple servers if you like, however. For example, you might run both *sshd1* and *sshd2*, or several versions of a server, each listening on a different TCP port.

5.2.1. Running as the Superuser

The SSH server is invoked by simply typing its name:

```
# SSH1, SSH2, OpenSSH
$ sshd
```

The server automatically runs in the background, so no ampersand is required at the end of the line.

To invoke the server when the host computer boots, add appropriate lines to */etc/rc.local* or the appropriate startup file on your system. For example:

```
# Specify the path to sshd.
SSHD=/usr/local/bin/sshd
# If sshd exists, run it and echo success to the system console.
if [ -x "$SSHD" ]
then
  $SSHD && echo 'Starting sshd'
fi
```

SSH2 comes with a sample SysV-style init control script, named *sshd2.startup*.

5.2.2. Running as an Ordinary User

Any user can run *sshd*, provided that several steps are completed beforehand:

* Or *sshd* can be invoked by inetd, creating one *sshd* process per connection. [5.4.3.2]

1. Get permission from your system administrator.
2. Generate a host key.
3. Select a port number.
4. Create a server configuration file (optional).

Before starting, ask your system administrator if you may run an SSH server. While this isn't necessary from a technical standpoint, it is a wise idea. An administrator might not appreciate your creating a new avenue for logins behind his back. Likewise, if the administrator has disabled SSH or certain SSH features, there's probably a good security reason, and you shouldn't just work around it!

Next, you must generate your own host key. Any other existing host key is probably readable only by the superuser. Host keys are generated with the program *ssh-keygen*. [6.2] For now, to create a 1024-bit host key and store it in the file *~/myserver/hostkey*, type the following for SSH1 or OpenSSH:

```
# SSH1, OpenSSH
$ ssh-keygen -N '' -b 1024 -f ~/myserver/hostkey
```

This command generates the files *hostkey* and *hostkey.pub* in the directory *~/myserver* (so make sure the directory exists). Here's the analogous command for SSH2:

```
# SSH2 only
$ ssh-keygen2 -P -b 1024 ~/myserver/hostkey
```

The *–P* and *–N* cause the generated key to be saved in plaintext, because *sshd* expects to read it without prompting someone for a passphrase.

Third, you must select a port number on which the SSH server listens for connections. The port number is set with the *–p* command-line option of *sshd* or the `Port` keyword in the configuration file, as we discuss later. Your server can't listen on port 22, the default, because only the superuser may run processes to listen on that port. Your port number must be greater than or equal to 1024, as lower port numbers are reserved by the operating system for use by privileged programs. [3.4.2.3] The port number also must not conflict with those in use by other programs on the server computer; if it does, you get an error message when you try to start the server:

```
error: bind: Address already in use
```

If you receive this error, try another integer in the free range (above 1024). Avoid numbers mentioned in the computer's services map (usually */etc/services* or the Network Information Service (NIS) "services" map, which you can view with the Unix command *ypcat –k* services). These numbers have been designated by the system administrator for use with particular programs or protocols, so you might be causing trouble if you steal one.

Finally, you must create your own SSH server configuration file. Otherwise, the server uses built-in defaults or a systemwide configuration file (if one exists) and might not operate as you intend.

Assuming you have generated a host key in *~/myserver/hostkey*, selected the port number 2345, and created a configuration file in *~/myserver/config*, the server is invoked with the command:

```
# SSH1, SSH2, OpenSSH
$ sshd -h ~/myserver/hostkey -p 2345 -f ~/myserver/config
```

A server run by an ordinary user has some disadvantages:

- It runs under the uid of the ordinary user, not root, so it can connect only to that user's account.
- It is invoked manually, rather than automatically when the computer boots. As a result, to run the server, you must connect once without SSH to the computer. And each time the computer is rebooted, the server dies, and you need to redo this step. Conceivably you can set up a *cron* job to keep it running automatically.
- While setting up a server, it's useful to read the diagnostic messages printed by the server, in case something isn't working right. Unfortunately, your server's log messages are written to the system log files, which you don't own and possibly can't access. Because *sshd* does its logging via the syslog service, an ordinary user can't control where the log messages are sent. To see them, you need to locate the system logs, which might be in */var/adm/messages*, */var/log/messages*, or someplace else depending on how *syslogd* is set up, and you need appropriate permissions to read these files. To get around this annoyance, consider running the server in debug mode, so messages will appear on your terminal (as well as in the system logs). [5.8] This way, you can more easily see error messages until you get the server working.

Nevertheless, for many users, the advantages of SSH outweigh these inconveniences. Assuming your system administrator approves, you can secure your logins with *sshd* even if you aren't a superuser.

5.3. Server Configuration: An Overview

As mentioned at the beginning of the chapter, the behavior of the server, *sshd*, may be controlled at three levels:

- *Compile-time configuration* (Chapter 4) is accomplished when *sshd* is built. For example, a server may be compiled with or without support for *rhosts* authentication.
- *Serverwide configuration*, the subject of this chapter, is performed by a system administrator and applies to a running instance of the server. For instance, an administrator may deny SSH access by all hosts in a given domain or make the server listen on a particular port.

  Serverwide configuration can be dependent on compile-time configuration. For example, a server's trusted-host authentication options work only if the server is compiled with trusted-host authentication support included. Otherwise, the options have no effect. We identify such dependencies throughout the book. Figure 5-1 highlights the serverwide configuration tasks.

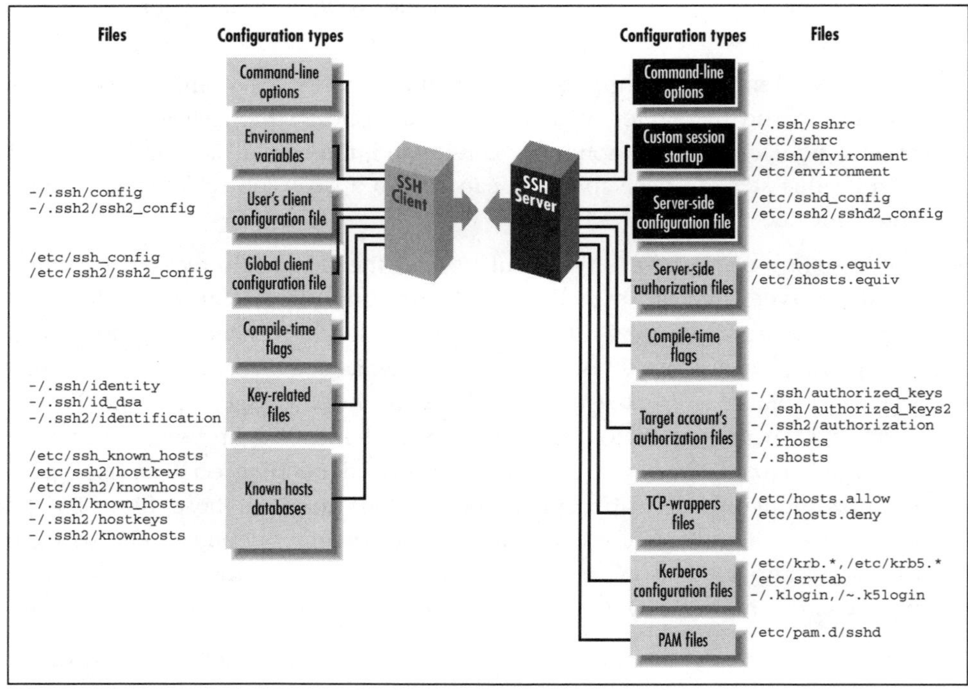

Figure 5-1. Serverwide configuration (highlighted parts)

- *Per-account configuration* (Chapter 8) is performed by the end user, specifically, the owner of the account to which an SSH connection has been requested. For example, users may permit or deny access to their own accounts from particular hosts, overriding the serverwide configuration.

Suppose user deborah on the machine *client.unc.edu* invokes an SSH client. The clients's behavior is determined by the compile-time options selected when the software was built, the machinewide client configuration file on *client.unc.edu*, deborah's own client configuration file, and the command-line options used by deborah when invoking the client. An SSH server running on *server.unc.edu* accepts deborah's connection to the account charlie. The server's behavior is determined by the compile-time options used when *sshd* was built, the machinewide server configuration file on *server.unc.edu*, the command-line options used when the SSH server was run, and charlie's personal server configuration file (e.g., an *authorized_keys* file), plus several files that set environment variables for the successful login session.

With three levels of server configuration, and multiple entry points for modifying the behavior at each level, things can get complicated. In particular, different options may work together or cancel each other. For example, user charlie can configure his account on *server.unc.edu* to accept connections from *client.unc.edu*, while the system administrator of *server.unc.edu* can configure the SSH server to reject them. (In this case, Charlie loses.) Administrators must understand not only how to configure the server themselves, but also how their choices interact with compile-time and per-account settings.

5.3.1. Server Configuration Files

Serverwide configuration is accomplished in two ways: through a server configuration file, or through command-line options. In a *server configuration file*, numerous configuration variables, called *keywords*, may have their values set. For example, to set the TCP port on which the server will listen, a configuration file can contain the line:

```
# SSH1, SSH2, OpenSSH
Port 1022
```

The configuration file is typically */etc/sshd_config* for SSH1 and OpenSSH or */etc/ssh2/sshd2_config* for SSH2. The file contains keywords and their values, as in the `Port` example, with one pair (keyword and value) per line. Keywords are case-insensitive: `Port`, `port`, and `PoRt` are all treated identically. Comments may appear in the file as well: any line beginning with a hash sign (#) is a comment:

```
# This is a comment
```

To use a configuration file other than the default, invoke *sshd* with the *–f* command-line option, providing the alternative filename as an argument:

```
# SSH1, SSH2, OpenSSH
$ sshd -f /usr/local/ssh/my_config
```

For SSH2, the configuration file format has the following extensions in addition to keywords:

Sections
: The label `*:` often appears at the beginning of the configuration file, since it is present in the sample configuration file distributed with SSH2. This actually serves no purpose and is confusing; see the following sidebar.

Subsystems
: Keywords beginning with the string "subsystem-", such as:

```
# SSH2 only
subsystem-sftp     sftp-server
```

indicate a subsystem, a predefined command that SSH2 clients may invoke by name. Subsystems are a layer of abstraction and a convenience feature. [5.7]

What's That *: ?

The *sshd2_config* file supplied with SSH2 contains the following lines at the top, just above the keyword settings:

```
# The "*" defines for all hosts
*:
```

This is unnecessary and misleading. In the client configuration file, a colon introduces a labelled *section* of the configuration file [7.1.3.3], which limits the following configuration statements (up to the next label, or the end of the file) to apply only when the client is connecting to a host whose name matches the label.

The section label syntax is also recognized in the server configuration file, but it serves no purpose. The way the code is written, the only label that can ever match on the server side is *, and that is the effective default label, anyway, so it is unnecessary.

The section label is misleading because it suggests you can label a section in the server configuration file like this:

```
client.host.net:
  AllowUsers smith
```

By analogy with the client configuration file, you might expect that this restricts logins from the machine *client.host.net* to only accessing the account "smith". This won't work. In fact, statements labelled with anything besides * will be silently ignored by *sshd*. Beware!

5.3.2. Command-Line Options

Additionally, when invoking the server, you may supply command-line options. For example, the port value may be specified on the command line with the *–p* option:

```
# SSH1, SSH2, OpenSSH
$ sshd -p 1022
```

Command-line options override settings in the configuration file. Thus, if the configuration file says port 1022 but the server is invoked with *–p 2468*, the port used will be 2468.

Most command-line options duplicate the features found in the configuration file, for convenience, while a few provide unique functionality. For instance, the *–f* option instructs *sshd* to use a different configuration file, a feature that's useless to put in a configuration file.

On the other hand, keywords don't necessarily have command-line equivalents. Most SSH1 and OpenSSH keywords don't. Any SSH2 keyword, however, may be set by the *–o* server command-line option. For example, to set the TCP port number by this method:

```
# SSH2 only
$ sshd2 -o "Port 1022"
```

5.3.3. Changing the Configuration

sshd reads its configuration file at startup. Therefore, if you modify the file while the server is running, the changes don't affect the server. You must force the server to reread the file in order accept the changes. This is done by sending a SIGHUP signal to the server process.* The pid of the server is found in a file, usually */etc/sshd.pid* for SSH1, */var/run/sshd2_22.pid* for SSH2, or */var/run/sshd.pid* for OpenSSH. [5.4.1.3]

Suppose the PID file is */etc/sshd.pid*, the default for *sshd1*. To send the SIGHUP signal, run the Unix *kill* command:

```
$ cat /etc/sshd.pid
119384
$ kill -HUP 119384
```

or more succinctly, with backquotes:

```
$ kill -HUP `cat /etc/sshd.pid`
```

* The SSH2 server supports SIGHUP restarts in Version 2.0.12 and up.

The SIGHUP signal restarts *sshd* (with a different pid) but doesn't terminate existing SSH connections, so the signal is safe to send while clients are connected. The new *sshd* process reads and conforms to the new configuration.

The SIGHUP technique works only for settings in the configuration file, not command-line options. To change those, you must kill and restart the server with the new options. For example:

```
# SSH1, SSH2, OpenSSH
$ kill 119384
$ sshd new_options
```

5.3.4. A Tricky Reconfiguration Example

Because command-line options override their configuration file equivalents, some interesting situations can arise. Suppose the configuration file defines the number of bits in the server key to be 1024:

```
# SSH1, OpenSSH
ServerKeyBits 1024
```

but the server is invoked with the *–b* command-line option, overriding this value with 512:

```
# SSH1, OpenSSH
$ sshd -b 512
```

The server uses a 512-bit key. Now, suppose you restart *sshd* with SIGHUP:

```
# SSH1 only
$ kill -HUP `cat /etc/sshd.pid`

# OpenSSH only
$ kill -HUP `cat /var/run/sshd.pid`
```

forcing *sshd* to reread the configuration file. What do you think happens to the key length? Does the server set the length to 1024 after rereading the configuration file, or does the command-line option remain in effect for a 512-bit key? In fact, the command-line option takes precedence again, and the key remains 512 bits. *sshd* saves its argument vector (argv) and reapplies it on restart.

5.4. Getting Ready: Initial Setup

We now embark on a detailed discussion of SSH server configuration, using both keywords and command-line options. Please keep in mind that SSH2 and OpenSSH are still evolving products and their features may change. Be sure to read their documentation for the latest information. SSH1 is no longer actively developed, so its feature set is unlikely to change.

We begin with initial setup decisions, such as: where should important files be kept? What should their permissions be? What TCP/IP settings should be used? What are the properties of the server key? Which encryption algorithms are supported?

5.4.1. File Locations

sshd expects certain files to exist, containing the server's host key, the random seed, and other data. The server looks for these files in default locations, or you may override them with keywords and command-line options as described later.

Although you may place these files anywhere you like, we strongly recommend keeping them on a local disk on your server machine, not on a remotely mounted disk (e.g., via NFS). This is for security reasons, as NFS will gleefully transmit your sensitive files unencrypted across the network. This would be especially disastrous for the unencrypted private host key!

As a running example, we use an invented directory, */usr/local/ssh*, as our preferred (nondefault) location for the SSH server's files.

5.4.1.1. Host key files

The host key of *sshd* uniquely identifies a server to SSH clients. The host key is stored in a pair of files, one containing the private key and the other the public key. For SSH1 and OpenSSH, the private key is stored in */etc/ssh_host_key* and is readable only by privileged programs such as the SSH server and clients. Its location may be changed with the `HostKey` keyword:

```
# SSH1, OpenSSH
HostKey /usr/local/ssh/key
```

The server's public key is stored in a second file with the same name but with *.pub* appended. So the default for SSH1 and OpenSSH is */etc/ssh_host_key.pub*, and the preceding `HostKey` example implies */usr/local/ssh/key.pub*.

The OpenSSH server also has an SSH-2 host key, located by default in */etc/ssh_host_dsa_key*, and its location may be moved with the `HostDsaKey` keyword:

```
# OpenSSH only
HostDsaKey /usr/local/openssh/key2
```

For SSH2, the default private key file is */etc/ssh2/hostkey* if the server is run by the superuser or *~/.ssh2/hostkey* if run by any other user. To specify a different private key file, use the `HostKeyFile` keyword:

```
# SSH2 only
HostKeyFile /usr/local/ssh/key
```

The server's public key file, normally */etc/ssh2/hostkey.pub* for superusers or *~/.ssh2/hostkey.pub* for others, may be changed independently with the **PublicHostKeyFile** keyword:

```
# SSH2 only
PublicHostKeyFile /usr/local/ssh/pubkey
```

If you prefer command-line options, *sshd* supports the *–h* command-line option to specify the private key file:

```
# SSH1, SSH2, OpenSSH
$ sshd -h /usr/local/ssh/key
```

Once again, the public key filename is derived by appending *.pub* to the private key filename, in this case, */usr/local/ssh/key.pub*.

5.4.1.2. Random seed file

The SSH server generates pseudo-random numbers for cryptographic operations. [3.7] It maintains a pool of random data for this purpose, derived either from the operating system if provided (e.g., */dev/random* on some Unix flavors) or from various bits of changing machine state (e.g., clock time, statistics on resource use by processes, etc.). This pool is called the *random seed.* SSH1 stores it in */etc/ssh_random_seed*, and its location may be changed with the **RandomSeed** keyword:

```
# SSH1 only
RandomSeed /usr/local/ssh/seed
```

Likewise for SSH2, the random seed is stored in */etc/ssh2/random_seed*, and the location may be overridden with the **RandomSeedFile** keyword:

```
# SSH2 only
RandomSeedFile /usr/local/ssh/seed2
```

If running on a system with a random-bit source, such as */dev/urandom*, OpenSSH doesn't create a random seed file.

5.4.1.3. Process ID file

We said earlier that the SSH1 server's pid is stored in */etc/ssh.pid*, and this location may be overridden with the **PidFile** keyword:

```
# SSH1, OpenSSH
PidFile /usr/local/ssh/pid
```

There is no corresponding keyword for SSH2. Its pid file is always named */var/run/sshd2_*`N.pid`, where `N` is the TCP port number of the server. Since the default port is 22, the default pid file is */var/run/sshd2_22.pid*. If multiple *sshd2* processes are run simultaneously on different ports of the same machine, their pid files can be distinguished by this naming convention.

5.4.1.4. Server configuration file

The server configuration file is normally */etc/sshd_config* for the SSH1 and OpenSSH servers and */etc/ssh2/sshd2_config* for the SSH2 server. An alternative configuration file can be specified with the *–f* command-line option:

```
# SSH1, SSH2, OpenSSH
$ sshd -f /usr/local/ssh/config
```

This is useful when testing a new server configuration: create a new file and instruct *sshd* to read it. It is also necessary if you are running multiple *sshd*s on the same machine and want them to operate with different configurations.

5.4.1.5. User SSH directory

sshd1 expects a user's SSH-related files to be found in the directory *~/.ssh*. This location can't be changed by serverwide configuration. (You have to modify the source code.)

sshd2 expects user files to be in the directory *~/.ssh2* by default, but this can be changed with the `UserConfigDirectory` keyword. The directory name may be literal, as in:

```
# SSH2 only
UserConfigDirectory /usr/local/ssh/my_dir
```

or it may be specified with `printf`-like patterns, as in:

```
# SSH2 only
UserConfigDirectory %D/.my-ssh
```

The `%D` pattern expands to the user's home directory. So the preceding example expands to *~/.my-ssh*. The following table shows the available patterns:

Pattern	Meaning
`%D`	User's home directory
`%U`	User's login name
`%IU`	User's uid (Unix user ID)
`%IG`	User's gid (Unix group ID)

For the system administrator, the `UserConfigDirectory` keyword provides a quick way to override all users' SSH2 preferences. Specifically, you can cause *sshd2* to ignore everybody's *~/.ssh2* directories, substituting your own instead. For instance, the line:

```
# SSH2 only
UserConfigDirectory /usr/sneaky/ssh/%IU/
```

tells *sshd2* to seek the preferences for each user in */usr/sneaky/ssh/<username>* instead of *~/.ssh*. This powerful feature can also be misused if your machine is compromised. If an intruder inserted the following line into *sshd2_config*:

```
# SSH2 only
UserConfigDirectory /tmp/hack
```

and uploaded his own public key file into */tmp/hack*, he would gain SSH2 access to every user's account.

5.4.1.6. Per-account authorization files

The SSH1 and OpenSSH servers expect to find a user's public-key authorization file in *~/.ssh/authorized_keys* (and *~/.ssh/authorized_keys2* for OpenSSH/2). These locations can't be changed by serverwide configuration.

The SSH2 server uses a different key file layout. [6.1.2] The authorization file, normally *~/.ssh2/authorization*, contains names of separate public key files, rather than the keys themselves. *sshd2* can be instructed to find the authorization file elsewhere via the keyword `AuthorizationFile`.

```
# SSH2 only
AuthorizationFile my_public_keys
```

Filenames can be absolute or are relative to the user's SSH2 directory. The preceding lines specifies the file *~/.ssh2/my_public_keys.*

5.4.2. File Permissions

As security products, SSH1, SSH2, and OpenSSH require certain files and directories on the server machine to be protected from unwanted access. Imagine if your *authorized_keys* or *.rhosts* file were world-writable; anyone on that host could modify them and gain convenient access to your account. *sshd* has several configuration keywords for reducing this risk.

5.4.2.1. Acceptable permissions for user files

Users aren't always careful to protect important files and directories in their accounts, such as their *.rhosts* file or personal SSH directory. Such lapses can lead to security holes and compromised accounts. To combat this, you can configure *sshd* to reject connections to any user account that has unacceptable permissions.

The `StrictModes` keyword, with a value of `yes` (the default), causes *sshd* to check the permissions of important files and directories. They must be owned by the account owner or by root, and group and world write permission must be disabled. For SSH1, `StrictModes` checks:

- User's home directory
- User's *~/.rhosts* and *~/.shosts* file

- User's SSH configuration directory, *~/.ssh*
- User's SSH *~/.ssh/authorized_keys* file

For OpenSSH, **StrictModes** checks the same files as for SSH1, plus the user's authorization file for SSH-2 connections, *~/.ssh/authorized_keys2.*

For SSH2, the list is smaller and is checked only for trusted-host authentication:* [3.4.2.3]

- User's home directory
- User's *~/.rhosts* and *~/.shosts* file

If any check fails, the server rejects SSH connection attempts to the account. If **StrictModes** is given the value **no**, these checks aren't performed.

```
# SSH1, SSH2, OpenSSH
StrictModes no
```

However, we strongly suggest you leave these checks enabled.

Even if **StrictModes** is enabled, though, it can be defeated in two ways. First, *sshd* can be compiled with the flag **--enable-group-writeability** [4.1.5.2], which makes group-writable files acceptable to **StrictModes**. This can be useful for shared accounts, permitting all members of a group to modify SSH-related files in an account. Second, you can use POSIX ACLs, which are supported in Solaris and some other flavors of Unix, to set file permissions with greater precision. *sshd* doesn't check ACLs, so one could argue that **StrictModes** is an incomplete test.

5.4.2.2. Permissions for newly created files

The *umask* of a Unix process determines the default permissions for files and directories that the process creates. *sshd1*'s umask may be specified with the keyword **Umask**, so any files it creates have the desired permissions. The value is an ordinary Unix umask value, usually given in octal:

```
# SSH1 only
# Create files rw-r--r-- and directories rwx-r-xr-x:
Umask 022
```

Remember that a leading zero is necessary for *sshd1* to interpret the value as octal. For more information on umasks, see the Unix manpages for *umask* or for most shells.

sshd1 creates a pid file (*/etc/sshd.pid* or the value of **PidFile**) and a random seed file (*/etc/ssh_random_seed* or the value of **RandomSeed**). Only the pid file is affected by the server's umask. The random seed file is explicitly created with

* The *sshd2_config* manpage for SSH2 2.2.0 says that **StrictModes** isn't implemented, but this statement is obsolete.

mode 0600, readable and writable only by the owner. Strictly speaking, this umask also applies to other processes spawned by *sshd1*—specifically, user shells—but the value is typically overridden by shells.

5.4.3. TCP/IP Settings

Since the SSH protocol operates over TCP/IP, *sshd* permits control over various parameters related to TCP/IP.

5.4.3.1. Port number and network interface

By default, *sshd* listens on TCP port 22. The port number may be changed with the `Port` keyword:

```
# SSH1, SSH2, OpenSSH
Port 9876
```

or the *–p* command-line option:

```
# SSH1, SSH2, OpenSSH
$ sshd -p 9876
```

The SSH1 and OpenSSH servers accept integers in decimal, octal, or hexadecimal, while the SSH2 server reads all numbers as decimal. See the sidebar "Numeric Values in Configuration Files."

You may also configure *sshd* to bind its listening port on a particular network interface. By default, the port is bound on all active network interfaces on the host. The **`ListenAddress`** keyword limits *sshd* to listen on only one interface, with default value 0.0.0.0.

For example, suppose a computer has two Ethernet cards and is attached to two different networks. One interface has the address 192.168.10.23, and the other, 192.168.11.17. By default, *sshd* listens on both interfaces; therefore, you can reach the server by connecting to port 22 at either address. However, this may not always be what you want; perhaps you want to provide SSH service only to hosts on one network and not the other:

```
# SSH1, SSH2, OpenSSH
ListenAddress 192.168.10.23
```

Of course, this represents a real restriction only if the two networks aren't otherwise connected together (say, by a router), so that port 22 on 192.168.10.23 is not reachable from the network 192.168.11/24.

OpenSSH permits more than one **`ListenAddress`** line in the configuration file, permitting listening on selected multiple interfaces:

```
# OpenSSH only
ListenAddress 192.168.10.23
ListenAddress 192.168.11.17
```

Numeric Values in Configuration Files

SSH1 and OpenSSH accept numeric values in decimal, octal, or hexadecimal, using standard C language notation. If a value begins with `0x`, it is treated as hexadecimal. If it begins with a leading zero, it is considered octal. Any other numeric value is read as decimal.

SSH2, in contrast, requires all numbers to be given in decimal.

5.4.3.2. Invocation by inetd

sshd normally runs as a daemon, spawning child processes to handle connections. Alternatively, the server may be invoked by *inetd* as are many other network daemons. In this case, *inetd* invokes a new instance of the server for each connection.

If the *inetd* behavior is desired, you must have an entry for SSH in the server machine's TCP/IP services map, either */etc/services* or */etc/inet/services*, such as:

```
ssh    tcp/22
```

and an appropriate line in the *inetd* configuration file, */etc/inetd.conf*, for the SSH service. This line must invoke *sshd* with the *–i* command-line option, which turns on *inetd* behavior:

```
ssh stream  tcp     nowait  root    /usr/local/sbin/sshd     sshd -i
```

What this means, exactly, is that *sshd* simply starts up and expects to handle a single connection on a TCP socket attached to its standard input and output. This is opposed to its behavior without *–i*, where it becomes a master server listening for TCP connections and starting subprocesses to handle individual connections.

The *inetd* approach has advantages and disadvantages. On the down side, *inetd*-based SSH connections are slower to start up if the session uses a server key, because *sshd* generates a new key each time. This applies to connections using the SSH-1 protocol, i.e., the servers of SSH1 and OpenSSH/1. [3.5.1.2] Whether that's an issue, of course, depends on the speed of the server machine in question. On the up side, the *inetd* approach allows using a wrapper program to invoke *sshd*, should that be needed. Also, *inetd* provides a single, centralized point of control for all types of network connections, which simplifies maintenance. If you want to forbid all types of TCP/IP connections, for example, you can simply disable *inetd* instead of running around killing other daemons.

5.4.3.3. Idle connections

Suppose an SSH connection is established between a server and a client, but no data passes over the connection for a long time. What should the server do: keep the connection alive, or terminate it?

SSH1 provides the `IdleTimeout` keyword, which tells the server what to do if a connection is idle, i.e., if the user doesn't transmit any data in a given period. If `IdleTimeout` is zero (the default), the server does nothing, leaving idle connections intact:

```
# SSH1 only
IdleTimeout 0
```

Otherwise, the server terminates the connection after a specified interval of idleness. In this case, the value of `IdleTimeout` is a positive integer, optionally followed by letter: `s` for seconds, `m` for minutes, `h` for hours, `d` for days, or `w` for weeks. If no letter is given, the number represents seconds.

Here are several ways to set an `IdleTimeout` of exactly one day:

```
# SSH1 only
IdleTimeout 1d
IdleTimeout 24h
IdleTimeout 1440m
IdleTimeout 86400s
IdleTimeout 86400
```

The idle timeout can also be set for a given key in a user's *authorized_keys* file using the idle-timeout option. [8.2.7] Notably, this option overrides the server's `IdleTimeout` value but only for that key. This is a rare instance of a per-account option overriding a serverwide option.

5.4.3.4. KeepAlive

`KeepAlive` is a related but distinct feature to `IdleTimeout`. Where `IdleTimeout` detects and ends healthy but unused connections, `KeepAlive` is concerned with recognizing when a connection has failed. Suppose a client establishes an SSH connection, and some time later, the client host crashes abruptly. If the SSH server has no reason to send unsolicited messages to the client, it may never notice the half-dead TCP connection to its partner, and the *sshd* remains around indefinitely, using up system resources such as memory and a process slot (and making the sysadmin's *ps* output messy).

The `KeepAlive` keyword instructs *sshd* how to proceed if a connection problem occurs, such as a prolonged network outage or a client machine crash:

```
# SSH1, SSH2, OpenSSH
KeepAlive yes
```

The value `yes` (the default) tells the server to set the TCP keepalive option on its connection to the client. This causes TCP to periodically transmit and expect keepalive messages. If it doesn't receive responses to these messages for a while, it returns an error to *sshd*, which then shuts down the connection. The value `no` means not to use keepalive messages.

The TCP keepalive feature, and hence SSH's `KeepAlive`, is intended to prevent half-dead connections from building up over time. The keepalive message interval and timeout period reflect this: they are quite long, typically on the order of hours. This is to minimize the network load imposed by the keepalive messages and also to prevent connections from being unnecessarily torn down because of transient problems, such as a temporary network outage or routing flap. These timers aren't set in SSH; they are properties of the host's TCP stack. They shouldn't be altered lightly, since they affect every TCP connection using keepalives on that host.

KeepAlive and connection timeouts. It's important to note that `KeepAlive` isn't intended to deal with the problem of losing connections due to firewall, proxying, NAT, or IP masquerading timeouts. This problem occurs when your SSH connection is going across one of these entities, which decides to tear it down because it's been idle for a while. Since this is done to conserve shared resources (such as a limited pool of external, routable IP addresses), these timeouts are typically quite short, perhaps a few minutes to an hour or so. The name "KeepAlive" suggests that it might be the right thing to use, since that's what you want to do—keep your connection alive. But really, `KeepAlive` is the wrong name for it; it would be better named "DetectDead" (but that sounds like a spell a second-level cleric would use to avoid being eaten by zombies). In order for `KeepAlive` to deal with this problem, you have to dramatically shorten the TCP keepalive interval on the SSH host. This is contrary to its purpose and unwise because it affects not only SSH connections, but every TCP connection using keepalives, even those that don't need it. Doing this on the server side is an especially bad idea as a general principle, since a busy server may be using lots of TCP connections, and enabling `KeepAlive` on many of them since it's supposed to be an inexpensive feature. This can impose an unnecessary and damaging additional network load, especially if it becomes a widespread practice.

It's good to remember that the timeout annoying you so much is there for a reason. You may like to leave an SSH connection up for a long time unused, but if it's occupying one of a limited number of simultaneous outbound Internet TCP connections for your company, perhaps it's better if you just suck it up for the common good. Typing `ssh` again once in a while is really not that hard; use your shell's alias feature if you find the number of keystrokes onerous. If you genuinely think the timeout is inappropriate or unnecessary, argue the case with the network administrator, and try to get it changed.

For the occasions when it's really necessary, the right way to accomplish this sort of keepalive behavior is with an application-level mechanism implemented in SSH—having it periodically send SSH protocol messages over the connection to make it appear nonidle. This feature isn't available in any SSH implementation we know of, but we encourage its addition. NAT, etc., timeouts are a common problem, and we would like to discourage the misuse of TCP keepalives as a solution. In the meantime, the better low-tech solution is simply to have something that sends characters over your connection once in a while. Run Emacs and have it display the time in the mode line. Run a program in the background that prints "Boo!" to your terminal if it's been idle for 20 minutes. You get the idea.

5.4.3.5. Failed logins

Suppose a user attempts to log in via SSH but fails to authenticate. What should the server do? The keywords `LoginGraceTime` and `PasswordGuesses` control the server's response.

Users are given a limited time to authenticate successfully, 10 minutes by default. This timeout is controlled by the `LoginGraceTime` keyword, given a value in seconds:

```
# SSH1, SSH2, OpenSSH
LoginGraceTime 60
```

or the *-g* command-line option:

```
# SSH1, SSH2, OpenSSH
$ sshd -g 60
```

To disable this feature, provide a `LoginGraceTime` value of zero:

```
# SSH1, SSH2, OpenSSH
LoginGraceTime 0
```

or by command-line option:

```
# SSH1, SSH2, OpenSSH
$ sshd -g 0
```

If password authentication is used for a connection request, *sshd2* permits a client only three tries to authenticate before dropping the connection. This restriction may be modified with the `PasswordGuesses` keyword:

```
# SSH2 only
PasswordGuesses 5
```

The situation with public-key authentication is slightly more complicated. There are two sorts of requests a client can make in this regard: a query whether a particular public key is authorized to log into the target account, and an actual authentication attempt including a signature of the corresponding private key. It's good to allow an unlimited number of queries, since otherwise it limits the number of keys one can have in an agent, for example. But it's reasonable to limit the number of failed attempts. None of the current SSH servers do what we consider to be the right thing. SSH1 and SSH2 simply allow an unlimited number of public-key queries or attempts. OpenSSH, on the other hand, limits the overall number of authentication attempts or queries of any kind, and it uses a built-in, nonconfigurable limit of 5 (the source code says 6, but the way it's coded it comes out to 5). So if you have five keys in your agent, you never get to use password authentication with the OpenSSH server, because it rejects your connection after determining that you can't use any of those keys. Or if you have six keys and the sixth is the one you need to use, you're out of luck; you have to remove some keys from your agent (or not use the agent) to get it to work (these numbers are one fewer for OpenSSH/2, by the way).

Of course, there's a security argument to be made here. It's better in a sense to not allow queries and always force the client to perform an attempt. That way, if it fails, the client doesn't know whether it was because the signature was wrong or the key is simply not authorized. This makes it harder for an attacker to determine which keys are the ones to try to steal. But in normal use it's computationally expensive for legitimate clients to do this, and so the protocol does allow queries.

5.4.3.6. Limiting simultaneous connections

sshd can handle an arbitrary number of simultaneous connections by default. SSH2 provides the `MaxConnections` keyword for limiting this number, say, if you want to conserve resources on the server machine:

```
# SSH2 only
MaxConnections 32
```

To specify an unlimited number of connections, provide a value of zero:

```
# SSH2 only
MaxConnections 0
```

Of course, the number of connections can also be limited by available memory or other operating system resources. `MaxConnections` has no effect on these other factors. (Sorry, you can't increase your CPU speed by setting a keyword!)

5.4.3.7. Reverse IP mappings

The SSH2 server optionally does a reverse DNS lookup on a client's IP address. That is, it looks up the name associated with the address, then looks up the addresses for that name and makes sure that the client's address is among them. If this check fails, the server refuses the connection.

sshd2 uses the `gethostbyname()` and `gethostbyaddr()` system services to perform these mappings, so the databases that are consulted depend on the host operating system configuration. It might use the DNS, the Network Information Service (NIS or YP), static files on server machine, or some combination.

To enable this check, use the **RequireReverseMapping** keyword with a value of **yes** or **no** (the default):

```
# SSH2 only
RequireReverseMapping yes
```

This feature is a bit of security-oriented consistency checking. SSH uses cryptographic signatures to determine a peer's identity, but the list of peer public keys (the known hosts database) is often indexed by hostname, and so SSH must translate the address to a name in order to check the peer's identity. Reverse mapping tries to ensure that someone isn't playing games with the naming service in a cracking attempt. There is a tradeoff, however, since in today's Internet, the DNS reverse-address mappings aren't always kept up to date. The SSH server might reject legitimate connection attempts because of poorly maintained reverse-address mappings over which you have no control. In general, we recommend turning off this feature; it isn't usually worth the hassle.

5.4.3.8. Controlling TCP_NODELAY

TCP/IP has a feature called the Nagle Algorithm, which is designed to reduce the number of TCP segments sent with very small amounts of data (e.g., one byte), usually as part of an interactive terminal session. Over fast links such as Ethernet, the Nagle algorithm generally isn't needed. Over a wide-area network, however, it can cause noticeable delays in the responsiveness of X clients and character terminal displays, as multibyte terminal control sequences may be transmitted inconveniently by the algorithm. In such cases, you should turn off the Nagle Algorithm using the **NoDelay** keyword:

```
# SSH2 only
NoDelay yes
```

NoDelay disables the Nagle Algorithm by toggling the TCP_NODELAY bit when requesting a TCP connection from the Unix kernel. Legal values are **yes** (to disable) and **no** (to enable; the default).

In order to work, this feature must be enabled at compile time using **--enable-tcp-nodelay**. [4.1.5.3] Note also that **NoDelay** can be enabled or disabled by the SSH2 client, rather than serverwide, using the client configuration keyword **NoDelay**. [7.4.4.4]

5.4.3.9. Discovering other servers

SSH2 2.1.0 adds a feature for seeking out and discovering SSH2 servers automatically. The keyword **MaxBroadcastsPerSecond**, when given an integer value greater than zero, causes an SSH2 server to listen to UDP broadcasts sent to port 22:

```
# SSH2 only
MaxBroadcastsPerSecond 10
```

A new program supplied with SSH2, *ssh-probe2*, sends broadcast queries and prints the locations and versions of any SSH2 servers it finds. The server only responds to this many queries per second; the rate-limiting prevents a denial-of-service attack that floods the server with queries, causing it to spend all its time replying to them.

MaxBroadcastsPerSecond and *ssh-probe2* are a rather ad hoc solution for locating SSH2 servers. Perhaps when Dynamic DNS and SRV records become more widely used, such tricks won't be necessary.

5.4.3.10. Agent forwarding

Agent forwarding permits a series of SSH connections (from one machine to another to another, ...) to operate seamlessly using a single agent. [6.3.5] Agent forwarding may be enabled or disabled in the SSH2 server using the keyword **ForwardAgent** or **AllowAgentForwarding** with a value of **yes** (the default) or **no**:

```
# SSH2 only
ForwardAgent no
```

It may also be enabled or disabled by the client. [6.3.5.3]

Agent forwarding is convenient, but in a security-sensitive environment, it might be appropriate to disable this feature. Because forwarded agent connections are implemented as Unix domain sockets, an attacker can conceivably gain access to them. These sockets are just nodes in the filesystem, protected only by file permissions that can be compromised.

For example, suppose you maintain a network of exposed, untrusted machines that you access from a more secure network using SSH. You might consider disabling agent forwarding on the untrusted machines. Otherwise, an attacker can compromise an untrusted machine; take control of a forwarded agent from a legitimate, incoming SSH connection; and use the agent's loaded keys to gain access to the secure network via SSH. (The attacker can't retrieve the keys themselves in this way, however.)

5.4.3.11. Forwarding

SSH's forwarding or tunneling feature protects other TCP/IP-based applications by encrypting their connections. We cover forwarding in great detail in Chapter 9, but we introduce here the serverwide configuration keywords for enabling and disabling it.

TCP port forwarding can be enabled or disabled by the keyword `AllowTcpForwarding` with the value `yes` (the default) or `no`:

```
# SSH1, SSH2, OpenSSH
AllowTcpForwarding no
```

or more selectively for particular users or Unix groups:

```
# SSH2 only
AllowTcpForwardingForUsers smith jones roberts
AllowTcpForwardingForGroups students faculty
DenyTcpForwardingForUsers badguys
DenyTcpForwardingForGroups bad*
```

Forwarding for X, the popular window system, can be separately enabled or disabled with the keyword `X11Forwarding` (SSH1, SSH2, OpenSSH), or `ForwardX11` or `AllowX11Forwarding` (SSH2 synonyms for `X11Forwarding`). The default value is `yes`, to enable forwarding:

```
# SSH1, SSH2, OpenSSH
X11Forwarding no

# SSH2 only: either will work
ForwardX11 no
AllowX11Forwarding no
```

5.4.4. Server Key Generation

All SSH servers maintain a host key, which is persistent, generated by the system administrator when installing SSH, and identifies the host for authentication purposes. [5.4.1.1]

Separately, an SSH-1 server maintains another key while running, called the server key, which protects client/server communications. This key is temporary and never explicitly stored on disk. The server generates it at startup, and regenerates it at regular intervals. SSH1 and OpenSSH can specify the length of the server key in bits. The key length is 768 bits by default, 512 bits at a minimum, and you may choose another length using the `ServerKeyBits` keyword:

```
# SSH1, OpenSSH
ServerKeyBits 1024
```

or the *–b* command-line option:

```
# SSH1, OpenSSH
$ sshd -b 1024
```

You may also specify the lifetime or *regeneration interval* of the server key. When the lifetime ends, another server key is generated and the process repeats, say, every 10 minutes. This is a security feature: if an intruder captures a server key, it can decrypt transmissions for only a limited time (10 minutes in our example).

Likewise, if an encrypted transmission is captured by a sniffer, the server key necessary to decrypt the session is destroyed in the server after 10 minutes.

Key regeneration is specified in seconds. Regeneration occurs every 3600 seconds (one hour) by default. The interval is specified with the **KeyRegenerationInterval** keyword:

```
# SSH1, OpenSSH
KeyRegenerationInterval 1200
```

or the *-k* command-line option:

```
# SSH1, OpenSSH
$ sshd -k 1200
```

A zero value turns off the key regeneration feature:

```
# SSH1, OpenSSH
KeyRegenerationInterval 0
```

or:

```
# SSH1, OpenSSH
$ sshd -k 0
```

The **RekeyIntervalSeconds** keyword specifies how often (in seconds) *sshd2* performs key exchange with the client to replace the session data-encryption and integrity keys. The default is 3600 seconds (one hour), and a zero value disables rekeying:*

```
# SSH2 only
RekeyIntervalSeconds 7200
```

5.4.5. Encryption Algorithms

The SSH server supports a number of data-encryption algorithms for its secure connection; the client selects a cipher to use from the list the server supports. SSH2 has a server configuration option to set the list of allowable ciphers, selected from those the server software supports. The **Ciphers** keyword serves this purpose. Its value may have two different forms:

- A comma-separated list of algorithm names (strings), indicating which algorithms are permissible. The following table displays the supported values.

* Note that at press time, you must disable session rekeying in the SSH2 server if you wish to use it with many other SSH clients, since the latter don't yet support session rekeying; the connection dies with an error once the rekeying interval expires.

Value	Meaning
`3des-cbc`	The 3DES (Triple DES) algorithm
`blowfish-cbc`	The Blowfish algorithm
`twofish-cbc`	The TwoFish algorithm
`arcfour`	The ARCFOUR algorithm
`none`	No encryption

The `none` algorithm is available only when SSH is compiled with the `--with-none` flag. The `-cbc` suffixes indicate cipher block chaining. These algorithms are in a class called *block ciphers*, which may operate in a variety of modes; CBC is one of them.

- A single string indicating a set of algorithms. The following table displays the supported values:

Value	Meaning
`none`	Unencrypted transmission
`any`	Any algorithm implemented in the server, including `none`
`anycipher`	Same as `any`, but excluding `none`
`anystd`	Any standard algorithm found in the IETF SecSH draft (assuming it is implemented in the server), including `none`
`anystdcipher`	Same as `anystd`, but excluding `none`

Here are some examples:

```
# SSH2, OpenSSH/2
Ciphers 3des-cbc
Ciphers 3des-cbc,blowfish-cbc,arcfour
Ciphers any
```

Individual algorithms and sets of algorithms can't be mixed:

```
# This is ILLEGAL
Ciphers 3des,anystd
```

The `Ciphers` keyword is useful for quickly disabling individual encryption algorithms, say, if a security hole is discovered in one of them. Just omit that algorithm from the `Ciphers` list and restart the server.

Support for some algorithms can be omitted from the SSH1 server at compile time. [4.1.5.6] In particular, support for the `none` cipher type is not compiled in by default. This omission is a security feature to make insecure SSH sessions more difficult to create. Otherwise, if an attacker gained access to your account for a few moments, he could add "Ciphers none" to your SSH client configuration file. You might never notice this small change, but all of your future SSH connections would be insecure.*

Use the none cipher only for testing. Using the SSH-1 protocol with no encryption seriously weakens it: not only do you lose data privacy, but also you effectively lose server authentication and integrity protection. SSH-2 doesn't suffer from these problems. In either case, however, password authentication isn't available, since the password would be sent in the clear.

5.4.5.1. MAC algorithms

The MAC keyword lets you select the allowed integrity-checking algorithms, known as the Message Authentication Code, used by *sshd2*. [3.2.3] Here are the available algorithms: [3.9.3]

```
hmac-sha1
hmac-md5
hmac-md5-96
```

The following table shows keywords with special meanings that can also be used:

Value	Meaning
any	Any supported algorithm
anymac	Any supported algorithm, except none
anystd	Any standard algorithm; that is, one defined in the current working draft of the SSH-2 protocol
anystdmac	Same as anystd, but excludes none
none	No MAC; this is insecure

5.4.6. SSH Protocol Selection

OpenSSH lets you limit its protocol support to SSH-1, SSH-2, or both, using the Protocol keyword. Permissible values are 1 (for SSH-1, the default), 2 (for SSH-2), or both 1 and 2 separated by a comma:

```
# OpenSSH only
Protocol 1,2
```

* If you do connect using the none cipher, *ssh* prints a warning message, "WARNING: Encryption is disabled!" Even so, an attacker can enable QuietMode in your clients and suppress this message. [5.8.1.3]

5.5. Letting People in: Authentication and Access Control

A large part of the SSH server's job is to grant or deny connection requests from clients. This is done at two levels: *authentication* and *access control* (a.k.a *authorization*).

Authentication, as we've seen, means verifying the identity of the user requesting a connection. Access control means permitting or denying SSH connections from particular users, machines, or Internet domains.

5.5.1. Authentication

sshd supports several different techniques for authentication that may be enabled or disabled. [3.1.3] [3.4.2] For example, if you don't trust password authentication, you can turn it off serverwide but still permit public-key authentication.

As SSH has evolved, the syntax for configuring authentication has changed several times. We cover not only the current keywords but also the deprecated or obsolete ones, in case you're running an older version of *sshd*.

In SSH1 and OpenSSH, different authentication techniques are turned on and off with keywords of the form:

```
Name_Of_TechniqueAuthentication
```

For example, password authentication is controlled by the keyword `PasswordAuthentication`, RSA public-key authentication by `RSA-Authentication`, and so forth, one keyword per technique. Values may be `yes` or `no`:

```
# SSH1, OpenSSH; deprecated for SSH2
RSAAuthentication yes
```

Early versions of SSH2 also used one keyword per authentication technique, but keywords were a bit more generic. Instead of `RSAAuthentication`, which mentions the algorithm RSA, the keyword was changed to `PubKeyAuthentication` without naming a specific algorithm.

```
# SSH2 only, but deprecated
PubKeyAuthentication yes
```

This left the door open for the support of other public key algorithms. The older keywords such as `RSAAuthentication` were still usable as synonyms for the more generic keywords.

SSH2 today uses an entirely different syntax. Instead of creating a new keyword for each technique, it uses only two keywords, `AllowedAuthentications` and

`RequiredAuthentications`. Each is followed by the names of one or more authentication techniques, for example:

```
# SSH2 only; recommended technique
AllowedAuthentications password,hostbased,publickey
```

`AllowedAuthentications` specifies which techniques can be used to connect to this SSH server.* In contrast, `RequiredAuthentications` specifies which ones must be used.† A configuration line like:

```
# SSH2 only; recommended technique
AllowedAuthentications publickey,password
RequiredAuthentications publickey,password
```

means that the server requires both public-key and password authentication before allowing a connection. The `RequiredAuthentications` list must be a subset of `AllowedAuthentications`: a required technique must also be allowed. By default, *sshd2* allows only password and public-key authentication.

If you think about it, these keywords are a little confusing, or at least not well-chosen. In practice, if you use `RequiredAuthentications` at all, it always has exactly the same value as `AllowedAuthentications`: there's no point in having a method allowed but not in the "required" set, since that method doesn't get you a connection. It would be more useful to be able to specify multiple subsets of the allowed methods, which are the combinations acceptable for authenticating a client.

Table 5-1 displays the authentication-related keywords.

Table 5-1. Authentication-Related Keywords

Type	SSH1	OpenSSH	New SSH2	Old SSH2
`AllowedAuthentications`	No	No	Yes	No
`DSAAuthentication`	No	Yes[a]	No	No
`KerberosAuthentication`	Yes	Yes	No	No
`PasswordAuthentication`	Yes	Yes	Deprecated	Yes
`PubKeyAuthentication`	No	No	Deprecated	Yes
`RequiredAuthentications`	No	No	Yes	No
`RhostsAuthentication`	Yes	Yes	No	Yes
`RhostsPubKeyAuthentication`	No	No	No	Yes
`RhostsRSAAuthentication`	Yes	Yes	No	Yes
`RSAAuthentication`	Yes	Yes	Deprecated	Yes

* The order is not significant, since the client drives the authentication process.

† `RequiredAuthentications` was broken in SSH2 2.0.13, causing authentication to always fail. The problem was fixed in 2.1.0.

Table 5-1. Authentication-Related Keywords (continued)

Type	SSH1	OpenSSH	New SSH2	Old SSH2
`SKeyAuthentication`	No	Yes	No	No
`TISAuthentication`	Yes	Yes[b]	No	No

[a] SSH-2 protocol only.
[b] Actually means S/Key authentication, not TIS.

We now describe how to enable and disable each type of authentication.

5.5.1.1. Password authentication

Password authentication accepts your login password as proof of identity. [3.4.2.1] In SSH1 and OpenSSH, password authentication is permitted or forbidden with the `PasswordAuthentication` keyword, given the value `yes` (the default) or `no`:

```
# SSH1, OpenSSH; deprecated for SSH2
PasswordAuthentication yes
```

`PasswordAuthentication` works for SSH2, but this keyword is discouraged. Instead, use the keyword `AllowedAuthentications` with a value of `password`:

```
# SSH2 only
AllowedAuthentications password
```

Normally, password authentication requires your ordinary login password. However, this may be changed by compile-time configuration. For SSH1, if Kerberos or SecurID support has been compiled into the server, password authentication changes to support Kerberos [5.5.1.7] or SecurID. [5.5.1.9]

5.5.1.2. Public-key authentication

Public-key authentication verifies a user's identity by way of cryptographic keys. [3.4.2.2] In SSH1 and OpenSSH/1, public-key authentication uses RSA encryption and is permitted or forbidden with the `RSAAuthentication` keyword. It may have the value `yes` (the default) or `no`:

```
# SSH1, OpenSSH; deprecated for SSH2
RSAAuthentication yes
```

The keyword `RSAAuthentication` works for SSH2, as does the more general-sounding keyword `PubKeyAuthentication`, which has the same function, but both are no longer recommended. Instead, use the keyword `AllowedAuthentications` with a value of `publickey`:

```
# SSH2 only
AllowedAuthentications publickey
```

OpenSSH provides public-key authentication for SSH-2 connections with the `DSAAuthentication` keyword:

```
# OpenSSH/2 only
DSAAuthentication yes
```

Public-key authentication is marvelously configurable for most Unix SSH implementations. See Chapter 8 for details on tailoring authentication for individual accounts.

5.5.1.3. Rhosts authentication

Trusted-host authentication verifies an SSH client's identity by checking the remote hostname and username associated with it. [3.4.2.3] In SSH1 and OpenSSH, two types of trusted-host authentication are supported. The weaker Rhosts authentication mimics the behavior of the Berkeley r-commands (*rsh*, *rcp*, *rlogin*), checking the server files */etc/hosts.equiv* and *~/.rhosts* for permission to authenticate and using the network naming service (e.g., DNS, NIS) and privileged TCP source port to verify the client host's identity. SSH2 doesn't support this insecure technique.

Rhosts authentication is permitted or forbidden with the `RhostsAuthentication` keyword, given the value `yes` (the default) or `no`:

```
# SSH1, OpenSSH
RhostsAuthentication yes
```

Rhosts authentication can be useful, but unfortunately it also enables connections via the insecure r-commands, since it uses the same permission files. To eliminate this potential security risk, use the SSH-specific files */etc/shosts.equiv* and *~/.shosts* instead, deleting */etc/hosts.equiv* and *~/.rhosts*. You can also tell the SSH server to ignore all users' *.rhosts* and *.shosts* files with the keyword `IgnoreRhosts`. Permissible values are `yes` (to ignore them) or `no` (the default):

```
# SSH1, SSH2, OpenSSH
IgnoreRhosts yes
```

Some subtleties: although the keyword name contains "Rhosts," remember that it applies to *.shosts* files as well. Also, although user files are ignored by `IgnoreRhosts`, */etc/hosts.equiv* and */etc/shosts.equiv* remain in force.

SSH1 and SSH2 also permit separate control over Rhosts authentication for root. The keyword `IgnoreRootRhosts` permits or prevents use of the superuser's *.rhosts* and *.shosts* files, overriding `IgnoreRhosts`:

```
# SSH1, SSH2
IgnoreRootRhosts yes
```

Values of `yes` (ignore the files) or `no` (don't ignore) are permitted. If not specified, the value of `IgnoreRootRhosts` defaults to that of `IgnoreRhosts`. For example, you can permit all *.rhosts* files except root's:

```
# SSH1 only
IgnoreRhosts no
IgnoreRootRhosts yes
```

You can also ignore all *.rhosts* files except root's:

```
# SSH1 only
IgnoreRhosts yes
IgnoreRootRhosts no
```

Again, `IgnoreRootRhosts` doesn't stop the server from considering */etc/hosts.equiv* and */etc/shosts.equiv*. For stronger security, it's best to disable *.rhosts* access entirely.

Rhosts authentication can be complicated by other aspects of your server machine's environment, such as DNS, NIS, and the ordering of entries in static host files. It may also open new avenues for attack on a system. [3.4.2.3]

5.5.1.4. Stronger trusted-host authentication

The second, stronger type of trusted-host authentication is supported by SSH1, SSH2, and OpenSSH. For SSH1 and OpenSSH/1, it is called RhostsRSA authentication, and for SSH2, hostbased authentication.* In either case, the less secure parts of *rhosts* authentication are supplemented by cryptographic tests of host keys. [3.4.2.3] The files */etc/hosts.equiv* and *~/.rhosts* (and the SSH-specific */etc/shosts.equiv* and *~/.shosts*) are still consulted, but they aren't sufficient to pass the test.

SSH1 and OpenSSH use the keyword `RhostsRSAAuthentication` (surprise!) to enable or disable this type of authentication:

```
# SSH1, OpenSSH; deprecated for SSH2
RhostsRSAAuthentication yes
```

The keyword `RhostsRSAAuthentication` is accepted by *sshd2*, as is the more general-sounding keyword `RhostsPubKeyAuthentication`, which has the same function; however, both keywords are considered obsolete. Instead, use the keyword `AllowedAuthentications` with the value `hostbased`:

```
# SSH2 only
AllowedAuthentications hostbased
```

5.5.1.5. Fetching public keys of known hosts

sshd2 needs the public keys of all hosts from which it accepts connections via hostbased authentication. These keys are kept in separate files in the directory */etc/ssh2/knownhosts*. A host's public key is fetched from this directory whenever that host requests a connection. Optionally, the server also searches the directory *~/.ssh2/knownhosts* in the target user's account. This optional feature is enabled with the keyword `UserKnownHosts`, with a value of `yes` (the default) or `no`:

---

* OpenSSH 2.3.0 doesn't yet support hostbased authentication for SSH-2 connections.

```
# SSH2 only
UserKnownHosts no
```

OpenSSH supports the same functionality, but reversed, with the **IgnoreUserKnownHosts** keyword. The value **yes** causes the user's known hosts database to be ignored; the default is **no**:

```
# OpenSSH only
IgnoreUserKnownHosts yes
```

Having *sshd* consult the user's known hosts database might be unacceptable in a security-conscious environment. Since hostbased authentication relies on the integrity and correct administration of the client host, the system administrator usually grants hostbased authentication privileges to only a limited set of audited hosts. If the user's file is respected, however, a user can extend this trust to a possibly insecure remote host. An attacker can then:

1. Compromise the insecure, remote host
2. Impersonate the user on the remote host
3. Access the user's local account via SSH, without needing a key passphrase or the local account password

5.5.1.6. PGP authentication

Pretty Good Privacy (PGP) is another security product employing public-key authentication. [1.6.2] PGP keys and SSH keys are implemented differently and aren't interchangeable. However, recent versions of SSH2 now support authentication by PGP key, following the OpenPGP standard. Yes, you can use your favorite PGP key to prove your identity to an SSH2 server (as long as the key file is OpenPGP-compatible; some PGP keys, especially those produced by older software versions, aren't). At press time, this feature is only sketchily documented. Here's how to make it work.

First, you need SSH2 2.0.13 or higher, or the corresponding version from F-Secure, installed on both the client and server machines. Also, both implementations must be compiled with PGP support included, using the compile-time flag **--with-pgp**. [4.1.5.7]

On the client machine, you need to make your PGP secret key ring and the desired secret key for authentication available to SSH2 clients. Here's how:

1. Copy your PGP secret key ring to your account's SSH2 directory, *~/.ssh2*. Suppose it is called *secring.pgp*.
2. In an identification file, either *~/.ssh2/identification* or another of your choice, indicate the secret key ring with the keyword **PgpSecretKeyFile**:

```
# SSH2 only
PgpSecretKeyFile secring.pgp
```

3. Identify the PGP key you wish to use for authentication. This may be done with any of three keywords:
   — To identify the key by name, use **IdPgpKeyName**:

   ```
   # SSH2 only
   IdPgpKeyName mykey
   ```

   — To identify the key by its PGP fingerprint, use **IdPgpKeyFingerprint**:

   ```
   # SSH2 only
   IdPgpKeyFingerprint 48 B5 EA 28 80 5E 29 4D 03 33 7D 17 5E 2E CD 20
   ```

   — To identify the key by its key ID, use **IdPgpKeyId**:

   ```
   # SSH2 only
   IdPgpKeyId 0xD914738D
   ```

For **IdPgpKeyId**, the leading **0x** is necessary, indicating that the value is in hexadecimal. You can give the value in decimal instead, without the leading **0x**, but since PGP displays the value in hex already, it's unlikely you'd want to do this.

On the server machine (say, *server.example.com*), you need to make your public key ring and the desired public key for authentication available to the SSH2 server:

1. Copy your public key ring from the client machine to the server machine. (Note that this is a key ring, not a lone public key.) Place the ring into your *~/.ssh2* directory on the server. Suppose it is called *pubring.pgp*.
2. In your authorization file, *~/.ssh2/authorization*, identify the public key ring with the keyword **PgpPublicKeyFile**:

   ```
   # SSH2 only
   PgpPublicKeyFile pubring.pgp
   ```

3. Identify the public key by name, fingerprint, or key ID as in the client's identification file. The relevant keywords are slightly different: **PgpKeyName**, **PgpKeyFingerprint**, and **PgpKeyId**, respectively. (The keywords for the identification file begin with "Id".)

   ```
   # SSH2 only: use any ONE of these
   PgpKeyName mykey
   PgpKeyFingerprint 48 B5 EA 28 80 5E 29 4D 03 33 7D 17 5E 2E CD 20
   PgpKeyId 0xD914738D
   ```

You are done! From the client, initiate an SSH2 session. Suppose you create an alternative identification file to use PGP authentication, called *~/.ssh2/idpgp*, containing your **PgpSecretKeyFile** and other lines. Use the *–i* flag to indicate this file, and initiate a connection:

```
$ ssh2 -i idpgp server.example.com
```

If everything is set up properly, you are prompted for your PGP passphrase:

```
Passphrase for pgp key "mykey":
```

Enter your PGP passphrase, and authentication should succeed.

5.5.1.7. Kerberos authentication

Kerberos can be used as an authentication mechanism by SSH1 and OpenSSH.* We summarize the Kerberos-related configuration keywords here and defer a more detailed treatment of the topic. [11.4] Just as this book went to press, SSH2 2.3.0 was released with "experimental" Kerberos-5 support, which we don't discuss here.

First, note that Kerberos authentication is supported only if it is enabled at compile time. Unless the configuration option `--with-kerberos5` (SSH1) or `--with-kerberos4` (OpenSSH) is used, Kerberos support isn't present in *sshd*.

Assuming the server supports it, Kerberos authentication is enabled or disabled by the keyword `KerberosAuthentication` with the value `yes` or `no`:

```
# SSH1, OpenSSH
KerberosAuthentication yes
```

The default is `yes` if Kerberos support has been compiled into the server; otherwise, the default is `no`.

Connections may be authenticated by Kerberos ticket or by password (authenticated by the Kerberos server) if password authentication is also enabled:

```
# SSH1, OpenSSH
KerberosAuthentication yes
PasswordAuthentication yes
```

Instead of checking against the local login password, *sshd* instead requests a Kerberos TGT for the user and allows login if the ticket matches the password.† It also stores that TGT in the user's credentials cache, eliminating the need to do a separate *kinit*.

If Kerberos fails to validate a password, the server optionally validates the same password by ordinary password authentication. This is useful in an environment where Kerberos is in use, but not by everyone. To enable this option, use the keyword `KerberosOrLocalPasswd` with a value of `yes`; the default is `no`:

```
# SSH1, OpenSSH
KerberosOrLocalPasswd yes
```

Finally, the keyword `KerberosTgtPassing` controls whether the SSH server does Kerberos ticket-granting-ticket (TGT) forwarding:

* They use different versions of Kerberos: Kerberos-5 for SSH1, and Kerberos-4 for OpenSSH.

† It also requires a successful granting of a host ticket for the local host as an antispoofing measure.

```
# SSH1, OpenSSH
KerberosTgtPassing yes
```

Its default value follows the same rule as `KerberosAuthentication`: if Kerberos support is compiled into the server, the default is `yes`, otherwise `no`.

OpenSSH adds the keyword `KerberosTicketCleanup`, which deletes the user's Kerberos ticket cache on logout. Values are `yes` and `no`, and the default is `yes`, to perform the deletion:

```
# OpenSSH only
KerberosTicketCleanup yes
```

5.5.1.8. TIS authentication

The SSH1 server may authenticate users via the Gauntlet firewall toolkit from Trusted Information Systems (TIS). When an SSH client tries to authenticate via Gauntlet, the SSH server communicates with Gauntlet's authentication server, *authsrv*, forwarding *authsrv*'s requests to the client, and the client's responses to *authsrv*.

TIS authentication is a compile-time option, controlled by the configuration flag `--with-tis`. [4.1.5.7] Assuming support has been compiled into *sshd*, TIS authentication is enabled and disabled by the keyword `TISAuthentication` with a value of `yes` or `no` (the default):

```
# SSH1 only
TISAuthentication yes
```

See the file *README.TIS* in the SSH1 distribution for further details about TIS authentication. Additional information on Trusted Information Systems and *authsrv* can be found at:

http://www.tis.com/
http://www.msg.net/utility/FWTK/
http://www.fwtk.org/

5.5.1.9. SecurID authentication

SecurID from Security Dynamics is a hardware-based authentication technique. Users need a physical card, called a SecurID card, in order to authenticate. The card contains a microchip that displays (on a little LCD) an integer that changes at regular intervals. To authenticate, you must provide this integer along with your password. Some versions of the SecurID card also have a keypad that supports entering a password, for two-factor authentication.

If the SSH1 server is compiled with support for SecurID, using `--with-securid`, password authentication is transformed into SecurID authentication. [4.1.5.7] Users must provide the current integer from their card in order to authenticate.

5.5.1.10. S/Key authentication

S/Key is a one-time password system, created by Bellcore, supported as an SSH authentication method only by OpenSSH. "One-time" means that each time you authenticate, you provide a different password, helping to guard against attacks, since a captured password will likely be useless. Here's how it works:

1. When you connect to a remote service, it provides you with an integer and a string, called the *sequence number* and the *key*, respectively.
2. You enter the sequence number and key into an *s/key calculator* program on your local machine.
3. You also enter a secret passphrase into the calculator, known only to yourself. This passphrase isn't transmitted over the network, only into the calculator on your local machine, so security is maintained.
4. Based on the three inputs you provided, the calculator produces your one-time password.
5. You enter the password to authenticate to the remote service.

The OpenSSH server optionally supports S/Key authentication if you set the keyword `SKeyAuthentication`. The default is `yes`, to support it. To turn it off, use `no`.

```
# OpenSSH only
SkeyAuthentication no
```

More information on one-time passwords is found at:

http://www.ietf.cnri.reston.va.us/html.charters/otp-charter.html

5.5.1.11. PAM authentication

The Pluggable Authentication Modules system (PAM) by Sun Microsystems is an infrastructure for supporting multiple authentication methods. Ordinarily when a new authentication mechanism comes along, programs need to be rewritten to accommodate it. PAM eliminates this hassle. Programs are written to support PAM, and new authentication mechanisms may be plugged in at runtime without further source-code modification. More PAM information is found at:

http://www.sun.com/solaris/pam/

OpenSSH includes support for PAM. SSH1 1.2.27 has been integrated with PAM by a third party, but the combination requires changes to the SSH1 source code. Details are found at:

http://diamond.rug.ac.be/sshd_PAM/

5.5.1.12. AFS token passing

The Andrew File System (AFS) is a distributed filesystem with goals similar to NFS, but more sophisticated and scalable. It uses a modified version of the Kerberos 4 protocol for authentication. OpenSSH can be compiled with support for AFS, using the compile-time flags **--with-afs** and **--with-kerberos4**. The keyword **AFSTokenPassing** controls this feature, given a value of **yes** (accept forwarded tokens, the default) or **no**:

```
# OpenSSH only
KerberosAuthentication  yes
KerberosTGTPassing      yes
AFSTokenPassing         yes
```

AFSTokenPassing causes OpenSSH to establish Kerberos/AFS credentials on the remote host, based on your existing credentials on the client (which you must have previously obtained using *klog* or *kinit*). This can be a necessity for using OpenSSH at all in an AFS environment, not just a convenience: if your remote home directory is on AFS, *sshd* needs AFS credentials to access your remote *~/.ssh* directory in order to perform public-key authentication, for example. In that case, you may also need to use AFS tools to adjust the permissions on the remote *~/.ssh* directory, to allow *sshd* to read what it needs to. Just make sure that others cannot read your sensitive files (*~/.ssh/identity*, any other private key files, and *~/.ssh/random_seed*). For more information on AFS, visit:

> *http://www.alw.nih.gov/Docs/AFS/AFS_toc.html*
> *http://www.faqs.org/faqs/afs-faq/*

5.5.2. Access Control

Serverwide access control permits or denies connections from particular hosts or Internet domains, or to specific user accounts on the server machine. It is applied separately from authentication: for example, even if a user's identity is legitimate, you might still want to reject connections from her computer. Similarly, if a particular computer or Internet domain has poor security policies, you might want to reject all SSH connection attempts from that domain.

SSH access control is scantily documented and has many subtleties and "gotchas." The configuration keywords look obvious in meaning, but they aren't. Our primary goal in this section is to illuminate the murky corners so you can develop a correct and effective access-control configuration.

Keep in mind that SSH access to an account is permitted only if both the server and the account are configured to allow it. If a server accepts SSH connections to all accounts it serves, individual users may still deny connections to their accounts. [8.2] Likewise, if an account is configured to permit SSH access, the SSH server on its host can nonetheless forbid access. This two-level system applies to all SSH access control, so we won't state it repeatedly. Figure 5-2 summarizes the two-level access control system.*

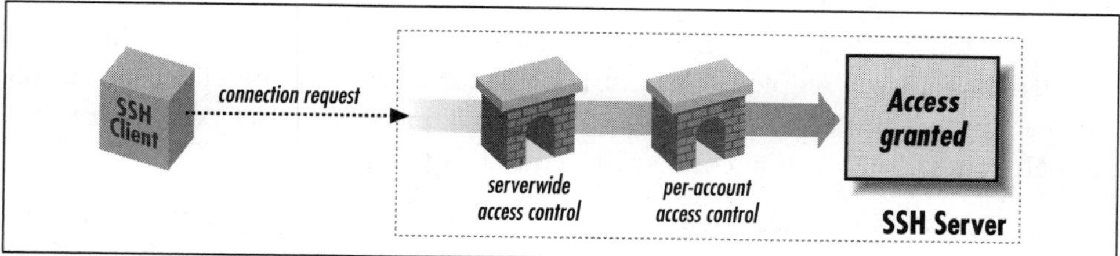

Figure 5-2. Access control levels

5.5.2.1. Account access control

Ordinarily, any account may receive SSH connections as long as it is set up correctly. This access may be overridden by the server keywords `AllowUsers` and `DenyUsers`. `AllowUsers` specifies that only a limited set of local accounts may receive SSH connections. For example, the line:

```
# SSH1, SSH2, OpenSSH
AllowUsers smith
```

permits the local smith account and *only* the smith account, to receive SSH connections. The configuration file may have multiple `AllowUsers` lines:

```
# SSH1, SSH2, OpenSSH
AllowUsers smith
AllowUsers jones
AllowUsers oreilly
```

in which case the results are cumulative: the local accounts smith, jones, and oreilly, and only those accounts, may receive SSH connections. The SSH server maintains a list of all `AllowUsers` values, and when a connection request arrives, it does a string comparison (really a pattern match, as we'll see in a moment) against the list. If a match occurs, the connection is permitted; otherwise, it is rejected.

A single `AllowUsers` keyword in the configuration file cuts off SSH access for all other accounts not mentioned. If the configuration file has no `AllowUsers` keywords, the server's `AllowUsers` list is empty, and connections are permissible to all accounts.

* This concept is true for the configuration keywords discussed in this section but not for trusted-host control files, e.g., *~/.rhosts* and */etc/hosts.equiv*. Each of these may in fact override the other. [3.4.2.3]

DenyUsers is the opposite of **AllowUsers**: it shuts off SSH access to particular accounts. For example:

```
# SSH1, SSH2, OpenSSH
DenyUsers smith
```

states that the smith account may not receive SSH connections. **DenyUsers** keywords may appear multiple times, just like **AllowUsers**, and the effects are again cumulative. As for **AllowUsers**, the server maintains a list of all **DenyUsers** values and compares incoming connection requests against them.

Both **AllowUsers** and **DenyUsers** can accept more complicated values than simple account names. An interesting but potentially confusing syntax supported by *sshd1* and *sshd2* is to specify both an account name and a hostname (or numeric IP address), separated by an @ symbol:

```
# SSH1, SSH2
AllowUsers jones@example.com
```

Despite its appearance, this string isn't an email address, and it doesn't mean "the user jones on the machine *example.com*." Rather, it describes a relationship between a *local* account, jones, and a *remote* client machine, *example.com*. The meaning is: "clients on *example.com* may connect to the server's jones account." Although this meaning is surprising, it would be even stranger if jones were a remote account, since the SSH server has no way to verify account names on remote client machines (except when using hostbased authentication).

For SSH1 and OpenSSH, wildcard characters are acceptable in the user and host portions of **AllowUsers** and **DenyUsers** arguments. The ? symbol represents any single character except @, and the * represents any sequence of characters, again not including @. For SSH2, you may use full regular expressions, although the syntax is a little different from usual to accommodate "fileglob" syntax as well; see Appendix A.

The SSH2 regular-expression language includes keywords with a colon character in them, such as `[:digit:]`. Using a colon in an SSH2 access-control pattern can cause a nasty, difficult-to-track-down problem: it is ignored, along with the rest of your configuration file! The problem is that the parser is a bit dumb and interprets the colon as introducing a labelled section of the file. The label doesn't match anything, and so the rest of the file, now included in the section, is silently ignored. You can avoid this problem simply by placing the pattern inside quotation marks:

```
AllowHosts "10.1.1.[:digit:]##"
```

Though undocumented, this quoting syntax works.

Here are some examples. SSH connections are permitted only to accounts with five-character names ending in "mith":

```
# SSH1, SSH2, OpenSSH
AllowUsers ?mith
```

SSH connections are permitted only to accounts with names beginning with the letter "s", coming from hosts whose names end in ".edu":

```
# SSH1, SSH2, OpenSSH
AllowUsers s*@*.edu
```

SSH2 connections are permitted only to account names of the form "test`N`" where `N` is a number, e.g., "test123".

```
# SSH2 only
AllowUsers test[0-9]##
```

One unfortunate, glaring omission is that you can't specify IP networks with traditional "address/masklength" syntax, e.g., 10.1.1.0/28 to mean the addresses 10.1.1.0 through 10.1.1.15.* To restrict connections to come from this range of addresses with **AllowHosts** [5.5.2.3] is rather more verbose:

```
# SSH1
AllowHosts *@10.1.1.? *@10.1.1.10 *@10.1.1.11 *@10.1.1.12 *@10.1.1.13
AllowHosts *@10.1.1.14 *@10.1.1.15
```

or complicated:

```
# SSH2
AllowHosts *@10.1.1.(?|(1[0-5]))
```

Restricting to a network that falls on an octet boundary, of course, is easier:

```
# SSH1, SSH2
# Allow connections only from 10.1.1.0/24
AllowHosts *@10.1.1.*
```

Note, though, that this can be easily circumvented; an attacker need only control a domain server somewhere and connect from a machine named 10.1.1.evil.org. A more effective statement is:

```
# SSH2 only
AllowUsers "*@10.1.1.[:isdigit:]##"
```

Even this isn't foolproof. Address and hostname-based restrictions are weak restrictions at best; they should be used only as an adjunct to a strong authentication method.

* In this notation, the mask specifies the number of 1 bits in the most-significant portion of the netmask. You might be more familiar with the older, equivalent notation giving the entire mask, e.g., 10.1.1.0/255.255.255.240.

Multiple strings may appear on a single **AllowUsers** line. SSH1 and OpenSSH separate strings with whitespace; however, the syntax differs between SSH1/OpenSSH and SSH2:

```
# SSH1, OpenSSH
AllowUsers  smith jones cs*
```

and SSH2 separates them with commas, no whitespace permitted:

```
# SSH2 only
AllowUsers  smith,jones,cs*
```

AllowUsers and **DenyUsers** may be combined effectively. Suppose you're teaching a course and want your students to be the only users with SSH access to your server. It happens that only student usernames begin with "stu", so you specify:

```
# SSH1, SSH2, OpenSSH
AllowUsers stu*
```

Later, one of your students, stu563, drops the course so you want to disable her SSH access. Simply change the configuration to:

```
# SSH1, SSH2, OpenSSH
AllowUsers stu*
DenyUsers stu563
```

Hmm... this seems strange. The two lines appear to conflict because the first permits stu563 but the second rejects it. The server handles this in the following way: if any line prevents access to an account, the account can't be accessed. So in the preceding example, stu563 is denied access by the second line.

Consider another example:

```
# SSH1, SSH2, OpenSSH
AllowUsers smith
DenyUsers s*
```

It permits SSH connections to the smith account but denies connections to any account beginning with "s". What does the server do with this clear contradiction? It rejects connections to the smith account, following the same rule: if any restriction prevents access, such as the **DenyUsers** line shown, access is denied. Access is granted only if there are no restrictions against it.

sshd can store at most 256 user strings for **AllowUsers** and 256 for **DenyUsers**. This undocumented static limit applies if the strings follow a single keyword (e.g., **AllowUsers** followed by 256 strings) or multiple keywords (e.g., 16 **AllowUsers** keywords with 16 strings each). That is, the limit is internal to the server, not related to the length of a line in the configuration file.

Finally, here is a useful configuration example, expressed in SSH1 syntax:

```
AllowUsers walrus@* carpenter@* *@*.beach.net
```

This restricts access for most accounts to connections originating inside the domain *beach.net*—except for the accounts "walrus" and "carpenter", which may be accessed from anywhere. The @* following walrus and carpenter isn't strictly necessary, but it helps make clear the intent of the line.

It's worth noting that hostnames in these access-control statements are dependent on the integrity of DNS, which is easily spoofed. If this is a concern, consider using IP addresses instead, even though maintenance might be more cumbersome.

5.5.2.2. Group access control

sshd may permit or deny SSH access to all accounts in a Unix group on the server machine. The keywords **AllowGroups** and **DenyGroups** serve this purpose. They are followed by one or more Unix group names:

```
# SSH1, OpenSSH (separation by whitespace)
AllowGroups faculty
DenyGroups students secretaries

# SSH2 only (separation by comma)
AllowGroups faculty
DenyGroups students,secretaries
```

These keywords operate much like **AllowUsers** and **DenyUsers**. SSH1 and OpenSSH accept the wildcards * and ? within group names, whereas SSH2 accepts its usual regular expressions (see Appendix A), and you may provide multiple strings per line:

```
# SSH1, OpenSSH
AllowGroups ?aculty s*s

# SSH2 only
AllowGroups ?aculty,s*s
```

Unfortunately, these directives apply only to the target user's *primary* group, the one listed in the *passwd* record for the account. An account may belong to other groups as well (e.g., by entry in the */etc/groups* file or NIS map), but SSH doesn't notice. It's a pity: if supplementary groups were supported, you could easily designate a subset of SSH-accessible accounts by defining a group—say, *sshusers*—and configure the SSH server with **AllowGroups sshusers**. This feature also automatically prevents access to system accounts such as *bin*, *news*, and *uucp* that don't require SSH. Perhaps some SSH implementors will fix this someday.

By default, access is allowed to all groups. If any **AllowGroups** keyword appears, access is permitted to only the primary groups specified (and may be further restricted with **DenyGroups**).

As was the case for **AllowUsers** and **DenyUsers**, conflicts are resolved in the most restrictive way. If any **AllowGroups** or **DenyGroups** line prevents access to a given group, access is denied to that group even if another line appears to permit it. Also as before, there is a static limit of 256 strings that may follow AllowGroups or DenyGroups keywords in the configuration file.

5.5.2.3. Hostname access control

In the discussion of AllowUsers and DenyUsers, we described how to permit or reject SSH-1 connections from a given host, say, *example.com*:

```
# SSH1, OpenSSH
AllowUsers *@example.com
DenyUsers *@example.com
```

SSH1 and SSH2 provide the keywords AllowHosts and DenyHosts to restrict access by s host more concisely, getting rid of the unnecessary account-name wildcard:

```
# SSH1, SSH2
AllowHosts example.com
DenyHosts example.com
```

The AllowHosts and DenyHosts keywords permit or prevent (respectively) SSH connections from given hosts.* As with AllowUsers and DenyUsers:

- Values may contain the wildcards ? and * (SSH1, OpenSSH) or regular expressions (SSH2, Appendix A).
- Values may contain multiple strings separated by whitespace (SSH1, OpenSSH) or commas (SSH2).
- Keywords may appear multiple times in the configuration file, and the results are cumulative.
- Hostnames or IP addresses may be used.
- At most 256 strings may follow AllowHosts or DenyHosts keywords in the configuration file.

AllowHosts and DenyHosts have a unique feature among the access-control keywords. If *sshd1* refuses a connection based on AllowHosts or DenyHosts, it optionally prints an informative message for the client:

```
Sorry, you are not allowed to connect.
```

This printing is controlled by the SilentDeny keyword. If its value is no (the default), the message is printed, but if the value is yes, the message is suppressed (i.e., silent denial):

* Finer-grained control is provided by the "from" option in *authorized_keys*. [8.2.5] Each public key may be tagged with a list of acceptable hosts that may connect via that key.

```
# SSH1 only
SilentDeny no
```

As a side effect, `SilentDeny` also prevents the failed connection attempt from appearing in the server's log messages. With `SilentDeny` turned off, you see this in the log:

```
log: Connection from client.marceau.net not allowed.
fatal: Local: Sorry, you are not allowed to connect.
```

When `SilentDeny` is turned on, these messages don't appear in the server logs. `SilentDeny` doesn't apply to any other access-control keywords (`DenyUsers`, `DenySHosts`, etc.), nor is it related to authentication.

5.5.2.4. shosts access control

`AllowHosts` and `DenyHosts` offer total hostname-based access control, regardless of the type of authentication requested. A similar but less restrictive access control is specific to trusted-host authentication. You can deny access to hosts that are named in *.rhosts*, *.shosts*, */etc/hosts.equiv*, and */etc/shosts.equiv* files. This is accomplished with the keywords `AllowSHosts` and `DenySHosts`.*

For example, the line:

```
# SSH1, SSH2
DenySHosts badguy.com
```

forbids access by connections from *badguy.com*, but only when trusted-host authentication is being attempted. Likewise, `AllowSHosts` permits access only to given hosts when trusted-host authentication is used. Values follow the same syntax as for `AllowHosts` and `DenyHosts`. As a result, system administrators can override values in users' *.rhosts* and *.shosts* files (which is good, because this can't be done via the */etc/hosts.equiv* or */etc/shosts.equiv* files).

As for `AllowHosts` and `DenyHosts`:

- Values may contain the wildcards ? and * (SSH1) or regular expressions (SSH2, Appendix A).
- Values may contain multiple strings separated by whitespace (SSH1) or commas (SSH2).
- Keywords may appear multiple times in the configuration file, and the results are cumulative.

---

* Even though the keywords have "SHosts" in their names, they apply also to *.rhosts* and */etc/hosts.equiv* files.

- Hostnames or IP addresses may be used.
- There is a static limit of 256 strings that may follow **AllowSHosts** or **DenySHosts** keywords in the configuration file.

5.5.2.5. Root access control

sshd has a separate access-control mechanism for the superuser. The keyword **PermitRootLogin** allows or denies access to the root account by SSH:

```
# SSH1, SSH2, OpenSSH
PermitRootLogin no
```

Permissible values for this keyword are **yes** (the default) to allow access to the root account by SSH, **no** to deny all such access, and **nopwd** (SSH1, SSH2) or **without-password** (OpenSSH) to allow access except by password authentication.

In SSH1 and OpenSSH, **PermitRootLogin** applies only to logins, not to forced commands specified in *authorized_keys*. [8.2.4] For example, if root's *authorized_keys* file contains a line beginning with:

```
command="/bin/dump" ....
```

then the root account may be accessed by SSH to run the *dump* command, no matter what the value of **PermitRootLogin**. This capability lets remote clients run superuser processes, such as backups or filesystem checks, but not unrestricted login sessions.

The server checks **PermitRootLogin** after authentication is complete. In other words, if **PermitRootLogin** is **no**, a client is offered the opportunity to authenticate (e.g., is prompted for a password or passphrase) but is shut down afterward regardless.

We've previously seen a similar keyword, **IgnoreRootRhosts**, that controls access to the root account by trusted-host authentication. It prevents entries in *~root/.rhosts* and *~root/.shosts* from being used to authenticate root. Because *sshd* checks **PermitRootLogin** after authentication is complete, it overrides any value of **IgnoreRootRhosts**. Table 5-2 illustrates the interaction of these two keywords.

Table 5-2. Can root Log In?

	IgnoreRootRhosts yes	IgnoreRootRhosts no
PermitRootLogin yes	Yes, except by trusted-host	Yes
PermitRootLogin no	No	No
PermitRootLogin nopwd (nopassword)	Yes, except by trusted-host or password	Yes, except by password

5.5.2.6. Restricting directory access with chroot

The Unix system call `chroot` causes a process to treat a given directory as the root directory. Any attempt to *cd* outside the subtree rooted at the given directory fails. This is useful for restricting a user or process to a subset of a filesystem for security reasons.

SSH2 provides two keywords for imposing this restriction on incoming SSH clients. **`ChRootUsers`** specifies that SSH clients, when accessing a given account, are restricted to the account's home directory and its subdirectories:

```
# SSH2 only
ChRootUsers smith
```

Several accounts may be specified on the same line, separated by commas, meaning that each of these accounts are individually restricted when accessed via SSH2:

```
# SSH2 only
ChRootUsers smith,jones,mcnally
```

The other keyword, **`ChRootGroups`**, works similarly but applies to all accounts in a given Unix group:

```
# SSH2 only
ChRootGroups users,wheel,mygroup
```

`ChRootGroups` only examines an account's *primary* group; supplementary groups aren't considered. This makes it a much less useful feature than it would otherwise be. Hopefully, a fuller implementation will come in the future.

To make this `chroot` functionality work, you might need to copy some system files into the account in question. Otherwise the login might fail because it can't access needed resources, such as shared libraries. On our Linux system, we needed to copy the following programs and libraries into the account:

/bin/ls
/bin/bash
/lib/ld-linux.so.2
/lib/libc.so.6
/lib/libtermcap.so.2

This sort of thing can be reduced by statically linking the SSH executables. SSH2 recently added a tool called *ssh-chrootmgr* to help with this process; unfortunately, it occurred too close to press time for us to review it. See the manpage for details.

5.5.2.7. Summary of authentication and access control

SSH provides several ways to permit or restrict connections to particular accounts or from particular hosts. Tables 5-3 and 5-4 summarize the available options.

Table 5-3. SSH1 and OpenSSH Summary of Authentication and Access Control

If you are...	And you want to allow or restrict...	Then use...
User	Connections to your account by public-key authentication	*authorized_keys* [8.2.1]
Administrator	Connections to an account	`AllowUsers`, `DenyUsers`
User	Connections by a host	*authorized_keys* from="..." option [8.2.5.1]
Administrator	Connections by a host	`AllowHosts`, `DenyHosts` (or `AllowUsers`, `DenyUsers`)
User	Connections to your account by trusted-host authentication	*.rhosts*, *.shosts*
Administrator	Trusted-host authentication	`RhostsAuthentication`, `RhostsRSAAuthentication`, `IgnoreRhosts`, `AllowSHosts`, `DenySHosts`, */etc/hosts.equiv*, */etc/shosts.equiv*
Administrator	Root logins	`IgnoreRootRhosts`, `PermitRootLogin`

Table 5-4. SSH2 Summary of Authentication and Access Control

If you are...	And you want to allow or restrict...	Then use...
User	Connections to your account by public-key authentication	*authorization* file [8.2.2]
Administrator	Connections to an account	`AllowUsers`, `DenyUsers`
User	Connections by a host	N/A
Administrator	Connections by a host	`AllowHosts`, `DenyHosts`
User	Connections to your account by trusted-host authentication	*.rhosts*, *.shosts*
Administrator	Trusted-host authentication	`AllowedAuthentications`, `AllowSHosts`, `DenySHosts`, */etc/hosts.equiv*, */etc/shosts.equiv*
Administrator	Root logins	`PermitRootLogin`

5.5.3. Selecting a Login Program

Another way to control authentication and access to a machine is to replace the Unix *login* program. SSH1 provides a hook for doing so, though it requires solid knowledge of your operating system's login procedure.

When an SSH1 client initiates a terminal session with the server, normally the server invokes the local account's login shell directly. You can override this choice by specifying `--with-login` [4.1.5.9] during compile-time configuration, causing the server to invoke a login program instead (e.g., */bin/login* or Kerberos's *login.krb5*).*

What's the difference? That depends on the operating system on the server machine. The login program might set some additional environment variables (such as DISPLAY for the X Windows system), perform additional auditing or logging, or take other actions a shell doesn't.

In order for the login program specified by `--with-login` to be invoked by *sshd1*, you must also set the undocumented keyword `UseLogin`. It takes a value of `yes` (to use an alternative login program) or `no`, the default:

```
# SSH1, OpenSSH
UseLogin yes
```

OpenSSH doesn't have `--with-login`, so you can't specify an alternative login program. The OpenSSH `UseLogin` statement chooses only between */bin/login* and a login shell.

The behavior of a login program versus a login shell is entirely implementation-specific, so we won't cover the intricacies. If you need to muck with `UseLogin`, you first need to understand the features of your operating system and your login program in detail.

5.6. User Logins and Accounts

When a login occurs, the SSH server can take special actions. Here, we discuss:

- Printing welcome messages for the user
- Handling expired accounts or passwords
- Handling empty passwords
- Taking arbitrary actions with */etc/sshrc*

* If */bin/login* is invoked, you might wonder why it doesn't prompt every SSH client for a login password. Well, the server runs */bin/login -f*, which disables *login*'s password authentication. The *–f* option is left unmentioned in the *login* manpage of many operating systems.

5.6.1. Welcome Messages for the User

When users log in, *sshd* prints informative messages such as the "message of the day" file (*/etc/motd*) and whether the user has email. This output may be turned on and off in the configuration file. Since most Unix shells print this information on login, these SSH features are frequently redundant and turned off.

To enable or disable the message of the day, use the `PrintMotd` keyword with the value `yes` (the default) or `no`:

```
# SSH1, SSH2, OpenSSH
PrintMotd no
```

Incidentally, *sshd* obeys the Unix "hushlogin" convention. If the file *~/.hushlogin* exists, */etc/motd* isn't printed on login, regardless of the `PrintMotd` value.

A message about email (e.g., "You have mail") is printed on login if the `CheckMail` keyword has the value of `yes` (the default), or the message is skipped if the value is `no`:

```
# SSH1, SSH2, OpenSSH
CheckMail yes
```

5.6.2. Expired Account or Password

If a user's password or computer account is expiring soon, *sshd1* can optionally print warning messages when the user logs in via SSH:

```
WARNING: Your password expires in 7 days
WARNING: Your account expires in 10 days
```

These messages are turned on and off by the keywords `PasswordExpireWarningDays` and `AccountExpireWarningDays`, respectively:

```
# SSH1 only
PasswordExpireWarningDays 7
AccountExpireWarningDays 10
```

The value following the keyword is a number of days, and by default, both values are 14. A zero value means that the warning message is suppressed. Note that account and password expiration aren't features of SSH, but of the host operating system.*

If a password has expired, the SSH1 server can prompt the user to change it upon login. This feature is controlled by the keyword `ForcedPasswdChange`, given a value of `yes` or `no` (the default). If the feature is enabled:

---

* Account expiration requires that your operating system support */etc/shadow*. Password expiration requires `struct passwd` to have a `pw_expire` field à la FreeBSD.

```
# SSH1 only
ForcedPasswdChange yes
```

the user is prompted to change a password if expired. Until this password is changed, SSH connections aren't accepted.

5.6.3. Empty Passwords

If password authentication is used, and an account has an empty password, the SSH server may refuse access to the account. This feature is controlled by the keyword `PermitEmptyPasswords` with a value of `yes` (the default) or `no`. If enabled:

```
# SSH1, SSH2, OpenSSH
PermitEmptyPasswords yes
```

empty passwords are permissible; otherwise not.

The SSH1 server additionally may require users with empty passwords to change them. The keyword `ForcedEmptyPasswdChange` controls this feature much like `ForcedPasswdChange` for expired passwords. The `ForcedEmptyPasswdChange` keyword may have a value of `yes` or `no` (the default):

```
# SSH1 only
ForcedEmptyPasswdChange yes
```

If the value is `yes` and the password is empty, then upon login, the user is prompted to change his or her password and can't log in until the change is made.

5.6.4. Arbitrary Actions with /etc/sshrc

When a user logs in, the normal Unix login system typically runs some shell scripts, such as */etc/profile*. In addition, *sshd* runs the script */etc/sshrc* for each SSH-based login. This feature lets the system administrator run special commands for SSH logins that don't occur for ordinary logins. For example, you can do some additional logging of SSH connections, print welcome messages for SSH users only, and set SSH-related environment variables.

In all three, SSH1, SSH2, and OpenSSH, */etc/sshrc* is processed by the Bourne shell (*/bin/sh*) specifically, rather than the user's shell, so that it can run reliably for all accounts regardless of their various shells. It is run for logins (e.g., *ssh my-host*) and remote commands (*ssh my-host /bin/who*), just before the user's shell or command is invoked. It runs under the target account's uid, so it can't take privileged actions. If the script exits due to an error (say, a syntax error), the SSH session continues normally.

Note that this file is run as input to the Bourne shell: *sshd* runs */bin/sh /etc/sshrc*, not */bin/sh –c /etc/sshrc*. This means that it can't be an arbitrary program; it must be a file containing Bourne-shell commands (and it doesn't need the execute mode bit set).

/etc/sshrc operates machinewide: it is run for every incoming SSH connection. For more fine-grained control, each user may create the script *~/.ssh/rc* to be run instead of */etc/sshrc*. [8.4] */etc/sshrc* isn't executed if *~/.ssh/rc* exists in the target account. Note that SSH *rc* files interact with X authentication. [9.3.5.2]

5.6.4.1. /etc/nologin

If the file */etc/nologin* exists, *sshd* allows only root to log in; no other accounts are allowed access. Thus, *touch /etc/nologin* is a quick way to restrict access to the system administrator only, without having to reconfigure or shut down SSH.

5.7. Subsystems

Subsystems are a (mostly undocumented) layer of abstraction for defining and invoking remote commands in SSH2 and OpenSSH/2. Normally you invoke remote commands ad hoc by providing them on the client command line. For instance, the following line invokes the Unix backup program *tar* remotely to copy the */home* directory to tape:

```
# SSH2, OpenSSH/2
$ ssh server.example.com /bin/tar c /home
```

Subsystems are a set of remote commands predefined on the server machine so they can be executed conveniently.* These commands are defined in the server configuration file, and the syntax is slightly different between OpenSSH and SSH2. A subsystem for invoking the preceding backup command is:

```
# SSH2
subsystem-backups        /bin/tar c /home

# OpenSSH/2
subsystem backups        /bin/tar c /home
```

Note that SSH2 uses a keyword of the form "subsystem-*name*" with one argument, whereas OpenSSH uses the keyword "subsystem" with two arguments. This SSH2 syntax is quite odd and unlike anything else in its configuration language; we don't know how it ended up that way.

To run this command on the server machine, invoke *ssh* with the *–s* option:

```
# SSH2, OpenSSH/2
$ ssh -s backups server.example.com
```

* Abstractly, a subsystem need not be a separate program; it can invoke a function built into the SSH server itself (hence the name). But there are no such implementations at the moment.

This command behaves identically to the previous one in which */bin/tar* was invoked explicitly.

The default *sshd2_config* file defines one subsystem:

```
subsystem-sftp     sftp-server
```

Don't remove the **subsystem-sftp** line from *sshd2_config*: it is required for *scp2* and *sftp* to work. Internally, both programs run *ssh2 –s sftp* to perform file transfers.

Subsystems are mainly a convenience feature to predefine commands for SSH clients to invoke easily. The additional level of abstraction can be helpful to system administrators, who can define and advertise useful subsystems for their users. Suppose your users run the Pine email reader to connect to your IMAP server using SSH2 to secure the connection. [11.3] Instead of telling everyone to use the command:

```
$ ssh2 server.example.com /usr/sbin/imapd
```

and revealing the path to the IMAP daemon, *imapd*, you can define a subsystem to hide the path in case it changes in the future:

```
# SSH2 only
subsystem-imap /usr/sbin/imapd
```

Now users can run the command:

```
$ ssh2 -s imap server.example.com
```

to establish secure IMAP connections via the subsystem.

5.7.1. Disabling the Shell Startup File

If your remote shell is C shell or *tcsh*, it normally reads your remote shell startup file (*.cshrc*, *.tcshrc*) at the beginning of the session. Some commands in these startup files, particularly those that write to standard output, may interfere with the file-copy commands *scp2* and *sftp*. In SSH2, file copying is accomplished by the *sftp-server* subsystem, so SSH2 disables reading of *.cshrc* and *.tcshrc* for subsystems. [3.5.2.4] You can reenable this with the keyword **AllowCshrcSourcingWithSubsystems**, providing a value of **yes** (permit *.cshrc* and *.tcshrc* sourcing) or **no** (the default):

```
# SSH2 only
AllowCshrcSourcingWithSubsystems yes
```

SSH2 disables the sourcing of remote *.cshrc* and *.tcshrc* files by passing the *–f* command-line option to the remote C shell or *tcsh* invocation.

5.8. History, Logging, and Debugging

As an SSH server runs, it optionally produces log messages to describe what it is doing. Log messages aid the system administrator in tracking the server's behavior and detecting and diagnosing problems. For example, if a server is mysteriously rejecting connections it should accept, one of the first places to seek the cause is the server's log output.

Logging works differently for the SSH1, SSH2, and OpenSSH servers, so we discuss each separately.

5.8.1. Logging and SSH1

By default, *sshd1* writes log messages to syslog, the standard Unix logging facility (see the sidebar, "The Syslog Logging Service"). For example, a server startup generates these syslog entries:

```
log: Server listening on port 22.
log: Generating 768 bit RSA key.
log: RSA key generation complete.
```

and a client connection and disconnection appear as:

```
log: Connection from 128.11.22.33 port 1022
log: Rhosts with RSA host authentication accepted for smith, smith on myhost.net
log: Closing connection to 128.11.22.33
```

sshd1 permits logging to be controlled in three ways:

Fascist Logging mode
: Prints additional debug messages to the system log file. Enabled by the `FascistLogging` keyword.

Debug mode
: A superset of Fascist Logging mode. Enabled by the *–d* command-line option.

Quiet mode
: Suppresses all log messages except fatal errors. Enabled by the `QuietMode` keyword or the *–q* command-line option.

5.8.1.1. SSH1 Fascist Logging mode

Fascist Logging mode causes *sshd1* to print debug messages to the system log file as it proceeds. For example:

```
debug: Client protocol version 1.5; client software version 1.2.26
debug: Sent 768 bit public key and 1024 bit host key.
debug: Encryption type: idea
debug: Received session key; encryption turned on.
```

The Syslog Logging Service

Syslog is the standard Unix logging service. Programs send their log messages to the syslog daemon, *syslogd*, which forwards them to another destination such as a console or a file. Destinations are specified in the syslog configuration file, */etc/syslog.conf*.

Messages received by *syslogd* are processed according to their facility, which indicates a message's origin. Standard syslog facilities include `KERN` (messages from the operating system kernel), `DAEMON` (messages from system daemons), `USER` (messages from user processes), `MAIL` (messages from the email system), and others. By default, the facility for SSH server messages is `DAEMON`. This choice may be changed with the SSH keyword `SyslogFacility`, which determines the syslog facility code for logging SSH messages:

```
# SSH1, SSH2, OpenSSH
SyslogFacility USER
```

Other possible values are `USER`, `AUTH`, `LOCAL0`, `LOCAL1`, `LOCAL2`, `LOCAL3`, `LOCAL4`, `LOCAL5`, `LOCAL6`, and `LOCAL7`. See the manpages for *syslog*, *syslogd*, and *syslog.conf* for more information about this logging service.

Fascist Logging mode is controlled by the `FascistLogging` keyword in the server configuration file, given an argument of `yes` or `no` (the default):*

```
# SSH1 (and SSH2)
FascistLogging yes
```

5.8.1.2. SSH1 Debug mode

Like Fascist Logging mode, Debug mode causes the server to print debug messages. It is disabled by default, and is enabled by the *–d* command-line option of *sshd*:

```
# SSH1, OpenSSH
$ sshd -d
```

Debug mode prints the same diagnostic messages as Fascist Logging mode but also echoes them to standard error. For example, a server run in Debug mode on TCP port 9999 produces diagnostic output like the following:

```
# SSH1, OpenSSH
$ sshd -d -p 9999
debug: sshd version 1.2.26 [sparc-sun-solaris2.5.1]
debug: Initializing random number generator; seed file /etc/ssh_random_seed
log: Server listening on port 9999.
```

* But it's barely supported in SSH2, as we'll see. [5.8.2.5]

```
log: Generating 768 bit RSA key.
Generating p:  .....++ (distance 100)
Generating q:  ............++ (distance 122)
Computing the keys...
Testing the keys...
Key generation complete.
log: RSA key generation complete.
```

The server then waits in the foreground for connections. When one arrives, the server prints:

```
debug: Server will not fork when running in debugging mode.
log: Connection from 128.11.22.33 port 1022
debug: Client protocol version 1.5; client software version 1.2.26
debug: Sent 768 bit public key and 1024 bit host key.
debug: Encryption type: idea
debug: Received session key; encryption turned on.
debug: Installing crc compensation attack detector.
debug: Attempting authentication for smith.
debug: Trying rhosts with RSA host authentication for smith
debug: Rhosts RSA authentication: canonical host myhost.net
log: Rhosts with RSA host authentication accepted for smith, smith on myhost.net
debug: Allocating pty.
debug: Forking shell.
debug: Entering interactive session.
```

When the client exits, the server exits as well, since (as the preceding messages show) the server doesn't fork subprocesses while running in Debug mode but handles a single connection within the one process:

```
debug: Received SIGCHLD.
debug: End of interactive session; stdin 13, stdout (read 1244, sent 1244), stderr
0 bytes.
debug: pty_cleanup_proc called
debug: Command exited with status 0.
debug: Received exit confirmation.
log: Closing connection to 128.11.22.33
```

Debug mode has the following features beyond those of Fascist Logging mode:

- It echoes log messages to standard error.
- It prints a few extra messages to standard error that aren't written to the log file, such as RSA key generation messages.
- It makes the server single-threaded, preventing it from forking subprocesses. (Hence the message "Server will not fork when running in debugging mode" in the preceding output.) The server exits after handling one connection request. This is helpful while troubleshooting so you can focus on a single client connection.
- It sets `LoginGraceTime` to zero, so the connection doesn't drop while you are debugging a problem. (Very sensible.)

- It causes a Unix SSH client, upon connection, to print the server-side environment variable settings on standard error. This can aid in debugging connection problems. For example, a connection on port 9999 to the server shown earlier produces diagnostic output like:

```
$ ssh -p 9999 myserver.net
[...login output begins...]
Environment:
HOME=/home/smith
USER=smith
LOGNAME=smith
PATH=/bin:/usr/bin:/usr/ucb
MAIL=/var/mail/smith
SHELL=/usr/bin/ksh
TZ=US/Eastern
HZ=100
SSH_CLIENT=128.11.22.33 1022 9999
SSH_TTY=/dev/pts/3
TERM=vt220
REMOTEUSER=smith
[...login output continues...]
```

Because of these convenience features, Debug mode is generally more useful than Fascist Logging mode.

5.8.1.3. SSH1 Quiet mode

Quiet mode suppresses some diagnostic messages from *sshd1*, depending on the settings of the Fascist Logging and Debug modes. Table 5-5 illustrates the behavior of Quiet mode when used in tandem with these modes.

Table 5-5. Behavior of SSH1 Quiet Mode

Quiet	Debug	Fascist Logging	Results
No	No	No	Default logging (syslog); no "debug:" messages
No	No	Yes	Fascist Logging mode (syslog)
No	Yes	Yes/No	Debug mode (syslog, stderr)
Yes	No	No	Log fatal errors only (syslog)
Yes	No	Yes	Log fatal errors only (syslog)
Yes	Yes	Yes/No	Log fatal errors (syslog, stderr) and key generation messages

Quiet mode is controlled by the `QuietMode` keyword in the server configuration file, given an argument of `yes` or `no` (the default):

```
# SSH1, SSH2
QuietMode yes
```

or by the *-q* command-line option:

```
# SSH1, SSH2, OpenSSH
$ sshd -q
```

5.8.2. Logging and SSH2

The logging modes for SSH2 differ from those of SSH1. The keywords and options appear mostly the same, but their behaviors are different:

Debug mode
: Prints debug messages on standard error. Enabled by the *-d* command-line option, followed by an integer (a debug level) or a module specification (for finer-grained logging).

Verbose mode
: A shorthand for Debug mode level 2. Enabled with the *-v* command-line option or the `VerboseMode` keyword.

Fascist Logging mode
: Undocumented and has almost no purpose. Enabled by the `FascistLogging` keyword.

Quiet mode
: Suppresses all log messages except fatal errors. Enabled by the `QuietMode` keyword or the *-q* command-line option.

We strongly recommend compiling SSH2 with heavy debugging turned on, using the flag `--enable-debug-heavy`. [4.1.5.14] The resulting log messages are far more detailed than those printed by default.

5.8.2.1. SSH2 Debug mode (general)

SSH2's Debug mode is enabled only by command-line option, not keyword. As is the case for SSH1, Debug mode is controlled by the *-d* command-line option. Unlike its SSH1 counterpart, the option requires an argument indicating the debug level, and output is sent to standard error (stderr).

A debug level may be indicated in two ways. The first is a nonnegative integer:

```
# SSH2 only
$ sshd2 -d 1
```

The integer levels supported at press time are illustrated in Example 5-1. Specifying a debug level of `n` means that messages for all levels less than or equal to `n` will be printed. For instance, a debug level of 9 means that debug messages for levels 0–9 are printed.

Example 5-1. SSH2 Debug Levels

```
Not to be used inside loops:

   0) Software malfunctions
   1)
   2) (0-2 should also be logged using log-event)
   3) External non-fatal high level errors
        - incorrect format received from an outside source
        - failed negotiation
   4) Positive high level info
        - succeeded negotiation
   5) Start of a high or middle level operation
        - start of a negotiation
        - opening of a device
        - not to be used by functions which are called from inside loops

Can be used inside loops:

   6) Uncommon situations which might be caused by a bug
   7) Nice-to-know info
        - Entering or exiting a function
        - A result of a low level operation
   8) Data block dumps
        - hash
        - keys
        - certificates
        - other non-massive data blocks
   9) Protocol packet dumps
        - TCP
        - UDP
        - ESP
        - AH
   10) Mid-results
        - inside loops
        - non-final results
   11-15) For programmers own debug use
        - own discretion
        - needed only by a person doing bughunt
```

5.8.2.2. SSH2 Debug mode (module-based)

Debug levels can also be set differently for each source code "module" of SSH2. This permits finer-grained control over logging, as well as producing tons of output. This type of debugging is documented only within the source code (*lib/sshutil/sshcore/sshdebug.h*), so to use this mode effectively, you should have some C programming knowledge.

A SSH2 source file is defined to be a "module" for debugging purposes, by defining SSH_DEBUG_MODULE within the file. For example, the file *apps/ssh/auths-passwd.c* has the module name Ssh2AuthPasswdServer because it contains the line:

```
#define SSH_DEBUG_MODULE "Ssh2AuthPasswdServer"
```

The complete set of module names for SSH2 2.3.0 is found in Table 5-6.

Table 5-6. SSH2 Module Names

ArcFour	GetOptCompat	Main
Scp2	Sftp2	SftpCwd
SftpPager	Ssh1KeyDecode	Ssh2
Ssh2AuthClient	Ssh2AuthCommonServer	Ssh2AuthHostBasedClient
Ssh2AuthHostBasedRhosts	Ssh2AuthHostBasedServer	Ssh2AuthKerberosClient
Ssh2AuthKerberosServer	Ssh2AuthKerberosTgtClient	Ssh2AuthKerberosTgtServer
Ssh2AuthPasswdClient	Ssh2AuthPasswdServer	Ssh2AuthPubKeyClient
Ssh2AuthPubKeyServer	Ssh2AuthServer	Ssh2ChannelAgent
Ssh2ChannelSession	Ssh2ChannelSsh1Agent	Ssh2ChannelTcpFwd
Ssh2ChannelX11	Ssh2Client	Ssh2Common
Ssh2PgpPublic	Ssh2PgpSecret	Ssh2PgpUtil
Ssh2Trans	Ssh2Transport	SshADT
SshADTArray	SshADTAssoc	SshADTList
SshADTMap	SshADTTest	SshAdd
SshAgent	SshAgentClient	SshAgentPath
SshAppCommon	SshAskPass	SshAuthMethodClient
SshAuthMethodServer	SshBufZIP	SshBuffer
SshBufferAux	SshConfig	SshConnection
SshDSprintf	SshDebug	SshDecay
SshDirectory	SshEPrintf	SshEncode
SshEventLoop	SshFCGlob	SshFCRecurse
SshFCTransfer	SshFSM	SshFastalloc
SshFileBuffer	SshFileCopy	SshFileCopyConn
SshFileXferClient	SshFilterStream	SshGenCiph
SshGenMP	SshGetCwd	SshGlob
SshInet	SshKeyGen	SshPacketImplementation
SshPacketWrapper	SshPgpCipher	SshPgpFile
SshPgpGen	SshPgpKey	SshPgpKeyDB
SshPgpPacket	SshPgpStringToKey	SshProbe
SshProtoSshCrDown	SshProtoSshCrup	SshProtoTrKex
SshReadLine	SshReadPass	SshRegex

Table 5-6. SSH2 Module Names (continued)

SshSPrintf	SshServer	SshServerProbe
SshSftpServer	SshSigner2	SshStdIOFilter
SshStream	SshStreamPair	SshStreamstub
SshTUserAuth	SshTime	SshTimeMeasure
SshTimeMeasureTest	SshTtyFlags	SshUdp
SshUdpGeneric	SshUnixConfig	SshUnixPtyStream
SshUnixTcp	SshUnixUser	SshUnixUserFiles
SshUserFileBuffer	SshUserFiles	Sshd2
TestMod	TestSshFileCopy	TestSshGlob
TestTtyFlags	t-fsm	

To extract the current set of module names from the source code, search for SSH_DEBUG_MODULE in all source files from the root of the SSH2 distribution:

```
$ find . -type f -exec grep SSH_DEBUG_MODULE '{}' \;
```

Once you have identified the name of your desired module, run the server in debug mode, providing the module's name and debug level:

```
$ sshd2 -d "module_name=debug_level_integer"
```

This causes the given module to print log messages at the given debug level. For example:

```
$ sshd2 -d "Ssh2AuthPasswdServer=2"
```

causes the Ssh2AuthPasswdServer module to log at debug level 2. The messages provide the name of the function in which they occur and the name of the source file in which the code is found.

Multiple modules may be specified, separated by commas, each set to individual debug levels:

```
$ sshd2 -d "Ssh2AuthPasswdServer=2,SshAdd=3,SshSftp=1"
```

Additionally, the wildcards * and ? can specify multiple module names:

```
$ sshd2 -d 'Ssh2*=3'
```

Remember to enclose the patterns in single quotes to prevent their expansion by the Unix shell.

Note that just because a source code file has a debugging module name associated with it, doesn't mean it actually logs any information that way. You may find that turning on debugging for specific modules doesn't produce any extra debugging output.

5.8.2.3. Debugging sshd2 -i

If you use SSH2 from *inetd*, debugging is a little tricky. If you don't take extra steps, the debugging output goes to the client along with the normal protocol conversation, messing it up and causing the connection to fail. What you need to do is redirect *sshd*'s standard error to a file. Ideally, you do this in */etc/inetd.conf*:

```
ssh stream tcp nowait root /bin/sh /bin/sh -c "/usr/sbin/sshd2 -i -d2 2> /tmp/foo"
```

However, many *inetd*'s don't allow embedded spaces in program arguments (i.e., they don't recognize the quoting used in this example). You can get around this using a separate script, like so:

```
/etc/inetd.conf
  ssh stream tcp nowait root /path/to/debug-sshd2-i debug-sshd2-i

debug-sshd2-i
  #!/bin/sh
  # redirect sshd2 standard error to a file
  exec /usr/local/sbin/sshd2 -i -d2 2> /tmp/sshd2.debug
```

5.8.2.4. SSH2 verbose mode

Verbose mode is exactly equivalent to Debug mode level two. It may be enabled by the *–v* command-line option of *sshd2*:

```
# SSH2 only
$ sshd2 -v          Using –v
$ sshd2 -d 2        Identical to the preceding line
```

or by the `VerboseMode` keyword in the server configuration file, with a value of `yes` or `no` (the default):

```
# SSH2 only
VerboseMode yes
```

5.8.2.5. SSH2 Fascist Logging mode

Fascist Logging mode is undocumented in SSH2. Its only purpose seems to be to override Quiet mode. [5.8.2.6] Permissible values are `yes` and `no` (the default):

```
# SSH1, SSH2
FascistLogging yes
```

5.8.2.6. SSH2 quiet mode

In Quiet mode, only fatal errors are logged. It can be overridden by the undocumented Fascist Logging mode. As in SSH1, Quiet mode is controlled by the `QuietMode` keyword in the serverwide configuration file, given an argument of `yes` or `no` (the default):

```
# SSH1, SSH2
QuietMode yes
```

Or by the *–q* command-line option of *sshd*:

```
# SSH1, SSH2, OpenSSH
$ sshd -q
```

5.8.3. Logging and OpenSSH

Logging in OpenSSH is done via syslog, and is controlled by two configuration keywords: `SyslogFacility` and `LogLevel`. `SyslogFacility` determines the "facility" code used when sending a message to the syslog service; depending on the syslog configuration, this helps determine what's done with the log messages (written to the console, stored in a file, etc.). `LogLevel` determines how much detail is supplied in the information logged. The values in order of increasing verbosity are:

QUIET, FATAL, ERROR, INFO, VERBOSE, DEBUG

Logging with level `DEBUG` violates user privacy and should be used only to diagnose problems, not for normal operation.

If *sshd* is run in debug mode (*–d*), logging goes to standard error instead of to syslog. Quiet mode (`LogLevel Quiet` or *sshd –q*) sends nothing to the system log (although some messages resulting from OpenSSH activity may still be recorded, such as those from PAM).

5.8.3.1. Absence of RSA support

OpenSSH doesn't need to be compiled with RSA support if restricted to protocol 2, but if this support is missing, *sshd* prints an error message. To suppress this error message, use the *–Q* option:

```
# OpenSSH only
$ sshd -Q
```

5.9. Compatibility Between SSH-1 and SSH-2 Servers

OpenSSH Version 2 has support for both the SSH-1 and SSH-2 protocols within a single daemon accepting both types of connections. For SSH1 and SSH2, however, the story is more complicated.

The SSH2 server can accept connections from SSH1 clients. This compatibility is achieved by having the SSH2 server run the SSH1 server program instead whenever an SSH-1 connection is requested. This compatibility feature is enabled and disabled with the SSH2 `Ssh1Compatibility` keyword, given a value of `yes` or `no`:

```
# SSH2 only
Ssh1Compatibility yes
```

When `Ssh1Compatibility` is enabled, and an SSH-1 client connects to the SSH2 server, the two programs exchange strings indicating their versions. [3.4.1] *sshd2* then locates the *sshd1* executable by examining the value of the `Sshd1Path` keyword:

```
# SSH2 only
Sshd1Path /usr/local/bin/sshd1
```

sshd2 then invokes an *sshd1* process, passing the client's version string to *sshd1* using the *–V* command-line option:*

```
# SSH2 only, invoked automatically by sshd2
/usr/local/bin/sshd1 -V "client version string" <other arguments>
```

The *–V* command-line option is for internal use only by *sshd2*. It is necessary because when *sshd1* starts this way, the client has already sent its initial version announcement, which *sshd1* needs to get somehow. We can't think of any practical reason to use this option manually, but we mention it here for completeness.

When you compile and install SSH2, if SSH1 is already installed, then the configure script [4.1.4] automatically sets the internal, compiled-in defaults for `Ssh1Compatibility` to `yes`, and for `Sshd1Path` to the correct path to *sshd1*. If SSH1 isn't installed, then the compiled defaults are `no` for `Ssh1Compatibility` and the null string for `Sshd1Path`.

The OpenSSH server also implements the *–V* option, so that you can use OpenSSH instead of SSH1 for SSH2 backward-compatibility mode.

Although *sshd2* can accept and reroute SSH1 client connections, the reverse isn't true: *sshd1* can't accept SSH2 connections.

5.9.1. Security Issues with SSH-1 Compatibility Mode in SSH2

There's one vital thing to keep in mind if you're using the SSH-1 compatibility feature in SSH2: you must maintain two separate SSH server configurations. When *sshd2* starts *sshd1*, it is an entirely new process, with its own SSH1 server configuration file. No restrictions set in your SSH2 server configuration apply to it. Even restrictions that could apply, such as `AllowHosts`, don't, because *sshd2* invokes *sshd1* before performing such checks.

* Note that you need at least Version 1.2.26 (F-Secure 1.3.6) of SSH1 to use the compatibility mode, since this option isn't implemented in earlier versions.

This means you must keep the two configurations synchronized with respect to your security intent. Otherwise, an attacker can circumvent your carefully crafted SSH2 configuration simply by connecting with an SSH-1 client.

5.10. Summary

As you can see, SSH servers have a tremendous number of configuration options, and in some cases, multiple ways to achieve the same results. All this power comes at a price, however. When setting up a secure system, it is vital to consider each option carefully and select appropriate values. Don't skimp on understanding: the security of your systems may depend on it. Chapter 10 lists configurations for SSH1, SSH2, and OpenSSH. In addition, all the keywords and options in this chapter appear in Appendix B.

Remember that serverwide configuration is only one avenue for affecting server behavior. We discuss compile-time configuration in Chapter 4 and per-account configuration in Chapter 8.

6

In this chapter:
- *What Is an Identity?*
- *Creating an Identity*
- *SSH Agents*
- *Multiple Identities*
- *Summary*

Key Management and Agents

Your SSH private key is a precious thing. When you use public-key authentication, your key proves your identity to SSH servers. We've encountered several programs related to keys:

ssh-keygen
: Creates key pairs

ssh-agent
: Holds private keys in memory, saving you from typing your passphrase repeatedly

ssh-add
: Loads private keys into the agent

However, we haven't gone into much depth, covering only the most basic operations with keys. Now it's time to examine these concepts and programs in detail.

We begin with an overview of SSH *identities* and the keys that represent them. After that, we thoroughly cover SSH agents and their many features. Finally, we extol the virtues of having multiple SSH identities. If you've been getting by with a single key and only light agent use, we have a lot of cool stuff in store for you. Figure 6-1 summarizes the role of key management in the overall configuration process.

This chapter is the first in a sequence on advanced SSH for end users, as opposed to system administrators. Once you've covered key management in this chapter, we'll take you through client configuration, server configuration, and forwarding.

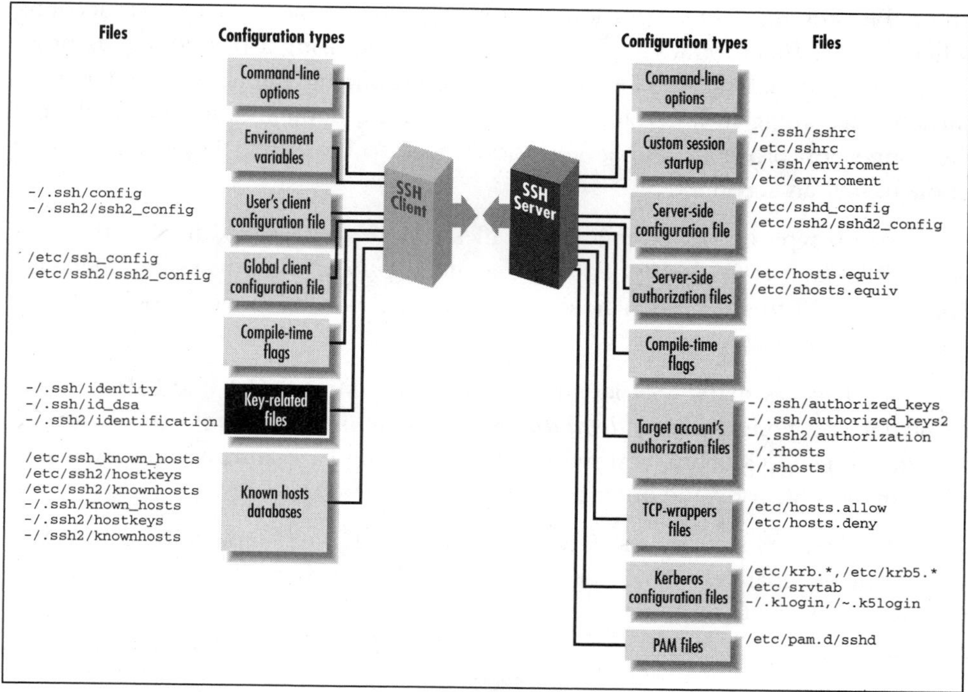

Figure 6-1. SSH user key and agent configuration (highlighted parts)

6.1. What Is an Identity?

An SSH identity is a sequence of bits that says, "I am really me." It is a mathematical construct that permits an SSH client to prove itself to an SSH server, so the SSH server will say, "Ah, I see, it's really you. You hereby are authenticated. Come in."

An identity consists of two parts, called the private key and the public key. Together, they are known as a key pair.

The private key represents your identity for outgoing SSH connections. When you run an SSH client in your account, such as *ssh* or *scp*, and it requests a connection with an SSH server, the client uses this private key to prove your identity to the server.

Private keys must be kept secret. An intruder with your private key can access your account as easily as you can.

The public key represents your identity for incoming connections to your account. When an SSH client requests access to your account, using a private key as proof of identity, the SSH server examines the corresponding public key. If the keys "match" (according to a cryptographic test [3.4.2.2]), authentication succeeds and the connection proceeds. Public keys don't need to be secret; they can't be used to break into an account.

A key pair is typically stored in a pair of files with related names.* In SSH, the public key filename is formed by adding the suffix *.pub* to the private key filename. For example, if the file *mykey* holds a private key, its corresponding public key is found in *mykey.pub*.†

You may have as many SSH identities as you like. Most SSH-1 and SSH-2 implementations let you specify a *default identity* clients use unless told otherwise. To use an alternative identity, you must change a setting by command-line argument, configuration file, or some other configuration tool.

The structure of identity files differs for SSH1, SSH2, and OpenSSH, so we will explain them separately. Their locations in the filesystem are shown in Figures 6-2 (private keys) and 6-3 (public keys).

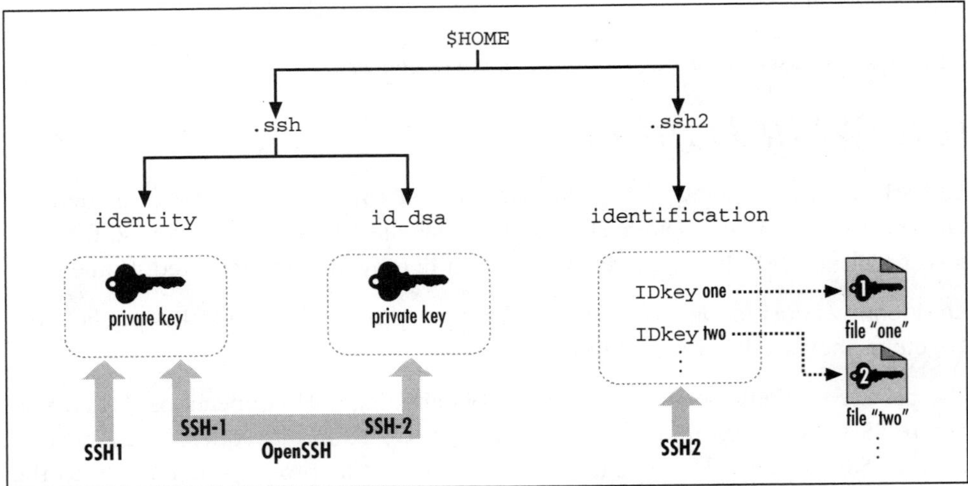

Figure 6-2. SSH identity files (private keys) and the programs that use them

* In contrast, some Windows implementations such as F-Secure SSH Client store keys in the Windows Registry.

† In fact, in SSH1, the so-called "private key file" contains the public key as well, for completeness, and only the part of the file containing the private key is encrypted with the passphrase. But the private key file is in a private binary format; the public key file is there for human convenience, to make it easy to add the public key to an *authorized_keys* file with a text editor, for example.

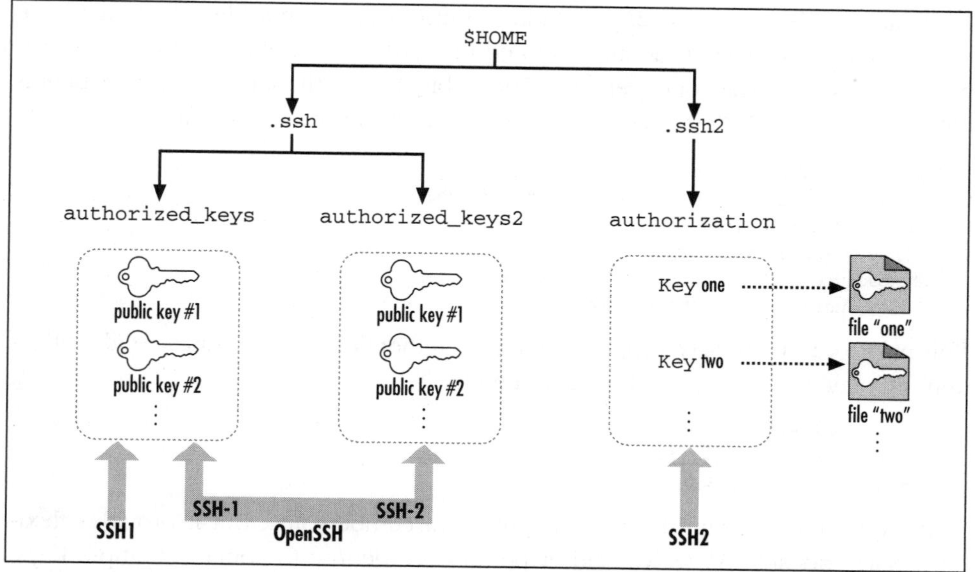

Figure 6-3. SSH authorization files (public keys) and the programs that use them

6.1.1. SSH1 Identities

An SSH1 identity is stored in two files. By default in SSH1, the private key is stored in the file *identity* and the public key in *identity.pub*. This key pair, which is kept in your *~/.ssh* directory, is your default identity clients use unless told otherwise.

The *.pub* file containing your public key has no function by itself. Before it can be used for authentication, this public key must be copied into an authorization file on an SSH-1 server machine, such as *~/.ssh/authorized_keys* for SSH1 or OpenSSH. Thereafter, when an SSH-1 client requests a connection to your server account using a private key as proof of identity, the SSH1 server consults your *authorized_keys* file to find the matching public key. [3.4.2.2]

6.1.2. SSH2 Identities

An SSH2 key pair, like its SSH1 ancestor, is stored in two files with the same relationship between their names (i.e., the private key filename plus *.pub* yields the public key filename). SSH2 key files are often named based on the key's cryptographic properties. For example, a 1024-bit, DSA-encrypted key is generated by default in the SSH2 files *id_dsa_1024_a* and *id_dsa_1024_a.pub*.

Unlike SSH1, however, an SSH2 identity is not a single key but a *collection* of keys. When an SSH2 client tries to authenticate, it may use all keys in the collection. If the first key fails to authenticate, the SSH2 client automatically tries the second, and so forth, until it succeeds or fails completely.

To create an identity in SSH2, private keys must be listed in a file called an *identification file*. Your default identity is stored in *~/.ssh2/identification*.* Inside the file, private keys are listed one per line. For public-key authentication, a line begins with the keyword **IdKey**, followed by the name of the private key file:

```
# SSH2 identification file
# The following names are relative to ~/.ssh2
IdKey id_dsa_1024_a
IdKey my-other-ssh2-key
# Absolute paths work for SSH2 2.1.0 and later
IdKey /usr/local/etc/third-key
```

You may recall that SSH2 supports PGP key authentication. [5.5.1.6] The identification file may also contain PGP-related keywords:

```
# SSH2 identification file
PgpSecretKeyFile my-file.pgp
IdPgpKeyName my-key-name
```

Using a separate identification file might seem cumbersome, but it provides flexibility SSH1 doesn't. As we've said, it permits an identity to contain multiple keys, any one of which may authenticate you. Another advantage of the SSH2 system is ease of deletion. To remove an SSH2 private key from consideration, simply delete or comment out its line from the identification file. To accomplish the same task with SSH1, you have to rename the private key file.

Like SSH1, SSH2 has an authorization file for incoming connections but with a difference. Instead of containing copies of public keys, the SSH2 authorization file merely lists the public key files using the **Key** keyword:

```
# SSH2 authorization file
Key id_dsa_1024_a.pub
Key something-else.pub
```

This is easier to maintain than SSH1's *authorized_keys* file because only one copy of each public key exists. For SSH1 and OpenSSH, in contrast, there are separate copies in the *.pub* and *authorized_keys* files. [8.2.2]

6.1.3. OpenSSH Identities

For SSH-1 connections, OpenSSH uses exactly the same identity and authorization files as SSH1. For SSH-2 connections, your default identity is stored in the file *~/.ssh/id_dsa* (private key) and *~/.ssh/id_dsa.pub* (public key). The SSH-2 authorization file for OpenSSH is *~/.ssh/authorized_keys2*, and its format is similar to that of *~/.ssh/authorized_keys*. [8.2.1]

* This default may be changed with the `IdentityFile` keyword. [7.4.2]

6.2. Creating an Identity

Most SSH implementations include a program for creating key pairs. We will cover *ssh-keygen* from SSH1, SSH2, and OpenSSH.

6.2.1. Generating RSA Keys for SSH1

SSH1 and its derivatives use the program *ssh-keygen1* to create key pairs. [2.4.2] The program might also be called *ssh-keygen*, depending on how SSH1 was installed. Let's go into more detail about this program than we have before. Appendix B summarizes the *ssh-keygen* options.

ssh-keygen1 can create new keys or modify existing keys. When creating a new key, you may indicate the following with command-line options:

- The number of bits in the key, using *–b*. The default is 1024 bits.

  ```
  $ ssh-keygen1 -b 2048
  ```

- The name of the private key file to be generated, using *–f*. The name is relative to your current directory. Recall that the public key file is named after the private one with *.pub* appended. If you omit this option, you are prompted for the information.

  ```
  $ ssh-keygen1 -f mykey          Creates mykey and mykey.pub
  $ ssh-keygen1
  Enter file in which to save the key (/home/barrett/.ssh/identity): mykey
  ```

- The passphrase to decode the key, using *–N*. If you omit this option, you'll be prompted after generation.

  ```
  $ ssh-keygen1 -N secretword
  $ ssh-keygen1
  Enter passphrase:                   [nothing is echoed]
  Enter the same passphrase again:    [nothing is echoed]
  ```

- A textual comment associated with the key, using *–C*. If you omit this option, the comment will be "username@host", where username is your username on the local machine and host is the fully qualified domain name of the local machine:

  ```
  $ ssh-keygen1 -C "my favorite key"
  ```

If you specify both *–f* (specify output file) and *–N* (specify password), *ssh-keygen1* issues no prompts. Therefore, you can automate key generation using these options (and perhaps redirecting output to */dev/null)*:

```
$ ssh-keygen1 -f mykey -N secretword
```

You might use this technique to automate generation of a large number of keys for some purpose. Use it carefully, though, on a secure machine. The password on the command line is probably visible to other users on the same Unix machine via *ps* or similar programs, and if you're scripting with this technique, obviously the passphrases shouldn't be kept in files for long.

In addition to creating keys, *ssh-keygen1* can modify existing keys in the following ways:

- By changing the passphrase of an existing key, using *–p*. You can specify the filename with *-f* and the old and new passphrases with *–P* and *–N*, respectively:

  ```
  $ ssh-keygen1 -p -f mykey -P secretword -N newword
  ```

  but if you omit them, you are prompted:

  ```
  $ ssh-keygen1 -p
  Enter file key is in (/home/barrett/.ssh/identity): mykey
  Enter old passphrase: [nothing is echoed]
  Key has comment 'my favorite key'
  Enter new passphrase: [nothing is echoed]
  Enter the same passphrase again:
  ```

  Note that this changes the passphrase but doesn't change the key, it just re-encrypts the key with the new passphrase. So, the corresponding public key file doesn't change or need to be replaced on the SSH server machines to which you've copied it.

Before using any option that places your passphrase on the shell command line, such as *–N* or *–P*, carefully consider the security implications. Because the passphrase appears on your screen, it may be visible to onlookers, and while running, it may be visible in the machine's process list. Because it is on the command line, it is visible to other users on the same host using the *ps* command. In addition, if your shell creates history files of the commands you type, the passphrase is inserted into a history file where it can be read by a third party.

Also, if you think have a good reason to just type `Return` and give your key no passphrase, think again. Doing that is essentially equivalent to putting your password in a file in your home directory named *MY-PASSWORD.PLEASE-STEAL-ME*. If you don't want to have to type a passphrase, the right thing to do is to use *ssh-agent*, trusted-host authentication, or Kerberos. There are very limited circumstances having to do with unattended usage (e.g., *cron* jobs) where a plaintext, passphrase-less client key might be acceptable. [11.1]

- By changing the comment of an existing key, using *–c*. You may specify the filename, passphrase, and new comment with *–f*, *–P*, and *–C*, respectively, or you are prompted for them:

```
$ ssh-keygen -c -f mykey -P secretword -C "my second-favorite key"
$ ssh-keygen -c
Enter file key is in (/home/barrett/.ssh/identity): mykey
Enter passphrase: [nothing is echoed]
Key now has comment 'my favorite key'
Enter new comment: my second-favorite key
The comment in your key file has been changed.
```

- By upgrading an old SSH1 key to work with the current version of SSH1, with *-u*. Older versions of SSH1 used the IDEA algorithm to encrypt a key with its passphrase, but nowadays SSH1 uses 3DES for this purpose, rendering these older keys unusable. The *-u* option causes *ssh-keygen1* to decrypt the key and reencrypt it with SSH1's default algorithm (normally 3DES) to use with the current version of SSH1:

```
$ ssh-keygen1 -u -f mykey -P secretword
$ ssh-keygen1 -u
Enter file key is in (/home/barrett/.ssh/identity): mykey
Enter passphrase: [nothing is echoed]
Key's cipher has been updated.
```

When you make changes to a key, such as its passphrase or comment, the changes are applied to the key file only. If you have keys loaded into an SSH agent, the copies in the agents aren't changed. For instance, if you list the keys in the agent with *ssh-add1 -l* (lowercase L) after changing the comment, you still see the old comment in the agent. To make the changes take effect in the agent, unload and reload the affected keys.

6.2.2. Generating RSA/DSA Keys for SSH2

SSH2 and its derivatives use the cleverly named program *ssh-keygen2* to create key pairs. The program might also be called *ssh-keygen*, depending on how SSH2 was installed. As with *ssh-keygen1*, you can create new keys or modify existing ones; however, the command-line options are significantly different. *ssh-keygen2* also has a few other options for printing diagnostics.

When creating a new key, you may choose the name of the private key file to be generated, by specifying the name at the end of the command line:

```
$ ssh-keygen2 mykey          creates mykey and mykey.pub
```

The name is relative to your current directory, and as usual, the public key file is named after the private one with *.pub* appended. If you omit this option, the key is saved in the directory *~/.ssh2*, in a file whose name indicates the encryption algorithm and number of bits. An example is *id_dsa_1024_a*, which was generated by the DSA algorithm with 1024 bits.

You also may indicate the following with command-line options:

- The number of bits in the key, using *–b*. The default is 1024 bits.

  ```
  $ ssh-keygen2 -b 2048
  ```

- The key type, such as DSA or RSA, using *–t*. The default—and only option—for SSH2 is DSA (given as "dsa"):*

  ```
  $ ssh-keygen2 -t dsa
  ```

- A textual comment associated with the key, using *–c*:

  ```
  $ ssh-keygen2 -c "my favorite SSH2 key"
  ```

  If you omit this option, the generated comment describes how and by whom the key was generated. For example:

  ```
  "1024-bit dsa, barrett@server.example.com, Tue Feb 22 2000 02:03:36"
  ```

- The passphrase to decode the key, using *–p*. If you omit this option, you are prompted after generation.

  ```
  $ ssh-keygen2 -p secretword
  ```

  You can also designate an empty password using *–P*. This shouldn't be done in general but is appropriate in some special cases. [11.1.2.2]

  ```
  $ ssh-keygen2 -P
  ```

In addition to creating keys, *ssh-keygen2* can operate on existing keys in the following ways:

- By changing the passphrase and comment of an existing key, using *–e*. This option causes *ssh-keygen2* to become interactive, prompting for the new information. This interactive mode is primitive and annoying, requiring nearly 10 user responses to change the passphrase and comment, but it does the job:

  ```
  $ ssh-keygen2 -e mykey
  Passphrase needed for key "my favorite SSH2 key"
  Passphrase : [nothing is echoed]
  Do you want to edit key "my favorite SSH2 key" (yes or no)? yes
  Your key comment is "my favorite SSH2 key".
   Do you want to edit it (yes or no)? yes
  New key comment: this is tedious
  Do you want to edit passphrase (yes or no)? yes
  New passphrase : [nothing is echoed]
  Again          : [nothing is echoed]
  Do you want to continue editing key "this is tedious" (yes or no)? god no
  (yes or no)? no
  Do you want to save key "this is tedious" to file mykey (yes or no)? yes
  ```

  As with *ssh-keygen1*, changes are applied to the key files but not propagated to the copies currently loaded in an agent. (So if you do an *ssh-add2 –l* to list the keys, for example, you see the old comment.)

---

* F-Secure SSH2 Server adds support for RSA (argument "rsa") but only in a limited sense. [3.9]

- By printing the public key, deriving it from the private key, with *-D*, in case you ever lose your private key file:

```
$ ssh-keygen2 -D mykeyfile
Passphrase : ********
Public key saved to mykeyfile.pub
```

- By converting an SSH-1 format key to SSH-2 format, using *-1* (that's the digit "one", not a lowercase L). This isn't currently implemented.

```
$ ssh-keygen2 -1 ssh1key
```

ssh-keygen2 also gives you some control over input, output and diagnostics:

- By printing the *fingerprint* of a given key file, with *-F*. See the sidebar "Key Fingerprints" for more information. The fingerprint can be calculated from the public key:

```
# SSH2 only
$ ssh-keygen2 -F stevekey.pub
Fingerprint for key:
xitot-larit-gumet-fyfim-sozev-vyned-cigeb-sariv-tekuk-badus-bexax
```

- By printing the program version number, with *-V*:

```
$ ssh-keygen2 -V
ssh2: SSH Secure Shell 2.1.0 (noncommercial version)
```

- By printing a help message, with *-h* or *-?*. Most Unix shells require you to escape the question mark, to prevent the shell from interpreting it as a wildcard.

```
$ ssh-keygen2 -h
$ ssh-keygen2 -\?        Escaping the question mark
```

- By suppressing the progress indicator, using *-q*. The progress indicator is a sequence of O's and periods that displays while *ssh-keygen2* runs, like this: .oOo.oOo.oOo.oOo.

```
$ ssh-keygen2
Generating 1024-bit dsa key pair
.oOo.oOo.oOo.oOo
Key generated.

$ ssh-keygen2 -q
Generating 1024-bit dsa key pair
Key generated.
```

- By displaying information about an existing key, using *-i*:

```
$ ssh-keygen2 -i mykey
```

  This isn't currently implemented.

Finally, *ssh-keygen2* has one guru-level advanced option, *-r*, for affecting the random numbers used for key generation. It causes *ssh-keygen2* to modify *~/.ssh2/random_seed* using data you enter on standard input. [3.7] The SSH2 manpages call this "stirring data into the random pool." Note that the program doesn't prompt you to enter data; it just sits there looking like it's hung. When this occurs, type as much data as you like and press the EOF character (`Control-D` in most shells).

```
$ ssh-keygen2 -r
I am stirring the random pool.
blah blah blah
^D
Stirred in 46 bytes.
```

6.2.3. Generating RSA/DSA Keys for OpenSSH

OpenSSH's *ssh-keygen* program supports all the same features and options of its SSH1 counterpart. It also adds the capability to generate DSA keys for SSH-2 connections and a few more options:

- *–d* generates a DSA key instead of an RSA key:

  ```
  # OpenSSH only
  $ ssh-keygen -d
  ```

- *–x*, *–X*, and *–y* convert between SSH2 and OpenSSH key-storage formats. The following table illustrates this:

Option	Extract/Convert from...	To...
–x	OpenSSH DSA private key file	SSH2 public key
–X	SSH2 public key file	OpenSSH DSA public key
–y	OpenSSH DSA private key file	OpenSSH DSA public key

  An OpenSSH "private" key file actually contains both the public and private keys of a pair, so the *–x* and *–y* options simply extract the public key and print it out in the desired format. Use *–x* to add an OpenSSH public key to your *~/.ssh2/authorization* file on an SSH2 server host and *–X* to do the opposite. The *–y* option is useful if you accidentally delete your OpenSSH public key file and need to restore it.

  A function that's missing is converting the *private* keys as well. This is useful if you have an OpenSSH server host on which you also want to also run SSH2, and you want the two SSH servers to share a host key.

- *–l* prints the *fingerprint* of a given key file. See the sidebar "Key Fingerprints" for more information. The fingerprint can be calculated from the public key:

  ```
  # OpenSSH only
  $ ssh-keygen -l -f stevekey.pub
  1024 5c:f6:e2:15:39:14:1a:8b:4c:93:44:57:6b:c6:f4:17 steve@sshbook.com
  ```

Key Fingerprints

Fingerprints are a common cryptographic feature for checking that two keys in different places are the same, when comparing them literally—bit by bit—is infeasible. OpenSSH and SSH2 can compute fingerprints.

Suppose Steve wants SSH access to Judy's account. He sends his public key to Judy by email, and she installs it in her SSH authorization file. While this key exchange seems straightforward, it is insecure: a hostile third party could intercept Steve's key and substitute his own, gaining access to Judy's account.

To prevent this risk, Judy needs some way to verify that the key she receives is Steve's. She could call Steve on the telephone and check, but reading a 500-byte encrypted public key over the phone is annoying and error-prone. This is why fingerprints exist.

A fingerprint is a short value computed from a key. It's analogous to a checksum, verifying that a string of data is unaltered—in our case, a key. To check the validity of a key using fingerprints, Steve and Judy can do the following:

1. Judy receives a public key that is supposed to be Steve's, storing it in the file *stevekey.pub*.
2. Separately, Judy and Steve view the fingerprint of the key:

   ```
   # OpenSSH only
   $ ssh-add -l stevekey.pub
   1024 5c:f6:e2:15:39:14:1a:8b:4c:93:44:57:6b:c6:f4:17 Steve@sshbook.com

   # SSH2 only
   $ ssh-keygen2 -F stevekey.pub
   Fingerprint for key:
   xitot-larit-gumet-fyfim-sozev-vyned-cigeb-sariv-tekuk-badus-bexax
   ```

3. Judy calls Steve on the telephone and asks him to read the fingerprint over the phone. Judy verifies that it matches the fingerprint of the key she received. Fingerprints aren't unique, but for any two keys, the probability that their fingerprints are identical is small. Therefore, keys are a quick and convenient method for checking that a key is unaltered.

As you can see, OpenSSH and SSH2 use different output formats for fingerprints. OpenSSH's numeric format is more traditional and should be familiar to users of PGP. SSH2 uses a textual format called "Bubble Babble" which is claimed to be easier to read and remember.

Fingerprints also surface when you connect to an SSH server whose host key has changed. In this case, OpenSSH prints a warning message and the fingerprint of the new key, which may be conveniently compared with the fingerprint of the real host key, should you have it.

- *-R* detects whether OpenSSH supports RSA keys or not. Because RSA was patented technology until September 2000, a particular installation of OpenSSH may or may not include this algorithm. [3.9.1.1] If you invoke *ssh-keygen* with this option, it immediately exits with a code of 0 if RSA is supported, or 1 if it isn't.

```
# OpenSSH only, with RSA support
$ ssh-keygen -R; echo $?
0

# OpenSSH only, without RSA support
$ ssh-keygen -R; echo $?
1
```

6.2.4. Selecting a Passphrase

Choose your passphrases carefully. Make them at least 10 characters long, containing a mix of uppercase and lowercase letters, digits, and nonalphanumeric symbols. At the same time, you want the passphrase to be easy to remember, but hard for others to guess. Don't use your name, username, phone number, or other easily guessed information in the passphrase. Coming up with an effective passphrase can be a chore, but the added security is worth it.

If you forget a passphrase, you are out of luck: the corresponding SSH private key becomes unusable because you can't decrypt it. The same encryption that makes SSH so secure also makes passphrases impossible to recover. You have to abandon your SSH key, generate a new one, and choose a new passphrase for it. You must also install the new public key on every machine that had your original.

6.3. SSH Agents

An SSH agent is a program that caches private keys and responds to authentication-related queries from SSH clients. [2.5] They are terrific labor-saving devices, handling all key-related operations and eliminating the need to retype your passphrase.

The programs related to agents are *ssh-agent* and *ssh-add*. *ssh-agent* runs an agent, and *ssh-add* inserts and removes keys from the agent's key cache. A typical use might look like this:

```
# Start the agent
$ ssh-agent $SHELL
# Load your default identity
$ ssh-add
Need passphrase for /home/barrett/.ssh/identity (barrett@example.com).
Enter passphrase: ********
```

By typing your passphrase a single time, you decrypt the private key which is then stored in memory by the agent. From now on, until you terminate the agent or log out, SSH clients automatically contact the agent for all key-related operations. You needn't type your passphrase again.

We now briefly discuss how agents work. After that we get practical and illustrate the two ways to start an agent, various configuration options, and several techniques for automatically loading your keys into the agent. Finally, we cover agent security, agent forwarding, and compatibility between SSH-1 and SSH-2 agents.

6.3.1. Agents Don't Expose Keys

Agents perform two tasks:

- Store your private keys in memory
- Answer questions (from SSH clients) about those keys

Agents don't, however, send your private keys anywhere. This is important to understand. Once loaded, private keys remain within an agent, unseen by SSH clients. To access a key, a client says, "Hey agent! I need your help. Please perform a key-related operation for me." The agent obeys and sends the results to the client (see Figure 6-4).

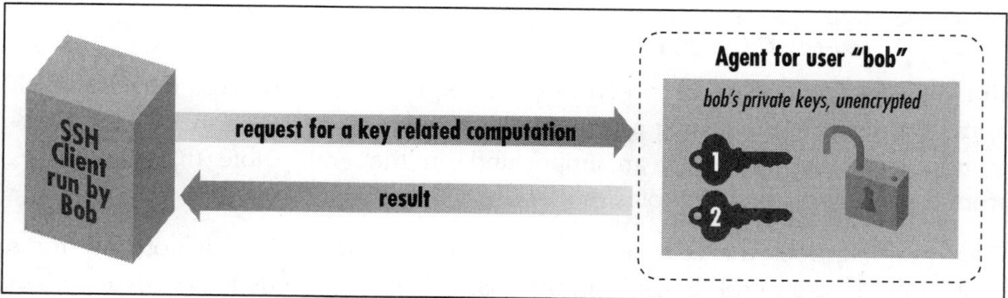

Figure 6-4. How an SSH agent works with its clients

For example, if *ssh* needs to sign an authenticator, it sends the agent a signing request containing the authenticator data and an indication of which key to use. The agent performs the cryptographic operation itself and returns the signature.

In this manner, SSH clients use the agent without ever seeing the agent's private keys. This technique is more secure than handing out keys to clients. The fewer places that private keys get stored or sent, the harder it is to steal them.*

* This design also fits well with *token-based key storage*, in which your keys are kept on a smart card carried with you. Examples are the U.S. government-standard Fortezza card or RSA Security's Keon system. Like agents, smart cards respond to key-related requests but don't give out keys, so integration with SSH would be straightforward. Though adoption of tokens has been slow, we believe it will be commonplace in the future.

6.3.2. Starting an Agent

There are two ways to invoke an agent in your login account:

- The *single-shell* method that uses your current login shell
- The *subshell* method that forks a subshell to facilitate the inheritance of some environment variables

Don't invoke an agent with the "obvious" but wrong command:

```
$ ssh-agent
```

Although the agent runs without complaint, SSH clients can't contact it, and the termination command (*ssh-agent -k*) doesn't kill it, because some environment variables aren't properly set.

6.3.2.1. Single-shell method

The single-shell method runs an agent in your current login shell. This is most convenient if you're running a login shell on a single terminal, as opposed to a Unix window system such as X. Type:

```
# SSH1, SSH2, OpenSSH
$ eval `ssh-agent`
```

and an *ssh-agent* process is forked in the background. The process detaches itself from your terminal, returning a prompt to you, so you needn't run it in the background manually (i.e., with an ampersand on the end). Note that the quotes around *ssh-agent* are backquotes, not apostrophes.

What purpose does the *eval* serve? Well, when *ssh-agent* runs, it not only forks itself in the background, it also outputs some shell commands to set several environment variables necessary for using the agent. The variables are SSH_AUTH_SOCK (for SSH1 and OpenSSH) or SSH2_AUTH_SOCK (SSH2), and SSH_AGENT_PID (SSH1, OpenSSH) or SSH2_AGENT_PID (SSH2).* The *eval* command causes the current shell to interpret the commands output by *ssh-agent*, setting the environment variables. If you omit the *eval*, these commands are printed on standard output as *ssh-agent* is invoked. For example:

* Older versions of SSH1 use SSH_AUTHENTICATION_SOCKET instead of SSH_AUTH_SOCK. If this applies to you, we recommend setting SSH_AUTH_SOCK yourself, for example (in C shell):

```
if ( "$SSH_AUTHENTICATION_SOCK" != "" ) then
  setenv SSH_AUTH_SOCK $SSH_AUTHENTICATION_SOCKET
endif
```

so your account continues to work if your SSH software is upgraded.

```
$ ssh-agent
SSH_AUTH_SOCK=/tmp/ssh-barrett/ssh-22841-agent; export SSH_AUTH_SOCK;
SSH_AGENT_PID=22842; export SSH_AGENT_PID;
echo Agent pid 22842;
```

Now you've got an agent running but inaccessible to the shell. You can either kill it using the pid printed in the previous output:

```
$ kill 22842
```

or connect your shell manually by setting the environment variables exactly as given:

```
$ SSH_AUTH_SOCK=/tmp/ssh-barrett/ssh-22841-agent; export SSH_AUTH_SOCK;
$ SSH_AGENT_PID=22842; export SSH_AGENT_PID;
```

Nevertheless, it's easier to use the single-shell form of the command so everything is set up for you.*

To terminate the agent, kill its pid:

```
# SSH1, SSH2, OpenSSH
$ kill 22842
```

and unset the environment variables:

```
$ unset SSH_AUTH_SOCK        # SSH2 uses SSH2_AUTH_SOCK instead
$ unset SSH_AGENT_PID        # SSH2 uses SSH2_AGENT_PID instead
```

Or for SSH1 and OpenSSH, use the more convenient *–k* command-line option:

```
# SSH1, OpenSSH
$ eval `ssh-agent -k`
```

This prints termination commands on standard output so the *eval* can invoke them. If you eliminate the *eval*, the agent is still killed, but your environment variables don't unset automatically:

```
# SSH1, OpenSSH
$ ssh-agent1 -k
unset SSH_AUTH_SOCK              # This won't get unset,
unset SSH_AGENT_PID              # and neither will this,
echo Agent pid 22848 killed      # but the agent gets killed.
```

Running an agent in a single shell, as opposed to the method we cover next (spawning a subshell), has one problem. When your login session ends, the *ssh-agent* process doesn't die. After several logins, you see many agents running, serving no purpose.†

* Why can't *ssh-agent* set its environment variables without all this trickery? Because under Unix, a program can't set environment variables in its parent shell.

† Actually, you can reconnect to an agent launched in a previous login by modifying your SSH_AUTH_SOCK variable to point to the old socket, but this is gross.

```
$ /usr/ucb/ps uax | grep ssh-agent
barrett   7833  0.4  0.4  828  608 pts/1    S 21:06:10  0:00 grep agent
barrett   4189  0.0  0.6 1460  844 ?        S   Feb 21  0:06 ssh-agent
barrett   6134  0.0  0.6 1448  828 ?        S 23:11:41  0:00 ssh-agent
barrett   6167  0.0  0.6 1448  828 ?        S 23:24:19  0:00 ssh-agent
barrett   7719  0.0  0.6 1456  840 ?        S 20:42:25  0:02 ssh-agent
```

You can get around this problem by running *ssh-agent –k* automatically when you log out. In Bourne style shells (*sh*, *ksh*, *bash*), this may be done with a trap of Unix signal 0 at the top of *~/.profile*:

```
# ~/.profile
trap '
  test -n "$SSH_AGENT_PID"  && eval `ssh-agent1 -k` ;
  test -n "$SSH2_AGENT_PID" && kill $SSH2_AGENT_PID
' 0
```

For C shell and *tcsh*, terminate the agent in your *~/.logout* file:

```
# ~/.logout
if ( "$SSH_AGENT_PID" != "" ) then
  eval `ssh-agent -k`
endif
if ( "$SSH2_AGENT_PID" != "" ) then
  kill $SSH2_AGENT_PID
endif
```

Once this trap is set, your *ssh-agent* process is killed automatically when you log out, printing a message like:

```
Agent pid 8090 killed
```

6.3.2.2. Subshell method

The second way to invoke an agent spawns a *subshell*. You provide an argument to *ssh-agent*, which is a path to a shell or shell script. Examples are:

```
$ ssh-agent /bin/sh
$ ssh-agent /bin/csh
$ ssh-agent $SHELL
$ ssh-agent my-shell-script          # Run a shell script instead of a shell
```

This time, instead of forking a background process, *ssh-agent* runs in the foreground, spawning a subshell and setting the aforementioned environment variables automatically. The rest of your login session runs within this subshell, and when you terminate it, *ssh-agent* terminates as well. This method, as you will see later, is most convenient if you run a window system such as X and invoke the agent in your initialization file (e.g., *~/.xsession*). However, the method is also perfectly reasonable for single-terminal logins.

When using the subshell method, invoke it at an appropriate time. We recommend the last line of your login initialization file (e.g., *~/.profile* or *~/.login*) or the first typed command after you log in. Otherwise, if you first run some background processes in your shell, and then invoke the agent, those initial background processes become inaccessible until you terminate the agent's subshell. For example, if you run the *vi* editor, suspend it, and then run the agent, you lose access to the editor session until you terminate the agent.

```
$ vi myfile                          # Run your editor
^Z                                   # Suspend it
$ jobs                               # View your background processes
[1] + Stopped (SIGTSTP) vi
$ ssh-agent $SHELL                   # Run a subshell
$ jobs                               # No jobs here! They're in the parent shell
$ exit                               # Terminate the agent's subshell
$ jobs                               # Now we can see our processes again
[1] + Stopped (SIGTSTP) vi
```

The advantages and disadvantages of the two methods are shown in Table 6-1.

Table 6-1. Pros and Cons of Invoking an Agent

Method	Pros	Cons
eval `ssh-agent`	Simple, intuitive	Must be terminated manually
ssh-agent $SHELL	Agent's environment variables are propagated automatically; terminates on logout	Your login shell becomes dependent on the agent's health; if the agent dies, your login shell may die

6.3.2.3. Format of environment variable commands

As we've said, *ssh-agent* prints a sequence of shell commands to set several environment variables. The syntax of these commands differs depending on which shell is being used. You can force the commands to use Bourne-style or C shell-style syntax with the *–s* and *–c* options, respectively:

```
# Bourne-shell style commands
$ ssh-agent -s
SSH_AUTH_SOCK=/tmp/ssh-barrett/ssh-3654-agent; export SSH_AUTH_SOCK;
SSH_AGENT_PID=3655; export SSH_AGENT_PID;
echo Agent pid 3655;

# C-shell style commands
$ ssh-agent -c
setenv SSH_AUTH_SOCK /tmp/ssh-barrett/ssh-3654-agent;
setenv SSH_AGENT_PID 3655;
echo Agent pid 3655;
```

Normally *ssh-agent* detects your login shell and prints the appropriate lines, so you don't need *–c* or *–s*. One situation where you need these options is if you invoke *ssh-agent* within a shell script, but the script's shell is not the same type as your login shell. For example, if your login shell is */bin/csh*, and you invoke this script:

```
#!/bin/sh
`ssh-agent`
```

ssh-agent outputs C shell-style commands, which will fail. So you should use:

```
#!/bin/sh
`ssh-agent -s`
```

This is particularly important if you run an agent under X, and your *~/.xsession* file (or other startup file) is executed by a shell different from your login shell.

6.3.2.4. SSH-1 and SSH-2 agent compatibility

An SSH-1 agent can't service requests from SSH-2 clients. The reverse, however, is supported by SSH2. If *ssh-agent2* is invoked with the *–1* option (that's a numeral one, not a lowercase L), the agent services requests from SSH-1 clients, even from *ssh-add1*. This works only for SSH-2 implementations that support RSA, because SSH-1 uses RSA keys. At press time, only F-Secure SSH2 Server is capable of SSH-1 agent compatibility.

```
# Invoke an SSH2 agent in SSH1 compatibility mode
$ eval `ssh-agent2 -1`

# Add an SSH1 key
$ ssh-add1
Need passphrase for /home/smith/.ssh/identity (smith SSH1 key).
Enter passphrase: ****
Identity added (smith SSH1 key).

# Add an SSH2 key
$ ssh-add2
Adding identity: /home/smith/.ssh2/id_dsa_1024_a.pub
Need passphrase for /home/smith/.ssh2/id_dsa_1024_a
 (1024-bit dsa, smith SSH2 key, Thu Dec 02 1999 22:25:09-0500).
Enter passphrase: ********

# ssh-add1 lists only the SSH1 key
$ ssh-add1 -l
1024 37 1425047358166328978851045774063877571270... and so forth

# ssh-add2 lists both keys
# F-Secure SSH Server only
$ ssh-add2 -l
Listing identities.
The authorization agent has 2 keys:
id_dsa_1024_a: 1024-bit dsa, smith SSH2 key, Thu Dec 02 1999 22:25:09-0500
smith SSH1 key
```

Now an SSH-1 client contacts *ssh-agent2* transparently, believing it to be an SSH-1 agent:

```
$ ssh1 server.example.com
[no passphrase prompt appears]
```

ssh-agent2 achieves compatibility by setting the same environment variables normally set by *ssh-agent1*: SSH_AUTH_SOCK and SSH_AGENT_PID. Therefore, any SSH-1 agent requests are directed to *ssh-agent2*.

If you have an *ssh-agent1* process running, and you invoke *ssh-agent2 -1*, your old *ssh-agent1* process becomes inaccessible as *ssh-agent2* overwrites its environment variables.

Agent compatibility works only if the SSH2 distribution is compiled with the flag `--with-ssh-agent1-compat`. [4.1.5.13] It also depends on the value of the client configuration keyword `Ssh1AgentCompatibility`. [7.4.14]

6.3.3. Loading Keys with ssh-add

The program *ssh-add* is your personal communication channel to an *ssh-agent* process. (Again, this command may be *ssh-add1* under SSH1 and *ssh-add2* under SSH2, with *ssh-add* a link to one program or the other.)

When you first invoke an SSH agent, it contains no keys. *ssh-add*, as you might guess from its name, can add private keys to an SSH agent. But the name is misleading, because it also controls the agent in other ways, such as listing keys, deleting keys, and locking the agent from accepting further keys.

If you invoke *ssh-add* with no arguments, your default SSH key is loaded into the agent, once you have typed its passphrase. For example:

```
$ ssh-add1
Need passphrase for /home/smith/.ssh/identity (smith@client).
Enter passphrase: ********
Identity added: /home/smith/.ssh/identity (smith@client).

$ ssh-add2
Adding identity: /home/smith/.ssh2/id_dsa_1024_a.pub
Need passphrase for /home/smith/.ssh2/id_dsa_1024_a
 (1024-bit dsa, smith@client, Thu Dec 02 1999 22:25:09-0500).
Enter passphrase: ********
```

Normally, *ssh-add* reads the passphrase from the user's terminal. If the standard input isn't a terminal, however, and the DISPLAY environment variable is set, *ssh-add* instead invokes an X window graphical program called *ssh-askpass* that pops up a window to read your passphrase. This is especially convenient in *xdm* start-up scripts.*

* X has its own security problems, of course. If someone can connect to your X server, they can monitor all your keystrokes, including your passphrase. Whether this is an issue in using *ssh-askpass* depends on your system and security needs.

Both *ssh-add1* and *ssh-add2* support the following command-line options for listing and deleting keys, and for reading the passphrase:

- List all identities loaded in the agent, with *–l*:

```
$ ssh-add1 -l
1024 35 1604921766775161379181745950571099412502846... and so forth
1024 37 1236194621955474376584658921922152150472844... and so forth

$ ssh-add2 -l
Listing identities.
The authorization agent has one key:
id_dsa_1024_a: 1024-bit dsa, smith@client, Thu Dec 02 1999 22:25:09-0500
```

  For OpenSSH, the *–l* option operates differently, printing the key's fingerprint rather than the public key (see the earlier sidebar "Key Fingerprints" for more detail):

```
# OpenSSH only
$ ssh-add -l
1024 1c:3d:cc:1a:db:74:f8:e6:46:6f:55:57:9e:ec:d5:fc smith@client
```

  To print the public key with OpenSSH, use *–L* instead:

```
# OpenSSH only
$ ssh-add -L
1024 35 1604921766775161379181745950571099412502846... and so forth
1024 37 1236194621955474376584658921922152150472844... and so forth
```

- Delete an identity from the agent, with *–d*:

```
$ ssh-add -d ~/.ssh/second_id
Identity removed: /home/smith/.ssh/second_id (my alternative key)

$ ssh-add2 -d ~/.ssh2/id_dsa_1024_a
Deleting identity: id_dsa_1024_a.pub
```

  If you don't specify a key file, *ssh-add1* deletes your default identity from the agent:

```
$ ssh-add -d
Identity removed: /home/smith/.ssh/identity (smith@client)
```

  ssh-add2, on the other hand, requires you to specify a key file:

```
$ ssh-add2 -d
(nothing happens)
```

- Delete all identities from the agent, with *–D*. This unloads every currently loaded key but leaves the agent running:

```
$ ssh-add -D
All identities removed.

$ ssh-add2 -D
Deleting all identities.
```

- Read the passphrase from standard input, with *–p*, as opposed to reading directly from your tty. This is useful if you want to send your passphrase to *ssh-add* in a program, as in this Perl fragment:

```
open(SSHADD,"|ssh-add -p") || die "can't start ssh-add";
print SSHADD $passphrase;
close(SSHADD);
```

In addition, *ssh-add2* has further features controlled by command-line options:

- Lock and unlock the agent with a password using *–L* and *–U*. A locked agent refuses all *ssh-add2* operations except an unlock request. Specifically:
  - If you try to modify the state of the agent (adding or deleting keys, etc.), you are told:

    ```
    The requested operation was denied.
    ```

  - If you try to list the keys in the agent, you are told:

    ```
    The authorization agent has no keys.
    ```

  To lock:

  ```
  $ ssh-add2 -L
  Enter lock password: ****
  Again: ****
  ```

  and to unlock:

  ```
  $ ssh-add2 -U
  Enter lock password: ****
  ```

  Locking is a convenient way to protect the agent if you step away from your computer but leave yourself logged in. You can unload all your keys with *ssh-add –D*, but then you'd have to reload them again when you return. If you have only one key, there's no difference, but if you use several, it's a pain. Unfortunately, the locking mechanism isn't tremendously secure. *ssh-agent2* simply stores the lock password in memory, refusing to honor any more requests until it receives an unlock message containing the same password. The locked agent is still vulnerable to attack: if an intruder gains access to your account (or the root account), he can dump the agent's process address space and extract your keys. The lock feature certainly deters casual misuse, but the potential for an attack is real. If you're seriously concerned about key disclosure, think twice before relying on locking. We prefer to see this feature implemented by encrypting all the agent's loaded keys with the lock password. This gives the same user convenience and provides better protection.

- Set a timeout on a key, with *–t*. Normally when you add a key, it remains loaded in the agent indefinitely, until the agent terminates or you unload the key manually. The *-t* option indicates the lifetime of a key, measured in minutes. After this time has passed, the agent automatically unloads the key.

```
# Unload this key after 30 minutes
$ ssh-add2 -t 30 mykey
```

- Place limits on agent forwarding with *-f* and *-F*. (Agent forwarding, which we'll cover soon, transmits agent requests between hosts.) The *-f* option lets you limit, for a given key, the distance that requests for this key may traverse. If a request is made from too far away, measured in hops from machine to machine, the request fails. A hop count of zero disables forwarding for this key alone:

```
# Load a key that may be used only  locally
$ ssh-agent2 -f 0 mykey

# Load a key and accept requests from up to 3 hops away
$ ssh-agent2 -f 3 mykey
```

The *-F* option lets you limit the set of hosts that may make requests relating to this key. It takes as an argument a set of hostnames, domains, and IP addresses that may make or forward requests. The argument is a comma-separated list of wildcard patterns, as for the serverwide configuration keywords `AllowHosts` and `DenyHosts`. [5.5.2.3]

```
# Permit request forwarding for a key only in the example.com domain
$ ssh-agent2 -F '*.example.com' mykey

# Permit forwarding from server.example.com and the harvard.edu domain
$ ssh-agent2 -F 'server.example.com,*.harvard.edu' mykey

# Same as the preceding command, but limit forwarding to 2 hops
$ ssh-agent2 -F 'server.example.com,*.harvard.edu' -f 2 mykey
```

SSH1 agents don't support this feature. If you use an SSH2 agent in SSH1 compatibility mode, these forwarding features won't necessarily work.

- Make the given key invisible to SSH-1 client requests if *ssh-agent2* is running in SSH1 compatibility mode, with *-1* (that's a one, not a lowercase L). It must be an RSA key, since all SSH1 public keys are RSA, and the only SSH-2 implementation that supports RSA keys (at press time) is F-Secure SSH2 Server. We demonstrate this feature by example:

  a. Generate an SSH2 RSA key, `my-rsa-key`:

  ```
  $ ssh-keygen2 -t rsa my-rsa-key
  ```

  b. Run an agent in SSH1 compatibility mode:

  ```
  $ eval `ssh-agent2 -1`
  ```

c. Load the key into the agent normally:

```
$ ssh-add2 my-rsa-key
Enter passphrase: ********
```

As the agent is running in SSH1 compatibility mode, notice that the key is visible to both SSH1 clients:

```
$ ssh-add1 -l
1023 33 753030143250178784431763590... my-rsa-key ...
```

and SSH2 clients:

```
$ ssh-add2 -l
Listing identities.
The authorization agent has one key:
my-rsa-key: 1024-bit rsa, smith@client, Mon Jun 05 2000 23:37:19 -040
```

Now let's unload the key and repeat the experiment:

```
$ ssh-add2 -D
Deleting all identities.
```

This time, load the key using the *–1* option, so SSH1 clients don't see it:

```
$ ssh-add2 -1 my-rsa-key
Enter passphrase: ********
```

Notice that the key is still visible to SSH2 clients:

```
$ ssh-add2 -l
Listing identities.
The authorization agent has one key:
my-rsa-key: 1024-bit rsa, smith@client, Mon Jun 05 2000 23:37:19 -040
```

But SSH1 clients can't see it:

```
$ ssh-add1 -l
The agent has no identities.
```

- Perform PGP key operations. The *ssh-add2* manpage documents the options *–R*, *–N*, *–P*, and *–F* for OpenPGP keyring operations, but at press time they aren't implemented.

6.3.3.1. Automatic agent loading (single-shell method)

It's a pain to invoke *ssh-agent* and/or *ssh-add* manually each time you log in. With some clever lines in your login initialization file, you can automatically invoke an agent and load your default identity. We demonstrate this with both methods of agent invocation, single-shell and subshell.

With the single-shell method, here are the major steps:

1. Make sure you're not already running an agent, by testing environment variable SSH_AUTH_SOCK or SSH2_AUTH_SOCK.
2. Run the agent, *ssh-agent1* or *ssh-agent2*, using *eval*.

3. If your shell is attached to a tty, load your default identity with *ssh-add1* or *ssh-add2*.

For the Bourne shell and its derivatives (*ksh*, *bash*), the following lines can be placed into *~/.profile*:

```
# Make sure ssh-agent1 and ssh-agent2 die on logout
trap '
  test -n "$SSH_AGENT_PID"  && eval `ssh-agent1 -k` ;
  test -n "$SSH2_AGENT_PID" && kill $SSH2_AGENT_PID
' 0

# If no agent is running and we have a terminal, run ssh-agent and ssh-add.
# (For SSH2, change this to use SSH2_AUTH_SOCK, ssh-agent2 and ssh-add2.)
if [ "$SSH_AUTH_SOCK" = "" ]
then
  eval `ssh-agent`
  /usr/bin/tty > /dev/null && ssh-add
fi
```

For the C shell and *tcsh*, the following lines can be placed into *~/.login*:

```
# Use SSH2_AUTH_SOCK instead for SSH2
if ( ! $?SSH_AUTH_SOCK  ) then
  eval `ssh-agent`
  /usr/bin/tty > /dev/null && ssh-add
endif
```

and termination code in *~/.logout*:

```
# ~/.logout
if ( "$SSH_AGENT_PID" != "" ) eval `ssh-agent -k`
if ( "$SSH2_AGENT_PID" != "" ) kill $SSH2_AGENT_PID
```

6.3.3.2. Automatic agent loading (subshell method)

The second way to load an agent on login uses the subshell method to invoke the agent. This time, you need to add lines to both your login initialization file (*~/.profile* or *~/.login*), an optional second file of your choice, and your shell initialization file (*~/.cshrc*, *~/.bashrc*, etc.). This method doesn't work for the Bourne shell, which has no shell initialization file.

1. In your *login* initialization file, make sure you're not already running an agent, by testing environment variable SSH_AUTH_SOCK or SSH2_AUTH_SOCK.
2. As the last line of your login initialization file, exec *ssh-agent*, which spawns a subshell. Optionally run a *second* initialization file to configure aspects of the subshell.
3. In your *shell* initialization file, check whether the shell is attached to a tty and that the agent has no identities loaded yet. If so, load your default identity with *ssh-add1* or *ssh-add2*.

Now let's see how to do this with Bourne shell and C shell families. For derivatives of Bourne shell (*ksh*, *bash*), put the following lines at the end of *~/.profile*:

```
test -n "$SSH_AUTH_SOCK" && exec ssh-agent $SHELL
```

This runs the agent, spawning a subshell. If you want to tailor the environment of the subshell, create a script (say, *~/.profile2*) to do so, and use this instead:

```
test -n "$SSH_AUTH_SOCK" && exec ssh-agent $SHELL $HOME/.profile2
```

Next, in your shell initialization file ($ENV for *ksh*, or *~/.bashrc* for *bash*), place the following lines to load your default identity only if it's not loaded already:

```
# Make sure we are attached to a tty
if /usr/bin/tty > /dev/null
then
  # Check the output of "ssh-add -l" for identities.
  # For SSH2, use the line:
  #  ssh-add2 -l | grep 'no keys' > /dev/null
  #
  ssh-add1 -l | grep 'no identities' > /dev/null
  if [ $? -eq 0 ]
  then
    # Load your default identity.  Use ssh-add2 for SSH2.
    ssh-add1
  fi
fi
```

6.3.3.3. Automatic agent loading (X Window System)

If you're using X and want to run an agent and load your default identity automatically, it's simple. Just use the single-shell method. For example, in your X startup file, usually *~/.xsession*, you can use these two lines:

```
eval `ssh-agent`
ssh-add
```

6.3.4. Agents and Security

As we mentioned earlier, agents don't expose private keys to SSH clients. Instead, they answer requests from clients about the keys. This approach is more secure than passing keys around, but it still has some security concerns. It is important to understand these concerns before completely trusting the agent model:

- Agents rely on external access control mechanisms.
- Agents can be cracked.

6.3.4.1. Access control

When your agent is loaded with private keys, a potential security issue arises. How does your agent distinguish between legitimate requests from your SSH clients and illegitimate requests from unauthorized sources? Surprisingly, the agent does not distinguish at all. Agents don't authenticate their clients. They will respond to any well-formed request received over their IPC channel, which is a Unix domain socket.

How is agent security maintained then? The host operating system is responsible for protecting the IPC channel from unauthorized access. For Unix, this protection is accomplished by the file permissions on the socket. SSH1 and SSH2 keep your agent sockets in a protected directory, */tmp/ssh-USERNAME*, where *USENRAME* is your login name, while OpenSSH names the directory */tmp/ssh-STRING*, where `STRING` is random text based on the agent's pid. In either case, the directory is protected from all other users (mode 700) and owned by you:

```
$ ls -la /tmp/ssh-smith/
drwx------    2 smith    smith         1024 Feb 17 18:18 .
drwxrwxrwt    9 root     root          1024 Feb 17 18:01 ..
srwx------    1 smith    smith            0 May 14  1999 agent-socket-328
s-w--w--w-    1 root     root             0 Feb 14 14:30 ssh-24649-agent
srw-------    1 smith    smith            0 Dec  3 00:34 ssh2-29614-agent
```

In this case, user smith has several agent-related sockets in this directory. The two sockets owned by smith were created by agents run and owned by smith. The third, which is world-writable and owned by root, was created by the SSH server to effect an agent forwarding.* [6.3.5]

This organization of a user's sockets into a single directory is not only for neatness but also for security and portability, because different operating systems treat socket permissions in different ways. For example, Solaris appears to ignore them completely; even a socket with permission 000 (no access for anyone) accepts all connections. Linux respects socket permissions, but a write-only socket permits both reading and writing. To deal with such diverse implementations, SSH keeps your sockets in a directory owned by you, with directory permissions that forbid anyone else to access the sockets inside.

Using a subdirectory of */tmp*, rather than */tmp* itself, also prevents a class of attacks called *temp races*. A temp-race attack takes advantage of race conditions inherent in the common setting of the "sticky" mode bit on the Unix */tmp* directory, allowing anyone to create a file there, but only allowing deletion of files owned by the same uid as the deleting process.

* Even though this socket is world-writable, only user smith can access it due to the permissions on the parent directory, */tmp/ssh-smith*.

6.3.4.2. Cracking an agent

If the machine running your agent is compromised, an attacker can easily gain access to the IPC channel and thus to your agent. This permits the interloper to make requests of the agent, at least for a time. Once you log out or unload your keys from the agent, the security hole is closed. Therefore, you should run agents only on trusted machines, perhaps unloading your keys (*ssh-agent –D*) if you're away from the computer for an extended time, such as overnight.

Since agents don't give out keys, your keys would seem safe from theft if the machine is compromised. Alas, that's not the case. An enterprising cracker, once logged into the machine, has other means for getting your keys, such as:

- Stealing your private key file and attempting to guess your passphrase
- Tracing processes that you're running, and catching your passphrase while you type it
- Trojan horse attacks: installing modified versions of system programs, such as the login program, shells, or the SSH implementation itself, that steal your passphrase
- Obtaining a copy of the memory space of your running agent and picking the keys out of it directly (this is a bit harder than the others)

The bottom line is this: run agents only on trusted machines. SSH does not excuse you from securing other aspects of your system.

6.3.5. Agent Forwarding

So far, our SSH clients have conversed with an SSH agent on the same machine. Using a feature called *agent forwarding*, clients can also communicate with agents on remote machines. This is both a convenience feature—permitting your clients on multiple machines to work with a single agent—and a means for avoiding some firewall-related problems.

6.3.5.1. A firewall example

Suppose you want to connect from your home computer, H, to a computer at work, W. Like many corporate computers, W is behind a network firewall and not directly accessible from the Internet, so you can't create an SSH connection from H to W. Hmm... what can you do? You call technical support and for once, they have good news. They say that your company maintains a gateway or "bastion" host, B, that is accessible from the Internet and runs an SSH server. This means you should be able to reach W by opening an SSH connection from H to B, and then from B to W, since the firewall permits SSH traffic. Tech support gives you an account on the bastion host B, and the problem seems to be solved... or is it?

For security reasons, the company permits access to its computers only by public-key authentication. So, using your private key on home machine H, you successfully connect to bastion host B. And now you run into a roadblock: also for security reasons, the company prohibits users from storing SSH keys on the exposed bastion host B, since they can be stolen if B were hacked. That's bad news, since the SSH client on B needs a key to connect to your work account on W. Your key is at home on H. (Figure 6-5 illustrates the problem.) What now?

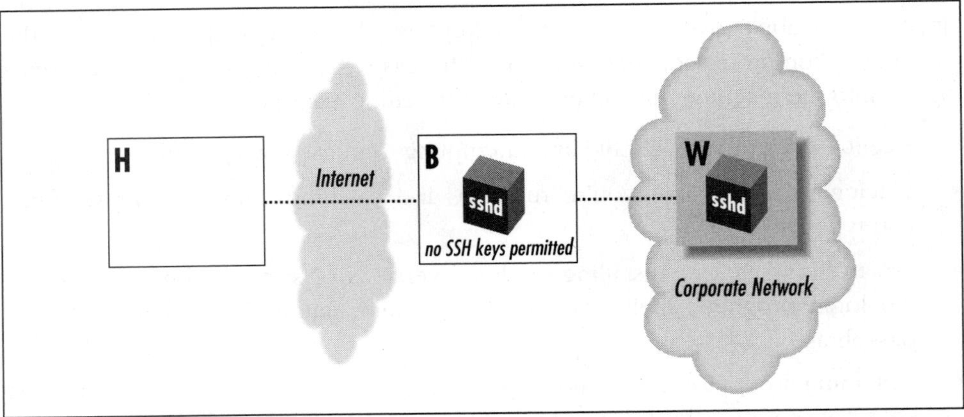

Figure 6-5. Bastion host scenario

Notice that this problem doesn't arise with *telnet* or *rsh*. You'd simply type your password to reach W (insecurely, of course).* For a solution, we turn to SSH agents and agent forwarding.

SSH agent forwarding allows a program running on a remote host, such as B, to access your *ssh-agent* on H transparently, as if the agent were running on B. Thus, a remote SSH client running on B can now sign and decrypt data using your key on H as shown in Figure 6-6. As a result, you can invoke an SSH session from B to your work machine W, solving the problem.

6.3.5.2. How agent forwarding works

Agent forwarding, like all SSH forwarding (Chapter 9), works "behind the scenes." In this case, an SSH client has its agent requests forwarded across a separate, previously established SSH session, to an agent holding the needed keys, shown in Figure 6-7. The transmission takes place over a secure SSH connection, of course. Let's examine, in detail, the steps that occur.

* This key-distribution problem can also be solved with network file-sharing protocols, such as NFS, SMB, or AFP, but these aren't usually available in the remote-access situation we're discussing.

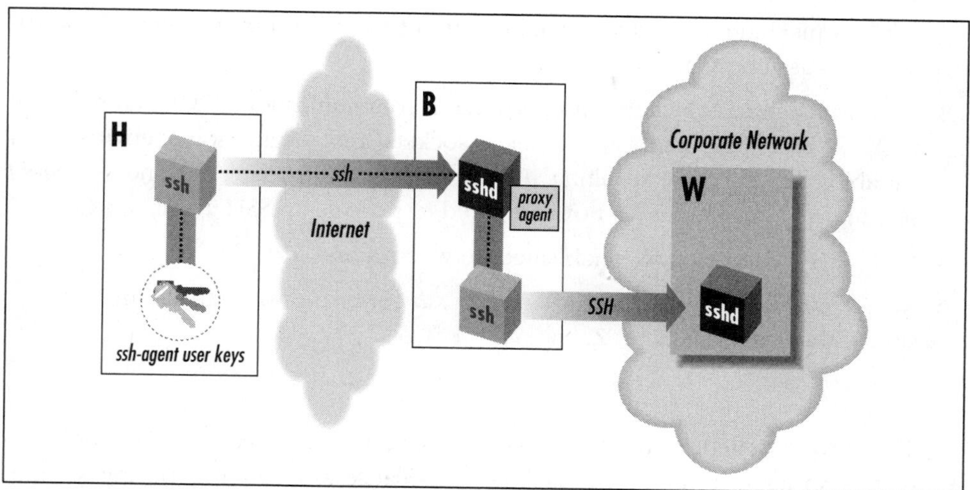

Figure 6-6. Solution with SSH agent forwarding

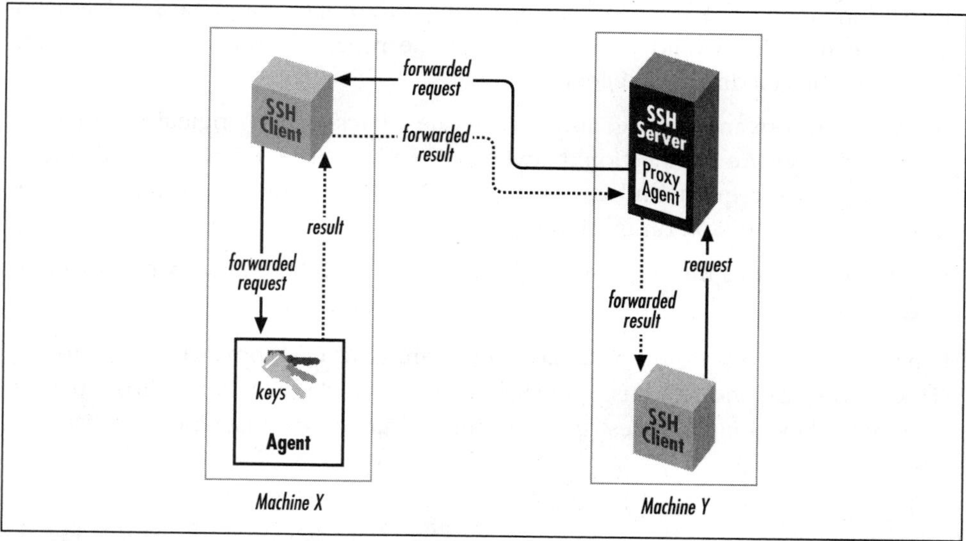

Figure 6-7. How agent forwarding works

1. Suppose you're logged onto machine X, and you invoke *ssh* to establish a remote terminal session on machine Y:

   ```
   # On machine X:
   $ ssh Y
   ```

2. Assuming that agent forwarding is turned on, the client says to the SSH server, "I would like to request agent forwarding, please," when establishing the connection.

3. *sshd* on machine Y checks its configuration to see if it permits agent forwarding. Let's assume that it's enabled.
4. *sshd* on machine Y sets up an interprocess communication (IPC) channel local to Y by creating some Unix domain sockets and setting some environment variables. [6.3.2.1] The resulting IPC mechanism is just like the one *ssh-agent* sets up. As a result, *sshd* is now prepared to pose as an SSH agent.
5. Your SSH session is now established between X and Y.
6. Next, from machine Y, you run another *ssh* command to establish an SSH session with a third machine, Z:

```
# On machine Y:
$ ssh Z
```

7. This new *ssh* client now needs a key to make the connection to Z. It believes there's an agent running on machine Y, because *sshd* on Y is posing as one. So, the client makes an authentication request over the agent IPC channel.
8. *sshd* intercepts the request, masquerading as an agent, and says, "Hello, I'm the agent. What would you like to do?" The process is transparent: the client believes it's talking to an agent.
9. *sshd* then forwards the agent-related request back to the original machine, X, over the secure connection between X and Y. The agent on machine X receives the request and accesses your local key, and its response is forwarded back to *sshd* on machine Y.
10. *sshd* on Y passes the response on to the client, and the connection to machine Z proceeds.

Thanks to agent forwarding, you have transparent access from machine Y to any SSH keys on machine X. Thus, any SSH clients on Y can access any hosts permitted by your keys on X. To test this, run this command on machine Y to list your keys:

```
# On machine Y:
$ ssh-agent -l
```

You will see all keys that are loaded in your agent on machine X.

It's worth noting that the agent-forwarding relationship is transitive: if you repeat this process, making a chain of SSH connections from machine to machine, then clients on the final host will still have access to your keys on the first host (X). (This assumes, of course, that agent forwarding is permitted by *sshd* on each intermediate host.)

6.3.5.3. Enabling agent forwarding

Before an SSH client can take advantage of agent forwarding, the feature must be turned on. SSH implementations vary in their default settings of this feature, and of course the system administrator can change it. If necessary, you can turn it on manually with the configuration keyword `ForwardAgent`* in the client configuration file *~/.ssh/config*, giving a value of `yes` (the default) or `no`:

```
# SSH1, SSH2, OpenSSH
ForwardAgent yes
```

Likewise, you can use command-line options. In addition to the *-o* command-line option, which accepts any configuration keyword and its value:

```
# SSH1, SSH2, OpenSSH
$ ssh -o "ForwardAgent yes" ...
```

The *ssh* option *-a* turns off agent forwarding:

```
# SSH1, SSH2, OpenSSH
$ ssh -a ...
```

In addition, *ssh2* and OpenSSH's *ssh* accept options to turn on agent forwarding, even though it's on by default:

```
# SSH2 only
$ ssh2 +a ...

# OpenSSH only
$ ssh -A ...
```

6.3.6. Agent CPU Usage

Before we leave our discussion of agents, we'll make one final note about performance. Agents carry out all cryptographic work that would otherwise be done by SSH clients. This means an agent can accumulate substantial CPU time. In one case we saw, some friends of ours were using SSH1 for a great deal of automation, running hundreds of short-lived SSH sessions in a row. Our friends were quite puzzled to find that the single *ssh-agent* used by all these processes was eating the lion's share of CPU on that machine.

6.4. Multiple Identities

Until now, we've assumed you have a single SSH identity that uniquely identifies you to an SSH server. You do have a default identity—our earlier *ssh-add* examples operated on it—but you may create as many other identities as you like.

---

* SSH2 supports the keyword `AllowAgentForwarding` as a synonym for `ForwardAgent`.

Why use several identities? After all, with a single SSH identity, you can connect to remote machines with a single passphrase. That's very simple and convenient. In fact, most people can survive perfectly well with just one identity. Multiple identities have important uses, however:

Additional security
: If you use different SSH keys for different remote accounts, and one of your keys is cracked, only some of your remote accounts will be vulnerable.

Secure batch processes
: Using an SSH key with an empty passphrase, you can create secure, automated processes between interacting computers, such as unattended backups. [11.1.2.2] However, you definitely don't want your regular logins to use an unencrypted private key, so you should create a second key for this purpose.

Different account settings
: You can configure your remote account to respond differently based on which key is used for connecting. For example, you can make your Unix login session run different startup files depending on which key is used.

Triggering remote programs
: Your remote account can be set up to run specific programs when an alternative key is used, via forced commands. [8.2.4]

In order to use multiple identities, you need to know how to switch between them. There are two ways: manually, and automatically with an agent.

6.4.1. Switching Identities Manually

ssh and *scp* let you switch your identity with the *–i* command-line option and the `IdentityFile` configuration keyword. For either of these techniques, you provide the name of your desired private key file (SSH1, OpenSSH) or identification file (SSH2). [7.4.2] Table 6-2 displays a summary of the syntax.

Table 6-2. Syntax Summary

Version	ssh	scp	IdentityFile Keyword
SSH1, OpenSSH	*ssh1 –i key_file ...*	*scp1 –i key_file ...*	`IdentityFile` *key_file*
SSH2	*ssh2 –i id_file ...*	*scp2 –i id_file ...*	`IdentityFile` *id_file*

6.4.2. Switching Identities with an Agent

If you use an SSH agent, identity-switching is handled automatically. Simply load all the desired identities into the agent using *ssh-add*. Thereafter, when you attempt a connection, your SSH client requests and receives a list of all your identities from the agent. The client then tries each identity in turn until one authenticates successfully, or they all fail. Even if you have 10 different identities for 10 different SSH servers, a single agent (containing these keys) provides appropriate key information to your SSH clients for seamless authentication with all 10 servers.

All this happens transparently with no effort on your part. Well, almost no effort. There are two potential problems that can strike if you have two SSH identities that can connect to the same SSH server.

The first problem occurs because the agent stores identities in the order in which it receives them from *ssh-add*. As we've said, the SSH client tries identities "in turn," i.e., in the order it gets them from the agent. Therefore, it is your responsibility to add identities to the agent in a careful, useful order. Otherwise, if two or more identities apply in a situation, an SSH client might authenticate with the wrong one.

For example, suppose you have two SSH1 identities stored in the files *id-normal* and *id-backups*. You use *id-normal* for normal terminal sessions to *server.example.com* and *id-backups* for invoking a remote backup program on *server.example.com* (e.g., using a forced command [8.2.4]). Each day when you log in, you load both keys into an agent, using a clever script that locates and loads all key files in a given directory:

```
#!/bin/csh
cd ~/.ssh/my-keys              # An example directory
foreach keyfile (*)
  ssh-add $keyfile
end
```

What happens when you invoke an SSH client?

```
$ ssh server.example.com
```

In this case, the remote backup program gets run, authenticating with the key in file *id-backups*. You see, the wildcard in your script returns a list of key files in alphabetical order, so *id-backups* is added before *id-normal*, as if you'd typed:

```
$ ssh-add id-backups
$ ssh-add id-normal
```

Therefore, your SSH clients will always use the key *id-backups* when connecting to *server.example.com* because the agent provides it first in response to a client request. This might not be what you intended.

The second problem only makes this behavior worse: identities in an agent take precedence over identities used manually. If an identity in the agent can successfully authenticate, there's no way to override the agent manually with the *–i* command-line option or the `IdentityFile` keyword. So in the earlier example, there is literally no way to use the identity *id-normal*. The obvious attempt:

```
$ ssh -i id-normal server.example.com
```

still authenticates with *id-backups* because it is loaded first into the agent. Even nonloaded identities can't override the agent's selection. For example, if you load only one identity into the agent and try authenticating with the other:

```
$ ssh-add id-normal
$ ssh -i id-backups server.example.com
```

your *ssh* connection authenticates with the loaded identity, in this case *id-normal*, regardless of the *–i* option.*

As a general rule, if you have two SSH identities valid on an SSH server, don't load either identity into an agent. Otherwise, one of those identities will be unable to access that server.

6.4.3. Tailoring Sessions Based on Identity

Despite the gloom and doom in the previous section, multiple identities can be extremely useful. In particular, you can configure your remote accounts to respond differently to different identities. This is a three-step process:

1. Generate a new SSH identity, as we have discussed in this chapter.
2. Set up a detailed client configuration that does what you want, using your new identity. This is the subject of Chapter 7.
3. Set up your account on the SSH server machine to respond to your new identity in a desired manner. This is covered in detail in Chapter 8.

We strongly encourage you to experiment with this technique. You can do some really powerful and interesting things with SSH this way. If you're just running simple terminal sessions with SSH, you are missing half the fun.

6.5. Summary

In this chapter, we've seen how to create and use SSH identities, represented by key pairs, either individually (SSH-1) or in collections (SSH-2). Keys are created by *ssh-keygen* and are accessed by clients as needed. SSH-2 provides an additional

* This undocumented behavior drove us insane until we figured out what was happening. Similar behavior occurs with Kerberos authentication in SSH1. If you have Kerberos credentials that allow you to connect, you aren't running an agent, and you specify a key with *–i*, that key isn't used unless you destroy your Kerberos credentials (or otherwise make them unusable, for instance, hiding them by setting the KRB5CCNAME variable), because Kerberos is tried first.

layer of configuration, the identification file, which lets you use a set of identities as a single identity. You may have as many identities as you like.

SSH agents are useful timesavers to avoid retyping passphrases. Their operation has numerous subtleties, but once you get the hang of it, running an agent should become second nature.

7

Advanced Client Use

In this chapter:

- *How to Configure Clients*
- *Precedence*
- *Introduction to Verbose Mode*
- *Client Configuration in Depth*
- *Secure Copy with scp*
- *Summary*

SSH clients are marvelously configurable. Chapter 2 introduced remote logins and file copying but covered only the tip of the iceberg. You can also connect with multiple SSH identities, use a variety of authentication and encryption techniques, exercise control over TCP/IP settings, and generally tailor the feel and operation of SSH clients to your liking. You can even save common collections of SSH settings in configuration files for ease of use.

We'll be focusing on *outgoing* SSH use, running SSH clients to connect to remote hosts, using the components highlighted in Figure 7-1. A related topic, not covered in this chapter, is how to control incoming SSH connections to your account. That sort of access control is a function of the SSH server, not the clients, and is covered in Chapter 8.

7.1. How to Configure Clients

The clients *ssh* and *scp* are quite configurable, with many settings that can be changed to suit your whim. If you want to modify the behavior of these clients, three general techniques are at your disposal:

Environment variables
: For minor changes to the behavior of *scp*

Command-line options
: For changing the behavior of *ssh* or *scp* for a single invocation

Configuration keywords
: For changes that remain in force until you change them again; these are stored in a *client configuration file*

We now present a general overview of these three methods.

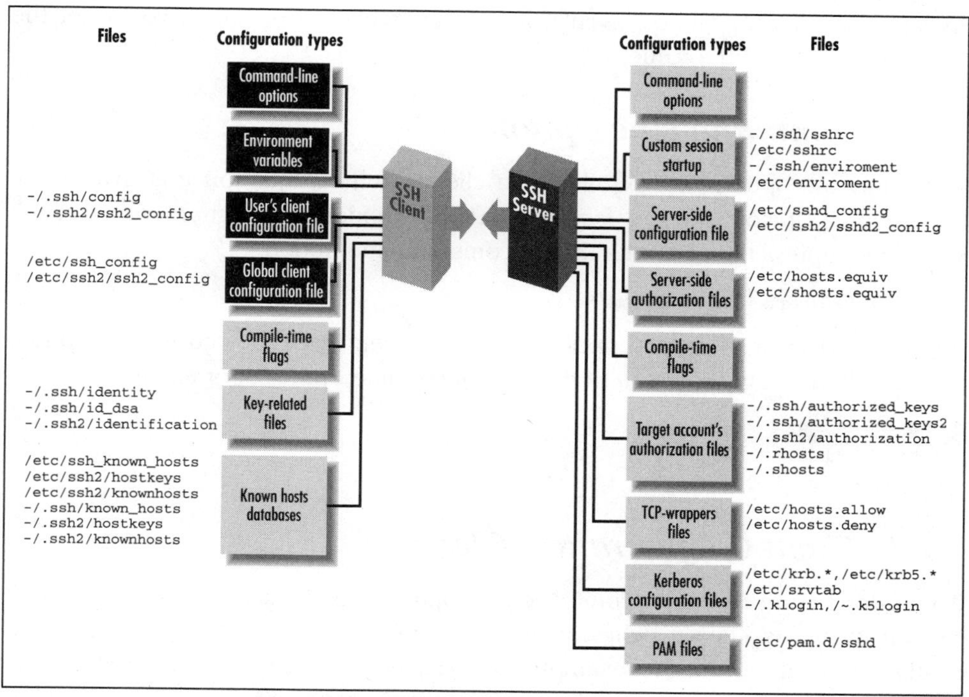

Figure 7-1. Client configuration (highlighted parts)

7.1.1. Environment Variables

Several client features are controlled by environment variables. For example, *scp* prints statistics about each file it transfers if the environment variable SSH_ALL_SCP_STATS is set. Environment variables may be set in your current shell by the standard methods:

```
# C shell family (csh, tcsh)
$ setenv SSH_ALL_SCP_STATS 1

# Bourne shell family (sh, ksh, bash)
$ SSH_ALL_SCP_STATS=1
$ export SSH_ALL_SCP_STATS
```

Alternatively, environment variables and values may be specified in a file. System administrators can set environment variables for all users in */etc/environment*, and users can set them in *~/.ssh/environment* (SSH1, OpenSSH) and *~/.ssh2/environment* (SSH2). These files contain lines of the format:

```
NAME=VALUE
```

where ***NAME*** is the name of an environment variable, and ***VALUE*** is its value. The value is taken literally, read from the equals sign to the end of the line. Don't enclose the value in quotes, even if it contains whitespace, unless you want the quotes to be part of the value.

7.1.2. Command-Line Options

Command-line options let you change a client's behavior just once at invocation. For example, if you're using *ssh1* over a slow modem connection, you can tell SSH1 to compress the data with the *–C* command-line option:

```
$ ssh1 -C server.example.com
```

ssh, *scp*, and most of their support programs, when invoked with the *–h* option, print a help message listing all of their command-line options. For example:

```
# SSH1, SSH2
$ ssh -h
$ ssh-keygen2 -h
```

7.1.3. Client Configuration Files

If you don't want to retype command-line options continually, *configuration files* let you change a client's behavior now and in the future, until you change the configuration file again. For example, you can enable compression for all clients you invoke by inserting this line into a client configuration file:

```
Compression yes
```

In a client configuration file, client settings are changed by specifying 276 keywords and values. In the example, the keyword is `Compression` and the value is `yes`. In SSH1 and OpenSSH, you may optionally separate the keyword and value with an equals sign:

```
Compression = yes
```

SSH2 doesn't support this syntax, however, so it can be easier always to use the "keyword <space> value" format to avoid confusion.

You may configure clients to behave differently for each remote host you visit. This can be done on the fly with command-line options, but for anything reasonably complex, you'll end up typing long, inconvenient command lines like:

```
$ ssh1 -a -p 220 -c blowfish -l sally -i myself server.example.com
```

Alternatively, you can set these options within a configuration file. The following entry duplicates the function of the command-line options above, collecting them under the name "myserver":

```
# SSH1, OpenSSH
Host myserver
 ForwardAgent no
```

```
Port 220
Cipher blowfish
User sally
IdentityFile myself
HostName server.example.com
```

To run a client with these options enabled, simply type:

```
$ ssh1 myserver
```

Configuration files take some time to set up, but in the long run they are significant timesavers.

We've given you a peek at the *structure* of a configuration file: a `Host` specification, followed by a bunch of keyword/value pairs. In the coming sections, we continue this philosophy, defining the structure and general rules before explaining the meanings of keywords. Once the generalities are covered, we'll dive into specific keywords. Sound good? Let's go.

7.1.3.1. Keywords versus command-line options

As we cover the many configuration keywords, note that all can be supplied on the command line if desired. The *–o* command-line option exists for this purpose. For any configuration line of the form:

```
Keyword Value
```

you may type:*

```
# SSH1, SSH2, OpenSSH
$ ssh -o "Keyword Value" ...
```

For example, the configuration lines:

```
User sally
Port 220
```

can be specified as:

```
# SSH1, SSH2, OpenSSH
$ ssh -o "User sally" -o "Port 220" server.example.com
```

SSH1 additionally permits an equals sign between the keyword and the value:

```
$ ssh1 -o User=sally -o Port=220 server.example.com
```

This example shows that the *–o* option may be specified multiple times on the command line. The option also works for *scp* in SSH1 and OpenSSH:

```
# SSH1, OpenSSH
$ scp -o "User sally" -o "Port 220" myfile server.example.com:
```

* Again, SSH1 and OpenSSH allow use of the equals sign (=) between the keyword and value, which allows you to omit the quotes on the command line: *ssh –o Keyword=Value.*

Another relationship between command-line options and configuration keywords is found in the *–F* option (SSH2 only). This option instructs an SSH2 client to use a different configuration file instead of *~/.ssh2/ssh2_config*. For example:

```
$ ssh2 -F ~/.ssh2/other_config
```

Unfortunately there's no equivalent option for SSH1 or OpenSSH clients.

7.1.3.2. Global and local files

Client configuration files come in two flavors. A single, *global* client configuration file, usually created by a system administrator, governs client behavior for an entire computer. The file is traditionally */etc/ssh_config* (SSH1, OpenSSH) or */etc/ssh2/ssh2_config* (SSH2). (Don't confuse these with the *server* configuration files in the same directories.) Each user may also create a *local* client configuration file within his or her account, usually *~/.ssh/config* (SSH1, OpenSSH) or *~/.ssh2/ssh2_config* (SSH2). This file controls the behavior of clients run in the user's login session.*

Values in a user's local file take precedence over those in the global file. For instance, if the global file turns on data compression, and your local file turns it off, the local file wins for clients run in your account. We cover precedence in more detail soon. [7.2]

7.1.3.3. Configuration file sections

Client configuration files are divided into *sections*. Each section contains settings for one remote host or for a set of related remote hosts, such as all hosts in a given domain.

The beginning of a section is marked differently in different SSH implementations. For SSH1 and OpenSSH, the keyword `Host` begins a new section, followed by a string called a *host specification*. The string may be a hostname:

```
Host server.example.com
```

an IP address:

```
Host 123.61.4.10
```

a nickname for a host: [7.1.3.5]

```
Host my-nickname
```

or a wildcard pattern representing a set of hosts, where ? matches any single character and * any sequence of characters (just like filename wildcards in your favorite Unix shell):

* The system administrator may change the locations of client configuration files, using the compile-time flag `--with-etcdir` [4.1.5.1] or the serverwide keyword `UserConfigDirectory`. [5.4.1.5] If the files aren't in their default locations on your computer, contact your system administrator.

```
Host *.example.com
Host 128.220.19.*
```

Some further examples of wildcards:

`Host *.edu`	*Any hostname in the edu domain*
`Host a*`	*Any hostname whose name begins with "a"*
`Host *1*`	*Any hostname (or IP address!) with 1 in it*
`Host *`	*Any hostname or IP address*

For SSH2, a new section is marked by a host specification string followed by a colon. The string, like the argument of **Host**, may be a computer name:

```
server.example.com:
```

an IP address:

```
123.61.4.10:
```

a nickname:

```
my-nickname:
```

or a wildcard pattern:

```
*.example.com:

128.220.19.*:
```

Following the host-specification line are one or more settings, i.e., configuration keywords and values, as in the example we saw earlier. The following table contrasts SSH1 and SSH2 configuration files:

SSH1, OpenSSH	SSH2

`Host myserver`
` User sally`
` IdentityFile myself`
` ForwardAgent no`
` Port 220`
` Cipher blowfish`
	`myserver:`
	` User sally`
	` IdentityFile myself`
	` ForwardAgent no`
	` Port 220`
	` Ciphers blowfish`

The settings apply to the hosts named in the host specification. The section ends at the next host specification or the end of the file, whichever comes first.

7.1.3.4. Multiple matches

Because wildcards are permitted in host specifications, a single hostname might match two or more sections in the configuration file. For example, if one section begins:*

```
Host *.edu
```

* We use only the SSH1 file syntax here to keep things tidy, but the explanation is true of SSH2 as well.

and another begins:

```
Host *.harvard.edu
```

and you connect to *server.harvard.edu,* which section applies? Believe it or not, they both do. Every matching section applies, and if a keyword is set more than once with different values, only one value applies. For SSH1 and OpenSSH, the earliest value takes precedence, whereas for SSH2 the latest value wins.

Suppose your client configuration file contains two sections to control data compression, password authentication, and password prompting:

```
Host *.edu
 Compression yes
 PasswordAuthentication yes

Host *.harvard.edu
 Compression no
 PasswordPromptLogin no
```

and you connect to *server.harvard.edu*:

```
$ ssh server.harvard.edu
```

Notice that the string `server.harvard.edu` matches both `Host` patterns, `*.edu` and `*.harvard.edu`. As we've said, the keywords in both sections apply to your connection. Therefore, the previous *ssh* command sets values for keywords `Compression`, `PasswordAuthentication`, and `PasswordPromptLogin`.

But notice, in the example, that the two sections set different values for `Compression`. What happens? The rule is that the first value prevails, in this case, `yes`. So in the previous example, the values used for *server.harvard.edu* are:

```
Compression yes                 The first of the Compression lines
PasswordAuthentication yes      Unique to first section
PasswordPromptLogin no          Unique to second section
```

and as shown in Figure 7-2. `Compression no` is ignored because it is the second `Compression` line encountered. Likewise, if 10 different `Host` lines match *server.harvard.edu,* all 10 of those sections apply, and if a particular keyword is set multiple times, only the first value is used.

While this feature might seem confusing, it has useful properties. Suppose you want some settings applied to all remote hosts. Simply create a section beginning with:

```
Host *
```

and place the common settings within it. This section should be either the first or the last in the file. If first, its settings take precedence over any others. This can be used to guard against your own errors. For example, if you want to make sure you never, ever, accidentally configure SSH sessions to fall back to the insecure *rsh* protocol, at the beginning of your configuration file put:

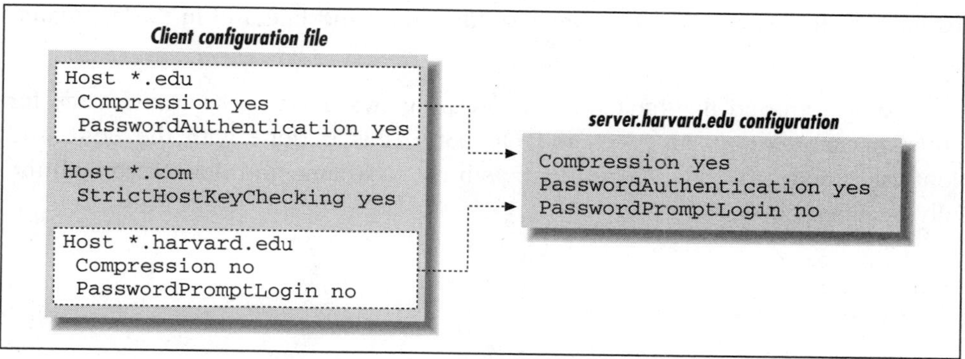

Figure 7-2. SSH1 client configuration file with multiple matches (SSH2 not shown)

```
# First section of file
Host *
 FallBackToRsh no
```

Alternatively, if you place `Host *` as the last section in the configuration file, its settings are used only if no other section overrides them. This is useful for changing SSH's default behavior, while still permitting overrides. For example, by default, data compression is disabled. You can make it enabled by default by ending your configuration file with:

```
# Last section of file
Host *
 Compression yes
```

Voilá, you have changed the default behavior of *ssh* and *scp* for your account! Any other section, earlier in the configuration file, can override this default simply by setting `Compression` to `no`.

7.1.3.5. Making nicknames for hosts

Suppose your client configuration file contains a section for the remote host *myserver.example.com*:

```
Host myserver.example.com
 ...
```

One day, while logged onto *ourclient.example.com*, you decide to establish an SSH connection to *myserver.example.com*. Since both computers are in the same domain, *example.com*, you can omit the domain name on the command line and simply type:

```
$ ssh myserver
```

This does establish the SSH connection, but you run into an unexpected nuance of configuration files. *ssh* compares the command-line string "myserver" to the Host string "myserver.example.com", determines that they don't match, and doesn't apply the section of the configuration file. Yes, the software requires an exact textual match between the hostnames on the command line and in the configuration file.

You can get around this limitation by declaring **myserver** to be a nickname for *myserver.example.com*. In SSH1 and OpenSSH, this is done with the `Host` and `HostName` keywords. Simply use `Host` with the nickname and `HostName` with the fully qualified hostname:

```
# SSH1, OpenSSH
Host myserver
 HostName myserver.example.com
 ...
```

ssh will now recognize that this section applies to your command *ssh myserver*. You may define any nickname you like for a given computer, even if it isn't related to the original hostname:

```
# SSH1, OpenSSH
Host simple
 HostName myserver.example.com
 ...
```

Then you can use the nickname on the command line:

```
$ ssh1 simple
```

For SSH2, the syntax is different but the effect is the same. Use the nickname in the host specification, and provide the full name to the `Host` keyword:

```
# SSH2 only
simple:
 Host myserver.example.com
 ...
```

Then type:

```
$ ssh2 simple
```

Nicknames are convenient for testing new client settings. Suppose you have an SSH1 configuration for *server.example.com*:

```
Host server.example.com
 ...
```

and you want to experiment with different settings. You can just modify the settings in place, but if they don't work, you have to waste time changing them back. The following steps demonstrate a more convenient way:

1. Within the configuration file, make a copy of the section you want to change:

```
# Original
Host server.example.com
 ...
```

```
# Copy for testing
Host server.example.com
 ...
```

2. In the copy, change "Host" to "HostName":

```
# Original
Host server.example.com
 ...
# Copy for testing
HostName server.example.com
 ...
```

3. Add a new **Host** line at the beginning of the copy, using a phony name, for example, "Host my-test":

```
# Original
Host server.example.com
...
# Copy for testing
Host my-test
 HostName server.example.com
 ...
```

4. Setup is done. In the copy (**my-test**), make all the changes you want and connect using *ssh my-test*. You can conveniently compare the old and new behavior by running *ssh server.example.com* versus *ssh my-test*. If you decide against the changes, simply delete the **my-test** section. If you like the changes, copy them to the original section (or delete the original and keep the copy).

You can do the same with SSH2:

```
# Original
server.example.com:
 ...
# Copy for testing
my-test:
 Host server.example.com
 ...
```

7.1.3.6. Comments, indenting, and style

You probably noticed in the previous examples that we are using the # symbol to represent comments:

```
# This is a comment
```

In fact, any line beginning with # in the configuration file is treated as a comment and ignored. Likewise, blank lines (empty or containing only whitespace) are also ignored.

You might also have noticed that the lines following a host specification are indented:

```
# SSH1, OpenSSH
Host server.example.com
 Keyword1 value1
 Keyword2 value2

# SSH2 only
server.example.com:
 Keyword1 value1
 Keyword2 value2
```

Indenting is considered good style because it visually indicates the beginning of a new section. It isn't required, but we recommend it.

7.2. Precedence

Perhaps you are wondering: what happens if some configuration settings conflict? For instance, if you use the `Compression` keyword to turn compression off, and also the *–C* command-line option to turn it on, who wins? In other words, who has *precedence*?

For SSH1, SSH2, and OpenSSH clients, the order of precedence is, from strongest to weakest:

1. Command-line options
2. The user's local client configuration file
3. The global client configuration file*

Command-line options have the highest precedence, overriding any client configuration files. The user's local file has next highest precedence, and the global file has lowest precedence. So in our compression example, *–C* takes precedence over the `Compression` keyword, and compression is enabled. If a setting isn't changed by any keyword or command-line option, the client's default setting is used.

Remember that we're speaking only of outgoing connections initiated by clients. Incoming connections, controlled by the SSH server, have other precedence rules. For servers, the user's local configuration file definitely doesn't override the global file; otherwise, users could override global server settings, creating security holes and wreaking other havoc. [8.1.1]

* Environment variables are not mentioned in this list because they don't compete for precedence. Environment variables control different features that don't overlap with command-line options and configuration files.

7.3. Introduction to Verbose Mode

Now that we've covered the generalities of command-line options and configuration files, we're about to launch into an extended discussion of configuration. Before we begin, let's practice some defense. As you try these options, occasionally you might see behavior that's not what you expected. Whenever this occurs, your first instinct should be: turn on verbose mode with the *–v* command-line option to track down the problem:

```
# SSH1, SSH2, OpenSSH
$ ssh -v server.example.com
```

In verbose mode, the client prints messages as it proceeds, providing clues to the problem. New SSH users (and quite a few experienced ones) frequently forget or neglect to use verbose mode when problems arise. Don't hesitate! Many questions we've seen in the Usenet SSH newsgroup, *comp.security.ssh* [12.3], could have been answered immediately by running *ssh –v* and examining the output.

Suppose you just installed your public key on *server.example.com* and are trying to authenticate with it. Strangely, you are prompted for your login password instead of your public-key passphrase:

```
$ ssh server.example.com
barrett@server.example.com's password:
```

Don't just sit there scratching your head in wonder. Let verbose mode come to the rescue:

```
$ ssh -v server.example.com
SSH Version 1.2.27 [sparc-sun-solaris2.5.1], protocol version 1.5.
client: Connecting to server.example.com [128.9.176.249] port 22.
client: Connection established.
client: Trying RSA authentication with key 'barrett@client'
client: Remote: Bad file modes for /users/barrett/.ssh              Uh oh!
client: Server refused our key.
client: Doing password authentication.
barrett@server.example.com's password:
```

These messages (which are abbreviated for this example) confirm that the SSH connection is succeeding, but public-key authentication is failing. The reason is "bad file modes": the remote SSH directory, */home/barrett/.ssh*, has incorrect permissions. A quick trip to the server and a well-placed *chmod* command later, the problem is solved:

```
# On the server
$ chmod 700 ~/.ssh
```

Verbose mode also works for *scp*:

```
$ scp -v myfile server.example.com:
Executing: host belvedere, user (unspecified), command scp -v -t .
SSH Version 1.2.27 [sparc-sun-solaris2.5.1], protocol version 1.5.
...
```

Verbose mode is your friend. Use it liberally. Now we're ready to learn those dozens of options.

7.4. Client Configuration in Depth

ssh and *scp* take their cues from command-line options, configuration-file keywords, and environment variables. SSH1, SSH2, and OpenSSH clients behave differently and obey different settings, but as usual, we cover them simultaneously. When a setting is supported by only some of these products, we'll say so.

7.4.1. Remote Account Name

ssh and *scp* assume that your local and remote usernames are the same. If your local username is henry and you run:

```
# SSH1, SSH2, OpenSSH
$ ssh server.example.com
```

ssh will assume your remote username is also henry and requests a connection to that account on *server.example.com*. If your remote account name differs from the local one, you must tell the SSH client your remote account name. For henry to connect to a remote account called sally, he can use the *–l* command-line option:

```
# SSH1, SSH2, OpenSSH
$ ssh -l sally server.example.com
```

If copying files with *scp*, the syntax is different for specifying the remote account name, looking more like an email address. [7.5.1] To copy the file *myfile* to the remote account sally on *server.example.com*:

```
# SSH1, SSH2, OpenSSH
$ scp myfile sally@server.example.com:
```

If you frequently connect to a remote machine using a different username, instead of monkeying with command-line options, specify the remote username in your client configuration file. The `User` keyword serves this purpose, and both *ssh* and *scp* pay attention to it. The following table shows how to declare that your remote username is sally on a given remote host:

SSH1, OpenSSH	SSH2
`Host server.example.com` ` User sally`	`server.example.com:` ` User sally`

Now, when connecting to *server.example.com*, you don't have to specify that your remote username is sally:

```
# The remote username sally will be used automatically
$ ssh server.example.com
```

7.4.1.1. Tricks with remote account names

With `User` and nicknames, you can significantly shorten the command lines you type for *ssh* and *scp*. Continuing the preceding example with "sally", if you have the configuration shown in this table:

SSH1, OpenSSH	SSH2

`Host simple`
`HostName server.example.com`
`User sally`
	`simple:`
	`Host server.example.com`
	`User sally`

then these long commands:

```
$ ssh server.example.com -l sally
$ scp myfile sally@server.example.com:
```

may be reduced to:

```
$ ssh simple
$ scp myfile simple:
```

This table shows how you can specify separately several different accounts names on different hosts, each in its own section of the configuration file:

SSH1, OpenSSH	SSH2

`Host server.example.com`
`User sally`
`...`
`Host another.example.com`
`User sharon`
`...`
	`server.example.com:`
	`User sally`
	`...`
	`another.example.com:`
	`User sharon`
	`...`

This technique is convenient if you have only one account on each remote machine. But suppose you have two accounts on *server.example.com*, called sally and sally2. Is there some way to specify both in the configuration file? The following attempt doesn't work (we show SSH1 syntax only):

```
# THIS WILL NOT WORK PROPERLY
Host server.example.com
 User sally
 User sally2
 Compression yes
```

because only the first value (sally) prevails. To get around this limitation, you can use nicknames to create two sections for the same machine in your configuration file, each with a different **User**:

```
# SSH1, OpenSSH
# Section 1: Convenient access to the sally account
Host sally-account
 HostName server.example.com
 User sally
 Compression yes

# Section 2: Convenient access to the sally2 account
Host sally2-account
 HostName server.example.com
 User sally2
 Compression yes
```

Now you can access the two accounts easily by nickname:

```
$ ssh sally-account
$ ssh sally2-account
```

This works, but it isn't ideal. You've duplicated your settings (**HostName** and **Compression**) in each section. Duplication makes a configuration file harder to maintain, since any future changes needs to be applied twice. (In general, duplication isn't good software engineering.) Are you doomed to duplicate? No, there's a better solution. Immediately after the two sections, create a third section with a **Host** wildcard that matches both sally-account and sally2-account. Suppose you use sally*-account and move all duplicated settings into this new section:

```
# SSH1, OpenSSH
Host sally*-account
 HostName server.example.com
 Compression yes
```

The end result is shown in this table:

SSH1, OpenSSH	SSH2

`Host sally-account`
` User sally`
 	
`Host sally2-account`
` User sally2`
`Host sally*-account`
` HostName server.example.com`
` Compression yes`
	`sally-account:`
	` Host server.example.com`
	` Compression yes`
	`sally2-account:`
	` User sally2`
	`sally*-account:`
	` User sally`

Since sally*-account matches both other sections, its full name and compression settings apply to both sally-account and sally2-account. Any settings that differ between sally-account and sally2-account (in this case, **User**) are kept in their respective sections. You've now achieved the same effect as in the previous example—two accounts with different settings on the same remote machine—but with no duplication of settings.

7.4.2. User Identity

SSH identifies you by an *identity* represented by a key pair (SSH-1) or a collection of key pairs (SSH-2). [6.1] Normally, SSH clients use your default key file (SSH1, OpenSSH) or default identification file (SSH2) to establish an authenticated connection. However, if you've created other keys, you may instruct SSH clients to use them to establish your identity. A command-line option (*–i*) and configuration keyword (`IdentityFile`) are available for this purpose.

In SSH1 and OpenSSH, for example, if you have a private key file called *my-key*, you can make clients use it with the commands:

```
$ ssh1 -i my-key server.example.com
$ scp1 -i my-key myfile server.example.com:
```

or with the configuration keyword:

```
IdentityFile my-key
```

The file location is assumed to be relative to the current directory, i.e., in these cases the file is *./my-key*.

SSH2 also has *–i* and `IdentityFile`, but their use is slightly different. Instead of a key file, you supply the name of an identification file:*

```
$ ssh2 -i my-id-file server.example.com
```

```
IdentityFile my-id-file
```

Take note of this difference between *ssh1* and *ssh2*. If you mistakenly provide a key filename to *ssh2*, the client attempts to read the key file as if it's an identification file, sending a random result to the SSH2 server. Authentication mysteriously fails, possibly with the log message "No further authentication methods available," or you may be prompted for your login password rather than your public key passphrase.

Multiple identities can be quite useful. [6.4] For example, you can set up your remote account to run specific programs when a second key is used. The ordinary command:

```
$ ssh server.example.com
```

* In SSH2 2.0.13 and earlier, the *–i* option and `IdentityFile` require the identity file to be in your SSH2 directory, *~/.ssh2*. SSH2 2.1.0 and later accept absolute pathnames; any path that doesn't begin with a slash (/) is treated as relative to *~/.ssh2*.

initiates a regular login session, but:

```
$ ssh -i other_identity server.example.com
```

can run a complex batch process on *server.example.com*. Using configuration keywords, you can accomplish the same effect by specifying an alternative identity as shown in this table:

SSH1, OpenSSH	SSH2

`Host SomeComplexAction`
`HostName server.example.com`
`IdentityFile other_identity`
`...`
	`SomeComplexAction:`
	`Host server.example.com`
	`IdentityFile other_identity`
	`...`

You can then invoke:

```
$ ssh SomeComplexAction
```

SSH1 and OpenSSH can specify multiple identities in a single command:*

```
# SSH1, OpenSSH
$ ssh -i id1 -i id2 -i id3 server.example.com
```

or:

```
# SSH1, OpenSSH
Host server.example.com
 IdentityFile id1
 IdentityFile id2
 IdentityFile id3
```

Multiple identities are tried in order until one successfully authenticates. However, SSH1 and OpenSSH limit you to 100 identities per command.

If you plan to use multiple identities frequently, remember that an SSH agent can eliminate hassle. Simply load each identity's key into the agent using *ssh-add*, and you won't have to remember multiple passphrases while you work.

7.4.3. Host Keys and Known-Hosts Databases

Every SSH server has a host key [3.3] that uniquely identifies the server to clients. This key helps prevent spoofing attacks. When an SSH client requests a connection and receives the server's host key, the client checks it against a local database of known host keys. If the keys match, the connection proceeds. If they don't, the client behaves according to several options you can control.

In SSH1 and OpenSSH, the host key database is maintained partly in a serverwide location (*/etc/ssh_known_hosts*) and partly in the user's SSH directory (*~/.ssh/*

* SSH2 accomplishes the same thing with identification files, which may contain multiple keys.

known_hosts).[*] In SSH2, there are two databases of host keys for authenticating server hosts (the "hostkeys" map in */etc/ssh2/hostkeys*) and client hosts (the "knownhosts" map); in this section we are concerned only with the former. Similar to its SSH1 counterpart, the SSH2 hostkeys map is maintained in a serverwide directory (*/etc/ssh2/hostkeys/*) and a per-account directory (*~/.ssh2/hostkeys/*). In this section, we refer to the SSH1, SSH2, and OpenSSH map simply as the *host key database.*

7.4.3.1. Strict host key checking

Suppose you request an SSH connection with *server.example.com,* which sends its host key in response. Your client looks up *server.example.com* in its host key database. Ideally, a match is found and the connection proceeds. But what if this doesn't happen? Two scenarios may arise:

SCENARIO 1
: A host key is found for *server.example.com* in the database, but it doesn't match the incoming key. This can indicate a security hazard, or it can mean that *server.example.com* has changed its host key, which can happen legitimately. [3.10.4]

SCENARIO 2
: No host key for *server.example.com* exists in the database. In this case, the SSH client is encountering *server.example.com* for the first time.

In each scenario, should the client proceed or fail? Should it store the new host key in the database, or not? These decisions are controlled by the keyword `StrictHostKeyChecking`, which may have three values:

`yes`
: Be strict. If a key is unknown or has changed, the connection fails. This is the most secure value, but it can be inconvenient or annoying if you connect to new hosts regularly, or if your remote host keys change frequently.

`no`
: Not strict. If a key is unknown, automatically add it to the user's database and proceed. If a key has changed, leave the known hosts entry intact, print a warning, and permit the connection to proceed. This is the least secure value.

`ask`
: Prompt the user. If a key is unknown, ask whether it should be added to the user's database and whether to connect. If a key has changed, ask whether to connect. This is the default and a sensible value for knowledgeable users.

[*] OpenSSH additionally keeps SSH-2 known host keys in the file *~/.ssh/known_hosts2.*

(Less experienced users might not understand what they're being asked and therefore may make the wrong decision.)

Here's an example:

```
# SSH1, SSH2, OpenSSH
StrictHostKeyChecking yes
```

Table 7-1 summarizes SSH's **StrictHostKeyChecking**'s behavior.

Table 7-1. StrictHostKeyChecking Behavior

Key Found?	Match?	Strict?	Action
Yes	Yes	–	Connect
Yes	No	Yes	Warn and fail
Yes	No	No	Warn and connect
Yes	No	Ask	Warn and ask whether to connect
No	–	Yes	Warn and fail
No	–	No	Add key and connect
No	–	Ask	Ask whether to add key and to connect

OpenSSH has an additional keyword, **CheckHostIP**, to make a client verify the IP address of an SSH server in the database. Its values may be **yes** (the default, to verify the address) or **no**. The value **yes** provides security against name service spoofing attacks. [3.10.2]

```
# OpenSSH only
CheckHostIP no
```

7.4.3.2. Moving the known hosts files

SSH1 and OpenSSH permit the locations of the host key database, both the serverwide and per-account parts, to be changed using configuration keywords. **GlobalKnownHostsFile** defines an alternative location for the serverwide file. It doesn't actually move the file—only the system administrator can do that—but it does force your clients to use another file in its place. This keyword is useful if the file is outdated, and you want your clients to ignore the serverwide file, particularly if you're tired of seeing warning messages from your clients about changed keys.

```
# SSH1, OpenSSH
GlobalKnownHostsFile /users/smith/.ssh/my_global_hosts_file
```

Similarly, you can change the location of your per-user part of the database with the keyword **UserKnownHostsFile**:

```
# SSH1, OpenSSH
UserKnownHostsFile /users/smith/.ssh/my_local_hosts_file
```

7.4.4. TCP/IP Settings

SSH uses TCP/IP as its transport mechanism. Most times you don't need to change the default TCP settings, but in such situations as the following, it's necessary:

- Connecting to SSH servers on other TCP ports
- Using privileged versus nonprivileged ports
- Keeping an idle connection open by sending keepalive messages
- Enabling the Nagle Algorithm (TCP_NODELAY)
- Requiring IP addresses to be Version 4 or 6

7.4.4.1. Selecting a remote port

Most SSH servers listen on TCP port 22, so clients connect to this port by default. Nevertheless, sometimes you need to connect to an SSH server on a different port number. For example, if you are a system administrator testing a new SSH server, you can run it on a different port to avoid interference with an existing server. Then your clients need to connect to this alternate port. This can be done with the client's `Port` keyword, followed by a port number:

```
# SSH1, SSH2, OpenSSH
Port 2035
```

or the *–p* command-line option followed by the port number:

```
# SSH1, SSH2, OpenSSH
$ ssh -p 2035 server.example.com
```

You can also specify an alternative port for *scp*, but the command-line option is *–P* instead of *–p*:*

```
# SSH1, SSH2, OpenSSH
$ scp -P 2035 myfile server.example.com:
```

In SSH2 2.1.0 and later, you can also provide a port number as part of the user and host specification, preceded by a hash sign. For example, the commands:

```
# SSH2 only
$ ssh2 server.example.com#2035
$ ssh2 smith@server.example.com#2035
$ scp2 smith@server.example.com#2035:myfile localfile
```

each create SSH-2 connections to remote port 2035. (We don't see much use for this alternative syntax, but it's available.)

After connecting to the server, *ssh* sets an environment variable in the remote shell to hold the port information. For SSH1 and OpenSSH, the variable is called SSH_

* *scp* also has a *–p* option with the same meaning as for *rcp*: "preserve file permissions."

CLIENT, and for SSH2 it is SSH2_CLIENT. The variable contains a string with three values, separated by a space character: the client's IP address, the client's TCP port, and the server's TCP port. For example, if your client originates from port 1016 on IP address 24.128.23.102, connecting to the server's port 22, the value is:

```
# SSH1, OpenSSH
$ echo $SSH_CLIENT
24.128.23.102 1016 22

# SSH2 only
$ echo $SSH2_CLIENT
24.128.23.102 1016 22
```

These variables are useful for scripting. In your shell's startup file (e.g., *~/.profile*, *~/.login*), you can test for the variable, and if it exists, take actions. For example:

```
#!/bin/sh
# Test for an SSH_CLIENT value of nonzero length
if [ -n "$SSH_CLIENT" ]
then
# We logged in via SSH.
  echo 'Welcome, SSH-1 user!'
  # Extract the IP address from SSH_CLIENT
  IP=`echo $SSH_CLIENT | awk '{print $1}'`
  # Translate it to a hostname.
  HOSTNAME=`host $IP | grep Name: | awk '{print $2}'`
  echo "I see you are connecting from $HOSTNAME."
else
  # We logged in not by SSH, but by some other means.
  echo 'Welcome, O clueless one. Feeling insecure today?'
fi
```

7.4.4.2. Forcing a nonprivileged local port

SSH connections get locally bound to a privileged TCP port, one whose port number is below 1024. [3.4.2.3] If you ever need to override this feature—say, if your connection must pass through a firewall that doesn't permit privileged source ports—use the *–P* command-line option:

```
# SSH1, SSH2, OpenSSH
$ ssh -P server.example.com
```

The *–P* option makes *ssh* select a local port that is nonprivileged.* Let's watch this work by printing the value of SSH_CLIENT on the remote machine, with and without *–P*. Recall that SSH_CLIENT lists the client IP address, client port, and server port, in order.

```
# Default: bind to privileged port.
$ ssh server.example.com 'echo $SSH_CLIENT'
```

* Yes, it's counterintuitive for *–P* to mean *non*privileged, but that's life.

```
128.119.240.87 1022 22                          1022 < 1024

# Bind to non-privileged port.
$ ssh -P server.example.com 'echo $SSH_CLIENT'
128.119.240.87 36885 22                         36885 >= 1024
```

The configuration keyword **UsePrivilegedPort** (SSH1, OpenSSH) has the same function as *–P*, with values **yes** (use a privileged port, the default) and **no** (use a nonprivileged port):

```
# SSH1, OpenSSH
UsePrivilegedPort no
```

scp also permits binding to nonprivileged ports with these configuration keywords. However, the command-line options are different from those of *ssh*. For *scp1*, the option *–L* means to bind to a nonprivileged port, the same as setting **UsePrivilegedPort** to **no**:*

```
# SSH1 only
$ scp1 -L myfile server.example.com:
```

scp2 has no command-line option for this feature.

For trusted-host authentication you must use a privileged port. In other words, if you use *–P* or **UsePrivilegedPort no**, you disable Rhosts and RhostsRSA authentication. [3.4.2.3]

7.4.4.3. Keepalive messages

The **KeepAlive** keyword instructs the client how to proceed if a connection problem occurs, such as a prolonged network outage or a server machine crash:

```
# SSH1, SSH2, OpenSSH
KeepAlive yes
```

The value **yes** (the default) tells the client to transmit and expect periodic *keepalive messages*. If the client detects a lack of responses to these messages, it shuts down the connection. The value **no** means not to use keepalive messages.

Keepalive messages represent a tradeoff. If they are enabled, a faulty connection is shut down, even if the problem is transient. However, the TCP keepalive timeout on which this feature is based is typically several hours, so this shouldn't be a big problem. If keepalive messages are disabled, an unused faulty connection can persist indefinitely.

KeepAlive is generally more useful in the SSH server, since a user sitting on the client side will certainly notice if the connection becomes unresponsive. However,

* The *–P* option was already taken for setting the port number. The source code suggests that *–L* can mean "large local port numbers."

SSH can connect two programs together, with the one running the SSH client waiting for input from the other side. In such a situation, it can be necessary to have a dead connection be eventually detected.

`KeepAlive` isn't intended to deal with the problem of SSH sessions being torn down because of firewall, proxying, NAT, or IP masquerading timeouts. [5.4.3.4]

7.4.4.4. Controlling TCP_NODELAY

TCP/IP has a feature called the Nagle Algorithm, an optimization for reducing the number of TCP segments sent with very small amounts of data. [4.1.5.3] SSH2 clients may also enable or disable the Nagle Algorithm using the **`NoDelay`** keyword:

```
# SSH2 only
NoDelay yes
```

Legal values are `yes` (to disable the algorithm) and `no` (to enable it; the default).

7.4.4.5. Requiring IPv4 and IPv6

OpenSSH can force its clients to use Internet Protocol Version 4 (IPv4) or 6 (IPv6) addresses. IPv4 is the current version of IP used on the Internet; IPv6 is the future, permitting far more addresses than IPv4 can support. For more information on these address formats visit:

> *http://www.ipv6.org*

To force IPv4 addressing, use the *–4* flag:

```
# OpenSSH only
$ ssh -4 server.example.com
```

or likewise for IPv6, use *–6*:

```
# OpenSSH only
$ ssh -6 server.example.com
```

7.4.5. Making Connections

Under the best conditions, an SSH client attempts a secure connection, succeeds, obtains your authentication credentials, and executes whatever command you've requested, be it a shell or otherwise. Various steps in this process are configurable, including:

- The number of times the client attempts the connection
- The look and behavior of the password prompt (for password authentication only)
- Suppressing all prompting
- Running remote commands interactively with a tty

- Running remote commands in the background
- Whether or not to fall back to an insecure connection, if a secure one can't be established
- The escape character for interrupting and resuming an SSH session

7.4.5.1. Number of connection attempts

If you run an SSH1 or OpenSSH client and it can't establish a secure connection, it will retry. By default, it tries four times in rapid succession. You can change this behavior with the keyword **ConnectionAttempts**:

```
# SSH1, OpenSSH
ConnectionAttempts 10
```

In this example, *ssh1* tries 10 times before admitting defeat, after which it either quits or falls back to an insecure connection. We'll come back to this when we discuss the keyword **FallBackToRsh**. [7.4.5.8]

Most people don't have much use for this keyword, but it might be helpful if your network is unreliable. Just for fun, you can force *ssh1* to give up immediately by setting **ConnectionAttempts** equal to zero:

```
# SSH1, OpenSSH
$ ssh -o ConnectionAttempts=0 server.example.com
Secure connection to server.example.com refused.
```

7.4.5.2. Password prompting in SSH1

If you're using password authentication in SSH1, clients prompt like this for your password:

```
smith@server.example.com's password:
```

You may tailor the appearance of this prompt. Perhaps for privacy reasons, you might not want your username or hostname appearing on the screen. The configuration keyword **PasswordPromptLogin**, with a value of **yes** (the default) or **no**, prints or suppresses the username. For example:

```
# SSH1 only
PasswordPromptLogin no
```

causes this prompt to appear without the username:

```
server.example.com password:
```

Likewise, **PasswordPromptHost** prints or suppresses the hostname, again with values of **yes** (the default) or **no**. The line:

```
# SSH1 only
PasswordPromptHost no
```

makes the prompt appear without the hostname:

```
smith's password:
```

If both keywords have value `no`, the prompt is reduced to:

```
Password:
```

Remember, this applies only to password authentication. With public-key authentication, the prompt for a passphrase is completely different and not controlled by these keywords:

```
Enter passphrase for RSA key 'Dave Smith's Home PC':
```

You may also control the number of times you are prompted for your password if mistyped. By default, you're prompted only once, and if you mistype the password, the client exits. The keyword `NumberOfPasswordPrompts` may change this to between one and five prompts:*

```
# SSH1, OpenSSH
NumberOfPasswordPrompts 3
```

Now your SSH clients provides three chances to type your password correctly.

7.4.5.3. Password prompting in SSH2

SSH2 adds flexibility to password prompting. Instead of preset prompt strings, you can design your own with the `PasswordPrompt` keyword:

```
# SSH2 only
PasswordPrompt Enter your password right now, infidel:
```

You can insert the remote username or hostname with the symbols `%U` (remote username) or `%H` (remote hostname). For example, to emulate the SSH1 prompt:

```
# SSH2 only
PasswordPrompt "%U@%H's password:"
```

Or you can be fancier:

```
# SSH2 only
PasswordPrompt "Welcome %U! Please enter your %H password:"
```

7.4.5.4. Batch mode: suppressing prompts

In some cases, you don't want to be prompted for your password or RSA passphrase. If *ssh* is invoked by an unattended shell script, for example, nobody will be at the keyboard to type a password. This is why SSH *batch mode* exists. In batch mode, all prompting for authentication credentials is suppressed. The

* The upper limit of five prompts is enforced by the SSH server.

keyword **BatchMode** can have a value of **yes** (disable prompting) or **no** (the default, with prompting enabled):

```
# SSH1, SSH2, OpenSSH
BatchMode yes
```

Batch mode may be enabled for *scp* also with the *–B* option:

```
# SSH1, SSH2, OpenSSH
$ scp1 -B myfile server.example.com:
```

Batch mode doesn't replace authentication. If a password or passphrase is required, you can't magically log in without it by suppressing the prompt. If you try, your client exits with an error message such as "permission denied." In order for batch mode to work, you must arrange for authentication to work without a password/passphrase, say, with trusted-host authentication or an SSH agent. [11.1]

7.4.5.5. Pseudo-terminal allocation (TTY/PTY/PTTY)

A Unix *tty* (pronounced as it's spelled, T-T-Y) is a software abstraction representing a computer terminal, originally an abbreviation for "teletype." As part of an interactive session with a Unix machine, a tty is allocated to process keyboard input, limit screen output to a given number of rows and columns, and handle other terminal-related activities. Since most terminal-like connections don't involve an actual hardware terminal, but rather a window, a software construct called a *pseudo-tty* (or *pty*, pronounced P-T-Y) handles this sort of connection.

When a client requests an SSH connection, the server doesn't necessarily allocate a pty for the client. It does so, of course, if the client requests an interactive terminal session, e.g., just *ssh host*. But if you ask *ssh* to run a simple command on a remote server, such as *ls*:

```
$ ssh remote.server.com /bin/ls
```

no interactive terminal session is needed, just a quick dump of the output of *ls*. In fact, by default *sshd* doesn't allocate a pty for such a command. On the other hand, if you try running an interactive command like the text editor Emacs in this manner, you get an error message:

```
$ ssh remote.server.com emacs -nw
emacs: standard input is not a tty
```

because Emacs is a screen-based program intended for a terminal. In such cases, you can request that SSH allocate a pty using the *–t* option:

```
# SSH1, SSH2, OpenSSH
$ ssh -t server.example.com emacs
```

SSH2 also has the keyword `ForcePTTYAllocation`, which does the same thing as *–t*.*

If SSH allocates a pty, it also automatically defines an environment variable in the remote shell. The variable is SSH_TTY (for SSH1 and OpenSSH) or SSH2_TTY (for SSH2) and contains the name of the character device file connected to the "slave" side of the pty, the side that emulates a real tty. We can see this in action with a few simple commands. Try printing the value of SSH_TTY on a remote machine. If no tty is allocated, the result is blank:

```
$ ssh1 server.example.com 'echo $SSH_TTY'
[no output]
```

If you force allocation, the result is the name of the tty:

```
$ ssh1 -t server.example.com 'echo $SSH_TTY'
/dev/pts/1
```

Thanks to this variable, you can run shell scripts on the remote machine that use this information. For example, here's a script that runs your default editor only if a terminal is available:

```
#!/bin/sh
if [ -n $SSH_TTY -o -n $SSH2_TTY ]; then
   echo 'Success!'
   exec $EDITOR
else
   echo "Sorry, interactive commands require a tty"
fi
```

Place this script in your remote account, calling it *myscript* (or whatever), and run:

```
$ ssh server.example.com myscript
Sorry, interactive commands require a tty
$ ssh -t server.example.com myscript
Success!
...Emacs runs...
```

7.4.5.6. Backgrounding a remote command

If you try running an SSH remote command in the background, you might be surprised by the result. After the remote command runs to completion, the client automatically suspends before the output is printed:

```
$ ssh server.example.com ls &
[1]  11910
$
... time passes ...
[1] + Stopped (SIGTTIN)        ssh server.example.com ls &
```

* In SSH1 and OpenSSH, the `no-pty` option in *authorized_keys* can override this request for a tty. [8.2.9]

This happens because *ssh* is attempting to read from standard input while in the background, which causes the shell to suspend *ssh*. To see the resulting output, you must bring *ssh* into the foreground:

```
$ fg
README
myfile
myfile2
```

ssh provides the *–n* command-line option to get around this problem. It redirects standard input to come from */dev/null*, which prevents *ssh* from blocking for input. Now when the remote command finishes, the output is printed immediately:

```
# SSH1, SSH2, OpenSSH
$ ssh -n server.example.com ls &
[1]  11912
$
... time passes ...
README
myfile
myfile2
```

SSH2 has a keyword `DontReadStdin` that does the same thing as *–n*, accepting the values `yes` or `no` (the default is `no`):

```
# SSH2 only
DontReadStdin yes
```

7.4.5.7. Backgrounding a remote command, take two

The preceding section assumed you didn't need to type a password or passphrase, e.g., that you're running an SSH agent. What happens if you use *–n* or `DontReadStdin` but the SSH client needs to read a password or passphrase from you?

```
$ ssh -n server.example.com ls &
$
Enter passphrase for RSA key 'smith@client':
```

STOP! Don't type your passphrase! Because the command is run in the background with *–n*, the prompt is also printed in the background. If you respond, you will be typing to the shell, not the *ssh* prompt, and anything you type will be visible.

You need a solution that not only disables input and sends the process into the background, but also permits *ssh* to prompt you. This is the purpose of the *–f* command-line option, which instructs *ssh* to do the following in order:

1. Perform authentication, including any prompting
2. Cause the process to read from */dev/null*, exactly like *–n*
3. Put the process into the background: no "&" is needed

Here's an example:

```
$ ssh -f server.example.com ls
Enter passphrase for RSA key 'smith@client': ********
$
... time passes...
README
myfile
myfile2
```

SSH2 has a keyword `GoBackground` that does the same thing, accepting the values `yes` or `no` (the default):

```
# SSH2 only
GoBackground yes
```

`GoBackground` and *–f* also set up any port forwardings you may have specified on the command line. [9.2.6] The setup occurs after authentication but before backgrounding.

7.4.5.8. RSH issues

Suppose a remote host isn't running an SSH server, but you try to log into it via SSH. What happens? Depending on your client configuration settings, three scenarios can occur:

Scenario 1

ssh attempts an SSH connection, fails, and then attempts an insecure *rsh* connection.* This is the default behavior, and it's a sensible guess of what a user might have done anyway. ("Hmm, I can't connect by SSH. I'll try *rsh* instead.") The connection attempt displays:

```
$ ssh no-ssh-server.com
Secure connection to no-ssh-server.com on port 22 refused; reverting to insecure
method.
Using rsh.  WARNING: Connection will not be encrypted.
```

Scenario 2

ssh attempts an SSH connection, fails, and stops. This behavior is best for security-conscious installations where *rsh* is simply not acceptable.

```
$ ssh no-ssh-server.com
Secure connection to no-ssh-server.com on port 22 refused.
```

* Only if *ssh* is compiled with support for *rsh*, using the compile-time flag `--with-rsh`. [4.1.5.12] If not, Scenario 2, fail and stop, is the only possibility.

Scenario 3

Rather than attempt an SSH connection at all, *ssh* immediately attempts an insecure *rsh* connection.* This is best if you know in advance that certain machines don't run SSH servers, and you find *rsh* acceptable.

```
$ ssh no-ssh-server.com
Using rsh.  WARNING: Connection will not be encrypted.
```

Two configuration keywords select the behavior you prefer. (And remember, you can configure them separately for each remote host you want to visit.) **FallBackToRsh** controls what happens when an SSH connection attempt fails: should it then try an *rsh* connection or not? **FallBackToRsh** may have the value **yes** (the default, to try *rsh*) or **no** (don't try *rsh*):

```
# SSH1, SSH2, OpenSSH
FallBackToRsh no
```

The keyword **UseRsh** instructs *ssh* to use *rsh* immediately, not even attempting an SSH connection. Permissible values are **yes** (to use *rsh*) and **no** (the default, to use *ssh*):

```
# SSH1, SSH2, OpenSSH
UseRsh yes
```

Therefore, here is how to create these three scenarios:.

Scenario 1: Try ssh first, then fall back to rsh

```
# SSH1, SSH2, OpenSSH
FallBackToRsh yes
UseRsh no
```

Scenario 2: Use ssh only

```
# SSH1, SSH2, OpenSSH
FallBackToRsh no
UseRsh no
```

Scenario 3: Use rsh only

```
# SSH1, SSH2, OpenSSH
UseRsh yes
```

Please be careful with the **UseRsh** keyword. Make sure to limit its effects to individual remote hosts in your configuration file, not to all hosts. The following table depicts an example that can disable encryption for all your SSH connections:

SSH1, OpenSSH	SSH2

`# Never do this! Security risk!!`
`Host *`
` UseRsh yes`
	`# Never do this! Security risk!!`
	`*:`
	` UseRsh yes`

* Again, only if *ssh* is compiled with `--with-rsh`.

7.4.5.9. Escaping

Recall that the *ssh* client has an *escape sequence* feature. [2.3.2] By typing a particular character, normally a tilde (~), immediately after a newline or carriage return, you can send special commands to *ssh*: terminate the connection, suspend the connection, and so forth. But sometimes the default escape character can cause a problem.

Suppose you connect by ssh from host A to host B, then from host B to host C, and finally from host C to host D, making a chain of *ssh* connections. (We represent the machines' shell prompts as A$, B$, C$, and D$.)

```
A$ ssh B
...
  B$ ssh C
  ...
    C$ ssh D
    ...
      D$
```

While logged onto host D, you press the Return key, then ~ `^Z` (tilde followed by `Control-Z`) to suspend the connection temporarily. Well, you've got three *ssh* connections active, so which one gets suspended? The first one does, and this escape sequence brings you back to the host A prompt. Well, what if you want to escape back to host B or C? There are two methods, one with forethought and one on the spur of the moment.

If you prepare in advance, you may change the escape character for each connection with the configuration keyword **EscapeChar**, followed by a character:

```
# SSH1, SSH2, OpenSSH
EscapeChar %
```

or the *-e* command-line option, followed again by the desired character (quoted if necessary to protect it from expansion by the shell):

```
# SSH1, SSH2, OpenSSH
$ ssh -e '%' server.example.com
```

So, going back to our example of hosts A through D, you want a different escape character for each segment of this chain of connections. For example,

```
# SSH1, SSH2, OpenSSH
A$ ssh B
...
  B$ ssh -e '$' C
  ...
    C$ ssh -e '%' D
    ...
      D$
```

Now, while logged onto host D, a tilde still brings you back to host A, but a dollar sign brings you back to host B, and a percent sign back to host C. The same effect can be achieved with the **EscapeChar** keyword, but the following table shows that more forethought is required to set up configuration files on three hosts.

SSH1, OpenSSH	SSH2

`# Host A configuration file`
`Host B`
` EscapeChar ~`
 	
`# Host B configuration file`
`Host C`
` EscapeChar ^`
 	
`# Host C configuration file`
`Host D`
` EscapeChar %`
	`# Host A configuration file`
	`B:`
	` EscapeChar ~`
	
	`# Host B configuration file`
	`C:`
	` EscapeChar ^`
	
	`# Host C configuration file`
	`D:`
	` EscapeChar %`

Even if you don't normally make chains of SSH connections, you might still want to change the escape character. For example, your work might require you to type a lot of tildes for other reasons, and you might accidentally type an escape sequence such as `~.` (tilde period) and disconnect your session. Oops!

The second method requires no forethought. Recall that typing the escape character twice sends it literally across the SSH connection. [2.3.2] Therefore, you can suspend the second SSH connection by typing two escapes, the third by typing three escapes, and so on. Remember you must precede your escape characters by pressing the Return key. While logged onto host D, you could escape back to host B, for example, by hitting the Return key, then typing two tildes, and `Control-Z`.

7.4.6. Proxies and SOCKS

SOCKS is an application-layer network proxying system supported by various SSH implementations. Proxying in general provides a way to connect two networks at the application level, without allowing direct network-level connectivity between them. Figure 7-3 shows a typical SOCKS installation.

The figure shows a private network and the Internet. The gateway machine is connected to both, but doesn't function as a router; there's no direct IP connectivity between the two networks. If a program running on H wants to make a TCP connection to a server on S, it instead connects to the SOCKS server running on G. Using the SOCKS protocol, H requests a connection to S. The SOCKS server makes a connection from G to S on behalf of H and then steps out of the way, passing data back and forth between H and S.

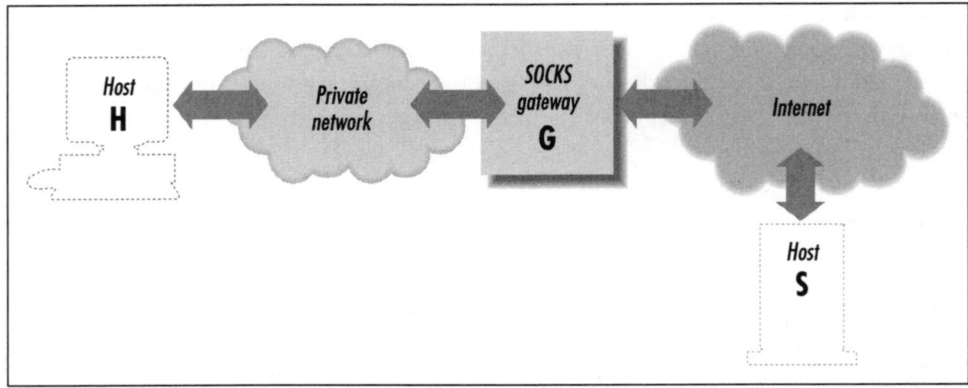

Figure 7-3. A typical SOCKS installation

A general drawback of application-level proxying is lack of transparency: only those programs written with support for the particular proxying scheme have network access. SOCKS, however, isn't specific to any higher-level protocol such as HTTP or SMTP. It provides general services: makes a TCP connection, pings a host, performs a traceroute, etc. Many of its services match the existing programming boundary between applications and network-services libraries. As a result, on modern computer systems employing dynamically linked libraries, it is often possible to extend SOCKS to non-SOCKS-aware applications, such as SSH, by replacing the right libraries with SOCKS-aware ones.

SOCKS comes in two versions, SOCKS4 and SOCKS5. The major difference between them is that SOCKS5 performs user authentication, whereas SOCKS4 doesn't. With SOCKS5, you can require the client to provide a username and password (or other authentication schemes) before accessing its network services.

7.4.6.1. SOCKS in SSH1

The following description assumes you've installed SSH1 with SOCKS support, using the NEC *socks5* package. [4.1.5.8] If you use a different package, the SOCKS-specific configuration details may differ from those we describe.

By the way, the names are a little confusing. Even though the NEC software is named "socks5," it implements both the SOCKS4 and SOCKS5 protocols. We write "socks5" in lowercase to refer to the NEC implementation.

Once you've installed your SOCKS-aware *ssh*, you can control its SOCKS-related behavior using environment variables. By default, *ssh* doesn't use SOCKS at all. If you set SOCKS_SERVER to "socks.shoes.com", *ssh* uses the SOCKS gateway running on *socks.shoes.com* for any connection to an SSH server outside the local host's subnet (as defined by netmask setting on the relevant network interface). If you want *ssh* to use SOCKS for all connections, even local-subnet ones, set the variable SOCKS5_NONETMASKCHECK. If your SOCKS gateway requires username/password authentication, set the variables SOCKS5_USER and SOCKS5_PASSWD with your username and password. SOCKS-specific debugging output is available by setting environment variables:

```
#!/bin/csh
setenv SOCKS5_DEBUG 3
setenv SOCKS5_LOG_STDERR
```

The documentation mentions debugging levels only up to 3, but in fact the code uses higher ones that are sometimes crucial to understanding a problem. Try cranking up the value if you're not getting enough information.

7.4.6.2. SOCKS in SSH2

SSH2 provides SOCKS4 support only. It is integrated into the SSH2 code, so you don't need to install a separate SOCKS package. You also don't need to enable SOCKS specifically when compiling; it is always included.

The SSH2 SOCKS feature is controlled with a single parameter, set with the **SocksServer** configuration keyword or the SSH_SOCKS_SERVER environment variable. The configuration option overrides the environment variable if both are present.

The **SocksServer** keyword is a string with the following format:

```
socks://[user]@gateway[:port]/[net1/mask1,net2/mask2,...]
```

Here, *gateway* is the machine running the SOCKS server, *user* is the username you supply for identification to SOCKS, and *port* is the TCP port for the SOCKS server (by default, 1080). The *net/mask* entries indicate netblocks that are to be considered local; that is, *ssh2* uses SOCKS only for connections lying outside the given network ranges. The mask is given as a number of bits, not an explicit mask, i.e., 192.168.10.0/24 instead of 192.168.10.0/255.255.255.0.

The parts of the string enclosed in square brackets are optional. So an SSH_SOCKS_SERVER value can be as simple as this:

```
socks://laces.shoes.net
```

With this value, *ssh2* uses SOCKS for all connections. It connects to a SOCKS server running on *laces.shoes.net*, port 1080, and it doesn't supply a username. You might wonder why there's a username but no password field. Recall that SOCKS4 doesn't support user authentication. The username is advisory only; the SOCKS server has no way of verifying your claimed identity.

You'll probably never want to use an SSH_SOCKS_SERVER setting as simple as this one, which uses the SOCKS server for all *ssh2* connections, even those connecting back to the same machine or to a machine on the same network. A better setup is to use SOCKS only for hosts on the other side of the gateway from you. Here's a more complete example:

```
socks://dan@laces.shoes.net:4321/127.0.0.0/8,192.168.10.0/24
```

With this value, *ssh2* connects directly to itself via its loopback address (127.0.0.1), or to hosts on the class C network 192.168.10.0. It uses SOCKS for all other connections, supplying the username "dan" and looking for the SOCKS server on port 4321.

7.4.6.3. SOCKS in OpenSSH

OpenSSH doesn't include explicit support for SOCKS. However, we have found that it works just fine with the *runsocks* program supplied with NEC's SOCKS5 package. *runsocks* is a wrapper that rearranges dynamic linking order so that sockets routines such as `bind`, `connect`, etc., are replaced by SOCKS-ified versions at runtime. On a Linux system, we found that setting the appropriate *socks5* environment variables as discussed earlier, and then running:

```
% runsocks ssh ...
```

caused OpenSSH to work seamlessly through our SOCKS server. One caveat, though: in order to work, the OpenSSH client must not be setuid. For obvious security reasons, shared-library loaders ignore the shenanigans of *runsocks* if the executable in question is setuid. And remember that setuid is required for trusted-host authentication. [3.4.2.3]

At one time, there was some code in OpenSSH for SOCKS support. However, it was removed and replaced by a recommendation to use the `ProxyCommand` feature instead. The idea is to have a little program that just takes a hostname and port number on the command line, connects to that socket via SOCKS, then acts as a pipe, passing data back and forth between the TCP connection and its standard input and output. If this program were called *ssh-proxy,* it can be used with OpenSSH like so:

```
% ssh -o 'ProxyCommand ssh-proxy %h %p' ...
```

This still doesn't work with SSH1 RhostsRSA authentication unless *ssh-proxy* is setuid root and written to use a privileged source port. It doesn't by itself interfere with SSH2 hostbased authentication, but it has a separate problem. [7.4.6.4]

We're sure such a SOCKS proxying widget must be available somewhere, but we haven't turned one up. You can't use the SOCKS-ified *telnet* that comes with *socks5* because it isn't transparent; bytes in the binary SSH protocol stream are interpreted as Telnet escape sequences and are munged. The authors did prove the concept, though, by taking a copy of *netcat* (*http://www.l0pht.com/~weld/netcat/*), and SOCKS-ifying it by linking against the *socks5* libraries. The *netcat* executable is named *nc*; using our altered version, the following worked for us, sending the SSH connection through our SOCKS gateway:

```
% ssh -o 'ProxyCommand nc %h %p' ...
```

Perhaps the OpenSSH folks will see fit to include such a utility at some point.

7.4.6.4. Other SOCKS issues

Keep in mind that an SSH connection through SOCKS appears to come from the SOCKS gateway, not from the originating client host. This causes a problem with trusted-host authentication. *sshd1* uses the source IP address of the connection to look up the client's host key, so RhostsRSA authentication will fail: it expects the gateway's host key, not that of the real client. You can get around this only by giving all the clients the same host key and associating that with the gateway in the SSH server's known-hosts database. That's not such a great arrangement, since if one host key is stolen, the thief can masquerade as any user on any of the clients, not just one. But it might be acceptable in some situations.

With SSH2, the problem should be gone; the SSH-2 protocol makes hostbased authentication independent of the client host address. However, SSH2 still implements it the old way, which still doesn't work through SOCKS. You might be tempted simply to disable the address/name check yourself in the source code. Don't do it. The issue is slightly more complicated. [3.5.1.6]

7.4.7. Forwarding

Port forwarding and X forwarding are covered in Chapter 9 and agent forwarding in Chapter 6. We mention them here only for completeness, since forwarding can be controlled in the client configuration file and on the command line.

7.4.8. Encryption Algorithms

When establishing a connection, an SSH client and server have a little conversation about encryption. The server says, "Hello client, here are the encryption algorithms I support." In return, the client says, "Hi there server, I'd like to choose this particular algorithm, please." Normally, they reach agreement, and the connection proceeds. If they can't agree on an encryption algorithm, the connection fails.

Most users let the client and server work things out themselves. But if you like, you may instruct the client to request particular encryption algorithms in its conversation with the server. In SSH1 and OpenSSH, this is done with the `Cipher` keyword followed by your encryption algorithm of choice:

```
# SSH1, OpenSSH
Cipher blowfish
```

or the *–c* command-line option:

```
# SSH1, SSH2, OpenSSH
$ ssh -c blowfish server.example.com
$ scp -c blowfish myfile server.example.com:
```

SSH2 is almost the same, but the keyword is **Ciphers** (note the final "s") and is followed by one or more encryption algorithms, separated by commas, indicating that any of these algorithms is acceptable:

```
# SSH2, OpenSSH/2
Ciphers blowfish,3des
```

SSH2 also supports the *–c* command-line option as previously, but it may appear multiple times to specify several acceptable ciphers:

```
# SSH2 only
$ ssh2 -c blowfish -c 3des -c idea server.example.com
$ scp2 -c blowfish -c 3des -c idea myfile server.example.com:
```

OpenSSH/2 permits multiple algorithms to follow a single *–c*, separated by commas, to achieve the same effect:

```
# OpenSSH/2 only
$ ssh -c 3des-cbc,blowfish-cbc,arcfour server.example.com
```

All ciphers acceptable by a server may be specified for the client. [5.4.5] Check the latest SSH documentation for a current list of supported ciphers.

7.4.8.1. MAC algorithms

The *–m* command-line option lets you select the integrity-checking algorithm, known as the MAC (Message Authentication Code), used by *ssh2*: [3.9.3]

```
# SSH2 only
$ ssh2 -m hmac-sha1 server.example.com
```

You can specify multiple algorithms on the command line, each preceded by a separate *–m* option:

```
# SSH2 only
$ ssh2 -m hmac-sha1 -m another-one server.example.com
```

and the SSH2 server selects one to use.

7.4.9. Session Rekeying

The **RekeyIntervalSeconds** keyword specifies how often (in seconds) the SSH2 client performs key exchange with the server to replace the session data-encryption and integrity keys. The default is 3600 seconds (one hour), and a zero value disables rekeying:*

```
# SSH2 only
RekeyIntervalSeconds 7200
```

7.4.10. Authentication

In a typical SSH setup, clients try to authenticate by the strongest methods first. If a particular method fails or isn't set up, the next one is tried, and so on. This default behavior should work fine for most needs.

Nevertheless, your clients may request specific types of authentication if they need to do so. For example, you might want to use public-key authentication only, and if it fails, no other methods should be tried.

7.4.10.1. Requesting an authentication technique

SSH1 and OpenSSH clients can request specific authentication methods by keyword. The syntax is the same as the server's in */etc/sshd_config*. [5.5.1] You can specify:

```
PasswordAuthentication
RhostsAuthentication
RhostsRSAAuthentication
RSAAuthentication
TISAuthentication
KerberosAuthentication
```

(The latter two keywords require TIS or Kerberos support compiled in, respectively.) Any or all of these keywords may appear with the value `yes` or `no`.

For SSH2, the `AllowedAuthentications` keyword selects one or more authentication techniques. Again, the keyword has the same use here as for the SSH2 server. [5.5.1]

OpenSSH accepts the same keywords as SSH1 except for `TISAuthentication`, and it adds `SkeyAuthentication` for one-time passwords. [5.5.1.10]

7.4.10.2. The server is the boss

When a client specifies an authentication technique, this is just a request, not a requirement. For example, the configuration:

```
PasswordAuthentication yes
```

* Note that at press time, you must disable session rekeying in the SSH2 client if you wish to use it with the OpenSSH server, because the latter doesn't yet support session rekeying. The connection dies with an error once the rekeying interval expires. This feature will likely be implemented soon, however.

informs the SSH server that you, the client, agree to participate in password authentication. It doesn't guarantee that you will authenticate by password, just that you are willing to do it if the server agrees. The server makes the decision and might still authenticate you by another method.

If a client wants to require an authentication technique, it must tell the server that one, and only one, technique is acceptable. To do this, the client must deselect every other authentication technique. For example, to force password authentication in SSH1 or OpenSSH:

```
# SSH1, OpenSSH
# This guarantees password authentication, if the server supports it.
PasswordAuthentication  yes
RSAAuthentication       no
RhostsRSAAuthentication no
RhostsAuthentication    no
KerberosAuthentication  no
# ... Add any other authentication methods, with value "no"
```

If the server doesn't support password authentication, however, this connection attempt will fail.

SSH2 has a better system: the `AllowedAuthentications` keyword, which has the same syntax and meaning as the server keyword of the same name: [5.5.1]

```
# SSH2 only
AllowedAuthentications password
```

7.4.10.3. Detecting successful authentication

SSH2 provides two keywords for reporting whether authentication is successful: `AuthenticationSuccessMsg` and `AuthenticationNotify`. Each of these causes SSH2 clients to print a message after attempting authentication.

`AuthenticationSuccessMsg` controls the appearance of the message "Authentication successful" after authentication, which is printed on standard error. Values may be `yes` (the default, to display the message) or `no`:

```
$ ssh2 server.example.com
Authentication successful.
Last login: Sat Jun 24 2000 14:53:28 -0400
...
$ ssh2 -p221 -o 'AuthenticationSuccessMsg no' server.example.com
Last login: Sat Jun 24 2000 14:53:28 -0400
...
```

`AuthenticationNotify`, an undocumented keyword, causes *ssh2* to print a different message, this time on standard output. If the authentication is successful, the message is "AUTHENTICATED YES", otherwise it's "AUTHENTICATED NO". Values may be `yes` (print the message) or `no` (the default):

```
$ ssh2 -q -o 'AuthenticationNotify yes' server.example.com
AUTHENTICATED YES
Last login: Sat Jun 24 2000 14:53:35 -0400
...
```

The behavior of these two keywords differs in the following ways:

- `AuthenticationSuccessMsg` writes to stderr; `AuthenticationNotify` writes to stdout.
- The *–q* command-line option [7.4.15] silences `AuthenticationSuccessMsg` but not `AuthenticationNotify`. This makes `AuthenticationNotify` better for scripting (for example, to find out if an authentication can succeed or not). Notice that *exit* is used as a remote command so the shell terminates immediately:

  ```
  #!/bin/csh
  # Get the AUTHENTICATION line
  set line = `ssh2 -q -o 'AuthenticationNotify yes' server.example.com exit`
  # Capture the second word
  set result = `echo $line | awk '{print $2}'`
  if ( $result == "YES" ) then
    ...
  ```

  In fact, `AuthenticationNotify` is used precisely in this manner by *scp2* and *sftp*, when these programs run *ssh2* in the background to connect to the remote host for file transfers. They wait for the appearance of the "AUTHENTICATED YES" message to know that the connection was successful, and they can now start speaking to the *sftp-server*.

`AuthenticationSuccessMsg` provides an additional safety feature: a guarantee that authentication has occurred. Suppose you invoke *ssh2* and are prompted for your passphrase:

```
$ ssh2 server.example.com
Passphrase for key "mykey": ********
```

You then see, to your surprise, a second passphrase prompt:

```
Passphrase for key "mykey":
```

You might conclude that you mistyped your passphrase the first time and type it again. But what if the second prompt came not from your *ssh2* client, but from the server, which has been hacked by an evil intruder? Your passphrase has just been stolen! To counteract this potential threat, *ssh2* prints "Authentication successful" after authentication, so the previous session actually looks like this:

```
$ ssh2 server.example.com
Passphrase for key "mykey": ********
Authentication successful.
Passphrase for key "mykey":
```

The second passphrase prompt is now revealed as a fraud.

7.4.11. Data Compression

SSH connections may be compressed. That is, data sent over an SSH connection may be compressed automatically before it is encrypted and sent, and automatically uncompressed after it is received and decrypted. If you're running SSH software on fast, modern processors, compression is generally a win. In an informal test between two Sun SPARCstation 10 workstations connected by Ethernet, we transmitted 12 MB of text from server to client over compressed and uncompressed SSH connections. With compression enabled at an appropriate level (explained later), the transmission time was halved.

To enable compression for a single session, use command-line options. Unfortunately, the implementations have incompatible syntax. For SSH1 and OpenSSH, compression is disabled by default, and the *–C* command-line option turns it on:

```
# SSH1, OpenSSH: turn compression ON
$ ssh1 -C server.example.com
$ scp1 -C myfile server.example.com:
```

For SSH2, however, *–C* means the opposite, turning compression off:

```
# SSH2 only: turn compression OFF
$ ssh2 -C server.example.com
```

and *+C* turns it on:

```
# SSH2 only: turn compression ON
$ ssh2 +C server.example.com
```

(There is no compression option for *scp2*.) To enable or disable compression for all sessions, use the `Compression` keyword, given a value of `yes` or `no` (the default):

```
# SSH1, SSH2, OpenSSH
Compression yes
```

SSH1 and OpenSSH may also set an integer *compression level* to indicate how much the data should be compressed. Higher levels mean better compression but slower performance. Levels may be from 0 to 9 inclusive, and the default level is 6.* The `CompressionLevel` keyword modifies the level:

```
# SSH1, OpenSSH
CompressionLevel 2
```

Changing the `CompressionLevel` can have a drastic effect on performance. Our earlier 12-MB test was run with the default compression level, 6, and took 42 seconds. With compression at various levels, the time ranged from 25 seconds to

* SSH's compression functionality comes from GNU Zip, a.k.a., *gzip*, a compression utility popular in the Unix world. The nine `CompressionLevel` values correspond to the nine methods supported by *gzip*.

nearly two minutes (see Table 7-2). With fast processors and network connections, `CompressionLevel 1` seems an obvious win. Experiment with `CompressionLevel` to see which value yields the best performance for your setup.

Table 7-2. Effect of Compression and CompressionLevel

Level	Bytes Sent	Time Spent (sec.)	Size Reduced (%)	Time Reduced (%)
None	12112880	55	0	0
1	2116435	25	82.5	55
2	2091292	25	82.5	55
3	2079467	27	82.8	51
4	1881366	33	84.4	40
5	1833850	36	84.8	35
6	1824180	42	84.9	24
7	1785725	48	85.2	13
8	1756048	102	85.5	–46
9	1755636	118	85.5	–53

7.4.12. Program Locations

The auxiliary program *ssh-signer2* is normally located in SSH2's installation directory, along with the other SSH2 binaries. [3.5.2.3] You can change this location with the undocumented keyword **SshSignerPath**:

```
# SSH2 only
SshSignerPath /usr/alternative/bin/ssh-signer2
```

If you use this keyword, be sure to set it to the fully qualified path of the program. If you use a relative path, hostbased authentication works only for users who have *ssh-signer2* in their search path, and *cron* jobs fail without *ssh-signer2* in their path.

7.4.13. Subsystems

Subsystems are predefined commands supported by an SSH2 server. [5.7] Each installed server can implement different subsystems, so check with the system administrator of the server machine for a list.*

* Or examine the server machine's configuration file */etc/ssh2/sshd2_config* yourself for lines beginning with *subsystem-*.

The *–s* option of *ssh2*, undocumented at press time, invokes a subsystem on a remote machine. For example, if the SSH2 server running on *server.example.com* has a "backups" subsystem defined, you run it as:

```
$ ssh2 -s backups server.example.com
```

7.4.14. SSH1/SSH2 Compatibility

SSH2 has a few keywords relating to SSH1 compatibility. If compatibility is enabled, when *ssh2* is asked to connect to an SSH-1 server, it invokes *ssh1* (assuming it is available).

The keyword **Ssh1Compatibility** turns on SSH1 compatibility, given the value **yes** or **no**. The default is **yes** if compatibility is compiled in; otherwise it is **no**:

```
# SSH2 only
Ssh1Compatibility yes
```

The keyword **Ssh1Path** locates the executable for *ssh1*, which by default is set during compile-time configuration:

```
# SSH2 only
Ssh1Path /usr/local/bin/ssh1
```

If you want SSH2 agents to store and retrieve SSH1 keys, turn on agent compatibility with the keyword **Ssh1AgentCompatibility**: [6.3.2.4]

```
# SSH2 only
Ssh1AgentCompatibility yes
```

Finally, *scp2* invokes *scp1* if the *–1* command-line option is present:

```
# SSH2 only
scp2 -1 myfile server.example.com:
```

In this case, *scp2 –1* simply invokes *scp1*, passing along all its arguments (except for the *–1* of course). We don't see much point to this option: if *scp1* is available, why not invoke it directly? But the option is there if you need it.

7.4.15. Logging and Debugging

Earlier in the chapter, we introduced the *–v* command-line option which causes SSH clients to print debugging messages. Verbose mode works for *ssh* and *scp*:

```
# SSH1, OpenSSH
$ ssh -v server.example.com
SSH Version 1.2.27 [sparc-sun-solaris2.5.1], protocol version 1.5.
client: Connecting to server.example.com [128.9.176.249] port 22.
client: Connection established.
...
```

Verbose mode can also be turned on for SSH2 with the (surprise!) **VerboseMode** keyword:

```
# SSH2 only
VerboseMode yes
```

If you ever encounter problems or strange behavior from SSH, your first instinct should be to turn on verbose mode.

SSH2 has multiple levels of debug messages; verbose mode corresponds to level 2. You can specify greater or less debugging with the *–d* command-line option, followed by an integer from 0 to 99:

```
$ ssh2 -d0        No debugging messages
$ ssh2 -d1        Just a little debugging
$ ssh2 -d2        Same as -v
$ ssh2 -d3        A little more detailed
$ ssh2 -d#        And so on...
```

The analogous feature in OpenSSH is the **LogLevel** directive, which takes one of six levels as an argument: **QUIET**, **FATAL**, **ERROR**, **INFO**, **VERBOSE**, and **DEBUG** (in order of increasing verbosity). So for example:

```
# OpenSSH
$ ssh -o LogLevel=DEBUG
```

is equivalent to *ssh –v*.

The *–d* option may also use the same module-based syntax as for server debugging: [5.8.2.2]

```
$ ssh2 -d Ssh2AuthPasswdServer=2 server.example.com
```

scp2 also supports this level of debugging, but the option is *–D* instead of *–d* since *scp –d* is already used to mean something else:

```
$ scp2 -D Ssh2AuthPasswdServer=2 myfile server.example.com
```

To disable all debug messages, use *–q*:

```
# SSH1, SSH2, OpenSSH
$ ssh -q server.example.com

# SSH2 only
$ scp2 -q myfile server.example.com:
```

or the **QuietMode** keyword:

```
# SSH2 only
QuietMode yes
```

Finally, to print the program version number, use *–V*:

```
# SSH1, SSH2, OpenSSH
$ ssh -V
```

```
# SSH2 only
$ scp2 -V
```

7.4.16. Random Seeds

SSH2 lets you change the location of your random seed file, which is *~/.ssh2/random_seed* by default: [5.4.1.2]

```
# SSH2 only
RandomSeedFile /u/smith/.ssh2/new_seed
```

7.5. Secure Copy with scp

The secure copy program, *scp*, obeys keywords in your client configuration file just as *ssh* does. In addition, *scp* provides other features and options that we'll cover in this section.

7.5.1. Full Syntax

So far, we've described the syntax of *scp* only in general: [2.2.1]

```
scp name-of-source name-of-destination
```

Each of the two names, or *path specifications*, on the command line represents files or directories in the following manner (it is fairly consistent with the behavior of Unix *cp* or *rcp*):

- If *name-of-source* is a file, *name-of-destination* may be a file (existing or not) or a directory (which must exist). In other words, a single file may be copied to another file or into a directory.
- If *name-of-source* is two or more files, one or more directories, or a combination, *name-of-destination* must be an existing directory into which the copy takes place.* In other words, multiple files and directories may be copied only into a directory.

Both *name-of-source* and *name-of-destination* may have the following form from left to right:

1. The *username* of the account containing the file or directory, followed by @. This part is optional and if omitted, the value is the username of the user invoking *scp*.

* We say "must," but technically you may specify a file as a destination in some cases. However, this behavior is probably not what you want. As your multiple files get copied into a single destination file, each is overwritten by the next.

2. The *hostname* of the host containing the file or directory, followed by a colon. This part is optional if the path is present, and the username isn't; if omitted, the value is *localhost*. SSH2 permits an optional *TCP port number* for the SSH connection to be inserted between the hostname and the colon, preceded by a hash sign.
3. The *directory path* to the file or directory. (Optional if the hostname is present.) Relative pathnames are assumed relative to the *default directory*, which is the current directory (for local paths) or the user's home directory (for remote paths). If omitted entirely, the path is assumed to be the default directory.

Although each field is optional, you can't omit them all at the same time, yielding the empty string. Either the hostname (2) or the directory path (3) must be present. Some examples:

MyFile
: The file *./MyFile* on *localhost*

MyDirectory
: The directory *./MyDirectory* on *localhost*

.
: The current directory on *localhost*

server.example.com:
: The directory *~username* on *server.example.com*

server.example.com
: A local file named "server.example.com" (oops: did you forget the trailing colon—a common mistake)

server.example.com:MyFile
: The file *MyFile* in the remote user's home directory on *server.example.com*

bob@server.example.com:
: The directory *~bob* on *server.example.com*

bob@server.example.com
: A local file named "bob@server.example.com" (oops; forgot the trailing colon again)

bob@server.example.com:MyFile
: The file *~bob/MyFile* on *server.example.com*

server.example.com:dir/MyFile
: The file *dir/MyFile* in the remote user's home directory on *server.example.com*

server.example.com:/dir/MyFile
: The file */dir/MyFile* on *server.example.com* (note the absolute path)

bob@server.example.com:dir/MyFile
: The file *~bob/dir/MyFile* on *server.example.com*

bob@server.example.com:/dir/MyFile
: The file */dir/MyFile* on *server.example.com* (although you authenticate as bob, the path is absolute)

server.example.com#2000:
: The remote user's home directory on *server.example.com*, via TCP port 2000 (SSH2 only)

Here are a few complete examples:

```
$ scp myfile myfile2                      A local copy just like cp
$ scp myfile bob@host1:                   Copy ./myfile to ~bob on host1
$ scp bob@host1:myfile .                  Copy ~bob/myfile on host1 to ./myfile
$ scp host1:file1 host2:file2             Copy file1 from host1 to file2 on host2
$ scp bob@host1:file1 jen@host2:file2     Same as above, but copying from bob's
                                          to jen's account
```

Table 7-3 summarizes the syntax of an *scp* path.

Table 7-3. scp Path Specifications

Field	Other Syntax	Optional?	Default for Local Host	Default for Remote Host
Username	Followed by @	Yes	Invoking user's username	Invoking user's username
Hostname	Followed by :	Only if username is omitted and path is present	None, file is accessed locally	N/A
Port number[a]	Preceded by #	Yes	22	22
Directory path	N/A	Only if hostname is present	Current (invoking) directory	Username's remote home directory

[a] SSH2 only.

7.5.2. Handling of Wildcards

scp for SSH1 and OpenSSH has no special support for wildcards in filenames. It simply lets the shell expand them:

```
$ scp *.txt server.example.com:
```

Watch out for wildcards in remote file specifications, as they are evaluated on the local machine, not the remote. For example, this attempt is likely to fail:

```
$ scp1 server.example.com:*.txt .              Bad idea!
```

The Unix shell attempts to expand the wildcard before *scp1* is invoked, but the current directory contains no filename matching "server.example.com:*.txt". C shell and its derivatives will report "no match" and not execute *scp1*. Bourne-style shells, noticing no match in the current directory, will pass the unexpanded wildcard to *scp1*, and the copy may succeed as planned, but this coincidental behavior shouldn't be relied on. Always escape your wildcards so they are explicitly ignored by the shell and passed to *scp1*:

```
$ scp1 server.example.com:\*.txt .
```

scp2 does its own regular expression matching after shell-wildcard expansion is complete. The *sshregex* manpage for SSH2 (see Appendix A) describes the supported operators. Even so, escape your wildcard characters if you want your local shell to leave them alone.

7.5.3. Recursive Copy of Directories

Sometimes you want to copy not just a single file but a directory hierarchy. In this case, use the *–r* option, which stands for recursive. If you are familiar with *rcp*, its *–r* option has the same effect.

For example, to securely copy the directory */usr/local/bin* and all its files and subdirectories to another machine:

```
# SSH1, SSH2, OpenSSH
$ scp -r /usr/local/bin server.example.com:
```

If you forget the *–r* option when copying directories, *scp* complains:

```
$ scp /usr/local/bin server.example.com:
/usr/local/bin: not a regular file
```

Although *scp* can copy directories, it isn't necessarily the best method. If your directory contains hard links or soft links, they won't be duplicated. Links are copied as plain files (the link targets), and worse, circular directory links cause *scp1* to loop indefinitely. (*scp2* detects symbolic links and copies their targets instead.) Other types of special files, such as named pipes, also aren't copied correctly.* A better solution is to use *tar*, which handles special files correctly, and send it to the remote machine to be untarred, via SSH:

```
$ tar cf - /usr/local/bin | ssh server.example.com tar xf -
```

* These limitations also are true when copying single files, but at least you see the erroneous result quickly. With directories, you can copy a hierarchy incorrectly and not notice.

7.5.4. Preserving Permissions

When *scp* copies files, the destination files are created with certain file attributes. By default, the file permissions adhere to a umask on the destination host, and the modification and last access times will be the time of the copy. Alternatively, you can tell *scp* to duplicate the permissions and timestamps of the original files. The *–p* option accomplishes this:

```
# SSH1, SSH2, OpenSSH
$ scp -p myfile server.example.com:
```

For example, if you transfer your entire home directory to a remote machine, you probably want to keep the file attributes the same as the original:

```
$ scp -rp $HOME server.example.com:myhome/
```

7.5.5. Automatic Removal of Original File

After copying a file, *scp2* can optionally remove the original if desired. The *–u* command-line option specifies this:*

```
# SSH2 only
$ scp2 myfile server.example.com:
$ ls myfile
myfile
$ scp2 -u myfile server.example.com:
$ ls myfile
myfile: No such file or directory
```

If you've ever wanted a "secure move" command in addition to secure copy, you can define one in terms of *scp2 –u*:

```
$ alias smv='scp2 -u'
```

7.5.6. Safety Features

scp has two features to protect you from running dangerous commands. Suppose you want to copy a local file *myfile* to a remote directory. You type:

```
# SSH1, SSH2, OpenSSH
$ scp2 myfile server.example.com:mydir
$ rm myfile
```

Then you connect to *server.example.com* and find, to your horror, that *mydir* was a file, not a directory, and you just overwrote it! The *–d* option prevents this tragedy. If the destination isn't a directory, *scp* complains and exits without copying the file.

* In some earlier versions of SSH2, this option has no effect.

```
# SSH1, SSH2, OpenSSH
$ scp2 -d myfile server.example.com:mydir
warning: Destination file is not a directory.
warning: Exiting.
```

This option is necessary only if you are copying a single file. If you are copying multiple files or a directory, all the *scp* implementations check by default that the remote destination is a directory.*

Another safety feature of *scp2* is the *–n* option, which instructs the program to describe its actions but not perform any copying. This is useful for verifying the behavior of *scp2* before executing a potentially risky command.

```
# SSH2 only
$ scp2 -n myfile server.example.com:
Not transferring myfile -> server.example.com:./myfile  (1k)
```

7.5.7. Statistics Display

As *scp* copies files, it may print statistics about its progress.

7.5.7.1. scp1 statistics

For *scp1*, the statistics display is configurable by command-line options and environment variables:†

```
$ scp1 myfile* server.example.com:
myfile1          |          50 KB |  50.0 kB/s | ETA: 00:00:00 | 100%
myfile2          |          31 KB |  31.3 kB/s | ETA: 00:00:00 | 100%
myfile3          |           3 KB |   3.8 kB/s | ETA: 00:00:00 | 100%
```

For each file, *scp1* displays the name, the size, the transfer rate, and a two-part progress meter about the transmission. "ETA" (Estimated Time of Arrival) is the estimated transfer time, and the final number is the percentage of the file transmitted so far. While the file is transferring, the ETA value counts down to zero and the percentage increases to 100, though you can't see this on the printed page.

Although the statistics are informative, you might want to change or disable them. For example, you might prefer to turn them off when *scp1* is part of a batch job that shouldn't produce screen output.

This statistics display can be configured in several ways, using command-line options and environment variables (see Table 7-4: note that command-line options take precedence over environment variables).

* There's one degenerate case. If your copy occurs on a single machine, e.g., *scp *.c mydir*, the *scp* client doesn't necessarily check that *mydir* is a directory.

† For starters, *scp1* must be compiled with the configuration flag `--with-scp-stats`, or else statistics will be unavailable. [4.1.5.11]

Table 7-4. Controlling Statistics in scp1

Desired Outcome	Using Options	Setting Environment Variables
No output[a]	*scp1 -q*	SSH_NO_SCP_STATS
Output, but not file-by-file	*scp1 –Q –A*	SSH_NO_ALL_SCP_STATS SSH_SCP_STATS
Output file-by-file	*scp1 –Q –a*	SSH_ALL_SCP_STATS SSH_SCP_STATS

[a] Also works for OpenSSH's *scp* client.

First, you may control the presence or absence of statistics at all. This is done with the options *–q* and *–Q*, or the environment variables SSH_SCP_STATS and SSH_NO_SCP_STATS. To disable statistics, use either of the following:

```
# SSH1, OpenSSH
$ scp -q myfile server.example.com:

# SSH1 only
$ setenv SSH_NO_SCP_STATS 1
$ scp1 myfile server.example.com:
```

To enable statistics, use either of these:

```
# SSH1 only
$ scp1 -Q myfile server.example.com:

# SSH1 only
$ setenv SSH_SCP_STATS 1
$ scp1 myfile server.example.com:
```

If statistics are enabled, you may also choose to print file-by-file statistics. This is done with the options *–a* and *–A*, or the environment variables SSH_ALL_SCP_STATS and SSH_NO_ALL_SCP_STATS. To print file-by-file statistics, use either of these:

```
# SSH1 only
$ scp1 -Q -a myfile server.example.com:

# SSH1 only
$ setenv SSH_ALL_SCP_STATS 1
$ scp1 myfile server.example.com:
```

or to print a single, cumulative statistic:

```
# SSH1 only
$ scp1 -Q -A myfile server.example.com:

# SSH1 only
$ setenv SSH_NO_ALL_SCP_STATS 1
$ scp1 myfile server.example.com:
```

7.5.7.2. scp2 statistics

The statistics display for *scp2* is configurable as well, but as of SSH2 2.1.0, this information is missing from the manpage. By default, the statistics display is enabled, and there's no compile-time option like SSH1's `--with-scp-stats` to disable it. The display looks different from that of *scp1*:

```
$ scp2 myfile* server.example.com:
Transfering myfile1 -> server.example.com:./myfile1  (50k)
|.........................................................|
51200 bytes transferred in 1.00 seconds [50.0 kB/sec].
Transfering myfile2 -> server.example.com:./myfile2  (30k)
|.........................................................|
31744 bytes transferred in 1.03 seconds [31.3 kB/sec].
Transfering myfile3 -> server.example.com:./myfile3  (3k)
|.........................................................|
3068 bytes transferred in 0.79 seconds [3.8 kB/sec].
```

The progress indicators (dotted lines) change as the files are transferred, but frankly we find them unintuitive. To suppress the statistics display, use the *–Q* command-line option (yes, it has the opposite meaning of SSH1's *–Q* option):

```
$ scp2 -Q myfile server.example.com:
```

7.5.8. Locating the ssh Executable

To copy files securely, *scp* invokes *ssh* internally. Therefore, *scp* needs to know where the *ssh* executable resides on disk. Normally, the path to *ssh* is made known to *scp* at compile time (by the compile-time flag `--prefix`), but you can specify the path manually if you like. [4.1.5.2] For instance, you can test a new version of *ssh* with an old version of *scp*. The command-line option *–S* specifies the path:

```
# SSH1, SSH2
$ scp -S /usr/alternative/bin/ssh myfile server.example.com:
```

7.5.9. For Internal Use Only

scp for SSH1 and OpenSSH has two undocumented options, *-t* and *-f*, for internal use. Most likely you will never need to use them explicitly. They inform *scp* of the direction of the copy: from the local to the remote machine, or from remote to local. The *–t* option means copying to a remote machine and *–f* means copying from a remote machine.

Whenever you invoke *scp*, it invisibly runs a second *scp* process on the remote host that includes either *–t* or *–f* on its command line. You can see this if you run *scp* in verbose mode. If copying from the local to the remote machine, you see:

```
$ scp -v myfile server.example.com:
Executing: host server.example.com, ..., command scp -v -t .
...
```

On the other hand, if you copy from the remote to the local machine, you see:

```
$ scp -v server.example.com:myfile .
Executing: host server.example.com, ..., command scp -v -f .
...
```

Again, it's likely you'll never use these options, but they're useful to know when reading *scp*'s output in verbose mode. Also, the *scp2* manpage mentions them, so it's good to understand what they are.

7.6. Summary

SSH clients can be configured with environment variables, command-line options, and keywords in configuration files. Command-line options have the highest precedence, followed by your local client configuration file, and finally the global client configuration file.

Client configuration files consist of sections, and multiple sections can apply to a single invocation. If the same keyword is set multiple times, the earliest (SSH1, OpenSSH) or latest (SSH2) value is the winner.

When experimenting with client configuration, remember verbose mode. If you experience unusual SSH behavior, your first instinct should be to add the *–v* option and run the client again, watching the debug output for clues.

In this chapter:

8

Per-Account Server Configuration

We've seen two techniques for controlling the SSH server's behavior globally: compile-time configuration (Chapter 4) and serverwide configuration (Chapter 5). These techniques affect all incoming SSH connections to a given server machine. Now it's time to introduce a third, finer-grained method of server control: *per-account configuration.*

As the name implies, per-account configuration controls the SSH server differently for each user account on the server machine. For example, a user account sandy can accept incoming SSH connections from any machine on the Internet, while rick permits connections only from the domain *verysafe.com*, and fraidycat refuses key-based connections. Each user configures his or her own account, using the facilities highlighted in Figure 8-1, without needing special privileges or assistance from the system administrator.

We have already seen a simple type of per-account configuration. A user may place a public key into her authorization file, instructing the SSH server to permit logins to her account by public-key authentication. But per-account configuration can go further, becoming a powerful tool for access control and playing some fun tricks with your account. Accepting or rejecting connections by particular keys or hosts is just the beginning. For instance, you can make an incoming SSH connection run a program of your choice, instead of the client's choice. This is called a *forced command*, and we'll cover quite a few interesting applications.

Per-account configuration may control only incoming SSH connections to your account. If you're interested in configuring outgoing SSH connections by running SSH clients, refer to Chapter 7.

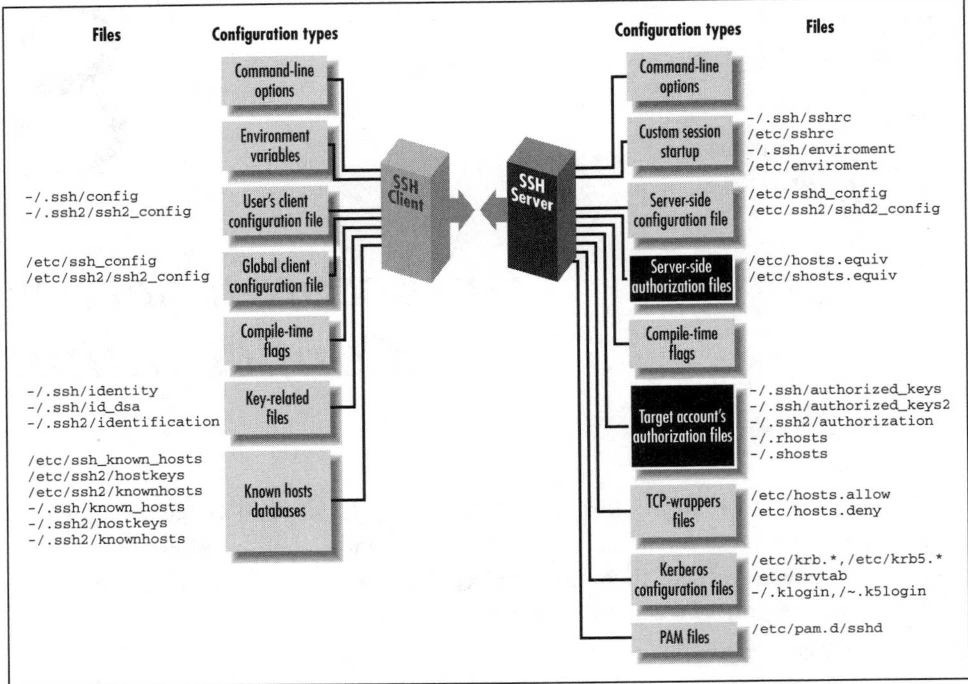

Figure 8-1. Per-account configuration (highlighted parts)

8.1. Limits of This Technique

Per-account configuration can do many interesting things, but it has some restrictions that we will discuss:

- It can't defeat security measures put in place by compile-time or serverwide configuration. (Thank goodness.)
- It is most flexible and secure if you use public-key authentication. Trusted-host and password authentication provide a much narrower range of options.

8.1.1. Overriding Serverwide Settings

SSH settings in a user's account may only restrict the authentication of incoming connections. They can't enable any SSH features that have been turned off more globally, and they can't permit a forbidden user or host to authenticate. For example, if your SSH server rejects all connections from the domain *evil.org*, you can't override this restriction within your account by per-account configuration.*

* There is one exception to this rule: trusted-host authentication. A user's *~/.shosts* file may override a restriction placed by the system administrator in */etc/shosts.equiv*. [8.3][3.4.2.3]

This limitation makes sense. No end-user tool should be able to violate a server security policy. However, end users should be (and are) allowed to restrict incoming connections to their accounts.

A few features of the server may be overridden by per-account configuration. The most notable one is the server's idle timeout, which may be extended beyond the serverwide setting. But such features can't coerce the server to accept a connection it has been globally configured to reject.

If you are an end user, and per-account configuration doesn't provide enough flexibility, you can run your own instance of the SSH server, which you may configure to your heart's content. [5.2.2] Be cautious, though, since this is seldom the right thing to do. The restrictions you're trying to circumvent are part of the security policy defined for the machine by its administrators, and you shouldn't run a program that flouts this policy just because you can. If the machine in question is under your administrative control, simply configure the main SSH server as you wish. If not, then installing and running your own *sshd* might violate your usage agreement and/or certainly annoy your sysadmin. And that's never a wise thing to do.

8.1.2. Authentication Issues

To make the best use of per-account configuration, use public-key authentication. Password authentication is too limited, since the only way to control access is with the password itself. Trusted-host authentication permits a small amount of flexibility, but not nearly as much as public-key authentication.

If you're still stuck in the password-authentication dark ages, let this be another reason to switch to public keys. Even though passwords and public-key passphrases might seem similar (you type a secret word, and *voilà*, you're logged in), public keys are far more flexible for permitting or denying access to your account. Read on and learn how.

8.2. Public Key-Based Configuration

To set up public-key authentication in your account on an SSH server machine, you create an authorization file, typically called *authorized_keys* (SSH1, OpenSSH/1), *authorized_keys2* (OpenSSH/2), or *authorization* (SSH2), and list the keys that provide access to your account. [2.4] Well, we've been keeping a secret. Your authorization file can contain not only keys but also other keywords or options to control the SSH server in powerful ways. We will discuss:

- The full format of an authorization file
- Forced commands for limiting the set of programs that the client may invoke on the server

- Restricting incoming connections from particular hosts
- Setting environment variables for remote programs
- Setting an idle timeout so clients will be forcibly disconnected if they aren't sending data
- Disabling certain features of the incoming SSH connection, such as port forwarding and tty allocation

As we demonstrate how to modify your authorization file, remember that the file is consulted by the SSH server only at authentication time. Therefore, if you change your authorization file, only new connections will use the new information. Any existing connections are already authenticated and won't be affected by the change.

Also remember that an incoming connection request won't reach your authorization file if the SSH server rejects it for other reasons, namely, failing to satisfy the serverwide configuration. If a change to your authorization file doesn't seem to be having an effect, make sure it doesn't conflict with a (more powerful) serverwide configuration setting.

8.2.1. SSH1 Authorization Files

Your SSH1 *authorized_keys* file, generally found in *~/.ssh/authorized_keys*, is a secure doorway into your account via the SSH-1 protocol. Each line of the file contains a public key and means the following: "I give permission for SSH-1 clients to access my account, in a particular way, using this key as authentication." Notice the words "in a particular way." Until now, public keys have provided unlimited access to an account. Now we'll see the rest of the story.

Each line of *authorized_keys* contains up to three items in order, some optional and some required:

- A set of *options* (optional, surprise, surprise).
- The *public key* (required). This appears in three parts: [3.4.2.2]
  - The *number of bits* in the key, typically a small integer such as 1024
  - The *exponent* of the key: an integer
  - The *modulus* of the key: a very large integer, typically several hundred digits long
- A descriptive *comment* (optional). This can be any text, such as "Bob's public key" or "My home PC using SecureCRT 3.1."

Public keys and comments are generated by *ssh-keygen* in *.pub* files, you may recall, and you typically insert them into *authorized_keys* by copying. [2.4.3] Options, however, are usually typed into *authorized_keys* with a text editor.*

An option may take two forms. It may be a keyword, such as:

```
# SSH1, OpenSSH: Turn off port forwarding
no-port-forwarding
```

or it may be a keyword followed by an equals sign and a value, such as:

```
# SSH1, OpenSSH: Set idle timeout to five minutes
idle-timeout=5m
```

Multiple options may be given together, separated by commas, with no whitespace between the options:

```
# SSH1, OpenSSH
no-port-forwarding,idle-timeout=5m
```

If you mistakenly include whitespace:

```
# THIS IS ILLEGAL: whitespace between the options
no-port-forwarding, idle-timeout=5m
```

your connection by this key won't work properly. If you connect with debugging turned on (*ssh1 –v*), you will see a "syntax error" message from the SSH server.

Many SSH users aren't aware of options or neglect to use them. This is a pity because options provide extra security and convenience. The more you know about the clients that access your account, the more options you can use to control that access.

8.2.2. SSH2 Authorization Files

An SSH2 authorization file, typically found in *~/.ssh2/authorization*,† has a different format from its SSH1 ancestor. Instead of public keys, it contains keywords and values, much like other SSH configuration files we've seen. Each line of the file contains one keyword followed by its value. The most commonly used keywords are `Key` and `Command`.

---

* When editing *authorized_keys*, be sure to use a text editor capable of handling long lines. The modulus of a key may be several hundred characters long. Some text editors can't display long lines, won't edit them properly, automatically insert line breaks, or wreak other sorts of havoc upon your nice public keys. (Aaargh. Don't get us started talking about brain-damaged text editors.) Use a modern editor, and turn off automatic line breaking. We use GNU Emacs.

† The name may be changed with the keyword `AuthorizationFile` in the serverwide configuration file. [5.4.1.6] Also, the *ssh2* manpage claims that `AuthorizationFile` can be set in the *client* configuration file, but as of SSH2 2.2.0 this setting has no effect. Since *sshd2* doesn't read the client configuration file, this is unsurprising.

Public keys are indicated using the **Key** keyword. **Key** is followed by whitespace, and then the name of a file containing a public key. Relative filenames refer to files in *~/.ssh2*. For example:

```
# SSH2 only
Key myself.pub
```

means that an SSH-2 public key is contained in *~/.ssh2/myself.pub*. Your *authorization* file must contain at least one **Key** line for public-key authentication to occur.

Each **Key** line may optionally be followed immediately by a **Command** keyword and its value. **Command** specifies a forced command, i.e., a command to be executed whenever the key immediately above is used for access. We discuss forced commands later in great detail. [8.2.4] For now, all you need to know is this: a forced command begins with the keyword **Command**, is followed by whitespace, and ends with a shell command line. For example:

```
# SSH2 only
Key somekey.pub
Command "/bin/echo All logins are disabled"
```

Remember that a **Command** line by itself is an error. The following examples are illegal:

```
# THIS IS ILLEGAL: no Key line
Command "/bin/echo This line is bad."
# THIS IS ILLEGAL: no Key line precedes the second Command
Key somekey.pub
Command "/bin/echo All logins are disabled"
Command "/bin/echo This line is bad."
```

8.2.2.1. SSH2 PGP key authentication

SSH2 Version 2.0.13 introduced support for PGP authentication. [5.5.1.6] Your *authorization* file may also include **PgpPublicKeyFile**, **PgpKeyName**, **PgpKeyFingerprint**, and **PgpKeyId** lines. A **Command** line may follow **PgpKeyName**, **PgpKeyFingerprint**, or **PgpKeyId**, just as it may follow **Key**:

```
# SSH2 only
PgpKeyName my-key
Command "/bin/echo PGP authentication was detected"
```

8.2.3. OpenSSH Authorization Files

For SSH-1 protocol connections, OpenSSH/1 uses the same *authorized_keys* file as SSH1. All configuration that's possible with SSH1 is available within OpenSSH/1.

For SSH-2 connections, OpenSSH/2 takes a new approach unlike SSH2's: a new authorization file, *~/.ssh/authorized_keys2*, with a format similar to that of *authorized_keys*. Each line may contain:

- Key authorization options (optional)
- The string "ssh-dss" (required)
- The DSA public key, represented as a long string (required)
- A descriptive comment (optional)

Here's an example with the long public key abbreviated:

```
host=192.168.10.1 ssh-dss AAAAB3NzaC1kc3MA... My OpenSSH key
```

8.2.4. Forced Commands

Ordinarily, an SSH connection invokes a remote command chosen by the client:

```
# Invoke a remote login shell
$ ssh server.example.com
# Invoke a remote directory listing
$ ssh server.example.com /bin/ls
```

A forced command transfers this control from the client to the server. Instead of the client's deciding which command will run, the owner of the server account decides. In Figure 8-2, the client has requested the command */bin/ls*, but the server-side forced command runs */bin/who* instead.

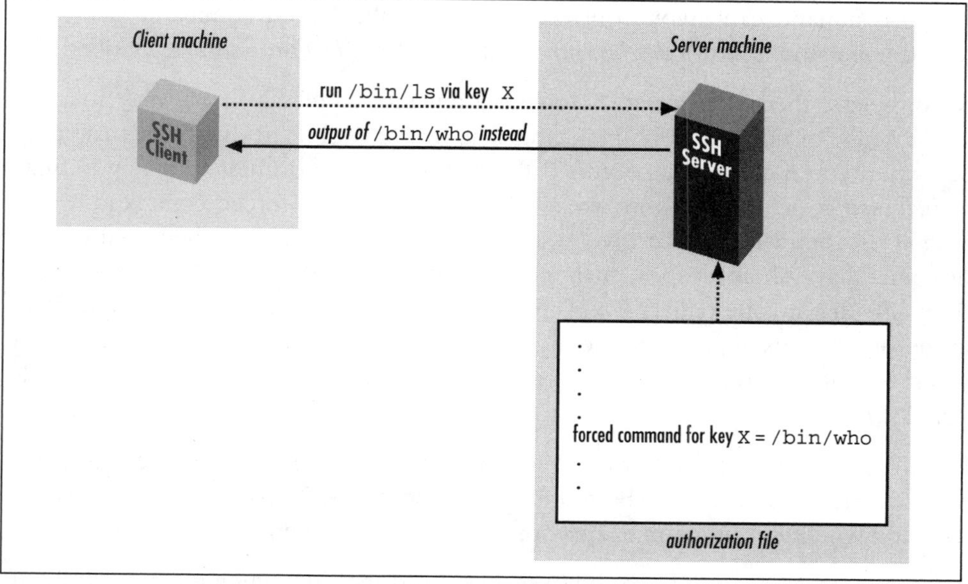

Figure 8-2. Forced command substituting /bin/who for /bin/ls

Forced commands can be quite useful. Suppose you want to give your assistant access to your account but only to read your email. You could associate a forced command with your assistant's SSH key to run only your email program and nothing else.

In SSH1 and OpenSSH, a forced command may be specified in *authorized_keys* with the "command" option preceding the desired key. For example, to run the email program *pine* whenever your assistant connects:

```
# SSH1, OpenSSH
command="/usr/local/bin/pine" ...secretary's public key...
```

In SSH2, a forced command appears on the line immediately following the desired `Key`, using the `Command` keyword. The previous example would be represented:

```
# SSH2 only
Key secretary.pub
Command "/usr/local/bin/pine"
```

You may associate at most one forced command with a given key. To associate multiple commands with a key, put them in a script on the remote machine and run the script as the forced command. (We demonstrate this in [8.2.4.3].)

8.2.4.1. Security issues

Before we begin in-depth examples of forced commands, let's discuss security. On first glance, a forced command seems at least as secure a "normal" SSH connection that invokes a shell. This is because a shell can invoke any program, while a forced command can invoke only one program, the forced command itself. If a forced command is */usr/local/bin/pine*, only */usr/local/bin/pine* can be invoked.

Nevertheless, there's a caveat. A forced command, carelessly used, may lull you into a sense of false security, believing that you have limited the client's capabilities when you haven't. This occurs if the forced command unintentionally permits a *shell escape*, i.e., a way to invoke a shell from within the forced command. Using a shell escape, a client can invoke any program available to a shell. Many Unix programs have shell escapes, such as text editors (*vi, Emacs*), pagers (*more, less*), programs that invoke pagers (*man*), news readers (*rn*), mail readers (such as Pine in the previous example!), and debuggers (*adb*). Interactive programs are the most common culprits, but even noninteractive commands may run shell commands (*find, xargs,* etc.).

When you define a forced command, you probably don't want its key used for arbitrary shell commands. Therefore, we propose the following safety rules for deciding whether a program is appropriate as a forced command:

- Avoid programs that have shell escapes. Read their documentation carefully. If you still aren't sure, get help.

- Avoid compilers, interpreters, or other programs that let the user generate and run arbitrary executable code.
- Treat very carefully any program that creates or deletes files on disk in user-specified locations. This includes not only applications (word processors, graphics programs, etc.) but also command-line utilities that move or copy files (*cp, mv, rm, scp, ftp*, etc.).
- Avoid programs with their setuid or setgid bits set, particularly setuid root.
- If using a script as a forced command, follow traditional rules of safe script writing. Within the script, limit the search path to relevant directories (omitting "."), invoke all programs by absolute path, don't blindly execute user supplied strings as commands, and don't make the script setuid anything.* And again, don't invoke any program that has a shell escape.
- Consider using a restricted shell to limit what the incoming client can do. For example, the restricted shell */usr/lib/rsh* (not to be confused with the r-command also called "rsh") can limit the remote directories the client can enter.
- Associate the forced command with a separate, dedicated SSH key, not the one used for your logins, so you can conveniently disable the key without affecting your login capability.
- Disable unnecessary SSH features using other options we cover later. Under SSH1, you may disable port forwarding with `no-port-forwarding`, agent forwarding with `no-agent-forwarding`, and tty allocation using `no-pty`.

Any program may be used as a forced command, but some may be risky choices. In the examples that follow, we cover several of these issues as they're encountered.

8.2.4.2. Rejecting connections with a custom message

Suppose you've permitted a friend to access your account by SSH, but now you've decided to disable the access. You can simply remove his key from your authorization file, but here's something fancier. You can define a forced command to print a custom message for your friend, indicating that his access has been disabled. For example:

```
# SSH1, OpenSSH
command="/bin/echo Sorry, buddy, but you've been terminated!" ...key...

# SSH2 only
Key friend.pub
Command "/bin/echo Sorry, buddy, but you've been terminated!"
```

* Modern Unix implementations often ignore the setuid bit on scripts for security reasons.

Any incoming SSH connection that successfully authenticates with this key causes the following message to be displayed on standard output:

```
Sorry, buddy, but you've been terminated!
```

and then the connection closes. If you'd like to print a longer message, which might be awkward to include in your authorization file, you can store it in a separate file (say, *~/go.away*) and display it using an appropriate program (e.g., *cat*):

```
# SSH1, OpenSSH
command="/bin/cat $HOME/go.away" ...key...

# SSH2 only
Key friend.pub
Command "/bin/cat $HOME/go.away"
```

Since the message is long, you might be tempted to display it one screenful at a time with a pager program such as *more* or *less*. Don't do it!

```
# SSH1: Don't do this!
command="/bin/more $HOME/go.away" ...key...
```

This forced command opens an unwanted hole into your account: the *more* program, like most Unix pager programs, has a shell escape. Instead of restricting access to your account, this forced command permits unlimited access.

8.2.4.3. Displaying a command menu

Suppose you want to provide limited access to your account, permitting the incoming SSH client to invoke only a few, specific programs. Forced commands can accomplish this. For instance, you can write a shell script that permits a known set of programs to be executed and then run the script as a forced command. A sample script, shown in Example 8-1, permits only three programs to be chosen from a menu.

Example 8-1. Menu Script

```
#!/bin/sh
/bin/echo "Welcome!
Your choices are:

1       See today's date
2       See who's logged in
3       See current processes
q       Quit"

/bin/echo "Your choice: \c"
read ans
while [ "$ans" != "q" ]
do
  case "$ans" in
```

Example 8-1. Menu Script (continued)

```
    1)
        /bin/date
        ;;
    2)
        /bin/who
        ;;
    3)
        /usr/ucb/w
        ;;
    q)
        /bin/echo "Goodbye"
        exit 0
        ;;
    *)
        /bin/echo "Invalid choice '$ans': please try again"
        ;;
  esac
  /bin/echo "Your choice: \c"
  read ans
done
exit 0
```

When someone accesses your account by public key and invokes the forced command, the script displays:

```
Welcome!
Your choices are:
 1        See today's date
 2        See who's logged in
 3        See current processes
 q        Quit

Your choice:
```

The user may then type `1`, `2`, `3`, or `q` to run the associated program. Any other input is ignored, so no other programs can be executed.

Such scripts must be written carefully to avoid security holes. In particular, none of the permitted programs should provide a means to escape to a shell, or else the user may execute any command in your account.

8.2.4.4. Examining the client's original command

As we've seen, a forced command gets substituted for any other command the SSH client might send. If an SSH client attempts to invoke the program *ps*:

```
$ ssh1 server.example.com ps
```

but a forced command is set up to execute "/bin/who" instead:

```
# SSH1, OpenSSH
command="/bin/who" ...key...
```

then *ps* is ignored and */bin/who* runs instead. Nevertheless, the SSH server does read the original command string sent by the client and stores it in an environment variable. For SSH1 and OpenSSH,* the environment variable is SSH_ORIGINAL_COMMAND, and for SSH2, it's SSH2_ORIGINAL_COMMAND. So in the our example, the value of SSH_ORIGINAL_COMMAND would be *ps*.

A quick way to see these variables in action is to print their values with forced commands. For SSH1, create a forced command like the following:

```
# SSH1 only
command="/bin/echo You tried to invoke $SSH_ORIGINAL_COMMAND" ...key...
```

Then connect with an SSH-1 client, supplying a remote command (which will not be executed), such as:

```
$ ssh1 server.example.com cat /etc/passwd
```

Instead of executing *cat*, the SSH1 server simply prints:

```
You tried to invoke cat /etc/passwd
```

and exits. Similarly, for SSH2, you can set up a forced command like this:

```
# SSH2 only
Key mykey.pub
Command "/bin/echo You tried to invoke $SSH2_ORIGINAL_COMMAND"
```

and then a client command like:

```
$ ssh2 server.example.com cat /etc/passwd
```

produces:

```
You tried to invoke cat /etc/passwd
```

8.2.4.5. Restricting a client's original command

Let's try a slightly more complex example using the environment variable SSH_ORIGINAL_COMMAND. We will create a forced command that examines the environment variable and turns a requested command into another of our choice. For example, suppose you want to permit a friend to invoke remote commands in your account, except for the *rm* (remove file) command. In other words, a command such as:

```
$ ssh server.example.com rm myfile
```

is rejected. Here's a script that checks for the presence of *rm* in the command string and, if present, rejects the command:

```
#!/bin/sh
# SSH1 only; for SSH2, use $SSH2_ORIGINAL_COMMAND.
#
```

* Older versions of OpenSSH didn't set SSH_ORIGINAL_COMMAND.

```
case "$SSH_ORIGINAL_COMMAND" in
  *rm*)
    echo "Sorry, rejected"
    ;;
  *)
    $SSH_ORIGINAL_COMMAND
    ;;
esac
```

Save this script in *~/rm-checker*, and define a forced command to use it:

```
# SSH1 only
command="$HOME/rm-checker" ...key...
```

Our script is just an example: it isn't secure. It can be easily bypassed by a clever command sequence to remove a file:

```
$ ssh server.example.com '/bin/ln -s /bin/r? ./killer && ./killer myfile'
```

which creates a link to */bin/rm* with a different name (`killer`) and then performs the removal. Nevertheless, the concept is still valid: you can examine SSH_ORIGINAL_COMMAND to select another command to execute instead.

8.2.4.6. Logging a client's original command

Another cool use of the "original command" environment variables is to keep a log of commands that are run using a given key. For example:

```
# SSH1 only
command="log-and-run" ...key...
```

where *log-and-run* is the following script. It appends a line to a log file, containing a timestamp and the command attempted:

```
#!/bin/sh
if [ -n "$SSH_ORIGINAL_COMMAND" ]
then
  echo "`/bin/date`: $SSH_ORIGINAL_COMMAND" >> $HOME/ssh-command-log
  exec $SSH_ORIGINAL_COMMAND
fi
```

8.2.4.7. Forced commands and secure copy (scp)

We've seen what happens when *ssh* encounters a key with a forced command. But what does *scp* do in this situation? Does the forced command run, or does the copy operation take place?

In this case, the forced command executes, and the original operation (file copy) is ignored. Depending on your needs, this behavior might be good or bad. In general, we do not recommend using *scp* with any key that has a forced command. Instead, use two keys, one for ordinary logins and file copying and the other for the forced command.

Now that we've thoroughly examined forced commands, let's move on to other features of per-account configuration.

8.2.5. Restricting Access by Host or Domain

Public-key authentication requires two pieces of information: the corresponding private key and its passphrase (if any). Without either piece, authentication can't succeed. Per-account configuration lets you add a third requirement for additional security: a restriction on the client's hostname or IP address. This is done with the `from` option. For example:

```
# SSH1, OpenSSH
from="client.example.com" ...key...
```

enforces that any SSH-1 connection must come from *client.example.com*, or else it is rejected. Therefore, if your private key file is somehow stolen, and your passphrase cracked, an attacker might still be stymied if he can't connect from the authorized client machine.

If the concept of "from" sounds familiar, you've got a good memory: it's the same access control provided by the `AllowUsers` keyword for serverwide configuration. [5.5.2.1] The `authorized_keys` option, however, is set by you within your account and applies to a single key, while `AllowUsers` is specified by the system administrator and applies to all connections to an account. Here's an example to demonstrate the difference. Suppose you want to permit connections from *remote.org* to enter the benjamin account. As system administrator, you can configure this within */etc/sshd_config*:

```
# SSH1, OpenSSH
AllowUsers benjamin@remote.org
```

Using per-account configuration, the user benjamin can configure the identical setting within his *authorized_keys* file, for a particular key only:

```
# SSH1, OpenSSH
# File ~benjamin/.ssh/authorized_keys
from="remote.org" ...key...
```

Of course, the serverwide setting takes precedence. If the system administrator had denied this access using the `DenyUsers` keyword:

```
# SSH1, OpenSSH
DenyUsers benjamin@remote.org
```

then user benjamin can't override this restriction using the `from` option in *authorized_keys*.

Just like `AllowUsers`, the `from` option can use the wildcard characters *, matching any string, and ?, matching any one character:

`from="*.someplace.org"`	*Matches any host in the someplace.org domain*
`from="som?pla?e.org"`	*Matches somXplaYe.org but not foo.someXplaYe.org or foo.somplace.org*

It can also match the client IP address, with or without wildcards (though this is not mentioned in the manpage):

```
from="192.220.18.5"
from="192.2??.18.*"
```

There may also be multiple patterns, this time separated by commas (`AllowUsers` employs spaces). No whitespace is allowed. You may also negate a pattern by prefixing it with an exclamation point (!). The exact matching rules are: every pattern in the list is compared to either the client's canonical hostname or its IP address. If the pattern contains only numerals, dots, and wildcards, it is matched against the address, otherwise, the hostname. The connection is accepted if and only if the client matches at least one positive pattern and no negated patterns. So for example, the following rule denies connections from *saruman.ring.org*, allows connections from other hosts in the domain *ring.org*, and denies everything else:

```
from="!saruman.ring.org,*.ring.org"
```

while this one again denies *saruman.ring.org* but allows all other clients:

```
from="!saruman.ring.org,*"
```

SSH1 unfortunately doesn't let you specify arbitrary IP networks using an address and mask, nor by *address/number of bits*. *libwrap* does [9.4], but its restrictions apply to all connections, not on a per-key basis.

Remember that access control by hostname may be problematic, due to issues with name resolution and security. [3.4.2.3] Fortunately, the `from` option is just an auxiliary feature of SSH-1 public-key authentication, which provides stronger security than would an entirely hostname-based solution.

8.2.5.1. Simulating "from" with SSH2

Although SSH2 doesn't support the `from` option, you can create your own host-based access control in SSH2 using a forced command. The trick is to examine the environment variable $SSH2_CLIENT [7.4.4.1] and create a script that performs the following steps:

1. From $SSH2_CLIENT, extract the IP address of the incoming client, which is the first value in the string.
2. Accept or reject the connection based on that IP address and any logic you like.

For example, suppose you want to permit connections from IP address 24.128.97.204 and reject them from 128.220.85.3. The following script does the trick when installed as a forced command:

```
#!/bin/sh
IP=`echo $SSH2_CLIENT | /bin/awk '{print $1}'`
case "$IP" in
  24.128.97.204)
    exec $SHELL
    ;;
  128.220.85.3)
    echo "Rejected"
    exit 1
    ;;
esac
```

Name the script (say) *~/ssh2from* and install it as an SSH2 forced command, and you're done:

```
# SSH2 only
Key mykey.pub
Command "$HOME/ssh2from"
```

This technique works reliably only for IP addresses, not hostnames. If you trust your name service, however, you can conceivably convert the IP address found in $SSH2_CLIENT to a hostname. On Linux you can use */usr/bin/host* for this purpose and, say, accept connections only from *client.example.com* or the domain *niceguy.org*:

```
#!/bin/sh
IP=`echo $SSH2_CLIENT | /bin/awk '{print $1}'`
HOSTNAME=`/usr/bin/host $IP | /bin/awk '{print $5}'`
case "$HOSTNAME" in
  client.example.com)
    exec $SHELL
    ;;
  *.niceguy.org)
    exec $SHELL
    ;;
  *)
    echo "Rejected"
    exit 1
    ;;
esac
```

8.2.6. Setting Environment Variables

The `environment` option instructs the SSH1 server to set an environment variable when a client connects via the given key. For example, the *authorized_keys* line:

```
# SSH1, OpenSSH
environment="EDITOR=emacs" ...key...
```

sets the environment variable EDITOR to the value **emacs**, thereby setting the client's default editor for the login session. The syntax following **environment=** is a quoted string containing a variable, an equals sign, and a value. All characters between the quotes are significant, i.e., the value may contain whitespace:

```
# SSH1, OpenSSH
environment="MYVARIABLE=this value has whitespace in it" ...key...
```

or even a double quote, if you escape it with a forward slash:

```
# SSH1, OpenSSH
environment="MYVARIABLE=I have a quote\" in my middle" ...key...
```

Also, a single line in *authorized_keys* may have multiple environment variables set:

```
# SSH1, OpenSSH
environment="EDITOR=emacs",environment="MYVARIABLE=26" ...key...
```

Why set an environment variable for a key? This feature lets you tailor your account to respond differently based on which key is used. For example, suppose you create two keys, each of which sets a different value for an environment variable, say, SPECIAL:

```
# SSH1, OpenSSH
environment="SPECIAL=1" ...key...
environment="SPECIAL=2" ...key...
```

Now, in your account's shell configuration file, you can examine $SPECIAL and trigger actions specific to each key:

```
# In your .login file
switch ($SPECIAL)
  case 1:
    echo 'Hello Bob!'
    set prompt = 'bob> '
    breaksw
  case 2:
    echo 'Hello Jane!'
    set prompt = jane> '
    source ~/.janerc
    breaksw
endsw
```

Here, we print a custom welcome message for each key user, set an appropriate shell prompt, and in Jane's case, invoke a custom initialization script, *~/.janerc*. Thus, the environment option provides a convenient communication channel between *authorized_keys* and the remote shell.

8.2.6.1. Example: CVS and $LOGNAME

As a more advanced example of the environment option, suppose a team of open source software developers around the Internet is developing a computer program. The team decides to practice good software engineering and store its code with CVS, the Concurrent Versions System version control tool. Lacking the funds to set up a server machine, the team places the CVS repository into the computer account of one of the team members, benjamin, since he has lots of available disk space. Benjamin's account is on the SSH server machine *cvs.repo.com.*

The other developers don't have accounts on *cvs.repo.com*, so benjamin places their public keys into his *authorized_keys* file so they can do check-ins. Now there's a problem. When a developer changes a file and checks the new version into the repository, a log entry is made by CVS, identifying the author of the change. But everyone is connecting through the benjamin account, so CVS always identifies the author as "benjamin," no matter who checked in the changes. This is bad from a software engineering standpoint: the author of each change should be clearly identified.*

You can eliminate this problem by modifying benjamin's file, preceding each developer's key with an environment option. CVS examines the LOGNAME environment variable to get the author's name, so you set LOGNAME differently for each developer's key:

```
# SSH1, OpenSSH
environment="LOGNAME=dan" ...key...
environment="LOGNAME=richard" ...key...
...
```

Now, when a given key is used for a CVS check-in, CVS identifies the author of the change by the associated, unique LOGNAME value. Problem solved!†

8.2.7. Setting Idle Timeout

The idle-timeout option tells the SSH1 server to disconnect a session that has been idle for a certain time limit. This is just like the `IdleTimeout` keyword for server-wide configuration but is set by you within your account, instead of by the system administrator. [5.4.3.3]

Suppose you let your friend Jamie access your account by SSH-1. Jamie works in an untrusted environment, however, and you are worried that he might walk away from his computer while connected to your account, and someone else might come by and use his session. One way to reduce the risk is to set an *idle timeout* on Jamie's key, automatically disconnecting the SSH-1 session after a given period of idle time. If the client stops sending output for a while, Jamie has probably walked away, and the session is terminated.

* In an industrial setting, each developer would have an account on the CVS repository machine, so the problem would not exist.

† Incidentally, the authors used this technique while collaborating on this book.

Timeouts are set in with the `idle-timeout` option. For example, to set the idle timeout to 60 seconds:

```
# SSH1, OpenSSH
idle-timeout=60s ...key...
```

`idle-timeout` uses the same notation for time as the `IdleTimeout` keyword: an integer, optionally followed by a letter indicating the units. For example, `60s` is 60 seconds, `15m` is fifteen minutes, `2h` is two hours, and so forth. If no letter appears, the default unit is seconds.

The `idle-timeout` option overrides any serverwide value set with the `IdleTimeout` keyword. For example, if the serverwide idle timeout is five minutes:

```
# SSH1, OpenSSH
IdleTimeout 5m
```

but your file sets it to 10 minutes for your account:

```
# SSH1, OpenSSH
idle-timeout=10m ...key...
```

then any connection using this key has an idle timeout of 10 minutes, regardless of the serverwide setting.

This feature has more uses than disconnecting absent typists. Suppose you're using an SSH-1 key for an automated process, such as backups. An idle timeout value kills the process automatically if it hangs due to an error.

8.2.8. Disabling Forwarding

Although you're permitting SSH-1 access to your account, you might not want your account to be used as a springboard to other machines by port forwarding. [9.2] To prevent this, use the `no-port-forwarding` option for that key:

```
# SSH1, OpenSSH
no-port-forwarding ...key...
```

Likewise, you can disable agent forwarding if you don't want remote users to travel through your account and onto other computers using the given key. [6.3.5] This is done with the `no-agent-forwarding` option:

```
# SSH1, OpenSSH
no-agent-forwarding ...key...
```

These aren't strong restrictions. As long as you allow shell access, just about anything can be done over the connection. The user need employ only a pair of custom programs that talk to each other across the connection and directly implement port forwarding, agent forwarding, or anything else you thought you were preventing. To be more than just a reminder or mild deterrent, these options must be used together with carefully restricted access on the server side, such as forced commands or a restricted shell on the target account.

8.2.9. Disabling TTY Allocation

Normally when you log in via SSH-1, the server allocates a pseudo-terminal (henceforth, tty) for the login session: [7.4.5.5]

```
# A tty is allocated for this client
$ ssh1 server.example.com
```

The server even sets an environment variable, SSH_TTY, with the name of the tty allocated. For example:

```
# After logging in via SSH-1
$ echo $SSH_TTY
/dev/pts/1
```

When you run a noninteractive command, however, the SSH server doesn't allocate a tty to set SSH_TTY:

```
# No tty is allocated
$ ssh1 server.example.com /bin/ls
```

Suppose you want to give someone SSH-1 access for invoking noninteractive commands but not for running an interactive login session. You've seen how forced commands can limit access to a particular program, but as an added safety precaution, you can also disable tty allocation with the `no-pty` option:

```
# SSH1, OpenSSH
no-pty ...key...
```

Noninteractive commands will now work normally, but requests for interactive sessions are refused by the SSH1 server. If you try to establish an interactive session, your client prints a warning message, such as:

```
Warning: Remote host failed or refused to allocate a pseudo-tty.
SSH_SMSG_FAILURE: invalid SSH state
```

or it appears to hang or fail altogether.

Just for fun, let's observe the effect of `no-pty` on the SSH_TTY environment variable with a simple experiment. Set up a public key and precede it with the following forced command:

```
# SSH1, OpenSSH
command="echo SSH_TTY is [$SSH_TTY]" ...key...
```

Now try connecting noninteractively and interactively, and watch the output. The interactive command gives SSH_TTY a value, but the noninteractive one doesn't:

```
$ ssh1 server.example.com
SSH_TTY is [/dev/pts/2]

$ ssh1 server.example.com anything
SSH_TTY is []
```

Next, add the `no-pty` option:

```
# SSH1, OpenSSH
no-pty,command="echo SSH_TTY is [$SSH_TTY]" ...key...
```

and try connecting interactively. The connection (properly) fails and SSH_TTY has no value:

```
$ ssh1 server.example.com
Warning: Remote host failed or refused to allocate a pseudo-tty.
SSH_TTY is []
Connection to server.example.com closed.
```

Even if a client requests a tty specifically (with *ssh -t*), the `no-pty` option forbids its allocation.

```
# SSH1, OpenSSH
$ ssh -t server.example.com emacs
Warning: Remote host failed or refused to allocate a pseudo-tty.
emacs: standard input is not a tty
Connection to server.example.com closed.
```

8.3. Trusted-Host Access Control

A limited type of per-account configuration is possible if you use trusted-host authentication rather than public-key authentication. Specifically, you can permit SSH access to your account based on the client's remote username and hostname via the system files */etc/shosts.equiv* and */etc/hosts.equiv*, and personal files *~/.rhosts* and *~/.shosts*. A line like:

```
+client.example.com jones
```

permits trusted-host SSH access by the user *jones@client.example.com.* Since we've already covered the details of these four files, we won't repeat the information in this chapter. [3.4.2.3]

Per-account configuration with trusted-host authentication is similar to using the `from` option of *authorized_keys* with public keys. Both may restrict SSH connections from particular hosts. The differences are shown in this table.

Feature	Trusted-Host	Public-Key from
Authenticate by hostname	Yes	Yes
Authenticate by IP address	Yes	Yes
Authenticate by remote username	Yes	No
Wildcards in hostnames and IP	No	Yes
Passphrase required for logins	No	Yes
Use other public-key features	No	Yes
Security	Less	More

To use trusted-host authentication for access control, all the following conditions must be true:

- Trusted-host authentication is enabled in the server, both at compile time and in the serverwide configuration file.
- Your desired client hosts aren't specifically excluded by serverwide configuration, e.g., by `AllowHosts` and `DenyHosts`.
- For SSH1, *ssh1* is installed setuid root.

Despite its capabilities, trusted-host authentication is more complex than one might expect. For example, if your carefully crafted *.shosts* file denies access to *sandy@trusted.example.com*:

```
# ~/.shosts
-trusted.example.com sandy
```

but your *.rhosts* file inadvertently permits access:

```
# ~/.rhosts
+trusted.example.com
```

then sandy will have SSH access to your account. Worse, even if you don't have a *~/.rhosts* file, the system files */etc/hosts.equiv* and */etc/shosts.equiv* can still punch a trusted-host security hole into your account against your wishes. Unfortunately, using per-account configuration, there's no way to prevent this problem. Only compile-time or serverwide configuration can disable trusted-host authentication.

Because of these issues and other serious, inherent weaknesses, we recommend against using the weak form of trusted-host authentication, Rhosts authentication, as a form of per-account configuration. (By default it is disabled, and we approve.) If you require the features of trusted-host authentication, we recommend the stronger form, called RhostsRSAuthentication (SSH1, OpenSSH) or hostbased (SSH2), which adds cryptographic verification of host keys. [3.4.2.3]

8.4. The User rc File

The shell script */etc/sshrc* is invoked by the SSH server for each incoming SSH connection. [5.6.4] You may define a similar script in your account, *~/.ssh/rc* (SSH1, OpenSSH) or *~/.ssh2/rc* (SSH2), to be invoked for every SSH connection to your account. If this file exists, */etc/sshrc* isn't run.

The SSH *rc* file is much like a shell startup file (e.g., *~/.profile* or *~/.cshrc*), but it executes only when your account is accessed by SSH. It is run for both interactive logins and remote commands. Place any commands in this script that you would like executed when your account is accessed by SSH, rather than an ordinary login. For example, you can run and load your *ssh-agent* in this file: [6.3.3]

```
# ~/.ssh/rc, assuming your login shell is the C shell
if ( ! $?SSH_AUTH_SOCK  ) then
  eval `ssh-agent`
  /usr/bin/tty | grep 'not a tty' > /dev/null
  if ( ! $status ) then
    ssh-add
  endif
endif
```

Like */etc/sshrc*, your personal *rc* file is executed just before the shell or remote command requested by the incoming connection. Unlike */etc/sshrc*, which is always processed by the Bourne shell (*/bin/sh*), your *rc* file is processed by your account's normal login shell.

8.5. Summary

Per-account configuration lets you instruct the SSH server to treat your account differently. Using public-key authentication, you can permit or restrict connections based on a client's key, hostname, or IP address. With forced commands, you can limit the set of programs that a client may run in your account. You can also disable unwanted features of SSH, such as port forwarding, agent forwarding, and tty allocation.

Using trusted-host authentication, you can permit or restrict particular hosts or remote users from accessing your account. This uses the files *~/.shosts* or (less optimally) *~/.rhosts*. However, the mechanism is less secure and less flexible than public-key authentication.

9

Port Forwarding and X Forwarding

In this chapter:

One of SSH's major benefits is *transparency.* A terminal session secured by SSH behaves like an ordinary, insecure one (e.g., created by *telnet* or *rsh*) once it has been established. Behind the scenes, however, SSH keeps the session secure via strong authentication, encryption, and integrity checking.

In some situations, however, transparency is hard to achieve. A network firewall might be in the way, interfering with certain network traffic you need. Corporate security policies might prohibit you from storing SSH keys on certain machines. Or you might need to use insecure network applications in an otherwise secure environment.

In this chapter, we'll discuss an important feature of SSH, called *forwarding* or *tunneling,* that addresses several concerns about transparency:

Securing other TCP/IP applications
: SSH can transparently encrypt another application's data stream. This is called *port forwarding.*

Securing X window applications
: Using SSH, you can invoke X programs on a remote machine and have them appear, securely, on your local display. (This feature of X is insecure ordinarily.) This is called *X forwarding,* a special case of port forwarding for which SSH has extra support.

SSH forwarding isn't completely transparent, since it occurs at the application level, not the network level. Applications must be configured to participate in forwarding, and a few protocols are problematic to forward (FTP data channels are a notable example). But in most common situations, once a secure tunnel is set up, the participating applications appear to the user to operate normally. For complete application-level transparency, you need a network-level technique, such as IPSEC [1.6.4] or a proprietary VPN (Virtual Private Network) technology available from various vendors, in host software or dedicated routers. While VPNs provide a more complete solution, they require significantly more work and expense to set up compared to SSH forwarding.

So, when we say "transparent" in this chapter, we mean "transparent to the application, once a little configuration has been done."

In this chapter, we discuss using SSH forwarding techniques to allow otherwise prohibited traffic across firewalls. This can be a perfectly legitimate and adequately safe practice if done properly: the firewall prevents unauthorized traffic, while SSH forwarding allows authorized users to bypass the restriction. However, don't forget you are bypassing a security restriction that is in place for a reason. Be sure to follow the guidelines we give for safe SSH forwarding. Also, take care that you aren't violating a company policy by using forwarding. Just because you *can* do something doesn't automatically mean that it's a good idea. If in doubt, consult with your system administrators.

9.1. What Is Forwarding?

Forwarding is a type of interaction with another network application, as shown in Figure 9-1. SSH intercepts a service request from some other program on one side of an SSH connection, sends it across the encrypted connection, and delivers it to the intended recipient on the other side. This process is mostly transparent to both sides of the connection: each believes it is talking directly to its partner and has no knowledge that forwarding is taking place. Even more powerfully, SSH forwarding can achieve certain types of communication that are impossible without it.

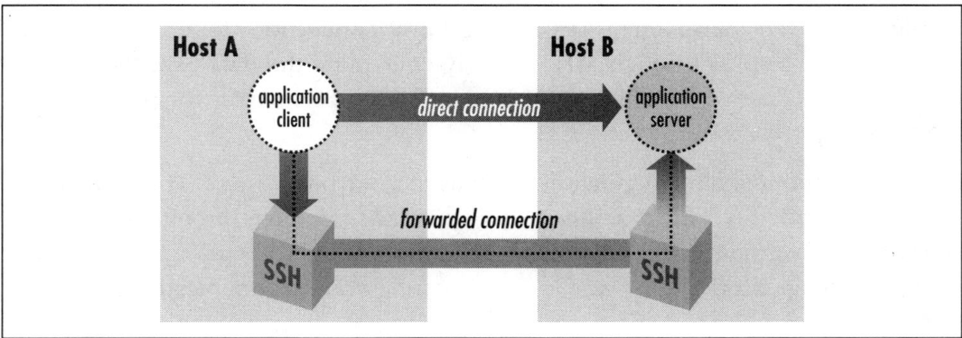

Figure 9-1. SSH forwarding

Forwarding isn't a new concept. The basic operation of a terminal connection over a network (say, using *telnet*) is also a kind of forwarding. In a *telnet* connection, you sit on one end, your remote shell is on the other, and both sides operate as if directly connected by a serial cable. Nevertheless, sitting in the middle is a cooperating *telnet* client and server, forwarding bytes back and forth. SSH forwarding is much the same, except SSH plays fancy tricks with the data to add security.

We have also seen another type of SSH forwarding, agent forwarding. [6.3.5] This let us create SSH connections from one computer, through a second computer, and onto a third using public-key authentication, but without installing our private key on the second machine. To accomplish this, an SSH server pretended to be an SSH agent, while transparently forwarding data to and from a remote agent. This paradigm holds true for TCP port forwarding and X forwarding, as the SSH server transparently masquerades as another network application.

9.2. Port Forwarding

SSH uses TCP/IP as its transport mechanism, usually TCP port 22 on the server machine, as it encrypts and decrypts the traffic passing over the connection. We will now discuss a cool feature that encrypts and decrypts TCP/IP traffic belonging to other applications, on other TCP ports, using SSH. This process, called port forwarding, is largely transparent and quite powerful. Telnet, SMTP, NNTP, IMAP, and other insecure protocols running over TCP can be made secure by forwarding the connections through SSH. Port forwarding is sometimes called tunneling because the SSH connection provides a secure "tunnel" through which another TCP/IP connection may pass.

Suppose you have a home machine H that runs an IMAP-capable email reader, and you want to connect to an IMAP server on machine S to read and send mail. Normally, this connection is insecure, with your mail account password transmitted as plaintext between your mail program and the server. With SSH port forwarding, you can transparently reroute the IMAP connection (found on server S's TCP port 143) to pass through SSH, securely encrypting the data over the connection.* The IMAP server machine must be running an SSH server for port forwarding to provide real protection.

In short, with minimal configuration changes to your programs, SSH port forwarding protects arbitrary TCP/IP connections by redirecting them through an SSH session. Port forwarding can even pass a connection safely through a firewall if you configure things properly. Once you start securing your communications with port

* Our port forwarding example protects your IMAP connection but doesn't truly protect your email messages. Before reaching your IMAP server, the messages pass through other mail servers and may be intercepted in transit. For end-to-end email security, you and your correspondent should use tools such as PGP or S/MIME to sign and/or encrypt the messages themselves.

forwarding, you'll wonder how you ever got along without it. Here are examples of what you can do:

- Access various kinds of TCP servers (e.g., SMTP, IMAP, POP, LDAP, etc.) across a firewall that prevents direct access.
- Provide protection for your sessions with these same TCP servers, preventing disclosure or alteration of passwords and other content that would otherwise be sent in the clear as part of the session.
- Tunnel the control connection of an FTP session, to encrypt your username, password, and commands. (It isn't usually possible to protect the data channels that carry the file contents, though. [11.2])
- Use your ISP's SMTP servers for sending mail, even if you're connected outside the ISP's network and the ISP forbids mail relaying from your current location. [11.3.2]

SSH port forwarding is a general proxying mechanism for TCP only. (See the sidebar "TCP Connections" for an overview of TCP concepts.) Forwarding can't work with protocols not built on TCP, such as the UDP-based DNS, DHCP, NFS, and NetBIOS,* or with non-IP-based protocols, such as AppleTalk or Novell's SPX/IPX.

9.2.1. Local Forwarding

In our earlier example, we had an IMAP server running on machine S, and an email reader on home machine H, and we wanted to secure the IMAP connection using SSH. Let's delve into that example in more detail.

IMAP uses TCP port 143; this means that an IMAP server will be listening for connections on port 143 on the server machine. To tunnel the IMAP connection through SSH, you need to pick a local port on home machine H (between 1024 and 65535) and forward it to the remote socket (S,143). Suppose you randomly pick local port 2001. The following command then creates the tunnel:†

```
$ ssh -L2001:localhost:143 S
```

* We're being a little imprecise here. DHCP is entirely based on UDP, so SSH port forwarding can't do anything with it. The others, however, either use both TCP and UDP for different purposes or can sometimes be configured to run over TCP, though they generally use UDP. Nevertheless, in most common situations, SSH can't forward them.

† You can also use *ssh –L2001:S:143 S*, substituting "S" for localhost, but we will discuss later why localhost is the better alternative when possible.

TCP Connections

To understand port forwarding, it's important to know some details about TCP, the Transmission Control Protocol. TCP is a fundamental building block of the Internet. Built on top of IP, it is the transport mechanism for many application-level Internet protocols such as FTP, Telnet, HTTP, SMTP, POP, IMAP, and SSH itself.

TCP comes with strong guarantees. A TCP connection is a virtual, full-duplex circuit between two communicating parties, acting like a two-way pipe. Either side may write any number of bytes at any time to the pipe, and the bytes are guaranteed to arrive unaltered and in order at the other side. The mechanisms that implement these guarantees, though, are designed to counter transmission problems in the network, such as routing around failed links, or retransmitting data corrupted by noise or lost due to temporary network congestion. They aren't effective against deliberate attempts to steal a connection or alter data in transit. SSH provides this protection that TCP alone lacks.

If an application doesn't need these guarantees about data integrity and order, or doesn't want the overhead associated with them, another protocol called User Datagram Protocol (UDP) often suffices. It is packet-oriented, and has no guarantees of delivery or packet ordering. Some protocols that run over UDP are NFS, DNS, DHCP, NetBIOS, TFTP, Kerberos, SYSLOG, and NTP.

When a program establishes a TCP connection to a service, it needs two pieces of information: the IP address of the destination machine and a way to identify the desired service. TCP (and UDP) use a positive integer, called a *port number*, to identify a service. For example, SSH uses port 22, *telnet* uses port 23, and IMAP uses port 143. Port numbers allow multiple services at the same IP address.

The combination of an IP address and a port number is called a *socket.* For example, if you run *telnet* to connect to port 23 on the machine at IP address 128.220.91.4, the socket is denoted "(128.220.91.4,23)." Simply put, when you make a TCP connection, its destination is a socket. The source (client program) also has a socket on its end of the connection, and the connection as a whole is completely defined by the pair of source and destination sockets.

In order for a connection attempt to a socket to succeed, something must be "listening" on that socket. That is, a program running on the destination machine must ask TCP to accept connection requests on that port and to pass the connections on to the program. If you've ever attempted a TCP connection and received the response "connection refused," it means that the remote machine is up and running, but nothing is listening on the target socket.

—Continued—

How does a client program know the target port number of a listening server? Port numbers for many protocols are standardized, assigned by the Internet Assigned Numbers Authority or IANA. (IANA's complete list of port numbers is found at *http://www.isi.edu/in-notes/iana/assignments/port-numbers.*) For instance, the TCP port number assigned to the NNTP (Usenet news) protocol is 119. Therefore, news servers listen on port 119, and newsreaders (clients) connect to them via port 119. More specifically, if a newsreader is configured to talk to a news server at IP address 10.1.2.3, it requests a TCP connection to the socket (10.1.2.3,119).

Port numbers aren't always hardcoded into programs. Many operating systems let applications refer to protocols by name, instead of number, by defining a table of TCP names and port numbers. Programs can then look up port numbers by the protocol name. Under Unix, the table is often contained in the file */etc/services* or the NIS services map, and queries are performed using the library routines `getservbyname()`, `getservbyport()`, and related procedures. Other environments allow servers to register their listening ports dynamically via a naming service, such as the AppleTalk Name Binding Protocol or DNS's WKS and SRV records.

So far, we've discussed the port number used by a TCP server when a TCP client program wants to connect. We call this the *target* port number. The client also uses a port number, called the *source* port number, so the server can transmit to the client. If you combine the client's IP address and its source port number, you get the client's socket.

Unlike target port numbers, source port numbers aren't standard. In most cases, in fact, neither the client nor the server cares which source port number is used by the client. Often a client will let TCP select an unused port number for the source. (The Berkeley r-commands, however, do care about source ports. [3.4.2.3]) If you examine the existing TCP connections on a machine with a command such as *netstat –a* or *lsof –i tcp*, you will see connections to the well-known port numbers for common services (e.g., 23 for Telnet, 22 for SSH), with large, apparently random source port numbers on the other end. Those source ports were chosen from the range of unassigned ports by TCP on the machines initiating those connections.

Once established, a TCP connection is completely determined by the combination of its source and target sockets. Therefore, multiple TCP clients may connect to the same target socket. If the connections originate from different hosts, the IP address portions of their source sockets will differ, distinguishing the connections. If they come from two different programs running on the same host, TCP on that host ensures they have different source port numbers.

The *-L* option specifies local forwarding, in which the TCP client is on the local machine with the SSH client. The option is followed by three values separated by colons: a local port to listen on (2001), the remote machine name or IP address (S), and the remote, target port number (143).

The previous command logs you into S, as it will if you just type **ssh S**. However, this SSH session has also forwarded TCP port 2001 on H to port 143 on S; the forwarding remains in effect until you log out of the session. To make use of the tunnel, the final step is to tell your email reader to use the forwarded port. Normally your email program connects to port 143 on the server machine, that is, the socket (S,143). Instead, it's configured to connect to port 2001 on home machine H itself, i.e., socket (localhost,2001). So the path of the connection is now as follows:

1. The email reader on home machine H sends data to local port 2001.
2. The local SSH client on H reads port 2001, encrypts the data, and sends it through the SSH connection to the SSH server on S.
3. The SSH server on S decrypts the data and sends it to the IMAP server listening on port 143 on S.
4. Data is sent back from the IMAP server to home machine H by the same process in reverse.

Port forwarding can be specified only when you create an SSH connection. You can't add a forwarding to an existing SSH connection with any SSH implementation we know of, though there's nothing intrinsic to the SSH protocol that would prevent it, and it would sometimes be a useful feature. Instead of using the *-L* option to establish a local forwarding, you can use the **LocalForward** keyword in your client configuration file:

```
# SSH1, OpenSSH
LocalForward 2001 localhost:143
# SSH2 only
LocalForward "2001:localhost:143"
```

Note the small syntactic differences. In SSH1 and OpenSSH, there are two arguments: the local port number, and the remote socket expressed as *host:port*. In SSH2, the expression is just as on the command line, except that it must be enclosed in double quotes. If you forget the quotes, *ssh2* doesn't complain, but it doesn't forward the port, either.

Our example with home machine H and IMAP server S can be set up like this:

```
# SSH1, OpenSSH
Host local-forwarding-example
 HostName S
 LocalForward 2001 localhost:143
# Run on home machine H
$ ssh local-forwarding-example
```

9.2.1.1. Local forwarding and GatewayPorts

In SSH1 and OpenSSH, by default, only the host running the SSH client can connect to locally forwarded ports. This is because *ssh* listens only on the machine's loopback interface for connections to the forwarded port; that is, it binds the socket (localhost,2001), a.k.a. (127.0.0.1,2001), and not (H,2001). So, in the preceding example, only machine H can use the forwarding; attempts by other machines to connect to (H,2001) get "connection refused." However, *ssh* for SSH1 and OpenSSH has a command-line option, *-g*, that disables this restriction, permitting any host to connect to locally forwarded ports:

```
# SSH1, OpenSSH
$ ssh1 -g -L<localport>:<remotehost>:<remoteport> hostname
```

The client configuration keyword `GatewayPorts` also controls this feature; the default value is `no`, and giving `GatewayPorts=yes` does the same thing as *-g*:

```
# SSH1, OpenSSH
GatewayPorts yes
```

There's a reason why `GatewayPorts` and *-g* are disabled by default: they represent a security risk. [9.2.4.2]

9.2.1.2. Remote forwarding

A remotely forwarded port is just like a local one, but the directions are reversed. This time the TCP client is remote, its server is local, and a forwarded connection is initiated from the remote machine.

Continuing with our example, suppose instead that you are logged into server machine S to begin with, where the IMAP server is running. You can now create a secure tunnel for remote clients to reach the IMAP server on port 143. Once again, you select a random port number to forward (say, 2001 again) and create the tunnel:

```
$ ssh -R2001:localhost:143 H
```

The *-R* option specifies remote forwarding. It is followed by three values, separated by colons as before but interpreted slightly differently. The *remote* port to be forwarded (2001) is now first, followed by the machine name or IP address (localhost) and port number (143). SSH can now forward connections from (H,2001) to (localhost,143).

Once this command has run, a secure tunnel has been constructed from the port 2001 on the remote machine H, to port 143 on the server machine S. Now any program on H can use the secure tunnel by connecting to (localhost,2001). As before, the command also runs an SSH terminal session on remote machine H, just as *ssh H* does.

As with local forwarding, you may establish a remote forwarding using a keyword in your client configuration file. The **RemoteForward** keyword is analogous to **LocalForward**, with the same syntactic differences between SSH1 and SSH2:

```
# SSH1, OpenSSH
RemoteForward 2001 S:143

# SSH2 only
RemoteForward "2001:S:143"
```

For example, here's the preceding forwarding defined in an SSH2-format configuration file:

```
# SSH2 only
remote-forwarding-example:
 Host H
 RemoteForward "2001:S:143"

$ ssh2 remote-forwarding-example
```

You might think that the **GatewayPorts** feature discussed in the last section applies equally well to remote port forwardings. This would make sense as a feature, but as it happens, it isn't done. The SSH-1 protocol lacks the ability to indicate this difference. SSH-2 can indicate it, but current clients always just request listening on all addresses, anyway. In SSH1 and SSH2, remotely forwarded ports always listen on all network interfaces and accept connections from anywhere. [9.4] The OpenSSH server does accept the **GatewayPorts** configuration option, and it applies globally to all remote forwardings established by that server.

9.2.2. Trouble with Multiple Connections

If you use **LocalForward** or **RemoteForward** in your configuration file, you might run into a subtle problem. Suppose you have set up a section in your configuration file to forward local port 2001 to an IMAP server:

```
# SSH1 syntax used for illustration
Host server.example.com
 LocalForward 2001 server.example.com:143
```

This configuration works fine if you connect once:

```
$ ssh server.example.com
```

But if you try to open a second *ssh* connection to *server.example.com* at the same time—perhaps to run a different program in another window of your workstation—the attempt will fail:

```
$ ssh server.example.com
Local: bind: Address already in use
```

Why does this happen? Because your configuration file section tries to forward port 2001 again but finds that port is already in use ("bound" for listening) by the first instance of *ssh*. You need some way to make the connection but omit the port forwarding.

SSH1 (but not OpenSSH) provides a solution, the client configuration keyword **ClearAllForwardings**. From the name, you might think it terminates existing forwardings, but it doesn't. Rather, it nullifies any forwardings specified in the current *ssh* command. In the previous example, you can connect without forwardings to *server.example.com* with:

```
# SSH1 only
$ ssh1 -o ClearAllForwardings=yes server.example.com
```

The original tunnel, set up by the first invocation, continues to exist, but **ClearAllForwardings** prevents the second invocation from attempting to recreate the tunnel. To illustrate the point further, here's a rather silly command:

```
$ ssh1 -L2001:localhost:143 -o ClearAllForwardings=yes mymachine
```

The *–L* option specifies a forwarding, but **ClearAllForwardings** cancels it. This silly command is identical in function to:

```
$ ssh1 mymachine
```

ClearAllForwardings may also be placed in your client configuration file, of course. It seems more useful on the command line, however, where it can be used on the fly without editing a file.

9.2.3. Comparing Local and Remote Port Forwarding

The differences between local and remote forwarding can be subtle. It can get a bit confusing to know which kind of forwarding to use in a given situation. The quick rule is look for the TCP client application.

If the TCP client application (whose connections you want to forward) is running locally on the SSH client machine, use local forwarding. Otherwise, the client application is on the remote SSH server machine, and you use remote forwarding.

The rest of this section is devoted to dissecting the forwarding process in detail and understanding where this rule comes from.

9.2.3.1. Common elements

Local and remote forwarding can be confusing because of overloaded terminology. In a given port forwarding situation, there are two clients and two servers lying around. We have the SSH client and server programs (e.g., *ssh* and *sshd*), plus the TCP application's client and server programs whose connection you want to protect by port forwarding.

An SSH session has a direction of establishment. That is, you run an SSH client on one machine, and it initiates a session with an SSH server on another. Likewise, a forwarded connection has a direction of establishment: you run an application client on one machine, and it initiates a session with a service on another. These two directions may or may not match. This is the difference between local and remote forwarding. Let's introduce some terminology and provide some diagrams to make sense of this.

To begin with, we have an application client and server running on two hosts, A and B (Figure 9-2).

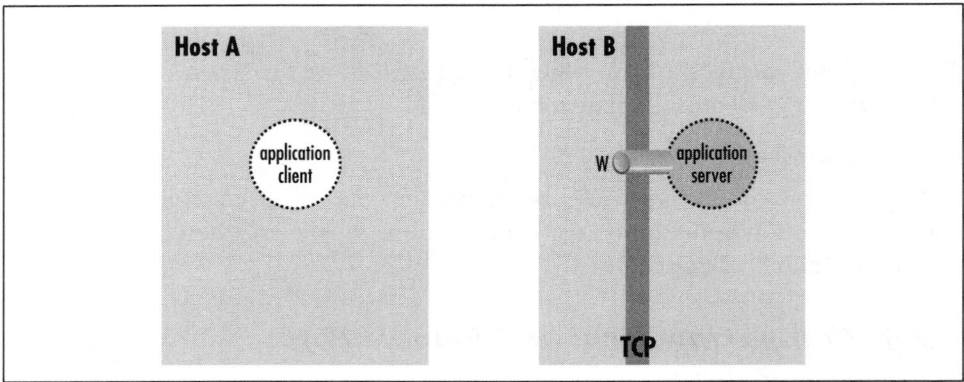

Figure 9-2. Application client and server

The application server is listening on a well-known port W for incoming client connections. Without SSH, you can tell the application client that its server is on host B, port W. The client makes a direct connection to the server, and all application protocol data go in the clear over the network (Figure 9-3).

To protect the application protocol data by forwarding, you establish an SSH session between these two hosts. When setting up the SSH session, you select an unused port number P on the application client side (host A), and request SSH port forwarding from the socket (A,P) to the socket (B,W). Once the session is established, the SSH process on A is listening for incoming TCP connection requests on port P. Tell the application client that its server is on (A,P) instead of (B,W), and the stage is now set for port forwarding (Figure 9-4).

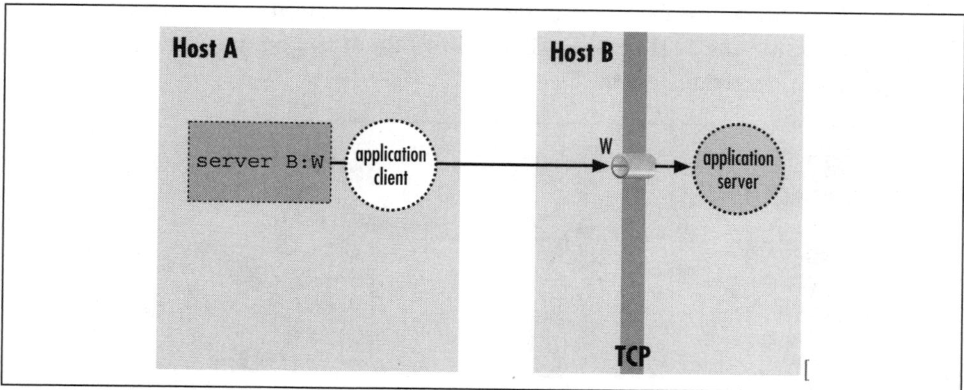

Figure 9-3. Direct client/server connection (no forwarding)

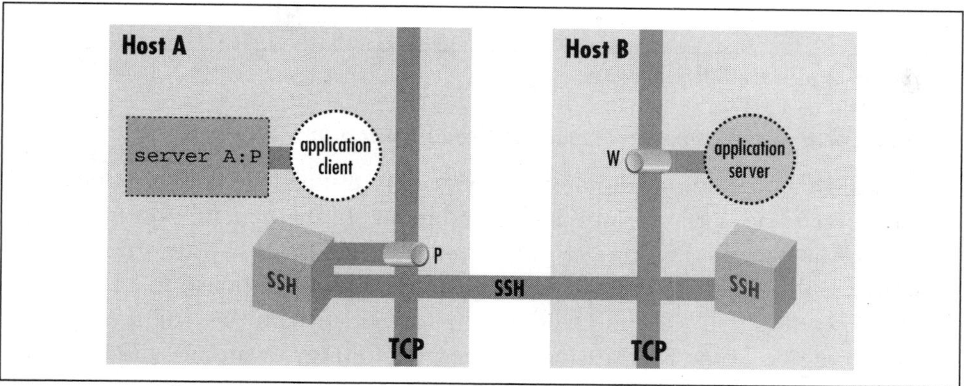

Figure 9-4. A forwarded port

There are now two cooperating SSH processes with an established, encrypted SSH session between them; you don't yet distinguish between the SSH client and server. Inside that session, SSH creates multiple *channels*, or logical streams for carrying data. It uses channels to carry and distinguish the input, output, and error streams for an interactive login or remote command run via SSH, and similarly creates a new channel for each use of a port forwarding, to carry the forwarded data inside the protected SSH session.

Figure 9-5 shows that now, when the application client tries to connect to its server, it connects instead to the listening SSH process (1). The SSH listener notices this and accepts the connection. It then notifies its partner SSH process that a new instance of this port forwarding is starting up, and they cooperate to establish a new channel for carrying the data for this forwarding instance (2). Finally, the partner SSH process initiates a TCP connection to the target of the port forwarding: the application server listening on (B,W) (3). Once this connection succeeds, the port forwarding instance is in place. The SSH processes cooperate to pass back and forth any data transmitted by the application client and server, over the channel inside the SSH session. This allows them to communicate and secures the application's activities on the network.

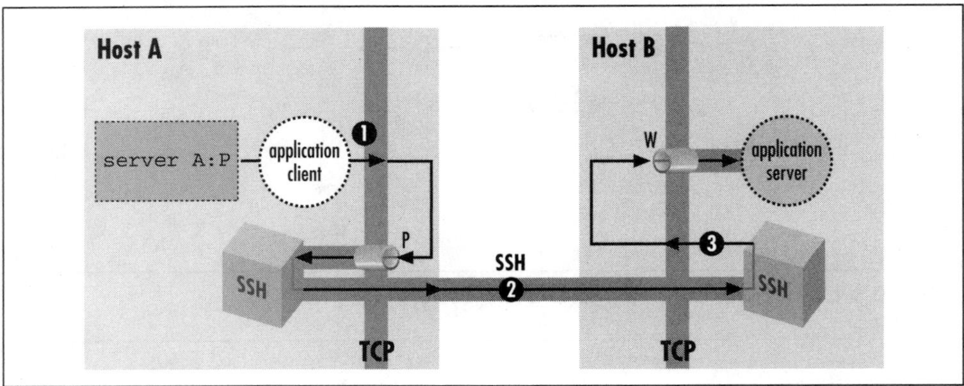

Figure 9-5. A forwarded connection

9.2.3.2. Local versus remote forwarding: the distinction

With this general framework in place, you can distinguish between local and remote forwarding. First we introduce some terms. In the generic port forwarding description in the last section, you saw that one SSH process listens for connections, while the other is ready to initiate connections in response to connections accepted on the other side, to complete the forwarded path. We call the first side the *listening* side of the SSH session with respect to this forwarding, and the other, the *connecting* side. For example, in Figure 9-4, host A is the listening side, while host B is the connecting side. Note that these terms aren't mutually exclusive. Since a single SSH session may have multiple forwardings in place, the same side of a session may be the listening side for some forwardings, and simultaneously the connecting side for others. But with respect to any particular forwarding, it is one or the other.

Now, recall that in the last section we didn't label the SSH processes according to which was the SSH client and which the SSH server, but simply referred to two cooperating SSH processes. We do so now, and can state succinctly the local versus remote distinction:

- In a *local* forwarding (Figure 9-6), the application client and hence the listening side are located with the SSH client. The application server and connecting side are located with the SSH server.
- In a *remote* forwarding (Figure 9-7), the situation is reversed: the application client and listening side are located with the SSH server, while the application server and connecting side are located with the SSH client.

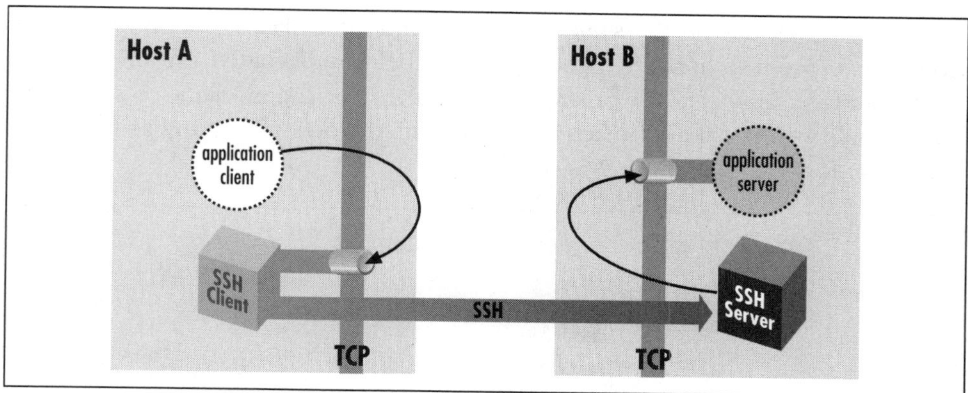

Figure 9-6. Local port forwarding

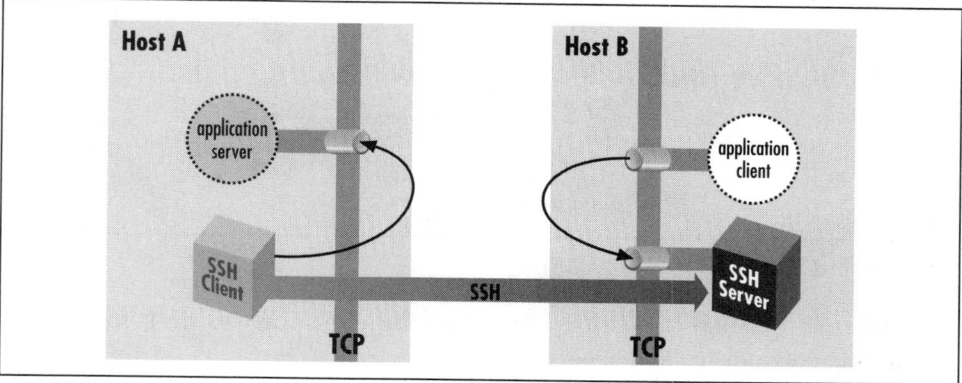

Figure 9-7. Remote port forwarding

So, as we said at the beginning of this section: use a local forwarding when the application client is on the local side of the SSH connection, and a remote forwarding when it's on the remote side.

9.2.4. Forwarding Off-Host

In all our discussions of port forwarding so far, the application client and server have been located on the machines on the ends of the SSH session. This is reflected in our always using "localhost" in naming the target socket of a forwarding:

```
$ ssh -L2001:localhost:143 server.example.com
```

Since the application server is located on the same machine as the connecting side of the SSH port forwarding, the target host can be "localhost." But the connections between the application client and the SSH listening side, and between the application server and the SSH connecting side, are themselves TCP connections. For convenience, TCP implementations allow programs to make connections between two sockets on the same host. The connection data is simply transferred from one process to another without actually being transmitted on any real network interface. However, in principle, either the application client or server—or both—could be on different machines, potentially involving as many as four hosts in a single forwarding (Figure 9-8).

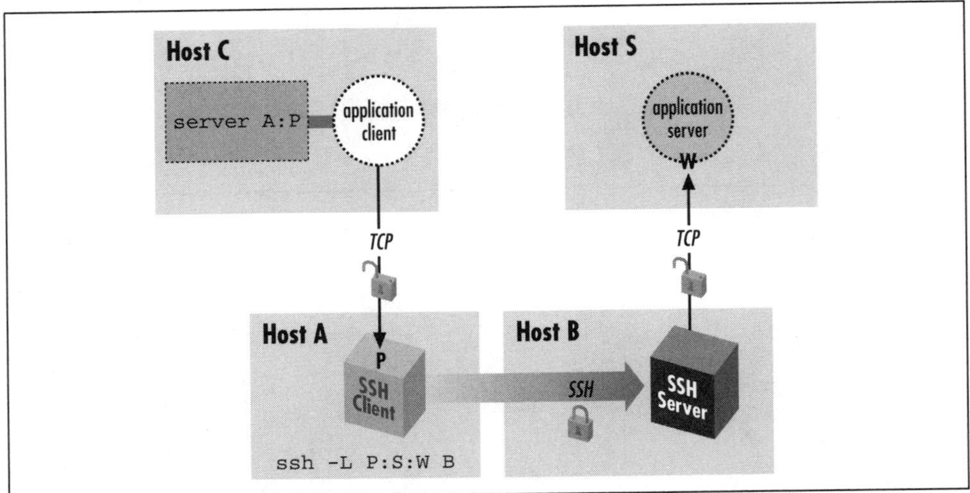

Figure 9-8. Off-host port forwarding

Although this situation is possible, you generally don't want to do it for security reasons, namely privacy and access control.

9.2.4.1. Privacy

As shown in Figure 9-8, the complete path followed by forwarded data includes three TCP connections. But only the second connection, between the two SSH processes, is protected as a channel inside the SSH session. The other two connections are just simple TCP connections. Normally each of these is on a single host, and is therefore protected from network snooping or interference, so the entire forwarding path is secure. But if either of these two connections is between different hosts, its data will be vulnerable in transit.

9.2.4.2. Access control and the loopback address

The other security problem of off-host forwarding concerns the listening side. In short, the listening side of a forwarding has no access control, so intruders may gain access to it. To explain this problem, we must first discuss the *loopback address* of a host.

In addition to any physical network interfaces it may have, a host running IP has also has a virtual one called the *loopback* interface. This is a software construct, not corresponding to any network hardware. Nonetheless, the loopback appears and responds like a real interface. Under Unix, it is often named *lo0* and is listed by *ifconfig*:

```
$ ifconfig -a
...
lo0: flags=849<UP,LOOPBACK,RUNNING,MULTICAST> mtu 8232
        inet 127.0.0.1 netmask ff000000
```

The loopback interface leads back to the host itself. A datagram "transmitted" on the loopback interface immediately appears as an incoming packet on the loopback interface and is picked up and processed by IP as being destined for the local host.

The loopback interface is always assigned the same IP address: 127.0.0.1, the loopback address,* and the local naming service provides the name "localhost" for that address. This mechanism gives a reliable way for processes to communicate with one another on the local host via IP, regardless of what IP addresses the host may have on real connected networks, or indeed if the host has no real network connections at all. You can always refer to your local host using the well-known loopback address.

By design, a loopback address is local to its host. One machine can't contact the loopback address of another. Since the loopback address 127.0.0.1 is standard on all IP hosts, any connection to 127.0.0.1 leads a machine to talk to itself. (Plus, the loopback network isn't routed on the Internet.)

9.2.4.3. Listening on ("binding") an interface

When a host listens on a TCP port, it establishes a potential endpoint for a TCP connection. But the endpoints of a TCP connection are sockets, and a socket is an (address,port) pair, not a (host,port) pair. Listening must take place on a particular socket and thus be associated with a particular address, hence a particular interface on the host. This is called *binding* the interface.† Unless otherwise specified, when asked to listen on a particular port, TCP binds all the host's interfaces and accepts connections on any of them. This is generally the right behavior for a server. It doesn't care how many network interfaces the local host has: it just accepts any connection made to its listening port, regardless of which host address was requested.

* Actually, the entire network 127.0.0.0/8—comprising 16 million addresses—is reserved for addresses that refer to the local host. Only the address 127.0.0.1 is commonly used, although we have seen devices use a handful of others for special purposes, such as "reject" interfaces on a terminal server or router.

† Named after the Berkeley sockets library routine *bind*, commonly used to establish the association.

Consider, however, what this means in the case of SSH port forwarding. There is no authentication or access control at all applied to the listening side of a forwarding; it simply accepts any connection and forwards it. If the listening side binds all the host's interfaces for the forwarded port, this means that anyone at all with network connectivity to the listening host—possibly the whole Internet!—can use your forwarding. This is obviously not a good situation. To address it, SSH by default binds only the loopback address for the listening side of a forwarding. This means that only other programs on the same host may connect to the forwarded socket. This makes it reasonably safe to use port forwarding on a PC or other single-user machine but is still a security problem on multiuser hosts. On most Unix machines, for example, a knowledgeable user can connect to any listening sockets and see what's on them. Keep this in mind when using port forwarding on a Unix machine.

If you want to allow off-host connections to your forwarded ports, you can use the *–g* switch or `GatewayPorts` option to have the listening side bind all interfaces, as we did in an earlier example: [9.2.4]

```
$ ssh -g -L P:S:W B
```

But be aware of the security implications! You may want to exercise more control over the use of forwarded ports in this situation by using TCP-wrappers, which we discuss later in this chapter.

9.2.5. Bypassing a Firewall

Let's tackle a more complicated example of port forwarding. Figure 9-9 returns us to the same company situation as in Figure 6-5 when we discussed agent forwarding. [6.3.5] Your home machine H talks to work machine W via a bastion host, B, and you want to access your work email from home. Machine W runs an IMAP server, and your home machine H has an IMAP-capable email reader, but you can't hook them up. Your home IMAP client expects to make a TCP connection directly to the IMAP server on W, but unfortunately that connection is blocked by the firewall. Since host B is inside the firewall, and it's running an SSH server, there should be some way to put all the pieces together and make the IMAP connection from H to W.

Port forwarding can solve this problem. As before, the IMAP server is on port 143, and we select a random local port number, 2001. This time, however, we use a slightly different command to set up forwarding:

```
# Executed on home machine H
$ ssh -L2001:W:143 B
```

This establishes an interactive SSH session from home machine H to bastion host B and also creates an SSH tunnel from local host H to the email server machine W.

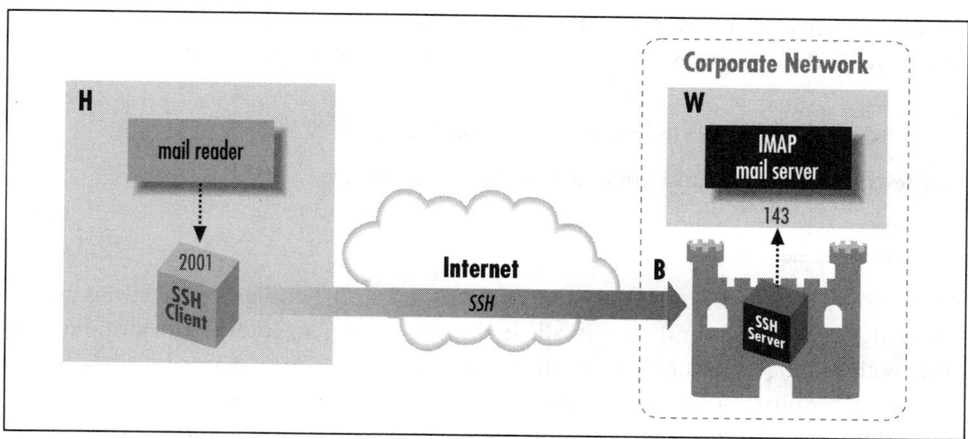

Figure 9-9. Port forwarding through a firewall

Specifically, in response to a connection on port 2001, the local SSH client directs the SSH server running on B to open a connection to port 143 on W, that is, socket W:143. The SSH server can do this because B is inside the firewall. If you configure your email reader to connect to local port 2001, as before, the communication path is now:

1. The email reader on home machine H sends data to local port 2001.
2. The local SSH client reads port 2001, encrypts the data, and sends it into the tunnel.
3. The tunnel passes through the firewall, because it is an SSH connection (port 22) that the firewall accepts.
4. The SSH server on bastion host B decrypts the data and sends it to port 143 on work machine W. This transmission isn't encrypted, but it's protected behind the firewall, so encryption isn't necessary. (Assuming you're not worried about snooping on your internal network.)
5. Data is sent back from the IMAP server to home machine H by the same process in reverse.

You have now bypassed the firewall by tunneling the IMAP traffic through SSH.

9.2.6. Port Forwarding Without a Remote Login

It may happen that you'd like to forward a port via SSH but don't want an SSH login session to the remote host. For example, if you're using the IMAP forwarding example we've been harping on, you may want only to read email, not open an unnecessary terminal connection at the same time. With SSH2, this is simple: just provide the *–f* option to *ssh2* in your port forwarding command:

```
# SSH2 only
$ ssh2 -f -L2001:localhost:143 server.example.com
```

or use the `GoBackground` keyword for the same effect:

```
# SSH2 only
GoBackground yes
```

As a result, *ssh2* puts itself into the background and handles connections to the forwarded port 2001, and that is all. It doesn't create an interactive terminal session with standard input, output, and error channels. The *–S* option also avoids starting a terminal session but unlike *–f*, it doesn't put the session in the background (in other words, the *–f* option implies *–S*):

```
# SSH2 only
$ ssh2 -S -L2001:localhost:143 server.example.com
```

The *–f* option is also supported by SSH1 and OpenSSH but its operation is different from that of SSH2. It is intended more for executing remote commands that don't require terminal interaction, such as graphical programs using X. Specifically:

- It causes the backgrounded *ssh* to connect the local end of the terminal session to */dev/null* (that is, *–f* implies the *–n* option).
- It requires you to specify a remote command, ideally one that doesn't read from standard input, since the backgrounded *ssh* connects the local end of the session channel to */dev/null* (that is, *–f* implies the *–n* option).

For example, if X forwarding is turned on (which we'll discuss later), the following command puts itself into the background, popping up a graphical clock on your local display, with the clock program running on the remote host *zwei.uhr.org*:

```
# SSH1, OpenSSH
$ ssh -f zwei.uhr.org xclock
```

This is equivalent to the background command:

```
# SSH1, OpenSSH
$ ssh -n zwei.uhr.org xclock &
```

In contrast, SSH2 doesn't require a remote command when using the *–f* option. You may provide one as earlier, and *ssh2* behaves in the same way as its SSH1 or OpenSSH counterparts:

```
$ ssh2 -f zwei.uhr.org xclock
```

but the remote command isn't necessary; you can set up a forwarding and put *ssh2* into the background conveniently:

```
$ ssh2 -f -L2001:localhost:143 server.example.com
```

If you tried this with SSH1 or OpenSSH, you see:

```
# SSH1, OpenSSH
$ ssh -f -L2001:localhost:143 server.example.com
Cannot fork into background without a command to execute.
```

To get around the nuisance of providing an unwanted remote command, use one that does nothing for a long time, such as *sleep*:

```
# SSH1, OpenSSH
$ ssh -f -L2001:localhost:143 server.example.com sleep 1000000
```

9.2.6.1. One shot forwarding

When invoked with *–f* or `GoBackground`, *ssh* persists until you explicitly kill it with the Unix *kill* command. (You can find its pid with the *ps* command.) Alternatively, you can request *one shot forwarding*, which causes the client to exit when forwarding is over with. Specifically, the client waits indefinitely for the first forwarded connection. After that, when the number of forwarded connections drops to zero, the client exits.

One shot forwarding is accomplished easily in SSH2 with the *–fo* command-line option, a variation on *–f* (the "o" stands for "one shot"):

```
# SSH2 only
$ ssh2 -fo -L2001:localhost:143 server
```

One shot forwarding isn't directly supported by SSH1 or OpenSSH, but you can get the same effect with the following method:

1. Set up the forwarding with *ssh –f*, and for the required remote command, use *sleep* with a short duration:

   ```
   $ ssh -f -L2001:localhost:143 server sleep 10
   ```

2. Before the sleep interval expires, use the forwarded connection:

   ```
   $ ssh -p2001 localhost
   ```

Once the *sleep* command finishes, the first *ssh* tries to exit, but it notices a forwarded connection is in use and refuses to exit, printing a warning you can ignore:

```
Waiting for forwarded connections to terminate...
The following connections are open:
  port 2001, connection from localhost port 143
```

ssh waits until that connection ends and then terminates, providing the behavior of one shot forwarding.

9.2.7. The Listening Port Number

Earlier, we suggested selecting any unused port for the listening side of a forwarding. Port numbers are encoded in a 16-bit field and can have any value from 1 to 65535 (port 0 is reserved). On multiuser operating systems such as Unix, ports 1 through 1023 are called *privileged* and are reserved for processes run by the superuser (user ID zero). If a nonprivileged process tries to bind a privileged port for listening, it will fail with an error message such as "insufficient permission."*

When setting up the listening side of a tunnel, you generally must select a port number between 1024 and 65535, inclusive. This is because an SSH program running under your user ID, not the superuser's, is responsible for listening on that port. If SSH reports that your chosen port is in already in use, just choose another; it shouldn't be hard to find a free one.

For the target side of the tunnel, you can specify any port number, privileged or not. You are attempting to connect to the port, not listen on it. In fact, most of the time the target side is a privileged port, since the most common TCP services have ports in the privileged range.

If you are the superuser on a machine with SSH clients, you can perform local forwarding with a privileged port. Likewise, you can forward a remote privileged port if your remote account has superuser privileges.

Some TCP applications hardcode the server port numbers and don't permit them to be changed. These applications aren't usable with port forwarding if the operating system has a privileged port restriction. For example, suppose you have an FTP client that's hardwired to connect to the server on the standard FTP control port, 21. To set up port forwarding, you have to forward the local port 21 to the remote port 21. But since port 21 is privileged, you can't use it as a listening port number unless you are the superuser. Fortunately, most Unix TCP-based programs let you set the destination port number for connections, and on PCs and Macs, there's no privileged port restriction.

9.2.8. Choosing the Target Forwarding Address

Suppose you want to forward a connection from your local machine to *remote.host.net*. The following two commands both work:

```
$ ssh -L2001:localhost:143 remote.host.net
$ ssh -L2001:remote.host.net:143 remote.host.net
```

* Microsoft Windows and MacOS have no privileged port restriction, so any user can listen on any free port.

The forwarded connection is made from the remote machine to either the loopback address or *remote.host.net*, and in either case, the connection stays on the remote machine and doesn't go over the network. However, the two connections are perceptibly different to the server receiving the forwarded connection. This is because the *source* sockets of the connections are different. The connection to localhost appears to come from source address 127.0.0.1, whereas the connection to *remote.host.net* is from the address associated with that name.

Most of the time this difference doesn't matter, but sometimes you must take it into account. The application server (e.g., the IMAP daemon) might be doing access control based on source address and not be configured to accept the loopback address. Or it might be running on a multihomed host and have bound only a subset of the addresses the host has, possibly not including the loopback address. Each of these situations is usually an oversight, but you might not be able to do anything about it. If you're getting "connection refused" from the connecting side of the forwarding, but you've verified that the server appears to be running and responding to normal clients, this might be the problem. If the server machine is running Unix, the command *netstat –a –n* should list all the network connections and listeners on that machine. Look for listeners on the relevant port, and the addresses on which they are listening.

Sometimes, the problem can be more acute if the server uses the source IP address itself as part of whatever protocol it's speaking. This problem crops up when trying to forward FTP over SSH. [11.2]

In general, we recommend using localhost as the forwarding target whenever possible. This way, you are less likely to set up an insecure off-host forwarding by accident.

9.2.9. Termination

What happens to forwardings when an SSH connection terminates? The ports simply cease being forwarded; that is, SSH is no longer listening on them, and connection attempts to those ports get "connection refused."

What happens if you try to terminate an SSH session while it still has active forwarded connections? SSH will notice and wait for them to disconnect before stopping the session. The details of this behavior differ among implementations.

In SSH2, if you log out of a session that has an active forwarded connection, the session stays open but sends itself into the background:

```
remote$ logout
warning: ssh2[7021]: number of forwarded channels still open, forked to background
to wait for completion.
local$
```

The *ssh2* process now waits in the background until the forwarded connections terminate, and then it exits. In contrast, with SSH1 and OpenSSH, if you disconnect a session with active forwardings, you get a warning, but the session stays in the foreground:

```
remote$ logout
Waiting for forwarded connections to terminate...
The following connections are open:
  port 2002, connection from localhost port 1465
```

To send it into the background and return to your local shell prompt, use the escape sequence return-tilde-ampersand: [2.3.2]

```
~& [backgrounded]
local$
```

and as with SSH2, the connection exits only after its forwarded connections terminate. Be careful not to use the SSH `^Z` escape for this purpose. That sends *ssh* into the background but suspended, unable to accept TCP connections to its forwarded ports. If you do this accidentally, use your shell's job control commands (e.g., *fg* and *bg*) to resume the process.

9.2.9.1. The TIME_WAIT problem

Sometimes a forwarded port mysteriously hangs around after the forwarding SSH session has gone away. You try a command you've used successfully several times in a row and suddenly get an error message:

```
$ ssh1 -L2001:localhost:21 server.example.com
Local: bind: Address already in use
```

(This happens commonly if you're experimenting with port forwarding, trying to get something to work.) You know that you have no active SSH command listening on port 2001, so what's going on? If you use the *netstat* command to look for other listeners on that port, you may see a connection hanging around in the TIME_WAIT state:

```
$ netstat -an | grep 2001
tcp    0   0   127.0.0.1:2001   127.0.0.1:1472    TIME_WAIT
```

The TIME_WAIT state is an artifact of the TCP protocol. In certain situations, the teardown of a TCP connection can leave one of its socket endpoints unusable for a short period of time, usually only a few minutes. As a result, you cannot reuse the port for TCP forwarding (or anything else) until the teardown completes. If you're impatient, choose another port for the time being (say, 2002 instead of 2001) and get on with your work, or wait a short time for the port to become usable again.

9.2.10. Configuring Port Forwarding in the Server

We've seen several keywords and command-line options for configuring SSH clients for port forwarding, such as *–L* and *–R*. In addition, the SSH server can be configured for port forwarding. We'll cover compile-time, serverwide, and per-account configuration.

9.2.10.1. Compile-time configuration

You can enable or disable port forwarding at compile time with *configure*. [4.1.5.5] It is enabled by default. For SSH1, the configure flags `--disable-server-port-forwardings` and `--disable-client-port-forwardings` turn off port forwarding capability for *sshd1* and SSH1 clients, respectively. For SSH2, the single flag `--disable-tcp-port-forwarding` disables port forwarding for both clients and servers.

9.2.10.2. Serverwide configuration

Port forwarding can be globally enabled or disabled in *sshd*. This is done with the serverwide configuration keyword `AllowTcpForwarding` in */etc/sshd_config*. The keyword may have the value `yes` (the default, enabling forwarding) or `no` (disabling forwarding):

```
# SSH1, SSH2, OpenSSH
AllowTcpForwarding no
```

In addition, SSH2 has the following options:

```
# SSH2 only
AllowTcpForwardingForUsers
AllowTcpForwardingForGroups
```

The syntax of these is the same as for the `AllowUsers` and `AllowGroups` options. [5.5.2.1] They specify a list of users or groups that are allowed to use port forwarding; the server refuses to honor port forwarding requests for anyone else. Note that these refer to the target account of the SSH session, not the client username (which is often not known).

F-Secure SSH1 Server supports the additional keywords `AllowForwardingPort`, `DenyForwardingPort`, `AllowForwardingTo`, and `DenyForwardingTo` for finer-grained control over forwarding. The two `...Port` keywords let you control remote forwardings for given TCP ports, with support for wildcards and numeric ranges. For example, to permit remote forwardings for ports 3000, 4000 through 4500 inclusive, 5000 and higher, and any port number ending in 7:

```
# F-Secure SSH1 only
AllowForwardingPort 3000 4000..4050 >5000 *7
```

The `...To` keywords are similar but control forwardings to particular hosts and ports (i.e., to particular sockets). Host and port specifications are separated by colons and use the same metacharacters as the `...Port` keywords:

```
# F-Secure SSH1 only
DenyForwardingTo server.example.com:80 other.net:* yoyodyne.com:<1024
```

The permissible metacharacters/wildcards are shown in the following table:

Metacharacter	Meaning	Example
`*`	Any digit	`300*`
`<`	All values less than	`<200`
`>`	All values greater than	`>200`
`..`	Range of values (inclusive)	`10..20`

It's important to realize that the directives in this section don't actually prevent port forwarding, unless you also disable interactive logins and restrict what programs may be run on the remote side. Otherwise, knowledgeable users can simply run their own port-forwarding application over the SSH session. These settings alone might be a sufficient deterrent in a nontechnical community, but they won't stop someone who knows what she's doing.

9.2.10.3. Per-account configuration

In your account, you can disable port forwarding for any client that connects via a particular key. Locate the public key in your *authorized_keys* file and precede it with the option `no-port-forwarding`:

```
# SSH1, OpenSSH
no-port-forwarding ...key...
```

(SSH2 doesn't currently have this feature.) Any SSH client that authenticates using this key can't perform port forwarding with your SSH server.

The same remarks we just made about serverwide port forwarding configuration apply here: the restriction isn't really meaningful unless you further restrict what this key is allowed to do.

9.3. X Forwarding

Now that you've seen general TCP port forwarding, we move to a new topic: forwarding of X protocol connections. X is a popular window system for Unix workstations, and one of its best features is its transparency. Using X, you can run remote X applications that open their windows on your local display (and vice versa, running local applications on remote displays). Unfortunately, the inter-machine communication is insecure and wide open to snoopers. But there's good news: SSH *X forwarding* makes the communication secure by tunneling the X protocol.

X forwarding also addresses some firewall-related difficulties. Suppose you're a system administrator with a set of exposed production machines on the other side of a firewall from you. You log into one of these machines using SSH, and want to run an graphical performance-monitoring tool, such as Solaris's *perfmon*, that uses the X Window System. You can't, though, because to do that, the external machine needs to make a TCP connection back to the internal machine you started on, and the firewall blocks it (as it should, since X is quite insecure). X forwarding solves this problem, permitting X protocol connections to pass through the firewall, securely tunneled via SSH.

Our discussion begins with a brief overview of X and then explains the details of X forwarding. In addition to explaining how to use X forwarding, we also expose the internals of X authentication and how it interacts with SSH, as well as other technical topics.

VNC Forwarding: An Alternative to X Forwarding

X forwarding is problematic from a security point of view, for the same reason as X itself. As we will see, the design of X means that remote programs must make separate network connections back to the user; this requires yet another layer of authentication and authorization, complicating the situation and opening an avenue of attack. SSH X forwarding tries to secure this as much as possible, but it may still be unacceptable in some environments.

An alternative technique is to use Virtual Network Computing (VNC) over SSH. VNC is free software developed by AT&T Laboratories in the United Kingdom, which provides remote GUI access for Unix and Windows platforms. With VNC, you can open a window on your Unix machine running X and have the desktop of a remote Windows machine appear there, so you can operate the Windows box remotely. Conversely, you can run the VNC client on a Windows machine and connect to a remote X display running on a Unix host. Since VNC involves only a single outbound connection, it is easier and safer to tunnel through SSH than X. You can find out more about VNC (and download the software) at:

http://www.uk.research.att.com/vnc/

9.3.1. The X Window System

The X Window System, or X, is the most widely used graphical display system for Unix machines. Like SSH, X has clients and servers. X clients are windowing application programs, such as terminal emulators, paint programs, graphical clocks, and so forth. An X server is the underlying display engine that processes requests from X clients, communicating via a network protocol called the *X protocol.* A machine typically runs a single X server but possibly many X clients.

Most important to our discussion, X supports sophisticated window management over a network. X clients can open windows not only on their local machine but also on other computers on the network, whether they are down the hall or across the globe. To accomplish this, an X client makes a network connection to a remote X server and carries on a conversation, using the X protocol to draw on the remote screen, receive remote keyboard events, learn the remote mouse location, and so on. This obviously requires some type of security, which we discuss soon.

A central concept of X is the *display*, an abstraction for the screen managed by an X server. When an X client is invoked, it needs to know which display to use. Displays are named by strings of the form *HOST:n.v*, where:

- *HOST* is the name of the machine running the X server controlling the display.
- *n* is the *display* number, an integer, usually 0. X allows for multiple displays controlled by a single server; additional displays are numbered 1, 2, and so on.
- *v* is the *visual* number, another integer. A visual is a virtual display. X supports multiple virtual displays on a single, physical display. If there's only one virtual display (which is the most common scenario), you omit the ".v", and the default is visual 0.

For example, on the machine *server.example.com,* display 0, visual 1 is represented by the display string "server.example.com:0.1".

Under Unix, most X client programs let you specify the display string in two ways: the *–d* or *–display* command-line option, or the environment variable DISPLAY. For example, to run the X client program *xterm* on the only X display of the workstation anacreon, use the command-line option:

```
$ xterm -d anacreon:0 &
```

or the environment variable:

```
$ setenv DISPLAY anacreon:0
$ xterm &
```

X is a large, deep software product whose documentation fills a dozen O'Reilly books. We've barely scratched the surface with our explanation, but you've now seen enough to understand X forwarding.

9.3.2. How X Forwarding Works

Although X clients can communicate with remote X servers, this communication isn't secure. All interactions between the X client and server, such as keystrokes and displayed text, can be easily monitored by network snooping because the connection isn't encrypted. In addition, most X environments use primitive authentication methods for connecting to a remote display. A knowledgeable attacker can get a connection to your display, monitor your keystrokes, and control other programs you're running.

Once again, SSH comes to the rescue. An X protocol connection can be routed through an SSH connection to provide security and stronger authentication. This feature is called X forwarding.

X forwarding works in the following way. (As illustration, please refer to Figure 9-10.) An SSH client requests X forwarding when it connects to an SSH server (assuming X forwarding is enabled in the client). If the server allows X forwarding for this connection, your login proceeds normally, but the server takes some special steps behind the scenes. In addition to handling your terminal session, it sets itself up as a proxy X server running on the remote machine and sets the DISPLAY environment variable in your remote shell to point to the proxy X display:

```
syrinx$ ssh sys1
Last login: Sat Nov 13 01:10:37 1999 from blackberry
Sun Microsystems Inc.   SunOS 5.6       Generic August 1997
You have new mail.
sys1$ echo $DISPLAY
sys1:10.0
sys1$ xeyes
The "xeyes" X client appears on the screen
```

The DISPLAY value appears to refer to X display #10 on sys1, but there's no such display. (In fact, there might be no true displays on sys1 at all.) Instead, the DISPLAY value points to the X proxy established by the SSH server, i.e., the SSH server is masquerading as an X server. If you now run an X client program, it connects to the proxy. The proxy behaves just like a "real" X server, and in turn instructs the SSH client to behave as a proxy X client, connecting to the X server on your local machine. The SSH client and server then cooperate to pass X protocol information back and forth over the SSH pipe between the two X sessions, and the X client program appears on your screen just as if it had connected directly to your display. That's the general idea of X forwarding.

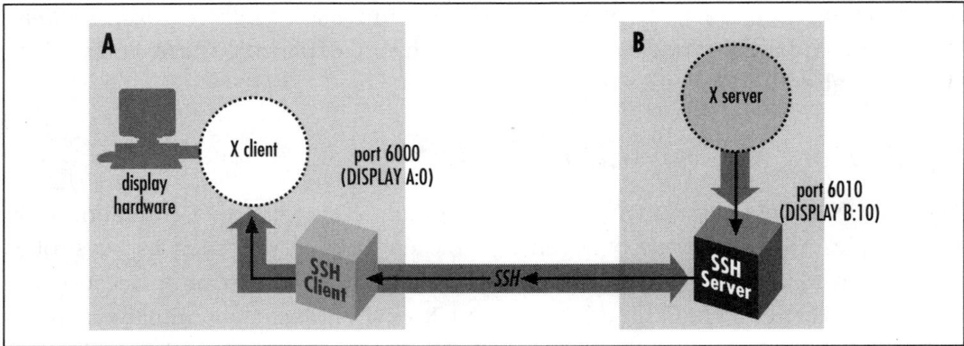

Figure 9-10. X forwarding

X forwarding can even solve the firewall problem mentioned earlier, as long as the firewall permits SSH connections to pass through. If a firewall sits between your local and remote machines, and you run an X client on the remote machine, X forwarding tunnels the X connection through the firewall's SSH port to the local machine. Therefore, the X client's windows can open on your local display. If X forwarding isn't present, the firewall blocks the connection.

Some aspects of X forwarding probably sound familiar from our earlier explanation of port forwarding. In fact, X forwarding is just a special case of port forwarding for which SSH has special support.

9.3.3. Enabling X Forwarding

X forwarding is on by default in SSH1 and SSH2, but off in OpenSSH. If you need to enable or disable X forwarding for your clients, here's how to do it. Unlike general port forwarding, which requires you to fiddle with TCP port numbers, X forwarding has only an on/off switch. In your SSH client configuration file, use the keyword **ForwardX11** with a value **yes** (the default, to enable) or **no** (to disable):

```
# SSH1, SSH2, OpenSSH
ForwardX11 yes
```

On the command line, you may also use *–x* to disable X forwarding:

```
# SSH1, SSH2, OpenSSH
$ ssh -x server.example.com
```

SSH2 and OpenSSH enables X forwarding with the following options:

```
# SSH2 only
$ ssh2 +x server.example.com

# OpenSSH only
$ ssh -X server.example.com
```

9.3.4. Configuring X Forwarding

The behavior of X forwarding can be modified through compile-time configuration, serverwide configuration, and per-account configuration.

9.3.4.1. Compile-time configuration

SSH1 and SSH2 can be compiled with or without X support. The compile-time flags `--with-x` and `--without-x` make this determination:

```
# SSH1, SSH2
$ configure ... --without-x ...
```

In addition, if you compile with X support, you may set the default behavior for X forwarding. In SSH1, you can enable or disable forwarding by default in the client and the server separately, using the compile-time flags `--enable-client-x11-forwarding` (or `--disable-client-x11-forwarding`) and `--enable-server-x11-forwarding` (or `--disable-server-x11-forwarding`):

```
# SSH1 only
$ configure ... --disable-server-x11-forwarding ...
```

In SSH2, you can enable or disable all X forwarding by default with `--enable-X11-forwarding` or `--disable-X11-forwarding`:

```
# SSH2 only
$ configure ... --enable-X11-forwarding ...
```

Remember, enable/disable flags simply set the default behavior. You can override these defaults with serverwide and per-account configuration.

9.3.4.2. Serverwide configuration

The serverwide configuration keywords `X11Forwarding` (SSH1, SSH2, OpenSSH) and its synonyms `ForwardX11` (SSH2) and `AllowX11Forwarding` (SSH2) enable or disable X forwarding in the SSH server. By default, it is enabled:

```
# SSH1, SSH2, OpenSSH
X11Forwarding no

# SSH2 only: either will work
ForwardX11 no
AllowX11Forwarding no
```

The `X11DisplayOffset` keyword lets you reserve some X11 display numbers so *sshd* can't use them. This keyword specifies the lowest display number SSH may use, preventing *sshd* from clashing with real X servers on the lower-numbered displays. For example, if you normally run actual X servers on displays 0 and 1, set:

```
# SSH1, OpenSSH
X11DisplayOffset 2
```

The `XAuthLocation` keyword specifies the path to the *xauth* program, which manipulates authorization records for X. We describe this keyword later, after we discuss *xauth*. [9.3.6.4]

```
# SSH1, OpenSSH
XAuthLocation /usr/local/bin/xauth
```

9.3.4.3. Per-account configuration

In your SSH1 or OpenSSH *authorized_keys* file, you may disallow X forwarding for incoming SSH connections that use a particular key for authentication. This is done with the option **no-X11-forwarding**: [8.2.8]

```
# SSH1, OpenSSH
no-X11-forwarding ...rest of key...
```

9.3.5. X Authentication

We've mentioned in passing that X performs its own authentication when X clients connect to X servers. Now we're going to dive into technical detail on the inner workings of X authentication, why it's insecure, and how SSH X forwarding builds on it to create a secure solution.

In most cases, X forwarding simply works, and you don't have to think about it. The following material is to aid your understanding and satisfy any intense cravings for tech talk (both yours and ours).

9.3.5.1. How X authentication works

When an X client requests a connection to an X server, the server authenticates the client. That is, the X server determines the client's identity to decide whether to allow a connection to the server's display. The current release of the X Window system (X11R6) provides two categories of authentication: host-based and key-based:

Host-based X authentication
: The simpler method. Using the program *xhost*, you indicate a list of hosts that may connect to your X display. Notice that connections are authenticated only by hostname, not by username. That is, any user on a listed host may connect to your display.

Key-based X authentication
: Uses the *xauth* program to maintain a list of X authentication keys, or *display keys*, for X clients. Keys are kept in a file, usually *~/.Xauthority*, along with other data associated with the various displays the client wants to access. When an X client connects to a server requiring authentication, the client supplies the appropriate credentials for that display from the *xauth* data. If

authentication is successful, the X client can then connect to the display managed by the X server.

Display keys are obtained from the X server in various ways depending on the environment. For example, if you start the server directly on the console of a machine using *xinit* or *startx*, these programs invoke an X server and insert a copy of the server's key directly into your *xauth* data. Alternatively, if you connect to a remote machine that runs the X Display Manager (XDM), the key is sent to your remote account when establishing your XDM session.

9.3.5.2. xauth and the SSH rc files

SSH has startup files that can be set to execute on the server side when a client logs in. These are the systemwide */etc/sshrc* and the per-account *~/.ssh/rc*. These can be shell scripts or any kind of executable program.

An important thing to note is that *sshd* runs *xauth* only to add the proxy display key if it doesn't run an *rc* program. If it does run an *rc* program, it feeds the key type and data to the program on a single line to its standard input, and it is up to the *rc* program to store the display key. This feature provides a way to customize handling the display key, in case just running *xauth* isn't the right thing to do in your situation.

9.3.5.3. Problems with X authentication

If you've used X, the authentication was probably transparent and seemed to work fine. Behind the scenes, however, the mechanism is insecure. Here are the major problems:

xhost is insecure
: Once you give permission for a remote host to connect to your display, any user on that host can connect. As with the r-commands, this authentication method depends on the network address of the connecting host, which can be easy for an attacker to usurp.

Key transfer may be manual and insecure
: Some remote-login protocols, such as *telnet*, don't assist with X authentication. If your display keys aren't available on a remote machine, you have to transfer them yourself, either manually or by automating the transfer, perhaps in your login script. This isn't only a nuisance but also insecure, since you're sending the key in plaintext over the network.

The most common key-based method, MIT-MAGIC-COOKIE-1, is insecure
: Although it uses a random string of bits, or *cookie*, as the *xauth* display key, this key is transmitted in plaintext at the beginning of every connection, where it can be intercepted and read.

The remote host might not support your chosen X authentication method
X11R6 supports other, more secure authentication methods. SUN-DES-1 employs Sun's secure RPC system, XDM-AUTHORIZATION-1 uses DES, and MIT-KERBEROS-5 involves Kerberos user-to-user authentication.* Unfortunately, these methods are often not available in particular instances of the X software. Sometimes they aren't compiled into X installations due to cryptographic export restrictions; other times, the X version is too old to support the more secure methods.

If the remote host is insecure, your display key can be compromised
In the best scenario, where the X server supports strong authentication and your key can be copied securely to the remote machine, you still have to store your sensitive display key there. If that machine is untrustworthy, your key can be at risk. (SSH doesn't have this problem, since only your public key is stored on the SSH server machine.)

9.3.5.4. SSH and authentication spoofing

Through X forwarding, SSH provides transparent, secure authentication and key transfer for X sessions. This is done by a technique called *authentication spoofing*, as depicted in Figure 9-11. Authentication spoofing involves a fake display key, which we call the *proxy key*, that authenticates access to the SSH X proxy server on the remote side. When relaying X traffic containing a key, SSH cleverly substitutes the real display key. Here's how it works.

The players begin in the following positions. You are logged into a local machine with a local display. The local machine runs an X server and SSH clients. On the other side of the network connection, an SSH server is running on a remote machine, where you invoke X clients. The goal is for the remote X clients to appear on your local display by way of SSH.

First, you run a local SSH client, asking it to set up X forwarding. The SSH client requests X forwarding from the remote SSH server, and it also reads your local display key from your *.Xauthority* file.

Next, the SSH client generates a proxy key. This is a string of random data of the same length as your local display key. The SSH client then sends the proxy key and its key type (e.g., MIT-MAGIC-COOKIE-1) to the remote machine, and the SSH server runs the *xauth* program on your behalf to associate the proxy key with your local display. The stage is now set for X forwarding.

* See the X11R6 *Xsecurity*(1) manpage for details on these methods. Also, remember that this is authentication only, not encryption. The contents of your X connection remain unencrypted and open to snooping or modification on the network.

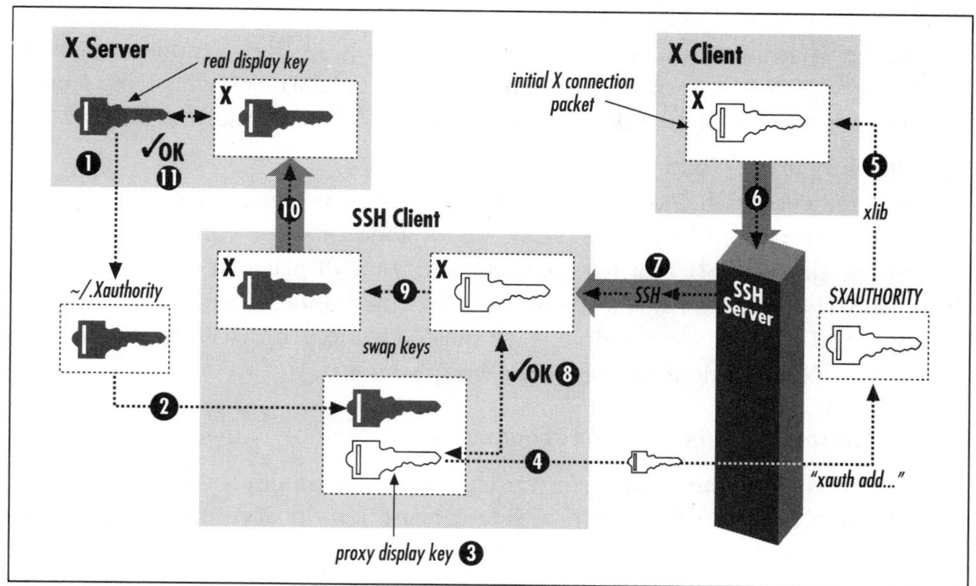

Figure 9-11. Authentication of forwarded X connections

When you start a remote X client, your local SSH client connects to your local X display. It then watches for the first X protocol message sent over the forwarded connection and treats it specially. Specifically, the SSH client parses the message, finds the X authentication key inside it, and compares it to the proxy key. If the keys don't match, the SSH client rejects and closes the connection. Otherwise, if the keys match, the SSH client substitutes the real display key in place of the proxy key and relays the modified message to your local X server. The X server, blissfully unaware that a key switch has taken place, reads the display key and proceeds normally with X authentication. The forwarded X connection is now established.

X forwarding with authentication spoofing solves all but one of the X authentication problems we raised earlier:

xhost
: X forwarding doesn't use *xhost*. (By the way, make sure to disable all *xhost* permissions when using X forwarding, or you will undermine the X security provided by SSH.)

Key transfer
: SSH transfers the X display key automatically and runs *xauth* on your behalf to install it on the remote side. The transfer is secure since the key travels over the encrypted SSH connection.

MIT-MAGIC-COOKIE-1 insecurity

The key transmitted at the beginning of every X session is now encrypted, along with the rest of the X traffic, inside the SSH session. This greatly increases the operational security of this common X authentication scheme.

Untrustworthy remote hosts

With authentication spoofing, only the proxy key, not the true display key, is sent to the remote host. The proxy key is good only for connecting to your display through SSH, not for connecting to your display directly. As soon as your SSH session ends, the proxy key becomes useless. Since SSH sessions come and go, but some people leave their X sessions up (with the same key) for days, X forwarding can be a great improvement.

9.3.5.5. Improving authentication spoofing

The remaining problem with X forwarding is the possibility of unsupported X authentication mechanisms. The local side can use a more sophisticated authentication method a remote host might not support.

In theory, SSH X forwarding can solve this problem by always installing a proxy key of type MIT-MAGIC-COOKIE-1, no matter what local authentication method is actually in use. After the SSH client has checked the X client's key against the proxy key for a match, its client could then generate and substitute whatever local authenticator is required using the true authentication type and key.

Unfortunately, SSH implementations don't go this far. The server compares keys literally as bit strings, and the SSH client substitutes keys verbatim, regardless of the key types. As a result, if you use a stronger X authentication method such as XDM-AUTHORIZATION-1, *sshd* blindly compares an encrypted authenticator with the proxy key, rightly determine that they don't match, and invalidly rejects the connection. The failure is silent and mysterious; we wish the software would detect the presence of an unsupported mode and issue a warning when setting up the connection.

If SSH knew the details of all X authentication modes, it could check the proxy authenticators on one side and generate correct ones for the X server on the other. However, this is a significant development effort, though perhaps one could link SSH against the X11 libraries to obtain the necessary algorithms. SSH would also have to deal with differing key data lengths, constructing a new X message to hold the proxy key instead of copying it to an existing message.

It would also be useful if X forwarding could be used without authentication spoofing. Then you could arrange your own security for the connection by, say, using *xhost* to allow any connection from your local machine (and hence the SSH X proxy), while still applying key-based authentication to X connections originating from elsewhere. You can accomplish this with general port forwarding, as discussed in the next section, but direct support is more convenient.

9.3.5.6. Nonstandard X clients

X clients generally do X *xauth*-style authentication by virtue of having been linked against Xlib, the common X programming library. Occasionally, though, you run across particular X client programs that don't use Xlib and simply ignore authentication issues. Since you can't turn off SSH X authentication spoofing, you can't use such programs across SSH X forwarding; you get this message:

```
X11 connection requests different authentication protocol: 'MIT-MAGIC-COOKIE-1'
vs. ''
```

You can, however, use a general port forwarding instead. For example:

```
foo% ssh -R6010:localhost:6000 bar
bar% setenv DISPLAY bar:10
```

Note that this bypasses the discipline imposed by X forwarding, of requiring *xauth* authentication on forwarded X connections. If your real X server is using *xhost* for access control, this port forwarding allows anyone on host foo to connect to your X server. Use this sort of thing with caution if you need to.

9.3.6. Further Issues

As we've said, X forwarding usually works fine without any special effort on your part. In some special situations, however, you might need to take some extra steps.

9.3.6.1. X server configuration

In order for X forwarding to work, your X server must accept the proxy X connections from your SSH client. This is sometimes not set up to begin with, because normal use doesn't require it. For example, if you're using an X server on a PC to access a remote Unix machine via XDM, you might never run local X clients at all, and they may not be allowed by default. You can run `xhost +localhost` to allow all connections from your PC, while still applying key-based authentication to connections from other sources. This allows SSH-forwarded (and authenticated) connections to be accepted.

9.3.6.2. Setting your DISPLAY environment variable

SSH sets the DISPLAY variable automatically only if X forwarding is in effect. If you don't use X forwarding but want to use X on a remote machine you logged into via SSH, remember that you have to set the DISPLAY variable yourself. You should do this only when both machines are on the same, trusted network, as the X protocol by itself is quite insecure.

Be careful not to set DISPLAY unintentionally! It is common for people to set the DISPLAY variable in a login command file or by other means. If you're not careful, this can make your X connections insecure without your noticing. If you use SSH to tunnel through a firewall that blocks normal X connections, then of course you'll notice because your X clients won't work. But if normal X connections are possible but undesirable, and X forwarding isn't in effect, your X programs will work but will (silently) not be secured. This is a good reason to block X traffic at the firewall if it presents a security risk or to configure your X server to accept connections only from the local host (the source of the SSH-forwarded X connections). If that's not feasible, you may want to put something like this in your login script:

```
#!/bin/csh
if ($?DISPLAY) then
   set display_host   = `expr "$DISPLAY" : '\(.*\):'`
   set display_number = `expr "$DISPLAY" : '.*:\([^.]*\)'`
   set my_host = `hostname`
   set result  = `expr '(' "$display_host" = "$my_host" ')' '&' '(' \
                 "$display_number" '>' "0" ')'`
   if ($result == 0) then
      echo "WARNING: X display $DISPLAY does not appear to be protected by SSH!"
      echo "unsetting DISPLAY variable just to be safe"
      unsetenv DISPLAY
   endif
endif
```

9.3.6.3. Shared accounts

If you share a single account among multiple people, you may have some trouble with X forwarding. For example, it is common for a group of sysadmins to share use of the root account. For each person to retain their own environment when using the root account, they may set their USER, LOGNAME, and HOME environment variables explicitly to reflect their personal accounts rather than the root account. If you use SSH to log into the root account with X forwarding turned on, though, it adds the proxy *xauth* key to root's *.Xauthority* file before the shell reads your login script and resets these environment variables. The result is that once you're logged in and try to use X, it fails: the X client looks in your *.Xauthority* file (because of the setting of your HOME variable), but the key isn't there.

You can deal with this problem by setting the XAUTHORITY variable to point to root's *.Xauthority* file, or by using code like the following in your login script to copy the needed key into your personal one:

```
if (($uid == 0) && ($?SSH_CLIENT) && ($?DISPLAY)) then
# If I do ssh -l root with X forwarding, the X proxy server's xauth key
```

```
# gets added to root's xauth db, not mine.  See if there's an entry for my
# display in root's xauth db...
  set key = `bash -c "xauth -i -f /.Xauthority list $DISPLAY 2> /dev/null"`
# ... and if so, copy it into mine.
  if ($? == 0) then
    xauth -bi add $key
    chown res ~res/.Xauthority >& /dev/null
  endif
endif
```

9.3.6.4. Location of the xauth program

Remember that *sshd* runs the *xauth* program on your behalf, to add the proxy key to your *.Xauthority* file on the remote side. The location of the *xauth* program is discovered when you configure the SSH package and compiled into the *sshd* executable. If *xauth* is subsequently moved, X forwarding won't work (*ssh –v* reveals this explicitly). For SSH1 and OpenSSH, the system administrator on the server side can use the serverwide configuration keyword `XAuthLocation` to set the path to the *xauth* program without having to recompile *sshd1*:

```
# SSH1, Open SSH
XAuthLocation /usr/local/bin/xauth
```

`XAuthLocation` can also appear in the client configuration file (OpenSSH only); the client uses *xauth* to get the local X display key.

9.3.6.5. X forwarding and the GatewayPorts feature

The `GatewayPorts` (*–g*) feature discussed earlier applies only to general port forwarding, not to X forwarding. The X proxies in SSH1, SSH2, and OpenSSH always listen on all network interfaces and accept connections from anywhere, though those connections are then subject to X authentication as described earlier. To restrict X client source addresses, use TCP-wrappers, which we discuss in the next section.

9.4. Forwarding Security: TCP-wrappers and libwrap

At several points in this chapter, we have talked about security issues and limitations of forwarding. So far, we've seen very little control over who can connect to a forwarded port. The SSH1 and OpenSSH default is to allow connections only from the local host, which is reasonably secure for a single-user machine. But if you need to allow connections from elsewhere, you have a problem, since it's all or nothing: to allow connections from elsewhere (using *–g* or `GatewayPorts=yes`), you must allow them from anywhere. And with SSH2 it's worse: forwarded ports will always accept connections from anywhere. X forwarding is in a slightly better position, since the X protocol has its own authentication, but you might still prefer to restrict access, preventing intruders from exploiting an unknown security flaw or performing a denial-of-service attack. SSH on the Unix platform provides an optional feature for access control based on the client address, called *TCP-wrappers*.

The term TCP-wrappers refers to software written by Wietse Venema. If it isn't already installed in your Unix distribution, you can get it at:

> *ftp://ftp.porcupine.org/pub/security/index.html*

TCP-wrappers are a global access control mechanism that integrates with other TCP-based servers, such as *sshd* or *telnetd*. Access control is based on the source address of incoming TCP connections. That is, a TCP-wrapper permits or denies connections based on their origin, as specified in the configuration files */etc/hosts.allow* and */etc/hosts.deny*. Figure 9-12 shows where TCP-wrappers fit into the scheme of SSH configuration.

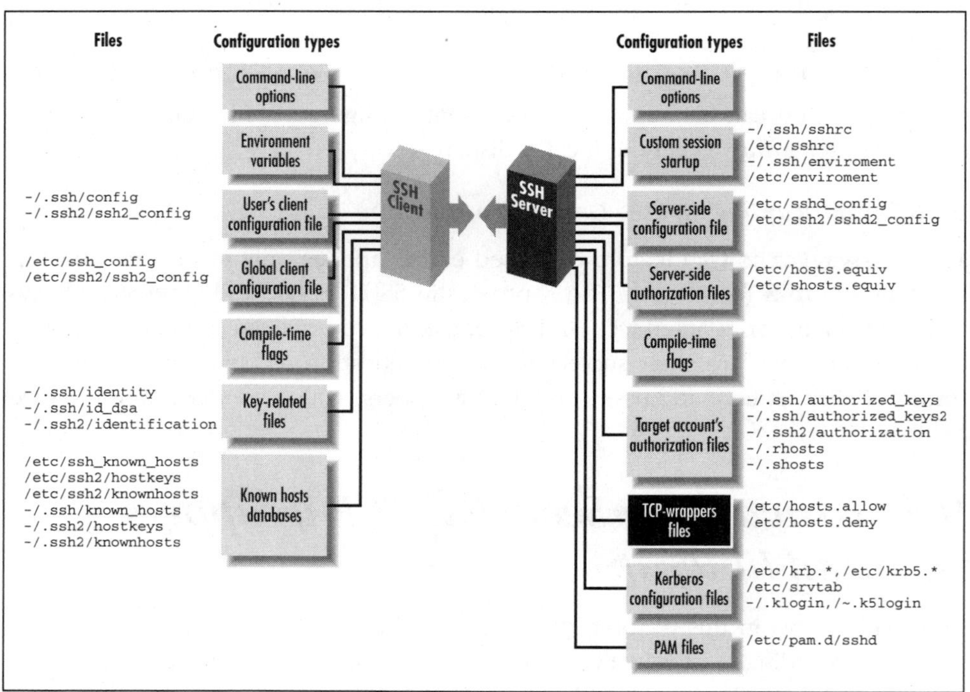

Figure 9-12. TCP-wrappers and SSH configuration (highlighted parts)

There are two ways to use TCP-wrappers. The most common method, *wrapping*, is applied to TCP servers that are normally invoked by *inetd*. You "wrap" the server by editing */etc/inetd.conf* and modifying the server's configuration line. Instead of invoking the server directly, you invoke the TCP-wrapper daemon, *tcpd*, which in turn invokes the original server. Then, you edit the TCP-wrapper configuration files to specify your desired access control. *tcpd* makes authorization decisions based on the their contents.

The *inetd* technique applies access control without having to modify the TCP server program. This is nice. However, *sshd* is usually not invoked by *inetd* [5.4.3.2], so the second method, *source code modification*, must be applied. To participate in TCP-wrapper control, the SSH server must be compiled with the flag `--with-libwrap` to enable internal support for TCP-wrappers. [4.1.5.3] *sshd* then invokes TCP-wrapper library functions to do explicit access-control checks according to the rules in */etc/hosts.allow* and */etc/hosts.deny*. So in a sense, the term "wrapper" is misleading since *sshd* is modified, not wrapped, to support TCP-wrappers. Figure 9-13 illustrates the process.

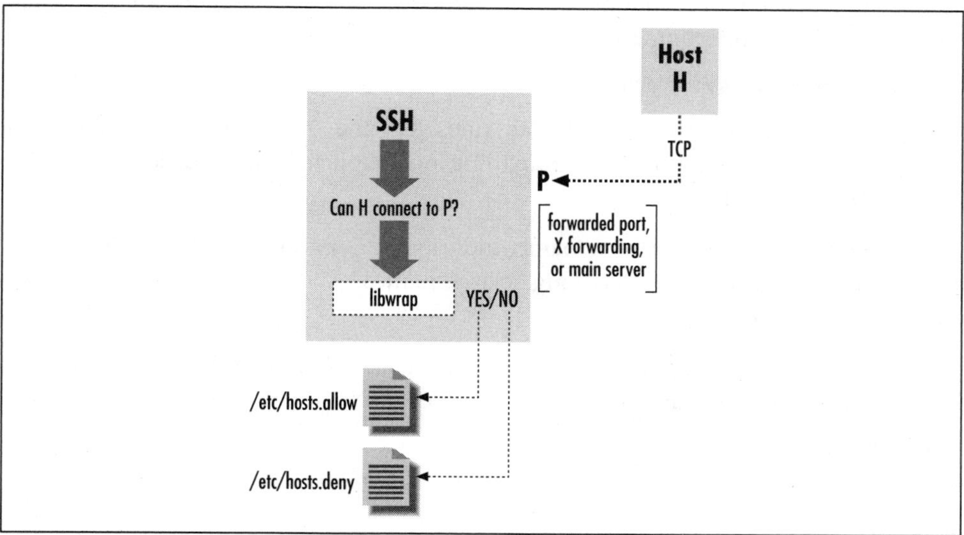

Figure 9-13. TCP-wrapper (libwrap) operation

9.4.1. TCP-wrappers Configuration

The access control language for TCP-wrappers has quite a few options and may vary depending on whose package you use and what version it is. We won't cover the language completely in this book. Consult your local documentation for a complete understanding: the manpages on *tcpd*(8), *hosts_access*(5), and *hosts_options*(5). We will just indicate some simple, common configurations.

The TCP-wrapper configuration is kept in the files */etc/hosts.allow* and */etc/hosts.deny*. These files contain patterns of the form:

```
service_1 [service_2 service_3 ...] : client_1 [client_2 client_3 ...]
```

Each pattern matches some (server,client) pairs, and hence may match a particular client/server TCP connection. Specifically, a connection between client C and server S matches this rule if some service *service_i* matches S, and some *client_j* matches C. (We explain the format and matching rules for these subpatterns shortly.) The *hosts.allow* file is searched first, followed by *hosts.deny*. If a matching pattern is found in *hosts.allow*, the connection is allowed. If none is found there, but one matches in *hosts.deny*, the connection is dropped. Finally, if no patterns match in either file, the connection is allowed. Nonexistence of either file is treated as if the file existed and contained no matching patterns. Note that the default, then, is to allow everything.

There is also an extended syntax, documented on the *hosts_options*(5) manpage. It may or may not be available, depending on how your TCP-wrapper library was built. It has many more options, but in particular, it allows tagging an individual rule as denying or rejecting a matching connection; for example:

```
sshd1 : bad.host.com : DENY
```

Using this syntax, you can put all your rules into the *hosts.allow* file, rather than having to use both files. To reject anything not explicitly allowed, just put `ALL:ALL:DENY` at the end of the file.

In a pattern, each service is a name indicating a server to which this pattern applies. SSH recognizes the following service names:

sshd
: The main SSH server. This can be *sshd*, *sshd1*, *sshd2*, or whatever name you invoke the daemon under (its *argv[0]* value).

sshdfwd-x11
: The X forwarding port.

sshdfwd-N
: Forwarded TCP port *N* (e.g., forwarded port 2001 is service `sshdfwd-2001`).

The X and port forwarding control features are available only in SSH1 and SSH2; OpenSSH uses only *libwrap* to control access to the main server.

Each *client* is a pattern that matches a connecting client. It can be:

- An IP address in dotted-quad notation (e.g., 192.168.10.1).
- A hostname (DNS, or whatever naming services the host is using).

- An IP network as network-number/mask (e.g., 192.168.10.0/255.255.255; note that the "/n-mask-bits" syntax, 192.168.10.0/24, isn't recognized).
- "ALL", matching any client source address.

Example 9-1 shows a sample */etc/hosts.allow* configuration. This setup allows connections to any service from the local host's loopback address, and from all addresses 192.168.10.x. This host is running publicly available servers for SSH1, POP, and IMAP, so we allow connections to these from anywhere, but SSH-2 clients are restricted to sources in another particular range of networks.

Example 9-1. Sample /etc/hosts.allow File

```
#
# /etc/hosts.allow
#
# network access control for programs invoked by tcpd (see inetd.conf) or
# using libwrap.  See the manpages hosts_access(5) and hosts_options(5).

# allow all connections from my network or localhost (loopback address)
#
ALL : 192.168.10.0/255.255.255.0 localhost

# allow connections to these services from anywhere
#
ipop3d imapd sshd1 : ALL

# allow SSH-2 connections from the class C networks
# 192.168.20.0, 192.168.21.0, ..., 192.168.27.0
#
sshd2 : 192.168.20.0/255.255.248.0

# allow connections to forwarded port 1234 from host blynken
sshdfwd-1234 : blynken.sleepy.net

# restrict X forwarding access to localhost
sshdfwd-x11 : localhost

# deny everything else
#
ALL : ALL : DENY
```

We allow connections to the forwarded port 1234 from a particular host, *blynken.sleepy.net*. Note that this host doesn't have to be on any of the networks listed so far but can be anywhere at all. The rules so far say what is allowed, but don't by themselves forbid any connections. So for example, the forwarding established by the command *ssh1 –L1234:localhost:21 remote* is accessible only to the local host, since SSH1 defaults to binding only the loopback address in any case. But *ssh1 –g –L1234:localhost:21 remote* is accessible to *blynken.sleepy.net* as well, as is either command using *ssh2* instead (since *ssh2* doesn't affect the localhost restriction and ignores the *–g* option). The important difference is that with this use of TCP-wrappers, *sshd* rejects connections to the forwarded port, 1234, from any other address.

The `sshdfwd-x11` line restricts X-forwarding connections to the local host. This means that if *ssh* connects to this host with X forwarding, only local X clients can use the forwarded X connection. X authentication does this already, but this configuration provides an extra bit of protection.*

The final line denies any connection that doesn't match the earlier lines, making this a default-to-closed configuration. If you wanted instead to deny some particular connections but allow all others, you would use something like this:

```
ALL : evil.mordor.net : DENY
telnetd : completely.horked.edu : DENY
ALL : ALL : ALLOW
```

The final line is technically not required, but it's a good idea to make your intentions explicit. If you don't have the *host_options* syntax available, you instead have an empty *hosts.allow* file and the following lines in *hosts.deny*:

```
ALL : evil.mordor.net
telnetd : completely.horked.edu
```

9.4.2. Notes About TCP-wrappers

Here are a few things to remember when using TCP-wrappers:

- You can't distinguish between ports forwarded by SSH1 and SSH2: the `sshdfwd-*` rules refer to both simultaneously. You can work around this limitation by linking each against a different *libwrap.a,* compiled with different filenames for the allow and deny files, or by patching the *ssh* and *sshd* executables directly, but then you have to keep track of these changes and extra files.
- The big drawback to TCP-wrappers is that it affects all users simultaneously. An individual user can't specify custom access rules for himself; there's just the single set of global configuration files for the machine. This limits its usefulness on multiuser machines.
- If you compile SSH with the `--with-libwrap` option, it is automatically and always turned on; there's no configuration or command-line option to disable the TCP-wrappers check. Remember that SSH does this check not only for forwarded ports and X connections but for connections to the main SSH server.

* SSH2 2.1.0 has a bug that causes an SSH session to freeze after it rejects a forwarded connection because of a TCP-wrappers rule, at least on some Unix systems. Until this bug is fixed, don't use TCP-wrappers for protecting forwarded ports (although using it to restrict access to the main *sshd2* server appears to work).

As soon as you install a version of *sshd* with TCP-wrappers, you must ensure that the TCP-wrappers configuration allows connections to the server, for instance with the rule `sshd1 sshd2 sshd : ALL` in */etc/hosts.allow*.

- Using hostnames instead of addresses in the TCP-wrappers rule set involves the usual security tradeoff. Names are more convenient, and their use avoids breakage in the future if a host address changes. On the other hand, an attacker can potentially subvert the naming service and circumvent the access control. If the host machine is configured to use only its */etc/hosts* file for name lookup, this may be acceptable even in a highly secure environment.
- The TCP-wrappers package includes a program called *tcpdchk*. This program examines the wrapper control files and reports inconsistencies that might signal problems. Many sites run this periodically as a safety check. Unfortunately, *tcpdchk* is written only with explicit wrapping via *inetd.conf* in mind. It doesn't have any way of knowing about programs that refer to the control files via the *libwrap* routines, as does *sshd*. When *tcpdchk* reads control files with SSH rules, it finds uses of the service names sshd1, sshdfwd-*n*, etc., but no corresponding wrapped services in *inetd.conf*, and it generates a warning. Unfortunately, we know of no workaround.

9.5. Summary

In this chapter, we discussed SSH port forwarding and X forwarding. Port forwarding is a general TCP proxying feature that tunnels TCP connections through an SSH session. This is useful for securing otherwise insecure protocols running on top of TCP or for tunneling TCP connections through firewalls that would otherwise forbid access. X forwarding is a special case of port forwarding for X Window System connections, for which SSH has extra support. This makes it easy to secure X connections with SSH, which is good because X, while popular and useful, is notoriously insecure. Access control on forwarded ports is normally coarse, but you can achieve finer control with the TCP-wrappers feature.

10

A Recommended Setup

In this chapter:

We've just covered a pile of chapters on SSH configuration: is your head spinning yet? With so many choices, you might be wondering which options you should use. How can system administrators secure their systems most effectively with SSH?

When set up properly, SSH works well and invisibly, but sometimes a good setup takes a few tries. In addition, there are some ways to configure the software that are simply wrong. If you're not careful, you can introduce security holes into your system.

In this chapter we present a recommended set of options for compilation, server configuration, key management, and client configuration. We assume:

- You're running SSH on a Unix machine.
- You want a secure system, sometimes at the expense of flexibility. For instance, rather than tell you to maintain your *.rhosts* files carefully, we recommend disabling Rhosts authentication altogether.

Of course, no single configuration covers all the possibilities; that is, after all, the point of configuration. This is just a sample setup, more on the secure side, to give you a starting point and cover some of the issues involved.

10.1. The Basics

Before you start configuring, make sure you're running an up-to-date SSH version. Some older versions have known security holes that are easily exploited. Always run the latest stable version, and apply updates or patches in a timely manner. (The same goes for your other security software.)

Always keep important SSH-related files and directories protected. The server's host key should be readable only by root. Each user's home directory, SSH configuration directory, and *.rhosts* and *.shosts* files should be owned by the user and protected against all others.

Also, remember that SSH doesn't and can't protect against all threats. It can secure your network connections but does nothing against other types of attacks, such as dictionary attacks against your password database. SSH should be an important part, but not the only part, of a robust security policy. [3.11]

10.2. Compile-Time Configuration

In Chapter 4, we covered many compile-time flags for building SSH distributions. Several flags should be carefully set to make your server machine maximally secure:

`--with-etcdir=...` *(SSH1, SSH2)*
: Make sure your *etc* directory is on a local disk, not an NFS-mounted partition. If the SSH server reads a file via NFS, the contents are transmitted in the clear across the network, violating security. This is especially true of the host key, which is stored unencrypted in this directory.

`--prefix=...` *(SSH1, SSH2, OpenSSH)*
: Likewise, make sure your SSH executables are installed on a local disk, as they can be spoofed if loaded over NFS.

`--disable-suid-ssh` *(SSH1)*
`--disable-suid-ssh-signer` *(SSH2)*
: Our recommended serverwide configuration disables trusted-host authentication, so there's no need for setuid permissions for *ssh1* and *ssh-signer2*.

`--without-none` *(SSH1)*
: You should disable the "none" cipher that permits unencrypted transmissions. An intruder with access to a user account for 10 seconds can add "Ciphers None" to its client configuration file, silently disabling encryption for the user's clients. If you need the none cipher for testing, build a separate server using `--with-none` and make it executable only by the system administrator.

`--without-rsh` *(SSH1, OpenSSH)*
: We don't recommend allowing *ssh* to fall back to *rsh*. You can enforce this restriction at compile time using `--without-rsh`, or at runtime in the serverwide configuration file. The choice is yours.

`--with-libwrap` *(SSH1, SSH2)*
`--with-tcp-wrappers` *(OpenSSH)*

libwrap affords more precise control over which client machines are allowed to connect to your server. It also makes port and X forwarding more flexible, since otherwise local forwardings are available either only to the local host or from anywhere at all. With `GatewayPorts` (or *ssh -g*) and *libwrap*, you can limit forwarding access to specific hosts. [9.2.1.1]

10.3. Serverwide Configuration

Chapter 5 was a detailed discussion of *sshd* and how to configure its runtime behavior. Now let's determine which configuration options are most important for security.

10.3.1. Disable Other Means of Access

SSH can provide a secure front door into your system but don't forget to close the back doors. If your system allows access via the infamous r-commands, disable them. This means:

- Remove the file */etc/hosts.equiv*, or make it a read-only empty file.
- Disable *rshd, rlogind,* and *rexecd* by removing or commenting out their lines in */etc/inetd.conf*:

  ```
  # turned off -- don't use!
  #shell   stream  tcp   nowait  root  /usr/sbin/in.rshd     in.rshd
  ```

  Make sure you restart *inetd* after doing this, so that the change takes effect (e.g., *skill –HUP inetd*).
- Educate users not to create *.rhosts* files.

You might also consider disabling *telnetd* and other insecure avenues for logging in, permitting logins only via SSH.

10.3.2. /etc/sshd_config

We'll now discuss our recommended *sshd_config* settings. We have omitted some keywords that aren't particularly security-related, such as `PrintMotd`, which simply prints a message after login. For any remaining keywords, use your judgment based on your system and needs.

The following files may be located anywhere on the machine's local disk. For security's sake, don't put them on an NFS-mounted partition. If you do, each time the files are accessed by the SSH server, their contents are transmitted in the clear over the network.

```
HostKey /etc/ssh_host_key
PidFile /etc/sshd.pid
RandomSeed /etc/ssh_random_seed
```

The following settings control file and directory permissions. The **StrictModes** value requires users to protect their SSH-related files and directories, or else they can't authenticate. The **Umask** value causes any files and directories created by *sshd1* to be readable only by their owner (the uid under which *sshd* is running).

```
StrictModes yes
Umask 0077
```

The following code represents the server's TCP settings. The **Port** and **ListenAddress** values are standard. We set an idle timeout to reduce the chances that an unattended terminal can be misused by an intruder. Fifteen minutes is short enough to be useful but long enough not to annoy users, though this depends on usage patterns. You may certainly use your judgment and set a different value, but do think about the issue. Also, we enable keepalive messages so connections to clients that have crashed or otherwise become unreachable will terminate rather than hang around and require manual reaping by the sysadmin.

```
Port 22
ListenAddress 0.0.0.0
IdleTimeout 15m
KeepAlive yes
```

For logins we allow 30 seconds for a successful authentication, which should be long enough for users and automated processes:

```
LoginGraceTime 30
```

The following settings control generation of the server key. We recommend at least 768 bits in your server key and that you regenerate the key at least once an hour (3600 seconds).

```
ServerKeyBits 768
KeyRegenerationInterval 3600
```

The following settings control authentication, and we enable only public-key authentication. Password authentication is disabled because passwords can be stolen and used more easily than public keys. This is a fairly harsh restriction, so you might want to leave it enabled depending on your needs. Without password authentication, you have a "chicken and egg" problem: how do users upload their public keys securely the first time? As system administrator, you have to institute a process for this transfer: for example, users can generate keys on a client machine and then request that you install them on the server machine. Rhosts authentication is disabled because it can be spoofed. RhostsRSA authentication is disabled too, because overall it is a medium-security method and this configuration is on the side of higher security.

```
PasswordAuthentication no
RhostsAuthentication no
RhostsRSAAuthentication no
RSAAuthentication yes
```

Although we've disabled trusted-host authentication already, we still forbid *sshd* to use *.rhosts* files at all (just in case you reenable trusted-host authentication):

```
IgnoreRhosts yes
IgnoreRootRhosts yes
```

UseLogin is disabled to prevent the unlikely but unwanted use of an alternative login program. (This isn't very useful. An intruder who can install an alternative login program probably can also edit *sshd_config* to change this line.)

```
UseLogin no
```

The following settings limit access to the server, permitting SSH connections only from within the local domain* (except for the account fred, which may receive connections from anywhere). If you want to restrict access to particular local accounts or Unix groups, add **AllowUsers** and **AllowGroups** lines (or **DenyUsers** and **DenyGroups**). We have set **SilentDeny** so that any rejections by **DenyHosts** produce no messages for the user. No sense in giving an intruder a clue about what happened, although this can make troubleshooting more difficult.

```
AllowHosts fred@* *.your.domain.com                Just an example
SilentDeny yes
```

We permit the superuser to connect via SSH but not by password authentication. This is redundant but consistent with turning off **PasswordAuthentication**.

```
PermitRootLogin nopwd
```

For logging error messages, we disable **FascistLogging** because it writes user-specific information to the log, such as the dates and times each person logged in. This information can be valuable to an intruder. We disable **QuietMode**, however, to receive more detailed (but less sensitive) log messages.

```
FascistLogging no
QuietMode no
```

We permit TCP port forwarding and X forwarding so users can secure their other TCP connections:

```
AllowTcpForwarding yes
X11Forwarding yes
```

* The reliability of this restriction depends on the integrity of DNS. Unfortunately, due to the implementation of AllowHosts, restriction by IP address is no more secure. [5.5.2.1]

10.3.3. /etc/ssh2/sshd2_config

We now move to our recommended *sshd2_config* settings. Again, we omitted some keywords that are not security-related.

As we have mentioned before, make sure all SSH-related files are on local disks, not remotely mounted partitions:

```
HostKeyFile /etc/ssh2/hostkey
PublicHostKeyFile /etc/ssh2/hostkey.pub
RandomSeedFile /etc/ssh2/random_seed
```

For the following settings, consider the pros and cons of storing user files on NFS-mounted filesystems: [10.7]

```
UserConfigDirectory
IdentityFile
AuthorizationFile
```

For this setting, see the discussion for SSH1:

```
StrictModes yes
```

For the first three settings, use the same reasoning as for SSH1. `RequireReverseMapping` is trickier, however. You might think that security would be increased by reverse DNS lookups on incoming connections, but in fact, DNS isn't secure enough to guarantee accurate lookups. Also, due to other issues in your Unix and network environment, reverse DNS mappings might not even work properly. [5.4.3.7]

```
Port 22
ListenAddress 0.0.0.0
KeepAlive yes
RequireReverseMapping no
```

For this setting, see the discussion for SSH1:

```
LoginGraceTime 30
```

In addition, since *sshd2* doesn't have a configuration keyword for the number of bits in the server key, run it with the *–b* option:

```
$ sshd2 -b 1024 ...
```

These settings mirror those for SSH1:

```
AllowedAuthentications publickey
RequiredAuthentications publickey
```

You disable `UserKnownHosts` to prevent users from extending trust to unknown hosts for the purpose of trusted-host authentication. The superuser can still specify trusted hosts in */etc/ssh2/knownhosts*.

```
IgnoreRhosts yes
UserKnownHosts no
```

See the discussion for SSH1 about this setting:

```
PermitRootLogin nopwd
```

Use either of the following settings as fits your needs. The notable feature is that they both exclude the none cipher which, as discussed for `--without-none`, may be a security risk.

```
Ciphers anycipher
Ciphers anystdcipher
```

The following settings produce enough logging information to be useful:

```
QuietMode no
VerboseMode yes
```

Since SSH-2 is a more secure protocol, we have disabled SSH-1 compatibility mode. However, this may not be an option for practical reasons; if you turn it on, set `Sshd1Path` to the pathname of your SSH1 server executable.

```
Ssh1Compatibility no
#Sshd1Path /usr/local/bin/sshd1   # commented out
```

10.4. Per-Account Configuration

Users should be instructed not to create *.rhosts* files. If trusted-host authentication is enabled in the local SSH server, advise users to create *.shosts* files instead of *.rhosts*.

For SSH1 and OpenSSH, each key in *~/.ssh/authorized_keys* should be restricted by appropriate options. First, use the `from` option to restrict access to particular keys by particular hosts when appropriate. For example, suppose your *authorized_keys* file contains a public key for your home PC, *myhome.isp.net*. No other machine will ever authenticate using this key, so make the relationship explicit:

```
from="myhome.isp.net" ...key...
```

Also set idle timeouts for appropriate keys:

```
from="myhome.isp.net",idle-timeout=5m ...key...
```

Finally, for each key, consider whether port forwarding, agent forwarding, and tty allocation are ever necessary for incoming connections. If not, disable these features with `no-port-forwarding`, `no-agent-forwarding`, and `no-pty`, respectively:

```
from="myhome.isp.net",idle-timeout=5m,no-agent-forwarding ...key...
```

10.5. Key Management

We recommend creating user keys at least 1024 bits long. Protect your key with a good passphrase. Make it lengthy and use a mixture of lowercase, uppercase, numeric, and symbolic characters. Don't use words found in a dictionary.

Empty passphrases should be avoided unless you absolutely need to use one, for example, in an automated batch script. [11.1.2.2]

10.6. Client Configuration

Most SSH security pertains to the server, but SSH clients have security-related settings too. Here are a few tips:

- Whenever you leave a computer while SSH clients are running, lock the computer's display with a password-protected screen locker. This is particularly important if you're running an agent that permits an intruder to access your remote accounts without a passphrase.
- In your client configuration file, turn on some safety features as mandatory values:

```
# SSH1, OpenSSH
# Put at the top of your configuration file
Host *
  FallBackToRsh no
  UseRsh no
  GatewayPorts no
  StrictHostKeyChecking ask

# SSH2 only
# Put at the bottom of your configuration file
*:
 GatewayPorts no
 StrictHostKeyChecking ask
```

  `FallBackToRsh` and `UseRsh` prevent the insecure r-commands from invocation by SSH without your knowledge. (These aren't present in SSH2.) The `GatewayPorts` value forbids remote clients from connecting to locally forwarded ports. Finally, rather than blindly connect, the `StrictHostKeyChecking` value warns you of any changed host keys and asks what you want to do.

10.7. Remote Home Directories (NFS, AFS)

We've mentioned NFS several times as a potential security risk for SSH installations. Now we delve into more detail on this topic.

In today's world of ubiquitous networking, it is common for your home directory to be shared among many machines via a network file-sharing protocol, such as SMB for Windows machines or NFS and AFS for Unix. This is convenient, but it does raise some issues with SSH, both technical and security-related.

SSH examines files in the target account's home directory in order to make critical decisions about authentication and authorization. For every form of authentication except password, the various control files in your home directory (*authorized_keys*, *.shosts*, *.k5login*, etc.) enable SSH access to your account. Two things are therefore important:

- Your home directory needs to be safe from tampering.
- SSH must have access to your home directory.

10.7.1. NFS Security Risks

The security of shared home directories is often not very high. Although the NFS protocol has versions and implementations that afford greater security, it is woefully insecure in most installations. Often, it employs no reliable form of authentication whatsoever, but rather uses the same scheme as *rsh*: the source IP address and DNS identify clients, and a privileged source port is proof of trustworthiness. It then simply believes the uid number encoded in NFS requests and grants access as that user. Breaking into a home directory can be as simple as:

1. Discover the uid, and create an account with that uid on a laptop running Unix.
2. Connect that machine to the network, borrowing the IP address of a trusted host.
3. Issue a *mount* command, *su* to the account with the uid, and start rifling through the files.

At this point, an intruder can easily add another public key to *authorized_keys*, and the account is wide open. The moral is that when designing a system, keep in mind that the security of SSH is no stronger than that of the home directories involved. You need at least to be aware of the trade-off between security and convenience involved here. If you are using an insecure NFS and want to avoid this weakness, you can:

- Use SSH2, which has the **UserConfigDirectory** option to place the per-user SSH configuration files, normally in *~/.ssh2*, elsewhere, say in */var/ssh/<username>*. You can still set the permissions so their owners can control them, but they won't be shared via NFS and thus not vulnerable. You can do the same with SSH1 or OpenSSH, but as they lack such a configuration option, you need to edit the source code.
- Turn off hostbased authentication, since the *~/.shosts* control file is vulnerable, and you can't change its location. Or, if you want to use hostbased authentication, set the **IgnoreRhosts** option. This causes *sshd* to ignore *~/.shosts*, relying instead solely on the systemwide */etc/shosts.equiv* file.
- If you are truly paranoid, disable swapping on your Unix machine. Otherwise, sensitive information such as server, host, and user keys, or passwords, may be written to disk as part of the normal operation of the Unix virtual memory system (should the running *sshd* be swapped out to disk). Someone with root access (and a lot of knowledge and luck) could read the swap partition and tease this information out of the mess there—though it's a difficult feat. Another option is to use an operating system that encrypts swap pages on disk, such as OpenBSD.

10.7.2. NFS Access Problems

Another problem that can arise with SSH and NFS is one of access rights. With the public-key or trusted-host methods, if the per-user control files are in the usual place, *sshd* must read the target account's home directory in order to perform authentication. When that directory is on the same machine as *sshd*, this isn't a problem. *sshd* runs as root, and therefore has access to all files. However, if the directory is mounted from elsewhere via NFS, *sshd* might not have access to the directory. NFS is commonly configured so the special access privileges accorded the root account don't extend to remote filesystems.

Now, this isn't a truly serious restriction. Since one of the root privileges is the ability to create a process with any uid, root can simply "become" the right user, and access the remote directory. SSH1 and SSH2 use this mechanism, but OpenSSH doesn't currently have it. [3.6]

You can work around the problem, but to do so you must make your *authorized_keys* file world-readable; the only way to let root read it remotely is to let everyone read it. This isn't too objectionable. The *authorized_keys* file contains no secrets; though you might prefer not to reveal which keys allow access to your account, thus advertising which keys to steal. However, to grant this access, you must make your home directory and *~/.ssh* world-searchable (that is, permissions at least 711). This doesn't allow other users to steal the contents, but it does allow them to guess at filenames and have those guesses verified. It also means that you must be careful about permissions on your files, since the top-level permissions on your directory don't prevent access by others.

All this may be entirely unacceptable or no problem at all; it depends on your attitude towards your files and the other users on the machines where your home directory is accessible.

10.7.3. AFS Access Problems

The Andrew File System, or AFS, is a file-sharing protocol similar in purpose to NFS, but considerably more sophisticated. It uses Kerberos-4 for user authentication and is generally more secure than NFS. The access problem discussed previously comes up for AFS, but it's more work to solve, and this time, OpenSSH is the winner.

Since AFS uses Kerberos, access to remote files is controlled by possession of an appropriate Kerberos ticket. There are no uid-switching games root can play; *sshd* must have an appropriate, valid AFS ticket in order to access your home directory. If you are logged into that machine, of course, you can use Kerberos and AFS commands to get such a ticket. However *sshd* needs it before you've logged in, so there's a bit of a quandary.

This need to transfer credentials from machine to machine isn't unique to SSH, of course, and there is a solution for it: ticket forwarding. It takes some special support, because it's sufficient to just copy the ticket over to the remote host; tickets are issued specifically for particular hosts. Ticket forwarding isn't a feature of Kerberos-4 generally (though it is in Kerberos-5), but AFS has implemented it specifically for Kerberos-4 TGTs and AFS access tokens, and OpenSSH performs this forwarding automatically. To use this feature, you must compile both the SSH client and server `--with-kerberos` and `--with-afs`, and turn on `AFSTokenPassing` on both sides (it is on by default). Then, if you have Kerberos-4 and AFS credentials when you log in via SSH, they are automatically transferred to the SSH server, permitting *sshd* access to your home directory to perform public-key or trusted-host authentication.

If you're not using OpenSSH, you might have trouble using SSH in an AFS environment. Patches for SSH1 are available from various sources on the Internet adding the same AFS forwarding features,* though we haven't had the opportunity to test them.

10.8. Summary

SSH1, SSH2, and OpenSSH are complex and have many options. It is vitally important to understand all options when installing and running SSH servers and clients, so their behavior will conform to your local security policy.

We have presented our recommended options for a high security setting. Your needs may vary. For instance, you might want the flexibility of other authentication methods that we have forbidden in our configuration.

* For example, Dug Song's *ssh-afs* patch; see *http://www.monkey.org/~dugsong/ssh-afs*.

11

In this chapter:
- *Unattended SSH: Batch or cron Jobs*
- *FTP Forwarding*
- *Pine, IMAP, and SSH*
- *Kerberos and SSH*
- *Connecting Through a Gateway Host*

Case Studies

In this chapter we'll delve deeply into some advanced topics: complex port forwarding, integration of SSH with other applications, and more. Some interesting features of SSH don't come to the surface unless examined closely, so we hope you get a lot out of these case studies. Roll up your sleeves, dive in, and have fun.

11.1. Unattended SSH: Batch or cron Jobs

SSH isn't only a great interactive tool but also a resource for automation. Batch scripts, *cron* jobs, and other automated tasks can benefit from the security provided by SSH, but only if implemented properly. The major challenge is authentication: how can a client prove its identity when no human is available to type a password or passphrase? (We'll just write "password" from now on to mean both.) You must carefully select an authentication method, and then equally carefully make it work. Once this infrastructure is established, you must invoke *ssh* properly to avoid prompting the user. In this case study, we discuss the pros and cons of different authentication methods for operating an SSH client unattended.

Note that any kind of unattended authentication presents a security problem and requires compromise, and SSH is no exception. Without a human present when needed to provide credentials (type a password, provide a thumbprint, etc.), those credentials must be stored persistently somewhere on the host system. Therefore, an attacker who compromises the system badly enough can use those credentials to impersonate the program and gain whatever access it has. Selecting a technique is a matter of understanding the pros and cons of the available methods, and picking your preferred poison. If you can't live with this fact, you shouldn't expect strong security of unattended remote jobs.

11.1.1. Password Authentication

Rule number 1: forget password authentication if you care about the security of your batch jobs. In order to use password authentication, you must embed the password within the batch script or put it in a file which the script reads, etc. Whatever you do, the location of the password will be obvious to anyone reading the script. We don't recommend this technique; the public-key methods coming up are more secure.

11.1.2. Public-Key Authentication

In public-key authentication, a private key is the client's credentials. Therefore the batch job needs access to the key, which must be stored where the job can access it. You have three choices of location for the key, which we discuss separately:

- Store the encrypted key and its passphrase in the filesystem.
- Store a plaintext (unencrypted) private key in the filesystem, so it doesn't require a passphrase.
- Store the key in an agent, which keeps secrets out of the filesystem but requires a human to decrypt the key at system boot time.

11.1.2.1. Storing the passphrase in the filesystem

In this technique, you store an encrypted key and its passphrase in the filesystem so a script can access them. We don't recommend this method, since you can store an unencrypted key in the filesystem with the same level of security (and considerably less complication). In either case, you rely solely on the filesystem's protections to keep the key secure. This observation is the rationale for the next technique.

11.1.2.2. Using a plaintext key

A plaintext or unencrypted key requires no passphrase. To create one, run *ssh-keygen* and simply press the Return key when prompted for a passphrase (or similarly, remove the passphrase from an existing key using *ssh-keygen –p*). You can then supply the key filename on the *ssh* command line using the *–i* option, or in the client configuration file with the `IdentityFile` keyword. [7.4.2]

Usually plaintext keys are undesirable, equivalent to leaving your password in a file in your account. They are never a good idea for interactive logins, since the SSH agent provides the same benefits in a much more secure fashion. But a plaintext key is a viable option for automation, since the unattended aspect forces us to rely on some kind of persistent state in the machine. The filesystem is one possibility.

Given that the situations of a plaintext key, encrypted key with stored passphrase, and stored password are in a sense all equivalent, there are still three reasons to prefer the plaintext key method:

- SSH provides much better control over account use on the server side with public-key authentication than with password; this is critical when setting up batch jobs, as we'll discuss shortly.
- All other things being equal, public-key authentication is more secure than password authentication, since it doesn't expose the authentication secret to theft by a malicious server.
- It is awkward to supply a password to SSH from another program. SSH is designed to take passwords from a user only: it doesn't read them from standard input but directly opens its controlling terminal to interact with the user. If there is no terminal, it fails with an error. In order to make this work from a program, you need to use a pseudo-terminal to interact with SSH (e.g., use a tool like Expect).

Plaintext keys are frightening, though. To steal the key, an attacker needs to override filesystem protections only once, and this doesn't necessarily require any fancy hacking: stealing a single backup tape will do. That's why for most cases, we recommend the next method.

11.1.2.3. Using an agent

The *ssh-agent* provides another, somewhat less vulnerable method of key storage for batch jobs. A human invokes an agent and loads the needed keys from passphrase-protected key files, just once. Thereafter, unattended jobs use this long-running agent for authentication.

In this case, the keys are still in plaintext but within the memory space of the running agent rather than in a file on disk. As a matter of practical cracking, it is more difficult to extract a data structure from the address space of a running process than to gain illicit access to a file. Also, this solution avoids the problem of an intruder's walking off with a backup tape containing the plaintext key.

Security can still be compromised by overriding filesystem permissions, though. The agent provides access to its services via a Unix-domain socket, which appears as a node in the filesystem. Anyone who can read and write that socket can instruct the agent to sign authentication requests and thus gain use of the keys. But this compromise isn't quite so devastating since the attacker can't get the keys themselves through the agent socket. She merely gains use of the keys for as long as the agent is running and as long as she can maintain her compromise of the host.

The agent method does have a down side: the system can't continue unattended after a reboot. When the host comes up again automatically, the batch jobs won't have their keys until someone shows up to restart the agent and provide the passphrases to load the keys. This is just a cost of the improved security, and you have a pager, right?

Another bit of complication with the agent method is that you must arrange for the batch jobs to find the agent. SSH clients locate an agent via an environment variable pointing to the agent socket, such as SSH_AUTH_SOCK for the SSH1 and OpenSSH agents. [6.3.2.1] When you start the agent for batch jobs, you need to record its output where the jobs can find it. For instance, if the job is a shell script, you can store the environment values in a file:

```
$ ssh-agent | head -2 > ~/agent-info
$ cat ~/agent-info
setenv SSH_AUTH_SOCK /tmp/ssh-res/ssh-12327-agent;
setenv SSH_AGENT_PID 12328;
```

You can add keys to the agent (assuming C shell syntax here):

```
$ source ~/agent-info
$ ssh-add batch-key
Need passphrase for batch-key (batch job SSH key).
Enter passphrase: **************
```

then instrument any scripts to set the same values for the environment variables:

```
#!/bin/csh
# Source the agent-info file to get access to our ssh-agent.
set agent = ~/agent-info
if (-r $agent) then
  source $agent
else
  echo "Can't find or read agent file; exiting."
  exit 1
endif
# Now use SSH for something...
ssh -q -o 'BatchMode yes' user@remote-server my-job-command
```

You also need to ensure that the batch jobs (and nobody else!) can read and write the socket. If there's only one uid using the agent, the simplest thing to do is start the agent under that uid (e.g., as root, do *su <batch_account> ssh-agent ...*). If multiple uids are using the agent, you must adjust the permissions on the socket and its containing directory so that these uids can all access it, perhaps using group permissions.

Some operating systems behave oddly with respect to permissions on Unix-domain sockets. Some versions of Solaris, for example, completely ignore the modes on a socket, allowing any process at all full access to it. To protect a socket in such situations, set the containing directory to forbid access. For example, if the containing directory is mode 700, only the directory owner may access the socket. (This assumes there's no other shortcut to the socket located elsewhere, such as a hard link.)

Using an agent for automation is more complicated and restrictive than using a plaintext key; however, it is more resistant to attack and doesn't leave the key on disk and tape where it can be stolen. Considering that the agent is still vulnerable to being misused via the filesystem, and that it is intended to run indefinitely, the advantages of this method are debatable. Still, we recommend the agent method as the most secure and flexible strategy for automated SSH usage in a security-conscious environment.

11.1.3. Trusted-Host Authentication

If security concerns are relatively light, consider trusted-host authentication for batch jobs. In this case, the "credentials" are the operating system's notion of a process's uid: the identity under which a process is running, which determines what rights it has over protected objects. An attacker need only manage to get control of a process running under your uid, to impersonate you to a remote SSH server. If he breaks root on the client, this is particularly simple, since root may create processes under any uid. The real crux, though, is the client host key: if the attacker gets that, he can sign bogus authentication requests presenting himself as any user at all, and *sshd* will believe them.

Trusted-host authentication is in many ways the least secure SSH authentication method. [3.4.2.3] It leaves systems vulnerable to transitive compromise: if an attacker gains access to an account on host H, she immediately has access to the same account on all machines that trust H, with no further effort. Also, trusted-host configuration is limited, fragile, and easy to get wrong. Public-key authentication affords both greater security and flexibility, particularly since you can restrict the commands that may be invoked and the client hosts that may connect, using its forced commands and other options in the authorization file.

11.1.4. Kerberos

Kerberos-5 [11.4] contains support for long-running jobs in the form of *renewable* tickets. While there's no explicit support for these in SSH, a batch job can be designed to use them. As with agent usage, a human performs an initial *kinit* to get a TGT for the batch account, using the *–r* switch to request a renewable ticket. Periodically, the batch job uses *kinit –R* to renew the TGT before it expires. This can be repeated up to the maximum renewable lifetime of the ticket, typically a few days.

Like trusted-host authentication, however, SSH Kerberos support lacks the close authorization controls provided by the public-key options. Even in an installation using Kerberos for user authentication, it's probably best to use some form of public-key authentication for unattended jobs instead. For more information on renewable tickets, see the Kerberos-5 documentation.

11.1.5. General Precautions for Batch Jobs

Regardless of the method you choose, some extra precautions will help secure your environment.

11.1.5.1. Least-privilege accounts

The account under which the automated job runs should have only those privileges needed to run the job, and no more. Don't run every batch job as root just because it's convenient. Arrange your filesystem and other protections so the job can run as a less privileged user. Remember that unattended remote jobs increase the risk of account compromise, so take the extra trouble to avoid the root account whenever possible.

11.1.5.2. Separate, locked-down automation accounts

Create accounts that are used solely for automation. Try not to run system batch jobs in a user account, since you might not be able to reduce its privileges to the small set necessary to support the job. In many cases, an automation account doesn't even need to admit interactive logins. If jobs running under its uid are created directly by the batch job manager (e.g., *cron*), the account doesn't need a password and should be locked.

11.1.5.3. Restricted-use keys

As much as possible, restrict the target account to perform only the work needed for the job. With public-key authentication, automated jobs should use keys that aren't shared by interactive logins. Imagine that someday you might need to eliminate the key for security reasons, and you don't want to affect other users or jobs by this change. For maximum control, use a separate key for each automated task. Additionally, place all possible restrictions on the key by setting options in the authorization file. [8.2] The `command` option restricts the key to running only the needed remote command, and the `from` option restricts usage to appropriate client hosts. Consider always adding the following options as well, if they don't interfere with the job:

```
no-port-forwarding,no-X11-forwarding,no-agent-forwarding,no-pty
```

These make it harder to misuse the key should it be stolen.

If you're using trusted-host authentication, these restrictions aren't available. In this case, it's best to use a special shell for the account, which limits the commands that may be executed. Since *sshd* uses the target account's shell to run any commands on the user's behalf, this is an effective restriction. One standard tool is the Unix "restricted shell." Confusingly, the restricted shell is usually named "rsh", but has nothing to do with the Berkeley r-command for opening a remote shell, *rsh*.

11.1.5.4. Useful ssh options

When running SSH commands in a batch job, it's a good idea to use these options:

```
ssh -q -o 'BatchMode yes'
```

The *–q* option is for quiet mode, preventing SSH from printing a variety of warnings. This is sometimes necessary if you're using SSH as a pipe from one program to another. Otherwise, the SSH warnings may be interpreted as remote program output and confuse the local program. [7.4.15]

The `BatchMode` keyword tells SSH not to prompt the user, who in this case doesn't exist. This makes error reporting more straightforward, eliminating some confusing SSH messages about failing to access a tty. [7.4.5.4]

11.1.6. Recommendations

Our recommended method for best security with unattended SSH operation is public-key authentication with keys stored in an agent. If that isn't feasible, trusted-host or plaintext-key authentication may be used instead; your local security concerns and needs will determine which is preferable, using the foregoing discussion as a guideline.

To the extent possible, use separate accounts and keys for each job. By doing so, you limit the damage caused by compromising any one account, or stealing any one key. But of course, there is a complexity trade-off here; if you have a hundred batch jobs, separate accounts or keys for each one may be too much to deal with. In that case, partition the jobs into categories according to the privileges they need, and use a separate account and/or key for each category of job.

You can ease the burden of multiple keys by applying a little automation to the business of loading them. The keys can all be stored under the same passphrase: a script prompts for the passphrase, then runs *ssh-add* multiple times to add the various keys. Or they have different passphrases, and the human inserts a diskette containing the passphrases when loading them. Perhaps the passphrase list itself is encrypted under a single password provided by the human. For that matter, the keys themselves can be kept on the key diskette and not stored on the filesystem at all: whatever fits your needs and paranoia level.

11.2. FTP Forwarding

One of the most frequently asked questions about SSH is, "How can I use port forwarding to secure FTP?" Unfortunately, the short answer is that you usually can't, at least not completely. Port forwarding can protect your account password, but usually not the files being transferred. Still, protecting your password is a big win, since the most egregious problem with FTP is that it reveals your password to network snoopers.*

Van Dyke's SecureFX (http://www.vandyke.com/)

Van Dyke Technologies, Inc. has a very useful Windows product, specifically designed to forward FTP over SSH, data connections and all. It is a specialized combination of SSH-2 and FTP clients. It connects to a server host via SSH-2, then connects to the FTP server (also running on that host) via a "tcpip-direct" channel in the SSH-2 session. This is the same mechanism used for local port forwarding in regular SSH-2 clients, but since this is a specially written application, it can talk to the server directly rather than go through a loopback connection to a locally forwarded TCP port.

SecureFX acts as a GUI FTP client. Whenever it needs an FTP data connection, it dynamically creates whatever channels or remote forwardings are necessary for the data ports (more outbound tcpip-direct channels for active FTP, or regular remote forwardings for passive mode). It works very smoothly and we recommend the product.

Note that at press time SecureFX runs only on Windows (98, 95, NT 4.0, and 2000) and requires an SSH-2 server; it doesn't speak SSH-1.

This section explains in detail what you can and can't do with FTP and SSH, and why. Some difficulties are due to limitations of FTP, not only when interacting with SSH, but also in the presence of firewalls and network address translation

* At least in its usual form. Some FTP implementations support more secure authentication methods, such as Kerberos. There are even protocol extensions that allow for encryption and cryptographic integrity checking of data connections. These techniques aren't widely implemented, however, and plaintext passwords with unprotected data connections are still the norm for FTP servers on the Internet.

(NAT). We will discuss each of these situations, since firewalls and NAT are common nowadays, and their presence might be the reason you're trying to forward FTP securely. If you are a system administrator responsible for both SSH and these networking components, we will try to guide you to a general understanding that will help you design and troubleshoot entire systems.

Depending on your network environment, different problems may arise when combining SSH with FTP. Since we can't cover every possible environment, we describe each problem in isolation, illustrating its symptoms and recommending solutions. If you have multiple problems occurring simultaneously, the software behavior you observe might not match the examples we've given. We recommend reading the entire case study once (at least cursorily) before experimenting with your system, so you will have an idea of the problems you might encounter. Afterward, go ahead and try the examples at your computer.

11.2.1. The FTP Protocol

To understand the problems between FTP and SSH, you need to understand a bit about the FTP protocol. Most TCP services involve a single connection from client to server on a known, server-side port. FTP, however, involves multiple connections in both directions, mostly to unpredictable port numbers:

- A single *control connection* for carrying commands from the client and responses from the server. It connects on TCP port 21 and persists for the entire FTP session.
- A number of *data connections* for transferring files and other data, such as directory listings. For each file transfer, a new data connection is opened and closed, and each one may be on a different port. These data connections may come from the client or the server.

Let's run a typical FTP client and view the control connection. We'll use debug mode (*ftp –d*) to make visible the FTP protocol commands the client sends on the control connection, since they aren't normally displayed. Debug mode prints these commands preceded by "--->", for example:

```
---> USER res
```

You'll also see responses from the server, which the client prints by default. These are preceded by a numerical code:

```
230 User res logged in.
```

Here's a session in which the user res connects to an FTP server, logs in, and attempts to change directory twice, once successfully and once not:

```
$ ftp -d aaor.lionaka.net
Connected to aaor.lionaka.net.
```

```
220 aaor.lionaka.net FTP server (SunOS 5.7) ready.
---> SYST
215 UNIX Type: L8 Version: SUNOS
Remote system type is UNIX.
Using binary mode to transfer files.
ftp> user res
---> USER res
331 Password required for res.
Password:
---> PASS XXXX
230 User res logged in.
ftp> cd rep
---> CWD rep
250 CWD command successful.
ftp> cd utopia
---> CWD utopia
550 utopia: No such file or directory.
ftp> quit
---> QUIT
221 Goodbye.
```

The control connection can be secured by standard port forwarding because it is on a known port (21). [9.2] In contrast, the destination port numbers for data connections are generally not known in advance, so setting up SSH forwarding for these connections is far more difficult. There's a second standard port number associated with FTP, the *ftp-data* port (20). But this is only the source port for data connections coming from the server; nothing ever listens on it.

Surprisingly, the data connections generally go in the opposite direction from the control one; that is, the server makes a TCP connection back to the client in order to transfer data. The ports on which these connections occur can be negotiated dynamically by the FTP client and server, and doing so involves sending explicit IP address information inside the FTP protocol. These features of usual FTP operation can cause difficulties when forwarding SSH connections and in other scenarios involving firewalls or NAT.

An alternative FTP mode, called *passive mode*, addresses one of these problems: it reverses the sense of the data connections, so that they go from the client to the server. Passive mode is a matter of FTP client behavior, and so is determined by a client setting. The behavior of setting up data connections from the server to the client, which we will call *active-mode* FTP, is traditionally the default in FTP clients, although that's changing. With a command-line client, the *passive* command switches to passive mode. The internal command that the client sends the server to tell it to enter passive mode is `PASV`. We discuss specific problems and how passive mode solves them, in upcoming sections. Figure 11-1 summarizes the workings of passive and active FTP.

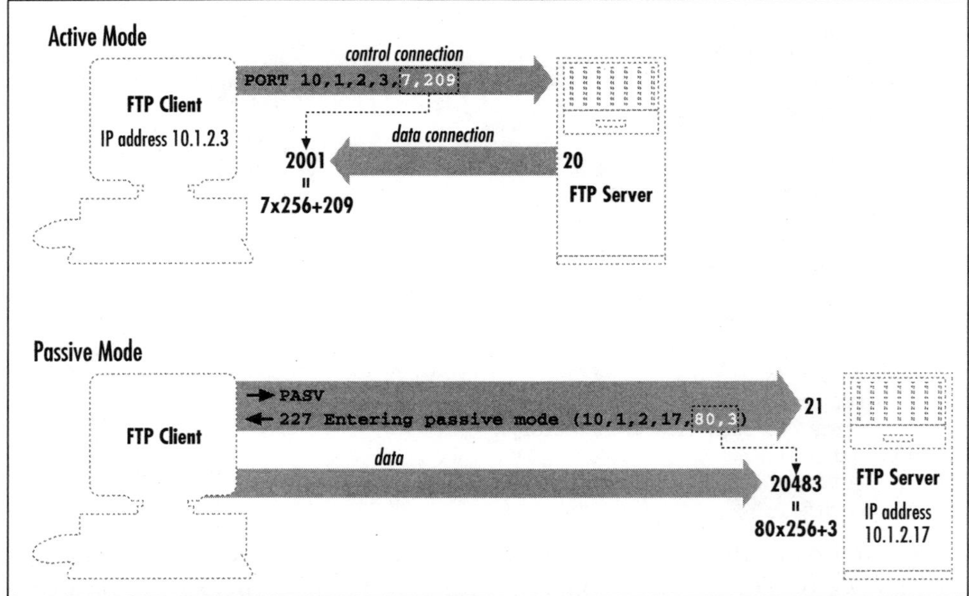

Figure 11-1. Basic FTP operation: control connection and active- versus passive-mode transfers

11.2.2. Forwarding the Control Connection

Since the FTP control connection is just a single, persistent TCP connection to a well-known port, you can forward it through SSH. As usual, the FTP server machine must be running an SSH server, and you must have an account on it that you may access via SSH (see Figure 11-2).

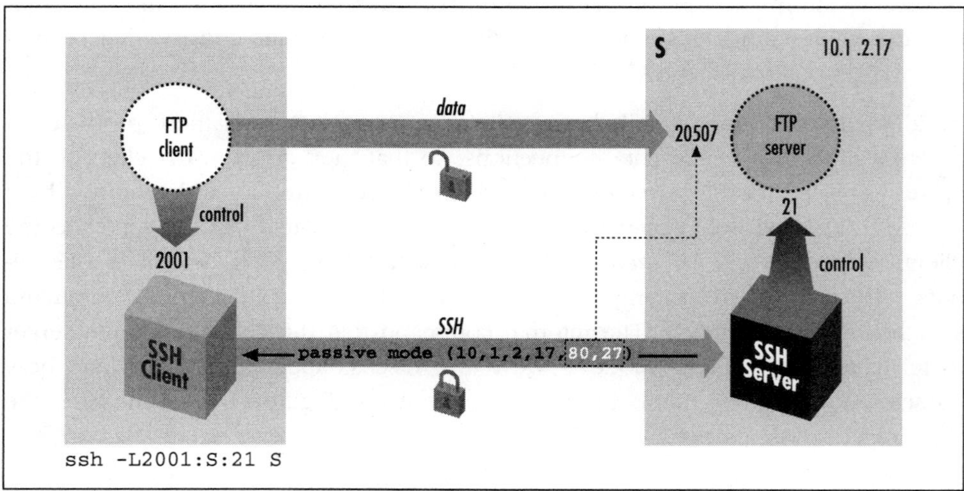

Figure 11-2. Forwarding the control connection

Suppose you are logged into the machine *client* and want to connect securely to an FTP server on the machine *server*. To forward the FTP control connection, run a port-forwarding command on *client*:*

```
client% ssh -L2001:server:21 server
```

Then, to use the forwarded port:

```
client% ftp localhost 2001
Connected to localhost
220 server FTP server (SunOS 5.7) ready.
Password:
230 User res logged in.
ftp> passive
Passive mode on.
ftp> ls
...and so on
```

There are two important things to notice about the commands we just recommended. We will discuss each.

- The target of the forwarding is *server*, not *localhost*.
- The client uses passive mode.

11.2.2.1. Choosing the forwarding target

We chose *server* as the target of our forwarding, not *localhost* (i.e., we didn't use *–L2001:localhost:21*). This is contrary to our previous advice, which was to use *localhost* where possible as the forwarding target. [9.2.8] Well, that technique isn't advisable here. Here's what can happen if you do:

```
client% ftp localhost 2001
Connected to client
220 client FTP server (SunOS 5.7) ready.
331 Password required for res.
Password:
230 User res logged in.
ftp> ls
200 PORT command successful.
425 Can't build data connection: Cannot assign requested address.
ftp>
```

The problem is a bit obscure but can be revealed by an execution trace of the FTP server as it responds to the *ls* command. The following output was produced by the Linux *strace* command:†

---

* If you're using the popular *ncftp* client, run this instead: *ncftp ftp://client:2001*.

† If you're on a Solaris 2 (SunOS 5) system, the corresponding operating system-supplied program is called *truss*. There is also an *strace* program with Solaris, but it is completely unrelated. Solaris 1 (SunOS 4 and earlier) has a *trace* command, and BSD has *ktrace*.

```
so_socket(2, 2, 0, "", 1)                     = 5
bind(5, 0x0002D614, 16, 3)                    = 0
        AF_INET  name = 127.0.0.1  port = 20
connect(5, 0x0002D5F4, 16, 1)                 Err#126 EADDRNOTAVAIL
        AF_INET  name = 192.168.10.1  port = 2845
write(1, " 4 2 5   C a n ' t   b u".., 67)    = 67
```

The FTP server is trying to make a TCP connection to the correct client address but from the wrong socket: the ftp-data port on its loopback address, 127.0.0.1. The loopback interface can talk only to other loopback addresses on the same machine. TCP knows this and responds with the error "address not available" (EADDRNOTAVAIL). The FTP server is being careful to originate the data connection from the same address to which the client made the control connection. Here, the control connection has been forwarded through SSH; so to the FTP server, it appears to come from the local host. And because we used the loopback address as the forwarding target, the source address of that leg of the forwarded path (from *sshd* to *ftpd*) is also the loopback address. To eliminate the problem, use the server's nonloopback IP address as the target; this causes the FTP server to originate data connections from that address.

You might try to solve this problem using passive mode, since then the server wouldn't originate any connections. But if you try:

```
ftp> passive
Passive mode on.
ftp> ls
227 Entering Passive Mode (127,0,0,1,128,133)
ftp: connect: Connection refused
ftp>
```

In this case, the failure is a slightly different manifestation of the same problem. This time, the server listens for an incoming data connection from the client, but again, it thinks the client is local so it listens on its loopback address. It sends this socket (address 127.0.0.1, port 32901) to the client, and the client tries to connect to it. But this causes the client to try to connect to port 32901 on the client host, not the server! Nothing is listening there, of course, so the connection is refused.

11.2.2.2. Using passive mode

Note that we had to put the client into passive mode. You will see later that passive mode is beneficial for FTP in general, because it avoids some common firewall and NAT problems. Here, however, it's used because of a specific FTP/SSH problem; if you didn't, here's what happens:

```
$ ftp -d localhost 2001
Connected to localhost.
220 server FTP server (SunOS 5.7) ready.
---> USER res
331 Password required for res.
```

```
Password:
---> PASS XXXX
230 User res logged in.
ftp> ls
---> PORT 127,0,0,1,11,50
200 PORT command successful.
---> LIST
425 Can't build data connection: Connection refused.
ftp>
```

This is a mirror image of the problem we saw when localhost was the forwarding target, but this time it happens on the client side. The client supplies a socket for the server to connect to, and since it thinks the server is on the local host, that socket is on the loopback address. This causes the server to try connecting to its local host instead of the client machine.

Passive mode can't always be used: the FTP client or server might not support it, or server-side firewall/NAT considerations may prevent it (you'll see an example of that shortly). If so, you can use the `GatewayPorts` feature of SSH and solve this problem as we did the previous one: use the host's real IP address instead of the loopback. To wit:

```
client% ssh -g -L2001:server:21 server
```

Then connect to the client machine by name, rather than to localhost:

```
client% ftp client 2001
```

This connects to the SSH proxy on the client's nonloopback address, causing the FTP client to listen on that address for data connections. The *–g* option has security implications, however. [9.2.1.1]

Of course, as we mentioned earlier, it's often the case that active-mode FTP isn't usable. It's perfectly possible that your local firewall/NAT setup requires passive mode, but you can't use it. In that case, you're just out of luck. Put your data on a diskette and contribute to the local bicycle-courier economy.

The various problems we have described, while common, depend on your particular Unix flavor and FTP implementation. For example, some FTP servers fail even before connecting to a loopback socket; they see the client's `PORT` command and reject it, printing "illegal PORT command". If you understand the reasons for the various failure modes, however, you will learn to recognize them in different guises.

11.2.2.3. The "PASV port theft" problem

Trying to use FTP with SSH can be sort of like playing a computer dungeon game: you find yourself in a twisty maze of TCP connections, all of which look alike and none of which seem to go where you want. Even if you follow all of our advice so far, and understand and avoid the pitfalls we've mentioned, the connection might still fail:

```
ftp> passive
Passive mode on.
ftp> ls
connecting to 192.168.10.1:6670
Connected to 192.168.10.1 port 6670
425 Possible PASV port theft, cannot open data connection.
! Retrieve of folder listing failed
```

Assuming you don't decide to give up entirely and move into a less irritating career, you may want to know, "What now?" The problem here is a security feature of the FTP server, specifically the popular *wu-ftpd* from Washington University. (See *http://www.wu-ftpd.org/*. This feature might be implemented in other FTP servers, but we haven't seen it.) The server accepts an incoming data connection from the client, then notices that its source address isn't the same as that of the control connection (which was forwarded through SSH and thus comes from the server host). It concludes that an attack is in progress! The FTP server believes someone has been monitoring your FTP control connection, seen the server response to the `PASV` command containing the listening socket, and jumped in to connect to it before the legitimate client can do so. So the server drops the connection and reports the suspected "port theft" (see Figure 11-3).

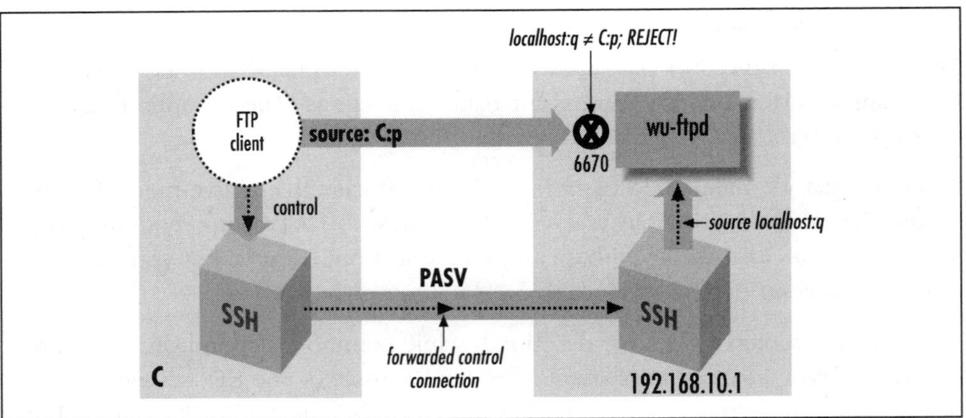

Figure 11-3. "PASV port theft"

There's no way around this problem but to stop the server from performing this check. It's a problematic feature to begin with, since it prevents not only attacks but also legitimate FTP operations. For example, passive-mode operation was originally intended to allow an FTP client to effect a file transfer between two remote servers directly, rather than first fetching the file to the client and then sending it to the second server. This isn't a common practice, but it is part of the protocol design, and the "port theft" check of *wu-ftpd* prevents its use. You can turn it off by recompiling *wu-ftpd* without FIGHT_PASV_PORT_RACE (use *configure --disable-pasvip*). You can also leave the check on but allow certain accounts to use alternate IP addresses for data connections, with the *pasv-allow* and *port-allow* configuration statements. See the *ftpaccess*(5) manpage for details. Note that these features are relatively recent additions to *wu-ftpd* and aren't in earlier versions.

11.2.3. FTP, Firewalls, and Passive Mode

Recall that in active mode, the FTP data connections go in the opposite direction than you might expect—from the server back to the client. This usual mode of operation (shown in Figure 11-4) often develops problems in the presence of a firewall. Suppose the client is behind a firewall that allows all outbound connections but restricts inbound ones. Then the client can establish a control connection to log in and issue commands, but data-transfer commands such as *ls*, *get*, and *put* will fail, because the firewall blocks the data connections coming back to the client machine. Simple packet-filtering firewalls can't be configured to allow these connections, because they appear as separate TCP destinations to random ports, with no obvious relation to the established FTP control connection.* The failure might happen quickly with the message "connection refused," or the connection might hang for a while and eventually fail. This depends on whether the firewall explicitly rejects the connection attempt with an ICMP or TCP RST message, or just silently drops the packets. Note that this problem can occur whether or not SSH is forwarding the control connection.

Passive mode usually solves this problem, reversing the direction of data connections so they go from the client to the server. Unfortunately, not all FTP client or servers implement passive-mode transfers. Command-line FTP clients generally use the `passive` command to toggle passive-mode transfers on and off; if it doesn't recognize that command, it probably doesn't do passive mode. If the client supports passive mode but the server doesn't, you may see a message like "PASV: command not understood" from the server. `PASV` is the FTP protocol command that instructs the server to listen for data connections. Finally, even if passive mode solves the firewall problem, it doesn't help with SSH forwarding, since the ports in question are still dynamically chosen.

---

* More sophisticated firewalls can take care of this problem. These products are a cross between an application-level proxy and a packet filter and are often called "transparent proxies" or "stateful packet filters." Such a firewall understands the FTP protocol and watches for FTP control connections. When it sees a `PORT` command issued by an FTP client, it dynamically opens a temporary hole in the firewall, allowing the specified FTP data connection back through. This hole disappears automatically after a short time and can only be between the socket given in the `PORT` command and the server's ftp-data socket. These products often also do NAT and can transparently deal with the FTP/NAT problems we describe next.

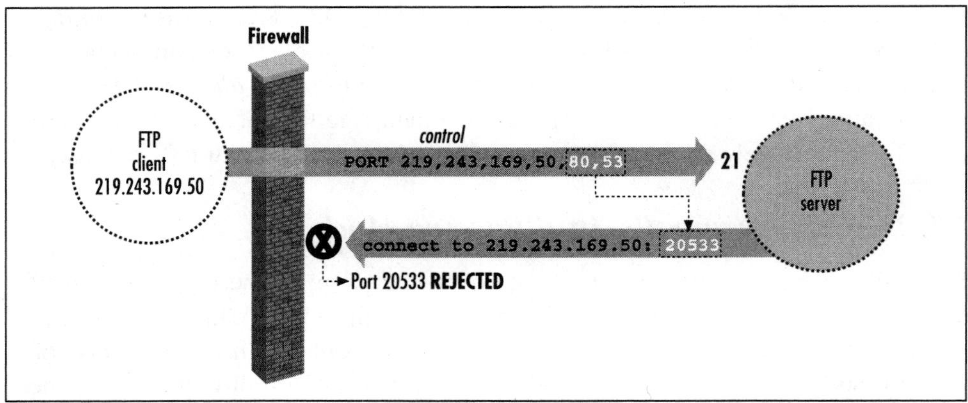

Figure 11-4. FTP client behind a firewall

Here is an example of the firewall problem, blocking the return data connections:

```
$ ftp lasciate.ogni.speranza.org
Connected to lasciate.ogni.speranza.org
220 ProFTPD 1.2.0pre6 Server (Lasciate FTP Server) [lasciate.ogni.speranza.org]
331 Password required for slade.
Password:
230 User slade logged in.
Remote system type is UNIX.
Using binary mode to transfer files.
ftp> ls
200 PORT command successful.
[...long wait here...]
425 Can't build data connection: Connection timed out
```

Passive mode comes to the rescue:

```
ftp> passive
Passive mode on.
ftp> ls
227 Entering Passive Mode (10,25,15,1,12,65)
150 Opening ASCII mode data connection for file list
drwxr-x--x  21 slade    web          2048 May  8 23:29 .
drwxr-xr-x 111 root     wheel       10240 Apr 26 00:09 ..
-rw-------   1 slade    other         106 May  8 15:22 .cshrc
-rw-------   1 slade    other       31384 Aug 18  1997 .emacs
226 Transfer complete.
ftp>
```

Now, in discussing the problem of using FTP through a firewall, we didn't mention SSH at all; it is a problem inherent in the FTP protocol and firewalls. However, even when forwarding the FTP control connection through SSH, this problem still applies, since the difficulty is with the data connection, not the control, and those don't go through SSH. So this is yet another reason why you will normally want to use passive mode with FTP and SSH.

11.2.4. FTP and Network Address Translation (NAT)

Passive-mode transfers can also work around another common problem with FTP: its difficulties with network address translation, or NAT. NAT is the practice of connecting two networks by a gateway that rewrites the source and destination addresses of packets as they pass through. One benefit is that you may connect a network to the Internet or change ISPs without having to renumber the network (that is, change all your IP addresses). It also allows sharing a limited number of routable Internet addresses among a larger number of machines on a network using private addresses not routed on the Internet. This flavor of NAT is often called *masquerading*.

Suppose your FTP client is on a machine with a private address usable only on your local network, and you connect to the Internet through a NAT gateway. The client can establish a control connection to an external FTP server. However, there will be a problem if the client attempts the usual reverse-direction data connections. The client, ignorant of the NAT gateway, tells the server (via a `PORT` command) to connect to a socket containing the client's private address. Since that address isn't usable on the remote side, the server generally responds "no route to host" and the connection will fail.* Figure 11-5 illustrates this situation. Passive mode gets around this problem as well, since the server never has to connect back to the client and so the client's address is irrelevant.

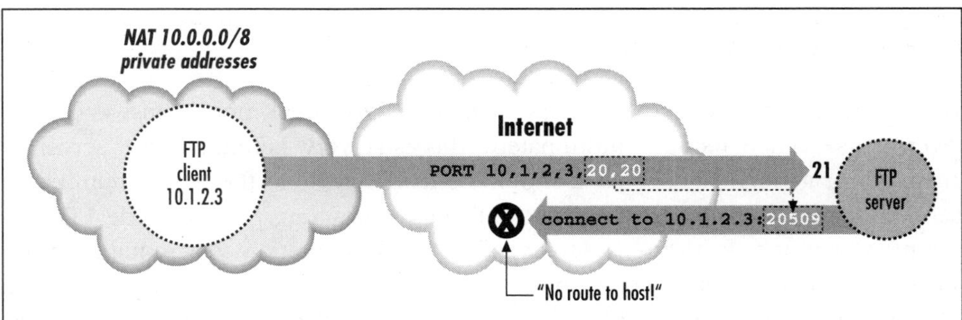

Figure 11-5. Client-side NAT prevents active-mode FTP transfers

So far, we've listed three situations requiring passive-mode FTP: control connection forwarding, client inside a firewall, and client behind NAT. Given these potential problems with active-mode FTP, and that there's no down side to passive mode we know of, we recommend always using passive mode FTP if you can.

* It could be worse, too. The server could also use private addressing, and if you're unlucky, the client's private address might coincidentally match a completely different machine on the server side. It's unlikely, though, that a server-side machine would happen to listen on the random port picked by your FTP client, so this would probably just generate a "connection refused" error.

11.2.4.1. Server-side NAT issues

The NAT problem we just discussed was a client-side issue. There is a more difficult problem that can occur if the FTP server is behind a NAT gateway, and you're forwarding the FTP control connection through SSH.

First, let's understand the basic problem without SSH in the picture. If the server is behind a NAT gateway, then you have the mirror-image problem to the one discussed earlier. Before, active-mode transfers didn't work because the client supplied its internal, non-NAT'd address to the server in the `PORT` command, and this address wasn't reachable. In the new situation, passive-mode transfers don't work because the server supplies its internal-only address to the client in the `PASV` command response, and that address is unreachable to the client (see Figure 11-6).

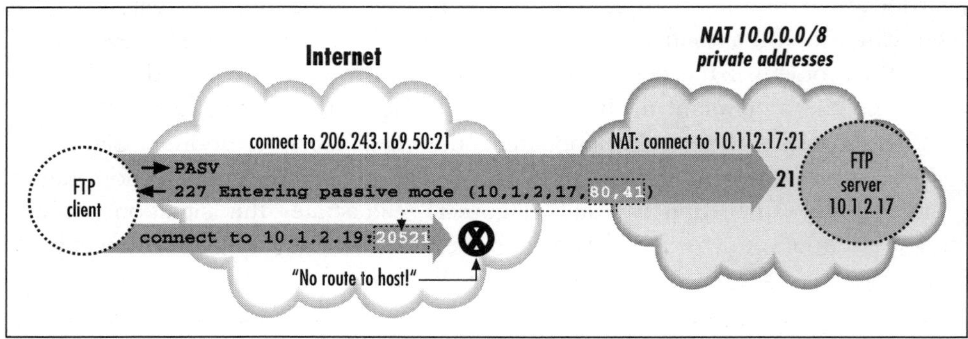

Figure 11-6. Server-side NAT prevents passive-mode FTP transfers

The earlier answer was to use passive mode; here the simplest answer is the reverse: use active mode. Unfortunately, this isn't very helpful. If the server is intended for general Net access, it should be made useful to the largest number of people. Since client-side NAT and firewall setups requiring passive-mode FTP are common, it won't do to use a server-side NAT configuration that requires active mode instead; this makes access impossible. One approach is to use an FTP server with special features designed to address this very problem. The *wu-ftpd* server we touched on earlier has such a feature. Quoting from the *ftpaccess*(5) manpage:

```
passive address <externalip> <cidr>
     Allows control of the address reported in response to
     a PASV command.  When any control connection matching
     the <cidr> requests a passive data connection (PASV),
     the  <externalip>  address  is  reported.  NOTE: this
     does not change the address the daemon actually lis-
     tens  on,  only  the  address reported to the client.
     This feature allows the daemon to  operate  correctly
     behind IP-renumbering firewalls.
```

```
For example:
 passive address 10.0.1.15   10.0.0.0/8
 passive address 192.168.1.5 0.0.0.0/0

Clients connecting from the class-A network 10 will be
told the passive connection is listening on IP-address
10.0.1.15 while all others will be told the connection is
listening on 192.168.1.5

Multiple passive addresses may be specified to handle com-
plex, or multi-gatewayed, networks.
```

This handles the problem quite neatly, unless you happen to be forwarding the FTP control connection through SSH. Site administrators arrange for FTP control connections originating from outside the server's private network to have external addresses reported in the PASV responses. But the forwarded control connection appears to come from the server host itself, rather than the outside network. Control connections coming from inside the private network *should* get the internal address, not the external one. The only way this will work is if the FTP server is configured to provide the external address to connections coming from itself as well as from the outside. This is actually quite workable, as there's little need in practice to transmit files by FTP from a machine back to itself. You can use this technique to allow control-connection forwarding in the presence of server-side NAT or suggest it to the site administrators if you have this problem.

Another way of addressing the server-side NAT problem is to use an intelligent NAT gateway of the type mentioned earlier. Such a gateway automatically rewrites the FTP control traffic in transit to account for address translation. This is an attractive solution in some respects, because it is automatic and transparent; there is less custom work in setting up the servers behind the gateway, and fewer dependencies between the server and network configurations. As it happens, though, this solution is actually worse for our purposes than the server-level one. This technique relies on the gateway's ability to recognize and alter the FTP control connection as it passes through. But such manipulation is exactly what SSH is designed to prevent! If the control connection is forwarded through SSH, the gateway doesn't know there is a control connection, because it's embedded as a channel inside the SSH session. The control connection isn't a separate TCP connection of its own; it's on the SSH port rather than the FTP port. The gateway can't read it because it's encrypted, and the gateway can't modify it even if the gateway can read it, because SSH provides integrity protection. If you're in this situation—the client must use passive-mode FTP, and the server is behind a NAT gateway doing FTP control traffic rewriting—you must convince the server administrator to use a server-level technique in addition to the gateway, specifically to allow forwarding. Otherwise, it's not going to happen, and we see trucks filled with tapes in your future, or perhaps HTTP over SSL with PUT commands.

We have now concluded our discussion of forwarding the control connection of FTP, securing your login name, password, and FTP commands. If that's all you want to do, you are done with this case study. We're going to continue, however, and delve into the murky depths of data connections. You'll need a technical background for this material as we cover minute details and little-known modes of FTP. (You might even wonder if we've accidentally inserted a portion of an FTP book into the SSH book.) Forward, brave reader!

11.2.5. All About Data Connections

Ask most SSH users about forwarding the FTP data connection, and they'll respond, "Sorry, it's not possible." Well, it *is* possible. The method we've discovered is obscure, inconvenient, and not usually worth the effort, but it works. Before we can explain it, we must first discuss the three major ways that FTP accomplishes file transfers between client and server:

- The usual method
- Passive-mode transfers
- Transfers using the default data ports

We'll just touch briefly on the first two, since we've already discussed them; we'll just amplify with a bit more detail. Then we'll discuss the third mode, which is the least known and the one you need if you really, really want to forward your FTP data connections.

11.2.5.1. The usual method of file transfer

Most FTP clients attempt data transfers in the following way. After establishing the control connection and authenticating, the user issues a command to transfer a file. Suppose the command is `get fichier.txt`, which asks to transfer the file *fichier.txt* from the server to the client. In response to this command, the client selects a free local TCP socket, call it C, and starts listening on it. It then issues a `PORT` command to the FTP server, specifying the socket C. After the server acknowledges this, the client issues the command `RETR fichier.txt`, which tells the server to connect to the previously given socket (C) and send the contents of that file over the new data connection. The client accepts the connection to C, reads the data, and writes it into a local file also called *fichier.txt*. When done, the data connection is closed. Here is a transcript of such a session:

```
$ ftp -d aaor.lionaka.net
Connected to aaor.lionaka.net.
220 aaor.lionaka.net FTP server (SunOS 5.7) ready.
---> USER res
331 Password required for res.
Password:
```

```
---> PASS XXXX
230 User res logged in.
---> SYST
215 UNIX Type: L8 Version: SUNOS
Remote system type is UNIX.
Using binary mode to transfer files.
ftp> get fichier.txt
local: fichier.txt remote: fichier.txt
---> TYPE I
200 Type set to I.
---> PORT 219,243,169,50,9,226
200 PORT command successful.
---> RETR fichier.txt
150 Binary data connection for fichier.txt (219.243.169.50,2530) (10876 bytes).
226 Binary Transfer complete.
10876 bytes received in 0.013 seconds (7.9e+02 Kbytes/s)
ftp> quit
```

Note the **PORT** command, `PORT 219,243,169,50,9,226`. This says the client is listening on IP address 219.243.169.50, port 2530 = (9<<8)+226; the final two integers in the comma-separated list are the 16-bit port number represented as two 8-bit bytes, most significant byte first. The server response beginning with "150" confirms establishment of the data connection to that socket. What isn't shown is that the source port of that connection is always the standard FTP data port, port 20 (remember that FTP servers listen for incoming control connections on port 21).

There are two important points to note about this process:

- The data connection socket is chosen on the fly by the client. This prevents forwarding, since you can't know the port number ahead of time to forward it with SSH. You can get around this problem by establishing the FTP process "by hand" using *telnet*. That is, choose a data socket beforehand and forward it with SSH, *telnet* to the FTP server yourself, and issue all the necessary FTP protocol commands by hand, using your forwarded port in the **PORT** command. But this can hardly be called convenient.
- Remember that the data connection is made in the *reverse direction* from the control connection; it goes from the server back to the client. As we discussed earlier in this chapter, the usual workaround is to use passive mode.

11.2.5.2. Passive mode in depth

Recall that in a passive-mode transfer, the client initiates a connection to the server. Specifically, instead of listening on a local socket and issuing a **PORT** command to the server, the client issues a **PASV** command. In response, the server selects a socket on its side to listen on and reveals it to the client in the response to the **PASV** command. The client then connects to that socket to form the data connection, and issues the file-transfer command over the control connection.

With command line-based clients, the usual way to do passive-mode transfers is to use the `passive` command. Again, an example:

```
$ ftp -d aaor.lionaka.net
Connected to aaor.lionaka.net.
220 aaor.lionaka.net FTP server (SunOS 5.7) ready.
---> USER res
331 Password required for res.
Password:
---> PASS XXXX
230 User res logged in.
---> SYST
215 UNIX Type: L8 Version: SUNOS
Remote system type is UNIX.
Using binary mode to transfer files.
ftp> passive
Passive mode on.
ftp> ls
---> PASV
227 Entering Passive Mode (219,243,169,52,128,73)
---> LIST
150 ASCII data connection for /bin/ls (219.243.169.50,2538) (0 bytes).
total 360075
drwxr-xr-x98   res      500         7168 May  5 17:13 .
dr-xr-xr-x   2 root     root           2 May  5 01:47 ..
-rw-rw-r--   1 res      500          596 Apr 25  1999 .FVWM2-errors
-rw-------   1 res      500          332 Mar 24 01:36 .ICEauthority
-rw-------   1 res      500           50 May  5 01:45 .Xauthority
-rw-r--r--   1 res      500         1511 Apr 11 00:08 .Xdefaults
226 ASCII Transfer complete.
ftp> quit
---> QUIT
221 Goodbye.
```

Note that after the user gives the *ls* command, the client sends PASV instead of PORT. The server responds with the socket on which it will listen. The client issues the LIST command to list the contents of the current remote directory, and connects to the remote data socket; the server accepts and confirms the connection, then transfers the directory listing over the new connection.

An interesting historical note, which we alluded to earlier, is that the PASV command wasn't originally intended for this use; it was designed to let an FTP client direct a file transfer between two remote servers. The client makes control connections to two remote servers, issues a PASV command to one causing it to listen on a socket, issues a PORT command to the other telling it to connect to the other server on that socket, then issues the data-transfer command (STOR, RETR, etc.). These days, most people don't even know this is possible, and will pull a file from one server to the local machine, and transfer it again to get it to the second remote machine. It's so uncommon that many FTP clients don't support this mode, and some servers prevent its use for security reasons. [11.2.2.3]

11.2.5.3. FTP with the default data ports

The third file-transfer mode occurs if the client issues neither a `PORT` nor a `PASV` command. In this case, the server initiates the data connection from the well-known ftp-data port (20) to the source socket of the control connection, on which the client must be listening (these sockets are the "default data ports" for the FTP session). The usual way to use this mode is with the FTP client command *sendport*, which switches on and off the client's feature of using a `PORT` command for each data transfer. For this mode, we want it turned off, and it is generally on by default. So the sequence of steps is this:

1. The client initiates the control connection from local socket C to server:21.
2. The user gives the *sendport* command, and then a data-transfer command, such as *put* or *ls*. The FTP client begins listening on socket C for an incoming TCP connection.
3. The server determines the socket C at the other end of the control connection. It doesn't need the client to send this explicitly via the FTP protocol, since it can just ask TCP for it (e.g., with the `getpeername()` sockets API routine). It then opens a connection from its ftp-data port to C, and sends or receives the requested data over that connection.

Now, this is certainly a simpler way of doing things than using a different socket for each data transfer, and so it begs the question of why `PORT` commands are the norm. If you try this out, you will discover why. First off, it might fail on the client side with the message "bind: Address already in use". And even if it does work, it does so only once. A second *ls* elicits another address-related error, this time from the server:

```
aaor% ftp syrinx.lionaka.net
Connected to syrinx.lionaka.net.
220 syrinx.lionaka.net FTP server (Version wu-2.5.0(1) Tue Sep 21 16:48:12 EDT
331 Password required for res.
Password:
230 User res logged in.
ftp> sendport
Use of PORT cmds off.
ftp> ls
150 Opening ASCII mode data connection for file list.
keep
fichier.txt
226 Transfer complete.
19 bytes received in 0.017 seconds (1.07 Kbytes/s)
ftp> ls
425 Can't build data connection: Cannot assign requested address.
ftp> quit
```

These problems are due to a technicality of the TCP protocol. In this scenario, every data connection is between the same two sockets, server:ftp-data and C.

Since a TCP connection is fully specified by the pair of source and destination sockets, these connections are indistinguishable as far as TCP is concerned; they are different incarnations of the same connection and can't exist at the same time. In fact, to guarantee that packets belonging to two different incarnations of a connection aren't confused, there's a waiting period after one incarnation is closed, during which a new incarnation is forbidden. In the jargon of TCP, on the side that performed an "active close" of the connection, the connection remains in a state called TIME_WAIT. This state lasts for a period that is supposed to be twice the maximum possible lifetime of a packet in the network (or "2MSL", for two times the Maximum Segment Lifetime). After that, the connection becomes fully closed, and another incarnation can occur. The actual value of this timeout varies from system to system, but is generally in the range of 30 seconds to 4 minutes.*

As it happens, some TCP implementations enforce even stronger restrictions. Often, a port that is part of a socket in the TIME_WAIT state is unavailable for use, even as part of a connection to a different remote socket. We have also run into systems that disallow listening on a socket that is currently an endpoint of some connection, regardless of the connection state. These restrictions aren't required by the TCP protocol, but they are common. Such systems usually provide a way to avoid the restrictions, such as the SO_REUSEADDR option of the Berkeley sockets API. An FTP client generally uses this feature, of course, but it doesn't always work!

This address-reuse problem comes up in two places in a default-port FTP transfer. The first one is when the client must start listening on its default data port, which by definition is currently the local endpoint of its control connection. Some systems simply don't allow this, even if the program requests address reuse; that's why the attempt might fail immediately with the message, "address already in use."

The other place is on a second data transfer. When the first transfer is finished, the server closes the data connection, and that connection on the server side moves into the TIME_WAIT state. If you try another data transfer before the 2MSL period has elapsed, the server tries to set up another incarnation of the same connection, and it will fail saying "cannot assign requested address." This happens regardless of the address reuse setting, since the rules of the TCP require it. You can transfer a file again within a few minutes, of course, but most computer users aren't good at waiting a few seconds, let alone minutes. It is this problem that prompts the use of a `PORT` command for every transfer; since one end of the connection is different every time, the TIME_WAIT collisions don't occur.

* See *TCP/IP Illustrated, Volume 1: The Protocols*, by W. Richard Stevens (Addison-Wesley), for more technical information about the TIME_WAIT state.

Because of these problems, the default-port transfer mode isn't generally used. It has, however, an important property for us: it is the only mode in which the data connection destination port is fixed and knowable before the data-transfer command is given. With this knowledge, some patience, and fair amount of luck, it is possible to forward your FTP data connections through SSH.

11.2.6. Forwarding the Data Connection

With all the foregoing discussion in mind, here we simply state the sequence of steps to set up data-connection forwarding. The tricky part is that SSH must request address reuse from TCP for forwarded ports. SSH2 and OpenSSH do this already, but SSH1 can't. It's is an easy source modification to make for SSH1, though. In the routine `channel_request_local_forwarding` in *newchannels.c*, add the following code right before the call to `bind()` (in Version 1.2.27, this is at line 1438):

```
...
sin.sin_port = htons(port);

{
  int flag = 1;
  setsockopt(sock, SOL_SOCKET, SO_REUSEADDR, (void *)&flag,
      sizeof(flag));
}

/* Bind the socket to the address. */
if (bind(sock, (struct sockaddr *)&sin, sizeof(sin)) < 0)
  packet_disconnect("bind: %.100s", strerror(errno));
...
```

Recompile and reinstall *sshd* on the server side. If you're not in a position to do that, you can copy your modified *ssh* client program to the server, and in the upcoming step (3), use *ssh –L* from the server to the client instead of *ssh –R* from client to server.

Another restriction is that the operating system in which the FTP client is running must allow a process to listen on a socket already in use as the endpoint of an existing connection. Some don't. To test this, try an FTP data transfer on the default data ports without SSH, just by using *ftp* as usual but giving the *sendport* command before *ls*, *get*, or whatever. If you get:

```
ftp: bind: Address already in use
```

then your operating system probably won't cooperate. There may be a way to alter this behavior; check the operating system documentation. Figure 11-7 illustrates the following steps.

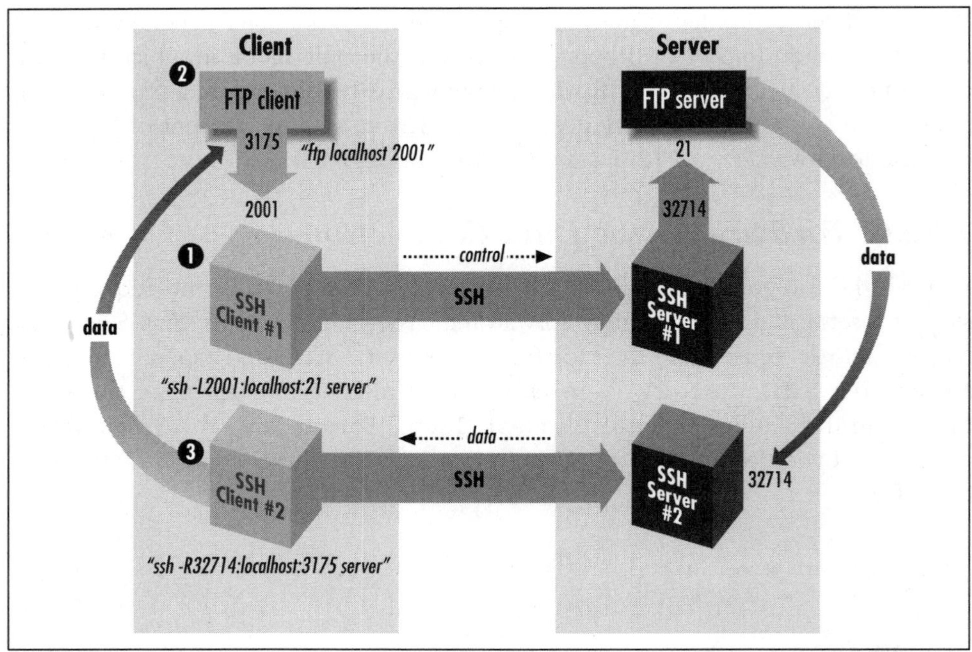

Figure 11-7. Forwarding the FTP data connection

1. Start an SSH connection to forward the control channel as shown earlier in this chapter, and connect with the FTP client. Make sure that passive mode is off.

   ```
   client% ssh1 -f -n -L2001:localhost:21 server sleep 10000 &
   ```

   or for SSH2:

   ```
   client% ssh2 -f -n -L2001:localhost:21 server
   ```

   Then:

   ```
   client% ftp localhost 2001
   Connected to localhost
   220 server FTP server (SunOS 5.7) ready.
   Password:
   230 User res logged in.
   ftp> sendport
   Use of PORT cmds off.
   ftp> passive
   Passive mode on.
   ftp> passive
   Passive mode off.
   ```

   Note that we are using localhost as the forwarding target here, despite our earlier advice. That's OK, because there won't be any `PORT` or `PASV` commands with addresses that can be wrong.

2. Now, we need to determine the real and proxy default data ports for the FTP client. On the client side, you can do this with *netstat*:

```
client% netstat -n | grep 2001
tcp        0       0 client:2001 client:3175 ESTABLISHED
tcp        0       0 client:3175 client:2001 ESTABLISHED
```

This shows that the source of the control connection from the FTP client to SSH is port 3175. You can do the same thing on the server side, but this time you need to know what's connected to the FTP server port (*netstat –n | egrep '\<21\>'*), and there may be many things connected to it. If you have a tool like *lsof*, it's better to find out the pid of the *ftpd* or *sshd* serving your connection and use *lsof –p <pid>* to find the port number. If not, you can do a *netstat* before connecting via FTP and then one right afterward, and try to see which is the new connection. Let's suppose you're the only one using the FTP server, and you get it this way:

```
server% netstat | grep ftp
tcp        0       0 server:32714 server:ftp   ESTABLISHED
tcp        0       0 server:ftp   server:32714 ESTABLISHED
```

So now, we have the FTP client's default data port (3175), and the source port of the forwarded control connection to the FTP server (32714), which we'll call the proxy default data port; it is what the FTP server thinks is the client's default data port.

3. Now, forward the proxy default data port to the real one:

```
# SSH1, OpenSSH
client% ssh1 -f -n -R32714:localhost:3175 server sleep 10000 &

# SSH2 only
client% ssh2 -f -R32714:localhost:3175 server
```

If, as we mentioned earlier, you don't replace *sshd* or run a second one, then you'd use the modified *ssh* on the server in the other direction, like this:

```
server% ./ssh -f -n -L32714:localhost:3175 client sleep 10000 &
```

4. Now, try a data-transfer command with *ftp*. If all goes well, it should work once, then fail with this message from the FTP server:

```
425 Can't build data connection: Address already in use.
```

(Some FTP servers return that error immediately; others will retry several times before giving up, so it may take a while for that error to appear.) If you wait for the server's 2MSL timeout period, you can do another single data transfer. You can use *netstat* to see the problem and track its progress:

```
server% netstat | grep 32714
127.0.0.1.32714     127.0.0.1.21        32768      0 32768       0 ESTABLISHED
127.0.0.1.21        127.0.0.1.32714     32768      0 32768       0 ESTABLISHED
127.0.0.1.20        127.0.0.1.32714     32768      0 32768       0 TIME_WAIT
```

The first two lines show the established control connection on port 21; the third one shows the old data connection to port 20, now in the TIME_WAIT state. When that disappears, you can do another data transfer command.

And there you have it: you have forwarded an FTP data connection through SSH. You have achieved the Holy Grail of FTP with SSH, though perhaps you agree with us and Sir Gawain that "it's only a model." Still, if you're terribly concerned about your data connections, have no other way to transfer files, can afford to wait a few minutes between file transfers, and are quite lucky, then this will work. It also makes a great parlor trick at geek parties.

11.3. Pine, IMAP, and SSH

Pine is a popular, Unix-based email program from the University of Washington (*http://www.washington.edu/pine/*). In addition to handling mail stored and delivered in local files, Pine also supports IMAP* for accessing remote mailboxes and SMTP† for posting mail.

In this case study, we integrate Pine and SSH to solve two common problems:

IMAP authentication
: In many cases, IMAP permits a password to be sent in the clear over the network. We discuss how to protect your password using SSH, but (surprisingly) not by port forwarding.

Restricted mail relaying
: Many ISPs permit their mail and news servers to be accessed only by their customers. In some circumstances, this restriction may prevent you from legitimately relaying mail through your ISP. Once again, SSH comes to the rescue.

We also discuss wrapping *ssh* in a script to avoid Pine connection delays and facilitate access to multiple mailboxes. This discussion will delve into more detail than the previous one on Pine/SSH integration. [4.5.4]

11.3.1. Securing IMAP Authentication

Like SSH, IMAP is a client/server protocol. Your email program (e.g., Pine) is the client, and an IMAP server process (e.g., *imapd*) runs on a remote machine, the *IMAP host*, to control access to your remote mailbox. Also like SSH, IMAP generally requires you to authenticate before accessing your mailbox, typically by password. Unfortunately, in many cases this password is sent to the IMAP host in the clear over the network; this represents a security risk (see Figure 11-8).‡

If you have an account on the IMAP host, and if it is running an SSH server, you can protect your password. Because IMAP is a TCP/IP-based protocol, one

---

* Internet Message Access Protocol, RFC-2060.

† Simple Mail Transfer Protocol, RFC-821.

‡ IMAP does support more secure methods of authentication, but they aren't widely deployed.

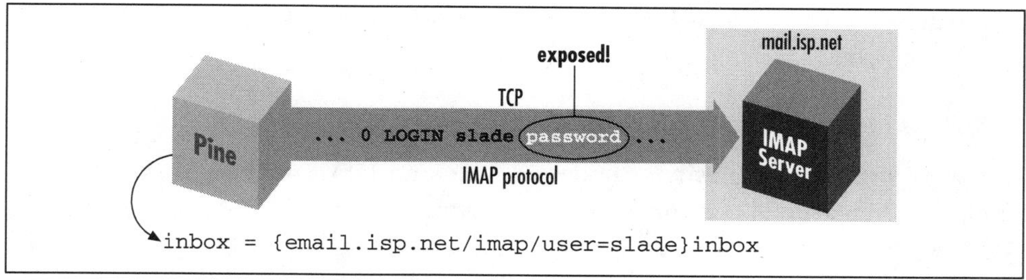

Figure 11-8. A normal IMAP connection

approach is to use SSH port forwarding between the machine running Pine and the IMAP host (see Figure 11-9). [9.2.1]

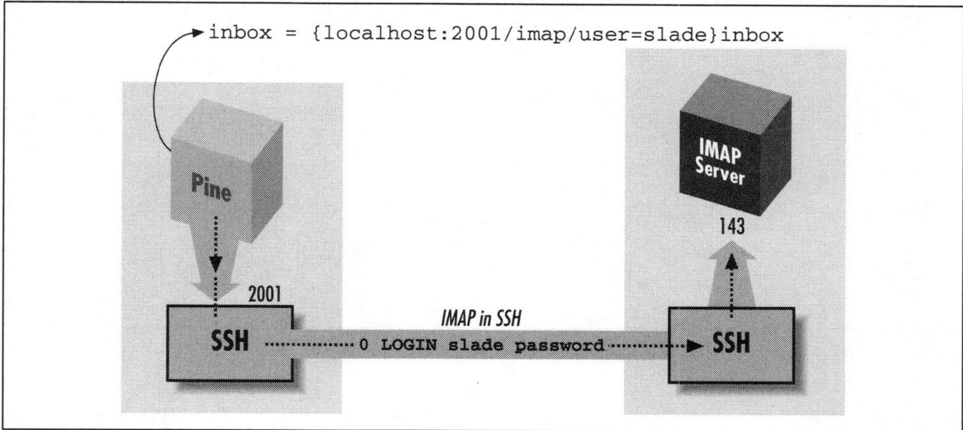

Figure 11-9. Forwarding an IMAP connection

However, this technique has two drawbacks:

Security risk
: On a multiuser machine, any other user can connect to your forwarded port. [9.2.4.3] If you use forwarding only to protect your password, this isn't a big deal, since at worst, an interloper could access a separate connection to the IMAP server having nothing to do with your connection. On the other hand, if port forwarding is permitting you to access an IMAP server behind a firewall, an interloper can breach the firewall by hijacking your forwarded port, a more serious security risk.

Inconvenience
: In this setup, you must authenticate twice: first to the SSH server on the IMAP host (to connect and to create the tunnel) and then to the IMAP server by password (to access your mailbox). This is redundant and annoying.

Fortunately, we can address both these drawbacks and run Pine over SSH securely and conveniently.

11.3.1.1. Pine and preauthenticated IMAP

The IMAP protocol defines two modes in which an IMAP server can start: normal and preauthenticated (see Figure 11-10). Normally, the server runs with special privileges to access any user's mailbox, and hence it requires authentication from the client. Unix-based IMAP servers enter this mode when started as root.

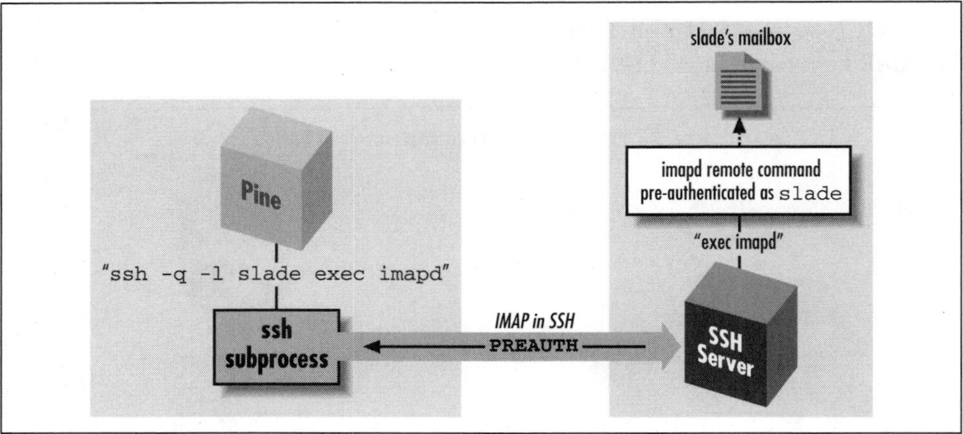

Figure 11-10. Pine/IMAP over SSH, preauthenticated

Here's a sample session that invokes an IMAP server, *imapd*, through *inetd* so it runs as root:

```
server% telnet localhost imap
* OK localhost IMAP4rev1 v12.261 server ready
0 login res password'
1 select inbox
* 3 EXISTS
* 0 RECENT
* OK [UIDVALIDITY 964209649] UID validity status
* OK [UIDNEXT 4] Predicted next UID
* FLAGS (\Answered \Flagged \Deleted \Draft \Seen)
* OK [PERMANENTFLAGS (\* \Answered \Flagged \Deleted \Draft \Seen)] Permanent
flags
1 OK [READ-WRITE] SELECT completed
2 logout
* BYE imap.example.com IMAP4rev1 server terminating connection
2 OK LOGOUT completed
```

Alternatively, in preauthenticated mode, the IMAP server assumes that authentication has already been done by the program that started the server and that it already has the necessary rights to access the user's mailbox. If you invoke *imapd* on the command line under a nonroot uid, *imapd* assumes you have already authenticated and opens your email inbox. You can then type IMAP commands and access your mailbox without authentication:

```
server% /usr/local/sbin/imapd
* PREAUTH imap.example.com IMAP4rev1 v12.261 server ready
0 select inbox
* 3 EXISTS
* 0 RECENT
* OK [UIDVALIDITY 964209649] UID validity status
* OK [UIDNEXT 4] Predicted next UID
* FLAGS (\Answered \Flagged \Deleted \Draft \Seen)
* OK [PERMANENTFLAGS (\* \Answered \Flagged \Deleted \Draft \Seen)] Permanent
flags
0 OK [READ-WRITE] SELECT completed
1 logout
* BYE imap.example.com IMAP4rev1 server terminating connection
1 OK LOGOUT completed
```

Notice the `PREAUTH` response at the beginning of the session, indicating pre-authenticated mode. It is followed by the command `select inbox`, which causes the IMAP server implicitly to open the inbox of the current user without demanding authentication.

Now, how does all this relate to Pine? When instructed to access an IMAP mailbox, Pine first attempts to log into the IMAP host using *rsh* and to run a preauthenticated instance of *imapd* directly. If this succeeds, Pine then converses with the IMAP server over the pipe to *rsh* and has automatic access to the user's remote inbox without further authentication. This is a good idea and very convenient; the only problem is that *rsh* is very insecure. However, you can make Pine use SSH instead.

11.3.1.2. Making Pine use SSH instead of rsh

Pine's *rsh* feature is controlled by three configuration variables in the *~/.pinerc* file: `rsh-path`, `rsh-command`, and `rsh-open-timeout`. `rsh-path` stores the program name for opening a Unix remote shell connection. Normally it is the fully qualified path to the *rsh* executable (e.g., */usr/ucb/rsh*). To make Pine use SSH, instruct it to use the *ssh* client rather than *rsh*, setting `rsh-path` to the location of the SSH client:

```
rsh-path=/usr/local/bin/ssh
```

`rsh-command` represents the Unix command line for opening the remote shell connection: in this case, the IMAP connection to the IMAP host. The value is a `printf`-style format string with four "%s" conversion specifications that are automatically filled in at runtime. From first to last, these four specifications stand for:

1. The value of `rsh-path`
2. The remote hostname

3. The username for accessing your remote mailbox
4. The connection method; in this case, "imap"

For example, the default value of **rsh-command** is:

```
"%s %s -l %s exec /etc/r%sd"
```

which can instantiate to:

```
/usr/ucb/rsh imap.example.com -l smith exec /etc/rimapd
```

To make this work properly with *ssh*, modify the default format string slightly, adding the *–q* option for quiet mode:

```
rsh-command="%s %s -q -l %s exec /etc/r%sd"
```

This instantiates to:

```
/usr/local/bin/ssh imap.example.com -w -l smith exec /etc/rimapd
```

The *–q* option is necessary so that *ssh* doesn't emit diagnostic messages that may confuse Pine, such as:

```
Warning: Kerberos authentication disabled in SUID client.
fwd connect from localhost to local port sshdfwd-2001
```

Pine otherwise tries to interpret these as part of the IMAP protocol. The default IMAP server location of */etc/r%sd* becomes */etc/rimapd.*

The third variable, **rsh-open-timeout**, sets the number of seconds for Pine to open the remote shell connection. Leave this setting at its default value, 15, but any integer greater than or equal to 5 is permissible.

So finally, the Pine configuration is:

```
rsh-path=/usr/local/bin/ssh
rsh-command="%s %s -q -l %s exec /etc/r%sd"
rsh-open-timeout=
```

Remote Usernames in Pine

By the way, it's not mentioned in the Pine manpage or configuration file comments, but if you need to specify a different username for connecting to a remote mailbox, the syntax is:

```
{hostname/user=jane}mailbox
```

This causes Pine to call the **rsh-command** with "jane" as the remote username (i.e., the third %s substitution).

Generally, you want to use an SSH authentication method that doesn't require typing a password or passphrase, such as trusted-host or public-key with an agent. SSH is run behind the scenes by Pine and doesn't have access to the terminal to prompt you. If you're running the X Window System, *ssh* can pop up an X widget instead to get input, *ssh-askpass*, but you probably don't want that either. Pine may make several separate IMAP connections in the course of reading your mail, even if it's all on the same server. This is just how the IMAP protocol works.

With the previous settings in your *~/.pinerc* file and the right kind of SSH authentication in place, you're ready to try Pine over SSH. Just start Pine and open your remote mailbox; if all goes well, it will open without prompting for a password.

11.3.2. Mail Relaying and News Access

Pine uses IMAP to read mail but not to send it. For that, it can either call a local program (such as *sendmail*) or use an SMTP server. Pine can also be a newsreader and use NNTP (the Network News Transfer Protocol, RFC-977) to contact a news server.

An ISP commonly provides NNTP and SMTP servers for its customers when connected to the ISP's network. However, for security and usage control reasons, the ISP generally restricts this access to connections originating within its own network (including its own dial-up connections). In other words, if you're connected to the Internet from elsewhere and try to use your ISP's services, the attempt will probably fail. Access to your usual servers can be blocked by a firewall, or if not, your outgoing mail can bounce with a message about "no relaying," and the news server rejects you with a message about "unauthorized use."

You are authorized to use the services, of course, so what do you do? Use SSH port forwarding! By forwarding your SMTP and NNTP connections over an SSH session to a machine inside the ISP's network, your connections appear to come from that machine, thus bypassing the address-based restrictions. You can use separate SSH commands to forward each port:

```
$ ssh -L2025:localhost:25 smtp-server ...
$ ssh -L2119:localhost:119 nntp-server ...
```

Alternatively, if you have a shell account on one of the ISP's machines running SSH but can't log into the mail or news servers directly, do this:

```
$ ssh -L2025:smtp-server:25 -L2119:nntp-server:119 shell-server ...
```

This is an off-host forwarding, and thus the last leg of the forwarded path isn't protected by SSH. [9.2.4] But since the reason for this forwarding isn't so much protection as it is bypassing the source-address restriction, that's OK. Your mail messages and news postings are going to be transferred insecurely once you drop them off, anyway. (If you want security for them, you need to sign or encrypt them separately, e.g., with PGP or S/MIME.)

In any case, now configure Pine to use the forwarded ports by setting the **smtp-server** and **nntp-server** configuration options in your *~/.pinerc* file:

```
smtp-server=localhost:2025
nntp-server=localhost:2119
```

11.3.3. Using a Connection Script

The Pine configuration option `rsh-path` can point not only to *rsh* or *ssh*, but also to any other program: most usefully, a script you've written providing any needed customizations. There are a couple of reasons why you might need to do this:

- The `rsh-path` setting is global, applying to every remote mailbox. That is, Pine tries to use this style of access either for every remote mailbox or for none. If you have multiple remote mailboxes but only some of them are accessible via SSH/*imapd*, this leads to annoyance. Pine falls back to a direct TCP connection if SSH fails to get an IMAP connection, but you have to wait for it to fail. If the server in question is behind a firewall silently blocking the SSH port, this can be a lengthy delay.
- The "multiple forwarding" problem. You might think to add forwarding options to Pine's `rsh-path` command, rather than run a separate SSH session to get them:

  ```
  rsh-command="%s %s -q -l %s -L2025:localhost:25 exec /etc/r%sd"
  ```

  This solution can get tricky if you're accessing multiple mailboxes, not only because the command is run for every mailbox, but also because it may run multiple times concurrently. Once the forwarded ports are already established, subsequent invocations will fail. More specifically, SSH1 and OpenSSH will fail altogether; SSH2 issues a warning but continues.

A custom connection script can solve these and other problems. The following Perl script examines the target server and returns failure immediately if it isn't among a small set of known names. This means that Pine moves quickly past the `rsh-path` command for other servers and attempts a direct IMAP connection. The script also discovers whether SMTP and NNTP forwardings are in place, and includes those in the SSH command only if they aren't. To use this script or another like it, point Pine's `rsh-path` option to your script, and set `rsh-command` to be compatible with your script:

```
rsh-path=/path/to/script
rsh-command=%s %s %s %s
```

Here is a sample implementation of the script, using Perl:

```
#!/usr/bin/perl

# TCP/IP module
use IO::Socket;

# get the arguments passed by Pine
($server,$remoteuser,$method) = @ARGV;

die "usage: $0 <server> <remote user> <method>"
    unless scalar @ARGV == 3;

if ($server eq "mail.isp.com") {
    # on this machine, I had to compile my own imapd
    $command = 'cd ~/bin; exec imapd';
} else if ($server eq "clueful.isp.com") {
    # on this box, the POP and IMAP servers are in the expected place
    $command = 'exec /etc/r${method}d';
} else {
    # signal Pine to move on
    exit 1;
}

$smtp = 25;  # well-known port for SMTP
$nntp = 119; # and NNTP
$smtp_proxy = 2025; # local port for forwarding SMTP connection
$nntp_proxy = 2119; # local port for forwarding NNTP connection
$ssh = '/usr/local/bin/ssh1'; # which SSH do I want to run?

# Try to connect to the forwarded SMTP port; only do forwarding if the
# attempt fails.  Also, do forwarding only if we're not in the domain
# "home.net".  The idea is that that's your home network, where you have
# direct access to your ISP's mail and news servers.

$do_forwards = !defined($socket = IO::Socket::INET->new("localhost:$smtp_proxy"))
    && `domainname` !~ /HOME.NET/i;

# be tidy
close $socket if $socket;

# Set the forwarding options if we're doing forwarding.  This assumes that
# the mail and news servers are called "mail" and "news", respectively, in
# your ISP's domain; a common and useful convention.

@forward = ('-L',"$smtp_proxy:mail:$smtp",'-L',"$nntp_proxy:news:$nntp");
    if ($do_forwards);

# prepare the arguments to ssh
@ssh_argv = ('-a','-x','-q',@forward,"$remoteuser\@$server");

# run ssh
exec $ssh, @ssh_argv, $command;
```

11.4. Kerberos and SSH

Kerberos is an authentication system designed to operate securely in an environment where networks may be monitored and user workstations aren't under central control. [1.6.3] It was developed as part of Project Athena, a wide-ranging research and development effort carried out at MIT between 1983 and 1991, funded primarily by IBM and Digital Equipment Corporation. Project Athena contributed many other pieces of technology to the computing world, including the well-known X Window System.

Kerberos is very different in character and design from SSH; each includes features and services the other lacks. In this study, we compare the two systems in detail, and then discuss how to combine them to obtain the advantages of both. If your site already uses Kerberos, you can add SSH while maintaining your existing account base and authentication infrastructure. (Figure 11-11 shows where Kerberos fits into the scheme of SSH configuration.) If you aren't using Kerberos, its advantages may also be compelling enough to motivate you to install it, especially for large computing environments.

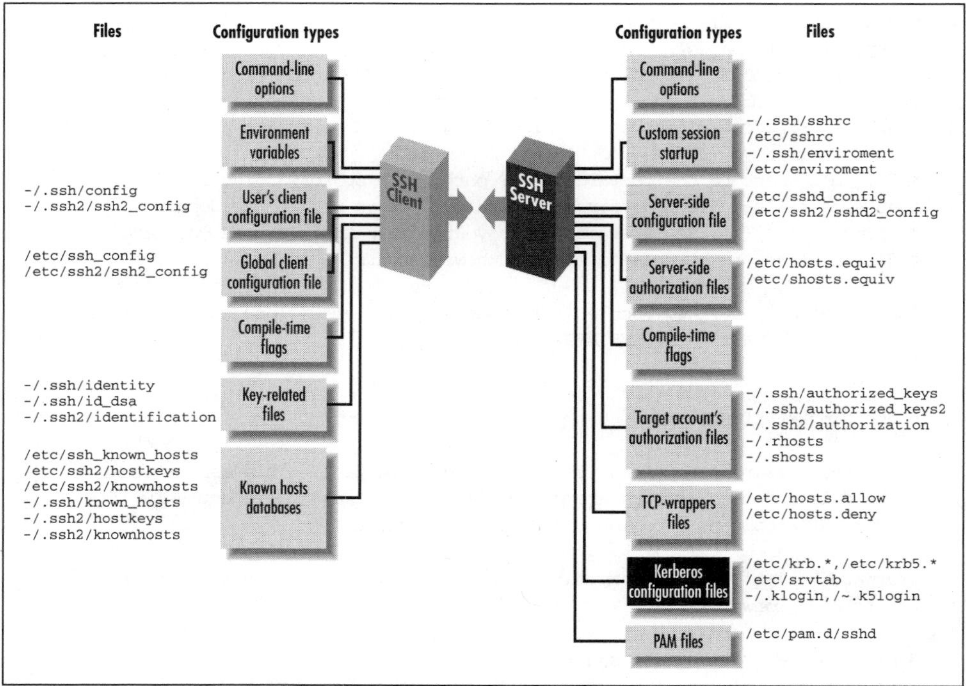

Figure 11-11. Kerberos configuration (highlighted parts)

There are two versions of the Kerberos protocol, Kerberos-4 and Kerberos-5. Free reference implementations of both are available from MIT:

ftp://athena-dist.mit.edu/pub/kerberos/

Kerberos-5 is the current version, and Kerberos-4 is no longer actively developed at MIT. Even so, Kerberos-4 is still in use in many contexts, especially bundled into commercial systems (e.g., Sun Solaris, Transarc AFS). SSH1 supports Kerberos-5, and OpenSSH/1 supports Kerberos-4. The current draft of the SSH-2 protocol doesn't yet define a Kerberos authentication method, but as this book went to press SSH 2.3.0 was released with "experimental" Kerberos-5 support, which we haven't covered here (but which should work substantially as described with SSH1).

11.4.1. Comparing SSH and Kerberos

While they solve many of the same problems, Kerberos and SSH are very different systems. SSH is a lightweight, easily deployed package, designed to work on existing systems with minimal changes. Kerberos, in contrast, requires you to establish a significant infrastructure before use.

11.4.1.1. Infrastructure

Let's consider an example: allowing users to create secure sessions between two machines. With SSH, you simply install the SSH client on the first machine and the server on the second, start the server, and you're ready to go. Kerberos, however, requires the following administrative tasks:

- Establish at least one Kerberos Key Distribution Center (KDC) host. The KDCs are central to the Kerberos system and must be heavily secured; typically they run nothing but the KDC, don't allow remote login access, and are kept in a physically secure location.* Kerberos can't operate without a KDC, so it is wise to establish backup or "slave" KDCs also, which then must be synchronized periodically with the master. A KDC host might also run a remote administration server, a credentials-conversion server for Kerberos-4 compatibility in a Kerberos-5 installation, and other server programs depending on your needs.
- For each Kerberos user, add an account (or "user principal") to the KDC database.
- For each application server that will use Kerberos to authenticate clients, add an account (or "service principal") to the KDC database. A separate principal is required for each server on each host.

* Although, if remote login access to a KDC is desired, SSH is a good way to do it!

- Distribute the service principal cryptographic keys in files on their respective hosts.
- Write a sitewide Kerberos configuration file (*/etc/krb5.conf*) and install it on all hosts.
- Install Kerberos-aware applications. Unlike SSH, Kerberos isn't transparent to TCP applications. For example, you might install a version of *telnet* that uses Kerberos to provide a strongly authenticated, encrypted remote login session similar to that of *ssh*.
- Deploy a clock-synchronization system such as Network Time Protocol (NTP). Kerberos relies on timestamps for proper operation.

Clearly, deploying Kerberos requires much more work and more changes to existing systems than SSH does.

11.4.1.2. Integrating with other applications

Another difference between SSH and Kerberos is their intended use. SSH is a set of programs that work together via the SSH protocol, designed to use in combination with existing applications with minimal changes. Consider programs like CVS [8.2.6.1] and Pine [11.3] that invoke the insecure *rsh* program internally to run remote programs. If configured to use *ssh* instead of *rsh*, the program's remote connections become secure; the introduction of *ssh* is transparent to the program and its remote partner. Alternatively, if an application makes a direct network connection to a TCP service, SSH port forwarding can secure that connection simply by telling the application to use a different server address and port.

Kerberos, on the other hand, is designed as an authentication infrastructure, together with a set of programming libraries.* The libraries are for adding Kerberos authentication and encryption to existing applications; this process is called *kerberizing* the application. The MIT Kerberos distribution comes with a set of common, kerberized services, including secure versions of *telnet*, *ftp*, *rsh*, *su*, etc.

11.4.1.3. Security of authenticators

The extra complexity of Kerberos provides properties and capabilities that SSH doesn't. One major win of Kerberos is its transmission and storage of authenticators (i.e., passwords, secret keys, etc.). To demonstrate this advantage, let's compare Kerberos's *ticket* system with SSH's password and public-key authentication.

SSH password authentication requires your password each time you log in, and it is sent across the network each time. The password isn't vulnerable during

* SSH2 has recently moved towards this model. It is similarly organized as a set of libraries implementing the SSH-2 protocol, accessed via an API by client and server programs.

transmission, of course, since SSH encrypts the network connection. However, it does arrive at the other side and exist in plaintext inside the SSH server long enough for authentication to occur, and if the remote host has been compromised, an adversary has an opportunity to obtain your password.

SSH cryptographic authentication, on the other hand, may require you to store your private keys on each client host, and you must have authorization files in each server account you want to access. This presents security and distribution problems. A stored key is protected by encryption with a passphrase, but having it stored at all on generally accessible hosts is a weakness Kerberos doesn't have. An adversary who steals your encrypted key may subject it to an offline dictionary attack to try to guess your passphrase. If successful, your adversary has access to your accounts until you notice and change all your key and authorization files. This change may be time-consuming and error-prone if you have several accounts on different machines, and if you miss one, you're in trouble.

Kerberos ensures that a user's password* travels as little as possible and is never stored outside the KDC. When a user identifies herself to the Kerberos system, the identifying program (*kinit*) uses her password for an exchange with the KDC, then immediately erases it, never having sent it over the network in any form nor stored it on disk. A client program that subsequently wants to use Kerberos for authentication sends a "ticket," a few bytes of data cached on disk by *kinit*, which convinces a kerberized server of the user's identity. Tickets are cached in files readable only by their users, of course, but even if they are stolen, they are of limited use: tickets expire after a set amount of time, typically a few hours, and they are specific to a particular client/server/service combination.

A stolen Kerberos ticket cache can be the target of a dictionary attack, but with an important difference: user passwords aren't present. The keys in the cache belong to server principals, and moreover, they are typically generated randomly and hence less vulnerable to a dictionary attack than user passwords. Sensitive keys are stored only on the KDCs, under the theory that it is much easier to effectively secure a small set of limited-use machines, rather than a large set of heterogeneous, multipurpose servers and workstations over which the administrator may have little control. Much of Kerberos's complexity results from this philosophy.

11.4.1.4. Account administration

Kerberos also serves other functions beyond the scope of SSH. Its centralized user account database can unify those of disparate operating systems, so you may administer one set of accounts instead of keeping multiple sets synchronized. Kerberos supports access control lists and user policies for closely defining which

* Actually, the secret key derived from the user's password, but the distinction isn't relevant here.

principals are allowed to do what; this is authorization, as opposed to authentication. Finally, a Kerberos service area is divided into realms, each with its own KDC and set of user accounts. These realms can be arranged hierarchically, and administrators can establish trust relationships between parent/child or peer realms, allowing automatic cross-authentication between them.

11.4.1.5. Performance

Kerberos authentication is generally faster than SSH public-key authentication. This is because Kerberos usually employs DES or 3DES, whereas SSH uses public-key cryptography, which is much slower in software than any symmetric cipher. This difference may be significant if your application needs to make many short-lived secure network connections and isn't running on the fastest hardware.

To sum up: Kerberos is a system of broader scope than SSH, providing authentication, encryption, key distribution, account management, and authorization services. It requires substantial expertise and infrastructure to deploy and requires significant changes to an existing environment for use. SSH addresses fewer needs, but has features that Kerberos installations typically don't, such as port forwarding. SSH is much more easily and quickly deployed and is more useful for securing existing applications with minimal impact.

11.4.2. Using Kerberos with SSH

Kerberos is an authentication and authorization (AA) system. SSH is a remote-login tool that performs AA as part of its operation, and one AA system it can use is (you guessed it) Kerberos. If your site already uses Kerberos, its combination with SSH is compelling, since you can apply your existing infrastructure of principals and access controls to SSH.

Even if you're not already using Kerberos, you might want to roll it out together with SSH as an integrated solution because of the advantages Kerberos provides. By itself, the most flexible SSH authentication method is public-key with an agent. Passwords are annoying and limited because of the need to type them repeatedly, and the trusted-host method isn't appropriate or secure enough for many situations. Unfortunately, the public-key method incurs substantial administrative overhead: users must generate, distribute, and maintain their keys, as well as manage their various SSH authorization files. For a large site with many nontechnical users, this can be a big problem, perhaps a prohibitive one. Kerberos provides the key-management features SSH is missing. SSH with Kerberos behaves much like public-key authentication: it provides cryptographic authentication that doesn't give away the user's password, and the ticket cache gives the same advantages as the key agent, allowing for single sign-on. But there are no keys to generate, authorization files to set up, or configuration files to edit; Kerberos takes care of all this automatically.

There are some disadvantages. First of all, only the Unix SSH packages have Kerberos support; we know of no Windows or Macintosh products containing it. Only the SSH-1 protocol currently supports Kerberos, although there is work in progress in the SECSH working group to add Kerberos to SSH-2. Second, public-key authentication is tied to other important features of SSH, such as forced commands in the authorization file, that can't be used with Kerberos authentication. This is an unfortunate artifact of the way Unix SSH has evolved. Of course, you can still use public-key authentication as needed. You may find the access controls of Kerberos adequate for most needs and use public-key for a few situations in which you need finer-grained control.

In the following sections, we explain how to use the SSH Kerberos support. If your site has a kerberized SSH installed, this should be enough to get you going. We can't discuss all the gory detail of building a Kerberos infrastructure, but we do give a quick outline of how to set up Kerberos from scratch, if you have your own systems and want to try it. However, these are just hints, and the description is incomplete. If you're going to use, install, and manage kerberized SSH, you need a more complete understanding of Kerberos than you will get here. A good place to start is:

http://web.mit.edu/kerberos/www/

11.4.3. A Brief Introduction to Kerberos-5

In this section, we introduce the important concepts of principals, tickets, and ticket-granting-tickets (TGTs), and follow them with a practical example.

11.4.3.1. Principals and tickets

Kerberos can authenticate a user or a piece of software providing or requesting a service. These entities have names, called *principals,* that consist of three parts: a name, an instance, and a realm, notated as *name/instance@REALM.** Specifically:

- The *name* commonly corresponds to a username for the host operating system.
- The *instance,* which may be null, typically distinguishes between the same name in different roles. For example, the user res might have a normal, user-level principal res@REALM (note the null instance), but he could have a

* This was the case in Kerberos-4. In fact, Kerberos-5 principals have a realm, plus any number of "components"—the first two of which are conventionally used as the name and instance, as in Kerberos-4.

second principal with special privileges, res/admin@REALM, for his role as a system administrator.

- The *realm* is an administrative division identifying a single instance of the Kerberos principal database (that is, a list of principals under common administrative control). Each host is assigned a realm, and this identification is relevant to authorization decisions, which we discuss shortly. Realms are always uppercase, by convention.

As we've discussed, Kerberos is based on tickets. If you want to use a network service—say, the *telnet* server on a host, to log in remotely—you must obtain a ticket for that service from the Kerberos Key Distribution Center, or KDC. The ticket contains an authenticator, proving your identity to the software providing the service. Since both you and the service must be identified to the KDC, both must have principals.

The system administrator establishes principals by adding them to the KDC database. Each principal has a secret key, known only to the principal owner and to the KDC; the operation of the Kerberos protocol is based on this fact. For instance, when you request a ticket for a service, the KDC gives you some bits that have been encrypted with the secret key of the service. Therefore, only the intended service can decrypt and verify the ticket. Moreover, a successful decryption proves that the KDC issued the ticket, since only the service and the KDC know the service's secret key.

For a user principal, the secret key is derived from the user's Kerberos password. Service principal keys are usually stored in the file */etc/krb5.keytab* on the host where the service runs, and the service calls a Kerberos library routine to read the file and extract its secret key. Obviously this file must be protected from general read access, since anyone who can read it can impersonate the service.

11.4.3.2. Obtaining credentials with kinit

Let's use an example to get a practical look at Kerberos. Suppose you are on a Unix host spot in the realm FIDO, and you want to use kerberized *telnet* to log into another host, *rover*. First, you obtain Kerberos credentials by running the command *kinit*:

```
[res@spot res]$ kinit
Password for res@FIDO: *********
```

kinit assumes that since your username is res and the host spot is in the realm FIDO, you want to obtain credentials for the principal res@FIDO. If you had wanted a different principal, you could have supplied it as an argument to *kinit*.

11.4.3.3. Listing credentials with klist

Having successfully gotten your credentials with *kinit*, you can examine them with the *klist* command, which lists all tickets you have obtained:

```
[res@spot res]$ klist
Ticket cache: /tmp/krb5cc_84629
Default principal: res@FIDO
Valid starting     Expires            Service principal
07/09/00 23:35:03  07/10/00 09:35:03  krbtgt/FIDO@FIDO
```

So far, you have only one ticket, for the service krbtgt/FIDO@FIDO. This is your Kerberos TGT, and it is your initial credential: proof to be presented later to the KDC that you have successfully authenticated yourself as res@FIDO. Note that the TGT has a validity period: it expires in 10 hours. After that, you must do another *kinit* to reauthenticate yourself.

11.4.3.4. Running a kerberized application

Having gotten your credentials, you now *telnet* to the remote host:

```
[res@spot res]$ telnet -a rover
Trying 10.1.2.3...
Connected to rover (10.1.2.3).
Escape character is '^]'.
[Kerberos V5 accepts you as "res@FIDO"]
Last login: Sun Jul  9 16:06:45 from spot
You have new mail.
[res@rover res]$
```

The *–a* option to this kerberized *telnet* client tells it to do auto-login: that is, it attempts to negotiate Kerberos authentication with the remote side. It succeeds: the remote side accepts your Kerberos identification, and allows you to log in without providing a password. If you return to spot and do a *klist*, you will see what happened:

```
[res@spot res]$ klist
Ticket cache: /tmp/krb5cc_84629
Default principal: res@FIDO
Valid starting     Expires            Service principal
07/09/00 23:35:03  07/10/00 09:35:03  krbtgt/FIDO@FIDO
07/09/00 23:48:10  07/10/00 09:35:03  host/rover@FIDO
```

Note that you now have a second ticket, for the service "host/rover@FIDO". This principal is used for remote login and command execution services on the host rover, such as kerberized *telnet*, *rlogin*, *rsh*, etc. When you ran *telnet –a rover*, the *telnet* client requested a ticket for host/rover@FIDO from the KDC, supplying your TGT with the request. The KDC validated the TGT, verifying that you had recently identified yourself as res@FIDO, and issued the ticket. *telnet* stored the new ticket in your Kerberos ticket cache, so that the next time you connect to rover, you can just use the cached ticket instead of contacting the KDC again (at least, until the ticket expires). It then presented the host/rover@FIDO ticket to the *telnet* server, which verified it and in turn believed that the client had been identified as res@FIDO to the KDC.

11.4.3.5. Authorization

So far we've taken care of authentication, but what about authorization? The *telnet* server on rover believes that you are res@FIDO, but why should res@FIDO be allowed to log in? This comes back to the host/realm correspondence we've mentioned. [11.4.3.2] Since you didn't specify otherwise, the *telnet* client told the server that you wanted to log into the account res on rover. (You could have changed that with *telnet –l username.*) Since rover is also in the realm FIDO, Kerberos applies a default authorization rule: if host H is in realm R, the Kerberos principal u@R is allowed access to the account u@H. Using this default rule implies that the system administrators are managing the correspondence between operating system (OS) usernames and Kerberos principals. If you had tried to log into your friend Bob's account instead, here's what would have happened:

```
[res@spot res]$ telnet -a -l bob rover
Trying 10.1.2.3...
Connected to rover (10.1.2.3).
Escape character is '^]'.
[Kerberos V5 accepts you as "res@FIDO"]
telnetd: Authorization failed.
```

Note that authentication was still successful: the *telnet* server accepted you as res@FIDO. The authorization decision failed, though: Kerberos decided that the principal res@FIDO was not allowed to access the account bob@rover. Bob can allow you to log into his account by creating the file *rover:~bob/.k5login*, and placing a line in it containing your principal name, res@FIDO. He would also have to place his own principal in there, since if a *.k5login* file exists, it overrides the default authorization rule, and Bob would be unable to log into his own account. So Bob's authorization file would look like this:

```
rover:~bob/.k5login:
  bob@FIDO
  res@FIDO
```

11.4.4. Kerberos-5 in SSH1

To enable Kerberos support in SSH1, compile it **--with-kerberos5**. [4.1.5.7] If your Kerberos support files (libraries and C header files) aren't in a standard place and *configure* can't find them, you can tell it where to look using:

```
# SSH1 only
$ configure ... --with-kerberos5=/path/to/kerberos ...
```

Two notes on doing this build:

- The MIT Kerberos-5 Release 1.1 renamed the library *libcrypto.a* to *libk5crypto.a*, and the SSH1 build files have not been updated to reflect this. You can either alter the SSH1 Makefile, or just use:

```
# cd your_Kerberos_library_directory
# ln -s libk5crypto.a libcrypto.a
```

- The routine `krb5_xfree()`, used in *auth-kerberos.c*, also appears to have disappeared in 1.1. Replacing all occurrences of `krb5_xfree` with `xfree` appears to work.

If you compile in Kerberos support, the resulting SSH programs work only on a system with Kerberos installed, even if you aren't using Kerberos authentication. The programs will likely refer to Kerberos shared libraries that must be present for the programs to run. Also, SSH performs Kerberos initialization on startup and expects a valid host Kerberos configuration file (*/etc/krb5.conf*).

After installation, we recommend setting the serverwide configuration keyword `KerberosAuthentication` in */etc/sshd_config* to "yes" for clarity, even though it is on by default:

```
# SSH1 only
KerberosAuthentication yes
```

Additionally, the host/server@REALM principal must be in the KDC database, and its key must be stored in */etc/krb5.keytab* on the server.

Once running with Kerberos support, SSH1 operates essentially as we described for kerberized *telnet*; Figure 11-12 illustrates the process. [11.4.3.4] On the client, simply run *kinit* to obtain your Kerberos TGT, and then try *ssh –v*. If Kerberos authentication succeeds, you will see:

```
$ ssh -v server
...
server: Trying Kerberos V5 authentication.
server: Kerberos V5 authentication accepted.
...
```

and in the server log:

```
Kerberos authentication accepted joe@REALM for login to account joe from client_
host
```

As with *telnet*, if you want to allow someone else to log into your account using Kerberos and *ssh –l your_username*, you must create a *~/.k5login* file and place their principal name in it, along with your own.

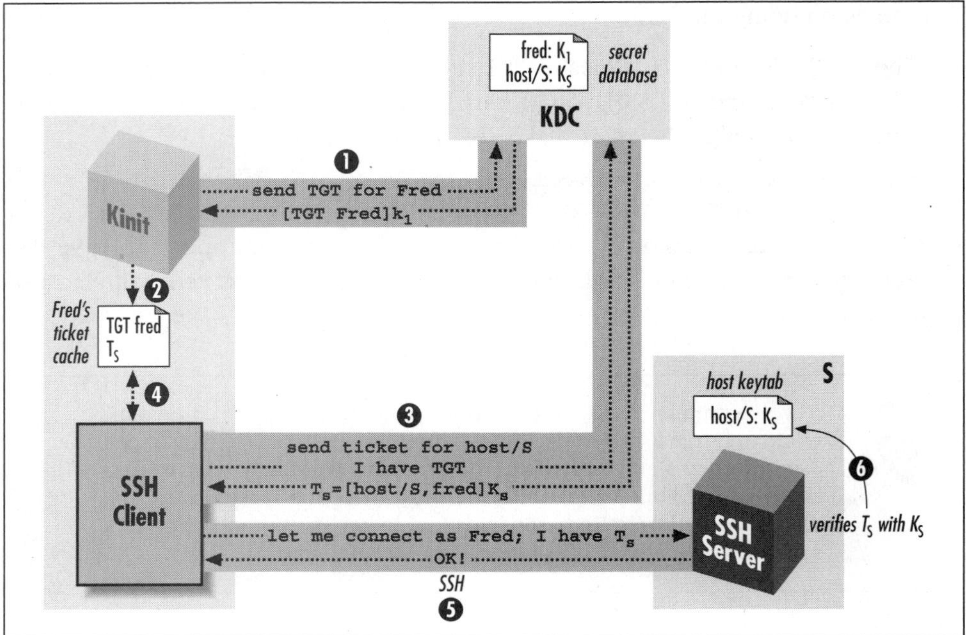

Figure 11-12. SSH with Kerberos authentication

11.4.4.1. Kerberos password authentication

If Kerberos authentication is enabled in the SSH server, password authentication changes in behavior. Passwords are now validated by Kerberos instead of the host operating system. This behavior is usually desired in a fully kerberized environment, where local passwords might not be usable at all. In a mixed environment, however, it may be useful to have SSH fall back on the operating system (OS) password if Kerberos validation fails. The SSH server option that controls this feature is `KerberosOrLocalPasswd`:

```
# SSH1, OpenSSH
KerberosOrLocalPasswd yes
```

This fallback is useful as a fail-safe: if the KDC isn't functioning, you can still authenticate by your OS password (although public-key would be a stronger fail-safe authentication method).

Another feature of kerberized password authentication is that *sshd* stores your TGT upon login, so you don't need to run *kinit* and retype your password to get Kerberos credentials on the remote host.

11.4.4.2. Kerberos and NAT

SSH is frequently used across firewalls, and these days such a boundary often includes network address translation. Unfortunately, Kerberos has a serious problem with NAT. Kerberos tickets usually include a list of IP addresses from which they are allowed to be used; that is, the client presenting the ticket must be transmitting from one of those addresses. By default, *kinit* requests a TGT limited to the IP addresses of the host it's running on. You can see this with the *–a* option to *klist*:

```
[res@spot res]$ klist -a -n
Ticket cache: /tmp/krb5cc_84629
Default principal: res@FIDO

Valid starting     Expires            Service principal
07/09/00 23:35:03  07/10/00 09:35:03  krbtgt/FIDO@FIDO
         Addresses: 10.1.2.1
07/09/00 23:48:10  07/10/00 09:35:03  host/rover@FIDO
         Addresses: 10.1.2.1
```

(The *–n* switch tells *klist* to display the addresses by number, rather than translating them to names.) Host spot's IP address is 10.1.2.1, and so the KDC issues the TGT limited to use from that address. If spot has multiple network interfaces or addresses, they are listed here as well. When you obtain subsequent service tickets based on this TGT, they are also limited to the same set of addresses.

Now, imagine you connect to an SSH server on the other side of a NAT gateway, which is rewriting your (the client's) IP address, but the KDC is inside the NAT boundary, with you.

When you obtain the service ticket from the KDC, it contains your real IP address. The SSH server, however, sees your NAT'd address as the source of the connection, notes that this doesn't match the address encoded in the ticket, and refuses authentication. In this case, *ssh –v* reports:

```
Trying Kerberos V5 authentication.
Kerberos V5: failure on credentials (Incorrect net address).
```

Figure 11-13 illustrates this problem. It has no good solution at the moment. One workaround is the undocumented *kinit –A* switch, which causes *kinit* to request a ticket with *no* addresses in it at all. This trick decreases security, because a stolen ticket cache can then easily be used from anywhere, but it gets around the problem.

11.4.4.3. Cross-realm authentication

Kerberos realms are distinct collections of principals under separate administrative control. For instance, you might have two departments, Sales and Engineering, that don't trust each other (just for the sake of example, of course). The Sales people don't want any of those weird Engineers to be able to create accounts in their space, and Engineering certainly doesn't want any sales-droids mucking about with their logins. So you create two Kerberos realms, SALES and ENGINEERING,

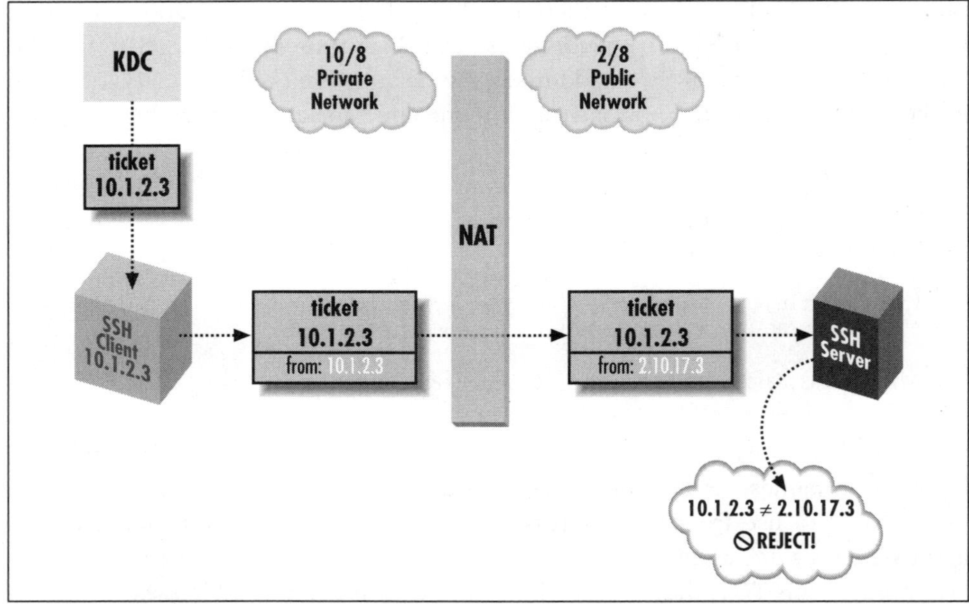

Figure 11-13. Kerberos and NAT

and have their respective administrators deal with account management in each realm.

The catch is, of course, that Sales and Engineering do need to work together. Sales guys need to log into Engineering machines to try out new products, and Engineering needs access to Sales desktops to fix the problems they constantly get into. Suppose Erin the engineer needs Sam from Sales to access her account on an Engineering machine, erin@bulwark. She can place Sam's principal name in her Kerberos authorization file, like so:

```
bulwark:~erin/.k5login:
  erin@ENGINEERING
  sam@SALES
```

However, this won't work. To log in, Sam needs a service ticket for host/bulwark@ENGINEERING. Only a KDC for the ENGINEERING realm can issue such a ticket, but an ENGINEERING KDC won't know the principal sam@SALES. In general, an ENGINEERING host has no way of authenticating a principal from the SALES realm. It looks as if Sam will need a principal in the ENGINEERING domain as well, but this poor solution violates the whole idea of having separate realms. It's also cumbersome, since Sam would have to do another *kinit* each time he wants to access resources in a different realm.

The solution to this problem is called *cross-realm authentication*. First, both realms must be described in the */etc/krb5.conf* files on all machines in both realms;

Kerberos knows only those realms listed in the configuration file. Then the administrators of the two realms establish a shared secret key between them, called a cross-realm key. The key is realized as a common key for two specially named principals, one in each realm. The key has a direction, and its existence allows one KDC to issue a TGT for the other realm; the other KDC can verify that this TGT was issued by its trusted peer realm using the shared key. With one cross-realm key in place, authentication in one realm provides a verifiable identity in the other realm as well. If the trust is symmetric—that is, if each realm should trust the other—then two cross-realm keys are needed, one for each direction.

Hierarchical Realms in Kerberos-5

For a large number of realms, the system as described quickly becomes unwieldy. If you want cross-realm trust between all of them, you must manually establish cross-realm keys for each pair of realms. Kerberos-5 supports hierarchical realms to address this problem. A realm name containing dots, such as ENGINEERING.BIGCORP.COM, implies the (possible) existence of realms BIGCORP.COM and COM. When attempting cross-realm authentication from SALES.BIGCORP.COM to ENGINEERING.BIGCORP.COM, if Kerberos doesn't find a direct cross-realm key, it attempts to navigate up and then down the realm hierarchy, following a chain of cross-realm relations to the target realm. That is, if there are cross-realm keys from SALES.BIGCORP.COM to BIGCORP.COM, and from BIGCORP.COM to ENGINEERING.BIGCORP.COM, the cross-realm authentication from SALES to ENGINEERING succeeds without needing an explicit cross-realm setup between them. This allows for scalable, complete, cross-realm relationships among a large collection of realms.

Note that Sam doesn't have a second principal now, sam@ENGINEERING. Rather, an ENGINEERING KDC can now verify that Sam was authenticated as sam@SALES by a SALES KDC and can therefore use the principal sam@SALES in authorization decisions. When Sam tries to log into bulwark using SSH, Kerberos notices that the target machine is in a different realm from Sam's principal and automatically uses the appropriate cross-realm key to obtain another TGT for him in the ENGINEERING realm. Kerberos then uses that to obtain a service ticket authenticating sam@SALES to host/bulwark@ENGINEERING. *sshd* on bulwark reads Erin's *~/.k5login* file, sees that sam@SALES is allowed access, and permits the login.

That's the basic idea. However, when SSH enters the picture, cross-realm authentication can fail due to a confusing catch. Suppose Sam uses bulwark so often that he's given an account there. The sysadmin puts "sam@SALES" into *bulwark:~sam/.k5login*, so that Sam can log in there with his SALES credentials. But, it doesn't work. Even with everything set up correctly so that cross-realm kerberized *telnet* works, SSH Kerberos authentication still fails for him. Even more mysteriously, every other form of authentication starts failing as well. Sam had public-key authentication set up and working before, and you'd expect it to try Kerberos, fail, then try public-key and succeed. But all the public-key attempts fail, too. Sam won't get much of a hint of what the problem is unless password authentication is turned on, and SSH eventually tries it:

```
[sam@sales sam]$ ssh -v bulwark
...
Trying Kerberos V5 authentication.
Kerberos V5 authentication failed.
Connection to authentication agent opened.
Trying RSA authentication via agent with 'Sam's personal key'
Server refused our key.
Trying RSA authentication via agent with 'Sam's work key'
Server refused our key.
Doing password authentication.
sam@SALES@bulwarks's password:
```

That last prompt doesn't look right at all: "sam@SALES@bulwark"? There's another hint from *sshd –d*:

```
Connection attempt for sam@SALES from sales
```

SSH is mistakenly using the principal name as if it were the account name—as if Sam had typed, *ssh –l sam@SALES bulwark*. Of course, there's no account named "sam@SALES"; there's one named "sam". And in fact, the quick fix for this problem is for Sam to specify his username explicitly, with *ssh –l sam bulwark*, even though this seems redundant.

The reason for this odd problem is a Kerberos-5 feature that SSH employs, called *aname→lname mapping* (authentication name to local name mapping). Kerberos can be used with a variety of operating systems, some of whose notions of a username don't correspond easily with Kerberos principal names. Perhaps the usernames allow characters that are illegal in principal names, or there are multiple operating systems with conflicting username syntaxes. Or perhaps when you merge two existing networks, you find username conflicts among existing accounts, so that the principal res@REALM must translate to the account res on some systems, but rsilverman on others. The Kerberos-5 designers thought it would be good if Kerberos could automate handling this problem itself, and so they included the aname → lname facility for translating principals to the correct local account names in various contexts.

SSH1 uses aname → lname. When doing Kerberos authentication, the SSH1 client supplies the principal name as the target account name by default, rather than the current local account name (that is, it behaves as if Sam had typed *ssh –l sam@SALES bulwark*). The server in turn applies the aname → lname mapping to this, to turn it into a local account name. When the principal name and the server host are in the same realm, this works automatically, because there is a default aname → lname rule that maps user@REALM to "user" if REALM is the host's REALM. However, Sam is doing cross-realm authentication, and so the two realms are different: his principal is sam@SALES, but the server's realm is ENGINEERING. So the aname → lname mapping fails, and *sshd* goes ahead with using "sam@SALES" as the local account name. Since there is no account with that name, every form of authentication is guaranteed to fail.

The system administrators of the ENGINEERING realm can fix this problem by configuring an aname → lname mapping for SALES. As it happens, though, the aname → lname facility in MIT Kerberos-5 Release 1.1.1 appears to be unfinished. It's almost entirely undocumented and includes references to utilities and files that don't appear to exist. However, we did manage to uncover enough information to give one example solution. From the comments in the source file *src/lib/krb5/os/an_to_ln.c*, we devised the following "auth_to_local" statements that can fix Sam's problem:

```
bulwark:/etc/krb5.conf:
    ...
    [realms]
        ENGINEERING = {
                     kdc = kerberos.engineering.bigcorp.com
            admin_server = kerberos.engineering.bigcorp.com
          default_domain = engineering.bigcorp.com

           auth_to_local = RULE:[1:$1]
           auth_to_local = RULE:[2:$1]
           auth_to_local = DEFAULT
        }
```

These rules cause the aname → lname function on this host to map principals of the form foo@REALM or foo/bar@REALM to the username "foo" for all realms, as well as applying the default translation rule for the host's realm.

11.4.4.4. TGT forwarding

Recall that Kerberos tickets are normally issued to be usable only from the requesting host. If you do a *kinit* on spot, then use SSH to log into rover, you are now stuck as far as Kerberos is concerned. If you want to use some Kerberos service on rover, you must run another kinit, because your credentials cache is stored on spot. And it won't help to copy the credentials cache file from spot to rover because the TGT won't be valid there; you need one issued for rover. If you do another *kinit*, your password is safe traveling over the network through SSH, but this is still not a single sign-on, and it's annoying.

SSH has an analogous problem with public-key authentication and solves it with agent forwarding. [6.3.5] Similarly, Kerberos-5 solves it with *TGT forwarding*. The SSH client asks the KDC to issue a TGT valid on the server host, based on the client's holding an existing valid TGT. When it receives the new TGT, the client passes it to *sshd*, which stores it in the remote account's Kerberos credentials cache. If successful, you'll see this message in the output from *ssh –v*:

```
Trying Kerberos V5 TGT passing.
Kerberos V5 TGT passing was successful.
```

and a *klist* on the remote host shows the forwarded TGT.

In order to use TGT forwarding, you must compile SSH with the switch `--enable-kerberos-tgt-passing`. You must also request a forwardable TGT with *kinit –f*; otherwise, you see:

```
Kerberos V5 krb5_fwd_tgt_creds failure (KDC can't fulfill requested option)
```

11.4.4.5. SSH1 Kerberos ticket-cache bug

Prior to Version 1.2.28, SSH1 had a serious flaw in its Kerberos ticket cache handling. Under some circumstances SSH1 mistakenly set the KRB5CCNAME environment variable on the remote side to the string "none". This variable controls where the ticket cache is stored. The ticket cache contains sensitive information; anyone who steals your ticket cache can impersonate you for the lifetime of its tickets. Normally, the ticket cache file is kept in */tmp*, which is reliably local to each machine. Setting KRB5CCNAME to `none` means that when the user does a *kinit*, the ticket cache is established in a file named *none* in the current working directory. This directory can easily be an NFS filesystem, allowing the tickets to be stolen by network snooping. Or it can be an inappropriate spot in the filesystem, perhaps one where inherited ACLs give someone else the right to read the file, regardless of the ownership and permissions set by SSH.

Don't use Kerberos authentication in SSH1 versions earlier than 1.2.28.

This bug was fixed by SSH Communications Security in Version 1.2.28 in response to our bug report. Note that this problem occurs if SSH1 is compiled with Kerberos support, even if Kerberos authentication isn't in use for the session at hand. The OpenSSH Kerberos-4 code has never had this bug.

11.4.4.6. Kerberos-5 setup notes

Here we present an abbreviated "quick-start" menu of steps to set up a working, one-host Kerberos system from scratch, using the MIT Kerberos-5 distribution Version 1.1.1. This is far from complete and might be wrong or misleading for some environments or builds. It's just meant to get you started, if you want to give Kerberos a try. Suppose the local host's name is *shag.carpet.net*, and your chosen realm name is FOO, and your username is "fred":

1. Compile and install krb5-1.1.1. We complied with `--localstatedir=/var` so the KDC database files go under */var*.
2. Run:

   ```
   $ mkdir /var/krb5kdc
   ```

3. Install an */etc/krb5.conf* file as follows. Note the log files; these will be useful to examine later in case of problems (or just for information):

   ```
   [libdefaults]
       ticket_lifetime = 600
       default_realm = FOO
       default_tkt_enctypes = des-cbc-crc
       default_tgs_enctypes = des-cbc-crc

   [realms]
       FOO = {
       kdc = shag.carpet.net
       admin_server = shag.carpet.net
       default_domain = carpet.net
       }

   [domain_realm]
       .carpet.net = FOO
        carpet.net = FOO

   [logging]
       kdc = FILE:/var/log/krb5kdc.log
       admin_server = FILE:/var/log/kadmin.log
       default = FILE:/var/log/krb5lib.log

   Install a file /var/krb5kdc/kdc.conf like this:

   [kdcdefaults]
       kdc_ports = 88,750

   [realms]
       FOO = {
       database_name        = /var/krb5kdc/principal
       admin_keytab         = /var/krb5kdc/kadm5.keytab
       acl_file             = /var/krb5kdc/kadm5.acl
       dict_file            = /var/krb5kdc/kadm5.dict
           key_stash_file       = /var/krb5kdc/.k5.FOO
       kadmind_port         = 749
   ```

```
    max_life           = 10h 0m 0s
    max_renewable_life = 7d 0h 0m 0s
    master_key_type    = des-cbc-crc
    supported_enctypes = des-cbc-crc:normal des-cbc-crc:v4
    }
```

4. Run:

   ```
   $ kdb5_util create
   ```

   This creates the KDC principal database in */var/krb5kdc*. You are prompted for the KDC master key, a password the KDC needs to operate. The key is stored in */var/krb5kdc/.k5.FOO*, which allows the KDC software to start without human intervention but which is obviously not wise unless the KDC machine is extremely well protected.

5. Run:

   ```
   $ kadmin.local
   This program modifies the principal database. Issue the following kadmin commands:
   kadmin.local: ktadd -k /var/krb5kdc/kadm5.keytab kadmin/admin kadmin/changepw
   Entry for principal kadmin/admin with kvno 4, encryption type DES cbc mode with
   CRC-32 added to keytab WRFILE:/var/krb5kdc/kadm5.keytab.
   Entry for principal kadmin/changepw with kvno 4, encryption type DES cbc mode with
   CRC-32 added to keytab WRFILE:/var/krb5kdc/kadm5.keytab.

   kadmin.local:  add_principal -randkey host/shag.carpet.net
   WARNING: no policy specified for host/shag.carpet.net@FOO; defaulting to no policy
   Principal "host/shag.carpet.net@FOO" created.

   kadmin.local:  ktadd -k /etc/krb5.keytab host/shag.carpet.net
   Entry for principal host/shag.carpet.net with kvno 3, encryption type DES cbc mode
   with CRC-32 added to keytab WRFILE:/etc/krb5.keytab.

   kadmin.local:  add_principal fred
   WARNING: no policy specified for fred@FOO; defaulting to no policy
   Enter password for principal "fred@FOO": ********
   Re-enter password for principal "fred@FOO": ********
   Principal "fred@FOO" created.

   kadmin.local: quit
   ```

6. Now, start the KDC and the *kadmin* daemons, *krb5kdc* and *kadmind.*

   If all goes well, you should be able to use *kinit* to get a TGT using the password you gave to *kadmin.local* when creating the "fred" principal, *klist* to see the TGT, and *kpasswd* to change your Kerberos password.

7. Try out kerberized SSH.

11.4.5. Kerberos-4 in OpenSSH

OpenSSH also supports Kerberos but only the older Kerberos-4 standard. The mechanics from a user perspective are mostly the same: in a functioning Kerberos realm, you use *kinit* to obtain a TGT, and then run the SSH client with `KerberosAuthentication` turned on (which it is by default). The sysadmin must compile OpenSSH using **`--with-kerberos4`**, ensure there is a Kerberos host principal with its keys installed on the SSH server machine, and turn on `KerberosAuthentication` in the SSH server configuration. The host principal is *rcmd.hostname@REALM*,* and the keytab file is */etc/srvtab*. `KerberosAuthentication` is on by default in the server only if */etc/srvtab* exists when it starts.

Access control for an account is via the file *~/.klogin*. With Kerberos-4, it isn't necessary to include the account's default principal in *~/.klogin* if that file exists; the default principal always has access.

Table 11-1 summarizes the salient differences between Kerberos-4 and Kerberos-5 with respect to SSH.

Table 11-1. Differences Between Kerberos-4 and Kerberos-5 with Respect to SSH

	Kerberos-4	Kerberos-5
Host principal	*rcmd.hostname@REALM*	*host/hostname@REALM*
Config files	*/etc/krb.conf*, */etc/krb.realms*	*/etc/krb5.conf*
Server principal keys	*/etc/srvtab*	*/etc/krb5.keytab*
Authorization file	*~/.klogin*	*~/.k5login*

11.4.5.1. Kerberos-4 compatibility mode in Kerberos-5

If you have a Kerberos-5 realm, you don't need to set up a separate Kerberos-4 KDC just to support OpenSSH. Kerberos-5 has a version 4 (v4) compatibility mode, in which the v5 KDC responds to v4 requests. If v4 compatibility is on, you can install v4 */etc/krb.conf* and */etc/krb.realms* files that point to your existing v5 KDC, and the v4 *kinit* can obtain a v4 TGT. Following the example in the previous section, these look like:

```
/etc/krb.conf:
FOO shag.carpet.net

/etc/krb.realms:
.carpet.net FOO
```

The KDC satisfies v4 requests for *rcmd.hostname@REALM* tickets, using the key of the corresponding v5 *host/hostname@REALM* principal, so you don't need to create separate "rcmd/hostname" principals in your v5 KDC. Since v4-only servers still need the principal key, you need to create a v4 version of the key file (*/etc/srvtab*)

* Principals in Kerberos-4 also include a name, optional instance, and realm, but are written *name.instance@REALM* instead of *name/instance@REALM* as in Kerberos-5.

with that key; you can do this with the v5 program *kutil* to read in an existing *krb5.keytab* and write out a v4 *srvtab*. Direct cross-realm authentication also automatically works using existing cross-realm keys; however, Kerberos-4 doesn't support hierarchical realms.

Using the Kerberos-5 credentials conversion service, you can even avoid having to do a separate v4 *kinit*. On the KDC, the separate server program *krb524d* must be running. Then, after doing a v5 *kinit*, the user simply runs the program *krb524init*. This obtains a v4 TGT using the v5 one, which you can verify with the v4 *klist* command.

Note that OpenSSH and SSH1 can't interoperate using Kerberos authentication. They use the same SSH protocol messages in each case but implicitly expect encapsulated Kerberos tickets of the appropriate Kerberos version. You can't use Kerberos-5 v4 compatibility mode to overcome this limitation. We hope OpenSSH will eventually add Kerberos-5 support.

Also note that Kerberos-4 doesn't have an analog to the Kerberos-5 *kinit –A* switch. We don't know of any way to overcome the Kerberos/NAT problem using Kerberos-4. [11.4.4.2] We have heard, however, that the Transarc AFS KDC ignores IP addresses in tickets, thus avoiding the problem.

11.4.5.2. Kerberos on Solaris

Sun Microsystems's Solaris operating system comes with a limited, special-purpose implementation of Kerberos-4, which supports Kerberos authentication for Sun's NFS and secure RPC. As far as we can tell, it doesn't suffice for compiling or running OpenSSH with Kerberos-4, so you probably want to install another Kerberos-4 package such as MIT's. Beware of confusion once you do so; the Solaris */bin/kinit*, for instance, won't have any effect on the MIT Kerberos-4 operation.

11.5. Connecting Through a Gateway Host

All along we've assumed that your outgoing connectivity is unlimited: that you can establish any outgoing TCP connection you desire. Even our discussions of firewalls have assumed that they restrict only incoming traffic. In more secure (or simply more regimented) environments, this might not be the case: in fact, you might not have direct IP connectivity at all to the outside world.

In the corporate world, companies commonly require all outgoing connections to pass through a proxy server or *gateway host*: a machine connected to both the company network and the outside. Although connected to both networks, a gateway host doesn't act as a router, and the networks remain separated. Rather, it allows limited, application-level access between the two networks.

In this case study, we discuss issues of SSH in this environment:

- Connecting transparently to external hosts using *ssh*
- Making *scp* connections
- Running SSH-within-SSH by port forwarding

11.5.1. Making Transparent SSH Connections

Suppose your company has a gateway host, G, which is your only gateway to the Internet. You are logged into a client host C and want to reach a server host S outside the company network, as shown in Figure 11-14. We assume that all three machines have SSH installed.

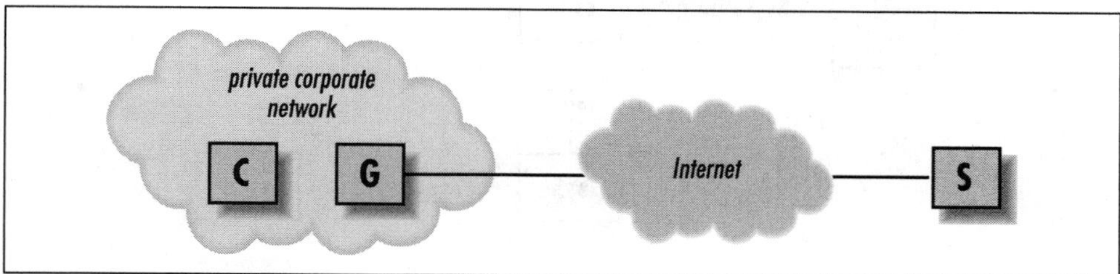

Figure 11-14. Proxy gateway

To make a connection from client C to server S now requires two steps:

1. Connect from C to gateway G:

```
# Execute on client C
$ ssh G
```

2. Connect from G to server S:

```
# Execute on gateway G
$ ssh S
```

This works, of course, but it requires an extra manual step on the gateway, a machine you don't care about. Using agent forwarding and public-key authentication, you can avoid entering a passphrase on gateway G, but even so, the additional hop ideally should be transparent.

Worse, you can't transparently execute remote commands on server S from client C. Instead of the usual:

```
# Execute on client C
$ ssh S /bin/ls
```

you must run a remote *ssh* on gateway G that in turn contacts server S:

```
# Execute on client C
$ ssh G "ssh S /bin/ls"
```

This isn't only annoying but also can complicate automation. Imagine rewriting all your SSH-based scripts to accommodate this environment.

Fortunately, SSH configuration is flexible enough to afford a neat solution, which we now present using SSH1 features and syntax. We use public-key authentication to take advantage of the options of the *authorized_keys* file, and *ssh-agent* with agent forwarding so that authentication passes on transparently to the second SSH connection (see Figure 11-15).

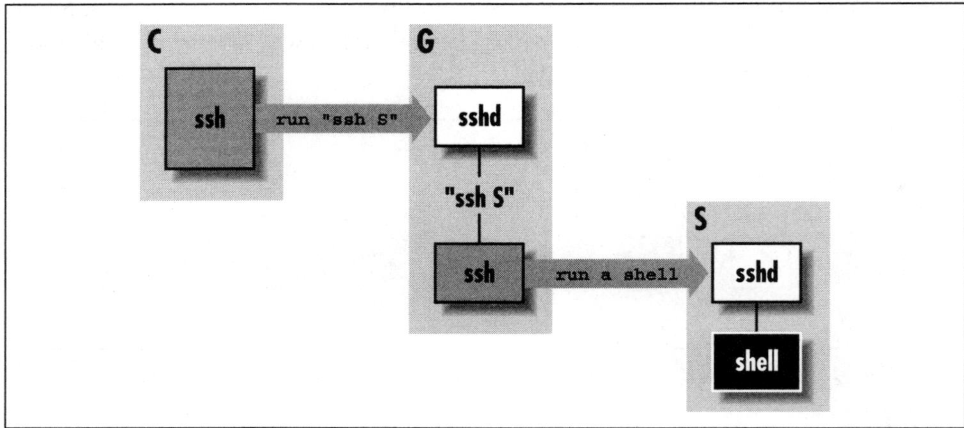

Figure 11-15. Chained SSH connections through a proxy gateway

Suppose your account on gateway G is gilligan, and on server S it is skipper. First, set up your SSH client configuration file so the name S is a nickname for accessing your account on gateway G:

```
# ~/.ssh/config on client C
host S
  hostname G
  user gilligan
```

Next, on gateway G, associate a forced command with your chosen key to invoke an SSH connection to server *S*: [8.2.4]

```
 # ~/.ssh/authorized_keys on gateway G
command="ssh -l skipper S" ...key..
```

Now, when you invoke the command *ssh S* on client C, it connects to gateway G, runs the forced command automatically, and establishes a second SSH session to server S. And thanks to agent forwarding, authentication from G to S happens automatically, assuming you've loaded the appropriate key. This can be the same key you used to access gilligan@*G* or a different one.*

This trick not only provides a transparent connection from client C to server S, it also sidesteps the fact that the name S might not have any meaning on client C. Often in this kind of network situation, your internal network naming scheme is cut off from the outside world (e.g., split DNS with internal roots). After all, what's the point of allowing you to name hosts you can't reach? Thanks to the `Host` configuration keyword for SSH clients, you can create a nickname S that instructs SSH to reach that host transparently via G. [7.1.3.5]

11.5.2. Using SCP Through a Gateway

Recall that the command:

```
$ scp ... S:file ...
```

actually runs *ssh* in a subprocess to connect to S and invoke a remote *scp* server. [3.8.1] Now that we've gotten *ssh* working from client C to server S, you'd expect that *scp* would work between these machines with no further effort. Well, it almost does, but it wouldn't be software if there weren't a couple of small problems to work around:

- Problems invoking the *ssh* subprocess, due to the forced command
- Authentication difficulties due to lack of a tty

11.5.2.1. Passing along the remote command

The first problem is that the *ssh* command on client C sends a command to be executed on server S, that starts the *scp* server, but now that command is ignored in favor of our forced command. You have to find a way to relay the intended *scp* server command to S. To accomplish this, modify the *authorized_keys* file on gateway G, instructing *ssh* to invoke the command contained in the environment variable SSH_ORIGINAL_COMMAND: [8.2.4.4]

```
# ~/.ssh/authorized_keys on gateway G
command="ssh -l skipper S $SSH_ORIGINAL_COMMAND" ...key...
```

Now the forced command invokes the proper *scp*-related command on server S. You aren't quite done, however, because this forced command unfortunately breaks our existing setup. It works fine for *ssh* invocations on client C that run a remote command (e.g., *ssh S /bin/ls*), but it fails when *ssh S* is invoked alone to run

* Note that if you want to use this setup for an interactive connection, you need to use the *–t* option to *ssh*, to force it to allocate a tty on *G*. It doesn't normally do that, because it doesn't have any way to know that the remote command—in this case, another instance of *ssh*—needs one.

a remote shell. You see, SSH_ORIGINAL_COMMAND is set only if a remote command is specified, so *ssh S* dies because SSH_ORIGINAL_COMMAND is undefined.

You can work around this problem using the Bourne shell and its parameter substitution operator `:-` as follows:

```
# ~/.ssh/authorized_keys on gateway G
command="sh -c 'ssh -l skipper S ${SSH_ORIGINAL_COMMAND:-}'" ...key...
```

The expression `${SSH_ORIGINAL_COMMAND:-}` returns the value of $SSH_ORIGINAL_COMMAND if it is set, or the empty string otherwise. (In general, `${V:-D}` means "return the value of the environment variable V or the string D if V isn't set." See the *sh* manpage for more information.) This produces precisely the desired behavior, and *ssh* and *scp* commands both work properly now from client C to server S.

11.5.2.2. Authentication

The second *scp*-related problem is authentication for the second SSH connection, from gateway G to server S. You can't provide a password or passphrase to the second *ssh* program, since it has no tty allocated.* So you need a form of authentication that doesn't require user input: either RhostsRSA, or public-key authentication with agent forwarding. RhostsRSA works as is, so if you plan to use it, you can skip to the next section. Public-key authentication, however, has a problem: *scp* runs *ssh* with the *–a* switch to disable agent forwarding. [6.3.5.3] You need to reenable agent forwarding for this to work, and this is surprisingly tricky.

Normally you could turn on agent forwarding in your client configuration file:

```
# ~/.ssh/config on client C, but this FAILS
ForwardAgent yes
```

but this doesn't help because the *–a* on the command line takes precedence. Alternatively, you might try the *–o* option of *scp*, which can pass along options to *ssh*, such as *–o ForwardAgent yes*. But in this case, *scp* places the *–a* after any *–o* options it passes where it takes precedence, so that doesn't work either.

There is a solution, though. *scp* has a *–S* option to indicate a path to the SSH client program it should use, so you create a "wrapper" script that tweaks the SSH command line as needed, and then make *scp* use it with *–S*. Place the following script in an executable file on client C, say *~/bin/ssh-wrapper*:

```
#!/usr/bin/perl
exec '/usr/local/bin/ssh1', map {$_ eq '-a' ? () : $_} @ARGV;
```

* Actually, you can hack your way around this, but it's ugly and we won't go into it.

This runs the real *ssh*, removing *–a* from the command line if it's there. Now, give your *scp* command like this:

```
scp -S ~/bin/ssh-wrapper ... S:file ...
```

and it should work.

11.5.3. Another Approach: SSH-in-SSH (Port Forwarding)

Instead of using a forced command, here's another way to connect by SSH through a gateway: forward a port on client C to the SSH server on S, using an SSH session from C to G, and then run a second SSH session through the first (see Figure 11-16).

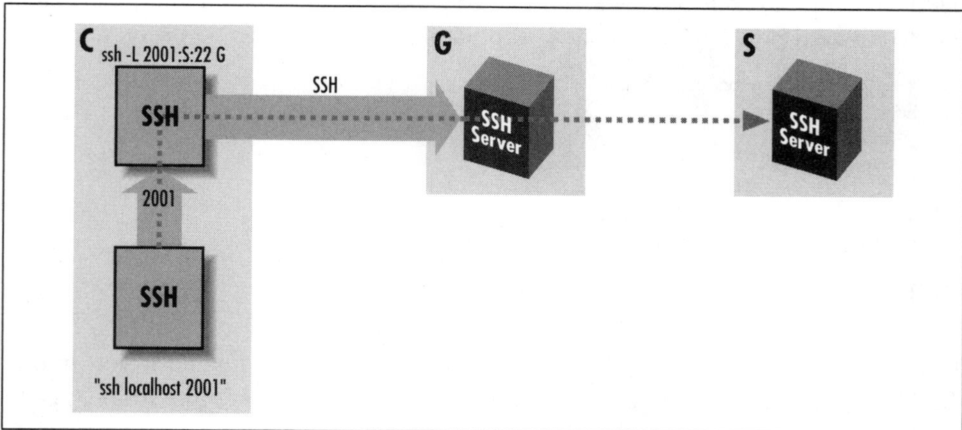

Figure 11-16. Forwarded SSH connection through a proxy gateway

That is:

```
# Execute on client C
$ ssh -L2001:S:22 G

# Execute on client C in a different shell
$ ssh -p 2001 localhost
```

This connects to server S by carrying the second SSH connection (from C to S) inside a port-forwarding channel of the first (from C to G). You can make this more transparent by creating a nickname S in your client configuration file:

```
# ~/.ssh/config on client C
host S
  hostname localhost
  port 2001
```

Now the earlier commands become:

```
# Execute on client C
$ ssh -L2001:S:22 G

# Execute on client C in a different shell
$ ssh S
```

Because this technique requires a separate, manual step to establish the port forwarding, it is less transparent than the one in [11.5.1]. However, it has some advantages. If you plan to use port or X forwarding between C and S with the first method, it's a little complicated. *scp* not only gives the *–a* switch to *ssh* to turn off agent forwarding, but also it gives *–x* and *–o* "ClearAllForwardings yes", turning off X and port forwarding. So you need to modify the earlier wrapper script to remove these unwanted options as well. [11.5.2.2] Then, for port forwarding you need to set up a chain of forwarded ports that connect to one another. For example, to forward port 2017 on client C to port 143 (the IMAP port) on server S:

```
# ~/.ssh/config on client C
host S
  hostname G
  user gilligan

# ~/.ssh/authorized_keys on gateway G
command="ssh -L1234:localhost:143 skipper@S" ...key...

# Execute on client C
$ ssh -L2017:localhost:1234 S
```

This works, but it's difficult to understand, error-prone, and fragile: if you trigger the TIME_WAIT problem [9.2.9.1], you have to edit files and redo the tunnel just to pick a new ephemeral port to replace 1234.

Using the SSH-in-SSH technique instead, your port and X-forwarding options operate directly between client C and server S in the usual, straightforward manner. The preceding example becomes:

```
# ~/.ssh/config on client C
host S
  hostname localhost
  port 2001

# Execute on client C
$ ssh -L2001:S:22 G

# Execute on client C in a different shell
$ ssh -L2017:localhost:143 S
```

This final command connects to server S, forwarding local port 2017 to the IMAP port on S.

11.5.4. Security Differences

The two methods just discussed differ in their security properties. Again, we assume the situation with machines *C*, *G*, and *S* as used earlier.

11.5.4.1. "Server-in-the-middle" attack

The first method was a chain of two SSH connections in series. The weakness with this is that if the SSH server in the middle (on G) has been compromised, the session data is exposed. Data from C is decrypted by that server and passed to the second SSH client (also on G), which then reencrypts it for transmission to S. So the session plaintext is recovered on G: a compromised server there has access to it and can read and alter it at will.

The second method, with port forwarding, doesn't suffer from this weakness. The server on G is in no special position with regard to observing the forwarded SSH connection from C to S. Any attempt to read or alter that session will fail, in the same way that network snooping or an active network attack will fail.

11.5.4.2. Server authentication

On the other hand, the port forwarding method is weaker than the chain-of-connections when implemented with SSH1 or OpenSSH, because it lacks server authentication. The reason for this is that the SSH1 and OpenSSH clients both behave specially when the server address is 127.0.0.1 ("localhost"): they force acceptance of the host key, regardless of what key is actually provided. More precisely: they omit checking the host key against the known-hosts list, behaving always as if the server-provided host key were associated with "localhost" in the list.

The reason for this feature is convenience. If a user's home directory is shared between machines, the SSH client on each machine sees the same per-user known-hosts file. But the name "localhost" is special, in that on each machine it means something different: that same host. So if the user employs *ssh localhost* on multiple machines, she will constantly get spurious warnings about the host key having changed. The known-hosts file maps "localhost" to the host key of the last host on which she did this, not the current one.

So the problem here is that, since the remote IP address of the SSH session from C to S is actually localhost, it effectively omits server authentication, and is thus vulnerable to a man-in-the-middle or spoofed server attack.

SSH2 doesn't have this special treatment of localhost and so doesn't exhibit the weakness. Its known-hosts list is also more fine-grained: it maps server *sockets* ([host,port] pairs) to keys, rather than server hosts. This means you can have separate keys for each locally forwarded port. So, to be as secure as possible, you don't just accept the server host key the first time you use *ssh2* to connect from C to S over the forwarded port 2001 on C. Doing so circumvents server authentication for that first connection. Instead, before making the first connection, you should copy S's host key into this file on *C: ~/.ssh2/hostkeys/key_2001_localhost.pub*. This associates S's host key with the socket (localhost,2001), and you will have proper server authentication for the initial forwarded connection.

In this chapter:
- *Debug Messages: Your First Line of Defense*
- *Problems and Solutions*
- *Other SSH Resources*
- *Reporting Bugs*

12
Troubleshooting and FAQ

SSH1, SSH2, and OpenSSH are complex products. When a problem occurs, your plan of action should be, in order:

1. Run the client and server in debug mode.
2. Consult archives of questions and answers to see if anyone else has encountered and solved this problem.
3. Seek help.

Many people jump immediately to Step 3, posting questions in public forums and waiting hours or days for a reply, when a simple *ssh –v* or FAQ can clarify the problem in moments. Be a smart and efficient technologist, and use your available resources before seeking help from the community. (Although the SSH community is eager to help if you've done your homework.)

12.1. Debug Messages: Your First Line of Defense

SSH1/SSH2 clients and servers have debugging built-in. When invoked with appropriate options, these programs emit messages about their progress and failures. You can use these messages to isolate problems.

12.1.1. Client Debugging

Most clients print debug messages when invoked with the *–v* (verbose mode) option: [7.4.15]

```
$ ssh -v server.example.com
$ scp -v myfile server.example.com:otherfile
```

So many problems can be identified in verbose mode. This should be your first instinct whenever you encounter a problem.

Please take a deep breath and repeat after us:
"*ssh –v* is my friend…"
"*ssh –v* is my friend…"
"*ssh –v* is my friend…"

12.1.2. Server Debugging

The SSH1, SSH2, and OpenSSH servers also print debug messages when asked:

```
# SSH1, OpenSSH
$ sshd -d

# SSH2 only
$ sshd2 -v
```

In either case, the server enters a special debugging mode. It accepts a single connection, operates normally until the connection terminates, and then exits. It doesn't go into the background or create a child process to handle the connection, and it prints information on its progress to the screen (that is, to the standard error stream).

SSH2 has a more complicated system for debugging: numeric debugging levels, specified with the *–d* option, where a higher number means more information. [5.8.2] In fact, *–v* for verbose mode is actually just a shorthand for *–d2*. At higher debug levels, the output is so huge that only SSH developers will likely find it of use in tracking down obscure problems. But you may need to crank up the level beyond 2 to see the information you need. For example, to have it report which algorithms are negotiated for a connection, use *–d3*. If you get the error message "TCP/IP Failure", turning up to *–d5* shows the more specific OS-level error message returned from the connection attempt.

When debugging a server, remember to avoid port conflicts with any other running SSH server. Either terminate the other server or use an alternative port number for debugging:

```
$ sshd1 -d -p 54321
```

Use the *–p* option in the client when testing this debugging instance of the server:

```
$ ssh -p 54321 localhost
```

This way, you don't interrupt or affect another *sshd* in use.

The Top Ten SSH Questions

Q: How do I install my public key file on the remote host the first time?

A: Connect by password authentication and use your terminal program's copy and paste feature. [12.2.2.4]

Q: I put my SSH public key file mykey.pub into my remote SSH directory, but public-key authentication doesn't work.

A: The public key must be referenced in your remote authorization file. [12.2.2.4]

Q: Public-key authentication isn't working.

A: Use *ssh –v*, and check your keys, files, and permissions. [12.2.2.4]

Q: Password authentication isn't working.

A: Use *ssh –v*. There are a variety of possible causes. [12.2.2.2]

Q: Trusted-host authentication isn't working (SSH1 RhostsRSA, SSH2 host-based).

A: Use *ssh –v*. Check your four control files, hostnames, and setuid status of the SSH client program or *ssh-signer2*. [12.2.2.3]

Q: How do I authenticate without typing a password or passphrase?

A: *ssh-agent*, unencrypted keys, trusted-host authentication, or Kerberos. [12.2.2.1]

Q: How do I secure FTP with port forwarding?

A: Forward a local port to port 21 on the FTP server for the control connection; the data connection is much harder. [12.2.5.6]

Q: X forwarding isn't working.

A: Don't set your remote DISPLAY variable manually. (And there are other things to check.) [12.2.5.6]

Q: Why don't wildcards or shell variables work on the scp command line?

A: Your local shell expands them before *scp* runs. Escape the special characters. [12.2.5.4]

Q: A feature of ssh or scp isn't working, but I'm sure I'm using it correctly.

A: Use *ssh –v*. Also the system configuration may be overriding your settings.

12.2. Problems and Solutions

In this section, we cover a wide range of difficulties, organized by category. The sidebar "The Top Ten SSH Questions" lists what, in our experience, are the most frequently asked of the frequently asked questions. We focus on problems that may occur in many versions of the SSH software on diverse operating systems. We don't address the following sorts of questions that rapidly become obsolete:

- Compilation problems specific to one operating system, such as "HyperLinux beta 0.98 requires the `--with-woozle` flag"
- Problems and bugs that are specific to one version of SSH1 or SSH2, particularly older versions

These types of problems are best solved by the SSH FAQ [12.3.1] or through discussion with other SSH users.

In all questions, we will assume you have already used debug or verbose mode (e.g., *ssh –v*) to isolate the problem. (If you haven't, you should!)

12.2.1. General Problems

Q: *The commands ssh, scp, ssh-agent, ssh-keygen, etc., aren't doing what I expect. Even the help messages look weird.*

A: Maybe they are SSH2 programs when you are expecting SSH1, or vice versa. Locate the executables and do an *ls –l*. If they are plain files, they are most likely from SSH1 or OpenSSH. If they are symbolic links, check whether they point to SSH1 or SSH2 files. (SSH2 files have names ending in "2".)

Q: *When I try to connect to an SSH server, I get the error "Connection refused."*

A: No SSH server is running where you tried to connect. Double-check the hostname and TCP port number: perhaps the server is running on a port different from the default?

Q: *When I log in, the message of the day (/etc/motd) prints twice.*

A: Both *sshd* and the *login* program are printing it. Disable *sshd*'s printing by setting the serverwide configuration keyword `PrintMotd` to `no`.

Q: *When I log in, I see two messages about email, such as "No mail" or "You have mail."*

A: Both *sshd* and the *login* program are checking for mail. Prevent *sshd* from checking by setting the serverwide configuration keyword `CheckMail` to `no`.

12.2.2. Authentication Problems

12.2.2.1. General authentication problems

Q: *The SSH1 server says "Permission denied" and exits.*

A: This occurs if all authentication techniques have failed. Run your client in debug mode and read the diagnostic messages, looking for clues. Also read our solutions to specific authentication problems in the rest of this section.

Q: *How do I authenticate without typing a password or passphrase?*

A: The four available authentication methods for this are:

— Public-key with *ssh-agent*

— Public-key with an unencrypted key on disk (empty passphrase)

— Trusted-host

— Kerberos (SSH1 and OpenSSH/1 only)

Automatic authentication has a number of important issues you should carefully consider before selecting from the preceding list. [11.1]

Q: *I get prompted for my password or passphrase, but before I have time to respond, the SSH server closes the connection.*

A: Your server's idle timeout value may be too short. If you are a system administrator of the server machine, set `IdleTimeout` to a larger value in the serverwide configuration file. [5.4.3.3] If you are an end user of SSH1 or OpenSSH, set an idle-timeout value in *authorized_keys*. [8.2.7]

Q: *RequiredAuthentications doesn't work.*

A: This feature was broken in SSH2 2.0.13, causing authentication always to fail. This problem was fixed in 2.1.0.

Q: *SilentDeny doesn't seem to work for any authentication method.*

A: `SilentDeny` has nothing to do with authentication. It applies only to access control using `AllowHosts` and `DenyHosts`. If a connection is denied access by an `AllowHosts` or `DenyHosts` value, `SilentDeny` controls whether the client sees an informative failure message or not.

12.2.2.2. Password authentication

Q: *Password authentication isn't working.*

A: Use *ssh –v*. If the connection is being refused altogether, the SSH server is probably not running, or you are connecting to the wrong port. Port 22 is the default, but the remote system administrator might have changed it. If you see "permission denied," password authentication might be disabled in the server.

Make sure the server permits password authentication in the serverwide configuration file ("PasswordAuthentication yes" for SSH1 and OpenSSH, "AllowedAuthentications password" for SSH2). Also check your client configuration file to make sure you don't have "PasswordAuthentication no".

If you are prompted for your password, but it is rejected, you might accidentally be connecting to the wrong account. Does your local username differ from the remote username? Then you must specify the remote username when connecting:

```
$ ssh -l my_remote_username server.example.com
$ scp myfile my_remote_username@server.example.com:
```

If this still doesn't work, check your local client configuration file (*~/.ssh/config* or *~/.ssh2/ssh2_config*) to make sure you haven't accidentally set the wrong value for the `User` keyword. In particular, if your configuration file contains `Host` values with wildcards, check that your current command line (the one that isn't working) isn't matching the wrong section in the file. [7.1.3.4]

One common problem on the server side involves OpenSSH and Pluggable Authentication Modules configuration. PAM is a general system for performing authentication, authorization, and accounting in an application-independent fashion. If your operating system supports PAM (as Linux and HPUX do, for example), OpenSSH will probably have been automatically compiled to use it. Unless you take the extra step of configuring PAM to support SSH, all password authentication will mysteriously fail. This is usually just a matter of copying the appropriate *sshd.pam* file from the *contrib* directory in the OpenSSH distribution, naming the copy "sshd" and placing it in the PAM configuration directory (usually */etc/pam.d*). The *contrib* directory contains several example files for different flavors of Unix. For example, on a RedHat Linux system:

```
# cp contrib/redhat/sshd.pam /etc/pam.d/sshd
# chown root.root /etc/pam.d/sshd
# chmod 644 /etc/pam.d/sshd
```

If OpenSSH isn't using PAM, and password authentication still isn't working, the compilation switches `--with-md5-passwords` or `--without-shadow` might be relevant. These make no difference if PAM support is enabled in OpenSSH, because they deal with how OpenSSH reads the Unix *passwd* map. When using PAM, the OpenSSH code doesn't read the *passwd* map directly; the PAM libraries do it instead. Without PAM, though, if your system is using MD5-hashed passwords instead of the more traditional *crypt* (DES) hash, you must use `--with-md5-passwords`. You can tell which hash your system is using by inspecting the */etc/passwd* and */etc/shadow* files. The hashed password is the second field in each entry; if the password field in */etc/passwd* is just "x", then the real entry is in */etc/shadow* instead. MD5 hashes are much longer and contain a wider range of characters:

```
# /etc/shadow, MD5 hash
test:$1$tEMXcnZB$rDEZbQXJzUz4g2J4qYkRh.:...

# /etc/shadow, crypt hash
test:JGQfZ8DeroV22:...
```

Finally, you can try `--without-shadow` if you suspect OpenSSH is trying to use the shadow password file, but your system doesn't use it.

Q: The server won't let me use an empty password.

A: Empty passwords are insecure and should be avoided. Nevertheless, you can set "PermitEmptyPasswords yes" in the serverwide configuration file. [5.6.3]

12.2.2.3. Trusted-host authentication

Q: Trusted-host authentication isn't working (SSH1 RhostsRSA, SSH2 hostbased).

A: Use *ssh –v*. If everything looks right, check the following. Suppose the client user is orpheus@earth, and the target account is orpheus@hades—that is, on host *earth*, user orpheus invokes *ssh hades*.

For SSH1 and OpenSSH/1:

- The SSH client program must be setuid root.
- "RhostsRSAAuthentication yes" belongs in the server and client configurations.
- The client's public host key must be in the server's known hosts list. In this case, *hades:/etc/ssh_known_hosts* must contain an entry associating the name "earth" with earth's public host key, like this:

  ```
  earth 1024 37 71641647885140363140390131934...
  ```

- The entry may be in the target account's known hosts file instead, i.e., in *hades:~orpheus/.ssh/known_hosts*. Take care that "earth" is the canonical name of the client host from the server's point of view. That is, if the SSH connection is coming from the address 192.168.10.1, then `gethostbyname(192.168.10.1)` on hades must return "earth", and not a nickname or alias for the host (e.g., if the hostname is *river.earth.net*, the lookup must not return just "river"). Note that this can involve multiple naming services, since `gethostbyname` can be configured to consult multiple sources to determine a translation (e.g., DNS, NIS, */etc/hosts*).

See */etc/nsswitch.conf*. If your systems don't agree on canonical hostnames, you'll have no end of trouble with RhostsRSA. You can work around such problems to an extent by manually adding extra host nicknames to the known hosts file, like this:

```
earth,gaia,terra 1024 37 71641647885140363140390131934...
```

— Edit *hades:/etc/shosts.equiv* or *hades:~orpheus/.shosts* to allow the login. Adding earth to *shosts.equiv* allows any nonroot user on earth to access the account by the same name on hades. Adding earth to *.shosts* allows orpheus@earth to access orpheus@hades.

— Some firewalls reject outbound connections from privileged ports. This prevents RhostsRSA authentication from working, since it relies on privileged source ports. You can use *ssh -P* to get a connection to the SSH server via a nonprivileged port, but you will have to use a different kind of authentication.

For SSH2:

— "AllowedAuthentications hostbased" in the server and client configurations.

— *ssh2* doesn't need to be setuid root, but *ssh-signer2* does. More precisely, it needs to be able to read the private host key, which in the normal installation means it must be setuid root.

— A copy of earth's public host key in *hades:/etc/ssh2/knownhosts/earth.ssh-dss.pub* (or *hades:~orpheus:/.ssh2/knownhosts/earth.ssh-dss.pub*, if you specified "UserKnownHosts yes" on the server).

— Regarding canonical hostnames, the same comments as for RhostsRSA apply.

For OpenSSH/2:

— "DSAAuthentication yes" belongs in the server and client configurations.

— *ssh* must be setuid root (or otherwise able to read the client hosts's private host key in */etc/ssh_host_dsa_key*; it doesn't require a privileged source port).

— A copy of earth's public host key in *hades:/etc/ssh_known_hosts2* (or *hades:~orpheus:/.ssh/known_hosts2*).

— The same comments as for RhostsRSA apply, regarding canonical hostnames.

12.2.2.4. Public-key authentication

Q: How do I install my public key file on the remote host the first time?

A: Here's the general method:

a. Generate a key pair.

b. Copy the text of the public key into your computer's clipboard or other cut/paste buffer.

c. Log into the remote host via SSH with password authentication, which doesn't require any special files in your remote account.

d. Edit the appropriate authorization and key files on the remote host:

— For SSH1 and OpenSSH/1, append the public key to *~/.ssh/authorized_keys*.

— For OpenSSH/2, append the public key to *~/.ssh/authorized_keys2*.

— For SSH2, paste the public key into a new *.pub* file in *~/.ssh2* (say, *newkey.pub*), and append the line "Key newkey.pub" to *~/.ssh2/authorization*.

e. Log out from the remote host.

f. Log back into the remote host using public-key authentication.

When editing the remote authorization file, make sure your text editor doesn't insert line breaks into the middle of a public key. SSH1 and OpenSSH public keys are very long and must be kept on a single line.

Q: I put my SSH public key file mykey.pub into my remote SSH directory, but public-key authentication doesn't work.

A: Placing a valid public key file (e.g., *mykey.pub*) in your SSH directory isn't sufficient. For SSH1 and OpenSSH/1, you must append the key (i.e., the contents of *mykey.pub*) to *~/.ssh/authorized_keys*. For OpenSSH/2, append the key to *~/.ssh/authorized_keys2*. For SSH2, you must add a line of text to *~/.ssh2/authorization*, `Key mykey.pub`.

Q: Public-key authentication isn't working.

A: Invoke the client in debug mode (*ssh –v*). Make sure:

— Your local client is using the expected identity file.

— The correct public key is on the remote host in the right location.

— Your remote home directory, SSH directory, and other SSH-related files have the correct permissions. [5.4.2.1]

Q: I'm being prompted for my login password instead of my public key passphrase. Or, my connection is rejected with the error message "No further authentication methods available." (SSH2)

A: There are several possible causes for both of these problems:

— Public-key authentication must be enabled in both the client and server (SSH1/OpenSSH "RSAAuthentication yes", SSH2 "AllowedAuthentications publickey").

— Specify your remote username with *–l* (lowercase L) if it differs from your local username, or else the SSH server will examine the wrong remote account:

```
$ ssh -l jones server.example.com
```

— Check the file permissions in your server account. If certain files or directories have the wrong owner or careless access permissions, the SSH server refuses to perform public-key authentication. This is a security feature. Run *ssh* in verbose mode to reveal the problem:

```
$ ssh -v server.example.com
...
server.example.com: Remote: Bad file modes for /u/smith/.ssh
```

In your server account, make sure that the following files and directories are owned by you and aren't world writable: ~, *~/.ssh*, *~/.ssh/authorized_keys*, *~/.ssh2*, *~/.rhosts*, and *~/.shosts*.

— For SSH2, if you use the *–i* option to specify an identification file:

```
$ ssh2 -i my-identity server.example.com
```

check that *my-identity* is an identification file, not a private key file. (In contrast, *ssh –i* for SSH1 and OpenSSH expects a private key file.) Remember that SSH2 identification files are text files containing the names of private keys.

Q: I'm being prompted for the passphrase of the wrong key.

A: Make sure your desired public key is in your authorization file on the SSH server machine.

Check for SSH agent problems. Are you running an agent and trying to specify another key with *ssh –i* or the `IdentityFile` keyword? The presence of an agent prevents *–i* and `IdentityFile` from working. Terminate your agent and try again.

For SSH1 and OpenSSH, if any options are specified in *~/.ssh/authorized_keys*, check for typographical errors. A mistyped option causes the associated key line to be skipped silently. Remember that options are separated by commas, not whitespace.

12.2.2.5. PGP key authentication

Q: After the PGP passphrase prompt, I am being prompted for my login password.

A: If you get prompted for your PGP key, and then your password:

```
Passphrase for pgp key "mykey": ********
smith's password:
```

and you know you're typing your passphrase correctly, then first make sure you're typing your PGP passphrase correctly. (For instance, encrypt a file with that public key and decrypt it.) If so, then there might be an incompatibility between the PGP implementations on your client and server machines. We've seen this behavior when the PGP key (generated on the client machine) doesn't have sufficient bits for the PGP implementation on the server machine. Generate a new key on the server machine.

Q: I get "Invalid pgp key id number '0276C297'"

A: You probably forgot the leading "0x" on the key ID, and SSH is trying to interpret a hexadecimal number as a decimal. Use `PgpKeyId 0x0276C297` instead.

12.2.3. Key and Agent Problems

12.2.3.1. General key/agent problems

Q: I generated a key with SSH1 and tried using it with another SSH1 client, such as NiftyTelnet SSH, F-Secure SSH Client, or SecureCRT, but the client complains that the key is in an invalid format.

A: First, make sure you generated the key using *ssh-keygen1*, not *ssh-keygen2*. SSH1 and SSH2 keys aren't compatible.

Next, make sure you transferred the key file using an appropriate file-transfer program. If you used FTP, confirm that the private key file was transferred in binary mode, or else the copy will contain garbage. The public key file should be transferred in ASCII mode.

Q: I generated an SSH1 key and tried using it with SSH2, but it didn't work. (Or vice versa.)

A: This is normal. SSH1 and SSH2 keys aren't compatible.

Q: I specified a key manually, using –i or IdentityFile, but it never gets used!

A: Are you running an agent? Then *–i* and `IdentityFile` don't have any effect. The first applicable key in the agent takes precedence.

12.2.3.2. ssh-keygen

Q: *Each time I run ssh-keygen, it overwrites my default identity file.*

A: Tell *ssh-keygen* to write its output to a different file. For *ssh-keygen* in SSH1 and OpenSSH, use the *–f* option. For *ssh-keygen2*, specify the filename as the last argument on the command line; no option is needed.

Q: *Can I change the passphrase for a key without regenerating the key?*

A: Yes. For *ssh-keygen* in SSH1 and OpenSSH, use the *–N* option, and for *ssh-keygen2*, use the *–p* option.

Q: *How do I generate a host key?*

A: Generate a key with an empty passphrase and install it in the correct location:

```
# SSH1, OpenSSH
$ ssh-keygen -N '' -b 1024 -f /etc/ssh_host_key

# SSH2 only
$ ssh-keygen2 -P -b 1024 /etc/ssh2/hostkey
```

Q: *Generating a key takes a long time.*

A: Yes it may, depending on the speed of your CPU and the number of bits you have requested. DSA keys tend to take longer than RSA keys.

Q: *How many bits should I make my keys?*

A: We recommend at least 1024 bits for strong security.

Q: *What does oOo.oOo.oOo.oOo mean, as printed by ssh-keygen2?*

A: The manpage calls it a "progress indicator." We think it's an ASCII representation of a sine wave. Or the sound of a chattering gorilla. You can hide it with the *–q* flag.

12.2.3.3. ssh-agent and ssh-add

Q: *My ssh-agent isn't terminating after I log out.*

A: If you use the single-shell method to start an agent, this is normal. You must terminate the agent yourself, either manually (bleah) or by including appropriate lines in your shell configuration files. [6.3.2.1] If you use the subshell method, the agent automatically terminates when you log out (actually, when you exit the subshell). [6.3.2.2]

Q: *When I invoke ssh-add and type my passphrase, I get the error message "Could not open a connection to your authentication agent."*

A: Follow this debugging process:

a. Make sure you are running an *ssh-agent* process:

```
$ /usr/bin/ps -ef | grep ssh-agent
smith 22719     1  0 23:34:44 ?        0:00 ssh-agent
```

If not, you need to run an agent before *ssh-add* will work.

b. Check that the agent's environment variables are set:

```
$ env | grep SSH
SSH_AUTH_SOCK=/tmp/ssh-barrett/ssh-22719-agent
SSH_AGENT_PID=22720
```

If not, then you probably ran *ssh-agent* incorrectly, like this:

```
# Wrong!
$ ssh-agent
```

For the single-shell method, you must use *eval* with backquotes:

```
  $ eval `ssh-agent`
```

Or for the subshell method, you must instruct *ssh-agent* to invoke a shell:

```
$ ssh-agent $SHELL
```

c. Make sure the agent points to a valid socket:

```
$ ls -lF $SSH_AUTH_SOCK
prwx------    1 smith   0 May 14 23:37 /tmp/ssh-smith/ssh-22719-agent|
```

If not, your SSH_AUTH_SOCK variable might be pointing to an old socket from a previous invocation of *ssh-agent*, due to user error. Terminate and restart the agent properly.

12.2.3.4. Per-account authorization files

Q: My per-account server configuration isn't taking effect.

A: Check the following:

- You might be confused about which versions of SSH use which files:
  - SSH1, OpenSSH/1: *~/.ssh/authorized_keys*
  - SSH2: *~/.ssh2/authorization*
  - OpenSSH/2: *~/.ssh/authorized_keys2* (note this isn't in *~/.ssh2*)
- Remember that the *authorized_keys* and *authorized_keys2* files contains keys, whereas the SSH2 *authorization* file contains directives referring to other key files.
- You might have a typographical error in one of these files. Check the spelling of options, and remember to separate SSH1 *authorized_keys* options with commas, not whitespace. For example:

```
# correct
no-x11-forwarding,no-pty 1024 35 8697511247987525784866526224505...
```

```
# INCORRECT (will silently fail)
no-x11-forwarding no-pty 1024 35 8697511247987525784866526224505...
# ALSO INCORRECT (note the extra space after "no-x11-forwarding,")
no-x11-forwarding, no-pty 1024 35 8697511247987525784866526224505...
```

12.2.4. Server Problems

12.2.4.1. sshd_config, sshd2_config

Q: How do I get sshd to recognize a new configuration file?

A: You can terminate and restart *sshd*, but there's quicker way: send the "hangup" signal (SIGHUP) to *sshd* with *kill –HUP*.

Q: I changed the sshd config file and sent SIGHUP to the server. But it didn't seem to make any difference.

A: *sshd* may have been invoked with a command-line option that overrides that keyword. Command line options remain in force and take precedence over configuration file keywords. Try terminating and restarting *sshd*.

12.2.5. Client Problems

12.2.5.1. General client problems

Q: A feature of ssh or scp isn't working, but I'm sure I'm using it correctly.

A: The feature might have been disabled by a system administrator, either when the SSH software was compiled (Chapter 4) or during serverwide configuration (Chapter 5). Compile-time flags cannot be checked easily, but serverwide configurations are found in the files */etc/sshd_config* (SSH1, OpenSSH) or */etc/ssh2/sshd2_config* (SSH2). Ask your system administrator for assistance.

12.2.5.2. Client configuration file

Q: ssh or scp is behaving unexpectedly, using features I didn't request.

A: The program might be responding to keywords specified in your client configuration file. [7.1.3] Remember that multiple sections of the *config* file apply if multiple `Host` lines match the remote machine name you specified on the command line.

Q: My SSH1 .ssh/config file doesn't seem to work right.

A: Remember that after the first use of a "Host" directive in the *config* file, all statements are inside some `Host` block, because a `Host` block is only terminated by the start of another `Host` block. The *ssh1* manpage suggests that you put defaults at the end of the *config* file, which is correct; when looking up a directive in the *config* file, *ssh1* uses the first match it finds, so defaults should go after any `Host` blocks. But don't let your own indentation or whitespace fool you. The end of your file might look like:

```
# last Host block
Host server.example.com
 User linda

# defaults
User smith
```

You intend that the username for logging into *server.example.com* is "linda", and the default username for hosts not explicitly listed earlier is "smith". However, the line "User smith" is still inside the "Host server.example.com" block. And since there's an earlier `User` statement for *server.example.com*, "User smith" doesn't ever match anything, and *ssh* appears to ignore it. The right thing to do is this:

```
# last Host block
Host server.example.com
 User linda

# defaults
Host *
 User smith
```

Q: *My .ssh2/ssh2_config file doesn't seem to work right.*

A: See our answer to the previous question for SSH1. However, SSH2 has the opposite precedence rule: if multiple configurations match your target, then the *last*, not the first, prevails. Therefore your defaults go at the beginning of the file.

12.2.5.3. ssh

Q: *I want to suspend ssh with the escape sequence but I am running more than two levels of ssh (machine to machine to machine). How do I suspend an intermediate ssh?*

A: One method is to start each *ssh* with a different escape character; otherwise, the earliest *ssh* client in the chain interprets the escape character and suspends.

Or you can be clever. Remember that if you type the escape character twice, that's the meta-escape: it allows you to send the escape character itself, circumventing its usual special function. So, if you have several chained *ssh* sessions all using the default escape character ~, you can suspend the *n*th one by pressing the Return key, then *n* tildes, then `Control-Z`.

Q: *I ran an ssh command in the background on the command line, and it suspended itself, not running unless I "fg" it.*

A: Use the *–n* command-line option, which instructs *ssh* not to read from stdin (actually, it reopens stdin on */dev/null* instead of your terminal). Otherwise, the shell's job-control facility suspends the program if it reads from stdin while in the background.

Q: *ssh prints "Compression level must be from 1 (fast) to 9 (slow, best)" and exits.*

A: Your `CompressionLevel` is set to an illegal value for this host, probably in your *~/.ssh/config* file. It must be an integer between 1 and 9, inclusive. [7.4.11]

Q: *ssh prints "rsh not available" and exits.*

A: Your SSH connection attempt failed, and your client was configured to fall back to an *rsh* connection. [7.4.5.8] However, the server was compiled without *rsh* fallback support or with an invalid path to the *rsh* executable. [4.1.5.12]

If you didn't expect your SSH connection to fail, run the client in debug mode and look for the reason. Otherwise, the SSH server is just not set up to receive *rsh* connections.

Q: *ssh1 prints "Too many identity files specified (max 100)" and exits.*

A: SSH1 has a hardcoded limit of 100 identity files (private key files) per session. Either you ran an *ssh1* command line with over 100 *–i* options, or your configuration file *~/.ssh/config* has an entry with over 100 `IdentityFile` keywords. You should never see this message unless your SSH command lines and/or config files are being generated automatically by another application, and something in that application has run amok. (Or else you're doing something *really* funky.)

Q: *ssh1 prints "Cannot fork into background without a command to execute" and exits.*

A: You used the *–f* flag of *ssh1*, didn't you? This tells the client to put itself into the background as soon as authentication completes, and then execute whatever remote command you requested. But, you didn't provide a remote command. You typed something like:

```
# This is wrong
$ ssh1 -f server.example.com
```

The *–f* flag makes sense only when you give *ssh1* a command to run after it goes into the background:

```
$ ssh1 -f server.example.com /bin/who
```

If you just want the SSH session for port-forwarding purposes, you may not want to give a command. You have to give one anyway; the SSH1 protocol requires it. Use *sleep 100000*. Don't use an infinite loop like the shell command *while true; do false; done*. This gives you the same effect, but your remote shell will eat all the spare CPU time on the remote machine, annoying the sysadmin and shortening your account's life expectancy.

Q: *ssh1 prints "Hostname or username is longer than 255 characters" and exits.*

A: *ssh1* has a static limit of 255 characters for the name of a remote host or a remote account (username). You instructed *ssh1*, either on the command line or in your configuration file, to use a hostname or username that's longer than this limit.

Q: *ssh1 prints "No host key is known for <server name> and you have requested strict checking (or 'cannot confirm operation when running in batch mode')," and exits.*

A: The client can't find the server's host key in its known-hosts list, and it is configured not to add it automatically (or is running in batch mode and so can't prompt you about adding it). You must add it manually to your per-account or systemwide known-hosts files.

Q: *ssh1 prints "Selected cipher type ... not supported by server" and exits.*

A: You requested that *ssh1* use a particular encryption cipher, but the SSH1 server doesn't support it. Normally, the SSH1 client and server negotiate to determine which cipher to use, so you probably forced a particular cipher by providing the *–c* flag on the *ssh1* command line or by using the `Cipher` keyword in the configuration file. Either don't specify a cipher and let the client and server work it out, or select a different cipher.

Q: *ssh1 prints "channel_request_remote_forwarding: too many forwards" and exits.*

A: *ssh1* has a static limit of 100 forwardings per session, and you've requested more.

12.2.5.4. scp

Q: *scp printed an error message: "Write failed flushing stdout buffer. write stdout: Broken pipe." or "packet too long".*

A: Your shell startup file (e.g., *~/.cshrc, ~/.bashrc*), which is run when *scp* connects, might be writing a message on standard output. These interfere with the communication between the two *scp1* programs (or *scp2* and *sftp-server*). If you don't see any obvious output commands, look for *stty* or *tset* commands that might be printing something.

Either remove the offending statement from the startup file or suppress it for noninteractive sessions:

```
if ($?prompt) then
  echo 'Here is the message that screws up scp.'
endif
```

The latest versions of SSH2 have a new server configuration statement, `AllowCshrcSourcingWithSubsystems`, which should be set to `no` to prevent this problem.

Q: *scp printed an error message, "Not a regular file."*

A: Are you trying to copy a directory? Use the *–r* option for a recursive copy. Otherwise, you may be trying to copy a special file that it doesn't make sense to copy, such as a device node, socket, or named pipe. If you do an *ls –l* of the file in question and the first character in the file description is something other than "–" (for a regular file) or "d" (for a directory), this is probably what's happening. You didn't really want to copy that file, did you?

Q: *Why don't wildcards or shell variables work on the scp command line?*

A: Remember that wildcards and variables are expanded by the *local* shell first, not on the remote machine. This happens even before *scp* runs. So if you type:

```
$ scp server.example.com:a* .
```

the local shell attempts to find local files matching the pattern `server.example.com:a*`. This is probably not what you intended. You probably wanted files matching `a*` on *server.example.com* to be copied to the local machine.

Some shells, notably C shell and its derivatives, simply report "No match" and exit. Bourne shell and its derivatives (*sh*, *ksh*, *bash*), finding no match, will actually pass the string `server.example.com:a*` to the server as you'd hoped.

Similarly, if you want to copy your remote mail file to the local machine, the command:

```
$ scp server.example.com:$MAIL .
```

might not do what you intend. $MAIL is expanded locally before scp executes. Unless (by coincidence) $MAIL is the same on the local and remote machines, the command won't behave as expected.

Don't rely on shell quirks and coincidences to get your work done. Instead, escape your wildcards and variables so the local shell won't attempt to expand them:

```
$ scp server.example.com:a\* .
$ scp 'server.example.com:$MAIL' .
```

See also Appendix A for specifics on *scp2*'s regular expressions.

Q: I used scp to copy a file from the local machine to a remote machine. It ran without errors. But when I logged into the remote machine, the file wasn't there!

A: By any chance, did you omit a colon? Suppose you want to copy the file *myfile* from the local machine to *server.example.com*. A correct command is:

```
$ scp myfile server.example.com:
```

but if you forget the final colon:

```
# This is wrong!
$ scp myfile server.example.com
```

myfile gets copied locally to a file called "server.example.com". Check for such a file on the local machine.

Q: How can I give somebody access to my account by scp to copy files but not give full login permissions?

A: Bad idea. Even if you can limit the access to *scp*, this doesn't protect your account. Your friend could run:

```
$ scp evil_authorized_keys you@your.host:.ssh/authorized_keys
```

Oops, your friend has just replaced your *authorized_keys* file, giving himself full login permissions. Maybe you can accomplish what you want with a clever forced command, limiting the set of programs your friend may run in your account. [8.2.4.3]

Q: scp –p preserves file timestamps and modes. Can it preserve file ownership?

A: No. Ownership of remote files is determined by SSH authentication. Suppose user smith has accounts on local computer *L* and remote computer *R*. If the local smith copies a file by *scp* to the remote smith account, authenticating by SSH, then the remote file is owned by the *remote* smith. If you want the file to be owned by a different remote user, *scp* must authenticate as that different user. *scp* has no other knowledge of users and uids, and besides, only root can change file ownership (on most modern Unix variants, anyway).

Q: OK, scp -p doesn't preserve file ownership information. But I am the superuser, and I'm trying to copy a directory hierarchy between machines (scp -r) and the files have a variety of owners. How can I preserve the ownership information in the copies?

A: Don't use *scp* for this purpose. Use *tar* and pipe it through *ssh*. From the local machine, type:

```
# tar cpf - local_dir | (ssh remote_machine "cd remote_dir; tar xpf -")
```

12.2.5.5. sftp2

Q: sftp2 reports "Cipher <name> is not supported. Connection lost."

A: Internally, *sftp2* invokes an *ssh2* command to contact *sftp-server*. [3.8.2] It searches the user's PATH to locate the *ssh2* executable rather than a hard-coded location. If you have more than one version of SSH2 installed on your system, *sftp2* might invoke the wrong *ssh2* program. This can produce the error message shown.

For example, suppose you have both SSH2 and F-Secure SSH2 installed. SSH2 is installed in the usual place, under */usr/local*, whereas F-Secure is installed under */usr/local/f-secure*. You ordinarily use SSH2, so */usr/local/bin* is in your PATH, but */usr/local/f-secure* isn't. You decide to use the F-Secure version of *scp2* because you want the CAST-128 cipher, which SSH2 doesn't include. First, you confirm that the SSH server in question supports CAST-128:

```
$ /usr/local/f-secure/bin/ssh2 -v -c cast server
  ...
debug: c_to_s: cipher cast128-cbc, mac hmac-sha1, compression none
debug: s_to_c: cipher cast128-cbc, mac hmac-sha1, compression none
```

Satisfied, you try *scp2* and get this:

```
$ /usr/local/f-secure/bin/scp2 -c cast foo server:bar
FATAL: ssh2: Cipher cast is not supported.
Connection lost.
```

scp2 is running the wrong copy of *ssh2* from */usr/local/bin/ssh2*, rather than */usr/local/f-secure/bin/ssh2*. To fix this, simply put */usr/local/f-secure/bin* earlier in your PATH than */usr/local/bin*, or specify the alternative location of *ssh2* with *scp2 –S*.

The same problem can occur in other situations where SSH programs run other ones. We have run afoul of it using hostbased authentication with both 2.1.0 and 2.2.0 installed. The later *ssh2* ran the earlier *ssh-signer2* program, and the client/signer protocol had changed, causing it to hang.

Q: sftp2 reports "ssh_packet_wrapper_input: invalid packet received."

A: Although this error appears mysterious, its cause is mundane. A command in the remote account's shell startup file is printing something to standard output, even though stdout isn't a terminal in this case, and *sftp2* is trying to interpret this unexpected output as part of the SFTP packet protocol. It fails and dies.

You see, *sshd* uses the shell to start the *sftp-server* subsystem. The user's shell startup file prints something, which the SFTP client tries to interpret as an SFTP protocol packet. This fails, and the client exits with the error message; the first field in a packet is the length field, which is why it's always that message.

To fix this problem, be sure your shell startup file doesn't print anything unless it's running interactively. *tcsh*, for example, sets the variable "$interactive" if stdin is a terminal. This problem has been addressed in SSH-2.2.0 with the `AllowCshrcSourcingWithSubsystems` flag, which defaults to `no`, instructing the shell not to run the user's startup file. [5.7.1]

12.2.5.6. Port forwarding

Q: I'm trying to do port forwarding, but ssh complains: "bind: Address already in use."

A: The port you're trying to forward is already being used by another program on the listening side (the local host if it's a *–L* forwarding or the remote host if it's a *–R*). Try using the *netstat –a* command, available on most Unix implementations and some Windows platforms. If you see an entry for your port in the LISTEN state, you know that something else is using that port. Check to see whether you've inadvertently left another *ssh* command running that's forwarding the same port. Otherwise, just choose another, unused port to forward.

This problem can occur when there doesn't appear to be any other program using your port, especially if you've been experimenting with the forwarding feature and have repeatedly used the same *ssh* to forward the same port. If the last one of these died unexpectedly (you interrupted it, or it crashed, or the connection was forcibly closed from the other side, etc.), the local TCP socket may have been left in the TIME_WAIT state (you may see this if you used the *netstat* program as described earlier). When this happens, you have to wait a few minutes for the socket to time out of this state and become free for use again. Of course, you can just choose another port number if you're impatient.

Q: How do I secure FTP with port forwarding?

A: This is a complex topic. [11.2] FTP has two types of TCP connections, control and data. The control connection carries your login name, password, and FTP commands; it is on TCP port 21 and can be forwarded by the standard method. In two windows, run:

```
$ ssh -L2001:name.of.server.com:21 name.of.server.com
$ ftp localhost 2001
```

Your FTP client probably needs to run in passive mode (execute the **passive** command). FTP data connections carry the files being transferred. These connections occur on randomly selected TCP ports and can't be forwarded in general, unless you enjoy pain. If firewalls or NAT (network address translation) are involved, you may need additional steps (or it may not be possible).

Q: X forwarding isn't working.

A: Use *ssh –v*, and see if the output points out an obvious problem. If not, check the following:

- Make sure you have X working before using SSH. Try running a simple X client such as *xlogo* or *xterm* first. Your local DISPLAY variable must be set, or SSH doesn't attempt X forwarding.
- X forwarding must be turned on in the client and server, and not disallowed by the target account (that is, with **no-X11-forwarding** in the *authorized_keys* file).
- *sshd* must be able to find the *xauth* program to run it on the remote side. If it can't, this should show up when running *ssh -v*. You can fix this on the server side with the **XAuthLocation** directive (SSH1, OpenSSH), or by setting a PATH (that contains *xauth*) in your remote shell startup file.
- Don't set the DISPLAY variable yourself on the remote side. *sshd* automatically sets this value correctly for the forwarding session. If you have commands in your login or shell startup files that unconditionally set DISPLAY, change the code to set it only if X forwarding isn't in use.
- OpenSSH sets the remote XAUTHORITY variable as well, placing the *xauth* credentials file under */tmp*. Make sure you haven't overridden this setting, which should look like:

  ```
  $ echo $XAUTHORITY
  /tmp/ssh-maPK4047/cookies
  ```

  Some flavors of Unix actually have code in the standard shell startup files (e.g., */etc/bashrc, /etc/csh.login*) that unconditionally sets XAUTHORITY to *~/.Xauthority*. If that's the problem, you must ask the sysadmin to fix it; the startup file should set XAUTHORITY only if the variable is unset.
- If you are using an SSH startup file (*/etc/sshrc* or *~/.ssh/rc*), *sshd* doesn't run *xauth* for you on the remote side to add the proxy key; one of these startup files must do it, receiving the proxy key type and data on standard input from *sshd*.

12.3. Other SSH Resources

If we haven't answered your questions in this chapter, try the following good sources of help available on the Internet.

12.3.1. Web Sites

The first place to turn when you run into trouble is the SSH FAQ, where many answers to common questions may be found:

http://www.employees.org/~satch/ssh/faq/

The SSH home page, maintained by SSH Communications Security, is also a good resource of general information and links to related content:

http://www.ssh.com/

as is the Secure Shell Community Site:

http://www.ssh.org/

A database of compilation errors for the SSH2 product is found at:

http://www.ssh.org/support.html

Information on OpenSSH can be found at:

http://www.openssh.com/

And of course, check out this book's web sites:

http://www.oreilly.com/catalog/sshtdg/
http://www.snailbook.com/

12.3.2. Usenet Newsgroups

On Usenet, the newsgroup *comp.security.ssh* discusses technical issues about SSH. If you don't have Usenet access, you can read and search for its articles on the Web at Deja.com:

http://www.deja.com/usenet/

or any other site that archives Usenet posts.

12.3.3. Mailing Lists

If you are a software developer interested in contributing to SSH or working with beta software, or if you want to discuss the installation or internals of SSH applications, consider joining the SSH mailing list. To subscribe, send an email message to *majordomo@clinet.fi* as follows:

```
To: majordomo@clinet.fi
Subject: (blank)
subscribe ssh
```

Please note that this list is for technical discussion, not for asking "Where can I find SSH for the Commodore 64?" Before subscribing, read the latest messages in the SSH mailing list archive to see if the list is appropriate for you:

http://www.cs.hut.fi/ssh-archive/

Before posting a troubleshooting question on this mailing list, run the SSH client and server in debug or verbose mode and include the full text of the debug messages in your note.

If you aren't interested in developing or testing SSH applications but want to receive major announcements about SSH, join the *ssh-announce* mailing list.

```
To: majordomo@clinet.fi
Subject: (blank)
subscribe ssh-announce
```

12.4. Reporting Bugs

If you believe that you've discovered a bug in an SSH implementation:

1. First check if the bug has already been reported, if there's a way to do this.
2. Report the bug to the vendor, including full details of your hardware and software configuration.

For SSH1 and SSH2, bugs should be reported by email to *ssh-support@ssh.com*. Additionally, SSH Communication Security has a web form for submitting SSH2 bug reports:

http://www.ssh.com/support/ssh/

For OpenSSH, bug reporting instructions are found on the web site:

http://www.openssh.com/

along with FAQs and subscription information for mailing lists.

F-Secure Corporation has support pages at:

http://www.f-secure.com/support/ssh/

and accepts bug reports at *F-Secure-SSH-Support@f-secure.com*.

In this chapter:
- *Common Features*
- *Covered Products*
- *Table of Products*
- *Other SSH-Related Products*

13
Overview of Other Implementations

SSH isn't just a Unix technology. It's been implemented also for Windows, Macintosh, Amiga, OS/2, VMS, BeOS, PalmOS, Windows CE, and Java. Some programs are original, finished products, and others are ports of SSH1 or SSH2 undertaken by volunteers and in various stages of completion.

For the remainder of this book, we cover several robust implementations of SSH for Windows (95, 98, NT, 2000) and the Macintosh. These are complete, usable products, in our opinions. We also provide pointers to other implementations if you wish to experiment with them.

We have set up a web page pointing to all SSH-related products that we know. From this book's catalog page:

http://www.oreilly.com/catalog/sshtdg/

follow the link labeled Authors' Online Resources, or visit us directly at:

http://www.snailbook.com/

Also check out this third-party page documenting free SSH implementations:

http://www.freessh.org/

13.1. Common Features

Every SSH implementation has a different set of features, but they all have one thing in common: a client program for logging into remote systems securely. Some clients are command-line based, and others operate like graphical terminal emulators, opening windows with dozens of configurable settings.

The remaining features vary widely across implementations. Secure file copy (*scp* and *sftp*), remote batch command execution, SSH servers, SSH agents, and particular authentication and encryption algorithms are found in only some of the products.

Nearly all implementations include a generator of public and private keys. For example, ports of SSH1/SSH2 have *ssh-keygen*, F-Secure SSH Client has Keygen Wizard, and SecureCRT has Key Generation Wizard. NiftyTelnet SSH for the Macintosh is a notable exception: it can't generate keys, but it accepts keys generated by other programs in the standard SSH-1 format.

13.2. Covered Products

For Windows, we cover:

- F-Secure SSH Client, a commercial SSH client by F-Secure Corporation, supporting SSH-1 and SSH-2 (a Macintosh version is also available)
- SecureCRT, a commercial SSH client by Van Dyke Technologies, supporting SSH-1 and SSH-2
- A Windows port of SSH1 by Sergey Okhapkin

For the Macintosh, we cover:

- NiftyTelnet SSH, a free SSH client by Jonas Walldén, implemented on top of the freeware Telnet client, NiftyTelnet

13.3. Table of Products

Unfortunately we can't cover every SSH implementation, but here are summaries to aid your explorations. The following tables list the major features of every SSH implementation we have encountered, sorted by platform, excluding the Unix products discussed in the previous part of the book (SSH1, SSH2, OpenSSH, F-Secure SSH). The meanings of the entries are described in this first table:

Feature	Meaning
Name	The product name. If followed by "(recommended)," we have evaluated the program and recommend its use. If a product isn't listed as recommended, it might still be good, but we didn't evaluate it thoroughly.
Platform	Does it run on Windows, Macintosh, Unix, etc.? We don't list specific Windows variants (NT, 98, 2000, etc.) because we couldn't test them all. Contact the vendor for details.
Version	What is the most recent version number at press time?

Feature	Meaning
License or distribution	How may this program be distributed? We provide only a summary of the licensing information; see the product documentation for full information.
Protocol	Does it implement SSH-1, SSH-2, or both?
Remote logins	Can the product open a login shell to a remote machine? We write either "ssh" to denote a command-line interface à la SSH1 or SSH2, or "terminal program" to denote a graphical interface
Remote commands	Can it invoke individual commands on a remote SSH server machine, in the manner of the *ssh* client (i.e., providing a command string as a final argument)?
File transfer	What program, if any, transmits files securely between machines?
Server	Does it include an SSH server?
Authentication	What forms of authentication are supported?
Key generation	Can it generate private/public key pairs?
Agent	Does it include an SSH agent?
Forwarding	Does it support port forwarding, X forwarding, both, or neither?
Notes	General information and supporting details.
Contact	URL to locate the software.

The remainder of this section is an extended table summarizing the many SSH implementations.

Name	AmigaSSH	SSH	JavaSSH	Java Telnet SSH Plug-in
Platform	Amiga	BeOS	Java	Java
Version	3.15	1.2.26-beos	20/07/1998	2.0 RC3
License or distribution	GNU Public License	Freeware	Freely distributable	GNU Public License
Protocol	SSH-1	SSH-1	SSH-1	SSH-1
Remote logins	Terminal program	*ssh*	Terminal program	Terminal program
Remote commands	No	*ssh*	No	No
File transfer	No	*scp*	No	No
Server	No	No	No	No
Authentication	Password, public-key	Password, public-key, trusted-host	Password, public-key	Password
Key generation	*ssh-keygen*	*ssh-keygen*	?	No
Agent	No	?	No	No
Forwarding	No	Port, X	No	No
Notes	Integration of NapsaTerm with SSH1 1.2.26; requires 68020 or greater CPU	Port of SSH1 1.2.26.	Requires Java AWT 1.1	Part of a Java Telnet applet
Contact	*http://www.lysator.liu.se/~lilja/amigassh/*	*http://www.bebits.com/app/703*	*http://www.cl.cam.ac.uk/~fapp2/software/java-ssh/*	*http://www.mud.de/se/jta/doc/plugins/SSH.html*

Name	MindTerm *(recommended)*	BetterTelnet	F-Secure SSH Client	NiftyTelnet SSH *(recommended)*
Platform	Java	Macintosh	Macintosh	Macintosh
Version	1.1	2.0fc1	2.1	1.1 R3
License or distribution	GNU Public License	GNU Public License	Commercial	Freeware
Protocol	SSH-1	See Notes	SSH-1, SSH-2	SSH-1
Remote logins	Terminal program	See Notes	Terminal program	Terminal program
Remote commands	Yes	See Notes	No	No
File transfer	*scp*, tunneled *ftp*	See Notes	Tunneled *ftp*	Graphical *scp*
Server	No	See Notes	No	No
Authentication	Password, public-key, trusted-host, TIS, sdi-token	See Notes	Password, public-key	public-key
Key generation	Yes	See Notes	Yes	No
Agent	No	See Notes	No	No (but can remember your passphrase)
Forwarding	Port, X	See Notes	Port, X	No
Notes	Can work as a standalone program or an applet; tested on many operating systems	SSH support is absent at press time (due to former export restrictions) but is due back soon	Windows version also available	Minimal but useful
Contact	*http://www.mindbright.se/*	*http://www.cstone.net/~rbraun/mac/telnet/*	*http://www.f-secure.com/*	*http://www.lysator.liu.se/~jonasw/freeware/niftyssh/*

Name	SSHDOS	SSHOS2	Top Gun SSH	lsh
Platform	MS-DOS	OS/2	PalmOS	Unix
Version	0.4	v03	1.2	1.0.3
License or distribution	GNU Public License	?	Freely distributable	GNU Public License
Protocol	SSH-1	SSH-1	SSH-1	SSH-2
Remote logins	Yes	*ssh*, terminal program	Terminal program	Yes
Remote commands	No	*ssh*	No	Yes
File transfer	No	*scp*	No	No
Server	No	Unfinished	No	Yes
Authentication	Password	Password, public-key, trusted-host	Password	Password, public-key, SRP
Key generation	No	Yes	No	Yes
Agent	No	Yes	No	No
Forwarding	No	Port, X	No	Port
Notes	Minimal; runs on low-end machines; based on PuTTY and SSH1 1.2.27	Based on SSH1 1.2.13	Based on Top Gun Telnet for the Palm Pilot	A promising work in progress, but not secure yet
Contact	*http://www.vein.hu/~nagyd/*	*ftp://ftp.cs.hut.fi/pub/ssh/old/os2/*	*http://www.isaac.cs.berkeley.edu/pilot/*	*http://www.net.lut.ac.uk/psst/*

Name	ossh	FISH	sshexec.com	AppGate
Platform	Unix	VMS	VMS	Windows, Unix, Macintosh
Version	1.5.6	0.6-1	5alpha1	
License or distribution	BSD License	Freely distributable	Freeware	Commercial
Protocol	SSH-1	SSH-1	SSH-1	
Remote logins	*ssh*	Yes	N/A	
Remote commands	*ssh*	Yes	N/A	
File transfer	*scp*	No	No	
Server	*sshd*	No	Yes	
Authentication	Password, public-key, trusted-host	Password, public-key, trusted-host, TIS (untested)	Password public-key	
Key generation	*ssh-keygen*	Yes	Yes	
Agent	*ssh-agent*	No	No	
Forwarding	Port, X	No	X	
Notes	Port of SSH1 1.2.12		A VMS server: a work in progress; not for novices	
Contact	*ftp://ftp.nada.kth.se/pub/krypto/ossh/*	*http://www.free.lp.se/fish/*	*http://www.er6.eng.ohio-state.edu/~jonesd/ssh/*	*http://www.appgate.com/*

Name	Chaffee Port	Free FiSSH	F-Secure SSH Client *(recommended)*	Mathur Port
Platform	Windows	Windows NT, 2000	Windows	Windows
Version	1.2.14a	?	4.1	1.2.22-Win32-beta1
License or distribution	?	Free for noncommercial use	Commercial	Some GNU Public License, some other
Protocol	SSH-1	SSH-1	SSH-1, SSH-2	SSH-1
Remote logins	*ssh*	Terminal program	Terminal program and ssh2 command-line client	*ssh*
Remote commands	*ssh*	?	*ssh2*	*ssh*
File transfer	*scp*	?	*scp2*, *sftp2*, graphical *sftp* client	*scp*
Server	No	?	No	*sshd*
Authentication	Password, public-key	?	Password, public-key	Password, public-key
Key generation	*ssh-keygen*	?	Yes	*ssh-keygen*
Agent	No	?	No	?
Forwarding	Port, X	?	Port, X	X, port
Notes	Undocumented; based on SSH1 1.2.14	Unstable, in our experience (hence much missing information in this entry)	Also available for Macintosh	Barely documented alpha software, from 1998; port of SSH1 1.2.22 with *cygnus dll*.
Contact	*http://bmrc.berkeley.edu/people/chaffee/winntutil.html*, *ftp://bmrc.berkeley.edu/pub/winnt/devel/ssh1.2.14a.exe*	*http://www.massconfusion.com/ssh/*	*http://www.f-secure.com/*	*ftp://ftp.cs.hut.fi/pub/ssh/contrib/*

Name	Metro State SSH (MSSH)	Okhapkin Port	PenguiNet	PuTTY *(recommended)*
Platform	Windows	Windows	Windows	Windows
Version	?	1.2.26, 1.2.27, 2.0.13	1.05	Beta 0.48
License or distribution	GNU Public License	Same as SSH1, SSH2	Shareware	Freely distributable
Protocol	SSH-1	SSH-1, SSH-2	SSH-1	SSH-1
Remote logins	See Notes	*ssh*	Terminal program	Terminal program
Remote commands	See Notes	*ssh*	No	No
File transfer	See Notes	*scp*	No	*scp*
Server	No	sshd (Windows NT only)	No	No
Authentication	Password	Password, public-key, trusted-host	Password, public-key, Rhosts, RhostsRSA	Password, TIS
Key generation	No	*ssh-keygen*	Yes	No
Agent	No	Nonfunctional	No	No
Forwarding	Port	Port, X	No	No
Notes	Does only TCP port forwarding, with specific support for Telnet and email connections	Includes two SSH1 ports and one SSH2 port		Popular; notable for including *scp*
Contact	*http://csi.mscd.edu/MSSH/*	*http://miracle.geol.msu.ru/sos/*	*http://www.siliconcircus.com/*	*http://www.chiark.greenend.org.uk/~sgtatham/putty/*

Name	SSH Secure Shell *(recommended)*	SecureCRT *(recommended)*	SecureFX *(recommended)*	SecureKoalaTerm
Platform	Windows	Windows	Windows	Windows
Version	2.1.0	3.1.2	1.0	1.0
License or distribution	Free for noncommercial use	Commercial	Commercial	Shareware
Protocol	SSH-2	SSH-1, SSH-2	SSH-2	SSH-1, SSH-2
Remote logins	Terminal program	Terminal program	No	Terminal emulator
Remote commands	No	No	No	No
File transfer	Graphical *scp2*	Zmodem (secure)	FTP (secure)	Zmodem (secure)
Server	No	No	No	No
Authentication	Password, public-key	Password, public-key, TIS	Password, public-key	Password, public-key
Key generation	Yes	RSA, DSA	Yes	Yes
Agent	No	No	No	No
Forwarding	Port, X	Port, X	No	No
Notes	This recent product could bring SSH2 to the masses; the scp2 client is particularly nice, emulating the Windows Explorer, permitting remote files to be dragged securely between machines; extensive documentation; SSH2 server is a separate product	A solid performer; our favorite of the commercial Windows clients	A secure, graphical FTP client for SSH2	Graphical terminal emulator with SSH support
Contact	*http://www.ssh.com/*	*http://www.vandyke.com/*	*http://www.vandyke.com/*	*http://www.midasoft.com/*

Name	therapy Port	TTSSH *(recommended)*	Zoc	sshCE
Platform	Windows	Windows	Windows	Windows CE
Version	0.2	1.5.1	3.14	1.00.40
License or distribution	See Notes	Freely distributable	Commercial	Freeware
Protocol	See Notes	SSH-1	SSH-1	SSH-1
Remote logins	See Notes	Terminal program	Terminal program	Terminal program
Remote commands	See Notes	No	No	No
File transfer	See Notes	Kermit, Xmodem, Zmodem, B-Plus, Quick-VAN (all secure)	Kermit, Ymodem, Zmodem	No
Server	See Notes	No	No	No
Authentication	See Notes	Password, public-key, trusted-host, TIS	Password	Password
Key generation	See Notes	No	No	No
Agent	See Notes	No	No	No
Forwarding	See Notes	Port, X	No	No
Notes	Unsupported and no longer in development; based on SSH1 1.2.20	Popular; an SSH extension to Teraterm Pro, a free terminal program	Full-featured terminal program	Currently this is beta software
Contact	*http://guardian.htu.tuwien.ac.at/therapy/ssh/*	*http://www.zip.com.au/~roca/ttssh.html*	*http://www.emtec.com/zoc/*	*http://www.movsoftware.com/sshce.htm*

13.4. Other SSH-Related Products

SecPanel is a graphical, point-and-click manager for SSH client connections; it's written in the programming language *tcl*:

> *http://www2.wiwi.uni-marburg.de/~leich/soft/secpanel/*

ssh.el is an Emacs interface for *ssh* client connections:

> *http://munitions.vipul.net/software/network/ssh/ssh.el*

ssh-keyscan is a replacement for *ssh-make-known-hosts*, purportedly much faster: [4.1.6]

> *ftp://cag.lcs.mit.edu/pub/dm/source/ssh-keyscan-0.3b.tar.gz*

In this chapter:
- *Obtaining and Installing Clients*
- *Client Use*
- *Obtaining and Installing the Server*
- *Troubleshooting*
- *Summary*

14

SSH1 Port by Sergey Okhapkin (Windows)

Numerous programmers have attempted to port SSH1 to Windows. Most ports that we've seen are unfinished, no longer in development, or distributed without source code. The best ports we've found are by Sergey Okhapkin, so we cover his work in this chapter. We'll call the software *Okhapkin's SSH1* to distinguish it from SSH1.

Okhapkin's software works fine, but installation is difficult. For this reason we recommend it for advanced Windows users only. Ideally you should be familiar with MS-DOS environment variables, *bzip2* compressed files, *tar* archives, the Windows NT Resource Kit, and most of all, installing applications manually on your PC. If these are alien concepts, consider a different SSH program for Windows. On the other hand, if you persevere through the installation, you get a powerful, command line-based SSH for free.

Okhapkin has done separate ports of SSH1 Versions 1.2.26 and 1.2.27, and SSH2 Version 2.0.13. We cover the 1.2.26 port since we had the least trouble installing it.

14.1. Obtaining and Installing Clients

Okhapkin's SSH1 is found on the author's web site in Russia:

> *http://miracle.geol.msu.ru/sos/*

The software is distributed in a format that is probably unfamiliar to most Windows users. First, the software has been packed into a *tar* archive, which is a common file format on Unix systems. Then the archive has been compressed with *bzip2*, a compression utility popular among Linux users. For example, the "bzipped" *tar* archive for Okhapkin's Version 1.2.26 port is *ssh-1.2.26-cygwinb20.tar.bz2*.

In this version of Okhapkin's SSH1, the clients (*ssh1, scp1*) run under 32-bit Windows systems; we installed them under Windows 95. The server (*sshd*) runs only on Windows NT.

For the conservative installation we describe, you need 40 MB of disk space to hold both SSH and the Cygwin support software and another 20 MB during installation, so make sure to have 60 MB free. SSH itself requires only 1 MB, so if you want to save space after the installation, you can delete most of Cygwin.

14.1.1. Prepare Folders

Before you start installing software, create the following folders on your C: drive:

```
C:\usr
C:\usr\local
C:\usr\local\bin
C:\etc
C:\home
C:\home\.ssh                    Note the period!
C:\tmp
```

To create *C:\home\.ssh* you must use the DOS *mkdir* command. Windows doesn't create folders with names beginning with a period.

```
C:\> mkdir C:\home\.ssh
```

14.1.2. Prepare autoexec.bat

You need to make two changes to your *autoexec.bat* file. First, add the folder *C:\usr\local\bin* to your MS-DOS search path. This is done by appending the following line to the file:

```
PATH=%PATH%;C:\usr\local\bin;C:\Cygwin\bin
```

Next, set the environment variable CYGWIN to have the value "tty":

```
SET CYGWIN=tty
```

This is required so the *ssh1* client can run interactively. Finally, save *autoexec.bat*, open an MS-DOS command line, and apply your changes:

```
C:\> C:\autoexec
```

14.1.3. Create a Password File

On Unix, the file */etc/passwd* contains login names, passwords, and other information about users. You must create a similar file on the PC to satisfy Okhapkin's SSH1 clients, because they need a login name to operate.

In the folder *C:\etc* you created earlier, create a one-line file called *passwd*. The line has seven fields, separated by colons:

1. A login name of your choice, which can be a string of letters and digits.
2. An asterisk.
3. An integer greater than 0.
4. An integer greater than 0.
5. Your full name.
6. The folder */home*, where your SSH folder is created. Note the direction of the slash; it's not the MS-DOS folder separator, but the slash on the question-mark key.
7. The program */command.com*. Again, note the slash.

This is the format of a *passwd* entry on Unix. For Okhapkin's SSH1, only fields 1 and 6 have any effect. The rest contain reasonable values should they ever be needed. Here's an example:

```
smith:*:500:50:Amy Smith:/home:/command.com
```

14.1.4. Install Cygwin

Cygwin is a wonderful collection of command-line programs. They are ports of GNU software (*http://www.gnu.org*) that run on Windows thanks to a library of code, the Cygwin DLL known as *cygwin1.dll*. Okhapkin's SSH1 requires this DLL, so after you install Cygwin, you may delete most of the other files. However, the whole Cygwin distribution is so useful we hope you'll keep it. The software is available from:

http://sourceware.cygnus.com/cygwin/

Install the binary release: the source code is unneeded for our purposes. The official download and installation can take quite some time, so you might consider downloading only *cygwin1.dll* and not the many accompanying programs. At press time, it is located on the Cygwin mirror machines (reachable from the URL above) in the */pub/cygwin/latest/cygwin* folder. The distribution is in gzipped *tar* format (*.tar.gz* filename suffix), which WinZip for Windows can unpack. Copy *cygwin1.dll* to the folder *C:\usr\local\bin* you created earlier.

14.1.5. Install bzip2

bzip2 is a program for compressing and uncompressing files. A Windows version is available from:

http://sourceware.cygnus.com/bzip2/

Download the program to the folder *C:\usr\local\bin.* The program is ready to run without any installation. Its name at press time is *bzip2095d_win32.exe,* but this could change as future revisions are released.

Rename the *bzip2* executable to *bzip2.exe*:

```
C:\> cd \usr\local\bin
C:\usr\local\bin> rename bzip2095d_win32.exe bzip2.exe
```

14.1.6. Install Okhapkin's SSH1

Download Okhapkin's SSH1 Version 1.2.26 from:

http://miracle.geol.msu.ru/sos/

The filename is *ssh-1.2.26-cygwinb20.tar.bz2.* Because the name has multiple periods, your download software might automatically rename the file, eliminating all periods but the last, e.g., *ssh-1_2_26-cygwinb20_tar.bz2.*

Uncompress the file with *bzip2* to produce a *tar* file:

```
C:\temp> bzip2 -d ssh-1_2_26-cygwinb20_tar.bz2
```

Extract the tar file in the root of the C: drive. This unpacks files into *C:\usr*:

```
C:\temp> cd \
C:\> tar xvf \temp\ssh-1_2_26-cygwinb20_tar
```

If you skipped installing the full Cygwin package, [14.1.4] you might not have a *tar* program. The popular WinZip program for Windows is also capable of unpacking the *tar* file (after you run *bzip2*). Be sure to unpack it into the root of the C: drive.

The SSH1 client software is now installed.

14.1.7. Create a Key Pair

Before running Okhapkin's SSH1 clients, set up your SSH folder and generate a key pair for public-key authentication. This is done by running *ssh-keygen1*:

```
C:\> ssh-keygen1
```

In the *C:\home\.ssh* folder, *ssh-keygen1* creates a private key file *identity* and public key file *identity.pub.* The output looks something like the following. Ignore the line `w: not found` caused by a harmless difference between Unix and Windows.

```
Initializing random number generator...
w: not found
Generating p:  ....................++ (distance 352)
Generating q:  ..........++ (distance 140)
Computing the keys...
Testing the keys...
Key generation complete.
```

ssh-keygen1 then prompts for a file in which to save the key. Accept the default by pressing the Enter key:

```
Enter file in which to save the key (/home/.ssh/identity): [press Enter]
```

You are then prompted for a passphrase for your private key. Choose a good one and type it twice. It doesn't display onscreen.

```
Enter passphrase: ********
Enter the same passphrase again: ********
```

Your key pair is now generated and saved in the folder *C:\home\.ssh*. Copy your public key (*identity.pub*) to any SSH server machine where you want to connect, appending it to your remote *~/.ssh/authorized_keys* file. [2.4.3]

14.1.8. Log into a Remote Host with ssh1

You are ready to connect! Run the *ssh1* client, providing your remote login name. Suppose it is "smith" on the SSH server machine *server.example.com*:

```
C:\> ssh1 -l smith server.example.com
```

On your first attempt, *ssh1* adds the remote host to its known hosts database. [2.3.1] Answer **yes** and continue:

```
Host key not found from the list of known hosts.
Are you sure you want to continue connecting (yes/no)? yes
Host 'relativity.cs.umass.edu' added to the list of known hosts.
```

Finally, you're prompted for your passphrase:

```
Enter passphrase for RSA key 'You@YourPC': ********
```

If all goes well, you are now logged into the remote host via SSH. You can also run individual commands by SSH in the usual way, providing a command at the end of the line:

```
C:\> ssh1 -l smith server.example.com  /bin/who
```

14.1.9. Copy Files Securely with scp1

Secure copying should also be possible with *scp1*. Try copying a file to the remote machine:

```
C:\> scp1 C:\autoexec.bat smith@server.example.com:
```

14.2. Client Use

Okhapkin's SSH1 supports most of the SSH1 features found in Chapters 5 through 7 and 9. Just substitute *C:\home\.ssh* wherever you see *~/.ssh*. For example, you can create a client configuration file in *C:\home\.ssh\config*. [7.1.3]

Unfortunately, the SSH agent doesn't run under Windows, so none of the information in Chapter 6 about *ssh-agent1* and *ssh-add1* applies.

14.3. Obtaining and Installing the Server

Okhapkin's SSH1 server, *sshd*, can run under Windows NT installed as a service. It supports most server configuration features from Chapter 5 with the notable exception of public-key authentication. NT login authentication requires an NT username and password, and SSH can't get around this barrier to provide authentication by public key.

Like the clients, the server requires tricky installation. We'll assume you have already installed the Cygwin library and the SSH1 clients.

14.3.1. Obtain sshd

Sergey Okhapkin makes *sshd* 1.2.26 available on his site in two forms: as a precompiled executable or as source code diffs. We used the executable. Additionally, some other folks have created packages containing Sergey's executable and other support files. One of our favorites is:

http://www.gnac.com/techinfo/ssh_on_nt/

14.3.2. Obtain the NT Resource Kit

To run sshd as an NT service, you need three programs from the NT Resource Kit: *instsrv.exe*, *srvany.exe*, and *kill.exe*. The first two are utilities for turning ordinary programs into NT services. The third is for killing processes that can't be killed by the NT Task Manager.

14.3.3. Create an Administrative User

sshd will be invoked as an NT service running under an administrative user's account, so now let's create that administrative user. Run User Manager and do the following:

1. Create a local user called (say) root.
2. Make root a member of the Administrators group.
3. Under "Options/User Rights", check the checkbox "Show Advanced User Rights".

Now grant root the following rights:

- Act as part of the operating system
- Increase quotas

- Log on as a service
- Replace a process level token

Close the application, and you're ready to continue.

14.3.4. Install the Server

First copy the server program, *sshd.exe*, to a folder of your choice, say, *C:\Bin*. To complete the installation, you must convert *sshd* to an NT service run by your new administrative user and create some registry entries:

1. To install the server as an NT service, run the following command, assuming your administrative user is root, your NT Resource Kit programs are in *C:\reskit*, and your computer's name is *mypc*. (This is one command on a single line.)

```
C:\> C:\reskit\instsrv.exe SecureShellDaemon
C:\reskit\srvany.exe -a mypc\root -p root
```

2. Create the following registry entries. HKLM means HKEY_LOCAL_MACHINE:
   — In *HKLM\SYSTEM\CurrentControlSet\Services\SecureShellDaemon*, create a string value called "ObjectName" with the value "LocalSystem".
   — In *HKLM\SYSTEM\CurrentControlSet\Services\SecureShellDaemon\Parameters*, create a string value "Application" with the value "C:\\Bin\\sshd.exe", and a string value "AppParameters" with value "–f /etc/sshd_config".

14.3.5. Generate Host Key

Your server needs a host key to identify it uniquely to SSH clients. [5.4.1.1] Use the *ssh-keygen1* program to generate it and store the key pair in *C:\etc*:

```
C:\> ssh-keygen1 -f /etc/ssh_host_key -N "" -C ""
```

14.3.6. Edit sshd_config

Your server is almost ready to run. Now it's time to create a server-wide configuration file so *sshd* behaves according to your system's security policy. [5.3.1] On NT this file resides in *C:\etc\sshd_config*. For our recommended settings, see Chapter 10.

Be sure to indicate the correct locations of files, such as the host key. In Cygwin, "/" stands for the root of your boot drive. For example:

```
HostKey /etc/ssh_host_key
PidFile /etc/sshd.pid
RandomSeed /etc/ssh_random_seed
```

If you make changes in *sshd_config* while the SSH server is running, you must terminate and restart *sshd* for those changes to take effect. [14.3.9] Stopping and restarting the service with the Services control panel isn't sufficient.

14.3.7. Run the Server

To run *sshd*, open the Services control panel and look for the service SecureShell-Daemon. Select it, and click the Start button. That's it! In the NT Task Manager, the process shows up as *sshd.exe*.

14.3.8. Test the Server

If you've installed both *sshd* and *ssh1* on your local PC, try connecting to yourself:

```
C:\> ssh1 localhost
smith@127.0.0.1's password: ********
```

Otherwise, try connecting from another site:

```
$ ssh1 -l smith mypc.mydomain.org
smith@mypc.mydomain.org's password: ********
```

If the connection doesn't work, use *ssh1 –v* to print diagnostic output and figure out the problem.

14.3.9. Terminate the Server

To terminate an NT service, one normally uses the Stop button on the Services control panel. Unfortunately, this doesn't work for *sshd* under NT, even though the service appear to have stopped in the control panel. You need to kill the process manually. This can be done with the program *kill.exe* from the NT Resource Kit. Get the pid of *sshd.exe* from the NT Task Manager (suppose it is 392), and then type:

```
C:\> kill 392
```

14.4. Troubleshooting

If *ssh1* or *scp1* doesn't work as expected, use the *–v* (verbose) option so the client prints debugging messages as it operates. These messages may provide a clue to the problem. Now for some specific problems:

Q: *When I run ssh1, it says "You don't exist, go away!"*

A: You probably didn't create *C:\etc\passwd* as directed. Also, make sure that you don't put drive specifications (C:) in the *passwd* file because the colon will be treated incorrectly as a field separator.

Q: *I can't create a folder called ".ssh" or any other name beginning with a period.*

A: You can't do it with Windows's graphical interface. Use an MS-DOS shell and the *mkdir* command (*mkdir .ssh*).

Q: *ssh1 says "Could not create directory /home/.ssh".*

A: You forgot to create *C:\home.*

Q: *scp1 complains that it can't find ssh1.*

A: Is *C:\usr\local\bin* (or wherever you put *ssh1.exe*) in your MS-DOS PATH?

Q: *ssh-agent1 doesn't work. It prints* `Bad modes or owner for directory '/tmp/ssh-smith'` *and exits.*

A: You're right. The SSH agent doesn't run under Windows, as it requires Unix domain sockets.

Q: *I can't connect via sshd to my NT account that's in another domain.*

A: That's right, you can't. NT *sshd* lets you connect to local accounts only, i.e., in the domain of the local machine.*

Q: *I am still having problems.*

A: Visit some of these fine sites for additional help:

http://miracle.geol.msu.ru/sos/ssh-without-cygwin.html
http://marvin.criadvantage.com/caspian/Software/SSHD-NT/
http://www.gnac.com/techinfo/ssh_on_nt/
http://www.onlinemagic.com/~bgould/sshd.html
http://v.iki.fi/nt-ssh.html

14.5. Summary

Sergey Okhapkin's port of SSH1 Version 1.2.26 is, in our experience, the best Windows port of SSH1 available. It provides a working *ssh1*, *scp1*, and *ssh-keygen1*, sufficient for a typical SSH environment; and as a bonus, *sshd* is available as well. Be aware that 1.2.26 isn't the most recent version of SSH1, however, so it may have security issues that are fixed in later official versions.

---

* We've heard reports that NT *sshd* authenticates accounts from any trusted domain, but we haven't verified this.

15 SecureCRT (Windows)

In this chapter:
- *Obtaining and Installing*
- *Basic Client Use*
- *Key Management*
- *Advanced Client Use*
- *Forwarding*
- *Troubleshooting*
- *Summary*

SecureCRT, created by Van Dyke Technologies, is a commercial SSH client for Microsoft Windows 9x, NT, and 2000. It is structured as a terminal program; in fact, it is based on the terminal program CRT, another Van Dyke product. As a result, SecureCRT's terminal capabilities are quite configurable. It includes emulation of several terminal types, logins via Telnet as well as SSH, a scripting language, a keymap editor, SOCKS firewall support, chat features, and much more. We will focus only on its SSH capabilities, however.

SecureCRT supports both SSH-1 and SSH-2 in a single program. Other important features include port forwarding, X11 packet forwarding, and support for multiple SSH identities. It doesn't include an agent. Secure file copy is accomplished not by an *scp*-type program, but by ZModem, the old protocol for uploading and downloading files. (The remote machine must have ZModem installed.) If ZModem is used while you're logged in via SSH, these file transfers are secure.

We've organized this chapter to mirror the first part of the book covering Unix SSH implementations. When appropriate, we refer you to the earlier material for more detailed information.

Our discussion of SecureCRT is based on Version 3.1.2, dated September, 2000.

15.1. Obtaining and Installing

SecureCRT may be purchased and downloaded from Van Dyke Technologies:

> *http://www.vandyke.com/*

A free evaluation version is available, expiring 30 days after installation, so you can try before you buy. Installation is straightforward and glitch-free. The software is distributed as a single *.exe* file; simply run it to install the program. You will need a serial number and license key to unpack the archive, and these are provided by Van Dyke to each registered user. Follow the onscreen instructions, installing the software in any folder you like. We accepted the default choices.

15.2. Basic Client Use

Once you've installed the program, it's time to set up a new *session*, which is SecureCRT's word for a collection of settings.* Choose "Connect..." from the File menu, and in the window that appears, click the Properties button. This opens the Session Options window shown in Figure 15-1. Select Connection, and enter the information as shown in the figure. Choose password authentication for now. Click OK to close the window, and in the Connect window, click the Connect button. You should be prompted for your login password on the remote machine, and then you'll be logged in via SSH.

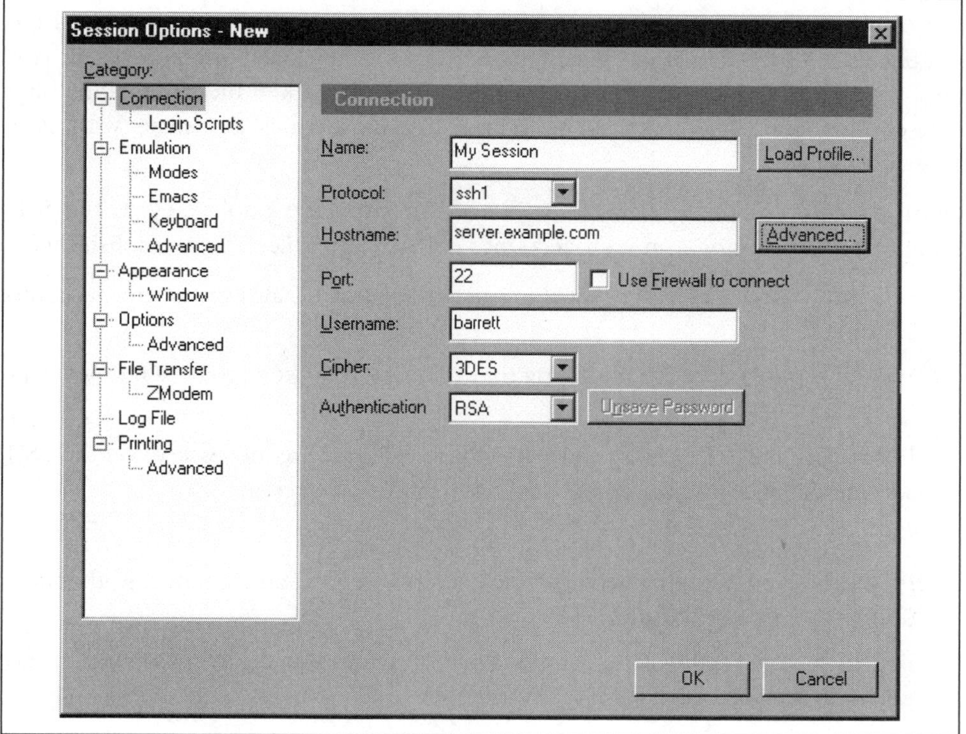

Figure 15-1. Secure CRT Session Options window

* "Session" is an unfortunate choice of term. Usually a session means an active SSH connection, not a static collection of settings.

Once you're logged in, the program operates just like a normal terminal program. SSH's end-to-end encryption is transparent to the user, as it should be.

15.3. Key Management

SecureCRT supports public-key authentication using RSA keys. It can generate keys with a built-in wizard or use existing SSH-1 and SSH-2 keys. It also distinguishes between two different types of SSH identities: *global* and *session-specific.*

15.3.1. RSA Key Generation Wizard

SecureCRT's RSA Key Generation Wizard creates key pairs for public-key authentication. The utility is run from the Session Options window, by clicking the Advanced button, the General tab, and then Create Identity File.

Operation is straightforward. All you need to supply is the passphrase, the number of bits in the key, and some random data by moving your mouse around the screen. RSA Key Generation Wizard then creates a key pair and stores it in two files. As with the Unix SSH implementations, the private key filename is anything you choose, and its corresponding public key filename is the same with *.pub* added.

Once your key pair is generated, you need to copy the public key to the SSH server machine, storing it in your account's authorization file. To accomplish this:

1. Log into to the SSH server machine using SecureCRT and password authentication.
2. View the public key file and copy the full text of the key to the Windows clipboard.
3. Install the public key (by pasting from the clipboard as necessary) on the SSH server machine in your remote account. [2.4.3]
4. Log out.
5. In the Session Options window, select Connection, and change Authentication from Password to RSA.
6. Log in again. SecureCRT prompts you for your public key passphrase, and you'll be logged in.

15.3.2. Using Multiple Identities

SecureCRT supports two types of SSH identities. Your global identity is the default for all SecureCRT sessions. You may override the default by using a session-specific identity that may differ (as the name implies) for each session you define.

In the Session Options window, click the Advanced button and the General tab. Under Identity Filename, you may select global and session-specific key files.

15.4. Advanced Client Use

SecureCRT lets you change settings for its SSH features and its terminal features. We will cover only the SSH-related ones. The others (and more details on the SSH features) are found in SecureCRT's online help.

SecureCRT calls a set of configuration parameters a session. It also distinguishes between *session options* that affect only the current session and *global options* that affect all sessions.

You can change session options before starting an SSH connection or while you are connected. Some options can't be changed while connected, naturally, such as the name of the remote SSH server machine. View the Session Options window (Figure 15-1) by selecting Session Options from the Options menu or clicking the Properties button on the button bar.

15.4.1. Mandatory Fields

To establish any SSH connection, you must fill in all the Connection fields in the Session Options window. These include:

Name
: A memorable name for your collection of settings. This can be anything, but it defaults to the name of the SSH server.

Protocol
: Either SSH-1 or SSH-2.

Hostname
: The name of the remote SSH server machine to which you want to connect.

Port
: The TCP port for SSH connections. Virtually all SSH clients and servers operate on port 22. Unless you plan to connect to a nonstandard SSH server, you won't need to change this. [7.4.4.1]

Username
: Your username on the remote SSH server machine. If you're using public key (RSA) authentication, this username must belong to an account that contains your public key.

Cipher
: The encryption algorithm to be used. Unless you have strong feelings about ciphers, use the default (3DES).

Authentication
How you identify yourself to the SSH server. This can be password authentication (using your remote login password), RSA authentication (public key), or TIS. [15.4.3] Trusted-host authentication isn't supported.

15.4.2. Data Compression

SecureCRT can transparently compress and uncompress the data traveling over an SSH connection. This can speed up your connection. [7.4.11]

In the Session Options window, choose Connection, and click the Advanced button and the General tab. The checkbox "Use Compression" enables data compression. You may also set a value for Compression Level. Its function is identical to the `CompressionLevel` keyword of SSH1. The higher the value, the better the compression, but the greater load on the CPU, potentially slowing your computer.

15.4.3. TIS Authentication

SecureCRT can authenticate you via the Gauntlet firewall toolkit from Trusted Information Systems (TIS). [5.5.1.8] In the Session Options window, under Connection, simply set Authentication to TIS.

15.4.4. Firewall Use

SecureCRT supports connections through several types of firewalls, such as the SOCKS4 and SOCKS5 firewalls supported by the SSH1 and SSH2 servers. Visit the Global Options window, select Firewall, and fill in the requested fields. You need to know the hostname or IP address of the firewall, and the TCP port on which to connect.

15.5. Forwarding

SecureCRT supports the SSH feature called forwarding (Chapter 9), in which another network connection can be passed through SSH to encrypt it. It is also called tunneling because the SSH connection provides a secure "tunnel" through which another connection may pass. Both TCP port forwarding and X forwarding are supported.

15.5.1. Port Forwarding

Port forwarding permits an arbitrary TCP connection to be routed through an SSH connection, transparently encrypting its data. [9.2] This turns an insecure TCP connection, such as Telnet, IMAP, or NNTP (Usenet news), into a secure one. Secure-

CRT supports local port forwarding, meaning that your local SSH client (SecureCRT) forwards the connection to a remote SSH server.

Each SecureCRT session you create may each have different port forwardings set up. To set up forwarding to a particular remote host, disconnect from that host (if you're connected) and open the Session Options window. Click the Advanced button and the Port Forwarding tab. Here's where you create port forwardings (see Figure 15-2).

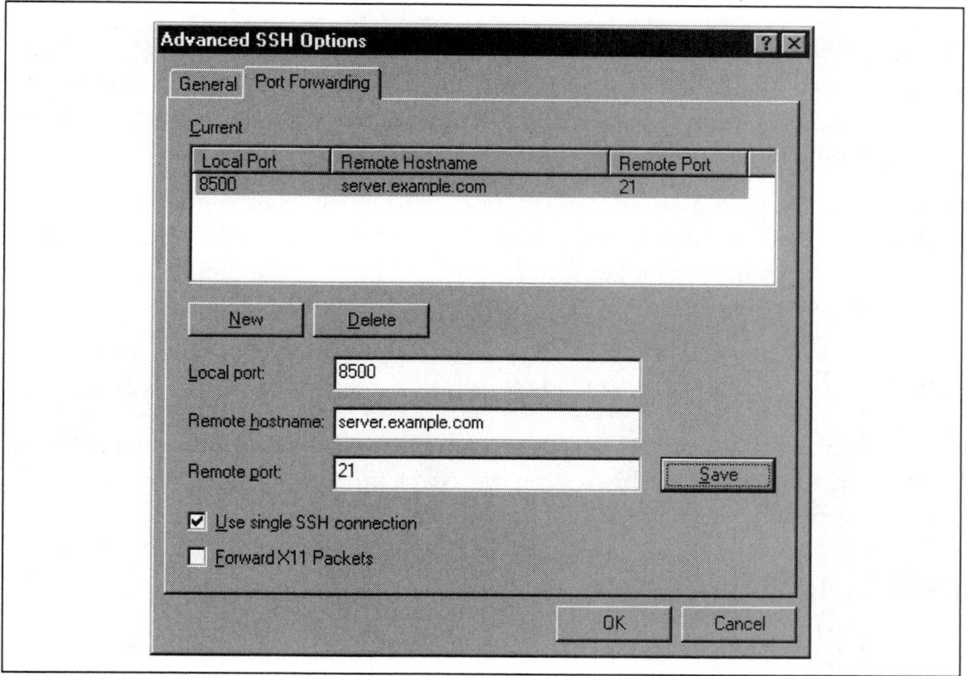

Figure 15-2. SecureCRT Port Forwarding tab

To create a new forwarding, first click the New button. Then fill in the name of the remote host where the TCP service (e.g., IMAP or NNTP) is found, the remote port number for that service, and finally, a local port number (on your PC) to use for the forwarding. This can be just about any number, but for tradition's sake, make it 1024 or higher. Choose a local port number that's not being used by any other SSH client on your PC

When you're done, click Save to save the forwarding. Then reopen your SSH connection, and your desired TCP port will be forwarded for the duration of your connection.

15.5.2. X Forwarding

The X Window System is the most popular windowing software for Unix machines. If you want to run remote X clients that open windows on your PC, you need:

- A remote host, running an SSH server, that has X client programs available
- An X server running on your PC under Windows, such as Hummingbird's eXceed

SSH makes your X connection secure by a process called X forwarding. [9.3] Turning on X forwarding is trivial in SecureCRT. Simply put a checkmark in the checkbox "Forward X11 Packets." It is found in the Session Options window: click the Advanced button, and select the Port Forwarding tab.

To secure an X connection by forwarding it through SSH, first run SecureCRT and establish a secure terminal connection to the SSH server machine. Then run your PC's X server, disabling its login features such as XDM. Now simply invoke X clients on the server machine.

15.6. Troubleshooting

ecureCRT, like any other SSH client, can run into unexpected difficulties interacting with an SSH server. In this section we cover problems specific to SecureCRT. For more general problems, see also Chapter 12.

15.6.1. Authentication

Q: When I use an RSA key, SecureCRT says "Internal error loading private key."

A: SecureCRT accepts only DSA keys for SSH2 (in conformance with the current draft SSH-2 standard). Some other SSH-2 implementations also support RSA keys; these don't work with SecureCRT at present. [3.9.1]

Q: I tried loading a key generated by another SSH-2 implementation, but SecureCRT says "The private key is corrupt."

A: While SSH protocol draft standard specifies how keys are represented within an SSH session, it doesn't cover formats for storing those keys in files. As a result, implementors are free to make up different, incompatible formats, making your life difficult. This is true of both SSH1 and SSH2, although there is less difference among SSH1 implementations than among SSH2. Since this may change, we will just say: "contact the vendor."

Q: *After typing my passphrase, I get a dialog box, "SSH_SMSG_FAILURE: invalid SSH state," and the session disconnects without logging me in.*

A: No pseudo-tty is being allocated. Possibly your remote account has the `no-pty` option set in its *authorized_keys* file. [8.2.9]

Q: *SSH-2 authentication fails with the message "SecureCRT is disconnecting from the SSH server for the following reason: reason code 2."*

A: At press time, some SSH-2 clients and servers from different vendors don't work together due to different interpretations of the SSH-2 draft standard. We hope such problems will have settled down by the time you read this. In the meantime, make sure you select the correct SSH Server in SecureCRT's Properties window, under Connection. To determine the type of server to which you are connecting, *telnet* to the server machine's SSH port (usually 22) and read the version string that appears. Using MS-DOS *telnet*, type:

```
telnet server.example.com 22
```

and a window opens with a response like:

```
SSH-1.99-2.0.13 F-SECURE SSH
```

indicating (in this case) F-Secure SSH Server Version 2.0.13.

15.6.2. Forwarding

Q: *I can't do port forwarding. I get a message that the port is already in use.*

A: Do you have another SecureCRT window open and connected with the same port forwarding setup? You can't have two connections forwarding the same local port. As a workaround, create a second session that duplicates the first, but with a different local port number. Now you can use both sessions simultaneously.

15.7. Summary

We have used SecureCRT for over a year and find it a solid, stable, and capable product with strong vendor support. Its shortcomings are that it lacks an agent and *scp*.

16

F-Secure SSH Client (Windows, Macintosh)

In this chapter:
- *Obtaining and Installing*
- *Basic Client Use*
- *Key Management*
- *Advanced Client Use*
- *Forwarding*
- *Troubleshooting*
- *Summary*

F-Secure Corporation, a distributor of commercial versions of SSH1 and SSH2 for Unix, also produces SSH clients for Windows and the Macintosh. [1.5] The client product line, cleverly named F-Secure SSH Client, is a windowing, VT100-style terminal emulator that permits logins via both SSH protocols, SSH-1 and SSH-2.

For Windows, we evaluated Version 4.1, which supports both protocols in a single product. Prior versions supported SSH-1 and SSH-2 in separate products. For Macintosh, we evaluated Versions 1.0 (SSH-1) and 2.0 (SSH-2), but at press time, they didn't run reliably on our system, so we won't cover them in this book. We experienced unexplained crashes that could have been due to our Macintosh configuration or to F-Secure. We had no such difficulties with the Windows client.

F-Secure SSH Client has a fairly rich set of features. Under SSH-1, it supports remote logins, port forwarding, X forwarding, key pair generation, and a selection of terminal program features. For SSH-2 only, it includes secure file copying by *scp2* and *sftp2*.

16.1. Obtaining and Installing

F-Secure's products may be purchased online at:

> *http://www.f-secure.com/*

Free evaluation versions are available. Installation is accomplished by a traditional Windows install program: you choose the destination directory and make a few other simple decisions.

16.2. Basic Client Use

Client behavior is set in the Properties window: visit the Edit menu and select Properties (Figure 16-1). Select Connection, and enter the information as shown in the figure. Click OK to close the window, and then in the File menu choose Connect. Since no public keys are known to the program yet, password authentication is used. If all goes well, you are prompted for your login password by the remote server, and then you're logged in via SSH.

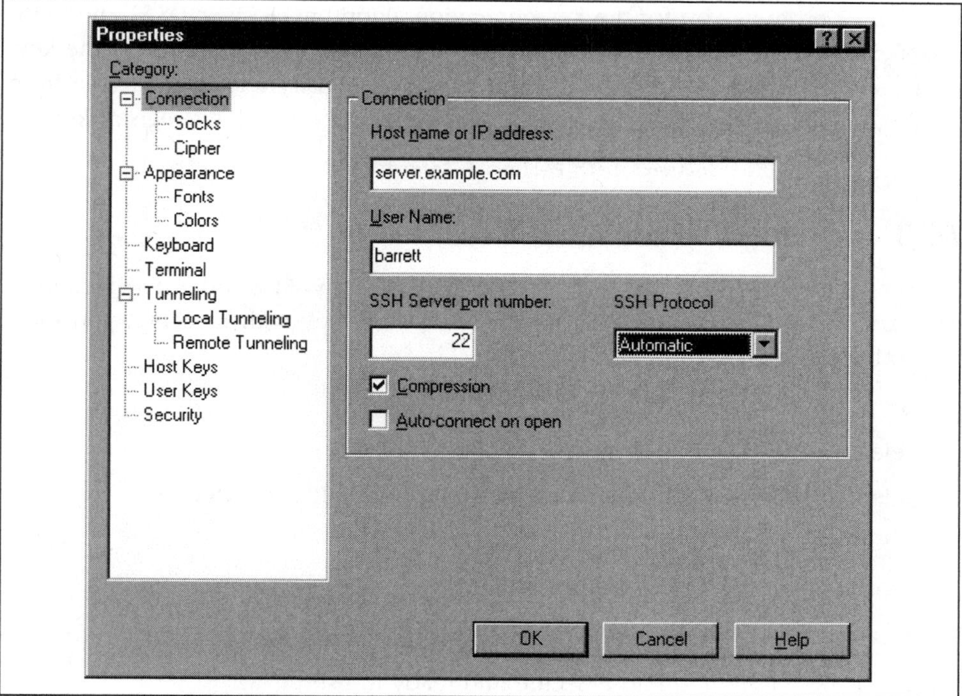

Figure 16-1. F-Secure SSH Client Connection properties window

Once logged in, the program operates just like a normal terminal program. SSH's end-to-end encryption is transparent to the user, as it should be.

When your settings are as you like them, create a *session file* to store them. Session files are named with *.ssh* extensions and may be saved and opened with (surprise, surprise) the Save and Open commands in the File menu.

16.3. Key Management

F-Secure SSH Client supports public-key authentication with RSA or DSA keys. It can generate keys with its built-in Key Generation Wizard or use existing SSH-1 or SSH-2 keys.

16.3.1. Generating Keys

The Key Generation Wizard is accessible within the program from the Tools menu. The wizard prompts you for the key-generation algorithm (RSA or DSA), the number of bits in the key, the key comment and passphrase, and the name of the key. After generation, the key is stored in the Windows registry and is accessible from the Properties window under User Keys. Incidentally, the Windows registry key is:

```
HKEY_CURRENT_USER\Software\Data Fellows\F-Secure SSH 2.0
```

16.3.2. Importing Existing Keys

F-Secure SSH Client stores keys in the Windows registry. Most other SSH products store keys in files, so if you want to use an existing key with F-Secure, you must *import* it into the registry:

1. Bring up the Properties window.
2. Select User Keys.
3. Select the RSA or DSA tab, if you are importing an RSA or DSA key.
4. Select the "Import..." button.
5. Browse to your key file, and select it.
6. Type the key's passphrase (for SSH-1 format keys only).

The key is now imported into F-Secure and ready to use.

16.3.3. Installing Public Keys

For SSH-2 public keys only, F-Secure SSH Client includes the Key Registration Wizard, which automatically uploads and installs your public key on an SSH-2 server machine where your remote account resides. What a great feature! Of course the operation is secure: it connects to your remote account by SSH-2 using password authentication.

SSH-1 public keys must be installed manually on the server. Connect the remote host using password authentication, and then open the Properties window and select User Keys. From here you have two choices:

- Export your public key to a file, using the "Export..." button, then transfer the file to the remote server machine, and copy its contents into your *authorized_keys* file.
- Copy your public key to the Windows clipboard, using the Copy To Clipboard button, and then paste it into your remote *authorized_keys* file.

16.3.4. Using Keys

Unlike most Unix SSH products, F-Secure SSH Client doesn't let you specify which key to use for a session. Instead, it tries each key in turn. When one matches a public key on the server, you are prompted for your passphrase. To reject F-Secure's choice of key and use a different one, press the Escape key or click Cancel, and the next key is selected and tried. If all keys fail, the program falls back to password authentication.

16.4. Advanced Client Use

To establish an SSH connection, you must fill in the following Connection fields in the Properties window. These include:

Host Name
: The name of the remote SSH server machine to which you want to connect.

User Name
: Your username on the remote SSH server machine. If you're using public key (RSA) authentication, this username must belong to an account that contains your public key.

Port Number
: The TCP port for SSH connections. Virtually all SSH clients and servers operate on port 22. Unless you plan to connect to a nonstandard SSH server, you don't need to change this. [7.4.4.1]

SSH Protocol
: You may require SSH-1 or SSH-2, or select Automatic to let the program figure it out based on the server's response.

Optionally, you may select the encryption cipher and an authentication method. In the Properties window, select Cipher to choose the set of encryption ciphers you will permit your client to use. (The default should be acceptable for most uses.) The SSH server negotiates with your client to choose a cipher they both support.

Your authentication method can be public key or password, which may be chosen in the login window. The program automatically tries to authenticate with each of your User Keys in order. [16.3.4]

16.4.1. Data Compression

F-Secure SSH can transparently compress and uncompress the data traveling over an SSH connection, which can speed up your connection. [7.4.11]

In the Properties window, choose Connection, and check the box labeled Compression. There's no way to set different compression levels as in SSH1.

16.4.2. Debugging with Verbose Mode

Is your SSH session not working as expected? Turn on verbose mode so status messages are printed in the window as your session runs. This can help you locate and solve problems.

In the Properties window, select Appearance and check the box labeled Verbose Mode. The next time you connect, you'll see messages like this:

```
debug: connecting ...
debug: addresses 219.243.169.50
debug: Registered connecting socket: 12
debug: Connection still in progress
debug: Marked name resolver 1 killed
debug: Replaced connected socket object 12 with a stream
```

Verbose mode is much like its counterpart in the Unix SSH products. [7.4.15] It can be an indispensable tool for diagnosing problems with your connection.

16.4.3. SOCKS Proxy Server

F-Secure SSH Client supports connecting through SOCKS Version 4 proxy servers. [4.1.5.8] On the Properties window, select Socks and fill in the hostname or IP address of the proxy server machine and the port number on the proxy (the usual SOCKS port is 1080).

16.4.4. Accepting Host Keys

Every SSH server has a unique host key that represents the server's identity, so SSH clients can verify that they are speaking with the actual server and not an impostor. [2.3.1] F-Secure SSH Client keeps track of all host keys it encounters. The keys are stored in the Windows registry.

If you want F-Secure SSH Client to reject host keys it hasn't seen before, visit the Properties window and select Security. A checkbox is available to set this option.

16.4.5. Additional Security Features

Normally, F-Secure SSH Client keeps track of hostnames, usernames, filenames, and terminal input and output that it encounters. Any time you want to purge this information from the program (say, to prevent a third party from viewing it on your computer), visit the Properties window and select Security. The buttons on this window will delete the information.

16.4.6. Secure File Transfer with SFTP

A graphical file transfer program, F-Secure SSH FTP, is also included. Its user interface should be familiar to anyone who has used a graphical FTP client, except that you must set up authentication via SSH. We don't document this program, as it comes with online help, but we did want to mention it.

16.4.7. Command-Line Tools

F-Secure SSH comes with a graphical terminal program as well as command-line clients using the SSH-2 protocol. These include *ssh2*, *scp2*, and *sftp2*. These programs are much the same as their counterparts in SSH2, as described in Chapter 2, except:

- Some of the Unix command-line options aren't supported. Type the program name by itself (e.g., *ssh2*) to see the current list of options.
- Key files aren't supported; these programs read keys from the Windows registry, just as F-Secure SSH Client does.

The command-line programs are useful for scripting and batch files, or for executing remote commands on the server machine:

```
C:\> ssh2 server.example.com mycommand
```

16.5. Forwarding

F-Secure SSH Client supports forwarding (Chapter 9), in which another network connection can be passed through SSH to encrypt it. It is also called tunneling because the SSH connection provides a secure "tunnel" through which another connection may pass. Both TCP port forwarding (local and remote) and X forwarding are supported.

16.5.1. Port Forwarding

Each F-Secure configuration you create may have different ports forwarded. To set up forwarding to a particular remote host, disconnect from that host (if you're connected), open the Properties window, and notice the Tunneling category. Select Local Tunneling to set up local forwarding (see Figure 16-2), or Remote Tunneling for remote forwarding, respectively. [9.2.3] Either way, you are prompted for similar information:

Source Port:
: The local port number

Destination Host:
: The remote hostname

Destination Port:
: The remote port number

Application to Start:
: An external application to be launched when this port is forwarded

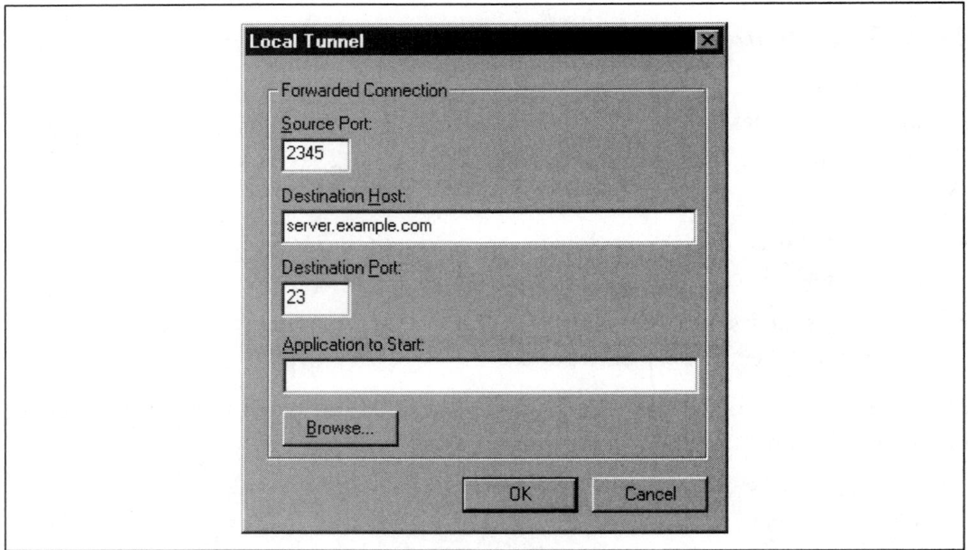

Figure 16-2. F-Secure SSH Client local port forwarding options

For example, to tunnel a *telnet* connection (TCP port 23) through SSH to connect to *server.example.com*, you can specify:

Source port: 8500 (any random port number)
Destination Host: *server.example.com*
Destination Port: 23
Application to Start: *c:\windows\telnet.exe*

Once you've made your choices, reopen the SSH connection, and the ports will be forwarded for the duration of your connection.

Note that F-Secure SSH Client forbids remote connections to locally forwarded ports. This security feature is analogous to specifying "GatewayPorts no". [9.2.1.1]

16.5.2. X Forwarding

The X Window System is the most popular windowing software for Unix machines. If you want to run remote X clients that open windows on your PC, you need:

- A remote host, running an SSH server, that has X client programs available
- An X server running on your PC under Windows, such as Hummingbird's eXceed

SSH makes your X connection secure by a process called X forwarding. [9.3] Turning on X forwarding is trivial in F-Secure SSH Client: open the Properties window, select Tunneling, and put a checkmark in the box Enable X11 Tunneling. You may also select the X display number, which you also may change during your SSH session.

To secure an X connection by forwarding it through SSH, first run F-Secure SSH Client and establish a secure terminal connection to the SSH server machine. Then run your PC's X server, disabling its login features such as XDM. Now simply invoke X clients on the server machine, and their windows will open on your local X display.

16.6. Troubleshooting

F-Secure SSH Client, like any other SSH client, can run into unexpected difficulties interacting with an SSH server. In this section we cover problems specific to F-Secure SSH. For more general problems, see also Chapter 12.

Q: Why is scrolling so slow for F-Secure SSH for Windows?

A: At press time, F-Secure's scrolling speed is quite poor, but you can speed it up somewhat by turning on jump scrolling, which is disabled by default. It can be enabled only through F-Secure's key-mapping facility. The following setup enables jump scrolling for one given Session File:

a. In your F-Secure installation directory, locate the file *Keymap.map*.

b. Edit this file and locate the line containing "enable fast-scroll-mapping".

c. Uncomment this line by removing any "#" symbols at the beginning of the line.

d. Save and close the file.

e. In the Edit menu, select Properties.

f. In the Properties window, select Keyboard.

g. Under Map Files, in the Keyboard blank, enter the path to the *Keymap.map* file you edited.

h. Click OK.

You can now toggle between smooth and jump scrolling by pressing `Control-Alt-F3`. Press this key sequence once in your F-Secure SSH session, and your scrolling will become speedy.

Q: *I got the error message "Warning: Remote host failed or refused to allocate a pseudo tty."*

A: Your server's SSH-1 *authorized_keys* file might have the `no-pty` option specified for the corresponding public key. [8.2.9]

Q: *I can't do port forwarding. I get a message that the port is already in use.*

A: Do you have another F-Secure window open and connected with the same port forwarding setup? You can't have two connections forwarding the same local port. As a workaround, create a second configuration that duplicates the first but with a different local port number. Now you can use both connections simultaneously.

Q: *I tried using the Key Registration Wizard but it didn't work. The Wizard said "Disconnected, connection lost."*

A: First, verify that your hostname, remote username, and remote password are given correctly. If they are definitely correct, click the Advanced button and check the information there. Is the SSH-2 server running on the default port, 22, or a different one? Do the SSH2 directory and authorization filenames you provided match the ones on the server?

Another possible (and more technical) cause is a missing or incomplete *sftp-server* subsystem entry in the server's */etc/sshd2_config* file. F-Secure recommends that the fully qualified path to *sftp-server2* appear in this entry, or else the SSH server possibly can't locate it. The Key Registration Wizard uses the SFTP protocol to transfer key files. The system administrator of the server machine needs to make this change.

Q: *How do I prevent the initial welcome window from being displayed in F-Secure SSH2?*

A: For Windows, modify the Registry value:

```
HKEY_CURRENT_USER\Software\Data Fellows\F-Secure SSH 2.0\TnT\Settings\ShowSplash
```

The default is `yes`; set it to `no`. The next time you run the program, no welcome window appears. (This is an undocumented feature.)

Q: How do I eliminate the Logon Information window that pops up when I run F-Secure SSH2 Client? I'm using public-key authentication so the window seems unnecessary.

A: In the Properties window, select Connection, and check the box Auto-Connect On Open.

16.7. Summary

Overall, F-Secure SSH Client for Windows is a good, solid product. The present version does have some long-standing weaknesses: no agent, no secure file copy in the SSH-1 products (though *sftp* is supported in the SSH-2 products), incomplete documentation (almost no mention of keyboard map files), and the inability to turn on jump scrolling in the Preferences window. Regardless, we've used the product reliably in various versions for over a year. F-Secure SSH is still in active development, so some of its limitations may still be overcome.

17

In this chapter:
- *Obtaining and Installing*
- *Basic Client Use*
- *Troubleshooting*
- *Summary*

NiftyTelnet SSH (Macintosh)

NiftyTelnet SSH is a minimal, freely distributable SSH client for the Macintosh by Jonas Walldén. Based on NiftyTelnet by Chris Newman, NiftyTelnet SSH is a graphical terminal program with SSH-1 support added. It supports remote logins and secure file copying. It also remembers your public key passphrase (i.e., caching it in memory) if you open multiple terminal windows. This isn't an agent, however.

NiftyTelnet's best features are that it is free, and it works pretty well. On the negative side, it doesn't support forwarding of any kind, and it can't generate SSH key pairs. In order to use public-key authentication, you need another SSH program to generate keys for your identity, such as *ssh-keygen1* from SSH1.

Our discussion of NiftyTelnet SSH is based on Version 1.1 R3.

17.1. Obtaining and Installing

NiftyTelnet SSH can be downloaded from:

> *http://www.lysator.liu.se/~jonasw/freeware/niftyssh/*

and unpacked with Stuffit Expander into a folder of your choice. You may copy the folder to any location on your Macintosh.

When NiftyTelnet SSH is run for the first time, it presents the New Connection dialog box shown in Figure 17-1. Click the New button to enter the settings for an SSH client/server connection. Figure 17-2 highlights the important fields for configuring SSH: Host Name, Protocol, and RSA Key File. For the Host Name, enter the name of a remote host running an SSH server, and set the Protocol to an SSH encryption algorithm (DES, 3DES, or Blowfish). If you plan to use password authentication, leave the RSA Key File line empty. Otherwise, if you have already installed a private key file on your Mac, fill in the location. You must list the entire path to the file, with folder names separated by colons. For example, if your key file *Identity* is found by opening the disk MyDisk, then the folder SSH, and then the folder NiftyTelnet, enter:

```
MyDisk:SSH:NiftyTelnet:Identity
```

Once your settings are complete, connect to the remote host using password authentication. Copy your public key onto the remote host, log out, and reconnect using public-key authentication.

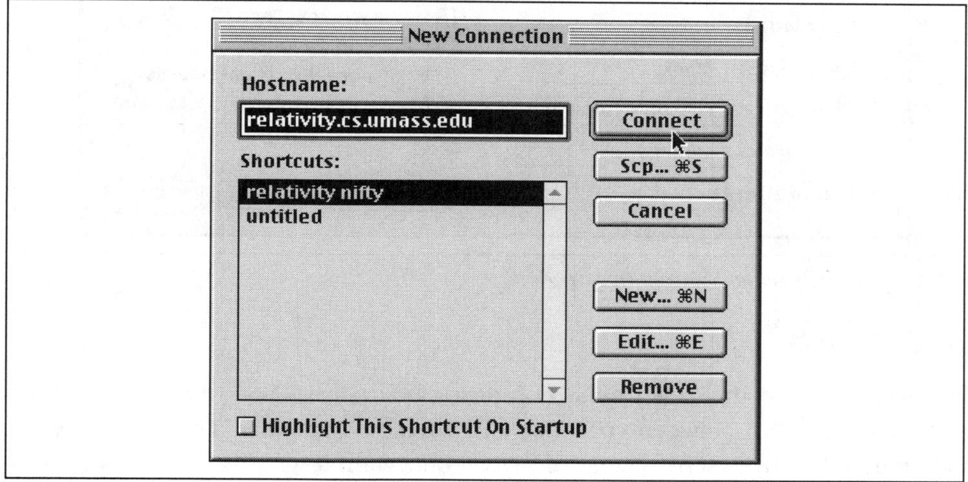

Figure 17-1. NiftyTelnet New Connection dialog box

17.2. Basic Client Use

NiftyTelnet SSH began life as NiftyTelnet, a Macintosh Telnet application, with SSH support added later by another programmer. Most of the configurable parameters relate to Telnet, so we don't cover them, just the SSH-specific ones.

17.2.1. Authentication

For SSH, you specify only your cipher (labeled "Protocol") and the path to your private key file (labeled "RSA Key File"), as shown in Figure 17-2. The default authentication method is public key, but if this fails or you have no key file, it falls back to password authentication.

The only tricky part is the path, which must be typed, rather than browsed by the usual Macintosh file selector. [17.3]

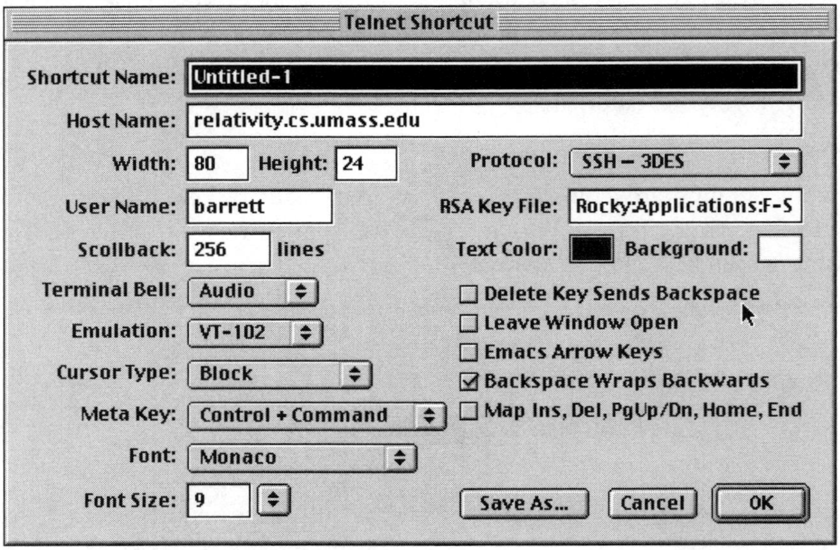

Figure 17-2. NiftyTelnet SSH Settings window

17.2.2. Scp

The Scp button on the New Connection dialog box permits secure copying of files and folders via SSH between your Mac and a remote computer. This feature operates much like the scp1 client of SSH1 but with a graphical interface (see Figure 17-3).

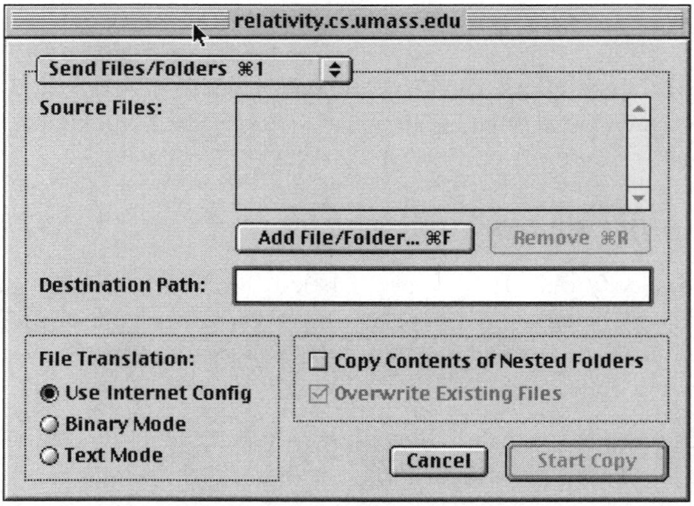

Figure 17-3. NiftyTelnet Scp window

Local files and folders may be selected by browsing, but remote files and folders must have their names entered manually. If you're used to Mac FTP clients such as Fetch, this interface might seem a bit spartan. Nonetheless, it works, and if you ask NiftyTelnet SSH to remember your password, you don't have to retype it for each file transfer.

17.2.3. Host Keys

Every SSH server has a unique host key that represents the server's identity, so clients such as NiftyTelnet SSH can verify that they are speaking with the actual server and not an impostor. [2.3.1]

NiftyTelnet keeps track of all server host keys it encounters. The keys are stored in a file called *NiftyTelnet SSH Known Hosts* in your Macintosh's *Preferences* folder within the *System* folder. The file has the same format as SSH1 known hosts files. [3.5.2.1]

17.3. Troubleshooting

Q: I want to do public-key authentication. How do I generate a key pair with NiftyTelnet SSH?

A: You can't. You must generate the key pair with a different SSH program, such as *ssh-keygen1* from SSH1 on a Unix machine. [2.4.2]

Q: What do I put in the "RSA Key File" blank?

A: The complete path to your private key file, folder by folder, with the folder names separated by colons. For example, if your key file *Identity* is found by opening the disk *MyDisk*, then the folder *SSH*, and then the folder *NiftyTelnet*, enter:

```
MyDisk:SSH:NiftyTelnet:Identity
```

Q: I cannot get the Scp feature to work. When I try to transfer a file, a window labeled "File: Waiting For Connection" appears for a few seconds and then disappears. No file is transferred.

A: According to the author, this problem sometimes occurs if NiftyTelnet SSH is communicating with an old SSH server. Reportedly, *sshd1* 1.2.25 and newer should work. We saw this problem initially with a 1.2.27 server, but it went away on its own, and we couldn't figure out the cause.

17.4. Summary

NiftyTelnet SSH is a fine choice for a Macintosh SSH client. It supports *scp*, a rarity among SSH-1 implementations for PCs and Macs, and it conveniently remembers your passphrase until the program exits. On the other hand, NiftyTelnet SSH has the fewest features of any SSH implementation we've seen and can't generate key pairs. If you need more bells and whistles, such as port forwarding and a wider set of options, consider F-Secure SSH Client for the Mac (Chapter 16).

SSH2 Manpage for sshregex

SSHREGEX(1) SSH2

Description

This document describes the regular expressions (or globbing patterns) used in filename globbing with *scp2* and *sftp2*.

Patterns

The escape character is a backslash "\". With this you can escape meta characters which you'd like to use in their plain character form.

In the following examples literal "E" and "F" denote any expression, be it a pattern or character, etc.

* Match any string consisting of zero or more characters. The characters can be any characters apart from slashes (/). However, the asterisk does not match a string if the string contains a dot (.) as its first character, or if the string contains a dot immediately after a slash. This means that the asterisk cannot be used to match filenames that have a dot as their first character.

   If the previous character is a slash (/), or the asterisk (*) is used to denote a match at the beginning of a string, it does match a dot (.).

   That is, the "*" functions as is normal in UNIX shell fileglobs.

? Match any single character except for a slash (/). However, do not match a dot (.) if located at the beginning of the string, or if the previous character is a slash (/).

   That is, "?" functions as is normal in Unix shell fileglobs (at least ZSH, although discarding the dot may not be a standard procedure).

***/* Match any sequence of characters that is either empty, or ends in a slash. However, the substring "/." is not allowed. This mimics ZSH's ingenious **/ construct. (Observe that "**" is equivalent to "*".)

E# Act as Kleene star, match E zero or more times.

E##
: Closure, match E one or more times.

(Start a capturing subexpression.

) End a capturing subexpression.

E|F
: Disjunction, match (inclusively) either E or F. E is preferred if both match.

[Start a character set. (See below).

Character Sets

A character set starts with "[" and ends at nonescaped "]" that is not part of a POSIX character set specifier and that does not follow immediately after "[".

The following characters have a special meaning and need to be escaped if meant literally:

– (minus sign)
: A range operator, except immediately after "[", where it loses its special meaning.

^ or !
: If immediately after the starting "[", denotes a complement: the whole character set will be complemented. Otherwise literal. "^".

[:alnum:]
: Characters for which "isalnum" returns `true` (see *ctype.h*).

[:alpha:]
: Characters for which "isalpha" returns `true` (see *ctype.h*).

[:cntrl:]
: Characters for which "iscntrl" returns `true` (see *ctype.h*).

[:digit:]
: Characters for which "isdigit" returns `true` (see *ctype.h*).

[:graph:]
: Characters for which "isgraph" returns `true` (see *ctype.h*).

[:lower:]
: Characters for which "islower" returns `true` (see *ctype.h*).

[:print:]
: Characters for which "isprint" returns `true` (see *ctype.h*).

[:punct:]
: Characters for which "ispunct" returns `true` (see *ctype.h*).

[:space:]
: Characters for which "isspace" returns `true` (see *ctype.h*).

[:upper:]
: Characters for which "isupper" returns `true` (see *ctype.h*).

[:xdigit:]
: Characters for which "isxdigit" returns `true` (see *ctype.h*).

Example

```
[[:xdigit:]XY] is typically equivalent to
[0123456789ABCDEFabcdefXY] .
```

Authors

SSH Communications Security Corp.

For more information, see *http://www.ssh.com/*.

See also

scp2(1), *sftp2*(1)

B

SSH Quick Reference

Legend

Mark	Meaning
✓	Yes: feature is supported/included
1	SSH-1 protocol only, not SSH-2
2	SSH-2 protocol only, not SSH-1
F	F-Secure SSH only
N	Not in F-Secure SSH

sshd Options

SSH1	SSH2	Open SSH	Option	Meaning
		✓	*–4*	Use IPv4 addresses only
		✓	*–6*	Use IPv6 addresses only
✓		✓	*–b bits*	# of bits in server key
✓		✓	*–d*	Verbose mode
	✓		*–d level*	Enable debug messages
	✓		*–d "module=level"*	Enable debug messages per module
✓	✓	✓	*–f filename*	Use other configuration file
✓	✓	✓	*–g time*	Set login grace time
✓	✓	✓	*–h filename*	Use other host key file
✓	✓	✓	*–i*	Use *inetd* for invocation
✓		✓	*–k time*	Key regeneration interval
	✓		*–o "keyword value"*	Set configuration keyword

SSH1	SSH2	Open SSH	Option	Meaning
✓	✓	✓	*–p port*	Select TCP port number
✓	✓	✓	*–q*	Quiet mode
		✓	*–Q*	Quiet if RSA support is missing
	✓		*–v*	Verbose mode
✓			*–V*	Print version number
		✓	*–V id*	OpenSSH SSH2 compatibility mode

sshd Keywords

SSH1	SSH2	Open SSH	Keyword	Value	Meaning
✓	✓	✓	#	Any text	Comment line
✓			`AccountExpireWarningDays`	# days	Warn user of expiration
		✓	`AFSTokenPassing`	Yes/no	Forward AFS tokens to server
	N		`AllowAgentForwarding`	Yes/no	Enable agent forwarding
	✓		`AllowedAuthentications`	Auth types	Permitted authentication techniques
	N		`AllowCshrcSourcingWith-Subsystems`	Yes/no	Source shell startup file
F			`AllowForwardingPort`	Port list	Permit forwarding for ports
F			`AllowForwardingTo`	Host/port list	Permit forwarding for hosts
✓	N	✓	`AllowGroups`	Group list	Access control by Unix group
✓	✓		`AllowHosts`	Host list	Access control by hostname
✓	✓		`AllowSHosts`	Host list	Access control via *shosts*
✓	N	✓	`AllowTcpForwarding`	Yes/no	Enable TCP port forwarding
	N		`AllowTcpForwardingFor-Users`	User list	Per user forwarding
	N		`AllowTcpForwardingFor-Groups`	Group list	Per group forwarding
✓	N	✓	`AllowUsers`	User list	Access control by username

SSH1	SSH2	Open SSH	Keyword	Value	Meaning
	N		`AllowX11Forwarding`	Yes/no	Enable X forwarding
	✓		`AuthorizationFile`	Filename	Location of authorization file
✓	✓	✓	`CheckMail`	Yes/no	Check new mail on login
	N		`ChRootGroups`	Group list	Run `chroot()` on login
	N		`ChRootUsers`	User list	Run `chroot()` on login
	✓	2	`Ciphers`	Cipher list	Select encryption ciphers
F			`DenyForwardingPort`	Port list	Forbid forwarding for ports
F			`DenyForwardingTo`	Host/port list	Forbid forwarding for hosts
✓	N	✓	`DenyGroups`	Group list	Access control by Unix group
✓	✓		`DenyHosts`	Host list	Access control by hostname
✓	✓		`DenySHosts`	Host list	Access control via *.shosts*
	N		`DenyTcpForwardingFor-Users`	User list	Per user forwarding
	N		`DenyTcpForwardingFor-Groups`	Group list	Per group forwarding
✓	N	✓	`DenyUsers`	User list	Access control by username
		2	`DSAAuthentication`	Yes/no	Permit SSH-2 DSA authentication
✓	✓		`FascistLogging`	Yes/no	Verbose mode
✓			`ForcedEmptyPasswdChange`	Yes/no	Change password if empty
✓			`ForcedPasswdChange`	Yes/no	Change password on first login
	✓		`ForwardAgent`	Yes/no	Enable agent forwarding
	✓		`ForwardX11`	Yes/no	Enable X forwarding
		✓	`GatewayPorts`	Yes/no	Gateway all locally forwarded ports
		2	`HostDSAKey`	Filename	Location of DSA key file

SSH1	SSH2	Open SSH	Keyword	Value	Meaning
✓		✓	`HostKey`	Filename	Location of host key file
	✓		`Hostkeyfile`	Filename	Location of host key file
✓			`IdleTimeout`	Time	Set idle timeout
✓	✓	✓	`IgnoreRhosts`	Yes/no	Ignore *.rhosts* files
✓	✓		`IgnoreRootRhosts`	Yes/no	Ignore */.rhosts* file
✓	✓		`IgnoreUserKnownHosts`	Yes/no	Ignore user's known-hosts keys
✓	✓	✓	`KeepAlive`	Yes/no	Send keepalive packets
✓		✓	`KerberosAuthentication`	Yes/no	Permit Kerberos authentication
✓		✓	`KerberosOrLocalPasswd`	Yes/no	Kerberos fallback authentication
✓		✓	`KerberosTgtPassing`	Yes/no	Support ticket-granting-tickets
		✓	`KerberosTicketCleanup`	Yes/no	Destroy ticket cache on logout
✓		✓	`KeyRegenerationInterval`	Time	Key regeneration interval
✓	✓	✓	`ListenAddress`	IP address	Listen on given interface
✓	✓	✓	`LoginGraceTime`	Time	Time limit for authentication
		✓	`LogLevel`	Syslog level	Set syslog level
	N		`Macs`	Algorithm	Select MAC algorithm
	N		`MaxBroadcastsPerSecond`	# broadcasts	Listen for UDP broadcasts
	✓		`MaxConnections`	# connections	Maximum # of simultaneous connections
	✓		`NoDelay`	Yes/no	Enable Nagle algorithm
✓	✓	✓	`PasswordAuthentication`	Yes/no	Permit password authentication
	✓		`PasswordGuesses`	# guesses	Limit # of password tries
✓			`PasswordExpireWarningDays`	# days	Warn user before expiration

SSH1	SSH2	Open SSH	Keyword	Value	Meaning
✓	✓	✓	`PermitEmptyPasswords`	Yes/no	Permit empty passwords
✓	✓	✓	`PermitRootLogin`	Yes/no/ nopwd	Permit superuser logins
	N		`PGPPublicKeyFile`	Filename	Default location of PGP public key file for authentication
✓		✓	`PidFile`	Filename	Location of pid file
✓	✓	✓	`Port`	Port number	Select server port number
✓	✓	✓	`PrintMotd`	Yes/no	Print message of the day
		✓	`Protocol`	1/2/1,2	Permit SSH-1 SSH-2 connections
	✓		`PubKeyAuthentication`	Yes/no	Permit public-key authentication
	✓		`PublicHostKeyFile`	Filename	Location of public host key
✓	✓		`QuietMode`	Yes/no	Quiet mode
✓			`RandomSeed`	Filename	Location of random seed file
	✓		`RandomSeedFile`	Filename	Location of random seed file
	N		`RekeyIntervalSeconds`	Seconds	Frequency of rekeying
	✓		`RequireReverseMapping`	Yes/no	Do reverse DNS lookup
	✓		`RequiredAuthentications`	Auth types	Required authentication techniques
✓	✓	✓	`RhostsAuthentication`	Yes/no	Permit *.rhosts* authentication
	✓		`RhostsPubKey-Authentication`	Yes/no	Permit combined authentication
✓	✓	✓	`RhostsRSAAuthentication`	Yes/no	Permit combined authentication
✓	✓	✓	`RSAAuthentication`	Yes/no	Permit public-key authentication
✓		✓	`ServerKeyBits`	# bits	# of bits in server key
		✓	`SkeyAuthentication`	Yes/no	Permit S/Key authentication

SSH1	SSH2	Open SSH	Keyword	Value	Meaning
	✓		`Ssh1Compatibility`	Yes/no	Enable SSH1 compatibility
	✓		`Sshd1Path`	Filename	Path to *sshd1*
✓			`SilentDeny`	Yes/no	`DenyHosts` prints no message
✓	✓	✓	`StrictModes`	Yes/no	Strict file/directory permissions
✓	✓	✓	`SyslogFacility`	Syslog level	Set syslog level
✓			`TISAuthentication`	Yes/no	Permit TIS authentication
✓			`Umask`	Unix umask	Set login umask
✓		✓	`UseLogin`	Yes/no	Select login program
	✓		`UserConfigDirectory`	Directory name	Location of user SSH2 directories
	✓		`UserKnownHosts`	Yes/no	Respect *~/.ssh2/knownhosts*
	✓		`VerboseMode`	Yes/no	Verbose mode
✓	N	✓	`X11Forwarding`	Yes/no	Enable X forwarding
✓		✓	`X11DisplayOffset`	# offset	Limit X displays for SSH
✓		✓	`XAuthLocation`	Filename	Location of *xauth*

ssh and scp Keywords

SSH1	SSH2	Open SSH	Keyword	Value	Meaning
✓	✓	✓	`#`	Any text	Comment line
		✓	`AFSTokenPassing`	Yes/no	Forward AFS tokens to server
	N		`AllowAgentForwarding`	Yes/no	Enable agent forwarding
	✓		`AllowedAuthentications`	Auth types	Permitted authentication techniques
	N		`AuthenticationNotify`	Yes/no	Print message on stdout on successful authentication
	N		`AuthenticationSuccessMsg`	Yes/no	Print message on stderr on successful authentication

SSH1	SSH2	Open SSH	Keyword	Value	Meaning
✓	✓	✓	`BatchMode`	Yes/no	Disable prompting
		✓	`CheckHostIP`	Yes/no	Detect DNS spoofing
✓		1	`Cipher`	Cipher	Request encryption cipher
	✓	2	`Ciphers`	Cipher_ list	Supported encryption ciphers
✓			`ClearAllForwardings`	Yes/no	Ignore any specified forwarding
✓	✓	✓	`Compression`	Yes/no	Enable data compression
✓		✓	`CompressionLevel`	0–9	Select compression algorithm
✓		✓	`ConnectionAttempts`	# attempts	# of retries by client
	N		`DefaultDomain`	Domain	Specify domain name
	✓		`DontReadStdin`	Yes/no	Redirect stdin from */dev/ null*
		2	`DSAAuthentication`	Yes/no	Permit SSH-2 DSA authentication
✓	✓	✓	`EscapeChar`	Character	Set escape character (^ = Ctrl key)
✓		✓	`FallBackToRsh`	Yes/no	Use *rsh* if *ssh* fails
	✓		`ForcePTTYAllocation`	Yes/no	Allocate a pseudo-tty
✓	✓	✓	`ForwardAgent`	Yes/no	Enable agent forwarding
✓			`ForwardX11`	Yes/no	Enable X forwarding
✓	✓	✓	`GatewayPorts`	Yes/no	Gateway locally forwarded ports
✓		1	`GlobalKnownHostsFile`	Filename	Location of global known hosts file
		2	`GlobalKnownHostsFile2`	Filename	Location of global known hosts file
	✓		`GoBackground`	Yes/no	Fork into background
✓	✓	✓	`Host`	Pattern	Begin section for this host
✓		✓	`HostName`	Hostname	Real name of host

SSH1	SSH2	Open SSH	Keyword	Value	Meaning
✓		1	`IdentityFile`	Filename	Name of private key file (RSA)
		2	`IdentityFile2`	Filename	Name of private key file (DSA)
✓	✓	✓	`KeepAlive`	Yes/no	Send keepalive packets
✓		✓	`KerberosAuthentication`	Yes/no	Permit Kerberos authentication
		✓	`KerberosTgtPassing`	Yes/no	Support ticket-granting-tickets
✓	✓	✓	`LocalForward`	Port, socket	Local port forwarding
	N		`Macs`	Algorithm	Select MAC algorithm
	✓		`NoDelay`	Yes/no	Enable Nagle algorithm
✓		✓	`NumberOfPasswordPrompts`	# prompts	# of prompts before failure
✓	✓	✓	`PasswordAuthentication`	Yes/no	Permit password authentication
	✓		`PasswordPrompt`	String	Password prompt
✓			`PasswordPromptHost`	Yes/no	Hostname for password prompt
✓			`PasswordPromptLogin`	Yes/no	Username for password prompt
✓	✓	✓	`Port`	Port number	Select server port number
✓		✓	`ProxyCommand`	Command	Connect to proxy server
	✓		`QuietMode`	Yes/no	Quiet mode
	✓		`RandomSeedFile`	Filename	Location of random seed file
✓	✓	✓	`RemoteForward`	Port, socket	Remote port forwarding
✓	✓	✓	`RhostsAuthentication`	Yes/no	Permit *.rhosts* authentication
	✓		`RhostsPubKey-Authentication`	Yes/no	Permit combined authentication
✓		✓	`RhostsRSAAuthentication`	Yes/no	Permit combined authentication
✓	✓	✓	`RSAAuthentication`	Yes/no	Permit public-key authentication

SSH1	SSH2	Open SSH	Keyword	Value	Meaning
	N		`PGPSecretKeyfile`	Filename	Default location of PGP private key file for authentication
		✓	`SkeyAuthentication`	Yes/no	Permit S/Key authentication
	N		`SocksServer`	Server	Specify SOCKS server
	✓		`Ssh1AgentCompatibility`	Yes/no	Enable SSH1 agent compatibility
	✓		`Ssh1Compatibility`	Yes/no	Enable SSH1 compatibility
	✓		`Ssh1Path`	Filename	Path to *ssh1*
	✓		`SshSignerPath`	Filename	Path to *ssh-signer2*
✓	✓	✓	`StrictHostKeyChecking`	Yes/no/ ask	Behavior on host key mismatch
✓			`TISAuthentication`	Yes/no	Permit TIS authentication
✓		✓	`UsePrivilegedPort`	Yes/no	Permit privileged port use
✓	✓	✓	`User`	Username	Remote username
✓		1	`UserKnownHostsFile`	Filename	Location of user known hosts file
		2	`UserKnownHostsFile2`	Filename	Location of user known hosts file
✓		✓	`UseRsh`	Yes/no	Use *rsh* instead of *ssh*
	✓		`VerboseMode`	Yes/no	Verbose mode
		✓	`XAuthLocation`	Filename	Location of *xauth*

ssh Options

SSH1	SSH2	Open SSH	Option	Meaning
		✓	*–2*	Use SSH-2 protocol only
		✓	*–4*	Use IPv4 addresses only
		✓	*–6*	Use IPv6 addresses only
✓			*–8*	No effect; simply passed along to *rsh* on fallback; signifies 8-bit clean connection
✓	✓	✓	*–a*	Disable agent forwarding
	✓		*+a*	Enable agent forwarding
		✓	*–A*	Enable agent forwarding

SSH1	SSH2	Open SSH	Option	Meaning
✓	✓	✓	–c *cipher*	Select encryption cipher
✓		✓	–C	Enable compression
	✓		–C	Disable compression
	✓		+C	Enable compression
	✓		–d *level*	Enable debug messages
	✓		–d *"module=level"*	Enable debug messages per module
✓	✓	✓	–e *character*	Set escape character (^ = Ctrl key)
✓	✓	✓	–f	Fork into background
	✓		–F *filename*	Use other configuration file
✓	✓	✓	–g	Gateway locally forwarded ports
	✓		–h	Print help message
✓	✓	✓	–i *filename*	Select identity file
✓		✓	–k	Disable Kerberos ticket forwarding
✓	✓	✓	–l *username*	Remote username
✓	✓	✓	–L *port1:host2: port2*	Local port forwarding
	N		–m *algorithm*	Select MAC algorithm
✓	✓	✓	–n	Redirect stdin from */dev/null*
		2	–N	Execute no remote command
✓	✓	✓	–o *"keyword value"*	Set configuration keyword
✓	✓	✓	–p *port*	Select TCP port number
✓	✓	✓	–P	Use nonprivileged port
✓	✓	✓	–q	Quiet mode
✓	✓	✓	–R *port1:host2: port2*	Remote port forwarding
	✓		–s *subsystem*	Invoke remote subsystem
	✓		–S	No session channel
✓	✓	✓	–t	Allocate tty
		2	–T	Don't allocate tty
✓	✓	✓	–v	Verbose mode
✓	✓	✓	–V	Print version number
✓	✓	✓	–x	Disable X forwarding
	✓		+x	Enable X forwarding
		✓	–X	Enable X forwarding

scp Options

SSH1	SSH2	Open SSH	Option	Meaning
	✓		*–1*	Enable *scp1* compatibility
		✓	*–4*	Use IPv4 addresses only
		✓	*–6*	Use IPv6 addresses only
✓		✓	*–a*	No file-by-file statistics
✓		✓	*–A*	Print file-by-file statistics
✓	✓	✓	*–B*	Disable prompting
✓	✓	✓	*–c cipher*	Select encryption cipher
✓		✓	*–C*	Enable compression
✓	✓	✓	*–d*	Require target to be a directory when copying a single file
	✓		*–D "module=level"*	Enable debug messages per module
✓	✓	✓	*–f*	Specify copy FROM (internal use)
	✓		*–h*	Print help message
✓	N	✓	*–i filename*	Select identity file
✓			*–L*	Use nonprivileged port
	✓		*–n*	Print actions, but don't copy
✓	N	✓	*–o "keyword value"*	Set configuration keyword
✓	✓	✓	*–p*	Preserve file attributes
✓	✓	✓	*–P port*	Select TCP port number
✓		✓	*–q*	Don't print statistics
	✓		*–q*	Quiet mode
✓			*–Q*	Print statistics
	✓		*–Q*	Don't print statistics
✓	✓	✓	*–r*	Recursive copy
✓	✓	✓	*–S filename*	Path to *ssh* executable
✓	✓	✓	*–t*	Specify copy TO (internal use)
	✓		*–u*	Remove original file
✓	✓	✓	*–v*	Verbose mode
	✓		*–V*	Print version number

ssh-keygen Options

SSH1	SSH2	Open SSH	Option	Meaning
	✓		*–1 filename*	Convert SSH1 key file to SSH2
✓	✓	✓	*–b bits*	# of bits in generated key
	N		*–B positive_integer* [a]	Specify numeric base for displaying key
✓		✓	*–c*	Change comment (with *–C*)
	✓		*–c comment*	Change comment
✓		✓	*–C comment*	Specify new comment (with *–c*)
		✓	*–d*	Generate DSA key
	N		*–D filename*	Derive public key from private key file
	✓		*–e filename*	Edit key file interactively
✓	b	✓	*–f filename*	Output filename
	✓		*–F filename*	Print fingerprint of public key
	✓		*–h*	Print help and exit
		✓	*–l*	Print fingerprint of public key
✓		✓	*–N passphrase*	Specify new passphrase
	✓		*–o filename*	Output filename
✓		✓	*–p*	Change passphrase (with *–P* and *–N*)
	F		*–p passphrase*	Change passphrase
✓		✓	*–P passphrase*	Specify old passphrase (with *–p*)
	✓		*–P*	Use empty passphrase
	✓	✓	*–q*	Quiet: suppress progress indicator
	✓		*–r*	Stir in data from random pool
		✓	*–R*	Detect RSA (exit code 0/1)
	✓		*–t algorithm*	Select key-generation algorithm
✓			*–u*	Change encryption algorithm
	F		*–v*	Print version string and exit
	N		*–V*	Print version string and exit
		✓	*–x*	Convert OpenSSH public key to SSH2
		✓	*–X*	Convert SSH2 public key to OpenSSH
		✓	*–y*	Derive public key from private key file
	✓		*–?* [c]	Print help and exit

[a] Undocumented
[b] The output filename is given as the final argument to *ssh-keygen2*
[c] You may need to escape the question mark in your shell, e.g., *–\?*

ssh-agent Options

SSH1	SSH2	Open SSH	Option	Meaning
	✓		*–1*	SSH1 compatibility mode
✓	✓	✓	*–c*	Print C shell-style commands
✓		✓	*–k*	Kill existing agent
✓	✓	✓	*–s*	Print *sh*-style commands

ssh-add Options

SSH1	SSH2	Open SSH	Option	Meaning
	✓		*–1*	Limit SSH1 compatibility
✓	✓	✓	*–d*	Unload key
✓	✓	✓	*–D*	Unload all keys
	✓		*–f step*	Limit agent-forwarding hops
	✓		*–F host_list*	Limit agent-forwarding hosts
	✓		*–I*	PGP keys are identified by ID
✓	✓		*–l*	List loaded keys
		✓	*–l*	List fingerprints of loaded keys
	✓		*–L*	Lock agent
		✓	*–L*	List loaded keys
	✓		*–N*	PGP keys are identified by name
✓	✓		*–p*	Read passphrase from stdin
	✓		*–P*	PGP keys are identified by fingerprint
	✓		*–R filename*	Specify PGP keyring file
	✓		*–t timeout*	Expire key after timeout
	✓		*–U*	Unlock agent

Identity and Authorization Files

~/.ssh/authorized_keys (SSH1, OpenSSH/1) and *~/.ssh/authorized_keys2* (OpenSSH/2): use one public key per line, preceded by options.

Option	Meaning
`command="`*`Unix shell command`*`"`	Specify a forced command
`environment="`*`variable=value`*`"`	Set environment variable
`from=`*`host_or_ip_address_specification`*	Limit incoming hosts

Option	Meaning
`idle-timeout=`*`time`*	Set idle timeout
`no-agent-forwarding`	Disable agent forwarding
`no-port-forwarding`	Disable port forwarding
`no-pty`	Don't allocate TTY

~/.ssh2/authorization (SSH2): use one keyword/value pair per line.

Keyword	Meaning
`Command` *`Unix_command`*	Specify a forced command
`Key` *`filename`*.pub	Location of public key file
`PgpPublicKeyFile` *`filename`*	Location of PGP public key file
`PgpKeyFingerprint` *`fingerprint`*	Select PGP key by fingerprint
`PgpKeyId` *`id`*	Select PGP key by ID
`PgpKeyName` *`name`*	Select PGP key by name

~/.ssh2/identification (SSH2): one keyword/value pair per line.

Keyword	Meaning
`IdKey` *`filename`*	Location of private key file
`IdPgpKeyFingerprint` *`fingerprint`*	Select PGP key by fingerprint
`IdPgpKeyId` *`id`*	Select PGP key by ID
`IdPgpKeyName` *`name`*	Select PGP key by name
`PgpSecretKeyFile` *`filename`*	Location of PGP private key file

Environment Variables

Variable	Set By	In	Meaning
SSH_AUTH_SOCK	*ssh-agent*	SSH1, OpenSSH	Path to socket
SSH2_AUTH_SOCK	*ssh-agent*	SSH2	Path to socket
SSH_CLIENT	*sshd*	SSH1, OpenSSH	Socket info
SSH2_CLIENT	*sshd*	SSH2	Socket info
SSH_ORIGINAL_COMMAND	*sshd*	SSH1	Client's remote command string
SSH_SOCKS_SERVER	*sshd*	SSH2	SOCKS firewall information
SSH_TTY	*sshd*	SSH1, OpenSSH	Name of allocated TTY
SSH2_TTY	*sshd*	SSH2	Name of allocated TTY

Index

Symbols

Numbers

A

D

F

G

H

I

P

T

U

V

W

X

Y

Z

About the Authors

Daniel J. Barrett, Ph.D., has been immersed in Internet technology since 1985. Currently a software engineer and vice president at a well-known financial services company, Dan has also been a heavy metal singer, Unix system administrator, university lecturer, web designer, and humorist.

Dan has written several other O'Reilly books, including *NetResearch: Finding Information Online* and *Bandits on the Information Superhighway*, as well as monthly columns for *Compute!* and *Keyboard Magazine*. He and his family reside in Boston.

You may write to Dan at *dbarrett@oreilly.com.*

Richard E. Silverman first touched a computer as a college junior in 1986, when he logged into a DEC-20, typed "MM" to send some mail, and was promptly lost to the world. He eventually resurfaced and discovered he had a career, which was convenient but somewhat disorienting, since he hadn't really been looking for one. Since earning his B.A. in computer science and M.A. in pure mathematics, Richard has worked in the fields of networking, formal methods in software development, public-key infrastructure, routing security, and Unix systems administration. Outside of work, he loves to read, study languages and mathematics, sing, dance, and exercise.

You may reach Richard at *res@oreilly.com.*

Colophon

Our look is the result of reader comments, our own experimentation, and feedback from distribution channels. Distinctive covers complement our distinctive approach to technical topics, breathing personality and life into potentially dry subjects.

The animal on the cover of *SSH, the Secure Shell: The Definitive Guide* is a land snail (*Mollusca gastropoda*).

A member of the mollusk family, a snail has a soft, moist body that is protected by a hard shell, into which it can retreat when in danger or when in arid or bright conditions. Snails prefer wet weather and, though not nocturnal, will stay out of bright sun. At the front of a snail's long body are two sets of tentacles: its eyes are at the end of one set, and the other set is used for smelling and navigation.

Land snails are hermaphrodites, each having both female and male sex organs, though a snail must mate with another snail in order for fertilization to occur. A snail lays eggs approximately six times a year, with almost 100 eggs each time. Young snails hatch in a month and become adults in two years. A snail's life span is approximately 5–10 years.

Known as a slow mover, a snail moves by muscles on its underside that contract and expand, propelling the snail along at a slow pace. It leaves a wet trail of mucus, which protects the snail from anything sharp it may need to crawl over as it searches for food. The snail's diet of plants, bark, and fruits causes it to be a pest in many parts of the world where it is notorious for destroying crops.

Mary Anne Weeks Mayo was the production editor and copyeditor for *SSH, the Secure Shell: The Definitive Guide.* Colleen Gorman proofread the book. Rachel Wheeler and Jane Ellin provided quality control. Matt Hutchinson and Lucy Muellner provided production assistance. John Bickelhaupt revised the index.

Ellie Volckhausen designed the cover of this book, based on a series design by Edie Freedman. The cover image is an original engraving from the book *Natural History of Animals* by Sanborn Tenney and Abby A. Tenney, published by Scribner, Armstrong & Co. in 1873. Emma Colby produced the cover layout with QuarkXPress 4.1 using Adobe's ITC Garamond font.

David Futato and Melanie Wang designed the interior layout based on a series design by Nancy Priest. Mike Sierra implemented the design in FrameMaker 5.5.6. The text and heading fonts are ITC Garamond Light and Garamond Book; the code font is Constant Willison. The illustrations that appear in the book were produced by Robert Romano using Macromedia FreeHand 8 and Adobe Photoshop 5. This colophon was written by Nicole Arigo.

Whenever possible, our books use a durable and flexible lay-flat binding. If the page count exceeds this binding's limit, perfect binding is used.

How to stay in touch with O'Reilly

1. Visit Our Award-Winning Web Site

http://www.oreilly.com/

★"Top 100 Sites on the Web" —*PC Magazine*
★"Top 5% Web sites" —*Point Communications*
★"3-Star site" —*The McKinley Group*

Our web site contains a library of comprehensive product information (including book excerpts and tables of contents), downloadable software, background articles, interviews with technology leaders, links to relevant sites, book cover art, and more. File us in your Bookmarks or Hotlist!

2. Join Our Email Mailing Lists

New Product Releases

To receive automatic email with brief descriptions of all new O'Reilly products as they are released, send email to:
ora-news-subscribe@lists.oreilly.com
Put the following information in the first line of your message (*not* in the Subject field):
subscribe ora-news

O'Reilly Events

If you'd also like us to send information about trade show events, special promotions, and other O'Reilly events, send email to:
ora-news-subscribe@lists.oreilly.com
Put the following information in the first line of your message (*not* in the Subject field):
subscribe ora-events

3. Get Examples from Our Books via FTP

There are two ways to access an archive of example files from our books:

Regular FTP

- ftp to:
  ftp.oreilly.com
  (login: anonymous
  password: your email address)
- Point your web browser to:
  ftp://ftp.oreilly.com/

FTPMAIL

- Send an email message to:
  ftpmail@online.oreilly.com
  (Write "help" in the message body)

4. Contact Us via Email

order@oreilly.com
To place a book or software order online. Good for North American and international customers.

subscriptions@oreilly.com
To place an order for any of our newsletters or periodicals.

books@oreilly.com
General questions about any of our books.

software@oreilly.com
For general questions and product information about our software. Check out O'Reilly Software Online at **http://software.oreilly.com/** for software and technical support information. Registered O'Reilly software users send your questions to: **website-support@oreilly.com**

cs@oreilly.com
For answers to problems regarding your order or our products.

booktech@oreilly.com
For book content technical questions or corrections.

proposals@oreilly.com
To submit new book or software proposals to our editors and product managers.

international@oreilly.com
For information about our international distributors or translation queries. For a list of our distributors outside of North America check out:
http://www.oreilly.com/distributors.html

5. Work with Us

Check out our website for current employment opportunites:
http://jobs.oreilly.com/

O'Reilly & Associates, Inc.
101 Morris Street, Sebastopol, CA 95472 USA
TEL 707-829-0515 or 800-998-9938
(6am to 5pm PST)
FAX 707-829-0104

International Distributors

http://international.oreilly.com/distributors.html

UK, Europe, Middle East and Africa (except France, Germany, Austria, Switzerland, Luxembourg, and Liechtenstein)

INQUIRIES
O'Reilly UK Limited
4 Castle Street
Farnham
Surrey, GU9 7HS
United Kingdom
Telephone: 44-1252-711776
Fax: 44-1252-734211
Email: information@oreilly.co.uk

ORDERS
Wiley Distribution Services Ltd.
1 Oldlands Way
Bognor Regis
West Sussex PO22 9SA
United Kingdom
Telephone: 44-1243-843294
UK Freephone: 0800-243207
Fax: 44-1243-843302 (Europe/EU orders)
or 44-1243-843274 (Middle East/Africa)
Email: cs-books@wiley.co.uk

France

INQUIRIES & ORDERS
Éditions O'Reilly
18 rue Séguier
75006 Paris, France
Tel: 33-1-40-51-52-30
Fax: 33-1-40-51-52-31
Email: france@oreilly.fr

Germany, Switzerland, Austria, Luxembourg, and Liechtenstein

INQUIRIES & ORDERS
O'Reilly Verlag
Balthasarstr. 81
D-50670 Köln, Germany
Telephone: 49-221-973160-91
Fax: 49-221-973160-8
Email: anfragen@oreilly.de (inquiries)
Email: order@oreilly.de (orders)

Canada (French language books)

Les Éditions Flammarion ltée
375, Avenue Laurier Ouest
Montréal (Québec) H2V 2K3
Tel: 00-1-514-277-8807
Fax: 00-1-514-278-2085
Email: info@flammarion.qc.ca

Hong Kong

City Discount Subscription Service, Ltd.
Unit A, 6th Floor, Yan's Tower
27 Wong Chuk Hang Road
Aberdeen, Hong Kong
Tel: 852-2580-3539
Fax: 852-2580-6463
Email: citydis@ppn.com.hk

Korea

Hanbit Media, Inc.
Chungmu Bldg. 210
Yonnam-dong 568-33
Mapo-gu
Seoul, Korea
Tel: 822-325-0397
Fax: 822-325-9697
Email: hant93@chollian.dacom.co.kr

Philippines

Global Publishing
G/F Benavides Garden
1186 Benavides Street
Manila, Philippines
Tel: 632-254-8949/632-252-2582
Fax: 632-734-5060/632-252-2733
Email: globalp@pacific.net.ph

Taiwan

O'Reilly Taiwan
1st Floor, No. 21, Lane 295
Section 1, Fu-Shing South Road
Taipei, 106 Taiwan
Tel: 886-2-27099669
Fax: 886-2-27038802
Email: mori@oreilly.com

India

Shroff Publishers & Distributors Pvt. Ltd.
12, "Roseland", 2nd Floor
180, Waterfield Road, Bandra (West)
Mumbai 400 050
Tel: 91-22-641-1800/643-9910
Fax: 91-22-643-2422
Email: spd@vsnl.com

China

O'Reilly Beijing
SIGMA Building, Suite B809
No. 49 Zhichun Road
Haidian District
Beijing, China PR 100080
Tel: 86-10-8809-7475
Fax: 86-10-8809-7463
Email: beijing@oreilly.com

Japan

O'Reilly Japan, Inc.
Yotsuya Y's Building
7 Banch 6, Honshio-cho
Shinjuku-ku
Tokyo 160-0003 Japan
Tel: 81-3-3356-5227
Fax: 81-3-3356-5261
Email: japan@oreilly.com

Singapore, Indonesia, Malaysia and Thailand

TransQuest Publishers Pte Ltd
30 Old Toh Tuck Road #05-02
Sembawang Kimtrans Logistics Centre
Singapore 597654
Tel: 65-4623112
Fax: 65-4625761
Email: wendiw@transquest.com.sg

All Other Asian Countries

O'Reilly & Associates, Inc.
101 Morris Street
Sebastopol, CA 95472 USA
Tel: 707-829-0515
Fax: 707-829-0104
Email: order@oreilly.com

Australia

Woodslane Pty., Ltd.
7/5 Vuko Place
Warriewood NSW 2102
Australia
Tel: 61-2-9970-5111
Fax: 61-2-9970-5002
Email: info@woodslane.com.au

New Zealand

Woodslane New Zealand, Ltd.
21 Cooks Street (P.O. Box 575)
Waganui, New Zealand
Tel: 64-6-347-6543
Fax: 64-6-345-4840
Email: info@woodslane.com.au

Argentina

Distribuidora Cuspide
Suipacha 764
1008 Buenos Aires
Argentina
Phone: 5411-4322-8868
Fax: 5411-4322-3456
Email: libros@cuspide.com